Introduction to Software Development

Learning to Program

Black & White Edition

Marwan Shaban

Icons by Google under Apache 2 license.

This product has no ISBN. It is a special black and white edition.

Library of Congress Control Number: 2021909532

About the cover: An astrolabe (ăs'trŭlāb) is an instrument probably used originally for measuring the altitudes of heavenly bodies and for determining their positions and movements. Although its origin is ancient and obscure, its invention is frequently ascribed either to Hipparchus or to Apollonius of Perga. For many centuries it was used by both astronomers and navigators (The Columbia Encyclopedia).

Cover design by Yasmeen Shaban.

Contents

List of Figures

List of Tables

List of Techniques

List of Tips

List of Examples

Preface

This book focuses on helping the reader develop an intuitive understanding of how to write good code. While learning Java, the reader will acquire principles and techniques that are presented in the context of realistic examples, with minimal jargon and constant reinforcement so that they're internalized and become habits. The techniques presented apply to any computer language, and have stood the test of time—techniques such as taking the extra time to simplify your code, starting your testing as soon as you can, and avoiding repeated code. Using a tutorial style and a steady progression from basic to advanced, the book allows the reader to follow along and try each example for him- or herself. The reader learns by doing.

Care was taken at each point to include only enough detail for the reader to progress to the next topic, avoiding discussion that would distract many readers from the main mission: learning how to write good code. As the focus is on learning to write code, software development processes and tools, such as source control and unit testing, aren't presented—indeed, it is my opinion that a good coder can easily learn those ancillary topics, while the reverse is not true.

The book is suitable for use in a two- or three-semester course on introductory programming.

My reviewers have saved me from many embarrassing oversights. I wish to thank professors Dick Grant, Lisa Macon, Ian O'Toole, Bill Gaught, Craig Tidwell, Adam Rocke, Mahendra Gossai, John Delgado, Ron Villmow, Holger Findling and Steven Zimmerman for their valuable feedback on early drafts of this book. I owe special thanks to professors Grant, Macon and O'Toole for their numerous insights and in-depth feedback. Any remaining shortcomings are mine alone. Error reports can be sent to ProfessorShaban@gmail.com.

I'm fortunate to have a family who are kind and supportive, and each inspirational in his or her own way—my wife Wyeleen, daughter Yasmeen, son Ramsey, parents Fuad and Mary, brothers Sami and Omar, and sister Rana. With gratitude, I dedicate this book to them.

Marwan Shaban
Orlando, May 2021

Introduction

Writing code is the essence of software development. This book is your introduction to the art of writing good code. After learning the materials in this book, you'll be able to move on to learn other kinds of programming or specialize in a particular language.

Some readers benefit more from in-depth discussion, while others need more of a tutorial style. I've tried to maintain a tutorial theme while covering essential information and avoiding programming topics that are best kept in reference texts. This allows the focus to remain on the main mission: developing solid coding skills.

How to use this book

You are encouraged to read the book's chapters sequentially; I have tried to introduce the reader to concepts when it makes sense to do so, and maintain a steady progression roughly in order of difficulty. Consequently, it didn't make sense to organize the book strictly in terms of language features, although each chapter has a focus and a theme.

Learning how to program is like learning to ride a bike. You can't learn it by reading a book. It takes constant practice for the ideas to take hold, and persistence is key. Learning the *syntax* is fast. Learning *how to program* takes time, and you can't expect it to be a fast process. As you study each chapter, you should follow along by typing in each example and making sure you get the expected output. Do each example over and over until you can write it without looking at the book. Your goal is to internalize the concepts and *get to the point where you are writing code easily without referring to examples*. You're not done until you reach that level of skill, and it's impossible to say how long this will take you, as each person is different—it takes as long as it takes. Remember, you don't learn programming by reading a book—you learn by doing!

Tip 1. Learning how to program is like learning to ride a bike. You must practice!

Syntax: The grammatical rules of a language.

Do each example over and over until you can write it without looking at the book. Your goal is to write code easily without referring to examples.

Tip 2. Copy/paste is the enemy of learning.

When addressing the danger of copy/paste, I'm referring to copying other people's code. Copying your own code is not only okay—you'll do it very often.

The book also tries to get you used to problem solving on your own. When studying or working on your homework, it's okay to search online now and then, but if you're a beginning programmer, you should avoid it to the extent possible. Conduct an Internet search only after you are stuck, and if you do use code that you find online, don't just copy and paste it into your program without understanding it. Copy/paste is the enemy of learning, because it makes it easy to skip ahead without going through the full learning process. It's important that you type the code yourself, to help you understand the details and help build that muscle memory. If you do copy code that you find online, be sure to understand how it works, and look up any language features that you don't recognize. Once you are past the learning stage and have completed this text, this advice no longer applies, and it's quite common for programmers to go online to look up techniques or languages features.

What you'll learn

The focus of this book is on learning the fundamentals. Thus, it doesn't teach how to build a graphical user interface. Rather, you will construct programs that interact with the user on the command line. This allows the focus to remain on learning core programming logic and programming basics. These core concepts apply to every kind of programming: desktop, database, cloud, web, enterprise, mobile, and more. What you learn here is a prerequisite to all those skills.

Since the book seeks to focus on teaching the basics and minimize distractions, you should consider each concept in the book to be essential. What's not in the book is as important as what's in it—if a language feature or programming technique is not covered, you can assume that it's not needed as part of the essential skill set. If you go through the book and master all its concepts, I believe you'll be done with the hard part, and all other software development skills will be relatively easy for you to master.

Unless you're already a programmer, resist the urge to skip sections. Don't rush it. If you learn the right way and get there in time, you'll have a solid foundation forever.

Getting Started | 1

1.1 Computer Languages and Compilers

Your computer executes machine language. Programming in such a low-level language is difficult for humans, so very early in the computer age, high-level languages were developed. The high-level language is translated into machine language by a compiler. When we create programs in high-level languages, there are many details of the program's execution that we don't need to worry about. The compiler takes care of those details for us. This is an example of abstraction, an important topic we'll discuss in later chapters.

In this book, the high-level language we use is Java. There are many high-level languages we could choose as a first language, but Java is a good choice due to its relative simplicity and also its prevalence, which makes it among the most in-demand language skills.

The Java compiler translates the Java source code into a machine language program. We make a distinction between compile-time, which is when the program is compiled, and run-time, which is when the program is executed. A program that is compiled once can be run many times, during which the program may interact with the user.

In this chapter, we'll download the tools needed to compile and run Java programs, and illustrate compiling and running a simple Java program. The main development tool that we'll interact with is Eclipse, which runs the Java compiler, and offers features that make Java development easier.

1.2 Hello World Program

The first program to write is customarily a simple program that outputs a simple message,

High-Level Language: A computer language that humans can read.

Machine Language: A computer's native language.

Compiler: A program that translates a high-level language into machine language.

Eclipse: An Integrated Development Environment (IDE) used to develop Java programs.

Example 1.1. Hello, World! program.

```
1  // main method
2  public static void main(String[] args) {
3    System.out.println("Hello, World!");
4  }
```

Above is the canonical Hello World program. You enter the program into Eclipse in preparation for compiling and running it. Here are a few things to note about the above code,

- A line that begins with two slashes (//) constitutes a comment. Comments don't cause the program to do anything - they're just there as clarifications for whoever reads the code.
- The main sequence of commands that make up the program is contained within { and } characters, which we call *curly braces* or *curly brackets*. In the above program, there's only one statement between the braces, which is the print statement.
- The word "main" is the name of the block of code enclosed within the curly braces. In Java, this is a special block of code, which will be executed when the program is started.
- The words "public", "static" and "void" will be explained in later chapters. They're keywords that denote properties of the main method.

JDK: The Java Development Kit that includes the Java compiler. It's used by Eclipse to compile Java programs.

Don't worry about the details at this point. Just know for now that the program will print the message "Hello, World!" when it runs. After installing JDK and Eclipse, we'll enter the above program and run it.

1.3 Installing the JDK

The first thing you need to download and install is the JDK (Java Development Kit). Installing the JDK also installs the Java compiler, which is invoked by Eclipse when it compiles your program. At the time of this writing, the JDK can be downloaded from this web page:

Web links that you see in this book may have changed by the time you read this. If that is the case, you should be able to easily search for the proper web page.

`https://www.oracle.com/java/technologies/javase-downloads.html`. Note that this is the Java SE edition. On this web page, you'll see a link to download the JDK (Figure 1.1).

Your operating system

The screen shots here show macOS. If you're on Windows, you

will choose the "Windows x64 Installer", and go through a typical Windows installation experience instead of using the standard macOS DMG file. Through the rest of the book, screen shots showing Eclipse on macOS should be very close to what a Windows user would see, as Eclipse looks the same on both operating systems.

Java editions

There are multiple editions of Java, including SE (Standard Edition), EE (Enterprise Edition) and ME (Micro Edition). In this book, we'll use the Standard Edition.

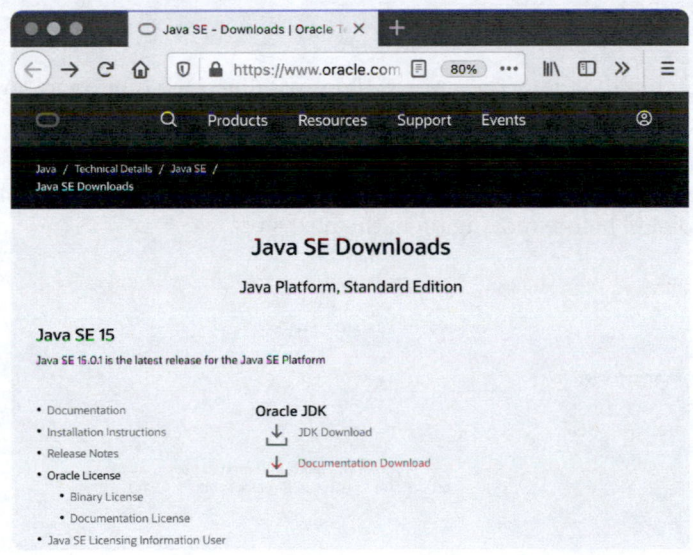

Screen shots that you see in this book may be different than what you see by the time you try this. If that is the case, do your best to use the new layouts to accomplish the same steps that you see here.

Figure 1.1: The JDK download page.

Clicking on the "JDK Download" link will take you to a second web page containing download links for each supported operating system (Figure 1.2).

Version numbers

By default, you should choose the latest version of software that you install. Here, we're installing JDK 15, which is the latest version at the time of this writing. Some programmers prefer to install the latest LTS (long term support) version of the JDK,

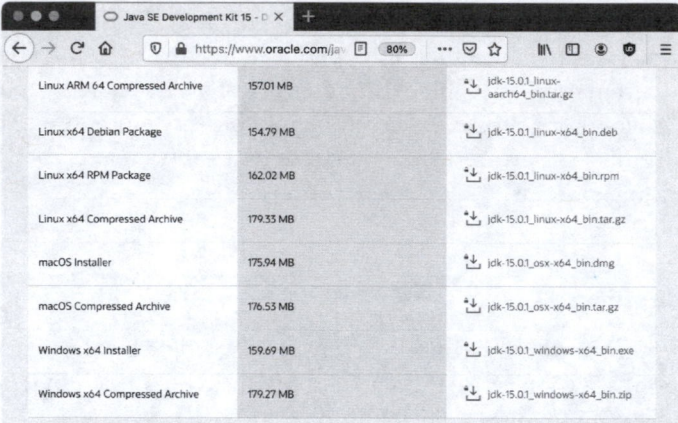

Figure 1.2: The JDK download page with download links for each operating system.

instead of the latest JDK version.

After downloading the appropriate installer for your operating system, you will start the installation process and go through a series of simple screens to complete the installation. Figure 1.3 shows the initial screen of the installer. Make sure the installer has completed before moving on to the next step.

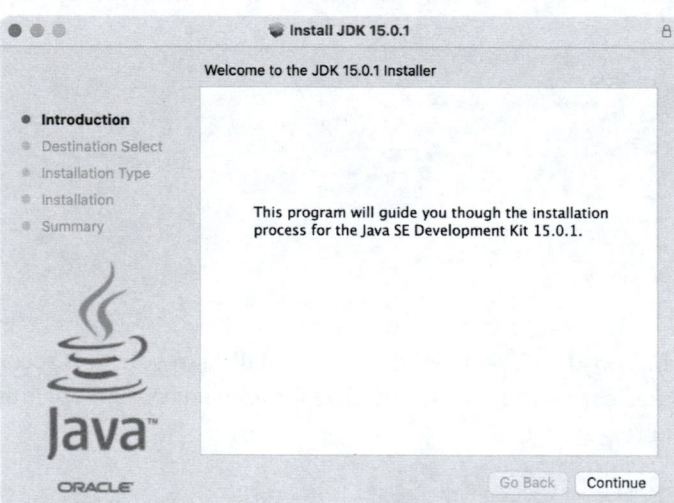

Figure 1.3: The JDK installer's initial screen.

1.4 Installing Eclipse

As we did with the JDK, we'll download and install Eclipse. Go to `https://www.eclipse.org/downloads/` and click the download link (see Figure 1.4). At the second download page, click Download again to start the download. Wait for the download to complete, and start the installation. The installer will show a number of different installation types. For our purposes, we need to choose the "Eclipse IDE for Java Developers" (see Figure 1.5).

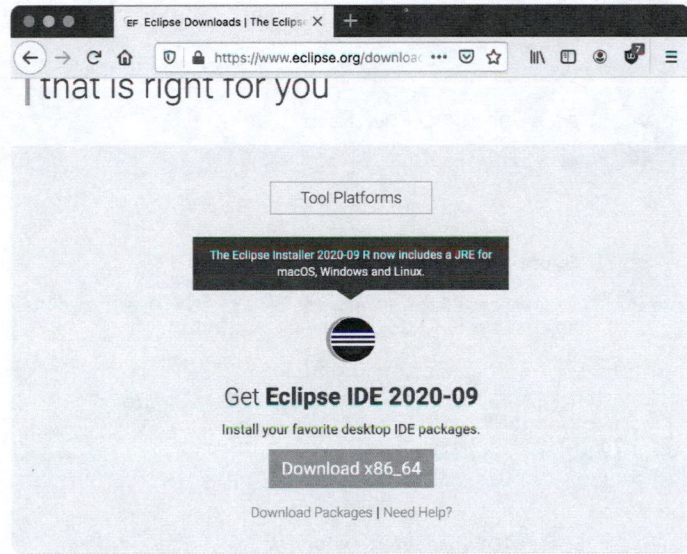

Figure 1.4: The Eclipse download page.

Next you will encounter the configuration screen which should show the path to the JDK that you just installed (Figure 1.6). Hit the Install button to start the installation. Wait for the installation process to finish, and then start Eclipse.

Upon launching Eclipse, you'll see the Eclipse workspace directory screen (Figure 1.7). Here you can override the location of the main Eclipse workspace, but we'll leave it with the default path and turn on the "Use this as the default and don't ask again" checkbox, then click Launch. The Eclipse main window is shown in Figure 1.8.

You'll learn what an Eclipse workspace is on page 40

At the moment, Eclipse is showing the Welcome view. Click on the "x" next to the tab's title to close the Welcome view. Also, close each of the Donate, Outline, Problems, Javadoc and Declaration views. You now have a minimal Eclipse window as shown in Figure 1.9.

View: A window within Eclipse.

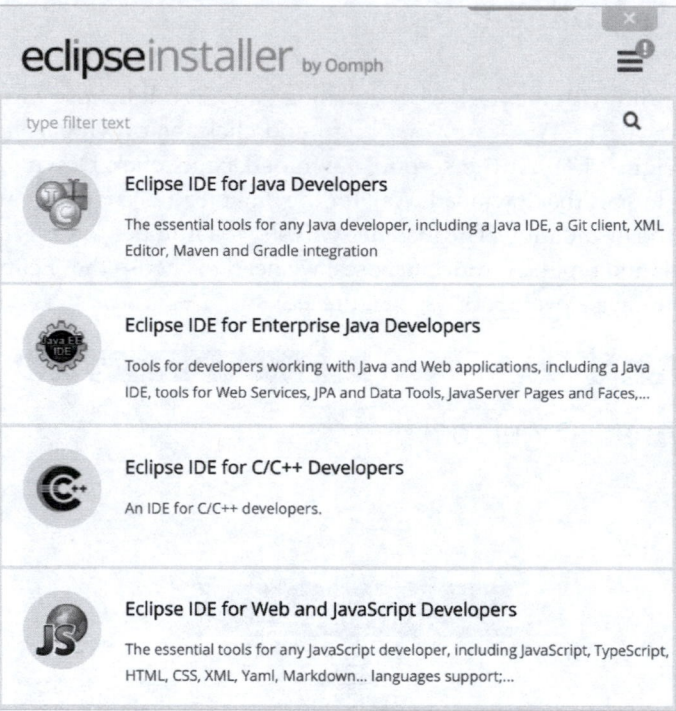

Figure 1.5: The Eclipse install options.

Figure 1.6: The Eclipse configuration screen.

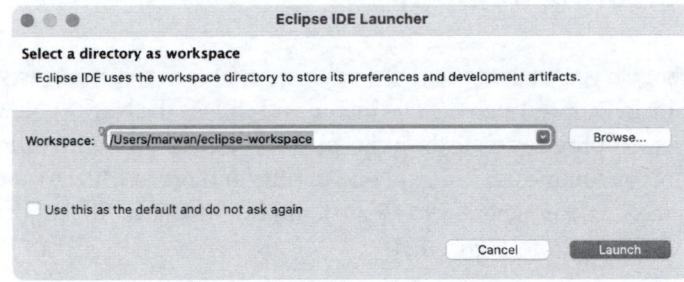

Figure 1.7: The Eclipse workspace directory screen.

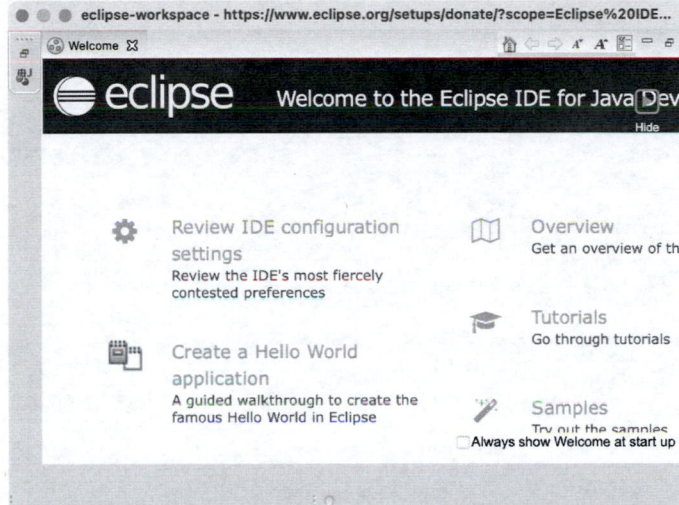

Figure 1.8: The Eclipse main window when started for the first time.

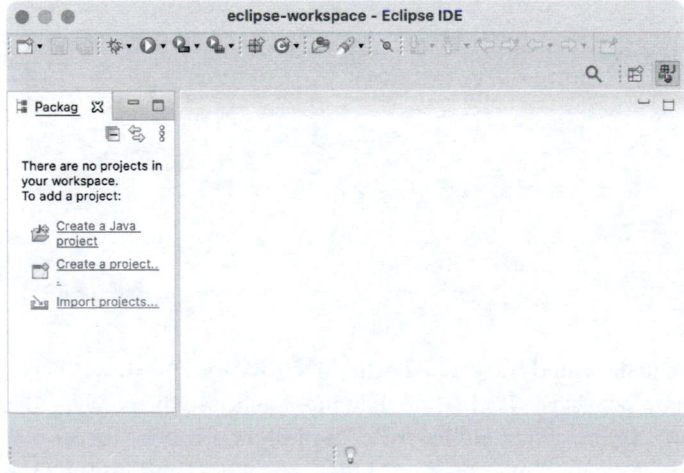

Figure 1.9: The Eclipse main window.

1.5 Creating a Program

Now that we've installed the JDK and Eclipse, we can create our first program. In Eclipse, open the File menu, and choose the New → New Java Project option to create the boilerplate project. Enter HelloWorld as the project name, and hit the Finish button (Figure 1.10). At the next screen, asking whether to create a module-info.java file, hit the Don't Create button (Figure 1.11).

Boilerplate: Standardized text used as a placeholder.

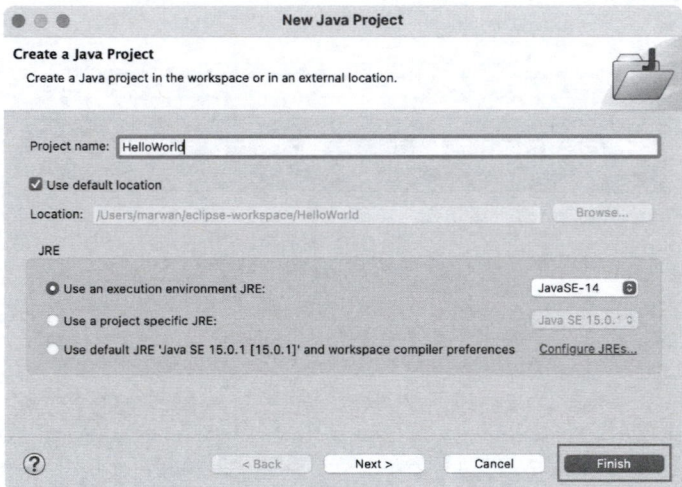

Figure 1.10: New Java Project window.

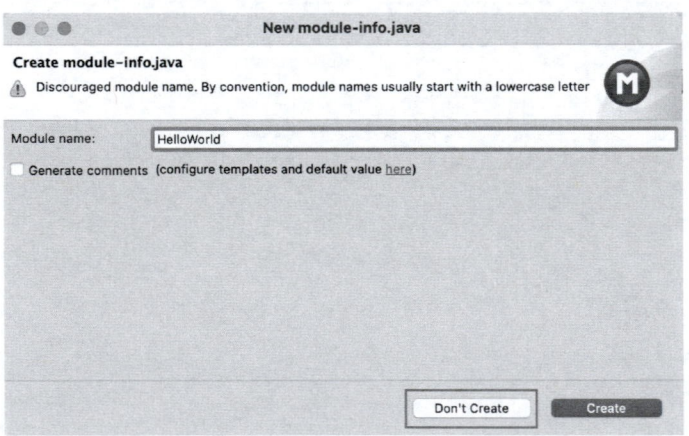

Figure 1.11: The module-info.java window.

You've just created the project called HelloWorld. Next, we'll create the main Java class. Back at the File menu, choose the New → Class option. Again, enter HelloWorld as the class name, turn on the "public static void main(String[] args)" checkbox, and hit the Finish button (Figure 1.12). At this point we've got a basic program with a class containing the `main` method (Figure 1.13).

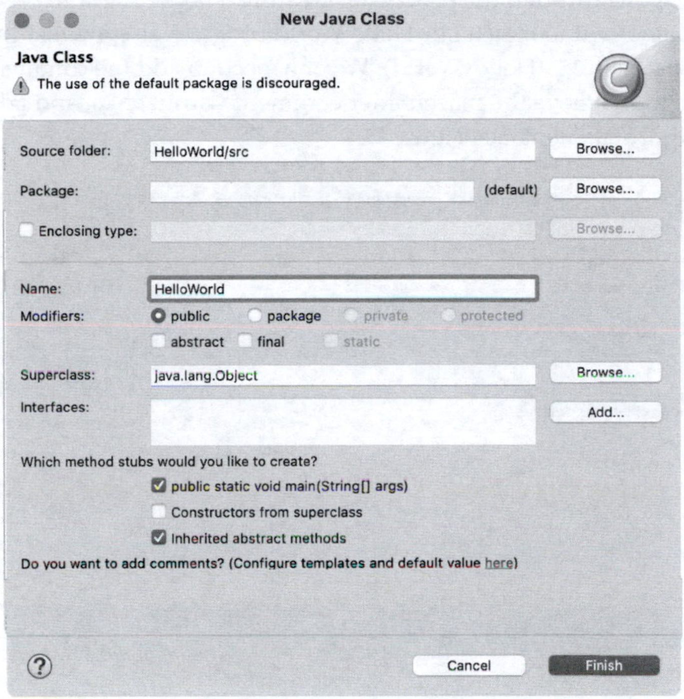

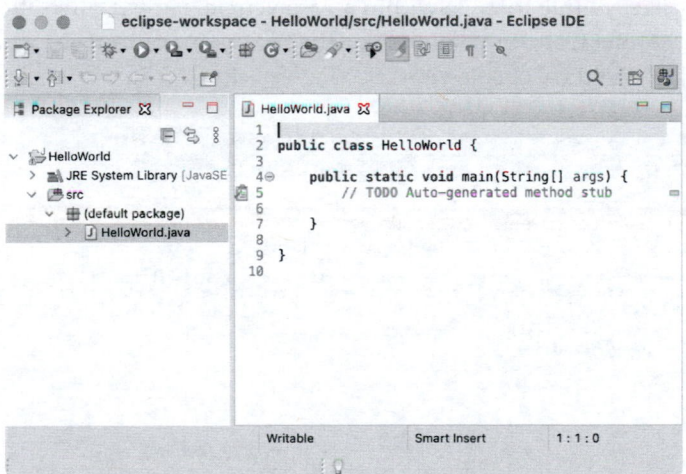

Figure 1.12: New Java Class window.

Figure 1.13: Boilerplate project with `main` method.

1.6 Running Programs

We've gone through the process of creating a new program. Next, we'll modify it to match our Hello World program as shown at the top of section 1.2 (Hello, World). We only need to add the comment at the top, remove the placeholder comment within `main`, and add the print statement. See Figure 1.14.

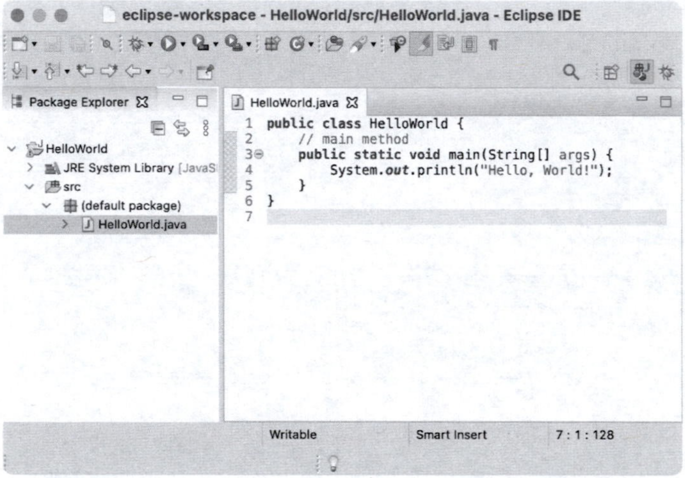

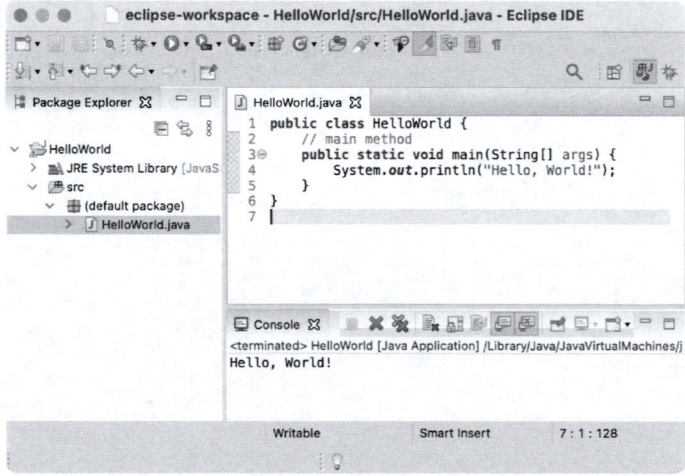

Figure 1.14: Eclipse with Hello World program.

Our program is now ready to test. The toolbar has a run button that looks like a white triangle within a green circle. Hit the run button on the toolbar, and you should see the program's output correctly displayed in the Console view. See Figure 1.15.

Figure 1.15: Hello World program's output correctly displayed in the Console view.

We'll have much more to say in chapter 3 about the various features available to you in Eclipse. Right now, it's time to move on to the next chapter and the basics of input and output in Java.

Exercises

1.1 Change the message that the program outputs, to print out your name. Run it and observe the output in the Console view.

1.2 Duplicate the print command (the entire line that prints Hello World) six times. Print out a different day of the week in each of the seven lines.

1.3 Create a new project by following the same process. You'll have to give the new project a different name. Test to make sure the second project also works.

Chapter Summary

- Install the JDK (Java Development Kit).
- Install Eclipse (the integrated development environment, or IDE).
- Use the New Java Project command in Eclipse to create a new program.
- Use the Run command in Eclipse to run a Java program. The output appears in Eclipse's Console view.
- The traditional "Hello, world" program is shown below with some of its notable components labeled:

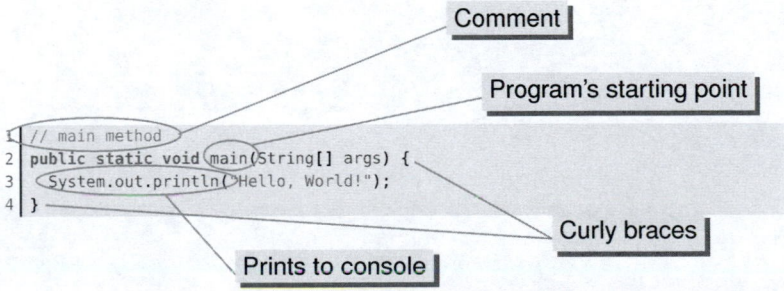

Exercise Solutions

1.1
```
1  // main method
2  public static void main(String[] args) {
3    System.out.println("Your Name");
4  }
```

```
Your Name
```

1.2
```
1   // main method
2   public static void main(String[] args) {
3     System.out.println("Sunday");
4     System.out.println("Monday");
5     System.out.println("Tuesday");
6     System.out.println("Wednesday");
7     System.out.println("Thursday");
8     System.out.println("Friday");
9     System.out.println("Saturday");
10  }
```

```
Sunday
Monday
Tuesday
Wednesday
Thursday
Friday
Saturday
```

1.3
```
1  public static void main(String[] args) {
2    System.out.println("Second Project");
3  }
```

Input, Processing and Output | 2

2.1 Variables

When your program runs, it stores its data in memory. It keeps track of the location within memory of each piece of data that is being processed. These memory locations can have names, and they can be referenced from the program's code. We call these variables. Example 2.1 shows an example of a variable,

```
1  public static void main(String[] args) {
2    int price;
3    price = 10;
4    System.out.println("The price is " + price);
5  }
```

In the above example, we have a variable called price, and its value is set to the number 10. A variable has a *type*. Our price has type `int`, which means it can store integers. Running this program produces the following output,

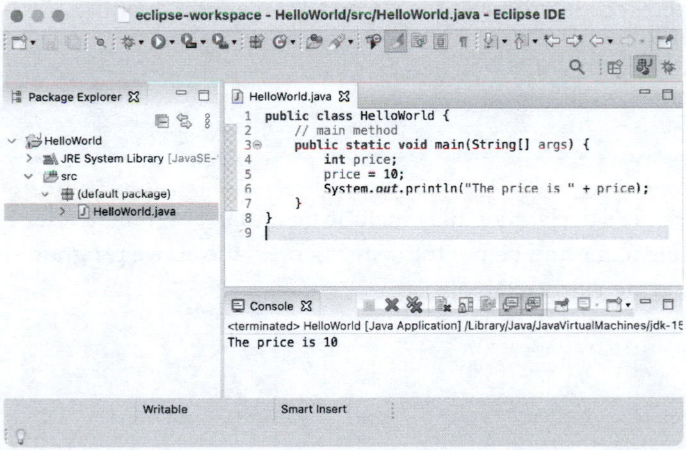

Figure 2.1: Using the variable `price`.

Henceforth, we'll save some space by illustrating program output inline, like this,

Example 2.1. Simple variable.

Variable: A location within memory that holds a data value.

Using the variable `price`.

```
The price is 10
```

Assignment: Changing the value contained within a variable.

Your program can change the value contained within a variable. One way to do this is to use the assignment operator. Technically, a variable is merely the name that we use to refer to the location within memory that contains the data. A variable name in Java can be any sequence of letters, numbers, the dollar sign symbol and underscore. It must begin with a letter. In addition, variable names are case sensitive, which means that uppercase and lowercase letters are different—so `price` and `Price` are different.

In your Java program, a variable is declared by stating its type, then its name. The semicolon is required at the end of the declaration. For example, the following program (example 2.2) displays remaining inventory after a sale,

Example 2.2. Computing remaining inventory after a sale.

```
1   int quantityOnHand;
2   quantityOnHand = 100;
3   int quantitySold;
4   quantitySold = 25;
5   int quantityRemaining;
6   quantityRemaining = quantityOnHand - quantitySold;
7   System.out.println("Quantity remaining = " + quantityRemaining);
```

I've omitted the main method's signature and braces, for brevity. The above code produces the expected remaining quantity,

```
Quantity remaining = 75
```

Initialization: assigning an initial value to a variable.

A variable's declaration may include an initial assignment after the variable name and before the semicolon. So the above program can be rewritten as in example 2.3,

Example 2.3. Simplified version.

```
1   int quantityOnHand = 100;
2   int quantitySold = 25;
3   int quantityRemaining = quantityOnHand - quantitySold;
4   System.out.println("Quantity remaining = " + quantityRemaining);
```

This form is preferred to the one above since it's shorter and, I would argue, clearer. This brings us to a very important principle, one that you should always remember and apply:

> **Technique 1. Simplify your code whenever you can**
>
> Always take the time to simplify your code before moving on. Code should be as brief as possible, without sacrificing clarity.

Your code is organized in blocks, delimited by the curly braces that we referred to earlier. For example, the `main` method defines a block of code that is run when the program is invoked, and when that block is finished executing, the program stops. Variables are declared within blocks, and their lifetimes end when the corresponding blocks finish executing. We say that the variable's *scope* is within the block in which it is defined.

Code block: Lines of code delimited by curly braces.

To **delimit** something is to surround it or mark its boundaries.

Variable scope: Variable use is limited to the blocks in which they're defined.

As you've noticed, variable names by convention begin with a lowercase letter, and each word after the first starts with an uppercase letter. This is called *camel case*.

> **Statements in Java**
>
> Most statements in Java have to end in a semicolon, as you've seen in example 2.3. A statement is not a line of code. Statements can span multiple lines, and one line can contain multiple statements. A statement corresponds to one valid Java instruction, such as the variable declaration on line 1 of example 2.3, or the assignment on line 3 of example 2.3.

2.2 Data Types

Each unit of data that your program processes has a particular type. Java makes sure that each variable only holds the type of data that it was declared as. For example, a variable declared as an integer only holds whole numbers in the proper range. Table 2.1 shows some of the basic data types in Java, with an example, and the range of possible values for each type.

Type	Example	Minimum value	Maximum value
int	1000	-2,147,483,648	2,147,483,647
float	3.14	$-3.4x10^{38}$	$3.4x10^{38}$
boolean	true	n/a	n/a
String	"Mary"	n/a	n/a

Table 2.1: Basic data types in Java.

Integer variables can have values in the range of $-2,147,483,648$ to $2,147,483,647$. Therefore, they can have $4,294,967,296$ different values, which is 2^{32}—because integers are represented with 32 bits, or 4 bytes.

Floating point variables are declared with the `float` keyword, and they hold decimal numbers in the range of approximately $-3.4x10^{38}$ to $3.4x10^{38}$.

Boolean variables only have a true or false value. They can be used in situations where data values determine different execution paths.

String variables contain text data, which can be of any length. Strings can be manipulated with Java code, for example to extract substrings, or concatenate (merge) different strings. Here is example code illustrating each of the above data types,

Example 2.4. Usage of `int`, `boolean`, `float` and `String`.

```
1  int quantitySold = 25;
2  boolean soldOut = false;
3  float taxRate = 0.06f;
4  String customerName = "John Doe";
5  System.out.println("Quantity sold: " + quantitySold);
6  System.out.println("Sold out: " + soldOut);
7  System.out.println("Tax rate: " + taxRate);
8  System.out.println("Customer name: " + customerName);
```

```
Quantity sold: 25
Sold out: false
Tax rate: 0.06
Customer name: John Doe
```

Hardcoded value: A constant value of a particular type in the program's source code.

Here we've declared four variables, each of a different type. Each of the four has been assigned a value of the appropriate type, then output to the console. Note that we've assigned specific values that are *hardcoded*, that is, specific values entered into the program's source code, as opposed to data that was entered by the user while the program is running. These are called *literal values* or *literal constants*.

Using string literals.

Note that the string literal is delimited by double quotes, and that these double quotes aren't part of the string data itself. Also note that the floating point literal is followed by lowercase "f". This is to distinguish it from a double-precision floating point literal which doesn't require the "f" suffix. We'll discuss the double precision floating point type in section 6.5.

Type Conversion

Some data types can be converted to one another. For example, an integer value can be assigned to a floating point variable, since the range of values for a floating point variable includes the possible integer values,

```
1  int intVariable = 123;
2  float floatVariable = intVariable;
3  System.out.println("floatVariable: " + floatVariable);
```

Example 2.5. Assigning an `int`'s value to a `float`.

```
floatVariable: 123.0
```

On the other hand, assigning a floating point value to an integer variable results in a compile error, but we can convert the floating point value to an integer value using an operation known as *type casting*, or just *casting*,

Casting: Converting a value from one type to another.

```
1  float floatVariable = 3.14f;
2  int intVariable = (int) floatVariable;
3  System.out.println("intVariable: " + intVariable);
```

Example 2.6. Type casting.

```
intVariable: 3
```

The cast operator is `(int)`. It converts the floating point value to an integer value. This is done by rounding down, not by rounding to the nearest integer.

Often you will need to extract numbers from strings. You can do this using Integer.parseInt() and Float.parseFloat(). For example,

```
1  String yearString = "2021";
2  int year = Integer.parseInt(yearString);
3
4  String taxRateString = "7.5";
5  float taxRate = Float.parseFloat(taxRateString);
6
7  System.out.println("The year is " + year + ", and the tax rate is " + taxRate
       + "%");
```

Example 2.7. Converting strings into numbers.

```
The year is 2021, and the tax rate is 7.5%
```

In example 2.7, the program creates two strings containing numbers, then converts them to numeric data types using `parseInt` and `parseFloat`.

2.3 Output

Method: A named block of code that can be executed from your Java code.

In Java, a *method* is a named block of code that you can execute just by invoking its name followed by a pair of parentheses. The `println` method is an example, and we've already seen how to execute `println` to print data to the Console view in Eclipse. We say that the section of code defined by the method is *executed*, *invoked*, or *called* when you use its name followed by parentheses. For example, `System.out.println("Hello, world!")` prints the string "Hello, world!". In the preceding example, the *literal string* contained within the pair of parentheses is called an *argument* that is passed to the method. A method can accept parameters and use their values within the method's block of code, or *body*. You can write your own methods; in fact, you've already written one: your `main()` method is called by the system when you tell Eclipse to run your program.

Calling a method: The act of using the method's name to execute its code.

Method argument: Data that you pass to a method.

Parameter: The name that we give to an argument within the method.

The `print()` method does the same thing as `println()`, except that it doesn't advance the output to the next line after printing. Both `print()` and `println()` can accept a parameter of various types, such as string, integer and float.

You can use `println()` without any parameters to move the output to the next line. If nothing has already been printed to the current line of output, this has the effect of printing an empty line. Together, `print()` and `println()` can be used to print almost anything you need to the Console view in Eclipse. Here's an example of using these two method together,

Example 2.8. Using `print` and `println`.

The `import` statement brings in a specific system identifier so that we can refer to it within a program.

```java
import static java.lang.System.out;

public class HelloWorld {
  public static void main(String[] args) {
    out.println("THE TEMPEST");
    out.println("");

    String playCharacter = "Master";
    out.print(playCharacter);
    out.println();
    out.print(1);
    out.println(" Boatswain!");
    out.println();
```

```
15      playCharacter = "Boatswain";
16      out.print(playCharacter);
17      out.println();
18      out.print(2);
19      out.println(" Here, master: what cheer?");
20      out.println();
21
22      playCharacter = "Master";
23      out.print(playCharacter);
24      out.println();
25      out.print(3);
26      out.println(" Good, speak to the mariners: fall to't, yarely,");
27      out.print(4);
28      out.println(" or we run ourselves aground: bestir, bestir.");
29      out.println();
30    }
31 }
```

```
THE TEMPEST

Master
1 Boatswain!

Boatswain
2 Here, master: what cheer?

Master
3 Good, speak to the mariners: fall to't, yarely,
4 or we run ourselves aground: bestir, bestir.
```

Note that we've added an `import` statement at the top, which allows us to use the syntax `out.println` instead of `System.out.println`. I like the short form better since it's less typing and less visual clutter.

As illustrated in the example above, `print` is used when we want to output bits of data that should all be on the same output line, whereas `println` is used when we want to output data, and then start a new line. The play script's line numbers 1, 2, 3 and 4 are printed, each followed by the script line. There is an empty line between the first character's lines and the second character's lines, which was produced using `out.println()`, that is, `println` with empty parentheses indicating no arguments are passed into the method.

Using `print` and `println`.

Note also that the default font used by Eclipse in the Console view is fixed-width, meaning each character takes up the same width. This allows you to play with ASCII art, which is one way we had fun with graphics before the advent of graphical user interfaces,

A **character** is a single letter, digit or symbol, not to be confused with the play characters in the last example.

Example 2.9. Fixed-width font in the Console view.

```
1  out.println("      oo0000");
2  out.println("     oo        _____");
3  out.println("    _I__n_n__||_||  _____");
4  out.println("   >(_____|_7_|-|_____|");
5  out.println("   /o ()() ()() o   oo  oo");
```

More ASCII art can be found at the ASCII Art Archive, https://www.asciiart.eu.

```
      oo0000
     oo        _____
    _I__n_n__||_||  _____
   >(_____|_7_|-|_____|
   /o ()() ()() o   oo  oo
```

Using `printf`.

Java helps you format output in various ways when printing out different data types. To do this, you can use the `printf` method. It differs from `print` and `println` in that it takes multiple parameters separated by commas. The first parameter is a string containing *format specifiers*, and the rest of the parameters are the data items to be printed. For example, `out.printf("%5.3f", interestRate)` prints out the value of a floating point variable called `interestRate`. It will use at least five characters to print the number, and will print three digits after the decimal point. If `interestRate` has more than three digits after the decimal point, `printf` will round up or down appropriately,

Example 2.10. Rounding with `printf`.

```
1  float interestRate = 3.1259f;
2  out.printf("%5.3f", interestRate);
```

```
3.126
```

Each parameter after the first needs its own format specifier within the format string. A format specifier begins with a percent sign (%) followed by optional modifiers then a character denoting the format type. Table 2.2 shows three of the most important format types that `printf` offers.

To left justify the output, add a hyphen before the number of characters, such as `%-5d`. To advance to a new line, add a %n within the format string. Example 2.11 shows another example of `printf`,

Example 2.11. Another `printf` example.

```
1  String customer = "John Doe";
2  float price = 48.99f;
3  float taxRate = 0.073f;
4  float total = price * (1 + taxRate);
5  out.printf("%s's total is $%.2f", customer, total);
```

```
John Doe's total is $52.57
```

Format	Type	Example	
s	String	%10s	Prints a string using at least ten characters.
d	int	%d	Prints an integer.
		%5d	Prints an integer, using at least five characters.
f	float	%5.3f	Prints a floating point number using at least five characters, and prints three digits after the decimal point.
		%.3f	Prints a floating point number with three digits after the decimal point.

Table 2.2: `printf` format specifiers.

2.4 Input

Your Java program can get input from the user, and store that input in data variables. For this, we'll use the **Scanner** class,

```java
1  import java.util.Scanner;
2  ...
3    Scanner input = new Scanner(System.in);
4
5    out.print("What's your name? ");
6    String name = input.nextLine();
7    out.print("Hello, " + name + "!");
8
9    input.close();
```

Example 2.12. Using `Scanner` to read input from the keyboard.

```
What's your name? Billy
Hello, Billy!
```

In the above example, we've created an object of type **Scanner**, and we've named it **input**. Note the new **import** statement that we've added to the top of our program. An import statement such as this allows us to abbreviate `java.util.Scanner` to `Scanner` when used in the rest of our program.

A method can **return** a value to the code that invoked it, which can be assigned to a variable or used in a computation.

To get input from the keyboard, we call the `nextLine` method of the `Scanner` object. This method returns a string which we then store in the `String` variable called `name`. The screen shot above shows the program's prompt followed by the user's input. The `nextLine` method suspends the program's execution and waits for the user's input. It doesn't return to the caller until the user has hit the enter key.

A `Scanner` object can be used to get keyboard input repeatedly, but in example 2.12 we've only used it to retrieve one string, the user's name. After our program has finished getting its input from the keyboard, the `Scanner` object is closed using the `input.close()` statement. If you don't close a `Scanner` object, your program will still work, but will contain a *resource leak*, and having too many resource leaks during runtime will affect your program's performance or cause it to stop working.

You can use the `Scanner` object to read integer and floating point input using its `nextInt` and `nextFloat` methods. The following (2.13) is an example program that reads string, integer and floating point data from the user (we've omitted the `Scanner` object's declaration as well as the call to its `close` method, for brevity),

Example 2.13. Getting input of different data types.

```
1   out.print("Enter product: ");
2   String product = input.nextLine();
3   out.print("Enter quantity: ");
4   int quantity = input.nextInt();
5   input.nextLine();
6   out.print("Enter price per unit: ");
7   float pricePerUnit = input.nextFloat();
8   input.nextLine();
9
10  out.printf("%d units of %s will cost $%.2f", quantity, product, pricePerUnit
        * quantity);
```

```
Enter product: 16 oz. Pepsi
Enter quantity: 3
Enter price per unit: 1.21
3 units of 16 oz. Pepsi will cost $3.63
```

Reading multiple types with `Scanner`

When reading both strings and numbers with an object of type `Scanner`, you should call `nextLine` after you read a number from the keyboard, as shown on line 8 of the above example. This is because `nextInt` and `nextFloat` only read the *number* from the keyboard. The following call to `nextLine` will instruct the `Scanner` object to *consume* the newline character generated by the enter key. Without the call to `nextLine` following `nextInt`, subsequent reading of string data with `nextLine` won't read the intended input properly.

2.5 Processing Numeric Data

Now that we know how to get input and generate output, it's time for our program to do something useful. A typical pattern is gathering input, processing the input and outputting a result. To process the input, our Java program will use data manipulation statements.

Numeric data is processed with mathematical expressions that combine numeric variables with mathematical operators. For example, `int birthYear = thisYear - age` will subtract your current age from this year to compute the year you were born,

```
1  import java.util.Calendar;
2  ...
3    out.print("Enter your age: ");
4    int age = input.nextInt();
5    input.nextLine();
6
7    int thisYear = Calendar.getInstance().get(Calendar.YEAR);
8    int birthYear = thisYear - age;
9
10   out.println("You were born in " + birthYear);
```

Example 2.14. Simple computation.

This simplistic formula doesn't take into account the month and day, so it may display an answer that is off by one year.

```
Enter your age: 31
You were born in 1989
```

`thisYear - age` is an example of an expression, and it computes the user's year of birth. An expression has inputs and produces an output. In this instance, the inputs are `thisYear` and `age`, both of which are of type `int`. The result of this expression is also of type `int` because the minus operator takes two integers and produces an integer. We say that the minus operator takes two *arguments*. Always keep in mind that an expression has a specific type, which is the type of data that it produces.

Expression: A formula that can include constants, variables and operators, which produces a result of a certain type.

We've already seen type conversion using casting. If we use the minus operator to subtract a floating point number from an integer, the minus operator automatically converts the integer to a floating point

Table 2.3: Common mathematical operators.

Operator	Example	
+	`birthYear + age`	Adds the user's age to his year of birth to get the current year.
-	`thisYear - age`	Subtracts the user's age from the current year to compute the user's year of birth.
*	`quantity * pricePerUnit`	Computes total price, given the price per unit and the number of units.
/	`miles / gallons`	Computes a vehicle's fuel efficiency (miles per gallon).
	`hours / 24`	Computes days from hours. This integer division returns the number of whole days without the remaining fraction, for example if hours is 36, the result is one day.
%	`hours % 24`	The *remainder* operator gives the remainder after performing integer division. For example, if hours is 36, the remainder is 12.

number, then performs the subtraction and produces a floating point result. Table 2.3 shows a list of some of the important operators.

Of course, expressions can be more complex than the example we just saw. Here's an example of converting temperature units,

```
1   out.print("Enter degrees Celsius: ");
2   int celsius = input.nextInt();
3   input.nextLine();
4
5   int fahrenheit = celsius * 9 / 5 + 32;
6
7   out.printf("%d Celsius is %d Fahrenheit", celsius, fahrenheit);
```

Example 2.15. Temperature conversion.

```
Enter degrees Celsius: 100
100 Celsius is 212 Fahrenheit
```

The formula to convert Celsius degrees to Fahrenheit is:

$Fahrenheit = 9/5 \, Celsius + 32$

which corresponds to our Java expression `celsius * 9 / 5 + 32`. The multiplication will be performed first, then the division and then the addition. In our test run above, `celsius` has the value 100. Since `celsius` is of type `int`, the multiplication will result in the integer value 900. The division is performed next, and will be integer division since both operands are integers (the two division operands being 900 and 5). The result of this integer division is the integer value 180. Then 180 is added to 32, resulting in 212.

Suppose our Java expression was `9 / 5 * celsius + 32`. Though that is equivalent mathematically to the previous expression, in practice the result will be different. The division operation occurs first, and since both operands are integers, the result of 1.8 will be rounded down to the integer value 1, which when multiplied by `celsius` is 100. Next 32 is added with a final result of 132. You should be aware of this pitfall with integer division. To force floating point division, one of the operands should be a floating point number. Two easy ways to fix this are,

Integer division: The division operator rounds down and produces an integer if both operands are integers.

- Use a floating point constant for one of the division arguments, and cast the final result to an integer: `int fahrenheit = (int) (9f / 5 * celsius + 32)`. This causes it to be a floating point division, producing a floating point result.
- Cast one of the division arguments to a floating point number, which again forces a floating point division: `int fahrenheit = (int) ((float) 9 / 5 * celsius + 32)`.

Our next example (2.16) involves adding the price of two items, multiplying the total by 1.05 to add 5% tax, and printing the total,

Example 2.16. Incorrect expression due to operator precedence.

```
1  float price1 = 19.95f;
2  float price2 = 2.80f;
3  float totalWithTax = price1 + price2 * 1.05f;
4  out.println("Total with tax is $" + totalWithTax);
```

```
Total with tax is $22.890001
```

The result is $22.89, which is incorrect. This is because we meant to add the tax to both prices. The tax was only added to `price2` due to *operator precedence*. The multiplication operator has higher precedence than the addition operator, so the multiplication is performed first, then the addition. To fix this, we must enclose the addition in parentheses,

Example 2.17. Corrected expression.

```
1  float price1 = 19.95f;
2  float price2 = 2.80f;
3  float totalWithTax = (price1 + price2) * 1.05f;
4  out.println("Total with tax is $" + totalWithTax);
```

```
Total with tax is $23.887499
```

This time, the addition was performed first, then the 5% sales tax was added to both prices. Operator precedence is another thing to keep in mind when working with numeric expressions. Table 2.4 shows operator precedence for the basic mathematical operators.

Table 2.4: Operator precedence in Java (abbreviated).

Precedence	Operator
1	cast operator
2	- (unary negation)
3	+, -
4	*, /, %

We'll add one more enhancement to example 2.17 by rounding the output to two decimal places using `printf`,

Example 2.18. After rounding to two decimal places.

```
1  float price1 = 19.95f;
2  float price2 = 2.80f;
3  float totalWithTax = (price1 + price2) * 1.05f;
4  out.printf("Total with tax is $%.2f", totalWithTax);
```

```
Total with tax is $23.89
```

Exercises

2.1 Write a program that converts miles to kilometers. Have the user enter the value in miles, multiply it by 1.61 and output the result.

2.2 Write a program that asks the user for a vehicle's fuel tank capacity in gallons and its fuel efficiency in miles per gallon. It should then output the vehicle's range, that is, the number of miles it can travel on a full tank.

2.3 Write a program that asks the user for three items' prices and a tax rate. Output the total price including tax.

2.4 Write a program that asks the user for his or her year of birth, and output how old he or she is.

2.5 Write a program that asks the user for a sphere's radius in inches, and output its volume in cubic inches using the formula $v = 4/3\pi r^3$.

2.6 Modify example 2.15 to use the expression `9 / 5 * celsius + 32`, then demonstrate both methods of forcing floating point division as discussed on page 27. Run your program and make sure it produces the correct result.

2.6 Processing String Data

Using the addition operator with two strings concatenates them, creating a new string with the combined contents of the two operands. We've done this earlier in this chapter,

```
1    out.print("What's your name? ");
2    String name = input.nextLine();
3    out.print("Hello, " + name + "!");
```

Example 2.19. String concatenation with the + operator.

```
What's your name? Billy
Hello, Billy!
```

Line 3 concatenates three strings, two literals and a `String` variable. After the three strings are concatenated, the resulting string is passed

String concatenation: Merging two strings to make a new combined string.

in to the `print` method as a parameter. Here's another example of string concatenation,

```
1   out.print("Enter your first name: ");
2   String firstName = input.nextLine();
3   out.print("Enter your last name: ");
4   String lastName = input.nextLine();
5   String fullName = firstName + " " + lastName;
6   out.printf("Hello, %s", fullName);
```

```
Enter your first name: Isaac
Enter your last name: Newton
Hello, Isaac Newton
```

We can extract first and last names from a string containing a full name. To do that, we look for the space character, then extract the first and last names separately,

Example 2.20. Extracting words from a string.

```
1   out.print("Enter your full name: ");
2   String name = input.nextLine();
3   int spaceIndex = name.indexOf(' ');
4   String firstName = name.substring(0, spaceIndex);
5   String lastName = name.substring(spaceIndex + 1);
6   out.printf("First name: %s, last name: %s", firstName, lastName);
```

```
Enter your full name: Isaac Newton
First name: Isaac, last name: Newton
```

`indexOf` and `substring` methods of the `String` class.

The `indexOf` method of the `String` class returns the index (position) of a certain character within the string. After we've retrieved the position of the space within the string containing first and last name, we extract the first and last name separately using the `substring` method of the `String` class. When passing one parameter into `substring()`, it returns the contents of the string starting at the specified index. When passing two parameters, it returns the contents of the string starting at the first index and ending at the second index. Note that the first character in a string has the index zero, thus we say that string indexing is zero-based.

String indexing is zero-based.

`char` data type.

One primitive data type in Java that we haven't seen yet is the `char` type. A variable of type `char` can hold a single character. `char` literals are enclosed in single quotes, and this is what we've passed into the `indexOf` method of the `String` class.

Exercises

2.7 Write a program that asks the user for his or her first, middle and last names, and outputs the full name.

2.8 Write a program that asks the user for three sentences separated by commas, then prints each sentence separately. Hint: you can do this by using `indexOf` to find the index of the first comma, then use `substring` to get a string containing the second and third sentences, then again use `indexOf` and `substring` to separate the second and third sentences.

2.9 Fix the two syntax errors in the following program, and test it with the retail price $15.50, which should produce a sale price of $16.27,

```
1  import static java.lang.System.out;
2  import java.util.Scanner;
3
4  public class Test {
5    public static void main(String[] args) {
6
7      Scanner input = new Scanner(System.in);
8
9      out.print("Enter retail price: ");
10     float retailPrice = input.nextFloat();
11     input.nextLine();
12
13     float taxRate = 0.05;
14     float sale Price = retailPrice * (1 + taxRate);
15
16     out.printf("The price with tax is %.2f", salePrice);
17
18     input.close();
19   }
20 }
```

2.7 Processing Dates

Occasionally your programs will need to process dates and times. Java provides the `LocalDate` and `LocalTime` classes to help with this. Let's suppose you want to display the current date and time. This can be done as in the following example (2.21),

Example 2.21. Printing current date and time.

```
1  import java.time.LocalDate;
2  import java.time.LocalTime;
3  ...
4
5    LocalDate date = LocalDate.now();
6    out.println("The date is " + date);
7
8    LocalTime time = LocalTime.now();
9    out.println("The time is " + time);
```

```
The date is 2021-02-16
The time is 20:19:58.868667
```

The `LocalDate` and `LocalTime` classes provide methods that retrieve the date and time's components (year, month, day, hour, minute, etc.), in case you need individual components or want to print it out in a different way than the output in the previous example. In the next example (2.22), you can see how to retrieve these individual components and use them to print the current date and time,

Example 2.22. Getting date and time components.

```
1    LocalDate date = LocalDate.now();
2    out.printf("The date is %d-%02d-%02d\n", date.getYear(), date.getMonthValue()
       , date.getDayOfMonth());
3
4    LocalTime time = LocalTime.now();
5    out.printf("The time is %02d:%02d:%02d\n", time.getHour(), time.getMinute(),
       time.getSecond());
```

```
The date is 2021-02-16
The time is 20:39:06
```

To initialize a `LocalDate` object with a specific day, you can use the `LocalDate.of()` method, passing it three integer parameters for the year, month and day. You can also use a string to initialize a `LocalDate` variable using the `LocalDate.parse()` method, which takes a string and optionally a date format. The following example (2.23) illustrates all three of these techniques of creating a date object,

Example 2.23. Initializing a `LocalDate` object.

```
1  import java.time.format.DateTimeFormatter;
2  ...
3    LocalDate date = LocalDate.of(2021, 7, 21);
4    out.printf("The date is %d-%02d-%02d\n", date.getYear(), date.getMonthValue()
       , date.getDayOfMonth());
5
6    LocalDate date2 = LocalDate.parse("2004-03-02");
7    out.println("The date is " + date2);
8
9    DateTimeFormatter formatter = DateTimeFormatter.ofPattern("MM/dd/yyyy");
10   LocalDate date3 = LocalDate.parse("04/03/2005", formatter);
```

```
11 │  out.println("The date is " + date3);
```

```
The date is 2021-07-21
The date is 2004-03-02
The date is 2005-04-03
```

`LocalDate` has many other useful features. Other common operations include,

- Adding a certain number of days to a `LocalDate` object can be done with the `plusDays()` method.
- Getting the number of days between two `LocalDate` objects can be done with the syntax `java.time.temporal.ChronoUnit.DAYS.between(date1, date2)`, which returns a long integer.

Chapter Summary

- Variables hold your programs' data. Your programs can read from and write to variables.
- Variables have specific data types.
- Data types have a range of allowed values.
- Output is displayed on the Console view in Eclipse. The `println` method allows you to write output, and the `printf` method allows greater flexibility in formatting output.
- The `Scanner` class allows your programs to get input from the user.
- Numeric data, string data and dates can be manipulated by your programs.
- A sample program is shown below, with labels for notable input, processing and output components:

```
1  import static java.lang.System.out;
2  import java.util.Calendar;
3  import java.util.Scanner;
4
5  public class Test {
6    public static void main(String[] args) {
7
8      Scanner input = new Scanner(System.in);
9
10     out.print("Enter your age: ");
11     int age = input.nextInt();
12     input.nextLine();
13
14     out.print("Enter your full name: ");
15     String name = input.nextLine();
16
17     int thisYear = Calendar.getInstance().get(Calendar.YEAR);
18     int birthYear = thisYear - age;
19
20     int spaceIndex = name.indexOf(' ');
21     String firstName = name.substring(0, spaceIndex);
22     String lastName = name.substring(spaceIndex + 1);
23
24     out.printf("First name: %s, last name: %s\n", firstName, lastName);
25     out.println("You were born in " + birthYear);
26
27     input.close();
28   }
29 }
```

Annotations:
- Import System.out
- Import Scanner class
- Creates Scanner object
- Read a number
- Read a string
- Numeric computation
- String manipulation
- Formatted output with `printf`
- Output with `println`
- Closing Scanner object

Exercise Solutions

2.1

```
1  out.print("Enter distance in miles: ");
2  float miles = input.nextFloat();
3  input.nextLine();
4
5  float kilometers = miles * 1.60934f;
6
7  out.printf("%.2f miles = %.2f kilometers", miles, kilometers);
```

```
Enter distance in miles: 3
3.00 miles = 4.83 kilometers
```

2.2

```
1  out.print("Enter fuel tank capacity in gallons: ");
2  float gallons = input.nextFloat();
3  input.nextLine();
4
```

```
5    out.print("Enter miles per gallon: ");
6    float mpg = input.nextFloat();
7    input.nextLine();
8
9    float range = mpg * gallons;
10
11   out.printf("Your vehicle's range is %.2f miles", range);
```

```
Enter fuel tank capacity in gallons: 13.3
Enter miles per gallon: 37
Your vehicle's range is 492.10 miles
```

2.3
```
1    out.print("Enter prices for three items: ");
2    float price1 = input.nextFloat();
3    float price2 = input.nextFloat();
4    float price3 = input.nextFloat();
5    input.nextLine();
6
7    out.print("Enter tax rate: ");
8    float taxRate = input.nextFloat();
9    input.nextLine();
10
11   float price = (price1 + price2 + price3) * (1 + taxRate);
12
13   out.printf("Total price = $%.2f", price);
```

```
Enter prices for three items: 1.99 12 5.99
Enter tax rate: 0.06
Total price = $21.18
```

2.4
```
1    out.print("What year were you born? ");
2    int birthYear = input.nextInt();
3    input.nextLine();
4
5    int thisYear = java.time.LocalDate.now().getYear();
6
7    out.println("You are " + (thisYear - birthYear) + " years old");
```

```
What year were you born? 2002
You are 19 years old
```

2.5
```
1    out.print("Enter sphere's radius in inches: ");
2    float radius = input.nextFloat();
3    input.nextLine();
4
5    float volume = radius * radius * radius * 3.14159f * 4 / 3;
6
7    out.printf("The sphere's volume is %.2f cubic inches", volume);
```

```
Enter sphere's radius in inches: 3
The sphere's volume is 113.10 cubic inches
```

2.6
```
1    out.print("Enter degrees Celsius: ");
2    int celsius = input.nextInt();
3    input.nextLine();
4
```

```
5    int fahrenheit = (int) (9f / 5 * celsius + 32);
6    out.printf("%d Celsius is %d Fahrenheit \n", celsius, fahrenheit);
7
8    fahrenheit = (int) ((float) 9 / 5 * celsius + 32);
9    out.printf("%d Celsius is %d Fahrenheit \n", celsius, fahrenheit);
```

```
Enter degrees Celsius: 100
100 Celsius is 212 Fahrenheit
100 Celsius is 212 Fahrenheit
```

2.7

```
1    out.print("Enter your first name: ");
2    String firstName = input.nextLine();
3    out.print("Enter your middle name: ");
4    String middleName = input.nextLine();
5    out.print("Enter your last name: ");
6    String lastName = input.nextLine();
7    String fullName = firstName + " " + middleName + " " + lastName;
8    out.printf("Hello, %s", fullName);
```

```
Enter your first name: Galileo
Enter your middle name: di Vincenzo
Enter your last name: Galilei
Hello, Galileo di Vincenzo Galilei
```

2.8

```
1    out.print("Enter a three-sentence poem: ");
2    String poem = input.nextLine();
3    int index = poem.indexOf(',');
4    String sentence1 = poem.substring(0, index);
5    poem = poem.substring(index+1);
6    index = poem.indexOf(',');
7    String sentence2 = poem.substring(0, index);
8    String sentence3 = poem.substring(index+1);
9    out.printf("%s\n%s\n%s", sentence1, sentence2, sentence3);
```

```
Enter a three-sentence poem: Everyone young or old, needs someone to listen, as their stories are told
Everyone young or old
 needs someone to listen
 as their stories are told
```

2.9

```
1    out.print("Enter retail price: ");
2    float retailPrice = input.nextFloat();
3    input.nextLine();
4
5    float taxRate = 0.05f;
6    float salePrice = retailPrice * (1 + taxRate);
7
8    out.printf("The price with tax is %.2f", salePrice);
```

```
Enter retail price: 15.50
The price with tax is 16.27
```

Working with the IDE (Integrated Development Environment)

3

3.1 Managing Programs

This isn't a book about Eclipse, so we won't go into too much detail here. We'll cover just what you need to learn about the IDE in order to move on to the next chapter.

The IDE (Integrated Development Environment) in our case is Eclipse, and its main window is shown in Figure 3.1.

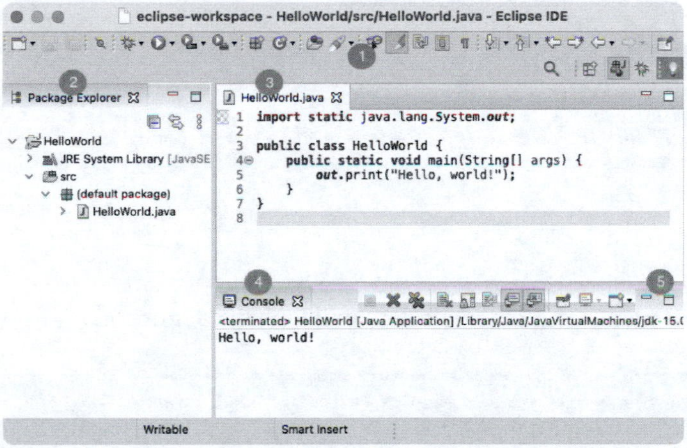

Figure 3.1: The Eclipse main window.

The toolbars (labeled 1 in the figure) each have a handle which looks like four vertical dots. You can grab toolbars by the handle and move them around the window. The Package Explorer view (2) shows a tree hierarchy of each of your projects. We only have one project so far, HelloWorld, and you can see its tree which contains HelloWorld.java under the "src" folder. The HelloWorld.java file (3) contains our main program's source code. The Console view (4) shows the program's output. Views such as Console and Package Explorer have their own minimize/maximize buttons on the top right (5). You can grab a view by its tab, where you see the view's name, and drag it around the window to dock it somewhere else. Views can be docked separately, and can also be docked together as tabs. You should practice moving some of the views around the window to get the hang of it.

If you accidentally minimize one of these views, you can get it back by clicking on its icon in the toolbar that it minimized to, or by choosing "Window → Show View" from the main menu, followed by the view that you want, e.g., "Window → Show View → Console".

You saw in section 1.5 how to create a new program. Follow the same process to create a second project, and name it "GeometryWiz". Add a class to your new project called "CircleArea", and enter the following code into the new file CircleArea.java,

Example 3.1. CircleArea class.

```
1  import static java.lang.System.out;
2  import java.util.Scanner;
3
4  public class CircleArea {
5
6    public static void main(String[] args) {
7      Scanner input = new Scanner(System.in);
8
9      out.print("Please enter circle's radius in feet: ");
10     float radius = input.nextFloat();
11     input.nextLine();
12     float area = radius * radius * 3.14f;
13     out.print("The circle with radius " + radius + " feet has an area of " +
         area + " square feet.");
14
15     input.close();
16   }
17 }
```

You can get a more accurate answer by using `(float) Math.PI` instead of 3.14f. We'll see `Math.PI` later on, in section 9.6.

At this point, your main window will look like Figure 3.2.

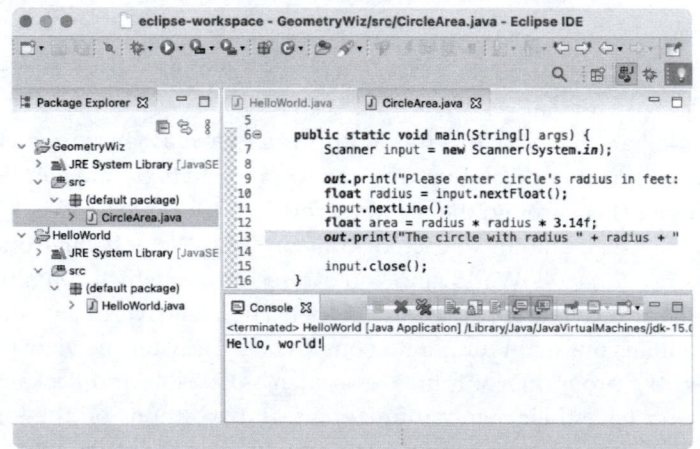

Figure 3.2: Eclipse window with two projects.

The Package Explorer window now has both of your projects, HelloWorld and GeometryWiz, each with its tree of assets. Hitting the

Run button in the toolbar will run your new class, CircleArea, *if you have its code in focus*. Click within the CircleArea.java window, then hit the Run button in the toolbar, to run it:

```
Please enter circle's radius in feet: 10
The circle with radius 10.0 feet has an area of 314.0 square feet.
```

Alternatively, you can right-click in the code window and choose "Run As → Java Application" from the context menu, or right-click on CircleArea.java in the Package Explorer view, then choose "Run As → Java Application". You can have multiple programs in your Eclipse workspace, and you need to make sure you're running the right one to avoid the confusion that can result if the wrong program runs in the Console view.

Above, I've used the terms *project* and *program* somewhat loosely. You run a program by invoking the `main` method belonging to one of your classes. A project can have many classes, and more than one of them can have a `main` method. If you aren't able to run the `main` method that you intend, you should go into the "Run Configurations" dialog box (colloquially, a *dialog box* is also called a *dialog*, a term we'll use occasionally), which you open using "Run → Run Configurations" from the main menu. The Run Configurations dialog is shown in Figure 3.3.

Run configuration: A definition telling Eclipse how to run your program. This definition is created automatically when you run your program for the first time.

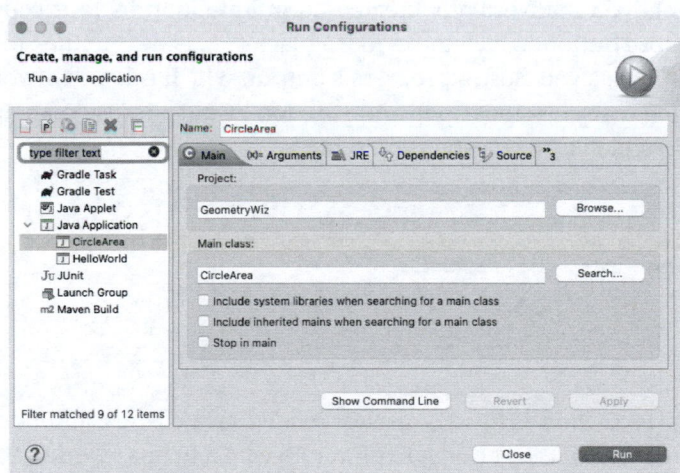

Figure 3.3: The Run Configurations dialog in Eclipse.

On the left-hand side of the Run Configurations dialog box, under Java Application, you will see the Java Application run configurations defined in your workspace (we'll deal with what a *workspace* is later in this chapter). If you're having trouble running your program, you can manually create a run configuration here, or delete a run configuration and re-create it. You can see in Figure 3.3 that the CircleArea run configuration invokes the `main` method in the CircleArea class of the GeometryWiz project.

If you have two programs running at the same time, the Console view shows both of them. To see how this works, run the CircleArea program and leave it waiting for user input. Then run the HelloWorld program. You'll see the Hello World output in the Console view, and the ▣▾ icon in its toolbar will become enabled. Clicking the triangle to its right brings up a menu of running programs, which you can use to switch between the different programs that are running simultaneously. See Figure 3.4.

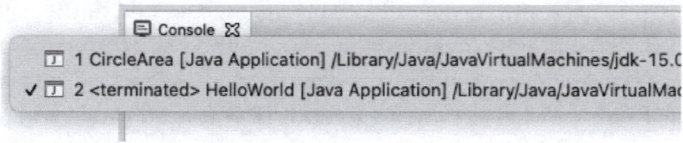

Figure 3.4: Multiple programs running in the Console view.

Two more toolbar buttons on the Console view that you should be aware of are the Stop and Close buttons (Figure 3.5). If a program is still running, the Stop button will be enabled (the one that looks like a red square). You can use it to force a program to stop, if for example you inadvertently created an infinite loop in your code. The Close button, which looks like a black "x", is next to the Stop button. It lets you close a program's output, which is handy if you have too many sessions open and you don't want confusion about which session is the most recent.

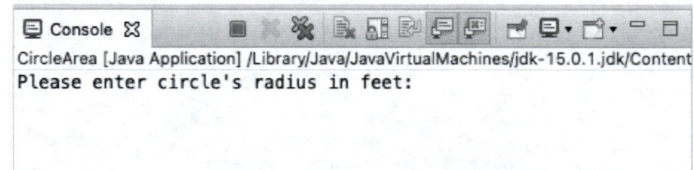

Figure 3.5: The Console view's toolbar.

Java Project: A collection of related Java classes in Eclipse.

Eclipse workspace: A collection of related Java projects along with Eclipse configuration settings.

A Java Project in Eclipse is a set of related Java classes, all under one tree within the Package Explorer view. An Eclipse workspace is the set of projects you currently have in Package Explorer, plus Eclipse's configuration settings. You can have multiple workspaces, for example, one for the assignments in your Java course, and another for the assignments in your Advanced Java course. You can switch workspaces at any time, using the "File → Switch Workspace" menu option. Choosing "Other" leads to the New Workspace dialog as shown in Figure 3.6. There, you can enter a directory to use as the root of a new workspace.

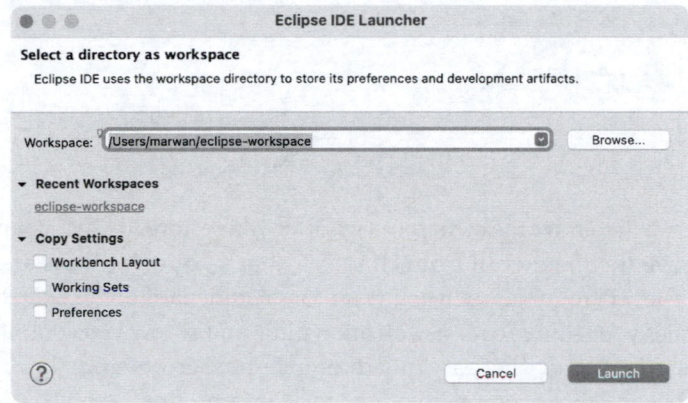

Figure 3.6: The New Workspace dialog in Eclipse.

The tree structure within the Package Explorer view is close but doesn't exactly mirror the tree of files and directories in your workspace. Rather, it's more of a logical organization of the files and other artifacts that make up a Java project. Occasionally you'll want to locate a Java file on disk. You can do that in Package Explorer by right-clicking on the Java file and choosing the "Show In $\rightarrow$ System Explorer" option. This opens a Windows Explorer window (or Finder window on MacOS) with the Java file selected.

Exercises

3.1   Refer to the bibliography and navigate to the Eclipse online help URL. Click around to familiarize yourself with the Eclipse help content.

3.2   Use the "Window $\rightarrow$ Show View" command on the main toolbar to open three or four views of your choosing, and peruse the views that appear.

3.2 Compile Errors

As you write code, Eclipse points out syntax errors. You'll see error symbols in the left margin, as well as red underlines where Eclipse thinks the error is. Hovering the mouse over either of those will show a tool tip with error information. I've illustrated this in Figure 3.7 by removing the semicolon at the end of the `print` statement.

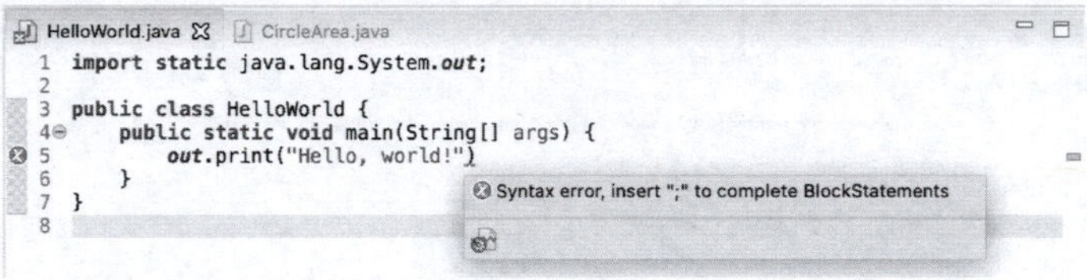

Figure 3.7: Compile-time error.

Eclipse will remove the error message after you restore the semicolon and save the file. Recall from chapter 1 that a compiler translates a high-level language such as Java into machine language. Eclipse compiles your source code as you are typing, and shows you compile errors in real-time. These are called compile-time errors since they're detected as Eclipse compiles your code. A Java program can't be run until all compile errors are fixed.

Often, multiple errors show up in your code. You should fix them one by one. Since coding mistakes sometimes result in more than one error message, sometimes it helps to fix the first error, which clears up other error messages in subsequent lines. Figure 3.8 shows an example of a single syntax error causing multiple error messages,

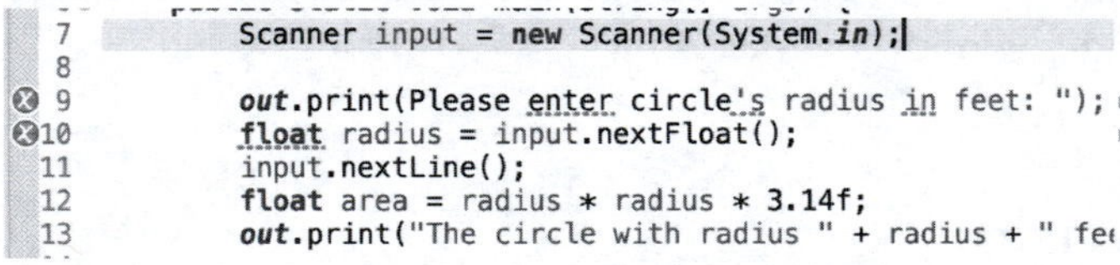

Figure 3.8: Multiple compile errors.

In figure 3.8, the missing double quote at the start of the string on line 9 caused several compile errors. There are four errors, three on line 9 and one on line 10. Hovering over each underlined section of code will show each of the four error messages, the first of which is shown below,

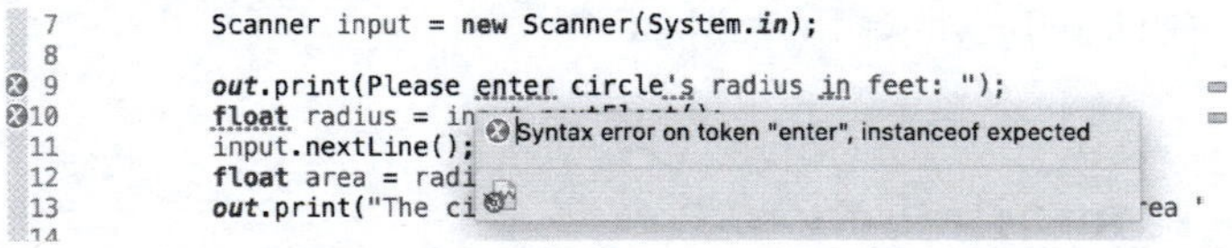

None of the four error messages actually says what the real problem is, but the first error message, "Syntax error on token "enter", instanceof expected", gives a hint that something is wrong near the word 'enter', and examining that area reveals the real problem. Adding double quotes after the opening parenthesis fixes the error. Compile errors aren't a bad thing—they're a normal part of software development. The compiler is helping you correct problems in your program.

Exercises

3.3 Enter the code in example 3.1. Remove the opening bracket that follows `public class CircleArea` on line 4 and read the compile error. Now restore the opening bracket and remove the corresponding closing bracket. Read the ensuing compile error.

3.4 Enter the following program, find the compile errors and fix them, then run it to make sure it works.

```
1  out.print("Enter your first name: ");
2  String firstName = input.nextLine;
3  out.print("Enter your last name: ");
4  String lastName = input.nextLine;
5  String fullName = firstName + " " + lastName;
6  out.printf("Hello, %s", fullName);
```

3.5 Enter the following program, find the compile errors and fix them, then run it to make sure it works.

```
1  float price1 = 19.95;
2  float price2 = 2.80;
3  float totalWithTax = price1 + price2 * 1.05;
4  out.println("Total with tax is " + totalWithTax);
```

3.3 Runtime Errors

Another kind of error you will encounter is the runtime error. These occur at runtime due to a variety of problems that can occur while your program is running. They can't be predicted by the compiler at compile-time. An example is when an integer is divided by another, and the denominator has the value zero at the time. The result is an error message at runtime, followed by the Java system terminating your program. Example 3.2 shows this,

Example 3.2. Runtime divide-by-zero error.

```
 1  import static java.lang.System.out;
 2  import java.util.Scanner;
 3
 4  public class HelloWorld {
 5    public static void main(String[] args) {
 6      Scanner input = new Scanner(System.in);
 7
 8      out.print("Please enter the rectangle's area: ");
 9      int area = input.nextInt();
10      input.nextLine();
11      out.print("Please enter the rectangle's height: ");
12      int height = input.nextInt();
13      input.nextLine();
14      int width = area / height;
15      out.print("The rectangle's width is: " + width);
16
17      input.close();
18    }
19  }
```

```
Please enter the rectangle's area: 10
Please enter the rectangle's height: 0
Exception in thread "main" java.lang.ArithmeticException: / by zero
        at HelloWorld.main(HelloWorld.java:14)
```

As you see in the above screen shot, the Java system produced an error message and the program terminated before reaching the `print` statement on line 15. Java refers to runtime errors as *exceptions*. The error message provides a lot of information about the error that occurred. From the error message in the screen shot above, we can get the following information,

Exception: An exceptional situation causing the Java program to terminate.

- The exception that occurred is of type "java.lang.ArithmeticException", and the specific error is "/ by zero".
- The error occurred in the thread called "main". Threads are simultaneous execution paths within your program, but in this simple program there is only one thread, the main thread.
- The error occurred in "HelloWorld.main", that is, the `main` method of the `HelloWorld` class.
- The error occurred in the file HelloWorld.java at line 14. Clicking the link in the error message will open that file, if it isn't already open, and highlight that line.

That's plenty to go on, and it doesn't take much detective work to get to the bottom of the issue. In chapter 4, you'll learn how to test for specific values and modify execution if a certain condition is met. In this case, the way to fix the problem is to test for the denominator being zero, and if it is, tell the user that zero is an invalid input value,

```
1   out.print("Please enter the rectangle's area: ");
2   int area = input.nextInt();
3   input.nextLine();
4   out.print("Please enter the rectangle's height: ");
5   int height = input.nextInt();
6   input.nextLine();
7   if (height == 0) {
8     out.print("The height can't be zero.");
9   }
10  else {
11    int width = area / height;
12    out.print("The rectangle's width is: " + width);
13  }
```

Example 3.3. Runtime divide-by-zero error averted.

```
Please enter the rectangle's area: 10
Please enter the rectangle's height: 0
The height can't be zero.
```

We'll leave the `if` statement's specifics for chapter 4. For now, we'll just say that the error condition was detected and the exception averted. We'll also discuss exceptions in more detail in chapter 12. In general, runtime errors are more difficult to correct than compile errors, but still are part of normal everyday life as a software developer. You'll get used to dealing with them with ease and they won't be a problem. Quite the opposite, these exceptions provide a lot of information that helps you to correct mistakes in your code.

3.4 Logic Errors

The last type of error we'll discuss is the logic error. Often, these are harder to detect and correct than compile or runtime errors, because they don't generate an error message. The program's logic is incorrect and the output will be wrong, at least for certain input values, but it's up to you to catch and correct them. We've already seen a good example of this in chapter 2, which we'll repeat here as example 3.4,

```
1   out.print("Enter degrees Celsius: ");
2   int celsius = input.nextInt();
3   input.nextLine();
4
5   int fahrenheit = 9 / 5 * celsius + 32;
6
7   out.printf("%d Celsius is %d Fahrenheit", celsius, fahrenheit);
```

Example 3.4. Example of a logic error.

```
Enter degrees Celsius: 100
100 Celsius is 132 Fahrenheit
```

This example implements the formula $Fahrenheit = 9/5\ Celsius +$ 32. One hundred degrees Celsius is 212 degrees Fahrenheit. But when we run our program and enter 100 as the Celsius temperature, the output is 132 degrees Fahrenheit. The problem as discussed in section 2.5 is that line 5 first divides 9 by 5, an integer division resulting in the value 1. To fix it, we change line 5 to use floating point division by using a floating point 9 (**9f**), then cast the final answer to an integer, as in example 3.5, which produces the right answer,

Example 3.5. Logic error corrected.

```
1   out.print("Enter degrees Celsius: ");
2   int celsius = input.nextInt();
3   input.nextLine();
4
5   int fahrenheit = (int) (9f / 5 * celsius + 32);
6
7   out.printf("%d Celsius is %d Fahrenheit", celsius, fahrenheit);
```

```
Enter degrees Celsius: 100
100 Celsius is 212 Fahrenheit
```

The programmer may not catch the erroneous computation without adequate testing. As the above example illustrates, you should carefully test your code before moving on to another task. Many professional software developers make a point to step through their code in the debugger at least once whenever they write new sections of code. We'll discuss the debugger later in the book.

Exercises

3.6   The following program has two syntax errors and one logic error. Fix them and test the program to make sure it works,

```
1   import static java.lang.System.out;
2   import java.util.Scannerr;
3
4   public class Test {
5     public static void main(String[] args) {
6
7       Scanner input = new Scanner(System.in);
8
9       out.print("Enter your full name: ");
10      String name = input.nextLine();
```

```
11    int spaceIndex = name.indexOf(' ');
12    String firstName = name.substring(0, spaceIndex));
13    String lastName = name.substring(spaceIndex + 1);
14    out.printf("First name: %s, last name: %s", lastName, firstName);
15
16    input.close();
17  }
18 }
```

Chapter Summary

- The Eclipse IDE calls your program a project. An Eclipse workspace can contain multiple projects.
- You can have multiple Eclipse workspaces, and switch between them using the "File → Switch Workspace" command.
- In Eclipse, a run configuration defines how your program is run.
- The Console view in Eclipse shows your program's output, and multiple programs can be run at once.
- Three common types of errors are:
    - Compile errors: Syntax errors in your Java code. Your program can't run while it has compile errors.
    - Runtime errors: Exceptions are thrown by your code in certain exceptional circumstances, such as attempting to divide by zero.
    - Logic errors: Mistakes in the code can cause the program to show incorrect output.

Exercise Solutions

3.4
```
1    out.print("Enter your first name: ");
2    String firstName = input.nextLine();
3    out.print("Enter your last name: ");
4    String lastName = input.nextLine();
5    String fullName = firstName + " " + lastName;
6    out.printf("Hello, %s", fullName);
```

```
Enter your first name: Rene
Enter your last name: Descartes
Hello, Rene Descartes
```

3.5
```
1    float price1 = 19.95;
2    float price2 = 2.80;
```

```
3    float totalWithTax = price1 + price2 * 1.05;
4    out.println("Total with tax is " + totalWithTax);
```

```
Total with tax is 22.890001
```

3.6

```
1  import static java.lang.System.out;
2  import java.util.Scanner;
3
4  public class Test {
5    public static void main(String[] args) {
6
7      Scanner input = new Scanner(System.in);
8
9      out.print("Enter your full name: ");
10     String name = input.nextLine();
11     int spaceIndex = name.indexOf(' ');
12     String firstName = name.substring(0, spaceIndex);
13     String lastName = name.substring(spaceIndex + 1);
14     out.printf("First name: %s, last name: %s", firstName, lastName)
         ;
15
16     input.close();
17   }
18 }
```

```
Enter your full name: Leonhard Euler
First name: Leonhard, last name: Euler
```

Conditionals | 4

4.1 Boolean Expressions

Conditional execution is when your program executes different code depending on some condition. A condition is evaluated using a boolean expression—an expression that evaluates to true or false. You saw the `boolean` data type in chapter 2. Variables of type `boolean` can only have a true or false value, and are initially false.

Several types of operators result in a boolean value. For example, we test whether two numbers are the same using the equals operator (==), which gives a boolean value that we can then use in an `if` statement. Another operator is `!=` which returns true if its two arguments are not equal. Table 4.1 shows more operators that return a boolean value.

Boolean Expression: An *expression* that has the value true or false.

Table 4.1: Common operators.

Operator	Example	
==	a == b	True if two numbers are equal.
!=	a != b	True if two numbers are not equal.
>	a > b	True if the first argument is larger than the second.
<	a < b	True if the first argument is smaller than the second.
>=	a >= b	True if the first argument is larger than or equal to the second.
<=	a <= b	True if the first argument is smaller than or equal to the second.
&&	(a > b) && (c > d)	and operator—True if a is bigger than b, *and* c is bigger than d.
||	(a > b) || (c > d)	or operator—True if a is bigger than b, *or* c is bigger than d.
!	!(a == b)	not operator—True if its argument is false.

All but the last operator in table 4.1 are *binary*. They each take two `arguments`, one on the left and one on the right. The last one is a *unary* operator, which takes a single argument. Using these operators, you can construct boolean expressions to test various conditions within your programs.

Exercises

4.1 Complete the following table,

Expression	Value
a	120
b	-12
c	0
d	31
a == b	*false*
a != b	
a > b	
a < b	
a >= b	
a <= b	
(a > b) && (c > d)	
(a > b) || (c > d)	
!(a == b)	

4.2 The `if` Statement

Here's an example of a basic `if` statement,

Example 4.1. == operator with a simple `if` statement.

```
1  boolean isEqual = false;
2  int number1 = 99 / 3;
3  int number2 = 22 + 11;
4  isEqual = number1 == number2;
5  if (isEqual) {
6    out.println("The numbers are equal");
7  }
```

```
The numbers are equal
```

Above, we declared a variable named `isEqual` of type `boolean`, and initialized its value to false. Then we declared two integer variables with values 99/3 and 22 + 11. The boolean variable is set to the result of the equality test `number1 == number2`. Since the two variables' values at runtime are equal, the boolean variable `isEqual` is assigned the value 'true'.

The `if` statement is on line 5 of example 4.1. An `if` statement must contain a boolean expression within parentheses, followed by a code block to execute if the expression evaluates to 'true'. In this case, the boolean expression consists of the single boolean variable `isEqual`, and its value is 'true', so the code within the block is executed. A code block is a set of statements enclosed by curly braces (above, this block starts on line 5 and ends on line 7).

Recall from Technique 1 on page 17 that we should always try to simplify our code. We can do this by noticing that `number1` and `number2` are only used in one place, on line 4, so we can combine lines 2-4 as shown in Example 4.2,

```
1  boolean isEqual = false;
2  isEqual = (99 / 3) == (22 + 11);
3  if (isEqual) {
4    out.println("The numbers are equal");
5  }
```

Example 4.2. Simplified version of example 4.1.

If you run the revised example, you'll see the same output. We've simplified our code while maintaining its clarity. But we can still simplify further, as shown in Example 4.3, since `isEqual` is only used in one place, on line 3, so we can get rid of the `isEqual` variable as well,

```
1  if ((99 / 3) == (22 + 11)) {
2    out.println("The numbers are equal");
3  }
```

Example 4.3. Simplified version of example 4.2.

Again, running the code produces the same output. Simplifying your code should be a natural and automatic practice as you write your programs.

An `if` statement has an optional `else` clause which is executed if its condition is false. To illustrate this, we modify our previous example to output 'not equal' in the case that the two numbers aren't equal. In addition, we'll change the program so that it prompts the user to enter the two numbers,

Example 4.4. Use of the `else` clause.

```
1  import static java.lang.System.out;
2  import java.util.Scanner;
3
4  public class HelloWorld {
5    public static void main(String[] args) {
6
7      Scanner input = new Scanner(System.in);
8
9      out.print("Enter first number: ");
10     int num1 = input.nextInt();
11     input.nextLine();
12     out.print("Enter second number: ");
13     int num2 = input.nextInt();
14     input.nextLine();
15
16     if (num1 == num2) {
17       out.println("The numbers are equal");
18     }
19     else {
20       out.println("The numbers are not equal");
21     }
22
23     input.close();
24   }
25 }
```

```
Enter first number: 17
Enter second number: 21
The numbers are not equal
```

Though we've gotten used to omitting the top few and bottom few lines of our programs in code examples, I've included them in example 4.4 to illustrate our next technique. Notice the deliberate use of blank lines between each group of related lines of code. The import statements at the top are grouped together. The declaration of the `Scanner` variable is by itself. The six lines that get the user's input are grouped together. And, the lines that make up the `if` block are grouped together. This logical grouping of lines is so that you can *quickly and easily* look at your code and visually see each section. Each section of your code is a distinct part that serves its own function within the overall *algorithm* that your code embodies. It's very important that your code be easy to traverse in this way. You will be making lots of changes as you develop and refine your programs, and having these visual groupings is essential both for the ease and speed with which you modify your program.

Technique 2. Group related code together

Organize the code within your program into logical groupings, separated by blank lines.

Another thing that you'll notice in example 4.4, as well as the other examples you've seen, is the consistent style of indenting lines of code. The lines within each block of code, delimited by curly braces, are indented one level deeper than the enclosing block. The outer block is the `class` declaration on line 4, and its curly braces are on lines 4 and 25. The next block is the `main` method declaration, starting on line 5 and ending on line 24. Notice that the entire `main` method is indented within the `class` block. Likewise, the contents of the `main` method are indented, and so are the contents of the `if` statement and its `else` clause. Eclipse by default indents blocks by four spaces, while code listings here display blocks indented only two spaces to save space. You should get used to maintaining consistent indentation at all times. Without correct indentation, you're more likely to introduce syntax or logical errors into your program.

Technique 3. Maintain proper indentation in your programs

Maintain proper indentation in your programs to keep the logical flow of the program clear, and help prevent syntax or logical errors.

Tip 3. Don't try to *memorize* techniques. Instead, *internalize* them by thinking about why we use each technique.

Eclipse can help fix your indentation via the "Source → Format" command.

Eclipse can help fix your indentation via the "Source → Format" command, but this feature usually doesn't work if you have compile errors in your code, because the compiler can't interpret the code properly in the presence of syntax errors. So we can't always rely on Eclipse to fix our indentation—we must do the work to keep our code tidy.

The two techniques you've just seen, as well as Technique 1 on page 17 are all meant to help you *quickly and easily* navigate and modify your programs. This is important, especially as your programs get longer and more sophisticated.

Java (and many other languages) allows you to omit the opening and closing braces in `if` and `else` blocks, if there is only one statement within the code block. Thus, example 4.4 can be revised as follows,

Example 4.5. Omitting opening-/closing braces when there's only one statement within the if or else code block.

```
1   out.print("Enter first number: ");
2   int num1 = input.nextInt();
3   input.nextLine();
4   out.print("Enter second number: ");
5   int num2 = input.nextInt();
6   input.nextLine();
7
8   if (num1 == num2)
9     out.println("The numbers are equal");
10  else
11    out.println("The numbers are not equal");
```

```
Enter first number: 15
Enter second number: 15
The numbers are equal
```

I prefer the final version to the one before it, since it has fewer lines, but clarity hasn't suffered. Note that the indentation as well as code block separation were maintained.

Compare strings using the equals() method instead of ==.

When comparing strings, the == operator shouldn't be used. Instead, the **equals** method of the String object should be used. For example, **str1.equals(str2)** returns true or false depending on whether the two strings are equal. The reason you can't use == is that it returns true when the two strings are *the same* string object, whereas **equals** returns true when the two string objects contain identical strings.

You can nest **if** statements to create a decision tree. Here's an example program that asks a series of questions to diagnose a medical condition,

Example 4.6. Nesting if statements.

```
1   out.print("Do you have a sore throat? ");
2   String answer = input.nextLine();
3   if (answer.equals("Yes")) {
4     out.print("Do you have a fever? ");
5     answer = input.nextLine();
6     if (answer.equals("Yes"))
7       out.print("Possibly the flu.");
8     else
9       out.print("Possibly strep throat.");
10  }
11  else {
12    out.print("are you in pain? ");
13    answer = input.nextLine();
14    if (answer.equals("Yes"))
15      out.print("Try Advil.");
16    else
17      out.print("You appear to be fine.");
18  }
```

```
Do you have a sore throat? No
are you in pain? Yes
Try Advil.
```

In this example of `if` statement nesting, the outer `if` statement, representing the question "do you have a sore throat" has two possible execution paths, one for a "yes" answer, and another for any other response. Each of the two execution paths has another `if` statement. Obviously, you could nest further `if` statements to create a more complex decision tree. Execution at runtime flows down through the decision tree based on the user's answers to each question. Note that we only declare the "answer" variable once, on line 2.

The next example (4.7) asks the user for the name of a country, and outputs its capital,

```
1   out.print("Enter country name: ");
2   String country = input.nextLine();
3
4   if (country.equals("United States"))
5     out.print("The capital is Washington, DC");
6   if (country.equals("Brazil"))
7     out.print("The capital is Brasilia");
8   if (country.equals("Canada"))
9     out.print("The capital is Ottawa");
10  if (country.equals("France"))
11    out.print("The capital is Paris");
12  if (country.equals("India"))
13    out.print("The capital is New Delhi");
```

Example 4.7. Printing the capital of a country.

```
Enter country name: France
The capital is Paris
```

Note the string comparison using the **equals** method. Also note that no output is generated if the user's input doesn't match the country name in any of the `if` statements. What if we want to output a default message, such as "not found", if the user entered an unrecognized country name? For this, we'll use **else**, as in the example 4.8,

```
1   out.print("Enter country name: ");
2   String country = input.nextLine();
3
4   if (country.equals("United States"))
5     out.print("The capital is Washington, DC");
6   else {
7     if (country.equals("Brazil"))
8       out.print("The capital is Brasilia");
9     else {
```

Example 4.8. Multiple nested `if` statements.

```
10        if (country.equals("Canada"))
11          out.print("The capital is Ottawa");
12        else {
13          if (country.equals("France"))
14            out.print("The capital is Paris");
15          else {
16            if (country.equals("India"))
17              out.print("The capital is New Delhi");
18            else
19              out.print("I don't know the capital of " + country);
20          }
21        }
22      }
23    }
```

```
Enter country name: New Zealand
I don't know the capital of New Zealand
```

Look carefully at the way each `if` statement is nested within the previous `if`'s `else` clause. If the user's input doesn't match any of the `if` statements, it keeps falling through the else clauses until it reaches the innermost else clause, where the "not found" message is printed. In Java (as well as similar languages), else clauses can be chained in a simpler way, as shown in example 4.9,

Example 4.9. Chaining `if` statements.

```
1   out.print("Enter country name: ");
2   String country = input.nextLine();
3
4   if (country.equals("United States"))
5     out.print("The capital is Washington, DC");
6   else if (country.equals("Brazil"))
7     out.print("The capital is Brasilia");
8   else if (country.equals("Canada"))
9     out.print("The capital is Ottawa");
10  else if (country.equals("France"))
11    out.print("The capital is Paris");
12  else if (country.equals("India"))
13    out.print("The capital is New Delhi");
14  else
15    out.print("I don't know the capital of " + country);
```

This syntax is equivalent to that in the prior example, but lacks the extra curly braces on each `else` clause. We're able to do this because each `else` clause only has one statement, which is the next `if` statement. Note that Java, and similar languages, consider `if` as a single statement, including its `else` clause. This syntax is preferable because it's more compact and easier to read—readability isn't sacrificed, nor is runtime efficiency since it generates the same machine code as the longer syntax.

In the above form of chaining `if` statements, each `else` clause is considered to belong to the `if` statement immediately preceding it. This is a language rule meant to clear up the ambiguity that results from omitting the curly braces. Without this rule, it would be unclear whether an else statement belongs to the first or second `if` in the following example:

```
1    if (condition1)
2    if (condition2)
3    {action 2}
4    else
5    {action 3}
```

Visualize the ambiguity in the above using each of the below indentation scenarios:

```
1    if (condition1)
2      if (condition2)
3        {action 1}
4    else
5      {action 2}
```

```
1    if (condition1)
2      if (condition2)
3        {action 1}
4      else
5        {action 2}
```

In the absence of curly braces, `else` belongs to the `if` immediately above it.

The language rule means the second scenario matches the correct runtime behavior. Note that using curly braces would remove the ambiguity, but would increase the number of lines. Also note that in Java, the compiler ignores indentation completely—indentation is there to make it easier for us humans to work with our code.

In some languages such as Python, indentation does affect the program's behavior.

The next example (4.10) shows a program that generates 10 random numbers between 1 and 100, and prints their average. After computing the average, if it's below 40, it prints "too low". If it's above 60, it prints "too high". Otherwise, it prints "normal". The `Math.random` method returns a random floating point number between 0 and 0.99999.... Multiplying it by 100 converts it to a random number between 0 and 99.99999..., then adding 1 makes a random number between 1 and 100.9999.... Finally, casting to an integer retains the integer portion, a random number between 1 and 100.

`Math.random()` generates random numbers.

```
1    int num1 = (int) (Math.random() * 100 + 1);
2    int num2 = (int) (Math.random() * 100 + 1);
3    int num3 = (int) (Math.random() * 100 + 1);
4    int num4 = (int) (Math.random() * 100 + 1);
5    int num5 = (int) (Math.random() * 100 + 1);
6    int num6 = (int) (Math.random() * 100 + 1);
7    int num7 = (int) (Math.random() * 100 + 1);
8    int num8 = (int) (Math.random() * 100 + 1);
```

Example 4.10. `if` statement example—averaging random numbers.

```
 9  int num9 = (int) (Math.random() * 100 + 1);
10  int num10 = (int) (Math.random() * 100 + 1);
11  int average = (num1 + num2 + num3 + num4 + num5 + num6 + num7 + num8 + num9 +
       num10) / 10;
12  out.println("The average is: " + average);
13  if (average < 40)
14    out.println("Too low");
15  else if (average > 60)
16    out.println("Too high");
17  else
18    out.println("Normal");
```

```
The average is: 61
Too high
```

Obviously, when you run this, you'll get different results since the program generates different random numbers each time it's run. Our last `if` statement example in this section will ask the user for the name of a country, and output the continent it's in,

Example 4.11. `if` statement example—output the continent.

```
 1  out.print("Enter country name: ");
 2  String country = input.nextLine();
 3
 4  if (country.equals("United States") || country.equals("Canada") || country.
       equals("Mexico"))
 5    out.print(country + " is in North America");
 6  else if (country.equals("Brazil") || country.equals("Chile") || country.
       equals("Argentina"))
 7    out.print(country + " is in South America");
 8  else if (country.equals("France") || country.equals("Belgium") || country.
       equals("Spain"))
 9    out.print(country + " is in Europe");
10  else if (country.equals("Egypt") || country.equals("South Africa") || country.
       equals("Kenya"))
11    out.print(country + " is in Africa");
12  else if (country.equals("China") || country.equals("India") || country.equals
       ("Cambodia"))
13    out.print(country + " is in Asia");
14  else
15    out.print("I don't know where " + country + " is.");
```

```
Enter country name: Belgium
Belgium is in Europe
```

Note the use of the *or* operator, `||`, to test whether the input matches any of a continent's countries.

Exercises

4.2   Write a program that asks the user for his car's mpg (miles per gallon). If it's below 20, the program should output 'not enough'. If it's between 20 and 30, it should output 'ok'. If it's above 30, it should output 'good'.

4.3   Write a program that asks the user for three numbers, and outputs the biggest one.

4.4   Write a program that greets the user with 'Good morning', 'Good afternoon' or 'Good evening', depending on the current hour of day. The current hour of day can be retrieved in Java using this syntax: `java.time.LocalTime.now().getHour()`.

4.5   Write a program that asks the user for a numeric grade between 0 and 100, and outputs the corresponding letter grade.

4.3 The `switch` Statement

The second most often used conditional statement in Java is `switch`. Its general format is,

```
 1  switch (expression) {
 2    case (literal value 1):
 3      (actions 1)
 4      break;
 5    case (literal value 2):
 6      (actions 2)
 7      break;
 8    case (literal value 3):
 9      (actions 3)
10      break;
11    default:
12      (actions 4)
13      break;
14  }
```

`switch` can be used when you want to compare an expression to several possible literal values. If `expression` matches `literal value 1`, then the actions under the corresponding `case` are executed. A `break` statement marks the end of the statements executed in each case block. The last `default` block is executed if none of the other `case` clauses match. Here is example 4.11, rewritten using a `switch` statement,

Example 4.12. `switch` statement example—output the continent.

```
1   out.print("Enter country name: ");
2   String country = input.nextLine();
3
4   switch (country) {
5     case "United States":
6     case "Canada":
7     case "Mexico":
8       out.print(country + " is in North America");
9       break;
10    case "Brazil":
11    case "Chile":
12    case "Argentina":
13      out.print(country + " is in South America");
14      break;
15    case "France":
16    case "Belgium":
17    case "Spain":
18      out.print(country + " is in Europe");
19      break;
20    case "Egypt":
21    case "South Africa":
22    case "Kenya":
23      out.print(country + " is in Africa");
24      break;
25    case "China":
26    case "India":
27    case "Cambodia":
28      out.print(country + " is in Asia");
29      break;
30    default:
31      out.print("I don't know where " + country + " is.");
32      break;
33  }
```

```
Enter country name: Chile
Chile is in South America
```

Note how the expression in the above example is the variable `country`, which is of type `String`. It's compared with the constant values representing country names in each `case` clause. Also note how multiple `case` clauses can be merged so that the same actions are executed if the value matches any of the constants in the `case` clauses. The `default` clause doesn't need a `break` statement, but it's frequently included. For an example like this one, using `if` and `switch` will both work, as you've seen, but I consider `switch` to be more natural, more readable and more maintainable. `switch` does have its limitations, for example, you can only compare the main expression to constant values, and you can only compare for an exact match, so something like example 4.10 that compares a value with a range can't be accomplished using `switch`.

What if the user entered "mexico" as the country name, instead of "Mexico"? If you try that with the above example, you'll see that the program doesn't recognize the country. That's because the `equals` method is *case sensitive*. To allow the program to recognize uppercase as well as lowercase input by the user, we can convert the user's input to lowercase, and compare it with the countries' names in lowercase,

Use `toLowerCase()` and `toUpperCase()` to convert a string to all lowercase or all uppercase.

```
1   out.print("Enter country name: ");
2   String country = input.nextLine();
3
4   switch (country.toLowerCase()) {
5     case "united states":
6     case "canada":
7     case "mexico":
8       out.print(country + " is in North America");
9       break;
10    case "brazil":
11    case "chile":
12    case "argentina":
13      out.print(country + " is in South America");
14      break;
15    case "france":
16    case "belgium":
17    case "spain":
18      out.print(country + " is in Europe");
19      break;
20    case "egypt":
21    case "south africa":
22    case "kenya":
23      out.print(country + " is in Africa");
24      break;
25    case "china":
26    case "india":
27    case "cambodia":
28      out.print(country + " is in Asia");
29      break;
30    default:
31      out.print("I don't know the capital of " + country);
32      break;
33  }
```

Example 4.13. Recognizing lowercase and uppercase input.

```
Enter country name: kenya
kenya is in Africa
```

Exercises

4.6   Write a program that asks the user for the name of a month, and uses a `switch` statement to output the number of days in that month.

4.7 Write a program that asks the user for a letter grade, and uses a `switch` statement to output the corresponding numeric grade range.

4.8 Fix the logic error in the following program, and test it to make sure it works,

```
1   out.print("Enter your car's miles-per-gallon: ");
2   int mpg = input.nextInt();
3   input.nextLine();
4
5   if (mpg < 25)
6     out.println("Too low");
7   if (mpg > 37)
8     out.println("Good");
9   else
10    out.println("Acceptable");
```

4.4 Conditional Expressions

Java has a way to conditionally assign one of two values to a variable based on a condition. A common pattern is using an `if` statement to assign one value or another to a variable based on a condition, such as this,

```
1   if (useSSL)
2     url = "https://" + webAddress;
3   else
4     url = "http://" + webAddress;
```

Java lets us abbreviate the above like this,

```
1   url = useSSL ? "https://" + webAddress : "http://" + webAddress;
```

This is called the question-mark-colon operator (`?:` operator). It's a ternary operator, meaning it takes three operands. The first is the condition, which must be a boolean expression, such as a boolean variable. The second operand is the result if the boolean expression is true, and the third is the result if the boolean expression is false. The question mark is positioned between the first and second operands, and the colon is positioned between the second and third operands. You'll encounter this operator occasionally, so you should be comfortable with its usage. Though it's strange at first, you'll eventually get comfortable using it, and there are times when it's natural to use it. Take for example the following line of code,

```
1   shiftsPerEmployee = numberOfEmployees == 0 ? 0 : numberOfShifts /
      numberOfEmployees;
```

This expression first checks that the number of employees isn't zero, and if so assigns a default value of zero thus avoiding a divide-by-zero exception. If the number of employees isn't zero, it divides the number of shifts by the number of employees to get the shifts per employee. The ternary operator is also useful when combined with certain features that you'll learn about in later chapters, such as testing whether a reference is null, giving a default value if it is, and following the reference if it isn't (more on that later).

You can use ?: to avoid runtime errors.

4.5 Shortcut Evaluation

We haven't yet discussed operator precedence with respect to boolean operators. Recall that in chapter 2 we listed the precedence of common arithmetic operators in table 2.4. We will now add the operators that test boolean conditions to that list:

Precedence	Operator
1	cast operator
2	- (unary negation), ! (logical 'not')
3	+, -
4	*, /, %
5	<, <=, >, >=
6	==, !=
7	&&
8	||
9	?:

Table 4.2: Operator precedence in Java.

With table 4.2 in mind, table 4.3 displays some sample expressions with the corresponding *implied* order of evaluation,

Expression	Implied evaluation order
x > 0 && y < 0	(x > 0) && (y < 0)
x > 10 || x > 0 && y < 0	(x > 10) || ((x > 0) && (y < 0))
x + y * 3 > 10 || x < 0	(x + (y * 3) > 10) || (x < 0)

Table 4.3: Operator precedence examples.

&& and \|\| are *shortcut* operators, meaning they evaluate the left-hand side only, if the right-hand side's value doesn't affect the expression's outcome. To see how this works, consider the following code,

```
1  if (age > 15 && passedDrivingTest) {
2    out.println("You can drive.");
3  }
```

The code checks two conditions, that the age is over 15 years old, and that the driving test has been passed. The code is equivalent to the following,

```
1   if (age > 15) {
2     if (passedDrivingTest) {
3       out.println("You can drive.");
4     }
5   }
```

You can see that the first condition is checked, and if it's true, the second condition is then checked, and if the second condition is also true, the message "you can drive" is printed. But, if the user's age is not over 15 years old, *the second condition isn't checked*. This is known as shortcut evaluation. The right-hand side of the && operator is only evaluated if it needs to be. This has practical implications if evaluating the right-hand side of the expression can have side effects. Consider the following code,

```
1   if (numberOfEmployees == 0 || numberOfShifts / numberOfEmployees > 2) {
2     out.println("Not enough employees are available.");
3   }
```

You can use shortcut evaluation to avoid runtime errors.

This code outputs a warning if there aren't enough employees to cover the shifts. Assuming the maximum number of shifts per employee is two, the code first checks that the number of employees is nonzero. If the number of employees is not zero, it divides the number of shifts by the number of employees, and if the result is more than two shifts per employee, the message "not enough employees" is printed. If the number of employees is zero, the right-hand side of the *or* operator isn't evaluated, thus avoiding a divide-by-zero exception.

4.6 Planning Your Projects

As you start each program, or each part of your program, you should plan ahead and break it down into simpler tasks, before you start writing code. To do this, you should write *pseudocode*, that is, an English description of what your program will do. It should have enough detail so that it's clear how to implement each part. It sounds like an obvious strategy, but it takes practice and discipline to get used to it. The pseudocode doesn't need to be elaborate—if you program is simple, the pseudocode will be quite short, which is fine. For example, consider the following exercise,

Pseudocode: An English description of the steps that make up a program's algorithm.

Write a program that accepts a date in the format "mm/dd/yyyy", and outputs the date in a long format such as "July 3, 2021".

To solve this exercise, we need to devise an algorithm that solves each requirement. We'll have to get input from the user in the required format, extract the month, day and year from the user's input, then output the month's name followed by the day and year. We could write the pseudocode as follows,

- Ask the user for the date string in the format "mm/dd/yyyy".
- Extract the month, day and year as integers from the date string that the user entered.
- Output the date in the required format, with the month name first, then day and year.

The above is perfectly good pseudocode for our program, but we should add more detail for how to accomplish the parts that aren't obvious. Specifically, how to extract the three integers from the string, and how to output the month's name given the month's number. After some thought, we can conclude that extracting three numbers from a date string in the format "mm/dd/yyyy" can be done using the two string methods `indexOf` and `substring`, as well as the `Integer.parseInt` method that we saw in chapter 2. And, printing the month's name given the month's number can be done with a `switch` statement. Our revised pseudocode might look like the following,

- Ask the user for the date string in the format "mm/dd/yyyy".
- Extract the month, day and year as integers from the date string that the user entered.
  - Extract three numbers, as strings, from the date string using indexOf() and substring().
  - Convert each of the three string numbers into integers using Integer.parseInt().
- Output the date in the required format, with the month name first, then day and year. The month's name can be output using a switch statement.

Example 4.14. Example pseudocode.

We wrote down enough detail to convince ourselves that we know how to accomplish the task, although we haven't written down *all* the details, and haven't written any code yet. You should get used to breaking down bigger tasks into smaller ones, and thinking through how a problem will be solved before writing code. How much detail to include in your pseudocode is subjective, and depends on your skill level. A rule of thumb is to omit details that are obvious to you.

> **Technique 4. Plan your projects**
>
> Break down projects into smaller tasks, and write down pseudocode before starting to implement your project. Include enough detail to convince yourself that each step can be accomplished. Think of it as the algorithm that your program will implement. It takes practice and discipline to plan your implementation before starting to write code, but you can't be a good developer without this skill. You will keep getting better the more you practice.

Exercises

4.9   Implement the pseudocode given in example 4.14: Write a program that accepts a date in the format "mm/dd/yyyy", and outputs the date in a long format such as "July 3, 2021".

4.10   Write pseudocode for example 4.6 on page 54.

Chapter Summary

- Boolean variables can have two values, true and false.
- Boolean expressions evaluate to true or false.
- The `if` statement evaluates a boolean expression and executes one of two blocks of code based on the result.
- The `switch` statement executes one of many blocks of code based on the result of an expression.
- The question-mark-colon operator (`?:`) produces one of two possible values, depending on the value of a boolean expression.

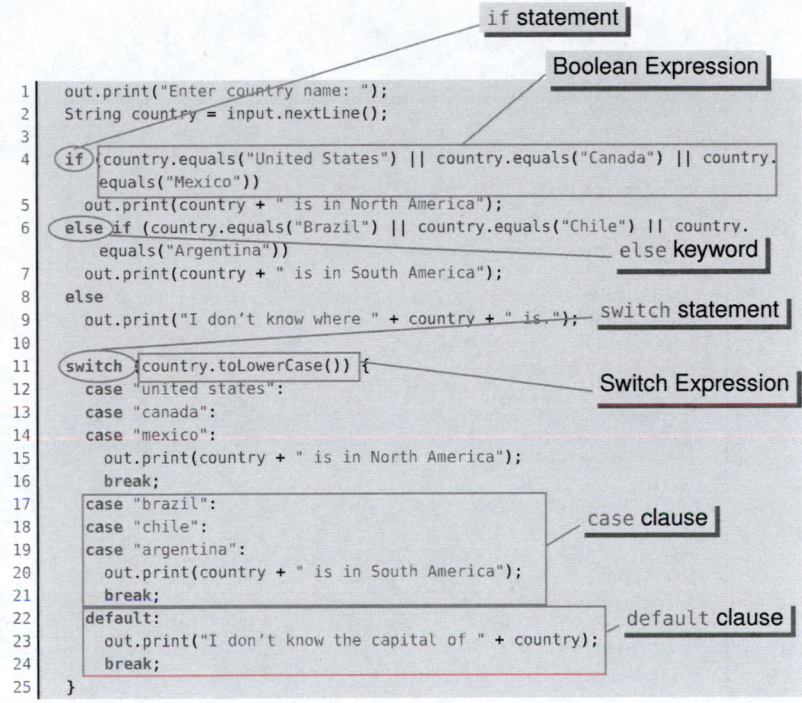

Exercise Solutions

4.1

Expression	Value
a	120
b	-12
c	0
d	31
a == b	*false*
a != b	*true*
a > b	*true*
a < b	*false*
a >= b	*true*
a <= b	*false*
(a > b) && (c > d)	*false*
(a > b) || (c > d)	*true*
!(a == b)	*true*

4.2

```
out.print("Enter miles per gallon: ");
float mpg = input.nextFloat();
```

```
3    if (mpg < 20)
4        out.println("Too low");
5    if (mpg >= 20 && mpg <= 30)
6        out.println("OK");
7    if (mpg > 30)
8        out.println("Good");
```

```
Enter miles per gallon: 37
Good
```

4.3
```
1    out.print("Enter three numbers: ");
2    float num1 = input.nextFloat();
3    float num2 = input.nextFloat();
4    float num3 = input.nextFloat();
5    out.print("The biggest is ");
6    if (num1 > num2) {
7        if (num1 > num3)
8            out.println(num1);
9        else
10           out.println(num3);
11   }
12   else {
13       if (num2 > num3)
14           out.println(num2);
15       else
16           out.println(num3);
17   }
```

```
Enter three numbers: 4 10 -2
The biggest is 10
```

4.4
```
1    int hour = java.time.LocalTime.now().getHour();
2    if (hour < 12)
3        out.print("Good morning");
4    else if (hour < 18)
5        out.print("Good afternoon");
6    else
7        out.print("Good evening");
```

```
Good evening
```

4.5
```
1    out.print("Enter grade (0-100): ");
2    int grade = input.nextInt();
3    if (grade < 60)
4        out.println("F");
5    else if (grade < 70)
6        out.println("D");
7    else if (grade < 80)
8        out.println("C");
9    else if (grade < 90)
10       out.println("B");
11   else
12       out.println("A");
```

```
Enter grade (0-100): 77
C
```

4.6

```
1    out.print("Enter a month: ");
2    String month = input.nextLine();
3    switch (month) {
4    case "February":
5      out.println(month + " has 28 days");
6      break;
7    case "January":
8    case "March":
9    case "May":
10   case "July":
11   case "August":
12   case "October":
13   case "December":
14     out.println(month + " has 31 days");
15     break;
16   default:
17     out.println(month + " has 30 days");
18     break;
19   }
```

```
Enter a month: June
June has 30 days
```

4.7

```
1    out.print("Enter a letter grade: ");
2    String month = input.nextLine();
3    switch (month) {
4    case "A":
5      out.println("90-100");
6      break;
7    case "B":
8      out.println("80-89");
9      break;
10   case "C":
11     out.println("70-79");
12     break;
13   case "D":
14     out.println("60-69");
15     break;
16   case "F":
17     out.println("0-59");
18     break;
19   default:
20     out.println("Unknown letter grade");
21     break;
22   }
```

```
Enter a letter grade: B
80-89
```

4.8

```
1    out.print("Enter your car's miles-per-gallon: ");
2    int mpg = input.nextInt();
3    input.nextLine();
4
5    if (mpg < 25)
```

```
6     out.println("Too low");
7   else if (mpg > 37)
8     out.println("Good");
9   else
10    out.println("Acceptable");
```

```
Enter your car's miles-per-gallon: 21
Too low
```

4.9

```
1   out.print("Enter date in the format 'mm/dd/yyyy': ");
2   String date = input.nextLine();
3
4   int index = date.indexOf('/');
5   int month = Integer.parseInt(date.substring(0, index));
6   date = date.substring(index+1);
7
8   index = date.indexOf('/');
9   int day = Integer.parseInt(date.substring(0, index));
10  int year = Integer.parseInt(date.substring(index+1));
11
12  String monthString = "";
13  switch (month) {
14  case 1: monthString = "January"; break;
15  case 2: monthString = "February"; break;
16  case 3: monthString = "March"; break;
17  case 4: monthString = "April"; break;
18  case 5: monthString = "May"; break;
19  case 6: monthString = "June"; break;
20  case 7: monthString = "July"; break;
21  case 8: monthString = "August"; break;
22  case 9: monthString = "September"; break;
23  case 10: monthString = "October"; break;
24  case 11: monthString = "November"; break;
25  case 12: monthString = "December"; break;
26  }
27  out.printf("%s %d, %d", monthString, day, year);
```

```
Enter date in the format 'mm/dd/yyyy': 04/21/2021
April 21, 2021
```

4.10

- Ask whether the user has a sore throat.
- If the user does have a sore throat, follow these steps:
  - Ask whether the user has a fever.
  - If the user reports having a fever, output 'Possibly the flu'.
  - If the user reports not having a fever, output 'Possibly strep throat'.
- If the user doesn't have a sore throat, follow these steps:
  - Ask whether the user is in pain.
  - If the user reports being in pain, output 'Try Advil'.

- If the user reports not being in pain, output 'You appear to be fine'.

Iteration 5

5.1 The `while` Loop

Often we need to repeat an action until a certain condition is met. Let's look back at example 4.6, which we've modified and reproduced here as example 5.1,

```
1   out.print("Do you have a sore throat? ");
2   String answer = input.nextLine().toLowerCase();
3   if (answer.equals("yes")) {
4     out.print("Do you have a fever? ");
5     answer = input.nextLine().toLowerCase();
6     if (answer.equals("yes"))
7       out.print("Possibly the flu.");
8     else
9       out.print("Possibly strep throat.");
10  }
11  else {
12    out.print("are you in pain? ");
13    answer = input.nextLine().toLowerCase();
14    if (answer.equals("yes"))
15      out.print("Try Advil.");
16    else
17      out.print("You appear to be fine.");
18  }
```

Example 5.1. Medical decision tree.

```
Do you have a sore throat? No
are you in pain? Yes
Try Advil.
```

We've modified the example from its original form by converting the user's input on lines 2, 5 and 13 to lowercase, and comparing it to a lowercase "yes". This lets our program recognize "YES" or "yes" in addition to "Yes". Suppose we want to further enhance the program so that the only acceptable inputs by the user are "yes" and "no." We would have to repeat the question until the user enters one of the acceptable answers. For this, we'll use a `while` loop,

Example 5.2. Basic while loop.

```
1  out.print("Do you have a sore throat (yes/no)? ");
2  String answer = input.nextLine().toLowerCase();
3  while (!answer.equals("yes") && !answer.equals("no")) {
4    out.print("Do you have a sore throat (yes/no)? ");
5    answer = input.nextLine().toLowerCase();
6  }
```

```
Do you have a sore throat (yes/no)? A little bit
Do you have a sore throat (yes/no)? maybe
Do you have a sore throat (yes/no)? no
are you in pain? yes
Try Advil.
```

The while statement.

The `while` statement accepts a boolean condition, just like the `if` statement does, and it has a body delimited by curly braces, just like `if`. The difference is that it executes the body repeatedly while the condition evaluates to "true", that is, until the condition evaluates to "false". In the above example, the condition checks that the answer is *not* "yes" and *not* "no". While the answer is neither yes nor no, the question is repeated and the user enters another response. Note that the variable `answer` is declared once on line 2, and used again on line 5, i.e., it's declared in one place and written to in multiple places.

There's another form of the `while` loop that checks the condition at the *bottom* of the code block, so that the code block is executed at least once. We have to add the **do** keyword before the code block, and we have to add a semicolon after the `while` condition. I'll illustrate this in example 5.3,

Example 5.3. do..while loop.

```
1  String answer;
2  do {
3    out.print("Do you have a sore throat (yes/no)? ");
4    answer = input.nextLine().toLowerCase();
5  } while (!answer.equals("yes") && !answer.equals("no"));
```

```
Do you have a sore throat (yes/no)? A little bit
Do you have a sore throat (yes/no)? maybe
Do you have a sore throat (yes/no)? no
are you in pain? yes
Try Advil.
```

This form of the `while` statement is more natural in this case, since we need to ask the question at least one time. The code block is executed, then the condition is checked, and the program repeats the question if necessary. The implementation in example 5.3 is preferable to that in example 5.1 because the two lines that print the prompt and get user input occur only once in example 5.3, but are repeated in example 5.1. Repeated code is bad for two reasons,

1. If you later need to modify the repeated code, for example by modifying the prompt in the above code, you would have to change it in two places instead of one place, and you run the risk of not making the same change, or forgetting to change one of them.
2. Repeated code usually results in a program that isn't as simple as it can be, which goes against technique 1 on page 17.

This brings us to our next technique:

> **Technique 5. Avoid repeating code**
>
> Avoid repeating code, to keep your program simple and maintainable.

You can think of this technique as a corollary to technique 1 (Simplify your code whenever you can), and is sometimes referred to as the DRY (Don't Repeat Yourself) principle.

Suppose we want to repeat an action a certain number of times. Here's an example of a loop that repeats exactly ten times,

```
1   int i = 1;
2   while (i <= 10) {
3     out.print(i + " ");
4     i = i + 1;
5   }
```

Example 5.4. Looping ten times using a `while` loop.

```
1 2 3 4 5 6 7 8 9 10
```

We've used a variable as a counter, starting with the value 1. Each time the loop's body executes, the current value is printed, followed by a space, and the counter's value is incremented by 1. Once the count reaches 11 at the end of the tenth iteration, the `while` loop's condition becomes false and the loop terminates.

It's customary to use i, j and k as loop counters. This custom dates back to the C language, which Java is derived from, and from there probably dates back to the field of mathematics where i, j and k are common variables in summations, such as $\sum_{i=1}^{10} i$.

Exercises

5.1 Write a program that accepts an integer from the user, and prints each digit on a line by itself. Use a `while` loop, repeatedly printing the number *mod* 10, then dividing it by 10, until the number reaches zero.

5.2 Write the program in example 5.1, and use the code in example 5.3 for each of the three diagnostic questions that the user is asked.

5.2 The `for` Loop

A more natural way to count to ten is using the `for` loop. The general structure of a `for` loop is as follows,

```
for ((start action); (loop condition); (end action)) {
    (statements)
}
```

where the "start action" is a statement that is executed once before the loop begins, the "loop condition" is the condition to keep looping, and the "end action" is code that gets executed *after each iteration*. Here's the previous example of counting to ten, rewritten as a `for` loop,

Example 5.5. Looping ten times using a `for` loop.

```
for (int i = 1; i <= 10; i = i + 1) {
    out.print(i + " ");
}
```

```
1 2 3 4 5 6 7 8 9 10
```

The code in examples 5.4 and 5.5 is equivalent. Each of them initializes the loop counter to 1, keeps looping while the loop counter is less than or equal to 10, increments the loop counter after each iteration, and prints the loop counter each time through the loop.

The `while` and `for` loops are like the `if` statement in that the curly braces can be omitted if code block only contains one statement. So, example 5.5 can be rewritten as follows,

```
1  for (int i = 1; i <= 10; i = i + 1)
2    out.print(i + " ");
```

Java has additional assignment operators that we haven't covered yet. If you're incrementing a variable, there's a shorter syntax. Instead of x = x + 10, we can use x += 10. And, if we're incrementing by one, we can use x++. So, the following three statements are equivalent,

```
1  x = x + 1;
2  x += 1;
3  x ++;
```

So the above loop can now be rewritten as,

```
1  for (int i = 1; i <= 10; i++)
2    out.print(i + " ");
```

Finally, it's customary in Java, and many other languages, to start the for-loop counter at zero. So the usual syntax is,

```
1  for (int i = 0; i < 10; i++)
2    out.print((i + 1) + " ");
```

```
1 2 3 4 5 6 7 8 9 10
```

The reason loop counters customarily start at zero is largely due to the fact that array indexes start at zero—we'll get to that in the next chapter.

Some of this may look strange at first, especially starting the loop counter at zero, but it's the most common pattern and you'll get used to it quickly.

Exercises

5.3 Write a for loop that prints the even numbers from 2 to 20.

5.4 Write a for loop that prints the square root of the integers from 1 to 10. To get the square root of an integer i, use the syntax Math.sqrt(i).

5.3 Loops and Math

Let's look at a few more examples of the for loop. The following program (example 5.6) uses the Math.pow method to calculate the first twenty powers of 2. Math.pow() takes two arguments, the

Math.pow() raises a number to a power.

base and the exponent, and returns the result as a floating point number,

Example 5.6. Using a loop to print the powers of 2.

```
1  for (int i = 0; i <= 20; i++)
2    out.print((int) Math.pow(2, i) + " ");
```

```
1 2 4 8 16 32 64 128 256 512 1024 2048 4096 8192 16384 32768 65536 13
```

The output starts with 1 since the loop counter is 0 the first time through the loop, and 2^0 is 1. Next we print the first ten negative powers of 2,

Example 5.7. Using a loop to print the negative powers of 2.

```
1  for (int i = 0; i >= -10; i--)
2    out.print(Math.pow(2, i) + " ");
```

```
1.0 0.5 0.25 0.125 0.0625 0.03125 0.015625 0.0078125 0.00390625 0.0019
```

This prints the values of $2^0, 2^{-1}, 2^{-2}$, and so on, so the loop counter starts at zero and is decremented by one each time through the loop, stopping at -10.

The next example (5.8) prints the value of π rounded to one digit, two digits, and so on,

Example 5.8. Using a loop to print the value of π rounded to one digit, two digits, and so on.

```
1  for (int i = 1; i <= 10; i++)
2    out.print(Math.round(Math.PI * Math.pow(10, i)) / Math.pow(10, i) + " ");
```

```
3.1 3.14 3.142 3.1416 3.14159 3.141593 3.1415927 3.14159265 3.1415926
```

The formula to round a floating point number x to i digits is:

$$Math.round(x * Math.pow(10, i))/Math.pow(10, i)$$

`Math.round()` rounds a floating point number to the nearest integer.

The number x is multiplied by 10 to the power i, rounded, then the result is divided by 10 to the power i. This is illustrated in table 5.1 by showing the intermediate values of the calculation where x is π and i is 3,

We saw in example 4.10 how to generate a random number between 1 and 100. With loops under our belt, we can write a program to print 100 random numbers,

Expression	Value
i	3
10^i	1000
π	3.141593
$\pi * 10^i$	3141.593
$Math.Round(\pi * 10^i)$	3142
$Math.Round(\pi * 10^i) / 10^i$	3.142

Table 5.1: The steps to compute the rounded π value.

```
1  for (int i = 1; i <= 100; i++) {
2     out.print((int) (Math.random() * 100 + 1) + " ");
3     if (i % 20 == 0)
4        out.println();
5  }
```

Example 5.9. Printing 100 random numbers.

```
23 70 99 88 77 3 41 21 88 78 77 84 82 36 89 51 1 79 44 78
26 52 87 60 7 62 12 82 83 57 57 5 96 9 68 53 32 45 58 8
57 22 5 42 73 48 7 40 19 12 59 93 41 84 88 40 49 37 2 46
79 18 54 39 82 28 91 46 77 96 13 72 100 59 100 49 8 88 35 19
8 25 71 79 3 57 34 6 58 46 53 75 44 53 19 55 6 21 26 28
```

We've added code to advance the output to the next line after every 20 random numbers. To do this, the `if` statement tests whether the loop counter is evenly divisible by 20, and if so, `println` is called. We'll enhance our program by computing the overall average of the 100 numbers, and print out the average before the program terminates,

```
1  int sum = 0;
2  for (int i = 1; i <= 100; i++) {
3     int number = (int) (Math.random() * 100 + 1);
4     sum += number;
5     out.print(number + " ");
6     if (i % 20 == 0)
7        out.println();
8  }
9  out.println("The average is: " + sum / 100);
```

Example 5.10. Printing 100 random numbers with their average.

```
46 12 77 52 34 88 18 59 92 47 66 83 23 69 69 5 71 95 13 17
18 38 31 81 91 82 52 21 76 36 4 90 10 89 80 91 38 76 63 89
73 83 5 25 47 16 86 8 37 97 93 88 50 98 62 100 3 65 4 23
77 3 46 25 6 22 62 54 94 20 59 71 46 43 13 70 73 42 38 76
40 79 38 97 45 19 99 5 43 6 39 87 13 58 55 96 62 1 29 91
The average is: 51
```

We've added code to add the random numbers by declaring a new variable, `sum`, initializing it to zero and adding each random number to it within the loop. Then after the loop terminates, we divide the sum by the number of random numbers to get the average.

Let's continue the example of producing an average of several numbers, but this time the user will be asked to enter each of the numbers. The user can enter a zero to exit the program,

Example 5.11. Printing the average of user-entered numbers.

```
1   int sum = 0;
2   int count = 0;
3   int number = 0;
4   do {
5     out.print("Enter a number (0 to exit): ");
6     number = input.nextInt();
7     input.nextLine();
8     if (number != 0) {
9       sum += number;
10      count ++;
11    }
12  } while (number != 0);
13  out.println("The average is: " + sum / count);
```

```
Enter a number (0 to exit): 55
Enter a number (0 to exit): 70
Enter a number (0 to exit): 59
Enter a number (0 to exit): 0
The average is: 61
```

This time, we use a `do...while` loop instead of a `for` loop, since we don't know beforehand how many numbers will be averaged. The user enters each number, entering 0 to exit from the loop. The sum is computed as before, and we've also keep a count of the numbers to be averaged. After the loop terminates, we divide the sum by the count to get the average.

Exercises

5.5 Use a while loop to print random numbers between 1 and 10 until the total of the random numbers exceeds 100.

5.6 Modify example 5.10 to accept a number from the user, and generate that many random numbers, printing the average after the loop terminates.

5.7 Fix the logic error in the following program, and test it to make sure it works,

```
1   int sum = 0;
2   for (int i = 1; i <= 10; i++) {
3     out.print((int) (Math.random() * 100 + 1) + " ");
4     sum += (int) (Math.random() * 100 + 1);
5   }
6   out.printf("\nThe sum of the above random numbers is %d", sum);
```

5.4 The break Statement

Using the break statement within a while or for loop causes it to
terminate immediately. We can rewrite the previous example as
follows,

```
1    int sum = 0;
2    int count = 0;
3    do {
4      out.print("Enter a number (0 to exit): ");
5      int number = input.nextInt();
6      input.nextLine();
7      if (number == 0)
8        break;
9      sum += number;
10     count ++;
11   } while (true);
12   out.println("The average is: " + sum / count);
```

Example 5.12. Using the break statement.

```
Enter a number (0 to exit): 55
Enter a number (0 to exit): 70
Enter a number (0 to exit): 59
Enter a number (0 to exit): 0
The average is: 61
```

When the user enters the value 0, the break statement is executed
to exit the loop. Note that the loop condition on line 11 has been
changed to true, since exiting the loop is done via break instead of
relying on a loop condition.

When using break to terminate a for loop, you may not need the
loop's condition anymore. Unlike while where we changed the loop
condition to 'true', a for loop's condition can be absent which has
the same effect. Note that the second semicolon is still required in
this situation,

```
1    for (int i = 1; ; i++) {
2      out.print(i + " ");
3      if (i == 10)
4        break;
5    }
```

Exercises

5.8 Rewrite example 5.2 to use a break statement when the user enters 'yes' or 'no' to terminate the loop.

5.9 Rewrite example 5.10 to use a break statement when the count reaches 100. The **for** loop's condition should be empty, so the **for** statement should look like this: *for (int i = 1; ; i++).*

5.5 The `continue` Statement

`continue` is another statement that is used to alter the normal flow of control in a loop. It's used to skip the rest of the *current* iteration of the loop, but doesn't cause the program to exit from the loop. It just skips the current iteration and causes the loop to begin the next iteration by evaluating the loop condition again. When used in a **for** loop, the **continue** statement causes the loop counter to be incremented before the loop condition is evaluated again. Example 5.13 loops through the numbers from 1 to 40, and prints those which aren't divisible by any number from 2 to 6,

Example 5.13. Using the `continue` statement.

```
for (int i = 1; i <= 40; i++) {
    if (i % 2 == 0 || i % 3 == 0 || i % 4 == 0 || i % 5 == 0 || i % 6 == 0)
        continue;
    out.println("The number " + i + " isn't divisible by 2, 3, 4, 5 or 6");
}
```

```
The number 1 isn't divisible by 2, 3, 4, 5 or 6
The number 7 isn't divisible by 2, 3, 4, 5 or 6
The number 11 isn't divisible by 2, 3, 4, 5 or 6
The number 13 isn't divisible by 2, 3, 4, 5 or 6
The number 17 isn't divisible by 2, 3, 4, 5 or 6
The number 19 isn't divisible by 2, 3, 4, 5 or 6
The number 23 isn't divisible by 2, 3, 4, 5 or 6
The number 29 isn't divisible by 2, 3, 4, 5 or 6
The number 31 isn't divisible by 2, 3, 4, 5 or 6
The number 37 isn't divisible by 2, 3, 4, 5 or 6
```

As the loop checks each number from 1 to 40, the "continue" statement is executed if the number is divisible by 2, 3, 4, 5 or 6. This causes the rest of the iteration (which is just the `println` statement in this case) to be skipped, and the loop counter is incremented then the loop condition is checked in preparation for the next iteration.

The `continue` statement is not used frequently, and you can usually get by without it with ease, but it's important to know and you'll find yourself using it occasionally.

5.6 Nested Loops

Loops are often nested, which allows the programmer to tackle many real-world situations. For example, suppose your program tracks airline flights. You might want to loop through a list of flights, and for each flight, loop through the list of passengers. This is done using a nested loop (that is, a loop within a loop), illustrated by the following pseudocode,

- Initialize total revenue r to zero.
- For each flight f, perform the following actions:
  - For each passenger p on flight f, perform the following actions:
    - Add passenger p's ticket price to the total revenue r.
- Output the total revenue r.

Example 5.14. Pseudocode for a nested loop.

Once we cover arrays and collections, we'll be able to implement the code illustrated by the pseudocode in example 5.14. Here's another simple example of a nested loop, constructing a multiplication table for numbers from 1 to 10,

```
for (int i = 1; i <= 10; i++) {
  for (int j = 1; j <= 10; j++)
    out.print(i * j + " ");
  out.println();
}
```

Example 5.15. Printing a multiplication table.

```
1 2 3 4 5 6 7 8 9 10
2 4 6 8 10 12 14 16 18 20
3 6 9 12 15 18 21 24 27 30
4 8 12 16 20 24 28 32 36 40
5 10 15 20 25 30 35 40 45 50
6 12 18 24 30 36 42 48 54 60
7 14 21 28 35 42 49 56 63 70
8 16 24 32 40 48 56 64 72 80
9 18 27 36 45 54 63 72 81 90
10 20 30 40 50 60 70 80 90 100
```

The multiplication table's rows are printed one at a time. The outer loop prints each row, with the loop counter `i` representing the row number, and the inner loop prints the columns, with the loop counter j representing the column number. Each iteration through the inner loop prints one number, the product of row and column numbers, followed by a space. After the inner loop terminates, `println` is called to advance to the next line.

We'll make a couple of improvements to this example. We'll print the row and column headers, and we'll use printf to pad each number so that it takes up four spaces—that way the columns will line up,

Example 5.16. Improved multiplication table.

```
 1   out.print("        ");
 2   for (int j = 1; j <= 10; j++)
 3     out.printf("%4d", j);
 4   out.println();
 5   out.println();
 6   for (int i = 1; i <= 10; i++) {
 7     out.printf("%4d    ", i);
 8     for (int j = 1; j <= 10; j++)
 9       out.printf("%4d", i * j);
10     out.println();
11   }
```

```
           1    2    3    4    5    6    7    8    9   10

      1    1    2    3    4    5    6    7    8    9   10
      2    2    4    6    8   10   12   14   16   18   20
      3    3    6    9   12   15   18   21   24   27   30
      4    4    8   12   16   20   24   28   32   36   40
      5    5   10   15   20   25   30   35   40   45   50
      6    6   12   18   24   30   36   42   48   54   60
      7    7   14   21   28   35   42   49   56   63   70
      8    8   16   24   32   40   48   56   64   72   80
      9    9   18   27   36   45   54   63   72   81   90
     10   10   20   30   40   50   60   70   80   90  100
```

Lines 1-3 print the header containing column numbers, followed by a blank line (lines 4 and 5). Line 7 prints the row header followed by blank spaces. Each number is now printed with `printf` with "%4d" as format specifier, which causes the number to be printed within four characters. The fixed-width font, which is the default for the Console view, helps to make each column line up correctly.

Here's another example of loop nesting which prints an asterisk if the row index is less than the column index. This produces a triangle,

```
1  for (int i = 0; i <= 8; i++) {
2    for (int j = 0; j <= 8; j++)
3      if (j < i)
4        out.print("*");
5    out.println();
6  }
```

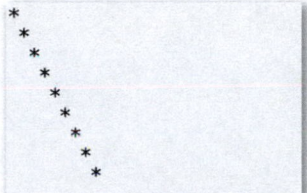

Example 5.17. Printing a triangle.

We could print just the diagonal line by printing an asterisk where j
== i, and a space character otherwise,

```
1  for (int i = 0; i <= 8; i++) {
2    for (int j = 0; j <= 8; j++)
3      if (j == i)
4        out.print("*");
5      else
6        out.print(" ");
7    out.println();
8  }
```

The other diagonal can be printed by changing our condition from
j == i to 8 - j == i (where 8 is one less than the number of
columns),

```
1  for (int i = 0; i <= 8; i++) {
2    for (int j = 0; j <= 8; j++)
3      if (8-j == i)
4        out.print("*");
5      else
6        out.print(" ");
7    out.println();
8  }
```

And, we can test for *either* j == i or 8 - j == i to print both
diagonals,

```
1  for (int i = 0; i <= 8; i++) {
2    for (int j = 0; j <= 8; j++)
3      if (j == i || 8-j == i)
4        out.print("*");
5      else
6        out.print(" ");
7    out.println();
8  }
```

There's one more thing I want to do—this code can be simplified by
combining lines 3-6 using the question-mark-colon operator,

```
1  for (int i = 0; i <= 8; i++) {
2    for (int j = 0; j <= 8; j++)
3      out.print((j == i || 8-j == i) ? "*" : " ");
4    out.println();
5  }
```

Example 5.18. Printing both diagonals.

Here, we've simplified our program without sacrificing clarity or runtime performance, applying technique 1 from page 17.

Exercises

5.10   Use the multiplication table code in example 5.16 to create a 5x5 table of powers. Use `Math.pow()` as in example 5.6 to generate `i` to the power `j` for each table cell. You'll have to cast the result of `Math.pow()` to an integer, and you'll have to increase the number of spaces used by each number to 5.

5.11   Use nested loops to print a two-dimensional grid representing a monthly calendar. Assume the first day of the month falls on a Sunday.

5.12   Modify example 5.18 to print an hourglass shape, as shown in this picture:

5.7 Printing Log Messages

A common technique for debugging programs is to generate logging output at different points of the program's execution. These are simple `println` statements inserted at key points within the code, to help the programmer find a particular bug. Let's use examples 5.1 and 5.3 to illustrate this. I've reproduced the code here as example 5.19 with an intentional mistake causing incorrect output,

```
1   String answer;
2   do {
3     out.print("Do you have a sore throat (yes/no)? ");
4     answer = input.nextLine().toLowerCase();
5   } while (!answer.equals("yes") || !answer.equals("no"));
6
7   if (answer.equals("yes")) {
8
9     do {
10      out.print("Do you have a fever? ");
11      answer = input.nextLine().toLowerCase();
12    } while (!answer.equals("yes") || !answer.equals("no"));
13
14    if (answer.equals("yes"))
15      out.print("Possibly the flu.");
16    else
17      out.print("Possibly strep throat.");
18  }
19  else {
20
21    do {
22      out.print("are you in pain? ");
23      answer = input.nextLine().toLowerCase();
24    } while (!answer.equals("yes") || !answer.equals("no"));
25
26    if (answer.equals("yes"))
27      out.print("Try Advil.");
28    else
29      out.print("You appear to be fine.");
30  }
```

Example 5.19. Program containing a bug.

```
Do you have a sore throat (yes/no)? No
Do you have a sore throat (yes/no)?
```

The problem is that the program won't let the user past the first question, even though the user's answer is valid. We add a diagnostic output message within the loop to check that our loop condition has the expected value, and then run the program again,

```
1   do {
2     out.print("Do you have a sore throat (yes/no)? ");
3     answer = input.nextLine().toLowerCase();
4
5     out.println("!answer.equals(\"yes\") || !answer.equals(\"no\") = " +
6       (!answer.equals("yes") || !answer.equals("no")));
7
8   } while (!answer.equals("yes") || !answer.equals("no"));
```

```
🖵 Console ✕              ▉ ✖ ✖ ᴇₓ 🔠 ᴇ₂ 🗗 🗗  🔏 🖳 ⋅ 🗗 ⋅  ▭
HelloWorld [Java Application] /Library/Java/JavaVirtualMachines/jdk-15.0.1.jdk/Contents/Home
Do you have a sore throat (yes/no)? No
!answer.equals("yes") || !answer.equals("no") = true
Do you have a sore throat (yes/no)? Yes
!answer.equals("yes") || !answer.equals("no") = true
Do you have a sore throat (yes/no)?
```

Infinite Loop: A loop that iterates forever, forcing the user to terminate the program.

As we test this program, we see the value of the loop condition printed out after each answer is entered. Once we've confirmed that the loop condition is true even when the input is valid, we know that's the cause of the infinite loop. Further inspection of the loop condition reveals that the *or* condition should be *and*. We can then correct the program and test it,

```
1   String answer;
2   do {
3     out.print("Do you have a sore throat (yes/no)? ");
4     answer = input.nextLine().toLowerCase();
5   } while (!answer.equals("yes") && !answer.equals("no"));
6
7   if (answer.equals("yes")) {
8
9     do {
10      out.print("Do you have a fever? ");
11      answer = input.nextLine().toLowerCase();
12    } while (!answer.equals("yes") && !answer.equals("no"));
13
14    if (answer.equals("yes"))
15      out.print("Possibly the flu.");
16    else
17      out.print("Possibly strep throat.");
18  }
19  else {
20
21    do {
22      out.print("are you in pain? ");
23      answer = input.nextLine().toLowerCase();
24    } while (!answer.equals("yes") && !answer.equals("no"));
25
26    if (answer.equals("yes"))
27      out.print("Try Advil.");
28    else
29      out.print("You appear to be fine.");
30  }
```

```
Do you have a sore throat (yes/no)? No
are you in pain? Yes
Try Advil.
```

Using log files.

A Production system runs on dedicated servers that are separate from development servers.

Log messages are commonly written to log files, which are particularly useful in production systems where the developer is typically unable to use the debugger (we discuss the debugger in the next section).

Technique 6. Use diagnostic output messages for debugging

Use diagnostic output messages to trace program execution and print values of expressions at runtime. This can help narrow down the cause of bugs in your code.

5.8 Using the Debugger

Another technique you should be familiar with is using the debugger
to follow program execution and examine the values of variables as
the program is running. To illustrate this, we return to the version
of the program containing a bug in example 5.19.

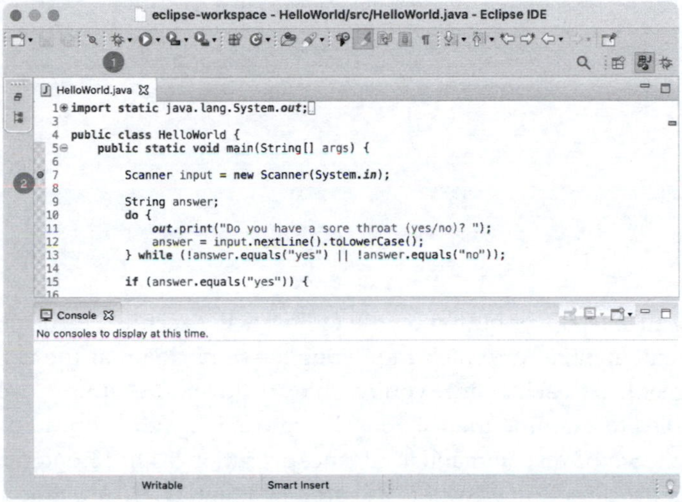

Figure 5.1: Eclipse with a breakpoint.

The blue left margin in the editor view within Eclipse can be double-
clicked to add a breakpoint at a line of code. This breakpoint appears
as a blue dot, highlighted as "2" in figure 5.1. A debugging session is
similar to running the program, but it puts Eclipse in debug mode,
and is initiated using the debug button on the toolbar, highlighted
as "1" in figure 5.1. Once debugging is started, the program runs
normally until it reaches a breakpoint, at which point it enters a
different *perspective* as shown in figure 5.2,

Perspective: An Eclipse layout showing certain views that are related to
each other.

The program is now in the debug perspective, and is stopped at
line 7 where we placed a breakpoint. The blue margin contains the
current execution point, shown as an arrow, partly obscured by the
breakpoint which is also on line 7 (label "1"). The call stack is in
the Debug view and shows the currently executing method, in our
case the `main` method (label "2"). The Variables view shows local
variables in the current stack frame, `args` being the only variable
currently shown here (label "3"). Finally, the toolbar sports buttons
useful in debug mode, such as Step Into, Step Over and Resume
(label "4").

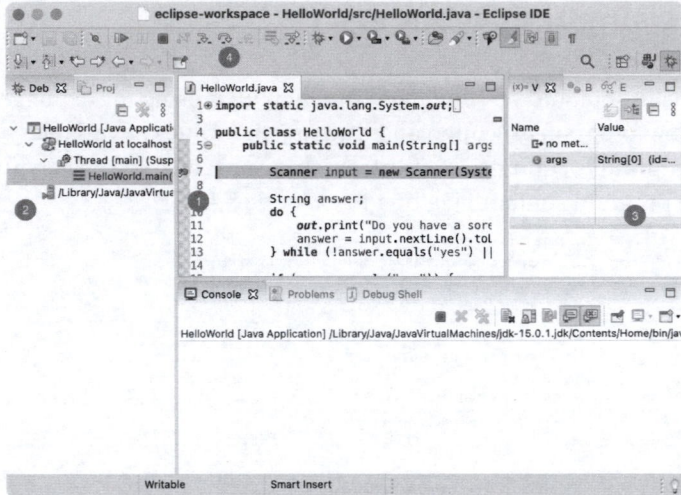

Figure 5.2: Eclipse in the debug perspective.

Using the Step Over button on the toolbar will execute the current Java statement, after which the debugger stops again at the next statement. At each point, you're able to hover the mouse over variables to examine their values. In figure 5.3, we've repeatedly used the Step Over command to advance execution to line 13, entering 'No' in the console in answer to the prompt at line 12. Once at line 13, we've hovered the mouse over the answer variable to see its value,

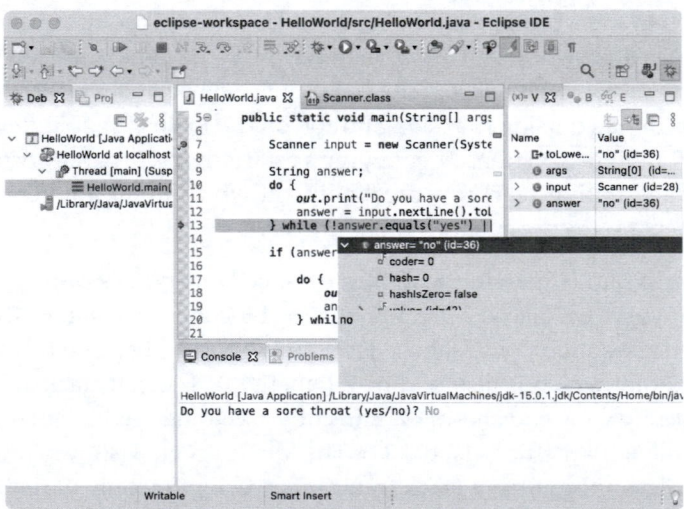

Figure 5.3: Stopped at a breakpoint to examine the value of answer.

We've entered the value "No", but hovering over the variable answer shows its value as "no", the result of calling toLowerCase(). answer's value can also be seen in the Variables view at this point.

We can also open the Expressions view, which initially is a tab to the right of the Variables view, and enter expressions of our choosing to evaluate them in real-time. Figure 5.4 shows the Expressions tab, which I've made wider for illustration, and I've entered a couple of expressions including the `while` loop's condition, to see their results,

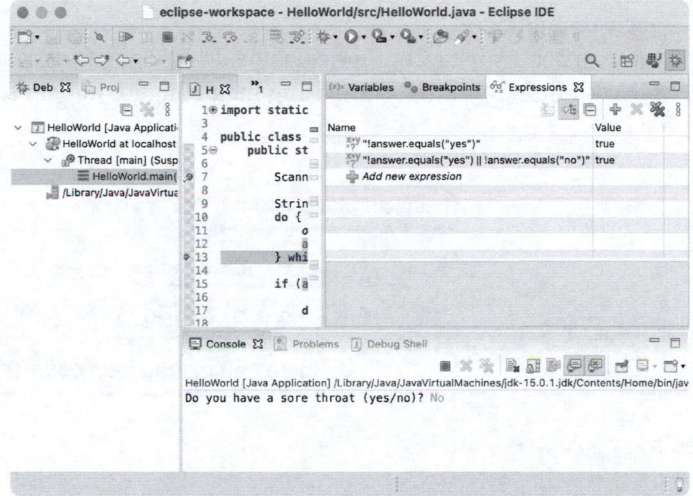

Figure 5.4: Evaluating expressions in the Expressions view of the debugger.

Stepping through the program and looking at variables' values, it doesn't take long for us to realize what's wrong with the `while` loop's condition and fix it. Once you're done with the debugger, you can switch back to the Java perspective using the "Window → Perspective → Open Perspective → Java" command.

> **Technique 7. Use the debugger to locate bugs at runtime**
>
> Use the debugger to locate bugs at runtime—it has a variety of features that allow you to control your program's execution, examine variables, navigate the call stack, and much more.

Chapter Summary

- The `while` statement executes a block of code repeatedly until a boolean expression evaluates to false. It's suitable for repetition when the number of iterations isn't known in advance.

- The `for` statement executes a block of code repeatedly until a boolean expression evaluates to false, while also maintaining a loop counter. It's useful for repeating a specific number of times.
- The `break` statement causes execution to exit from a loop immediately.
- The `continue` statement causes execution to skip the rest of the current iteration.
- Common debugging techniques include using log messages as well as stepping through code using the debugger in Eclipse.

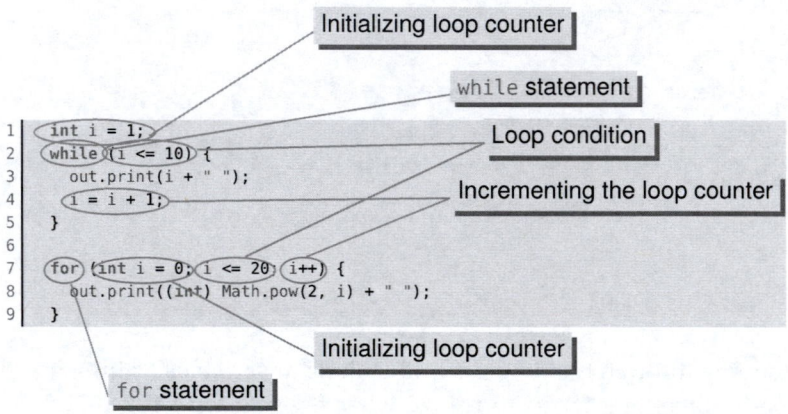

Exercise Solutions

5.1

```
1   out.print("Enter a number: ");
2   int number = input.nextInt();
3   input.nextLine();
4
5   while (number > 0) {
6       out.println(number % 10);
7       number = number / 10;
8   }
```

```
Enter a number: 431
1
3
4
```

5.2

```
1   String answer;
2   do {
3       out.print("Do you have a sore throat (yes/no)? ");
4       answer = input.nextLine().toLowerCase();
```

```
 5      } while (!answer.equals("yes") && !answer.equals("no"));
 6
 7      if (answer.equals("yes")) {
 8        do {
 9          out.print("Do you have a fever? ");
10          answer = input.nextLine().toLowerCase();
11        } while (!answer.equals("yes") && !answer.equals("no"));
12        if (answer.equals("yes"))
13          out.print("Possibly the flu.");
14        else
15          out.print("Possibly strep throat.");
16      }
17      else {
18        do {
19          out.print("are you in pain? ");
20          answer = input.nextLine().toLowerCase();
21        } while (!answer.equals("yes") && !answer.equals("no"));
22        if (answer.equals("yes"))
23          out.print("Try Advil.");
24        else
25          out.print("You appear to be fine.");
26      }
```

```
Do you have a sore throat (yes/no)? nope
Do you have a sore throat (yes/no)? no
are you in pain? no
You appear to be fine.
```

5.3
```
1   for (int i = 2; i <= 20; i = i + 2)
2     out.print(i + " ");
```

```
2 4 6 8 10 12 14 16 18 20
```

5.4
```
1   for (int i = 1; i <= 10; i++)
2     out.printf("%.3f ", Math.sqrt(i));
```

```
1.000 1.414 1.732 2.000 2.236 2.449 2.646 2.828 3.000 3.162
```

5.5
```
1   int sum = 0;
2   while (sum <= 100) {
3     int number = (int) (Math.random() * 10 + 1);
4     sum += number;
5     out.print (number + " ");
6   }
```

```
8 5 2 7 1 10 1 5 1 4 6 8 10 8 3 5 3 2 5 3 8
```

5.6
```
1   out.print("How many random numbers do you want? ");
2   int count = input.nextInt();
3   input.nextLine();
4   int sum = 0;
5   for (int i = 1; i <= count; i++) {
6     int number = (int) (Math.random() * 100 + 1);
7     sum += number;
```

```
8    out.print(number + " ");
9    if (i % 20 == 0)
10     out.println();
11   }
12   out.printf("\nThe average is: %.2f", (float) sum / count);
```

```
How many random numbers do you want? 30
12 74 69 79 47 23 100 97 30 60 5 41 26 89 88 77 41 41 6 32
14 25 60 59 32 86 15 93 25 67
The average is: 50.43
```

5.7

```
1    int sum = 0;
2    for (int i = 1; i <= 10; i++) {
3      int number = (int) (Math.random() * 100 + 1);
4      out.print(number + " ");
5      sum += number;
6    }
7    out.printf("\nThe sum of the above random numbers is %d", sum);
```

```
10 78 30 70 88 28 10 55 18 7
The sum of the above random numbers is 394
```

5.8

```
1    out.print("Do you have a sore throat (yes/no)? ");
2    String answer = input.nextLine().toLowerCase();
3    while (true) {
4      out.print("Do you have a sore throat (yes/no)? ");
5      answer = input.nextLine().toLowerCase();
6      if (answer.equals("yes") || answer.equals("no"))
7        break;
8    }
```

```
Do you have a sore throat (yes/no)? a little bit
Do you have a sore throat (yes/no)? yes
```

5.9

```
1    int sum = 0;
2    for (int i = 1; ; i++) {
3      int number = (int) (Math.random() * 100 + 1);
4      sum += number;
5      out.print(number + " ");
6      if (i % 20 == 0)
7        out.println();
8      if (i == 100)
9        break;
10   }
11   out.println("The average is: " + sum / 100);
```

```
16 29 37 78 12 84 41 26 18 78 46 10 27 77 56 94 18 16 51 86
97 18 53 8 80 87 1 80 59 13 36 82 88 62 47 18 91 8 92 45
38 50 23 50 3 12 68 35 69 11 93 44 76 89 35 36 58 36 36 79
52 83 34 32 84 94 47 41 47 93 86 94 37 73 59 33 16 25 87 37
29 32 31 73 95 80 51 18 25 65 54 37 5 60 53 47 26 56 66 45
The average is: 50
```

5.10

```
1    out.print("      ");
2    for (int j = 1; j <= 5; j++)
3      out.printf("%5d", j);
```

```
 4    out.printtln();
 5    out.println();
 6    for (int i = 1; i <= 5; i++) {
 7      out.printf("%5d   ", i);
 8      for (int j = 1; j <= 5; j++)
 9        out.printf("%5d", (int) Math.pow(i, j));
10      out.println();
11    }
```

```
          1    2    3    4    5

    1     1    1    1    1    1
    2     2    4    8   16   32
    3     3    9   27   81  243
    4     4   16   64  256 1024
    5     5   25  125  625 3125
```

5.11

```
 1    out.println("Sun  Mon  Tue  Wed  Thu  Fri  Sat");
 2    out.println();
 3    for (int day = 1; day <= 31; day++) {
 4      out.printf("%2d   ", day);
 5      if (day % 7 == 0)
 6        out.println();
 7    }
```

```
Sun  Mon  Tue  Wed  Thu  Fri  Sat

 1    2    3    4    5    6    7
 8    9   10   11   12   13   14
15   16   17   18   19   20   21
22   23   24   25   26   27   28
29   30   31
```

5.12

```
 1    for (int i = 0; i <= 8; i++) {
 2      for (int j = 0; j <= 8; j++)
 3        if ((j >= i && 8-j >= i) || (j <= i && 8-j <= i))
 4          out.print("*");
 5        else
 6          out.print(" ");
 7      out.println();
 8    }
```

```
*********
 *******
  *****
   ***
    *
   ***
  *****
 *******
*********
```

Arrays | 6

6.1 Creating Arrays

Arrays are collections of variables of the same type, and each member of the array can be referenced using its sequence number, which we call its *index*. The items in an array are called its *elements*, and they all have unique indexes, starting with zero and ending with one less than the array size. For example, in an array of five integers, the individual integers have indexes 0 through 4. An array itself is a variable, and has to be declared and initialized before you use it.

Arrays in Java are *zero-based*.

The syntax to declare an array is

$$type[] \; arrayname;$$

where *type* is the type of each element of the array, and *arrayname* is the array variable's name. The syntax to initialize an array is

$$arrayname = \text{new } type[count];$$

where *count* is the size of the array. Once you've initialized an array, you can access (that is, read from or write to) each element of the array using the syntax

$$arrayname[index]$$

Let's look at this in action,

Example 6.1. Array syntax.

```
1   String[] names;
2   names = new String[7];
3   names[0] = "Ronald";
4   out.println("The first name is " + names[0]);
```

```
The first name is Ronald
```

Example 6.1 declares an array of strings called `names`, assigns the string `"Ronald"` to the first element of the array, the first element having index 0, and then prints the value of the first element of the array. The elements of an array can't be accessed before the array is initialized, since the array's elements haven't been created yet.

Let's suppose you want a program that stores student names and ID numbers. Without using an array, you could do something like this,

```
1    String student1 = "Ronald";
2    String student2 = "Mike";
3    String student3 = "Cindy";
4    String student4 = "Tammy";
5    String student5 = "Blake";
6    String student6 = "Martha";
7    String student7 = "Sam";
8
9    int id1 = 7103;
10   int id2 = 4933;
11   int id3 = 6548;
12   int id4 = 6830;
13   int id5 = 711;
14   int id6 = 8937;
15   int id7 = 2002;
16
17   out.println("The first student is " + student1 + " with ID " + id1);
18   out.println("The second student is " + student2 + " with ID " + id2);
19   out.println("The third student is " + student3 + " with ID " + id3);
20   out.println("The fourth student is " + student4 + " with ID " + id4);
21   out.println("The fifth student is " + student5 + " with ID " + id5);
22   out.println("The sixth student is " + student6 + " with ID " + id6);
23   out.println("The seventh student is " + student7 + " with ID " + id7);
```

```
The first student is Ronald with ID 7103
The second student is Mike with ID 4933
The third student is Cindy with ID 6548
The fourth student is Tammy with ID 6830
The fifth student is Blake with ID 711
The sixth student is Martha with ID 8937
The seventh student is Sam with ID 2002
```

Arrays allow us to simplify this and organize our data in a much more manageable way. Using a string array for student names, and

an integer array for student ID numbers, we can rewrite the above
example as follows,

```
1   String[] students;
2   students = new String[7];
3   students[0] = "Ronald";
4   students[1] = "Mike";
5   students[2] = "Cindy";
6   students[3] = "Tammy";
7   students[4] = "Blake";
8   students[5] = "Martha";
9   students[6] = "Sam";
10
11  int[] IDs;
12  IDs = new int[7];
13  IDs[0] = 7103;
14  IDs[1] = 4933;
15  IDs[2] = 6548;
16  IDs[3] = 6830;
17  IDs[4] = 711;
18  IDs[5] = 8937;
19  IDs[6] = 2002;
20
21  for (int i = 0; i < 7; i++)
22    out.println("Student " + (i+1) + " is " + students[i] + " with ID " + IDs[i
        ]);
```

Example 6.2. Using arrays to store
student names and ID numbers.

```
Student 1 is Ronald with ID 7103
Student 2 is Mike with ID 4933
Student 3 is Cindy with ID 6548
Student 4 is Tammy with ID 6830
Student 5 is Blake with ID 711
Student 6 is Martha with ID 8937
Student 7 is Sam with ID 2002
```

Putting our student names and IDs in arrays has allowed us to
simplify the code that prints the data. We've replaced all seven
`println` statements with just one `println` statement within a loop.
Note that the number of array elements is 7, and the indexes are 0
through 6. We've used the array accessor syntax students[] and IDs[]
for both writing to the arrays, and reading from them. Note that
we use *(i+1)* in the `println` statement to print the sequence number
starting at 1.

There's an alternate syntax that can be used to initialize arrays, as
shown in the following example (6.3),

```
1   String[] students = new String[] { "Ronald", "Mike", "Cindy", "Tammy", "Blake
        ", "Martha", "Sam" };
2   int[] IDs = new int[] {7103, 4933, 6548, 6830, 711, 8937, 2002};
3
4   for (int i = 0; i < 7; i++)
5     out.println("Student " + (i+1) + " is " + students[i] + " with ID " + IDs[i
        ]);
```

Example 6.3. Array initializer syntax.

```
Student 1 is Ronald with ID 7103
Student 2 is Mike with ID 4933
Student 3 is Cindy with ID 6548
Student 4 is Tammy with ID 6830
Student 5 is Blake with ID 711
Student 6 is Martha with ID 8937
Student 7 is Sam with ID 2002
```

Using the alternate initializer syntax shown in example 6.3, the array size isn't provided between the square brackets in the `new` statement, and the `new` statement ends with a list of values within curly braces. This syntax is useful when the initial values of the array's elements are known at compile time. Java also allows you to omit the `new` operator if you're initializing the array when declaring it. Thus, the following is acceptable,

$$int[]\ IDs = \{7103,\ 4933,\ 6548,\ 6830,\ 711,\ 8937,\ 2002\}$$

Null: An array reference has the value `null` prior to the array being created.

Null reference exception: Dereferencing an array reference before the array is created results in a null reference exception.

Once an array is created, its size can't be changed. The array variable is just a reference to the actual array, and it's initially null. The "new" statement is what actually creates the array. Using the array accessor syntax (`[]`) with the array variable is called *dereferencing* the array. If an array variable is dereferenced before an array is created, a null reference exception occurs.

Exercises

6.1   Modify example 6.3. Add an array of seven student grades, and print the grades along with the students' names and IDs.

6.2   Modify the loop in example 6.3. Put an `if` statement in the loop, to print only students with an ID number under 6000.

6.2 Looping Through Arrays

In example 6.3, we used a loop to print the student names and ID numbers. We'll add a new array for student grades, and print those as well,

```
1   String[] students = new String[] { "Ronald", "Mike", "Cindy", "Tammy", "Blake
       ", "Martha", "Sam" };
2   int[] IDs = new int[] {7103, 4933, 6548, 6830, 711, 8937, 2002};
3   int[] grades = new int[] {95, 98, 100, 71, 89, 75, 90};
4
5   for (int i = 0; i < 7; i++)
6     out.printf("%s (%d): %d\n", students[i], IDs[i], grades[i]);
```

Example 6.4. Looping through an array.

```
Ronald (7103): 95
Mike (4933): 98
Cindy (6548): 100
Tammy (6830): 71
Blake (711): 89
Martha (8937): 75
Sam (2002): 90
```

We've replaced `println` on line 6 with `printf`, since it's easier to read what is being output. The "\n" at the end of the format string causes the output to advance to the next line.

Combining this with the code in example 5.10, we can print the average grade by keeping a running total of the grades, and dividing the total by the number of students after the loop completes,

```
1    String[] students = new String[] { "Ronald", "Mike", "Cindy", "Tammy", "Blake
        ", "Martha", "Sam" };
2    int[] IDs = new int[] {7103, 4933, 6548, 6830, 711, 8937, 2002};
3    int[] grades = new int[] {95, 98, 100, 71, 89, 75, 90};
4
5    int total = 0;
6    for (int i = 0; i < 7; i++) {
7      out.printf("%s (%d): %d\n", students[i], IDs[i], grades[i]);
8      total += grades[i];
9    }
10   out.println("The average grade is " + (total / 7));
```

Example 6.5. Computing an average.

```
Ronald (7103): 95
Mike (4933): 98
Cindy (6548): 100
Tammy (6830): 71
Blake (711): 89
Martha (8937): 75
Sam (2002): 90
The average grade is 88
```

Note in example 6.5 that the literal number 7 occurs in two places, on lines 6 and 10. If we add a student to this program, we would have to update that number on both lines 6 and 10 to account for the new array size, which is error-prone because we may forget to do it in one or both of those places. An important improvement is to replace the hardcoded 7 with the size of the array, as in example 6.6,

Example 6.6. Removing hardcoded array lengths.

```
1   String[] students = new String[] { "Ronald", "Mike", "Cindy", "Tammy", "Blake
        ", "Martha", "Sam" };
2   int[] IDs = new int[] {7103, 4933, 6548, 6830, 711, 8937, 2002};
3   int[] grades = new int[] {95, 98, 100, 71, 89, 75, 90};
4
5   int total = 0;
6   for (int i = 0; i < students.length; i++) {
7     out.printf("%s (%d): %d\n", students[i], IDs[i], grades[i]);
8     total += grades[i];
9   }
10  out.println("The average grade is " + (total / students.length));
```

```
Ronald (7103): 95
Mike (4933): 98
Cindy (6548): 100
Tammy (6830): 71
Blake (711): 89
Martha (8937): 75
Sam (2002): 90
The average grade is 88
```

An array's size can be obtained at runtime by using the `length` property of the array using the syntax `students.length`. Replacing the hardcoded array size with that expression makes our program more resilient to change.

> **Technique 8. Avoid hardcoded values when they can be replaced by computed values**
>
> Avoiding hardcoded values can make your program more resilient to change.

Let's update example 6.6 to also print the maximum and minimum grade. To compute the maximum grade, we need a new variable to hold the largest grade seen so far. Within the loop, if the student being processed has a bigger grade than the largest so far, we replace the largest so far with the current grade. Similar logic is used for the minimum grade except that its initial value needs to be large.

Example 6.7. Computing maximum and minimum.

```
1   String[] students = new String[] { "Ronald", "Mike", "Cindy", "Tammy", "Blake
        ", "Martha", "Sam" };
2   int[] IDs = new int[] {7103, 4933, 6548, 6830, 711, 8937, 2002};
3   int[] grades = new int[] {95, 98, 100, 71, 89, 75, 90};
4
5   int total = 0;
6   int maxGrade = 0;
7   int minGrade = 100;
8   for (int i = 0; i < students.length; i++) {
9     out.printf("%s (%d): %d\n", students[i], IDs[i], grades[i]);
10    total += grades[i];
11    if (grades[i] > maxGrade)
```

```
12      maxGrade = grades[i];
13    if (grades[i] < minGrade)
14      minGrade = grades[i];
15  }
16  out.println("The average grade is " + (total / students.length));
17  out.println("The maximum grade is " + maxGrade);
18  out.println("The minimum grade is " + minGrade);
```

```
Ronald (7103): 95
Mike (4933): 98
Cindy (6548): 100
Tammy (6830): 71
Blake (711): 89
Martha (8937): 75
Sam (2002): 90
The average grade is 88
The maximum grade is 100
The minimum grade is 71
```

Our next example is a program that reverses the contents of an array. Before we can do this, we need to know how to swap the values of two variables. To do that, we use a temporary variable to hold the value of the first, copy the value in the second to the first, then replace the value of the second with the temporary variable's value. For example, the following code swaps the values in `number1` and `number2`,

```
1  int temp;
2  temp = number1;
3  number1 = number2;
4  number2 = temp;
```

To reverse the contents of an array, we loop from the start of the array to its midpoint. Each time through the loop, we swap the current array element with its counterpart in the second half of the array, which is the array element in the second half of the array that has equal distance to the midpoint,

```
1   int[] numbers = new int[] { 23, 87, 55, 9, 53, 27 };
2
3   out.print("Array before reversing: ");
4   for (int i = 0; i < numbers.length; i++)
5     out.print(numbers[i] + " ");
6   out.println();
7
8   for (int i = 0; i < numbers.length / 2; i++) {
9     int temp = numbers[i];
10    numbers[i] = numbers[numbers.length - 1 - i];
11    numbers[numbers.length - 1 - i] = temp;
12  }
13
14  out.print("Array after reversing: ");
15  for (int i = 0; i < numbers.length; i++)
16    out.print(numbers[i] + " ");
```

Example 6.8. Reversing the contents of an array.

```
Array before reversing: 23 87 55 9 53 27
Array after reversing: 27 53 9 55 87 23
```

The first time through the loop, "i" is 0, and "numbers.length - 1 - i" is 5. The second time through the loop, "i" is 1, and "numbers.length - 1 - i" is 4. You can see the pairs in the below diagram. Since the array has six elements, the loop executes three times, reversing each of the three pairs.

Pairs of array elements that are processed each time through the loop.

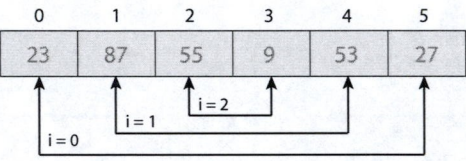

The code in example 6.8 is worth studying, since it exemplifies many situations you will encounter in the future. Pay special attention to the loop's upper limit, the code to swap two values, and array indexes on lines 10 and 11. If you have to, use the debugger to step through the code and examine the values of variables and expressions within the loop.

Tip 4. Pay special attention to array indexes and loop limits.

Note that this code works without any changes when the length of the array is odd, since the loop's upper limit is "numbers.length / 2", which performs integer division. For example, an array of size 5 would cause the loop to have an upper limit of 2, looping twice with "i" having values 0 and 1.

Our last example shows how to sort an array. In example 6.9, we've modified example 6.8 to sort the array instead of reversing it. Sorting is accomplished by calling the **sort** method of the **Arrays** class,

Example 6.9. Sorting an array.

```
1   String[] teams = new String[] { "Red Sox", "Yankees", "White Sox", "Vikings",
        "Jaguars", "Patriots", "Cowboys" };
2
3   out.print("Teams before sorting the array: ");
4   for (int i = 0; i < teams.length; i++)
5     out.print(teams[i] + " ");
6   out.println();
7
8   java.util.Arrays.sort(teams);
9
10  out.print("Teams after sorting the array: ");
11  for (int i = 0; i < teams.length; i++)
12    out.print(teams[i] + " ");
```

```
Teams before sorting the array: Red Sox Yankees White Sox Vikings Jaguars Patriots Cowboys
Teams after sorting the array: Cowboys Jaguars Patriots Red Sox Vikings White Sox Yankees
```

Exercises

6.3   Write a program that prompts the user for high temperatures for seven days (Sunday through Saturday). Store those temperatures in an array, and use a loop to find the highest temperature of the week.

6.4   Create an array of city names. Write a loop that goes through the array and tells whether it's sorted.

- Hint 1: You'll have to compare each element of the array to the one before it.
- Hint 2: You can compare two strings using this syntax: str1.compareTo(str2). This method returns a positive number if str1 is after str2 alphabetically, a negative number if str1 is before str2 alphabetically, and zero if they're equal.

6.5   Combine the code from examples 6.8 and 6.9 to sort the team names, then reverse them so that the output shows the team names in reverse alphabetical order.

6.3 Two-Dimensional Arrays

You can think of a two-dimensional array as an array of arrays. The syntax to declare it reflects that. A 2-D array is declared as "(type)[][]". Allocating a two-dimensional array with three rows and four columns is done with this syntax,

```
int[][] array;
array = new int[3][4];
```

The initializer syntax also works for two-dimensional arrays. Example 6.10 declares a 2-D array of integers that contains student grades, six grades per student. After creating the array, it prints them all out.

Example 6.10. 2-D array of student grades.

```
1   int[][] grades = new int[][] {
2       { 65, 100, 82, 97, 100, 75 },
3       { 99, 50, 100, 89, 71, 95 },
4       { 81, 85, 93, 99, 84, 85 }
5   };
6
7   for (int i = 0; i < grades.length; i++) {
8       out.print("Student " + i + ": ");
9       for (int j = 0; j < grades[i].length; j++)
10          out.print(grades[i][j] + " ");
11      out.println();
12  }
```

```
Student 0: 65 100 82 97 100 75
Student 1: 99 50 100 89 71 95
Student 2: 81 85 93 99 84 85
```

There is a duality between arrays and loops. Loops are the fundamental way that we process arrays. In the same way, nested loops are the algorithmic counterpart of multidimensional arrays.

Just as we used the `new` keyword to define a one-dimensional array, we use it to define a two-dimensional array, and in example 6.10 we use the same initializer syntax, except that the array elements are themselves arrays (lines 2-4). The nested loops are reminiscent of example 5.15, where we printed a multiplication table. Each iteration of the outer loop prints one row, while the inner loop prints one cell at a time, thus the outer loop corresponds to rows and the inner loop corresponds to columns. The row header is printed within the outer loop, before the inner loop is invoked, and we use a `println` statement after the inner loop to advance the output to the next line.

As we've seen in prior examples, example 6.10 uses the customary "i" and "j" variable names for the loop counters. More appropriate names would have been "student" and "assignment". Along with changing these loop counter names, our next example adds an array containing the student names, and uses the student names as the row headers,

Example 6.11. Adding student names to the grade output.

```
1   String[] students = new String[] { "Paul", "Tabatha", "Elaine" };
2   int[][] grades = new int[][] {
3       { 65, 100, 82, 97, 100, 75 },
4       { 99, 50, 100, 89, 71, 95 },
5       { 81, 85, 93, 99, 84, 85 }
6   };
7
8   for (int student = 0; student < grades.length; student++) {
9       out.print(students[student] + ": ");
10      for (int assignment = 0; assignment < grades[student].length; assignment++)
11          out.print(grades[student][assignment] + " ");
12      out.println();
13  }
```

```
Paul: 65 100 82 97 100 75
Tabatha: 99 50 100 89 71 95
Elaine: 81 85 93 99 84 85
```

The code is a bit longer using "student" and "assignment" as loop counters, but the change was worthwhile, since the code is clearer that way. Identifiers should help document the code as much as possible.

Technique 9. Use descriptive names for identifiers

Use descriptive names for variables, classes, and other identifiers. This helps make your code self-documenting, and helps you to quickly understand the code when you return to it later.

Next we enhance our example so that it prints out the average of grades for each student, and the overall average grade. For this, we use similar code to that in example 6.6, by keeping a running total of the grades and dividing the total by the number of grades to get the average,

```
1   String[] students = new String[] { "Paul", "Tabatha", "Elaine" };
2   int[][] grades = new int[][] {
3     { 65, 100, 82, 97, 100, 75 },
4     { 99, 50, 100, 89, 71, 95 },
5     { 81, 85, 93, 99, 84, 85 }
6   };
7
8   int overallSum = 0;
9   int overallCount = 0;
10  for (int student = 0; student < grades.length; student++) {
11    out.print(students[student] + ": ");
12    int sum = 0;
13    for (int assignment = 0; assignment < grades[student].length; assignment++)
      {
14      out.print(grades[student][assignment] + " ");
15      sum += grades[student][assignment];
16    }
17    out.println(". Average: " + sum / grades[student].length);
18    overallSum += sum;
19    overallCount += grades[student].length;
20  }
21  out.println("Class average is " + overallSum / overallCount);
```

Example 6.12. Adding grade averages.

```
Paul: 65 100 82 97 100 75 . Average: 86
Tabatha: 99 50 100 89 71 95 . Average: 84
Elaine: 81 85 93 99 84 85 . Average: 87
Class average is 86
```

In example 6.12 we compute the student's average by adding up the grades for the student, that is, the grades on the student's row, and then divide the sum by the number of grades on that row. The number of grades on the row is the upper limit of the inner loop's counter, `grades[student].length`. Similarly, the overall average is computed on line 21 by dividing the overall sum of grades by the total number of grades.

The rows in a two-dimensional array don't have to have the same number of columns. That's because the two-dimensional array is technically an array of arrays, each having its own length. This is called a *jagged* array, sometimes also called a *ragged* array. Exercise 6.8 shows an example of an array with a different number of columns in each row. Because Java allows jagged arrays, you should be careful to use the length of each row in an inner loop's upper limit, instead of the length of the first row in all iterations of the inner loop.

Jagged array: A two-dimensional array in which different rows have different lengths.

Your programs can have multi-dimensional arrays beyond two dimensions, if needed, and the syntax is similar, for example, "int[][][] a = new int[2][2][2]" defines a 2x2x2 array of integers.

Table 6.1 shows some of the common loop patterns.

Table 6.1: Some common loop patterns.

Pattern	Example
`for`	Reversing the contents of an array (example 6.8)
`for` `if`	Finding the biggest item in an array (example 6.7)
`for` `for`	Print a 2-D array (example 6.10)

`for`
  `for`
    `if`
	Finding the biggest item in a 2-D array

Exercises

6.6 Write a program that computes airline revenue. It should have a two-dimensional array of integers, each row being one flight on a particular day and each cell containing the price that a particular passenger paid. Iterate through the array to compute the total revenue for the day.

6.7 Create a two-dimensional array of strings. Each row should represent a state, and contains a list of cities. Use `Arrays.sort` as in example 6.9 to sort the cities of each state alphabetically. After sorting the contents of each row, print out the cities.

6.8 Fix the logic error in the following program, and test it to make sure it works,

```
// each row is a class containing an array of student IDs
int[][] classEnrollments = new int[][] {
  { 101, 2101, 412, 625, 420, 5561, 823, 99 },
  { 72, 518, 602, 3097, 421 },
  { 809, 393, 521, 345, 299, 711 }
};

int overallCount = 0;
for (int i = 0; i < classEnrollments.length; i++) {
  int count = 0;
  for (int student = 0; student < classEnrollments[i].length; student
      ++) {
    out.print(classEnrollments[i][student] + " ");
    count += classEnrollments[i][student];
  }
  out.println(". Students in this class: " + count);
  overallCount += count;
}
out.println("Total number of enrollments is " + overallCount);
```

6.4 Garbage Collection

As noted in section 6.1, the `new` keyword is what we use to allocate memory for an array, and the variable we use to refer to the array is merely a reference, initially having the null value. An array that has been allocated resides in an area of memory called the *heap*. An array's size can't change once it's been allocated, and it remains in the heap until it's no longer needed, at which time its memory is deallocated and can be reused for another purpose. An array can have more than one reference. For example, consider the following code,

```
String[] staff = new String[30];
String[] fullTimeStaff = staff;
```

Line 1 in the above code allocates space for an array of thirty strings, and points the variable `staff` at that array. The variable `staff` is merely a reference that we use to read from and write to the array. Line 2 creates a new variable of type `String[]` and points it to the existing array. Both `staff` and `fullTimeStaff` are *references* to the same array.

Garbage collection occurs automatically at certain intervals throughout the lifetime of your program.

An array can have any number of references pointing to it. A reference in your code is a variable that points to the actual memory holding the array's contents. In the above section of code, we have two references pointing to one array. Can an array have no references pointing to it? Yes, and that's what occurs when the block of code defining the reference finishes executing. The reference, like any variable, is limited in *scope* to the block of code in which it's defined.

A variable's scope is limited to the block of code in which it's defined.

Once all references to an array are out of scope, the array can no longer be accessed, and Java deallocates the array through a process called garbage collection. Java keeps a running count of references that are pointing to a given array, and garbage collection is performed at certain intervals throughout the lifetime of your program. You don't need to worry about cleaning up the memory that you allocate using the `new` keyword—Java does that for you automatically.

6.5 Comments

Comments start with two slashes, //.

Our examples have reached a level of complexity that warrants adding clarifying comments. Comments in Java start with a double forward-slash (//), and are meant for the software developer to leave notes to him- or herself. These aid him or her when going over the code at a later date to make changes or perform other types of maintenance. The Java compiler ignores a comment, starting with the forward slashes, up to the end of the line that it occurs on. Comments should be used to label sections of code, or clarify code sections whose functions aren't immediately obvious. When deciding whether a comment is needed, ask yourself whether it's faster to read the code to understand its purpose, or read the comment associated with that code. This is highly subjective, so every developer will have a different style with regard to comments. Furthermore, you'll find that your own commenting habits change over time. In example 6.13 we have added comments to the code from example 6.12,

Example 6.13. Adding comments.

```
1   String[] students = new String[] { "Paul", "Tabatha", "Elaine" };
2
3   // each row has one student's grades
4   int[][] grades = new int[][] {
5     { 65, 100, 82, 97, 100, 75 },
6     { 99, 50, 100, 89, 71, 95 },
7     { 81, 85, 93, 99, 84, 85 }
8   };
9
10  // print grades for each student
```

```
11   int overallSum = 0, overallCount = 0;
12   for (int student = 0; student < grades.length; student++) {
13     out.print(students[student] + ": "); // row header
14     int sum = 0;
15     for (int assignment = 0; assignment < grades[student].length; assignment++)
         {
16       out.print(grades[student][assignment] + " ");
17       sum += grades[student][assignment];
18     }
19     out.println(". Average: " + sum / grades[student].length); // student's
       average
20     overallSum += sum;
21     overallCount += grades[student].length;
22   }
23   out.println("Class average is " + overallSum / overallCount);
```

```
Paul: 65 100 82 97 100 75 . Average: 86
Tabatha: 99 50 100 89 71 95 . Average: 84
Elaine: 81 85 93 99 84 85 . Average: 87
Class average is 86
```

In example 6.13, we've also merged the declaration of overallSum and overallCount into one line, on line 11. Java lets us do this if the types are the same. The two variables are separated by a comma, and can still be initialized individually. Note that comments are used sparingly—not every section of code needs a comment. Remember that the comments are there to help you when you look at your code later, and only need to be there if they help you read the code faster, or if they help you locate a certain section of code faster. Comments are also often used to document formulas or algorithms.

> **Technique 10. Add comments to help you navigate your code later**
>
> Comments should help you locate a section of code faster when you later read your code. They're also used to help someone else understand your code.

Before moving on, I want to show a different **for** loop syntax, one that is often used when you don't need to use the array index within the loop (e.g., to modify the array). Example 6.14 has the rewritten code with the new loop syntax,

```
1   String[] students = new String[] { "Paul", "Tabatha", "Elaine" };
2
3   // each row has one student's grades
4   int[][] grades = new int[][] {
5     { 65, 100, 82, 97, 100, 75 },
6     { 99, 50, 100, 89, 71, 95 },
```

Example 6.14. Using the enhanced for loop syntax.

```
 7    { 81, 85, 93, 99, 84, 85 }
 8    };
 9
10    // print grades for each student
11    int overallSum = 0, overallCount = 0;
12    for (int student = 0; student < grades.length; student++) {
13      out.print(students[student] + ": "); // row header
14      int sum = 0;
15      for (int grade : grades[student]) {
16        out.print(grade + " ");
17        sum += grade;
18        }
19      out.println(". Average: " + sum / grades[student].length); // student's
         average
20      overallSum += sum;
21      overallCount += grades[student].length;
22    }
23    out.println("Class average is " + overallSum / overallCount);
```

```
Paul: 65 100 82 97 100 75 . Average: 86
Tabatha: 99 50 100 89 71 95 . Average: 84
Elaine: 81 85 93 99 84 85 . Average: 87
Class average is 86
```

The modified code is on lines 15-17. This syntax is clearer but doesn't provide the actual index, which we didn't need in the inner `for`-loop. Instead of "for (int assignment = 0; assignment < grades[student].length; assignment++)", we have "for (int grade : grades[student])". This declares the integer variable `grade`, and assigns it in turn to each integer element of the `grades[student]` array. Within the loop, we use `grade` in the call to `print`, as well as to increment `sum`. Note that we can't use this enhanced `for` syntax in the outer loop since we need the index in order to access the student name from the `students` array.

Our last example uses a two-dimensional array of floating point numbers to hold coordinates of a list of destinations. Each row contains the latitude and longitude of one city. We loop through the cities and compute the distance from each city to the next. This time, we don't want to process each row, but rather we want to process each *pair* of rows. So, the number of loop iterations is *one less* than the number of rows, and the code in the loop looks at the current row and the next row,

Example 6.15. Showing distances between cities on a trip.

```
1    double[][] points = new double[][] {
2      { 28.53, -81.38 },   // Orlando
3      { 29.75, -95.39 },   // Houston
4      { 32.21, -110.93 },  // Tucson
5      { 32.71, -117.15 },  // San Diego
6      { 40.71, -74.00 },   // New York
7      { 42.35, -71.07 }    // Boston
```

```
 8    };
 9
10    double tripLength = 0;
11    for (int i = 0; i < points.length - 1; i++) {
12      double[] point1 = points[i];
13      double[] point2 = points[i+1];
14
15      // distance between two points = square root of (latitude difference
         // squared + longitude difference squared)
16      double leg = Math.sqrt(
17        Math.pow(point1[0] - point2[0], 2) +
18        Math.pow(point1[1] - point2[1], 2));
19
20      /* Convert degrees to miles. 69 miles per degree longitude,
21       * and 55 miles per degree latitude (approximate for the
22       * United States). So we'll use 62 miles per degree as a
23       * very approximate average */
24      leg *= 62;
25
26      out.printf("Next leg: %.2f miles\n", leg);
27      tripLength += leg;
28    }
29    out.printf("Trip length = %.2f miles", tripLength);
```

```
Next leg: 871.91 miles
Next leg: 975.48 miles
Next leg: 386.88 miles
Next leg: 2720.89 miles
Next leg: 208.18 miles
Trip length = 5163.34 miles
```

Note the use of comments in three places, where they're necessary to clarify the programmer's intent:

- Each latitude/longitude pair has a comment containing the city's name.
- The formula for distance between two points.
- The conversion of degrees to miles, with explanation of how the formula was derived. Here we use a different comment notation which starts with /* and ends with */, and can span multiple lines.

A common practice when a developer wants to remove code from the program, but keep it around for use later, is to convert it into a comment by surrounding it with the /* and */ delimiters, or preceding each line with //. This is often because the code isn't working yet and the developer wants to focus on other parts of the program, or because the code is complicating a test case that he or she is working on. A quick way to comment out a block of code is to select it and use the Ctrl+/ shortcut (Cmd+/ on Mac). The same action will uncomment a block of code.

Colloquially, converting a section of code into a comment is known as *commenting out* the code.

Note in example 6.15 the `double` type which we're seeing for the first time. `double` works like `float`, except that it uses twice as many bits, resulting in more precise calculations. That's not why we've used it here in place of `float`. We're using it because `Math.pow()` and `Math.sqrt()` take parameters of type `double` and return a `double` value, and it would entail more code to cast values between the `float` and `double` types.

Chapter Summary

- An array is a sequence of variables that are accessed by index. Arrays are allocated with a specific number of elements, and an array's size can't be changed after it's been allocated.
- An array's elements all have the same type.
- Loops are commonly used to iterate through arrays, to performa an operation on each array element, or find an array element with a certain property.
- A two-dimensional array corresponds to a grid of items, all of the same type.

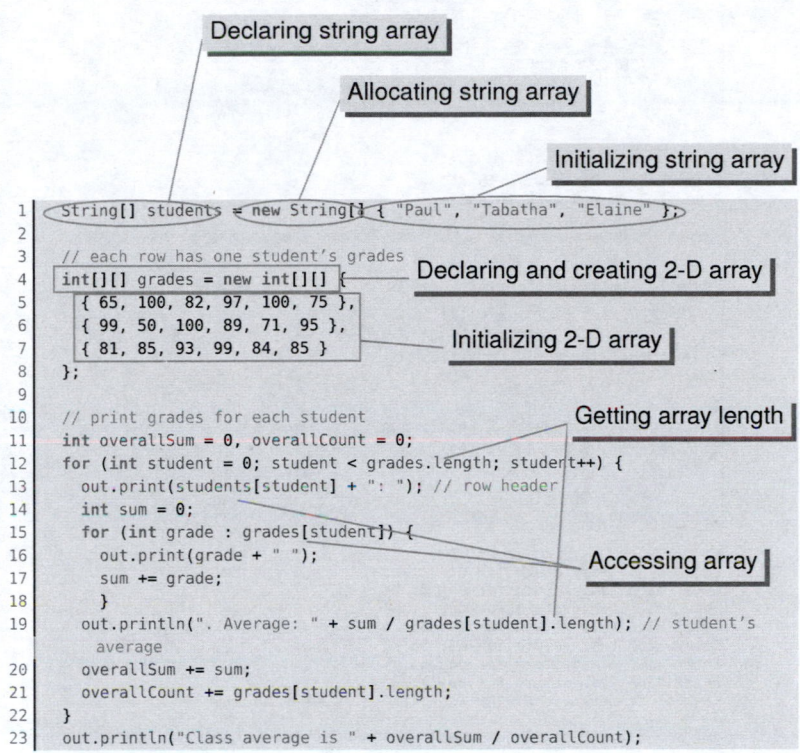

```
1   String[] students = new String[] { "Paul", "Tabatha", "Elaine" };
2
3   // each row has one student's grades
4   int[][] grades = new int[][] {
5       { 65, 100, 82, 97, 100, 75 },
6       { 99, 50, 100, 89, 71, 95 },
7       { 81, 85, 93, 99, 84, 85 }
8   };
9
10  // print grades for each student
11  int overallSum = 0, overallCount = 0;
12  for (int student = 0; student < grades.length; student++) {
13      out.print(students[student] + ": "); // row header
14      int sum = 0;
15      for (int grade : grades[student]) {
16          out.print(grade + " ");
17          sum += grade;
18      }
19      out.println(". Average: " + sum / grades[student].length); // student's
            average
20      overallSum += sum;
21      overallCount += grades[student].length;
22  }
23  out.println("Class average is " + overallSum / overallCount);
```

Labels in figure:
- Declaring string array
- Allocating string array
- Initializing string array
- Declaring and creating 2-D array
- Initializing 2-D array
- Getting array length
- Accessing array

Exercise Solutions

6.1
```
1   String[] students = new String[] { "Ronald", "Mike", "Cindy", "
        Tammy", "Blake", "Martha", "Sam" };
2   int[] IDs = new int[] {7103, 4933, 6548, 6830, 711, 8937, 2002};
3   char[] grades = new char[] {'C', 'A', 'A', 'B', 'A', 'C', 'A'};
4
5   for (int i = 0; i < 7; i++)
6       out.println("Student " + (i+1) + " is " + students[i] + " with
            ID " + IDs[i] + " and grade " + grades[i]);
```

```
Student 1 is Ronald with ID 7103 and grade C
Student 2 is Mike with ID 4933 and grade A
Student 3 is Cindy with ID 6548 and grade A
Student 4 is Tammy with ID 6830 and grade B
Student 5 is Blake with ID 711 and grade A
Student 6 is Martha with ID 8937 and grade C
Student 7 is Sam with ID 2002 and grade A
```

6.2
```
1   String[] students = new String[] { "Ronald", "Mike", "Cindy", "
        Tammy", "Blake", "Martha", "Sam" };
2   int[] IDs = new int[] {7103, 4933, 6548, 6830, 711, 8937, 2002};
```

```
3
4      for (int i = 0; i < 7; i++)
5        if (IDs[i] < 6000)
6          out.println("Student " + (i+1) + " is " + students[i] + " with
             ID " + IDs[i]);
```

```
Student 2 is Mike with ID 4933
Student 5 is Blake with ID 711
Student 7 is Sam with ID 2002
```

6.3
```
1    int[] temps = new int[7];
2    for (int i = 0; i < 7; i++) {
3      out.print("Enter high temperature for day " + (i+1) + ": ");
4      temps[i] = input.nextInt();
5    }
6
7    int high = Integer.MIN_VALUE;
8    for (int i = 0; i < 7; i++)
9      if (temps[i] > high)
10       high = temps[i];
11   out.println("Highest temperature of the week: " + high);
```

```
Enter high temperature for day 1: 81
Enter high temperature for day 2: 83
Enter high temperature for day 3: 88
Enter high temperature for day 4: 75
Enter high temperature for day 5: 79
Enter high temperature for day 6: 80
Enter high temperature for day 7: 81
Highest temperature of the week: 88
```

6.4
```
1    String[] cities = new String[] { "Atlanta", "Baltimore", "DC", "
       Buffalo", "Phoenix" };
2    boolean sorted = true;
3    for (int i = 1; i < cities.length; i++)
4      if (cities[i-1].compareTo(cities[i]) > 0) {
5        sorted = false;
6        break;
7      }
8
9    if (sorted)
10     out.println("City names are sorted");
11   else
12     out.println("City names are not sorted");
```

```
City names are sorted
```

6.5
```
1    String[] teams = new String[] { "Red Sox", "Yankees", "White Sox",
       "Vikings", "Jaguars", "Patriots", "Cowboys" };
2
3    java.util.Arrays.sort(teams);
4    for (int i = 0; i < teams.length / 2; i++) {
5      String temp = teams[i];
6      teams[i] = teams[teams.length - 1 - i];
7      teams[teams.length - 1 - i] = temp;
8    }
9
10   out.print("Teams in reverse alphabetical order: ");
```

```
11   for (int i = 0; i < teams.length; i++)
12     out.print(teams[i] + " ");
```

Teams in reverse alphabetical order: Yankees White Sox Vikings Red Sox Patriots Jaguars Cowboys

6.6
```
 1   int[][] prices = {
 2       { 294, 279, 288, 164, 186, 217, 202, 237, 273, 107 },
 3       { 109, 214, 111, 157, 208, 142 },
 4       { 84, 65, 58, 130, 77, 67, 135, 163, 76 },
 5   };
 6
 7   int sum = 0;
 8   for (int flight = 0; flight < prices.length; flight++)
 9     for (int passenger = 0; passenger < prices[flight].length;
         passenger ++)
10       sum += prices[flight][passenger];
11
12   out.println("Total revenue is $" + sum);
```

Total revenue is $4043

6.7
```
 1   String[][] cities = {
 2       { "Cupertino", "Pasadena", "Los Angeles", "San Diego" },
 3       { "Buffalo", "NYC", "Albany" },
 4       { "Tampa", "Orlando", "Miami", "Jacksonville" },
 5   };
 6
 7   for (int state = 0; state < cities.length; state++) {
 8     java.util.Arrays.sort(cities[state]);
 9     for (int city = 0; city < cities[state].length; city++)
10       out.print(cities[state][city] + " ");
11     out.println();
12   }
```

Cupertino Los Angeles Pasadena San Diego
Albany Buffalo NYC
Jacksonville Miami Orlando Tampa

6.8
```
 1   // each row is a class containing an array of student IDs
 2   int[][] classEnrollments = new int[][] {
 3     { 101, 2101, 412, 625, 420, 5561, 823, 99 },
 4     { 72, 518, 602, 3097, 421 },
 5     { 809, 393, 521, 345, 299, 711 }
 6   };
 7
 8   int overallCount = 0;
 9   for (int i = 0; i < classEnrollments.length; i++) {
10     int count = 0;
11     for (int student = 0; student < classEnrollments[i].length;
         student++) {
12       out.print(classEnrollments[i][student] + " ");
13       count++;
14       }
15     out.println(". Students in this class: " + count);
16     overallCount += count;
17   }
18   out.println("Total number of enrollments is " + overallCount);
```

```
101 2101 412 625 420 5561 823 99 . Students in this class: 8
72 518 602 3097 421 . Students in this class: 5
809 393 521 345 299 711 . Students in this class: 6
Total number of enrollments is 19
```

Methods | 7

7.1 Methods

Methods are simply blocks of code that you can execute from other parts of your program. Consider the following example,

```
1  public static void main(String[] args) {
2    sayHello();
3  }
4
5  public static void sayHello () {
6    out.println("Hello, User!");
7  }
```

```
Hello, User!
```

Lines 5-7 define the method `sayHello`. This method contains one line which prints the greeting. A method's name conforms to the same rules as variable names, and by convention is in camel case. The sayHello definition resembles that of `main`, with the keywords `public static void`. We'll get to `public` and `static` in chapter 8. The `void` keyword is the return type, and indicates no return value. Invoking the `sayHello` method is done in the `main` method by using its name followed by a pair of parentheses. When a method is called, the calling code is suspended, and will resume when the called method returns. We can invoke the method repeatedly using a loop,

```
1  public static void main(String[] args) {
2    for (int i = 0; i < 10; i++)
3      sayHello();
4  }
5
6  public static void sayHello () {
7    out.println("Hello, User!");
8  }
```

```
Hello, User!
Hello, User!
Hello, User!
Hello, User!
Hello, User!
Hello, User!
Hello, User!
Hello, User!
Hello, User!
Hello, User!
```

If `sayHello` contained more than one line, say a ten-line sequence of code, we would save a significant number of lines by calling it from multiple places rather than pasting its code into those places. This brings us to the first main benefit of using methods—they allow us to consolidate repeated segments of code, an application of technique 5 on page 75. Organizing your code to group related functionality takes practice. Methods are one of the main tools you have to keep your code organized and maintainable, and you'll see examples of this throughout the rest of the book.

Reorganizing a program's code so that it's more maintainable is sometimes called *refactoring*.

7.2 Parameters

The code that invokes a method can pass information into the method in the form of parameters. These are given between the opening and closing parentheses. In example 7.1, we modify the above program to pass a string into the `sayHello` method, which is used in the greeting message,

Example 7.1. Passing a parameter.

```
1   public static void main(String[] args) {
2       sayHello("Grumpy");
3       sayHello("Dopey");
4       sayHello("Happy");
5       sayHello("Bashful");
6       sayHello("Sneezy");
7       sayHello("Sleepy");
8       sayHello("Doc");
9   }
10
11  public static void sayHello (String name) {
12      out.println("Hello, " + name + "!");
13  }
```

```
Hello, Grumpy!
Hello, Dopey!
Hello, Happy!
Hello, Bashful!
Hello, Sneezy!
Hello, Sleepy!
Hello, Doc!
```

A method's definition can contain any number of parameters between the parentheses, separated by commas. The `sayHello` method requires one parameter called name, of type `String`. Each call to the method (lines 2 through 8) contains the required name parameter between the parentheses. Calls to a method must pass the correct number of parameters, and the parameter types must match the method's definition, or you'll get a compile error.

A parameter is the variable in the method's declaration, whereas an argument is the *value* passed in to the parameter.

In example 7.2, the methods `printMax` and `printAverage` each take two numbers as parameters, and print the larger one and their average, respectively,

```
1   public static void main(String[] args) {
2       printMax(5, 15);
3       printAverage(5, 15);
4       printMax(37, -11);
5       printAverage(37, -11);
6   }
7
8   public static void printMax (int number1, int number2) {
9       if (number1 > number2)
10          out.println(number1);
11      else
12          out.println(number2);
13  }
14
15  public static void printAverage (int number1, int number2) {
16      out.println((double) (number1 + number2) / 2);
17  }
```

Example 7.2. Passing multiple parameters.

```
15
10.0
37
13.0
```

7.3 Return Types

The point of having methods is to make code reusable. Having a method that takes two parameters and prints the average is not very reusable, so we'll fix that in example 7.3,

Example 7.3. Methods with return values.

```
1   public static void main(String[] args) {
2     printStatistics(5, 15);
3     printStatistics(37, -11);
4   }
5
6   public static void printStatistics (int number1, int number2) {
7     int maxNumber = getMax(number1, number2);
8     out.println(maxNumber);
9     double average = getAverage(number1, number2);
10    out.println(average);
11  }
12
13  public static int getMax (int number1, int number2) {
14    if (number1 > number2)
15      return number1;
16    else
17      return number2;
18  }
19
20  public static double getAverage (int number1, int number2) {
21    return (double) (number1 + number2) / 2;
22  }
```

```
15
10.0
37
13.0
```

The `printMax` and `printAverage` methods have been changed to `getMax` and `getAverage`, and they don't actually print anything. Rather, they return the results of the calculations. That way, they're much more reusable, for two reasons,

- The code that calls each of them may want the output to have a different format.
- The code that calls each of them may want to use the results (maximum or average) in different ways.

Stack Frame: The memory space containing a method's parameters and local variables.

Call Stack: The memory space where stack frames are allocated.

Stack Overflow: When the call stack runs out of memory because of too many nested method invocations.

A method can call another one, and the second method can in turn call a third. This nesting of method invocations can be arbitrarily deep as long as your program doesn't run out of memory. In our example, `main` calls `printStatistics`, which in turn calls `getMax` and `getAverage`. When a method calls another, Java allocates memory for the new method's local variables including parameters, and this memory block is called the stack frame. When the invoked method returns, the stack frame is deallocated. It's called a stack frame because these frames are stacked on one another when methods call each other (this is called pushing a frame onto the stack), and when methods return, their frames are deallocated (this is called popping the frame from the stack). If too many nested method invocations are made, the stack's memory runs out, and this is known as stack overflow. You shouldn't worry about stack overflows as the stack memory is large, and it doesn't run out unless a bug in your code caused an infinite recursion situation, where a bug causes a method to call itself repeatedly without breaking out of that loop.

Recursion is when a method calls itself. We'll discuss recursion in detail in chapter 15

Each method can return a value of a particular type, or may not return a value at all if its return type is declared as `void`. The return type is declared in the *method declaration* right before the method name. In the above example, `getMax` returns an integer, and `getAverage` returns a double precision floating point number. The `return` statement actually causes the method to terminate and return the value specified. Note that a `void` method can also use the return statement to return to the caller, but may not specify a value to return.

return statement.

Our final version of this example will prompt the user for two integers, then call the `printStatistics` method to print the maximum and average,

```java
public static void main(String[] args) {
    Scanner input = new Scanner(System.in);
    out.print("Enter two numbers separated by spaces: ");
    int first = input.nextInt();
    int second = input.nextInt();
    printStatistics(first, second);
    input.close();
}

public static void printStatistics (int number1, int number2) {
    int maxNumber = getMax(number1, number2);
    out.println(maxNumber);
    double average = getAverage(number1, number2);
    out.println(average);
}

public static int getMax (int number1, int number2) {
    if (number1 > number2)
        return number1;
    else
        return number2;
}

public static double getAverage (int number1, int number2) {
    return (double) (number1 + number2) / 2;
}
```

Example 7.4. Calculating statistics from user input.

```
Enter two numbers separated by spaces: 21 42
The maximum is 42
The average is 31.5
```

Now that we know how to pass parameters into methods and return results from methods, we have a powerful tool to simplify our programs. Let's look back at examples 5.1 and 5.3 which we combine now as example 7.5,

Example 7.5. Medical diagnosis program before simplification.

```
1   String answer;
2
3   do {
4     out.print("Do you have a sore throat (yes/no)? ");
5     answer = input.nextLine().toLowerCase();
6   } while (!answer.equals("yes") && !answer.equals("no"));
7
8   if (answer.equals("yes")) {
9
10    do {
11      out.print("Do you have a fever? ");
12      answer = input.nextLine().toLowerCase();
13    } while (!answer.equals("yes") && !answer.equals("no"));
14
15    if (answer.equals("yes"))
16      out.print("Possibly the flu.");
17    else
18      out.print("Possibly strep throat.");
19  }
20  else {
21
22    do {
23      out.print("Are you in pain? ");
24      answer = input.nextLine().toLowerCase();
25    } while (!answer.equals("yes") && !answer.equals("no"));
26
27    if (answer.equals("yes"))
28      out.print("Try Advil.");
29    else
30      out.print("You appear to be fine.");
31  }
```

```
Do you have a sore throat (yes/no)? Yes
Do you have a fever? No
Possibly strep throat.
```

The repeated sections (lines 3-6, 10-13 and 22-25) can be moved out into a new method that takes two parameters, the **Scanner** object and the question to ask, and returns the user's answer,

```
1   public static void main(String[] args) {
2
3     Scanner input = new Scanner(System.in);
4
5     String answer = askQuestion(input, "Do you have a sore throat (yes/no)? ");
6     if (answer.equals("yes")) {
7
8       answer = askQuestion(input, "Do you have a fever? ");
9       if (answer.equals("yes"))
10        out.print("Possibly the flu.");
11      else
12        out.print("Possibly strep throat.");
```

```
13      }
14      else {
15
16        answer = askQuestion(input, "Are you in pain? ");
17        if (answer.equals("yes"))
18          out.print("Try Advil.");
19        else
20          out.print("You appear to be fine.");
21      }
22
23      input.close();
24    }
25
26    public static String askQuestion(Scanner input, String question) {
27      String answer = "";
28      do {
29        out.print(question);
30        answer = input.nextLine().toLowerCase();
31      } while (!answer.equals("yes") && !answer.equals("no"));
32      return answer;
33    }
```

```
Do you have a sore throat (yes/no)? Yes
Do you have a fever? No
Possibly strep throat.
```

This hasn't saved us too many lines of code, but the repeated sections are gone and adding more questions will cause us to add far fewer lines to the program as opposed to the previous version. But, we shouldn't stop there, as we can simplify the program further. We don't need to return the actual user's input, which is a string. We can simply return true or false. In fact, we really should make this change because these are yes/no questions and true/false is the natural representation of the user's answer. So, our next version is as follows,

```
1   public static void main(String[] args) {
2
3     Scanner input = new Scanner(System.in);
4
5     if (askQuestion(input, "Do you have a sore throat (yes/no)? ")) {
6       if (askQuestion(input, "Do you have a fever? "))
7         out.print("Possibly the flu.");
8       else
9         out.print("Possibly strep throat.");
10    }
11    else {
12      if (askQuestion(input, "Are you in pain? "))
13        out.print("Try Advil.");
14      else
15        out.print("You appear to be fine.");
16    }
17
18    input.close();
19  }
20
```

```
21  public static boolean askQuestion(Scanner input, String question) {
22    String answer = "";
23    do {
24      out.print(question);
25      answer = input.nextLine().toLowerCase();
26    } while (!answer.equals("yes") && !answer.equals("no"));
27    return answer.equals("yes");
28  }
```

```
Do you have a sore throat (yes/no)? Yes
Do you have a fever? No
Possibly strep throat.
```

Since the `askQuestion` method now returns a boolean, we were able to call it within the *if* statement, saving space and making the program easier to read. In addition, we could also use the question-mark-colon operator to combine the inner `if` statements, as follows,

Example 7.6. Medical diagnosis program after simplification.

```
1   public static void main(String[] args) {
2
3     Scanner input = new Scanner(System.in);
4
5     if (askQuestion(input, "Do you have a sore throat (yes/no)? "))
6       out.print(askQuestion(input, "Do you have a fever? ") ? "Possibly the flu.
        " : "Possibly strep throat.");
7     else
8       out.print(askQuestion(input, "Are you in pain? ") ? "Try Advil." : "You
        appear to be fine.");
9
10    input.close();
11  }
12
13  public static boolean askQuestion(Scanner input, String question) {
14    String answer = "";
15    do {
16      out.print(question);
17      answer = input.nextLine().toLowerCase();
18    } while (!answer.equals("yes") && !answer.equals("no"));
19    return answer.equals("yes");
20  }
```

This is a worthwhile change, as it reduces the number of lines of code, and doesn't affect the clarity or runtime efficiency.

Tip 5. You should get used to the kind of code simplification that we performed to get from example 7.5 to example 7.6, and make it part of your routine.

7.4 Variable Scope

When a method is called from another, variables in the calling method aren't visible in the method that was called. For example, when `printStatistics` is called from `main` in example 7.4, the variables "first" and "second" in `main` aren't available to the `printStatistics` method. That is, their scope is limited to the method in which they're defined.

Furthermore, even if we renamed the parameters `number1` and `number2` in `printStatistics` to be `first` and `second` instead, they would be unrelated to the variables `first` and `second` in `main`. Each variable in Java has a distinct scope, and can only be referenced within that scope. In general, the scope of a variable begins at the line on which it's defined and ends at the end of the block in which it's defined. So the variable `first` in example 7.4 is accessible only between lines 4 and 8. `second` is accessible only between lines 5 and 8, and the variable `args` is accessible only between lines 1 and 8.

7.5 Modifying Parameters

In Java, parameters are passed *by value*. This means that the parameter received by the method is a `copy` of the parameter passed in by the caller. So modifying the parameter within the method doesn't change the variable specified in the method call, as example 7.7 shows,

```
1    public static void main(String[] args) {
2       int number = 26;
3       out.println("Before calling the method, the number is " + number);
4       method(number);
5       out.println("After calling the method, the number is " + number);
6    }
7
8    public static void method (int parameter) {
9       out.println("  Before changing the parameter, its value is " + parameter);
10      parameter = 0;
11      out.println("  After changing the parameter, its value is " + parameter);
12   }
```

Example 7.7. Parameters are passed by value.

```
Before calling the method, the number is 26
  Before changing the parameter, its value is 26
  After changing the parameter, its value is 0
After calling the method, the number is 26
```

As you can see from the output, changing the value of `parameter` within `method` doesn't change the value of the variable `number` which is passed into `method` as a parameter. Java copied the value contained within `number`, assigning that value to a new variable named `parameter` within the method.

When a reference type is passed in to a method as a parameter, a copy of the *reference* is passed in, meaning the parameter is pointing to the same structure that the caller is. To understand this, consider example 7.8,

Example 7.8. Modifying an array parameter's contents.

```java
public static void main(String[] args) {
    int[] numbers = { 1, 2, 3 };
    out.print("Before calling the method, the numbers are ");
    printNumbers(numbers);
    method(numbers);
    out.print("After calling the method, the numbers are ");
    printNumbers(numbers);
}

public static void method (int[] numbers) {
    out.print("  Before changing the parameter, its value is ");
    printNumbers(numbers);
    numbers[0] = 999;
    out.print("  After changing the parameter, its value is ");
    printNumbers(numbers);
}

public static void printNumbers(int[] numbers) {
    for (int number : numbers)
        out.print(number + " ");
    out.println();
}
```

```
Before calling the method, the numbers are 1 2 3
  Before changing the parameter, its value is 1 2 3
  After changing the parameter, its value is 999 2 3
After calling the method, the numbers are 999 2 3
```

As you can see from the output, the array belonging to the *caller* has been modified by *called* method. This illustrates the nature of reference variables. The variable "numbers" defined in `main` is a reference, or a *pointer* to the real location of the array. The array's location (the reference) has been copied into the `numbers` parameter, and used to modify the contents of the array belonging to the caller. In Java, arrays and classes (discussed in chapter 8) are reference types, in other words, any variable that is assigned a value by the "new" operator contains a reference to data, not actual data.

7.6 Overloading

In Java, as with many other languages, different methods can have the same name as long as they have a different number of parameters, or parameters of different types. To illustrate this, example 7.9 shows a program that computes the largest among a group of numbers,

```java
public static void main(String[] args) {

    out.println("The maximum of 31 and 35 is " + getMax(31, 35));

    int[] numbers = new int[] { 70, 75, 90 };
    out.println("The maximum number in the array is " + getMax(numbers));
}

public static int getMax(int number1, int number2) {
    return number1 > number2 ? number1 : number2;
}

public static int getMax(int[] numbers) {
    int result = Integer.MIN_VALUE;
    for (int number : numbers)
        if (number > result)
            result = number;
    return result;
}
```

Example 7.9. Overloading a method.

```
The maximum of 31 and 35 is 35
The maximum number in the array is 90
```

Example 7.9 has two different methods with the same name, `getMax`. In this situation, we say that `getMax` is overloaded. This isn't a syntax error because the two methods have different numbers of parameters, so Java can tell which one is being called by the number of parameters supplied. The call to `getMax` on line 3 refers to the instance having two parameters, and the call on line 6 refers to the instance having one parameter. Similarly, we could have defined a third `getMax` method with two parameters of type `float`, which would be allowed because the new method's parameters have different types from the existing method's parameters' types.

Method overloading: two or more methods having the same name.

The combination of a method's name, the number of parameters that it has, and the *types* of its parameters is called a method's *signature*. Java allows multiple methods with the same name in the same class as long as they all have different signatures. Note that the names of the parameters doesn't matter. It's the *types* of the parameters that make up its signature. Also note that the method's return type isn't part of its signature. Overloading is a common technique, and you will find yourself using it occasionally.

Method signature: the combination of a method's name and the types of each parameter that it takes.

Note how we've simplified the code in example 7.9. The `getMax` method that takes two parameters uses the ternary operator to keep the code brief, and the `getMax` method that takes one parameter

Integer.MIN_VALUE has the value −2,147,483,648 as shown in table 2.1.

uses a for-if pattern to get the largest number in the array using a minimal set of lines while keeping the code clear and without sacrificing runtime efficiency. The `result` variable starts with the value `Integer.MIN_VALUE` so that the answer is correct even when the input array contains only negative numbers. `Integer.MIN_VALUE` is a constant provided by Java's `Integer` class, having the smallest possible integer value. Note that the method returns `Integer.MIN_VALUE` if the input array is empty.

Our examples have grown to a nontrivial size. If you're thinking at this point that it's taking a long time to type them in, you might consider using a typing tutor to increase your speed. There are many good free typing tutors online, and anyone can increase his or her typing speed. Use a typing tutor until your speed is at least 60 words per minute for standard English practice phrases. You can't be a top performing software developer without this skill, as it will help you in more than one way:

Tip 6. Use a typing tutor to increase your typing speed.

- It will significantly increase your productivity.
- More importantly, it will buy you time. As a software developer, your multiple commitments and deadlines will often be out of your control. Being a fast coder gives you time to improve your code before you have to move on to the next project, thus improving the quality of your code and helping you to improve as a developer.

7.7 `main` Method Arguments

An **Argument** is the value passed in to a method's parameter.

The "args" parameter of the `main` method passes in command-line arguments. Many command-line programs use arguments that modify their behavior in different ways. Depending on what your program does, it may or may not use these command-line arguments. If it does, it reads them from the `args` parameter, a string array. In Eclipse, you can pass in arguments to your program via the run configuration mentioned in section 3.1. The second tab of the Run Configurations dialog contains the Program Arguments text field where arguments are specified, as shown in figure 7.1.

Having specified "-a" as the command-line argument in the Run Configuration dialog, we can modify our program to read this argument in the `main` method, and act on it,

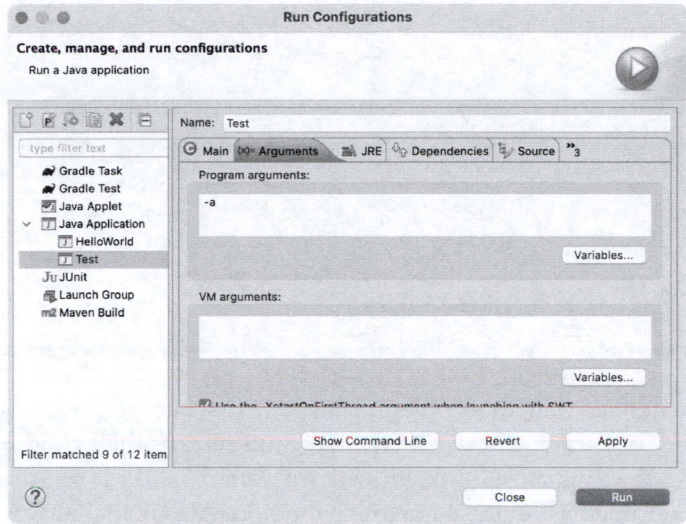

```
1  public static void main(String[] args) {
2    if (args.length > 0 && args[0].equals("-a"))
3      out.println("HELLO FROM main()");
4    else
5      out.println("Hello from main()");
6  }
```

Example 7.10. Using `args` parameter in `main` method.

```
HELLO FROM main()
```

Note that we've used the shortcut-and operator (`&&`) to ensure there is at least one argument, then read the first argument and if it's a dash followed by lowercase "a", we print the greeting in all-uppercase.

7.8 Variable-Length Arguments

In Java, a method can accept a variable number of parameters. This feature is not used too often, but we'll put it to good use in chapter 15. The notation "(type) ... (variable)" in the parameter list means that the caller can pass in an arbitrary number of arguments of the specified type. Within the method, they appear as an array of the specified type. Example 7.11 shows this in action,

Example 7.11. Using variable-length arguments.

```
1   public static void main(String[] args) {
2     out.println("The product of 1, 3, 5 and 7 is " + productOf(1, 3, 5, 7));
3   }
4
5   public static int productOf(int... numbers) {
6     int result = 1;
7     for (int number : numbers)
8       result *= number;
9     return result;
10  }
```

```
The product of 1, 3, 5 and 7 is 105
```

We've defined a method called `productOf` that accepts a variable number of parameters, all of type `int`, and returns their product. Note that we initialize the result with the value 1, and 1 is returned if no arguments are passed in to the method. Also note that we're using the `*=` operator which works like `+=` but does multiplication instead of addition. A method can have other parameters as well, but if it takes a variable number of parameters, the varargs parameter has to be the last one.

Exercises

7.1   Rewrite example 6.8 to use a method that swaps two elements in the array. It should receive the array and the indexes of the two elements to be swapped as parameters.

7.2   Rewrite example 6.12 to use a method that prints the grades for one student. It should receive as parameters the student's name and the student's grades (an array). It should print the student's grades and then return their sum.

7.3   Rewrite example 6.15 to use a method that calculates the distance between two points. It should receive two parameters, each representing one latitude/longitude coordinate pair, and should return the distance between the two points.

7.4   Fix the syntax errors in the following program, and test it to make sure it works,

```
1   public static void main(String[] args) {
2     int[] grades = new int[] { 70, 75, 90 };
3     out.println("The average of 70, 75, 90 is " +
4       getAverage(grades));
5   }
```

```
 6
 7    public static float getAverage(int[] numbers) {
 8      int sum = 0;
 9      for (int number : grades)
10        sum += number;
11      return sum / grades.length;
12    }
```

Chapter Summary

- A method is a block of code that is identified by name, and can be invoked from other places in your program.
- A method can receive parameters, which are local variables that have types. These parameters are passed into the method by the calling code.
- A method can optionally return a value to the calling code, representing the result of some computation that the method performs.
- Parameters are passed by value and not by reference. This means that when the method modifies its parameter's value, the corresponding parameter passed in by the caller isn't changed.

```
 1   public static void main(String[] args) {
 2
 3     Scanner input = new Scanner(System.in);
 4
 5     if (askQuestion(input, "Do you have a sore throat (yes/no)? "))
 6       out.print(askQuestion(input, "Do you have a fever? ") ? "Possibly the flu.
         " : "Possibly strep throat.");
 7     else
 8       out.print(askQuestion(input, "Are you in pain? ") ? "Try Advil." : "You
         appear to be fine.");
 9
10     input.close();
11   }
12
13   public static boolean askQuestion(Scanner input, String question) {
14     String answer = "";
15     do {
16       out.print(question);
17       answer = input.nextLine().toLowerCase();
18     } while (!answer.equals("yes") && !answer.equals("no"));
19     return answer.equals("yes");
20   }
```

Method call

Passing parameters

Method definition

Parameter definitions

Return statement

Exercise Solutions

7.1

```
1   public static void main(String[] args) {
2
3     Scanner input = new Scanner(System.in);
4
5     int[] numbers = new int[] { 23, 87, 55, 9, 53, 27 };
6
7     out.print("Array before reversing: ");
8     for (int i = 0; i < numbers.length; i++)
9       out.print(numbers[i] + " ");
10    out.println();
11
12    for (int i = 0; i < numbers.length / 2; i++)
13      swap(numbers, i, numbers.length - 1 - i);
14
15    out.print("Array after reversing: ");
16    for (int i = 0; i < numbers.length; i++)
17      out.print(numbers[i] + " ");
18
19    input.close();
20  }
21
22  public static void swap(int[] array, int index1, int index2) {
23    int temp = array[index1];
24    array[index1] = array[index2];
25    array[index2] = temp;
26  }
```

```
Array before reversing: 23 87 55 9 53 27
Array after reversing: 27 53 9 55 87 23
```

7.2

```
1   public static void main(String[] args) {
2
3     String[] students = new String[] { "Paul", "Tabatha", "Elaine"
        };
4     int[][] grades = new int[][] {
5       { 65, 100, 82, 97, 100, 75 },
6       { 99, 50, 100, 89, 71, 95 },
7       { 81, 85, 93, 99, 84, 85 }
8     };
9
10    int overallSum = 0;
11    int overallCount = 0;
12    for (int student = 0; student < grades.length; student++) {
13      int sum = processStudent(students[student], grades[student]);
14      overallSum += sum;
15      overallCount += grades[student].length;
16    }
17    out.println("Class average is " + overallSum / overallCount);
18  }
19
20  public static int processStudent(String name, int[] studentGrades)
        {
21    out.print(name + ": ");
22    int sum = 0;
```

```
23    for (int assignment = 0; assignment < studentGrades.length;
        assignment++) {
24      out.print(studentGrades[assignment] + " ");
25      sum += studentGrades[assignment];
26      }
27    out.println(". Average: " + sum / studentGrades.length);
28    return sum;
29  }
```

```
Paul: 65 100 82 97 100 75 . Average: 86
Tabatha: 99 50 100 89 71 95 . Average: 84
Elaine: 81 85 93 99 84 85 . Average: 87
Class average is 86
```

7.3
```
1   public static void main(String[] args) {
2
3     double[][] points = new double[][] {
4       { 28.53, -81.38 },  // Orlando
5       { 29.75, -95.39 },  // Houston
6       { 32.21, -110.93 }, // Tucson
7       { 32.71, -117.15 }, // San Diego
8       { 40.71, -74.00 },  // New York
9       { 42.35, -71.07 }   // Boston
10    };
11
12    double tripLength = 0;
13    for (int i = 0; i < points.length - 1; i++) {
14      double leg = distance(points[i], points[i+1]);
15      out.printf("Next leg: %.2f miles\n", leg);
16      tripLength += leg;
17    }
18    out.printf("Trip length = %.2f miles", tripLength);
19  }
20
21  public static double distance(double[] point1, double[] point2) {
22
23    // distance between two points = square root of (latitude
          difference squared + longitude difference squared)
24    double distance = Math.sqrt(
25        Math.pow(point1[0] - point2[0], 2) +
26        Math.pow(point1[1] - point2[1], 2));
27
28    /* Convert degrees to miles. 69 miles per degree longitude,
29     * and 55 miles per degree latitude (approximate for the
30     * United States). So we'll use 62 miles per degree as a
31     * very approximate average */
32    distance *= 62;
33
34    return distance;
35  }
```

```
Next leg: 871.91 miles
Next leg: 975.48 miles
Next leg: 386.88 miles
Next leg: 2720.89 miles
Next leg: 208.18 miles
Trip length = 5163.34 miles
```

7.4
```
1   public static void main(String[] args) {
2     int[] grades = new int[] { 70, 75, 90 };
```

```
3       out.println("The average of 70, 75, 90 is " +
4           getAverage(grades));
5   }
6
7   public static float getAverage(int[] numbers) {
8     int sum = 0;
9     for (int number : numbers)
10        sum += number;
11      return sum / numbers.length;
12  }
```

```
The average of 70, 75, 90 is 78.0
```

Classes | 8

8.1 Defining a Class

Classes are a way to group related data and functionality. Let's suppose you're writing a program to keep track of inventory. Each product in inventory has a name, a price, quantity on hand, and so on. Using a class allows us to group all these attributes together, along with code that performs computations related to inventory items.

Encapsulation refers to the bundling of an object's data and methods that operate on that data in a single place.

We'll start with example 8.1 by creating a new class, `Test`, in a new file, Test.java. Within this same java file, we add the new class, `Inventory`, which contains its data elements.

By convention, class names start with a capital letter.

```
1   public class Test {
2     public static void main(String[] args) {
3       InventoryItem item = new InventoryItem();
4       item.product = "Jenga Classic Game";
5       item.price = 9.50;
6       item.quantityOnHand = 80;
7     }
8   }
9
10  class InventoryItem {
11    String product;
12    double price;
13    int quantityOnHand;
14  }
```

Example 8.1. Inventory class.

The inventory class is in the same file as the `Test` class, but it can have its own file—we have them in the same file for convenience. The three data elements are defined, each with its own type. The `Test` class's `main` method creates a new instance of `InventoryItem`, and assigns values to each of its data members.

A class's data elements are variables declared within the class. They're variously known as class variables, instance variables, data elements, attributes or data members.

A class defines a new type, and objects (*instances*) of that type are created using the "new" keyword. As with arrays, variables of a class's type are references, and start out having the `null` value. Dereferencing an object reference without assigning an object instance to it results in a null pointer exception.

Creating a class instance.

To **dereference** is to access an object or array instance using a reference to that object or array.

As with arrays, an object created using the "new" keyword is stored in a special area of memory called the heap, and Java maintains a count of active references to it. Java also frees its memory once the number of references to an object reaches zero, through the garbage collection process that runs periodically throughout the lifetime of a Java program.

Data members of a class instance can be accessed using the dot notation. In example 8.1 we used the syntax "item.price = 9.50" to assign a value to the `price` data member of the `item` class instance.

The next example (8.2) defines a class to represent a car, with make, model, tankCapacity and mpg (miles per gallon) data members. The `main` method creates a `Car` instance, initializes its data and computes the vehicle's range in miles.

Example 8.2. Car class.

```
1  public class Test {
2    public static void main(String[] args) {
3      Car car = new Car();
4      car.mpg = 34;
5      car.make = "Honda";
6      car.model = "Civic";
7      car.tankCapacity = 21;
8      double range = car.tankCapacity * car.mpg;
9      out.println("The range is " + range + " miles.");
10   }
11 }
12
13 class Car {
14   double mpg;
15   String make;
16   String model;
17   double tankCapacity;
18 }
```

```
The range is 714.0 miles.
```

Note that the `main` method writes to the `car` object's instance variables on lines 4-7, and reads from them on line 8.

Exercises

8.1   Create a class that represents a television program, with data members for title, genre, production year, actors' names (an array) and director's name.

8.2   Create a class that represents a news story, with data members for title, summary, author and publication year.

8.2 Class Methods

A class not only contains data members, but also methods that operate on those data members. Consider example 8.3 which revises example 8.2 by adding the `printRange` instance method to the `Car` class, which computes and prints the vehicle's range in miles. The `main` method uses `printRange` to calculate and output the vehicle's range, instead of performing that computation itself.

```
1  public class Test {
2    public static void main(String[] args) {
3      Car car = new Car();
4      car.mpg = 34;
5      car.make = "Honda";
6      car.model = "Civic";
7      car.tankCapacity = 21;
8      car.printRange();
9    }
10 }
11
12 class Car {
13   double mpg;
14   String make;
15   String model;
16   double tankCapacity;
17
18   void printRange() {
19     double range = tankCapacity * mpg;
20     out.println("The range is " + range + " miles.");
21   }
22 }
```

Example 8.3. Instance methods.

```
The range is 714.0 miles.
```

The printRange() method is called using the class instance and dot notation, the same way you would access its instance variables. An instance's methods have direct access to its data members, so the dot notation isn't used within `printRange` when accessing `tankCapacity` and `mpg`.

The implementation in example 8.3 is better than that in example 8.2, because it's preferable to calculate the range within the "Car" class than in the `main` method of the "Test" class. In general, performing calculations related to the entity represented by a class should be within the class's code. This causes the code related to the class to be localized within the class, and makes it easier to maintain the application. If the vehicle's range was needed in two different places, each would call `printRange`, and the needed calculations would only exist in on place, within `printRange`. This is a special case of technique 2 on page 53, but deserves to be called out as its own technique:

> **Technique 11. Keep computations related to a class within the class**
>
> Keeping computations related to a class's functionality within the class promotes maintainability and modularity.

Example 8.3 is further refined in example 8.4, where `printRange` is replaced with `getRange`. The `main` method gets the range by calling `getRange` and then prints out the range instead of allowing an instance method of `Car` to print the range.

Example 8.4. User interaction in high-level code.

```java
public class Test {
  public static void main(String[] args) {
    Car car = new Car();
    car.mpg = 34;
    car.make = "Honda";
    car.model = "Civic";
    car.tankCapacity = 21;
    out.println("The range is " + car.getRange() + " miles.");
  }
}

class Car {
  double mpg;
  String make;
  String model;
  double tankCapacity;

  double getRange() {
    return tankCapacity * mpg;
  }
}
```

```
The range is 714.0 miles.
```

Printing the range in `main` is better than printing it within a method belonging to the `Car` class. The reason has to do with reusability. Having a `getRange` method that returns the range allows more than one caller to get the range and print it out, or use it in other ways. In contrast, the `printRange` method of example 8.3 isn't as useful because it doesn't give the calling method the option of printing the range in a different way. In general, performing input and output within a class's instance methods makes code less reusable. Instead, input and output functionality should gravitate to high-level code, and algorithms should gravitate to low-level code. Low-level code is within classes, and should be more generic in nature, so that it can be more useful to a variety of callers. High-level code, in contrast, is code that utilizes classes to implement the high-level objectives of an application.

Caller: Colloquially, the code that calls a method.

Tip 7. As you work on your application, always maintain an awareness of which part of your code is high-level and which is low-level. As you gain experience, keeping your code organized will get easier.

Technique 12. Don't perform input or output in low-level code

A class's instance methods should allow the calling code to retrieve or change the class's data. User interaction (input and output) shouldn't be done at a low level, but rather at a higher level such as the `main` method. This makes a class's methods more reusable.

Exercises

8.3   Create a class that represents a baseball game. Add data elements for the two team names, number of innings, the first team's total runs and the second team's total runs. Add a method that returns the name of the winning team. Test the method to make sure it works.

8.4   Create a class that represents a calendar event. It should contain the event's name and the event's date (day, month and year). Add a method that tells the user how many days remain until the event occurs.

- Hint 1: Create two instances of the `java.time.LocalDate` class, one representing today's date, and one representing the calendar event's date.
- Hint 2: Get today's date with `LocalDate.now()`.

- Hint 3: Convert the event's date to a `LocalDate` using `LocalDate.of(year, month, day)`.
- Hint 4: You can get the number of days between two `LocalDate`s with the syntax `java.time.temporal.ChronoUnit.DAYS.between(date1, date2)`, which returns a long integer.

8.3 Constructors

A class in Java can be initialized more easily using a constructor, which is a special method that has the same name as the class and has no return type, not even `void`. The constructor's parameters provide initial data that is used by the constructor to initialize the instance data. Next, we revise example 8.4 by adding a constructor to the `Car` class, and using it to initialize the data instead of initializing each piece of data separately within the `main` method,

Example 8.5. Class constructors.

```java
public class Test {
  public static void main(String[] args) {
    Car car = new Car(34, "Honda", "Civic", 21);
    out.println("The range is " + car.getRange() + " miles.");
  }
}

class Car {
  double mpg;
  String make;
  String model;
  double tankCapacity;

  public Car(double mpg, String make, String model, double tankCapacity) {
    this.mpg = mpg;
    this.make = make;
    this.model = model;
    this.tankCapacity = tankCapacity;
  }

  double getRange() {
    return tankCapacity * mpg;
  }
}
```

```
The range is 714.0 miles.
```

The constructor is called when an object is created using the "new" keyword, as on line 3 of example 8.5, and the parameters provided in the object creation must match the parameters that the constructor expects.

Line 15 shows the initialization of the instance variable mpg using the parameter having the same name. Since the parameter mpg has the same name as the instance variable mpg, it *hides* it. All references to mpg within the constructor will refer to the parameter instead of the instance variable. But, the instance variable can still be accessed using the "this.mpg" notation. Thus, we initialize the instance variable with the syntax "this.mpg = mpg".

Identifier hiding: when an identifier from an enclosing scope isn't accessible because another variable having the same name is declared in an inner scope.

In the same way, the other three data members are initialized on lines 16-18. Thus, the `Car` constructor initializes all four instance variables using the data passed into the constructor as parameters. If needed, additional initialization can be performed within constructors, although we didn't need to do that in this example.

A constructor that takes no parameters is called the default constructor. It's called when you create an object with the syntax "new Car()". If you don't declare any constructors, a default constructor is implicitly created for you, which is why the code in example 8.1 is able to create a new `InventoryItem` object in the statement "InventoryItem item = new InventoryItem()".

Default constructor: The constructor that takes no parameters. If no constructors are defined, Java creates an implicit default constructor.

Multiple constructors can be declared when you want to provide different ways of creating objects of a class. Consider example 8.6 where the class allows a caller to create a `Car` object by specifying all four attributes, or just the make and model,

Example 8.6. Multiple constructors.

```java
public class Test {
  public static void main(String[] args) {
    Car car1 = new Car(34, "Honda", "Civic", 21);
    out.println("The " + car1.model + "'s range is " + car1.getRange() + "
      miles.");
    Car car2 = new Car("Ford", "Fiesta");
    out.println("The " + car2.model + "'s range is " + car2.getRange() + "
      miles.");
  }
}

class Car {
  double mpg;
  String make;
  String model;
  double tankCapacity;

  public Car(double mpg, String make, String model, double tankCapacity) {
    this.mpg = mpg;
    this.make = make;
    this.model = model;
    this.tankCapacity = tankCapacity;
```

```
21    }
22
23    public Car(String make, String model) {
24      this.mpg = 20; // default mpg is 20 miles per gallon
25      this.make = make;
26      this.model = model;
27      this.tankCapacity = 15; // default tank capacity is 15 gallons
28    }
29
30    double getRange() {
31      return tankCapacity * mpg;
32    }
33 }
```

```
The Civic's range is 714.0 miles.
The Fiesta's range is 300.0 miles.
```

When the caller (the `main` method in this case) uses the constructor that accepts only make and model, the mpg and tankCapacity attributes are initialized to default values.

It's good practice to declare values that don't change, such as the default mpg and tankCapacity, as named constants. Example 8.7 does just that,

Example 8.7. Using named constants.

```
1  class Car {
2    double mpg;
3    String make;
4    String model;
5    double tankCapacity;
6
7    final double DEFAULT_MPG = 20;
8    final double DEFAULT_TANK_CAPACITY = 15;
9
10   public Car(double mpg, String make, String model, double tankCapacity) {
11     this.mpg = mpg;
12     this.make = make;
13     this.model = model;
14     this.tankCapacity = tankCapacity;
15   }
16
17   public Car(String make, String model) {
18     this.mpg = DEFAULT_MPG;
19     this.make = make;
20     this.model = model;
21     this.tankCapacity = DEFAULT_TANK_CAPACITY;
22   }
23
24   double getRange() {
25     return tankCapacity * mpg;
26   }
27 }
```

```
The Civic's range is 714.0 miles.
The Fiesta's range is 300.0 miles.
```

Note the use of the `final` keyword, which indicates that the default values are *constants*, that is, they can't be changed after being assigned a value in the initialization on lines 7 and 8 of example 8.7. When a constant value is used in more than one place within a program, having it declared as a named constant helps by ensuring that its value is only specified in one place, an application of technique 5 on page 75.

Constants in Java are in uppercase with underscores by convention.

Technique 13. Use named constants

Use named constants for values that don't change.

The next example (8.8) further simplifies the code in example 8.7 by consolidating the repeated code within the two constructors of the `Car` class,

```
1  class Car {
2    double mpg;
3    String make;
4    String model;
5    double tankCapacity;
6
7    static final double DEFAULT_MPG = 20;
8    static final double DEFAULT_TANK_CAPACITY = 15;
9
10   public Car(double mpg, String make, String model, double tankCapacity) {
11     this.mpg = mpg;
12     this.make = make;
13     this.model = model;
14     this.tankCapacity = tankCapacity;
15   }
16
17   public Car(String make, String model) {
18     this(DEFAULT_MPG, make, model, DEFAULT_TANK_CAPACITY);
19   }
20
21   double getRange() {
22     return tankCapacity * mpg;
23   }
24 }
```

Example 8.8. Constructor chaining.

```
The Civic's range is 714.0 miles.
The Fiesta's range is 300.0 miles.
```

There are two things to note about example 8.8,

- The constructor that accepts only make and model has *called* the constructor that accepts all four attributes as parameters. To call one constructor from another, the `this` keyword is used as the method name. By passing the default values for mpg and tank capacity on line 18, we've consolidated the repeated code in the two constructors by having the first constructor do the second constructor's work. This is another application of technique 5 on page 75.
- To use the named constants `DEFAULT_MPG` and `DEFAULT_TANK_-CAPACITY` as parameters to another constructor, we've had to add the `static` keyword to the two constants. The `static` keyword associates the constant with the class, and not the instance of the class. We'll explain the `static` keyword in detail later on, in section 9.6.

Constructor chaining: Having one constructor call another to increase code reuse and decrease code duplication.

This way of consolidating code within constructors by having one constructor call another is called *constructor chaining*. Any number of constructors can be chained, typically where each constructor calls the one that's slightly more specific.

> **The `this` keyword**
>
> Code within a class's methods can use the `this` keyword to refer to the object whose context the method is running in. Using "this." is like using the dot qualifier on an object reference. Thus, "car.mpg" in `main` is similar to using "this.mpg" in an instance method belonging to the `Car` class. The "this" keyword isn't needed except in certain situations,
>
> - The identifier being referenced is hidden by another identifier of the same name, as in "mpg" in the constructor on line 15 of example 8.5.
> - A constructor needs to call another constructor, as in example 8.8.

Exercises

8.5   Use example 8.8 as a starting point. Create an array of four cars in the `main` method. Add a method that takes an array of cars as a parameter, and returns the average miles per gallon for all of them. Print the average in the `main` method.

8.4 UML

The Unified Modeling Language (UML) Provides many types of diagrams that help document software programs. Its class diagram is a standard way to visually represent a class. It depicts the class's name, its attributes and their types, and its methods along with each method's return type and its parameters with the type of each parameter. Figure 8.1 shows a UML diagram of the `Car` class in example 8.8. The class name is at the top of the diagram. The next section shows the class's attributes, each with a name and a type. The final section of the diagram shows the class's methods, each with the method's name, return type, parameter names and the type of each parameter. The two constructors don't have a return type.

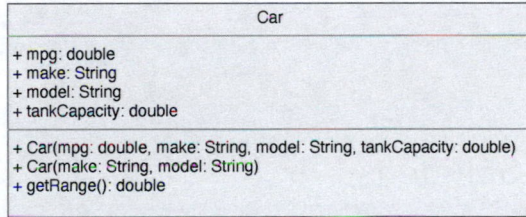

Figure 8.1: UML diagram of the `Car` class.

UML diagrams are commonly used to document a class so that consumers of that class know what it offers as far as attributes and methods. They can also be used to provide specifications for classes that a system requires, as documentation for the programmer who is tasked with implementing the class.

The excellent and free `https://diagrams.net` website supports various UML diagram types.

Chapter Summary

- A class encapsulates the data elements and code that relate to a particular domain entity. A class defines a type, and instances of that class can be created using the `new` keyword.
- A class can contain data elements and methods that operate on the data elements.

- A class's constructor is a special method that allows it to initialize its data. The caller can provide initial data values as arguments to the constructor.

```
1  public class Test {
2    public static void main(String[] args) {
3      Employee susan = new Employee(1001, "Susan");
4      out.println("Susan's information is: " + susan);
5    }
6  }
7
8  class Employee {
9
10     int id;
11     String name;
12
13     public Employee (int id, String name) {
14       this.id = id;
15       this.name = name;
16     }
17
18     @Override
19     public String toString() {
20       return name + " (ID " + id + ")";
21     }
22 }
```

Creating class instance

Class declaration

Class variables

Constructor

Exercise Solutions

8.1
```
1  class TelevisionProgram {
2    String title;
3    String genre;
4    int productionYear;
5    String[] actors;
6    String director;
7  }
```

8.2
```
1  class NewsStory {
2    String title;
3    String summary;
4    String author;
5    int publicationYear;
6  }
```

8.3
```
1  import static java.lang.System.out;
2
3  public class Test {
4    public static void main(String[] args) {
5      BaseballGame game = new BaseballGame();
6      game.team1Name = "Red Sox";
7      game.team2Name = "Yankees";
8      game.numberOfInnings = 11;
9      game.team1Runs = 3;
```

```
10       game.team2Runs = 4;
11
12       out.print("The winning team is: " + game.winningTeam());
13     }
14   }
15
16   class BaseballGame {
17     String team1Name, team2Name;
18     int numberOfInnings;
19     int team1Runs, team2Runs;
20
21     String winningTeam() {
22       if (team1Runs > team2Runs)
23         return team1Name;
24       else
25         return team2Name;
26     }
27   }
```

```
The winning team is: Yankees
```

8.4
```
1    import static java.lang.System.out;
2
3    import java.time.LocalDate;
4
5    public class Test {
6      public static void main(String[] args) {
7        Event event = new Event();
8        event.day = 1;
9        event.month = 1;
10       event.year = 2025;
11
12       out.print("Days until New Year's day 2025: " + event.daysUntil()
           );
13     }
14   }
15
16   class Event {
17     String name;
18     int day, month, year;
19
20     int daysUntil() {
21       LocalDate today = LocalDate.now();
22       LocalDate date = LocalDate.of(year, month, day);
23       return (int) java.time.temporal.ChronoUnit.DAYS.between(today,
           date);
24     }
25   }
```

```
Days until New Year's day 2025: 1419
```

8.5
```
1      public static void main(String[] args) {
2
3        Car[] carArray = {
4            new Car(34, "Honda", "Civic", 15),
5            new Car(39, "Toyota", "Corola", 16),
6            new Car(32, "Ford", "F350", 25),
7            new Car(26, "Jeep", "Cherokee", 21),
```

```
 8      };
 9      out.println("Average miles per gallon = " + AverageMpg (carArray
        ));
10    }
11
12    private static double AverageMpg (Car[] cars)
13    {
14      double total = 0;
15      for (Car car : cars)
16        total += car.getMpg();
17      return total / cars.length;
18    }
```

```
Average miles per gallon = 32.75
```

Inheritance | 9

9.1 Enumerations

An important Java feature we haven't seen yet is enumerations. An enumeration is a way to define a type whose instances can only have a certain set of possible values. For example, we could define an enumeration to represent a color,

```java
enum Color { BLUE, RED, GREEN, YELLOW, MAGENTA, BLACK,
                WHITE, GRAY };
```

By convention, enumeration values are uppercase, since they're essentially constants.

Having defined the `Color` enumeration, we can use it as a type,

```java
Color backgroundColor = Color.GREEN;
```

This defines a variable called `backgroundColor` of type `Color`, and initializes its value to `Color.GREEN`. We would further be able to test an enum variable's value with an `if` or `switch` statement,

```java
if (backgroundColor == Color.RED)
```

We could have used `String` as the type of this variable, but that wouldn't constrain the variable's possible values. By using an enumeration as the color variable's type, we guard against accidentally mistyping the color, and that reduces the number of bugs in the long run.

To show enumerations in action, the next example (9.1) has a class representing different types of employees,

Example 9.1. Using an enumeration.

```java
1   import static java.lang.System.out;
2
3   public class Test {
4     public static void main(String[] args) {
5
6       Employee susan = new Employee(1001, "Susan", EmployeeType.FULL_TIME, 52000,
          0, 0);
7       Employee irene = new Employee(1002, "Irene", EmployeeType.FULL_TIME, 36000,
          0, 0);
8       Employee phil = new Employee(1003, "Phil", EmployeeType.CONTRACT, 0, 40,
          45);
9       Employee william = new Employee(1004, "William", EmployeeType.PART_TIME, 0,
          15, 28);
10
11      out.printf("Susan's weekly salary is $%.2f\n", susan.getWeeklySalary());
12      out.printf("Irene's weekly salary is $%.2f\n", irene.getWeeklySalary());
13      out.printf("Phil's weekly salary is $%.2f\n", phil.getWeeklySalary());
14      out.printf("William's weekly salary is $%.2f\n", william.getWeeklySalary())
          ;
15    }
16  }
17
18  enum EmployeeType { FULL_TIME, PART_TIME, CONTRACT };
19
20  class Employee {
21
22    EmployeeType type;
23    int id;
24    String name;
25    int yearlySalary;    // for full-time employees
26    int hourlySalary;    // for part-time and contract employees
27    int hoursPerWeek;    // for part-time and contract employees
28    double taxRate = 0.205; // for full-time and part-time employees
29
30    public Employee (int id, String name, EmployeeType type, int yearlySalary,
          int hoursPerWeek, int hourlySalary) {
31      this.id = id;
32      this.name = name;
33      this.type = type;
34      this.yearlySalary = yearlySalary;
35      this.hoursPerWeek = hoursPerWeek;
36      this.hourlySalary = hourlySalary;
37    }
38
39    double getWeeklySalary () {
40      switch (type) {
41      case FULL_TIME:
42        return (double) yearlySalary / 52 * (1 - taxRate);
43      case PART_TIME:
44        return (double) hoursPerWeek * hourlySalary * (1 - taxRate);
45      case CONTRACT:
46        return (double) hoursPerWeek * hourlySalary;
47      default:
48        return 0;
49      }
50    }
51  }
```

```
Susan's weekly salary is $795.00
Irene's weekly salary is $550.38
Phil's weekly salary is $1800.00
William's weekly salary is $333.90
```

The `Employee` class encapsulates data related to employees, such as ID and name, as well as algorithms such as the code that calculates weekly salary in `getWeeklySalary()`. In the example, only full-time and part-time employees have taxes deducted from their pay. In addition, only part-time and contract employees are paid by the hour. This is a good example of how to isolate code related to an entity (an employee in this case) within the class representing that entity.

The `EmployeeType` enumeration is defined on line 18 of example 9.1. Note the role that this enumeration plays in the example. It's used by the `Employee` class to define the employee's type, and to calculate weekly salaries appropriately for each type of employee. An invalid employee type, e.g., as a parameter to the `Employee` constructor on line 6, or in a case clause of the switch statement on line 40, will result in a compile-time error, so the syntactic support that enumerations provides is significant.

Finally, note the `default` clause of the `switch` statement within `getWeeklySalary`. Without it, Java generates a compile error because it's doesn't recognize that all possible enumeration values have been handled by the `switch`. It's awkward, but the only obvious alternatives are to add a "return 0;" after the `switch` or replace the `switch` statement with a series of `if` statements.

Object Oriented Programming

Java supports object oriented programming, as do many other languages including C++, from which Java is derived. Object oriented programming refers to arranging code in classes that represent real-world entities, which helps to keep related code together in the same area of a program.

9.2 Inheritance

A Java class can extend another, and when it does, it inherits all of the base class's data members and instance methods. This allows

Creating a new class by extending another is sometimes called *subclassing*. The new class is the subclass, and the class that has been extended is called the *superclass*, the *base class* or the *parent class*.

you to extend the functionality of a class without modifying that class. This is usually used to create a new class that represents a more specific entity than the entity that the parent class represents. For example, a class representing a vehicle can be extended by a class representing a sedan. Extending a class is accomplished with the following syntax,

```
class Sedan extends Vehicle { }
```

We'll demonstrate inheritance by transforming example 9.1 so that each of the employee types has its own class,

Example 9.2. Using inheritance.

```java
 1  import static java.lang.System.out;
 2
 3  public class Test {
 4    public static void main(String[] args) {
 5
 6      FullTimeEmployee susan = new FullTimeEmployee(1001, "Susan", 52000);
 7      FullTimeEmployee irene = new FullTimeEmployee(1002, "Irene", 36000);
 8      ContractEmployee phil = new ContractEmployee(1003, "Phil", 40, 45);
 9      PartTimeEmployee william = new PartTimeEmployee(1004, "William", 15, 28);
10
11      out.printf("Susan's weekly salary is $%.2f\n", susan.getWeeklySalary());
12      out.printf("Irene's weekly salary is $%.2f\n", irene.getWeeklySalary());
13      out.printf("Phil's weekly salary is $%.2f\n", phil.getWeeklySalary());
14      out.printf("William's weekly salary is $%.2f\n", william.getWeeklySalary())
          ;
15    }
16  }
17
18  class Employee {
19
20    int id;
21    String name;
22
23    public Employee (int id, String name) {
24      this.id = id;
25      this.name = name;
26    }
27  }
28
29  class FullTimeEmployee extends Employee {
30
31    int yearlySalary;
32    double taxRate = 0.205;
33
34    public FullTimeEmployee (int id, String name, int yearlySalary) {
35      super(id, name);
36      this.yearlySalary = yearlySalary;
37    }
38
39    double getWeeklySalary () {
40      return (double) yearlySalary / 52 * (1 - taxRate);
41    }
42  }
43
```

```
44  class PartTimeEmployee extends Employee {
45
46    int hourlySalary;
47    int hoursPerWeek;
48    double taxRate = 0.205;
49
50    public PartTimeEmployee (int id, String name, int hoursPerWeek, int
          hourlySalary) {
51      super(id, name);
52      this.hoursPerWeek = hoursPerWeek;
53      this.hourlySalary = hourlySalary;
54    }
55
56    double getWeeklySalary () {
57      return (double) hoursPerWeek * hourlySalary * (1 - taxRate);
58    }
59  }
60
61  class ContractEmployee extends Employee {
62
63    int hourlySalary;
64    int hoursPerWeek;
65
66    public ContractEmployee (int id, String name, int hoursPerWeek, int
          hourlySalary) {
67      super(id, name);
68      this.hoursPerWeek = hoursPerWeek;
69      this.hourlySalary = hourlySalary;
70    }
71
72    double getWeeklySalary () {
73      return (double) hoursPerWeek * hourlySalary;
74    }
75  }
```

```
Susan's weekly salary is $795.00
Irene's weekly salary is $550.38
Phil's weekly salary is $1800.00
William's weekly salary is $333.90
```

Note the following details concerning the class inheritance in example 9.2,

- There are three types that each extend `Employee`. The `Employee` base class contains data and functionality that is common to all employee types (in this case, the employee's ID and name).
- Each of the three derived types, `FullTimeEmployee`, `PartTimeEmployee` and `ContractEmployee` inherit the `Employee` base class's data members (employee ID and name), and add their own data members, for example the yearly salary in the case of `FullTimeEmployee`.
- Each derived type's constructor calls the `Employee` constructor using the keyword `super`, passing it the parameters relevant

to the superclass. This is similar to the constructor chaining we saw earlier in chapter 8.

- Each derived type implements its own `getWeeklySalary` method, which is called from the `main` method.

Let us contrast examples 9.1 and 9.2 with respect to the distribution of data and code. When we switched to subclassing, the data and code specific to each type of employee migrated into the respective subclasses. This consolidated the data and code related to each subclass, but also broke apart the code which previously had computed weekly salaries for all employee types. We know from technique 2 on page 53 that related code should be together, so from first principles, it's not entirely clear that the move to subclassing is the better approach. There are pros and cons, as you can see, but on the whole it's better in example 9.2. It all depends on whether the new arrangement of data and code is more readable and more maintainable.

Exercises

9.1   Create classes for Animal, Dog, Cat and Mouse. The Dog, Cat and Mouse classes should extend Animal. Add a name variable to Animal. Add a method named speak() to each animal's class, which print out its sound. Create one object of each animal type, and make it speak.

9.3 The `Object` Class

You can have a class extend another, which itself extends a third class, and so on. Each subclass inherits all the data elements and methods in its direct superclass and each of its indirect superclasses.

In Java, all classes are ultimately derived from the built-in `Object` class, either directly or indirectly. If your class doesn't explicitly extend another class, it automatically extends the `Object` class. `Object` implements a small number of methods. A few of these are noteworthy:

- `toString()` returns a string representing the object, which is useful if you want to print the object to the console.

- `hashCode()` returns an integer that represents the object's data, and is meant to distinguish objects that contain different data. It's used internally in certain situations, and we'll deal with it in chapter 14.
- `equals()` returns true or false depending on whether the object's data is identical to the data within another object of the same type. For example, two strings should be compared for equality using the `equals()` method instead of the equality operator (==). We'll deal with `equals()` in chapter 14 as well.

Since every class extends `Object`, either directly or indirectly, every class inherits its methods, which includes `toString`. To see `toString` in action, let's print an employee's information,

```
1  ...
2    FullTimeEmployee susan = new FullTimeEmployee(1001, "Susan", 52000);
3    out.printf("Susan's information is: " + susan.toString());
4  ...
```

Example 9.3. Default `toString()`.

```
Susan's information is: FullTimeEmployee@4b1210ee
```

The output from example 9.3 shows the object's class name followed by its location in memory, which is the string that the `Object` class's `toString` implementation returns. The return value from the `toString` method is concatenated with the literal string by the + operator, after which the concatenated string is output by `printf`. Since the expression on the left of the + operator is a string, the operator converts the expression on its right to a string, so the explicit call to `toString` isn't actually necessary. If `susan.toString()` is replaced with `susan`, the `toString` method is invoked implicitly to convert the object to a string,

Calling `toString` implicitly.

```
1  ...
2    FullTimeEmployee susan = new FullTimeEmployee(1001, "Susan", 52000);
3    out.printf("Susan's information is: " + susan);
4  ...
```

Example 9.4. Implicitly calling `toString()`.

```
Susan's information is: FullTimeEmployee@4b1210ee
```

A class can choose to *override* a method that's defined by its superclass. In example 9.5, the `Employee` class overrides `toString` to provide a more appropriate representation of the object,

Overriding a method.

Example 9.5. Overriding
toString().

```
1  ...
2  FullTimeEmployee susan = new FullTimeEmployee(1001, "Susan", 52000);
3  out.printf("Susan's information is: " + susan);
4  ...
5  class Employee {
6
7    int id;
8    String name;
9
10   public Employee (int id, String name) {
11     this.id = id;
12     this.name = name;
13   }
14
15   @Override
16   public String toString() {
17     return name + " (ID " + id + ")";
18   }
19 }
20 ...
```

```
Susan's information is: Susan (ID 1001)
```

By providing its own implementation of the `toString` method,
the `Employee` class has hidden the base class's implementation.
When `printf` calls `toString`, the implementation within `Employee`
is called, instead of the implementation in `Object`. Note the `@Over-`
`ride` keyword before the `toString` implementation, which tells Java
that it's meant to override a method that's defined in the base class.
The code will work without this `@Override` keyword, but in the
presence of `@Override`, the compiler generates an error if there is
no such method in the base class, which guards against a mistyped
method name.

This isn't quite enough, as we want to add the data contained in `Full-`
`TimeEmployee`, not just `Employee`, so we must override `toString`
in the `FullTimeEmployee` class, which is done in the next example
(9.6),

Example 9.6. Chaining toString().

```
1  ...
2  class FullTimeEmployee extends Employee {
3
4    int yearlySalary;
5    double taxRate = 0.205;
6
7    public FullTimeEmployee (int id, String name, int yearlySalary) {
8      super(id, name);
9      this.yearlySalary = yearlySalary;
10   }
11
12   double getWeeklySalary () {
13     return (double) yearlySalary / 52 * (1 - taxRate);
```

```
14    }
15
16    @Override
17    public String toString() {
18      return super.toString() + " [$" + yearlySalary + "/year]";
19    }
20 }
21 ...
```

```
Susan's information is: Susan (ID 1001) [$52000/year]
```

Note the new `toString` implementation in `FullTimeEmployee`, which calls its superclass's `toString` implementation, and adds its own information to it. Calling the superclass's `toString` implementation is done using the `super` keyword, just as we do in the constructor to call the base class's constructor. Without the `super` keyword, calling `toString` won't call the implementation within `Employee`, but rather will call the `toString` method in the `FullTimeEmployee` class. This is because defining `toString` in `Full-TimeEmployee` hides the base class's implementation of that same method.

Note that we could have output all the data items within the `toString` method of the `FullTimeEmployee` class, including data items defined in `Employee`. But it's better to structure our code as in the above example, so that code related to the `Employee`'s data is within the `Employee` class, in keeping with technique 11 on page 140.

After making a similar change in the other two classes, `PartTimeEmployee` and `ContractEmployee` to include hourly salary, our example is as follows,

```
 1 import static java.lang.System.out;
 2
 3 public class Test {
 4   public static void main(String[] args) {
 5
 6     FullTimeEmployee susan = new FullTimeEmployee(1001, "Susan", 52000);
 7     FullTimeEmployee irene = new FullTimeEmployee(1002, "Irene", 36000);
 8     ContractEmployee phil = new ContractEmployee(1003, "Phil", 40, 45);
 9     PartTimeEmployee william = new PartTimeEmployee(1004, "William", 15, 28);
10
11     out.println("Susan's information is: " + susan);
12     out.println("Irene's information is: " + irene);
13     out.println("Phil's information is: " + phil);
14     out.println("William's information is: " + william);
15   }
16 }
17
```

Example 9.7. Employee example using `toString()`.

```
18  class Employee {
19
20    int id;
21    String name;
22
23    public Employee (int id, String name) {
24      this.id = id;
25      this.name = name;
26    }
27
28    @Override
29    public String toString() {
30      return name + " (ID " + id + ")";
31    }
32  }
33
34  class FullTimeEmployee extends Employee {
35
36    int yearlySalary;
37    double taxRate = 0.205;
38
39    public FullTimeEmployee (int id, String name, int yearlySalary) {
40      super(id, name);
41      this.yearlySalary = yearlySalary;
42    }
43
44    double getWeeklySalary () {
45      return (double) yearlySalary / 52 * (1 - taxRate);
46    }
47
48    @Override
49    public String toString() {
50      return super.toString() + " [$" + yearlySalary + "/year]";
51    }
52  }
53
54  class PartTimeEmployee extends Employee {
55
56    int hourlySalary;
57    int hoursPerWeek;
58    double taxRate = 0.205;
59
60    public PartTimeEmployee (int id, String name, int hoursPerWeek, int
          hourlySalary) {
61      super(id, name);
62      this.hoursPerWeek = hoursPerWeek;
63      this.hourlySalary = hourlySalary;
64    }
65
66    double getWeeklySalary () {
67      return (double) hoursPerWeek * hourlySalary * (1 - taxRate);
68    }
69
70    @Override
71    public String toString() {
72      return super.toString() + " [$" + hourlySalary + "/hour]";
73    }
74  }
75
76  class ContractEmployee extends Employee {
77
78    int hourlySalary;
```

```
79    int hoursPerWeek;
80
81    public ContractEmployee (int id, String name, int hoursPerWeek, int
          hourlySalary) {
82      super(id, name);
83      this.hoursPerWeek = hoursPerWeek;
84      this.hourlySalary = hourlySalary;
85    }
86
87    double getWeeklySalary () {
88      return (double) hoursPerWeek * hourlySalary;
89    }
90
91    @Override
92    public String toString() {
93      return super.toString() + " [$" + hourlySalary + "/hour]";
94    }
95  }
```

```
Susan's information is: Susan (ID 1001) [$52000/year]
Irene's information is: Irene (ID 1002) [$36000/year]
Phil's information is: Phil (ID 1003) [$45/hour]
William's information is: William (ID 1004) [$28/hour]
```

Figure 9.1 shows the UML diagram for the four classes in example 9.7. Inheritance is depicted with an arrow from the derived class to the extended class.

Exercises

9.2   Extend your solution to exercise 9.1 on page 156. Add a constructor that initializes the name, and override the toString method in Animal to print the animal's name. Create one object of each animal type, and print them out.

9.3   Extend your solution to exercise 9.2. Print the animal type along with the animal's name, and make each animal speak.

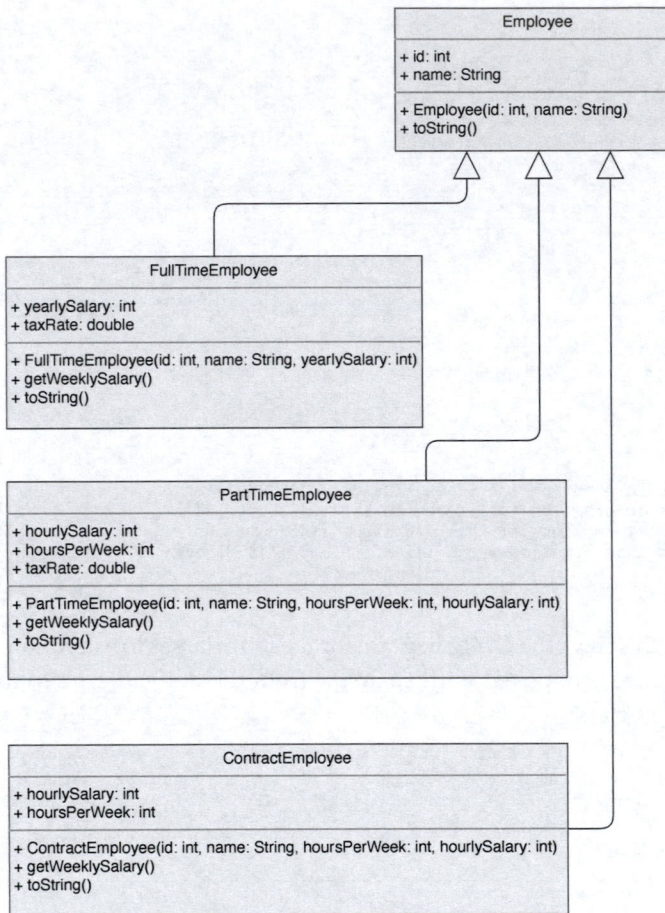

Figure 9.1: UML diagram of the `Employee` class and the classes that extend it.

9.4 Access Modifiers

Three common levels of access are provided by Java: `public`, `private` and `protected`. They're optionally used in the declaration of data elements and methods of a class.

- `public`: allows any code to access the data element or method.
- `private`: allows only code within the class itself to access the data element or method.
- `protected`: allows only code within the class or its subclasses to access the data element or method.

These access modifiers are meant to restrict access to certain data and functionality within a class in order to enforce a particular way of using the class or enforce rules imposed by the problem domain. The following example (9.8) illustrates this,

```java
1  public static void main(String[] args) {
2    PartTimeEmployee william = new PartTimeEmployee(1004, "William", 15, 12);
3    out.println("William's information is: " + william);
4  }
5  ...
6  class PartTimeEmployee extends Employee {
7
8    final int MINIMUM_WAGE = 15;
9
10   private int hourlySalary;
11   private int hoursPerWeek;
12   private double taxRate = 0.205;
13
14   public PartTimeEmployee (int id, String name, int hoursPerWeek, int
         hourlySalary) {
15     super(id, name);
16     setHoursPerWeek(hoursPerWeek);
17     setHourlySalary(hourlySalary);
18   }
19
20   public int getHourlySalary () {
21     return hourlySalary;
22   }
23
24   public void setHourlySalary (int hourlySalary) {
25     if (hourlySalary < MINIMUM_WAGE)
26       hourlySalary = MINIMUM_WAGE;
27     this.hourlySalary = hourlySalary;
28   }
29
30   public int getHoursPerWeek () {
31     return hoursPerWeek;
32   }
33
34   public void setHoursPerWeek (int hoursPerWeek) {
35     this.hoursPerWeek = hoursPerWeek;
36   }
37
38   double getWeeklySalary () {
39     return (double) hoursPerWeek * hourlySalary * (1 - taxRate);
40   }
41
42   @Override
43   public String toString() {
44     return super.toString() + " [$" + hourlySalary + "/hour]";
45   }
46 }
```

Example 9.8. Defining getters and setters.

```
William's information is: William (ID 1004) [$15/hour]
```

Example 9.8 adds four new methods to the `PartTimeEmployee` class, two for each of the class variables `hourlySalary` and `hoursPerWeek`. For each of those variables, *get* and *set* methods have been defined. The *get* methods return the respective variables, and the

Defining *getters* and *setters*.

set methods modify the variables by assigning new values. For example, `getHourlySalary` returns the value of `hourlySalary` and `setHourlySalary` sets the value of `hourlySalary` to a new value. These methods are commonly known as *getters* and *setters*.

Also note in example 9.8 that the variables `hourlySalary` and `hoursPerWeek` are now `private`, while the getters and setters are `public`. The getters and setters can be used from outside the class, while code outside the class can't directly access the class variables. Thus, the getters and setters manage access to these variables. This is useful for two reasons,

This is an example of how object oriented techniques are meant to minimize the effects of future changes in the code.

- If the internal implementation of a particular algorithm changes, and a class's variables change as a result, the getters and setters can often be adjusted without changing their signatures. Since calling code, that is, code that uses the class, can't directly access the class variables and only uses the getters and setters, the programmer is guaranteed that his or her internal changes to the class won't result in external code having to be adjusted.

Depending on the problem domain, these domain rules are sometimes called *business rules*.

- If the particular problem domain has rules that the program needs to enforce, setters provide a place to consolidate the enforcement of those rules, and that way the programmer doesn't need to enforce the rules in each section of code where the relevant data value is changed. In the above example, `setHourlySalary` checks to make sure that the hourly salary is at least equal to the minimum wage.

Note that the constructor also calls the two setters. That way, each class variable is only modified directly in one place, the setter.

> **Technique 14. Use getters and setters to manage access to class variables**
>
> Getters and setters don't have to be used for every class variable, but they should be used when either of the above two benefits applies. This is subjective, and involves anticipating the future needs of your program.

UML diagrams document access levels. The plus or minus sign to the left of each attribute and method indicate a public or private access level, respectively.

9.5 Abstract Classes

An abstract class is one that represents a real-world entity that has multiple flavors, such as the `Employee` class in example 9.7. In example 9.7, Instances of the `Employee` class itself aren't created directly. We only create instances of the subclasses of `Employee`. Thus, `Employee` is only there to define the common attributes that its subclasses share. We'll illustrate how abstract classes are defined in Java with example 9.9,

```java
1  import static java.lang.System.out;
2
3  public class Test {
4    public static void main(String[] args) {
5
6      FullTimeEmployee susan = new FullTimeEmployee(1001, "Susan", 52000);
7      FullTimeEmployee irene = new FullTimeEmployee(1002, "Irene", 36000);
8      ContractEmployee phil = new ContractEmployee(1003, "Phil", 40, 45);
9      PartTimeEmployee william = new PartTimeEmployee(1004, "William", 15, 28);
10
11     out.println("Susan's information is: " + susan);
12     out.println("Irene's information is: " + irene);
13     out.println("Phil's information is: " + phil);
14     out.println("William's information is: " + william);
15   }
16 }
17
18 abstract class Employee {
19
20   int id;
21   String name;
22
23   public Employee (int id, String name) {
24     this.id = id;
25     this.name = name;
26   }
27
28   @Override
29   public String toString() {
30     return name + " (ID " + id + ")";
31   }
32
33   abstract double getWeeklySalary();
34 }
35
36 class FullTimeEmployee extends Employee {
37
38   int yearlySalary;
39   double taxRate = 0.205;
40
41   public FullTimeEmployee (int id, String name, int yearlySalary) {
42     super(id, name);
43     this.yearlySalary = yearlySalary;
44   }
45
46   double getWeeklySalary () {
47     return (double) yearlySalary / 52 * (1 - taxRate);
48   }
```

Example 9.9. Abstract classes.

```
49
50    @Override
51    public String toString() {
52      return super.toString() + " [$" + yearlySalary + "/year]";
53    }
54  }
55
56  class PartTimeEmployee extends Employee {
57
58    final int MINIMUM_WAGE = 15;
59
60    private int hourlySalary;
61    private int hoursPerWeek;
62    private double taxRate = 0.205;
63
64    public PartTimeEmployee (int id, String name, int hoursPerWeek, int
          hourlySalary) {
65      super(id, name);
66      setHoursPerWeek(hoursPerWeek);
67      setHourlySalary(hourlySalary);
68    }
69
70    public int getHourlySalary () {
71      return hourlySalary;
72    }
73
74    public void setHourlySalary (int hourlySalary) {
75      if (hourlySalary < MINIMUM_WAGE)
76        hourlySalary = MINIMUM_WAGE;
77      this.hourlySalary = hourlySalary;
78    }
79
80    public int getHoursPerWeek () {
81      return hoursPerWeek;
82    }
83
84    public void setHoursPerWeek (int hoursPerWeek) {
85      this.hoursPerWeek = hoursPerWeek;
86    }
87
88    double getWeeklySalary () {
89      return (double) hoursPerWeek * hourlySalary * (1 - taxRate);
90    }
91
92    @Override
93    public String toString() {
94      return super.toString() + " [$" + hourlySalary + "/hour]";
95    }
96  }
97
98  class ContractEmployee extends Employee {
99
100   int hourlySalary;
101   int hoursPerWeek;
102
103   public ContractEmployee (int id, String name, int hoursPerWeek, int
          hourlySalary) {
104     super(id, name);
105     this.hoursPerWeek = hoursPerWeek;
106     this.hourlySalary = hourlySalary;
107   }
108
```

```
109    double getWeeklySalary () {
110      return (double) hoursPerWeek * hourlySalary;
111    }
112
113    @Override
114    public String toString() {
115      return super.toString() + " [$" + hourlySalary + "/hour]";
116    }
117 }
```

```
Susan's information is: Susan (ID 1001) [$52000/year]
Irene's information is: Irene (ID 1002) [$36000/year]
Phil's information is: Phil (ID 1003) [$45/hour]
William's information is: William (ID 1004) [$28/hour]
```

Note that the `Employee` class now has the `abstract` keyword (line 18), and has the new `getWeeklySalary` method definition with the abstract keyword and no body (line 33). We say that the method `getWeeklySalary` is *abstract*, as it has no body defined, thus each non-abstract class derived from `Employee` must define it (otherwise, the compiler will generate an error). We also say that the `Employee` class is abstract, as it can't be instantiated directly. The main benefit of abstract classes is to declare the methods that must be implemented by concrete classes that extend the abstract class.

Concrete class: a class that is not abstract.

9.6 The Static Keyword

A static variable is a variable that doesn't belong to an *instance* of the class. Rather, it belongs to the class itself. The class doesn't need to have any instances defined in order for a static variable of that class to exist and hold a value. This is useful, for example, to define constants, such as `Math.PI`, which is a constant defined in the built-in `Math` class. To use `Math.PI`, we didn't have to create an instance of the `Math` class. Instead, to reference a static variable, constant or method in a class, we use the class name followed by a dot, then the name of the variable, constant or method.

Declaring a static variable or constant is done by adding the `static` keyword before the type of that variable or constant. Initialization of static variables or constants is accomplished with the usual initialization syntax. Note that static variables or constants are initialized when the program starts, as opposed to class variables which are initialized when each instance of the class is created.

Static methods are defined by adding the `static` keyword before the return type. Static methods can't refer to instance variables, since a static method isn't defined in the context of an instance, but rather in the context of the class itself. Static methods allow a class to offer functionality that doesn't require instance data. An example of this is the `Math.random()` method that we used in chapters 4 and 5. Here again, it's not necessary to create an instance of the `Math` class in order to use its static methods. We just prefix the static method's name with the class name. Example 9.10 defines a static method that converts miles per hour to kilometers per hour,

Example 9.10. Static methods.

```java
 1  import static java.lang.System.out;
 2  import java.util.Scanner;
 3
 4  public class Test {
 5    public static void main(String[] args) {
 6
 7      Scanner input = new Scanner(System.in);
 8      out.print("Enter miles per hour: ");
 9      double milesPerHour = input.nextDouble();
10
11      out.printf("%.2f miles per hour is equal to %.2f kilometers per hour",
12          milesPerHour, Car.kmPerHour(milesPerHour));
13
14      input.close();
15    }
16  }
17
18  class Car {
19
20    public static double KM_PER_MILE = 1.60934;
21
22    public static double kmPerHour(double milesPerHour) {
23      return milesPerHour * KM_PER_MILE;
24    }
25  }
```

```
Enter miles per hour: 80
80.00 miles per hour is equal to 128.75 kilometers per hour
```

Chapter Summary

- Classes can extend one another. A class that extends another class inherits its data elements and functionality, and can override the base class's functionality with its own implementation.
- All classes ultimately extend the built-in `Object` class, either directly or indirectly.

- A class's data elements and methods can have access modifiers that prevent code outside the class from accessing them.

```java
1  public class Test {
2    public static void main(String[] args) {
3      FullTimeEmployee susan = new FullTimeEmployee(1001, "Susan", 52000);   ← Creating class instance
4      out.println("Susan's information is: " + susan);
5    }
6  }
7
8  class Employee {                                                            ← Class declaration
9
10     int id;                                                                 ← Class variables
11     String name;
12
13     public Employee (int id, String name) {                                 ← Constructor
14       this.id = id;
15       this.name = name;
16     }
17
18     @Override
19     public String toString() {                                              ← Overriding base class method
20       return name + " (ID " + id + ")";
21     }
22  }
23                                                                             ← One class extending another
24  class FullTimeEmployee extends Employee {
25
26     int yearlySalary;
27     double taxRate = 0.205;
28
29     public FullTimeEmployee (int id, String name, int yearlySalary) {
30       super(id, name);                                                      ← Constructor chaining
31       this.yearlySalary = yearlySalary;
32     }
33
34     double getWeeklySalary () {
35       return (double) yearlySalary / 52 * (1 - taxRate);
36     }
37                                                                             ← Calling base class method
38     @Override
39     public String toString() {
40       return super.toString() + " [$" + yearlySalary + "/year]";
41     }
42  }
```

Exercise Solutions

9.1
```java
1  ...
2    public static void main(String[] args) {
3      Cat cat = new Cat();
4      Mouse mouse = new Mouse();
5      Dog dog = new Dog ();
6
7      cat.speak();
8      mouse.speak();
9      dog.speak();
```

```
10    }
11 ...
12
13 class Animal {
14   String name;
15 }
16
17 class Cat extends Animal {
18   public void speak() {
19     out.println("meow!");
20   }
21 }
22
23 class Dog extends Animal {
24   public void speak() {
25     out.println("bark!");
26   }
27 }
28
29 class Mouse extends Animal {
30   public void speak() {
31     out.println("squeak!");
32   }
33 }
```

```
meow!
squeak!
bark!
```

9.2

```
 1 ...
 2   public static void main(String[] args) {
 3     Cat cat = new Cat("Skip");
 4     Mouse mouse = new Mouse("Flash");
 5     Dog dog = new Dog ("Trick");
 6
 7     out.println(cat);
 8     out.println(mouse);
 9     out.println(dog);
10   }
11 ...
12
13 class Animal {
14   String name;
15
16   public Animal (String name) {
17     this.name = name;
18   }
19
20   @Override
21   public String toString() {
22     return "name=" + name;
23   }
24 }
25
26 class Cat extends Animal {
27   public Cat (String name) {
28     super (name);
29   }
30
31   public void speak() {
32     out.println("meow!");
```

```
33      }
34    }
35
36    class Dog extends Animal {
37      public Dog (String name) {
38        super (name);
39      }
40
41      public void speak() {
42        out.println("bark!");
43      }
44    }
45
46    class Mouse extends Animal {
47      public Mouse (String name) {
48        super (name);
49      }
50
51      public void speak() {
52        out.println("squeak!");
53      }
54    }
```

```
name=Skip
name=Flash
name=Trick
```

9.3

```
1    ...
2      public static void main(String[] args) {
3        Cat cat = new Cat("Skip");
4        Mouse mouse = new Mouse("Flash");
5        Dog dog = new Dog ("Trick");
6
7        out.println(cat);
8        cat.speak();
9        out.println(mouse);
10       mouse.speak();
11       out.println(dog);
12       dog.speak();
13     }
14   ...
15
16   class Animal {
17     String name;
18
19     public Animal (String name) {
20       this.name = name;
21     }
22
23     @Override
24     public String toString() {
25       return "name=" + name;
26     }
27   }
28
29   class Cat extends Animal {
30     public Cat (String name) {
31       super (name);
32     }
33
34     @Override
```

```java
35    public String toString() {
36       return "Cat: " + super.toString();
37    }
38
39    public void speak() {
40      out.println("meow!");
41    }
42 }
43
44 class Dog extends Animal {
45    public Dog (String name) {
46       super (name);
47    }
48
49    @Override
50    public String toString() {
51       return "Dog: " + super.toString();
52    }
53
54    public void speak() {
55       out.println("bark!");
56    }
57 }
58
59 class Mouse extends Animal {
60    public Mouse (String name) {
61       super (name);
62    }
63
64    @Override
65    public String toString() {
66       return "Mouse: " + super.toString();
67    }
68
69    public void speak() {
70       out.println("squeak!");
71    }
72 }
```

```
Cat: name=Skip
meow!
Mouse: name=Flash
squeak!
Dog: name=Trick
bark!
```

Collections | 10

10.1 The `ArrayList` Class

The size of a native array in Java can't be changed after it's been created. An array is allocated with a particular size, and any attempt to read or write past the end of the array results in an `ArrayIndex-OutOfBoundsException`. This can be seen in example 10.1,

```java
import static java.lang.System.out;

public class Test {
  public static void main(String[] args) {

    String[] names = new String[3];
    names[0] = "Corrine";
    names[1] = "Steph";
    names[2] = "Zoe";
    names[3] = "Krich";

    out.print("The first name is: " + names[0]);
  }
}
```

Example 10.1. Writing past the end of an array.

```
Exception in thread "main" java.lang.ArrayIndexOutOfBoundsException: Index 3 out of bounds for length 3
        at Test.main(Test.java:10)
```

Example 10.1 creates an array of three strings. After writing the three strings, it attempts to write a fourth string, which causes the exception on line 10, as seen in the output. The string `names` in the example is a *native* Java array. Java provides a collection class called `ArrayList` which is more convenient than native arrays when the size of the data can change at runtime. This class contains a native array internally, and the class resizes that native array when needed, so that the array can grow dynamically. It resizes the native array by allocating a new, larger, native array and copying the contents of the existing array to the new one. Using an `ArrayList` is slightly different than using a native array because different syntax is required, but most of the concepts involved are the same. Example 10.1 can be rewritten as in example 10.2 to use the `ArrayList` class,

Example 10.2. Using `ArrayList`.

```
1  import static java.lang.System.out;
2  import java.util.ArrayList;
3
4  public class Test {
5    public static void main(String[] args) {
6
7      ArrayList<String> names = new ArrayList<>();
8      names.add("Corrine");
9      names.add("Steph");
10     names.add("Zoe");
11     names.add("Krich");
12
13     out.print("The first name is: " + names.get(0));
14   }
15 }
```

```
The first name is: Corrine
```

`ArrayList` is one of Java's collection classes, and we'll have more to say about the rest of the collection classes later. The `names` variable is now a collection, that is, it's a reference to an object of the `ArrayList` class. Note the following differences between examples 10.1 and 10.2,

- The native array and the collection are declared differently:
  - The native array is declared with the syntax

    `String[] names`

    This declares `names` as a reference to an array of `String` objects.
  - The collection is declared with the syntax

    `ArrayList<String> names`

    This declares `names` as a reference to an object of type `ArrayList<String>`. This is read as "array list of strings", where `ArrayList` is a parameterized class, and `String` is the parameter. We'll explain parameterized classes later in this chapter.
- The native array and the collection are created differently:
  - The native array is created with the syntax

    `new String[3]`

    This allocates an array of three `String` references.
  - The collection is created with the syntax

```
new ArrayList<>()
```

This creates an object of type `ArrayList<String>`.

- The native array is created with a specific size of 3, and can't grow beyond that. The collection is created with an initial size of zero, and can grow to an unlimited size, constrained only by the available memory space.
- We write to the native array with the syntax `names[0] = "Corrine"`, using the index to specify the array element that we want to write to. In contrast, we add items to the collection using the `add` method.
- We read from the native array with the syntax `names[0]`. In contrast, we read from the collection using the `get` method.

As you see, declaring a collection, allocating it, writing to it and reading from it all use syntax that is different from the syntax you use when working with arrays, but conceptually the two are similar in that we allocate a variable to hold strings, and then write strings and read them. The main difference is that we don't need to track the maximum size of a collection, since it will grow as needed. But, we still need to take into account the *current* size of a collection, and if we attempt to read beyond the current size, a runtime exception will occur.

The current size of an `ArrayList` is retrieved with the `size` method (as opposed to using `.length` for arrays). Consider the following example (10.3) which reads an arbitrary number of integers from the user, and then outputs the sum of those numbers,

```
1   Scanner input = new Scanner(System.in);
2   ArrayList<Integer> numbers = new ArrayList<>();
3   int number = 0;
4   do {
5     out.print("Enter a number (-1 to exit): ");
6     number = input.nextInt();
7     input.nextLine();
8     if (number != -1)
9       numbers.add(number);
10  } while (number != -1);
11
12  int sum = 0;
13  for (int i = 0; i < numbers.size(); i++)
14    sum += numbers.get(i);
15  out.println("The sum is " + sum);
16
17  input.close();
```

Example 10.3. Processing an arbitrary number of integers.

```
Enter a number (-1 to exit): 13
Enter a number (-1 to exit): 14
Enter a number (-1 to exit): 15
Enter a number (-1 to exit): -1
The sum is 42
```

Example 10.3 creates a collection of integers then asks the user to enter numbers one after another. The user can enter −1 to terminate the loop, after which the sum of all numbers that were entered will be displayed. Note that the loop on lines 13 and 14 looks the same as many looping examples we've already seen, except that the collection's size is retrieved using the `size` method, and the elements of the collection are retrieved with the `get` method. However, the loop's essence remains the same as loops we've already written, and we track and use array indexes in the same way.

Writing to an existing index in a collection.

We saw how to add new items to the end of a collection using the `add` method. We haven't yet seen how to modify existing elements of a collection. That's easy to do with the `set` method, which takes two parameters, the index to write to, and the data to write to that index in the collection.

Exercises

10.1 Create an `ArrayList` of strings and try to add an integer to it. Does this result in a compile-time error, or run-time error?

10.2 Create an `ArrayList` of ten random numbers between 1 and 50. Then, iterate over the `ArrayList` and compute their average.

10.2 Generics

Generic classes, or *generics* for short, are classes that accept one or more parameters, the parameters themselves being classes. Java's collection classes are examples of such parameterized types. As seen in the previous section, `ArrayList` accepts a type as a parameter, which is the type of item to be held in the collection. The parameter must be a class, and can't be a native type, thus `ArrayList<Integer>` is a valid type definition, but `ArrayList<int>` is not. `Integer` is what we call a wrapper class. It's a class that encapsulates an integer value and provides additional useful functionality, such as the

`Integer.parseInt` method that we used in chapter 2. Table 10.1 shows some of the available wrapper classes that Java provides,

Native Type	Wrapper Class
int	Integer
long	Long
float	Float
double	Double
char	Character
boolean	Boolean

Table 10.1: Wrapper classes.

When creating an instance of a generic class, the syntax is `new ArrayList<Integer>()`, but `new ArrayList<>()` is also permitted, since the compiler can infer the parameter's type from the type of reference the collection will be assigned to. Thus the statement:

```
ArrayList<Integer> numbers = new ArrayList<>();
```

creates a new `ArrayList<Integer>` and assigns it to `numbers`, which is a reference to an `ArrayList<Integer>`.

Java uses the type's parameter (`Integer` in the above example) to enforce at compile time the parameter types for the collection's `add` and `set` methods, and the return type of the `get` method. In the case of an `ArrayList<Integer>`, the `add` method accepts a parameter of type `Integer`, and the `get` method returns a value of type `Integer`. Looking at the UML class definition for `ArrayList` in figure 10.1, you can see the type parameter is referred to simply as `E`.

`E` and `T` are common placeholders for the class parameter.

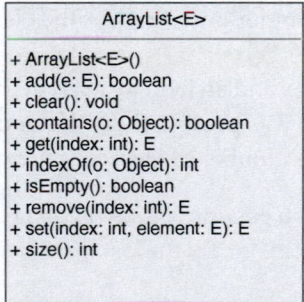

```
ArrayList<E>

+ ArrayList<E>()
+ add(e: E): boolean
+ clear(): void
+ contains(o: Object): boolean
+ get(index: int): E
+ indexOf(o: Object): int
+ isEmpty(): boolean
+ remove(index: int): E
+ set(index: int, element: E): E
+ size(): int
```

Figure 10.1: `ArrayList`'s partial class diagram.

While the class diagram for `ArrayList` has the placeholder `E` in place of the actual type parameter, your code will specify an actual type for the parameter and Java reflects that in the compilation and the editor's autocompletion support, which you can see in figure 10.2, where Eclipse shows that **add** accepts one parameter of type **Integer**,

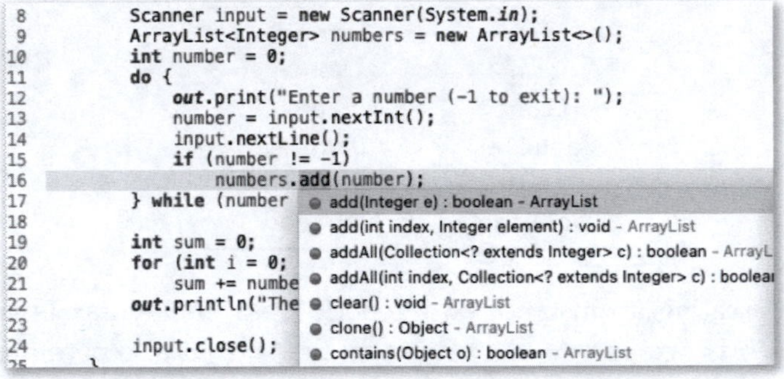

```
 8    Scanner input = new Scanner(System.in);
 9    ArrayList<Integer> numbers = new ArrayList<>();
10    int number = 0;
11    do {
12        out.print("Enter a number (-1 to exit): ");
13        number = input.nextInt();
14        input.nextLine();
15        if (number != -1)
16            numbers.add(number);
17    } while (number    ● add(Integer e) : boolean - ArrayList
18                        ● add(int index, Integer element) : void - ArrayList
19    int sum = 0;        ● addAll(Collection<? extends Integer> c) : boolean - ArrayL
20    for (int i = 0;     ● addAll(int index, Collection<? extends Integer> c) : boolea
21        sum += numbe    ● clear() : void - ArrayList
22    out.println("The    ● clone() : Object - ArrayList
23                        ● contains(Object o) : boolean - ArrayList
24    input.close();
25    }
```

Figure 10.2: Eclipse's autocompletion helper shows the declared parameter type.

Figure 10.1 shows some of **ArrayList**'s most important methods. Let's take a closer look at them,

You don't need to memorize these, but you should remember that they are there, so you can look up their details later when you need to use them. You will eventually use all of these methods.

- **add** takes one parameter, the new element to add to the list. It appends the item to the end of the list, increasing the list's size by one, and returns **true**.
- **clear** removes all items from the list.
- **contains** returns true or false depending on whether a specific item is in the list or not.
- **get** takes an index, and returns the element at that index in the list.
- **indexOf** takes an item and returns the first index at which that item occurs in the list, or -1 if the item isn't in the list.
- **isEmpty** returns **true** or **false** depending on whether the list is empty or not.
- **remove** takes an index and removes the element at that index, returning it.
- **set** takes an index and an item to insert at that index. It returns the element that was previously at that index.
- **size** returns the number of elements currently in the list.

You can create your own generic classes if you need to. Example 10.4 is a generic class that remembers the last three items that it's given,

Example 10.4. Defining your own generic class.

```
1  class LimitedMemory <E> {
2    private E item1 = null, item2 = null, item3 = null;
3
4    public void remember(E newItem) {
5      item3 = item2;
6      item2 = item1;
```

```
 7      item1 = newItem;
 8    }
 9
10    public ArrayList<E> getLastThree() {
11      ArrayList<E> result = new ArrayList<>();
12      result.add(item3);
13      result.add(item2);
14      result.add(item1);
15      return result;
16    }
17  }
```

The class definition **class LimitedMemory** is followed by the type parameter **<E>**, and the type **E** is used within the class as the type of three data items that this class can remember. The caller can keep sending it new items to remember, but it will only remember the last three items it has been given. The method **getLastThree** returns these three in an **ArrayList**. Now we can use this class to remember items of different types, as in example 10.5,

```
 1    Scanner input = new Scanner(System.in);
 2
 3    LimitedMemory<Integer> memory = new LimitedMemory<>();
 4    int number = 0;
 5    do {
 6      out.print("Enter a number (-1 to exit): ");
 7      number = input.nextInt();
 8      input.nextLine();
 9      if (number != -1)
10        memory.remember(number);
11    } while (number != -1);
12    out.println("The last three are: " + memory.getLastThree());
13    out.println();
14
15    LimitedMemory<String> memory2 = new LimitedMemory<>();
16    String name = "";
17    do {
18      out.print("Enter a name ('exit' to exit): ");
19      name = input.nextLine();
20      if (!name.equals("exit"))
21        memory2.remember(name);
22    } while (!name.equals("exit"));
23    out.println("The last three are: " + memory2.getLastThree());
24
25    input.close();
```

Example 10.5. Using your own generic class.

```
Enter a number (-1 to exit): 91
Enter a number (-1 to exit): 24
Enter a number (-1 to exit): -3
Enter a number (-1 to exit): 75
Enter a number (-1 to exit): 200
Enter a number (-1 to exit): -1
The last three are: [-3, 75, 200]

Enter a name ('exit' to exit): Larry
Enter a name ('exit' to exit): Bill
Enter a name ('exit' to exit): Nitro
Enter a name ('exit' to exit): Wolf
Enter a name ('exit' to exit): Yuri
Enter a name ('exit' to exit): exit
The last three are: [Nitro, Wolf, Yuri]
```

There are some things you aren't allowed to do within generic types, such as creating a new instance of the generic type E, and creating an array of the generic type E.

You probably won't need to define your own generic types often. Rather, you'll use them mostly by consuming the generic collection classes. Still, you should know that it's possible to create your own generics if you need to.

10.3 Iterating Over an `ArrayList`

There are several ways to iterate over an `ArrayList` collection.

for **Loop**

We saw in example 10.3 how to use a for-loop to get the sum of numbers in a list. Example 10.6 creates ten random numbers between 1 and 100, adds them to a list, then uses a **for** loop to print them out, followed by another **for** loop to compute the sum,

Example 10.6. Iterating over a list using a `for` loop.

```
1  import static java.lang.System.out;
2  import java.util.ArrayList;
3
4  public class Test {
5    public static void main(String[] args) {
6
7      // generate 10 random numbers, each between 1 and 100
8      ArrayList<Integer> numbers = new ArrayList<>();
9      for (int i = 0; i < 10; i++)
10       numbers.add((int) (Math.random() * 100) + 1);
11
12     printNumbers(numbers);
13     out.println("The sum is " + getSum(numbers));
14   }
```

```
15
16   public static void printNumbers(ArrayList<Integer> numbers) {
17     out.print("The list is ");
18     for (int i = 0; i < numbers.size(); i++)
19       out.print(numbers.get(i) + " ");
20     out.println();
21   }
22
23   public static int getSum(ArrayList<Integer> numbers) {
24     int sum = 0;
25     for (int i = 0; i < numbers.size(); i++)
26       sum += numbers.get(i);
27     return sum;
28   }
29 }
```

```
The list is 8 23 69 34 62 48 43 44 19 44
The sum is 394
```

Enhanced `for` Loop Syntax

The alternate `for` syntax that we first saw in example 6.14 can also be used to iterate through lists. This is called the *enhanced* for-loop syntax. Example 10.7 revises example 10.6 to use the enhanced `for` syntax,

```
1    public static void printNumbers(ArrayList<Integer> numbers) {
2      out.print("The list is ");
3      for (int number : numbers)
4        out.print(number + " ");
5      out.println();
6    }
7
8    public static int getSum(ArrayList<Integer> numbers) {
9      int sum = 0;
10     for (int number : numbers)
11       sum += number;
12     return sum;
13   }
```

Example 10.7. Iterating over a list using the enhanced `for` syntax.

```
The list is 34 24 87 7 55 74 79 60 26 54
The sum is 500
```

Using Iterators

An iterator is a class that helps us to iterate over the contents of a collection. The `iterator` method of the `ArrayList` class returns an object that is used to do the iteration. The iterator class has a `next` method that returns the next item in the collection, and a `hasNext` method that returns "true" as long as there are items remaining to be processed. Using an iterator is illustrated in the next example (10.8),

Example 10.8. Iterating over a list using an iterator class.

```java
1  import java.util.Iterator;
2  ...
3    public static void printNumbers(ArrayList<Integer> numbers) {
4      out.print("The list is ");
5      Iterator<Integer> iterator = numbers.iterator();
6      while (iterator.hasNext())
7        out.print(iterator.next() + " ");
8      out.println();
9    }
10
11   public static int getSum(ArrayList<Integer> numbers) {
12     int sum = 0;
13     Iterator<Integer> iterator = numbers.iterator();
14     while (iterator.hasNext())
15       sum += iterator.next();
16     return sum;
17   }
```

```
The list is 85 20 84 56 99 98 28 22 21 79
The sum is 592
```

Note that the iterator class is generic. Since `numbers` is of type `ArrayList<Integer>`, its `iterator` method on lines 5 and 13 each return an iterator of type `Iterator<Integer>`. The `while` loops continue calling `iterator.next()` until `iterator.hasNext()` returns false. The `next` method returns the next element of the list, in this case an `Integer` value.

Using `forEach`

The last way that we'll show to iterate over a list is to use its `forEach` method. This method takes a single parameter which contains a method. `forEach` will call this method once for each item contained in the list. The method receives the data item (of type `Integer` in this case) as a parameter, and can perform operations on that parameter. Example 10.9 shows this in action,

```java
public static void printNumbers(ArrayList<Integer> numbers) {
  out.print("The list is ");
  numbers.forEach((e) -> { out.print(e + " "); });
  out.println();
}

private static int sum = 0;
public static int getSum(ArrayList<Integer> numbers) {
  numbers.forEach((e) -> { sum += e; });
  return sum;
}
```

Example 10.9. Iterating over a list using `forEach`.

```
The list is 38 68 41 33 50 74 58 82 44 63
The sum is 551
```

As mentioned above, the parameter to `forEach` contains a method. The syntax `(e) -> { out.print(e + " "); }` is called a *lambda expression*, or *lambda* for short, which is code that is passed around like data. The syntax is shorthand for a method that takes a single parameter called `e`, and executes the statements contained within the curly braces. It's important for you to eventually be comfortable with lambda expressions, but it's more important for us at this point to focus on the basics. For that reason, this technique should be considered less important than the above three iteration techniques.

Lambda expression: a piece of code that's passed around like data.

The way `forEach` is being used to print the list is fine, but there's a problem with the way it's being used to compute the sum. The `sum` variable is declared as static because it can't be a local variable within `getSum`. If declared as a local variable in `getSum`, we get a compile-time error stating that accessing a variable declared in an enclosing scope from within this lambda expression requires it to be declared as `final`, which wouldn't work in our case because we need to increment the `sum` variable. Having `sum` as static at the class level lets us access it from within the lambda expression, because it technically wouldn't be in an enclosing scope. But the problem with using a static variable in this way is that there's only one instance of this variable, effectively making it a global variable. Unless you are using global variables as a place to store global settings, they're undesirable for two reasons,

Global variable: A variable that's available to all the code within a program. Using global variables tends to make tracing code dependencies more difficult.

Local variable: A variable that's defined in a local scope, such as a method.

- Global variables can be accessed from anywhere, so they can create a situation with subtle dependencies between different parts of a program. To reduce complexity and increase maintainability, we want different parts of the program to be self contained and independent, to the extent possible.

- If the `getSum` method was running more than once in parallel, it wouldn't work because all running instances share the same sum value. A single method can run multiple times in parallel if your code is multithreaded, such as code running on a web server with multiple web requests being processed simultaneously. A piece of code that uses a global variable in this way is called *non-reentrant*.

Technique 15. Avoid using global variables

Global variables should be avoided unless they hold data that's meant to be shared, such as global settings.

Now that we've explained why the code in example 10.9 is undesirable, we can show a slightly more complex implementation that doesn't have the drawback of using a static variable,

Example 10.10. Second attempt of iterating over a list using `forEach`.

```
1   public static void printNumbers(ArrayList<Integer> numbers) {
2     out.print("The list is ");
3     numbers.forEach((e) -> { out.print(e + " "); });
4     out.println();
5   }
6
7   public static int getSum(ArrayList<Integer> numbers) {
8     final ArrayList<Integer> sumList = new ArrayList<>();
9     sumList.add(0);
10    numbers.forEach((e) -> { sumList.set(0, sumList.get(0) + e); });
11    return sumList.get(0);
12  }
```

```
The list is 88 38 24 5 98 50 60 45 31 95
The sum is 534
```

The code in `getSum` within example 10.10 effectively uses an `ArrayList` as a container to hold the sum. It can be declared as `final` while still allowing the lambda expression's code to update its contents.

Exercises

10.3 Create an `ArrayList` of student names, and another `ArrayList` of grades, one grade per student. Iterate over both lists, and print each student's name with his or her grade on a separate line.

10.4 Modify your program from the previous exercise. Create a `Student` class that contains the student's name and grade. Create an `ArrayList` of `Student` objects and print each student's name with his or her grade on a separate line.

10.4 Example Project: Flight Database

We've got enough under our belt to attempt a slightly larger project now, putting together many of the concepts we've already learned. Along the way, we'll discuss some common practices with regard to the process of making software.

We'll write a program that allows the user to track airline flights, with features such as searching for flight by flight number or by destination. The program won't actually save the flights to a database (we'll add that in chapter 12).

It's important to keep in mind the phases of a project. First you should identify the requirements, then design the implementation, and finally implement the program.

The first thing to do is identify the list of features that your program needs. This shouldn't include technical details. It's a list of requirements. In the real world, sometimes you are given the requirements, and sometimes it's up to you to elicit them. Either way, it's important to have the requirements in writing, so that there's no ambiguity and you have a clear task to accomplish. Requirements shouldn't be too elaborate. Keep it brief and to the point. For this example project, we'll use the following list of features:

CRUD is a commonly used acronym that refers to the four basic operations offered in a software application, the ability to *create*, *read*, *update* and *delete* records.

- The user can add a new flight to the flight list.
- The user can delete a flight from the flight list.
- The user can change a flight's details.

- The user can display all flights.
- The user can look up a flight by airline and flight number.
- The user can search for flights by destination.
- Each flight record contains the airline, flight number, origin, destination, departure time, and arrival time.
- The program assumes every flight flies daily.

Just as you shouldn't start the coding before identifying the requirements, you shouldn't start coding before designing your program. The design doesn't contain requirements. Rather, it documents how each requirement will be implemented. As with the requirements, it should be brief and to the point. It's also important not to spend too much time on the design. It's just a starting point. As you write the code, your plan will often change, which is okay. The design doesn't have to conform to a specific format or list the design points in a specific order. Here's our design for implementing the above list of requirements,

- Repeatedly present a menu of choices with options for adding a flight, deleting a flight, changing a flight, displaying all flights, searching by flight number, searching by destination, and exiting from the program.
- Use three-letter airport codes for origin and destination.
- Create a class, `Flight`, to represent a flight.
- Use an `ArrayList` of `Flight` objects to contain the flights.
- The flights in the `ArrayList` aren't sorted in a particular order.
- When adding a new flight, gather the flight's data from the user and add the new `Flight` object to the `ArrayList`. Don't allow the user to add the flight if there's already a flight with the same airline and flight number.
- When deleting a flight, ask for the airline and flight number, locate the flight object's index in the `ArrayList`, then delete it using the index.
- Use hour and minute for the departure and arrival times.
- When changing a flight's details, ask for the airline and flight number, locate the flight in the `ArrayList`, then change the object's details. Don't allow the change if there's another flight in the list with the same airline and flight number.

Note that the design adds technical details, such as the class name (`Flight`) and the collection class to use (`ArrayList`). It also adds some details which may sound like requirements but weren't listed in the requirement list. For example, the design stipulates that no two flights in the list can have the same airline and flight number. It's okay to add details such as these as long as you notify the domain experts so that they can correct you if your assumption is wrong.

Although the design looks like a list of tasks, it's unordered. It also contains many details that aren't themselves tasks. So it's helpful to write down an abbreviated list of tasks in the order that you think will be easiest to implement,

- Write the `Flight` class.
- Create the application class and add a loop that displays the menu.
- Add the 'add flight' feature.
- Add the 'display all flights' feature.
- Add the 'look up by airline and flight number' feature.
- Add the 'delete flight' feature.
- Add the 'change a flight' feature.
- Add the 'search by destination' feature.

The above process is designed to help you think through the project. At this point, we have a good idea what code is needed, and a roadmap to write it. The first part is the `Flight` class, shown in example 10.11.

Getters and Setters

In most of our examples, we gloss over the use of getters and setters, to save some space. Since this is a larger example project, we will define getters and setters in the `Flight` class, and mark the instance variables as `private`.

Separate Java Files

In most of our examples, we have multiple Java classes in the same Java file, to keep things simple. Since this is a larger example project, we will put the `Flight` class in its own file, and mark it as `public`.

```java
public class Flight {
  public String origin;
  public String destination;
  public String airline;
  public int flightNumber;
  public int departureHour, departureMinute;
```

Example 10.11. The `Flight` class in `Flight.java`.

```
 7   public int arrivalHour, arrivalMinute;
 8
 9   public Flight (String origin, String destination, String airline,
10       int flightNumber, int departureHour, int departureMinute,
11       int arrivalHour, int arrivalMinute) {
12     this.origin = origin;
13     this.destination = destination;
14     this.airline = airline;
15     this.flightNumber = flightNumber;
16     this.departureHour = departureHour;
17     this.departureMinute = departureMinute;
18     this.arrivalHour = arrivalHour;
19     this.arrivalMinute = arrivalMinute;
20   }
21
22   public String getOrigin() {
23     return origin;
24   }
25
26   public void setOrigin(String origin) {
27     this.origin = origin;
28   }
29
30   public String getDestination() {
31     return destination;
32   }
33
34   public void setDestination(String destination) {
35     this.destination = destination;
36   }
37
38   public String getAirline() {
39     return airline;
40   }
41
42   public void setAirline(String airline) {
43     this.airline = airline;
44   }
45
46   public int getFlightNumber() {
47     return flightNumber;
48   }
49
50   public void setFlightNumber(int flightNumber) {
51     this.flightNumber = flightNumber;
52   }
53
54   public int getDepartureHour() {
55     return departureHour;
56   }
57
58   public void setDepartureHour(int departureHour) {
59     this.departureHour = departureHour;
60   }
61
62   public int getDepartureMinute() {
63     return departureMinute;
64   }
65
66   public void setDepartureMinute(int departureMinute) {
67     this.departureMinute = departureMinute;
68   }
```

```
69
70    public int getArrivalHour() {
71      return arrivalHour;
72    }
73
74    public void setArrivalHour(int arrivalHour) {
75      this.arrivalHour = arrivalHour;
76    }
77
78    public int getArrivalMinute() {
79      return arrivalMinute;
80    }
81
82    public void setArrivalMinute(int arrivalMinute) {
83      this.arrivalMinute = arrivalMinute;
84    }
85
86    @Override
87    public String toString() {
88      return String.format("%s %d (%s %02d:%02d -> %s %02d:%02d)", airline,
89        flightNumber, origin, departureHour, departureMinute, destination,
90        arrivalHour, arrivalMinute);
     }
}
```

Note that we're using the static method `String.format` in our `toString` method, which is like `printf` in that it uses format specifiers for greater control over the format of the output, but unlike `printf`, it writes the result to a string.

Using `String.format`.

We can't run the program yet, because we need to add the menu loop before there's anything that can be tested. But, we should aim to create a minimal program so that we can start testing it. Next is the menu loop,

```
1  import static java.lang.System.out;
2  import java.util.ArrayList;
3  import java.util.Scanner;
4
5  public class Test {
6    public static void main(String[] args) {
7
8      Scanner input = new Scanner (System.in);
9      ArrayList<Flight> flights = new ArrayList<>();
10
11     boolean done = false;
12     while (!done) {
13       out.println();
14       out.println("(A)dd flight");
15       out.println("(D)elete flight");
16       out.println("(C)hange a flight");
17       out.println("(L)ist all flights");
18       out.println("(1)Search by airline and flight number");
19       out.println("(2)Search by destination");
20       out.println("(E)xit");
21
22       String choice = input.nextLine();
23       switch (choice.toLowerCase()) {
```

Example 10.12. The menu loop in `Test.java`.

```
24        case "a":
25          addFlight(input, flights);
26          break;
27        case "d":
28          deleteFlight(input, flights);
29          break;
30        case "c":
31          modifyFlight(input, flights);
32          break;
33        case "l":
34          listFlights(flights);
35          break;
36        case "1":
37          showFlightDetails(input, flights);
38          break;
39        case "2":
40          searchByDestination(input, flights);
41          break;
42        case "e":
43          done = true;
44          break;
45        default:
46          out.println("Please try again");
47          break;
48      }
49    }
50
51    input.close();
52  }
53
54  private static void addFlight(Scanner input, ArrayList<Flight> flights) {
55  }
56
57  private static void deleteFlight(Scanner input, ArrayList<Flight> flights) {
58  }
59
60  private static void modifyFlight(Scanner input, ArrayList<Flight> flights) {
61  }
62
63  private static void listFlights(ArrayList<Flight> flights) {
64  }
65
66  private static void showFlightDetails(Scanner input, ArrayList<Flight>
        flights) {
67  }
68
69  private static void searchByDestination(Scanner input, ArrayList<Flight>
        flights) {
70  }
71 }
```

```
(A)dd flight
(D)elete flight
(C)hange a flight
(L)ist all flights
(1)Search by airline and flight number
(2)Search by destination
(E)xit
2

(A)dd flight
(D)elete flight
(C)hange a flight
(L)ist all flights
(1)Search by airline and flight number
(2)Search by destination
(E)xit
e
```

Note that we've added our `flights` object, of type `ArrayList<Flight>` on line 9. Note also that we've added empty placeholder methods for each option, so that we can begin testing right away. The loop looks like it's working, so we can move on to the 'add flight' and 'display all flights' features,

```
1  private static void addFlight(Scanner input, ArrayList<Flight> flights) {
2    out.print("Airline: ");
3    String airline = input.nextLine();
4    out.print("Flight Number: ");
5    int flightNumber = input.nextInt();
6    input.nextLine();
7    out.print("Origin: ");
8    String origin = input.nextLine();
9    out.print("Destination: ");
10   String destination = input.nextLine();
11
12   out.print("Departure time (hour:minute): ");
13   String departure = input.nextLine();
14   int colonIndex = departure.indexOf(':');
15   int departureHour = -1, departureMinute = -1;
16   if (colonIndex > 0) {
17     departureHour = Integer.parseInt(departure.substring(0, colonIndex));
18     departureMinute = Integer.parseInt(departure.substring(colonIndex + 1));
19   }
20
21   if (departureHour == -1 || departureMinute == -1) {
22     out.println("Invalid departure time");
23     return;
24   }
25
26   out.print("Arrival time (hour:minute): ");
27   String arrival = input.nextLine();
28   colonIndex = arrival.indexOf(':');
29   int arrivalHour = -1, arrivalMinute = -1;
30   if (colonIndex > 0) {
31     arrivalHour = Integer.parseInt(arrival.substring(0, colonIndex));
32     arrivalMinute = Integer.parseInt(arrival.substring(colonIndex + 1));
33   }
34
35   if (arrivalHour == -1 || arrivalMinute == -1) {
36     out.println("Invalid arrival time");
```

Example 10.13. 'Add flight' feature.

```
37      return;
38    }
39
40    Flight flight = new Flight(origin, destination, airline, flightNumber,
          departureHour, departureMinute, arrivalHour, arrivalMinute);
41    flights.add(flight);
42  }
43
44  private static void listFlights(ArrayList<Flight> flights) {
45    for (Flight flight : flights)
46      out.println(flight);
47  }
```

```
a
Airline: Delta
Flight Number: 1100
Origin: JFK
Destination: MCO
Departure time (hour:minute): 13:30
Arrival time (hour:minute): 16:11

(A)dd flight
(D)elete flight
(C)hange a flight
(L)ist all flights
(1)Search by airline and flight number
(2)Search by destination
(E)xit
l
Delta 1100 (JFK 13:30 -> MCO 16:11)
```

The last menu selection here is a lowercase L, not a digit 1.

We've added the **AddFlight** and **listFlights** implementations and finally were able to see some real results. When writing code, you should try to get something minimal working so that you can test it, then as you add each feature, test it before moving on to the next feature. This way of working incrementally has several benefits,

- If you have a design problem, you will discover it earlier if you work incrementally instead of trying to write everything first, and then start testing.
- Testing each feature directly after it's written allows you to more accurately predict when you will finish the implementation. You uncover and fix bugs before moving on. On the other hand, if you write a lot of code that's yet to be tested, you are far less certain of how many problems remain and how much longer you need to work before you're done.

Technique 16. Start testing as soon as you can

Try to write something that can be tested right away, so you don't write too much code before you can begin testing.

> **Technique 17. Test each feature right after you write it**
>
> After you write a feature, test it before moving on to the next feature.

As mentioned in tip 7 and technique 12 (page 141), you should always maintain an awareness of which parts of your code are higher level, and which are lower level. So far, it's pretty simple—the low-level code is in the `Flight` class, and the high-level code is in the `Test` class. All the input and output is performed in the high-level code (the `Test` class).

Keep in mind how your code is structured.

We won't add thorough error checking of the user's input until we've covered exceptions in chapter 12. We also won't be storing our data in a file until chapter 12, which means that the program won't read the flights from a saved file when it starts. So when testing each feature, we'll have to add two or three flights to the list each time we run the program. That's a little time consuming, so to avoid having to do that, we'll hardcode some test data. That way, the program will have some flights in the list when it starts, and we can save some time when testing. Near the top of our `main` method, we'll add code that adds flights after creating the flight list,

Adding test data.

```
1   ArrayList<Flight> flights = new ArrayList<>();
2   flights.add(new Flight("JFK", "MCO", "Delta", 1100, 13, 30, 16, 11));
3   flights.add(new Flight("LGA", "LAX", "United", 29, 6, 0, 9, 21));
4   flights.add(new Flight("CLE", "PDX", "Delta", 412, 9, 59, 11, 15));
5   flights.add(new Flight("SAT", "BWI", "American", 11, 20, 42, 1, 2));
6   flights.add(new Flight("LFT", "ATL", "Delta", 90, 12, 0, 15, 57));
7   flights.add(new Flight("SNA", "CVG", "Southwest", 170, 10, 30, 12, 28));
```

```
Delta 1100 (JFK 13:30 -> MCO 16:11)
United 29 (LGA 06:00 -> LAX 09:21)
Delta 412 (CLE 09:59 -> PDX 11:15)
American 11 (SAT 20:42 -> BWI 01:02)
Delta 90 (LFT 12:00 -> ATL 15:57)
Southwest 170 (SNA 10:30 -> CVG 12:28)
```

Everything looks good so far, so we're gaining confidence that we're on the right track. Since 'delete flight' and 'look up by airline and flight number' share the code that prompts for the airline and flight number, we'll add those next,

```
1   private static int findFlight(Scanner input, ArrayList<Flight> flights) {
2       out.print("Airline: ");
3       String airline = input.nextLine();
4       out.print("Flight number: ");
5       int flightNumber = input.nextInt();
```

Example 10.14. Adding features to delete a record and show a record's details.

```
6      input.nextLine();
7
8      for (int i = 0; i < flights.size(); i++)
9        if (airline.toLowerCase().equals(flights.get(i).getAirline().toLowerCase
       ()) &&
10           flightNumber == flights.get(i).getFlightNumber())
11         return i;
12
13     return -1;
14   }
15
16   private static void deleteFlight(Scanner input, ArrayList<Flight> flights) {
17     int index = findFlight(input, flights);
18     if (index == -1) {
19       out.println("Not found");
20       return;
21     }
22
23     flights.remove(index);
24     out.println("Deleted");
25   }
26
27   private static void showFlightDetails(Scanner input, ArrayList<Flight>
         flights) {
28     int index = findFlight(input, flights);
29     if (index == -1) {
30       out.println("Not found");
31       return;
32     }
33     out.println(flights.get(index));
34   }
```

```
d
Airline: united
Flight number: 29
Deleted

(A)dd flight
(D)elete flight
(C)hange a flight
(L)ist all flights
(1)Search by airline and flight number
(2)Search by destination
(E)xit
l
Delta 1100 (JFK 13:30 -> MCO 16:11)
Delta 412 (CLE 09:59 -> PDX 11:15)
American 11 (SAT 20:42 -> BWI 01:02)
Delta 90 (LFT 12:00 -> ATL 15:57)
Southwest 170 (SNA 10:30 -> CVG 12:28)
```

```
1
Airline: delta
Flight number: 90
Delta 90 (LFT 12:00 -> ATL 15:57)
```

Next is searching by destination, which bears some resemblance to searching by airline and flight number,

```
1   private static void searchByDestination(Scanner input, ArrayList<Flight>
        flights) {
2     out.print("Destination: ");
3     String destination = input.nextLine();
4
5     for (int i = 0; i < flights.size(); i++)
6       if (destination.toLowerCase().equals(flights.get(i).getDestination().
      toLowerCase()))
7         out.println(flights.get(i));
8   }
```

Example 10.15. Search by destination feature.

```
(A)dd flight
(D)elete flight
(C)hange a flight
(L)ist all flights
(1)Search by airline and flight number
(2)Search by destination
(E)xit
2
Destination: BWI
American 11 (SAT 20:42 -> BWI 01:02)
```

Next, the 'change a flight' feature,

```
1    private static void modifyFlight(Scanner input, ArrayList<Flight> flights) {
2      int index = findFlight(input, flights);
3      if (index == -1) {
4        out.println("Not found");
5        return;
6      }
7
8      Flight flight = flights.get(index);
9
10     // gather new flight data
11
12     out.print("Airline [" + flight.getAirline() + "]: ");
13     String airline = input.nextLine();
14     if (airline.isEmpty())
15       airline = flight.getAirline();
16
17     out.print("Flight Number [" + flight.getFlightNumber() + "]: ");
18     int flightNumber = 0;
19     String flightNumberString = input.nextLine();
20     if (flightNumberString.isEmpty())
21       flightNumber = flight.getFlightNumber();
22     else
23       flightNumber = Integer.parseInt(flightNumberString);
24
25     Flight foundFlight = getFlight(flights, airline, flightNumber);
26     if (foundFlight != null && foundFlight != flight) {
27       out.println("Airline and flight number already used.");
28       return;
29     }
30
31     out.print("Origin [" + flight.getOrigin() + "]: ");
32     String origin = input.nextLine();
33     if (origin.isEmpty())
34       origin = flight.getOrigin();
35
```

Example 10.16. Change flight details feature.

```
36    out.print("Destination [" + flight.getDestination() + "]: ");
37    String destination = input.nextLine();
38    if (destination.isEmpty())
39      destination = flight.getDestination();
40
41    String timeString = String.format("%02d:%02d", flight.getDepartureHour(),
        flight.getDepartureMinute());
42    out.print("Departure time (hour:minute) [" + timeString + "]: ");
43    String departure = input.nextLine();
44    int departureHour = flight.getDepartureHour(), departureMinute = flight.
        getDepartureMinute();
45    if (!departure.isEmpty()) {
46      int colonIndex = departure.indexOf(':');
47      if (colonIndex > 0) {
48        departureHour = Integer.parseInt(departure.substring(0, colonIndex));
49        departureMinute = Integer.parseInt(departure.substring(colonIndex + 1))
        ;
50      }
51      if (departureHour == -1 || departureMinute == -1) {
52        out.println("Invalid departure time");
53        return;
54      }
55    }
56
57    timeString = String.format("%02d:%02d", flight.getArrivalHour(), flight.
        getArrivalMinute());
58    out.print("Arrival time (hour:minute) [" + timeString + "]: ");
59    String arrival = input.nextLine();
60    int arrivalHour = flight.getArrivalHour(), arrivalMinute = flight.
        getArrivalMinute();
61    if (!arrival.isEmpty()) {
62      int colonIndex = arrival.indexOf(':');
63      if (colonIndex > 0) {
64        arrivalHour = Integer.parseInt(arrival.substring(0, colonIndex));
65        arrivalMinute = Integer.parseInt(arrival.substring(colonIndex + 1));
66      }
67      if (arrivalHour == -1 || arrivalMinute == -1) {
68        out.println("Invalid arrival time");
69        return;
70      }
71    }
72
73    // update flight's data
74    flight.setAirline(airline);
75    flight.setFlightNumber(flightNumber);
76    flight.setOrigin(origin);
77    flight.setDestination(destination);
78    flight.setDepartureHour(departureHour);
79    flight.setDepartureMinute(departureMinute);
80    flight.setArrivalHour(arrivalHour);
81    flight.setArrivalMinute(arrivalMinute);
82  }
83
84  private static Flight getFlight(ArrayList<Flight> flights, String airline,
        int flightNumber) {
85    for (Flight flight : flights)
86      if (flight.getAirline().toLowerCase().equals(airline) &&
87          flight.getFlightNumber() == flightNumber)
88        return flight;
89    return null;
90  }
```

```
c
Airline: delta
Flight number: 412
Airline [Delta]:
Flight Number [412]:
Origin [CLE]:
Destination [PDX]: JFK
Departure time (hour:minute) [09:59]:
Arrival time (hour:minute) [11:15]:

(A)dd flight
(D)elete flight
(C)hange a flight
(L)ist all flights
(1)Search by airline and flight number
(2)Search by destination
(E)xit
l
Delta 1100 (JFK 13:30 -> MCO 16:11)
United 29 (LGA 06:00 -> LAX 09:21)
Delta 412 (CLE 09:59 -> JFK 11:15)
American 11 (SAT 20:42 -> BWI 01:02)
Delta 90 (LFT 12:00 -> ATL 15:57)
Southwest 170 (SNA 10:30 -> CVG 12:28)
```

The code in example 10.16 allows the user to select a flight, then change any of its details. The user is able to hit the enter key to leave particular fields unchanged. The `modifyFlight` method checks to make sure the specified combination of airline and flight number aren't already used by a different flight. All that remains is to add the same checking to the `addFlight` method, which is left as an exercise for the reader.

A class can contain a collection as an attribute, in fact that's common. Table 10.2 shows some of the common patterns involving objects and collections.

Table 10.2: Some common collection patterns.

Pattern	Example
Object Object	Team object contains a Coach object
Object Collection Object	Team object contains a collection of Player objects
Collection Object Collection Object	A list of flights, each containing a list of passengers

Exercises

10.5   Create a program that manages sales at a convenience store. It should track a list of inventory items, with each inventory item containing a name, barcode, quantity available, quantity sold, and price. The user should be able to add a new inventory item to the list, delete an inventory item from the list, change an inventory item, list all inventory items, find an inventory item by barcode or find an inventory item using a partial name search.

   - Hint: For the partial name search, use the `String.contains` method to determine whether the user's input is part of the product name.

10.5 Other Collection Classes

Table 10.3 shows some of the collection classes that Java provides. As you can see from the table, `ArrayList` is used far more often than the others. Each has its own pros and cons, which we'll explore in detail in chapters 13 and 14.

Table 10.3: Some of Java's collection classes.

Class	Brief Description	Usage Frequency
ArrayList	Encapsulates an array of objects.	Very common
LinkedList	Each element points to the next one, forming a chain.	Rare
HashMap	Maps keys to values, where the key and value are arbitrary classes.	Somewhat common
HashSet	Contains distinct instances of an arbitrary class.	Rare

Chapter Summary

- The Java collection classes encapsulate native data structures such as arrays.
- Java collection classes grow automatically as more data is added to them.
- `ArrayList` is the most commonly used collection class, and encapsulates a native Java array.
- Collection classes are *generic*. They require a parameter specifying the type of data that will be contained.
- Collection classes offer methods to add data, remove data, find data items, iterate over the collection, and so on.

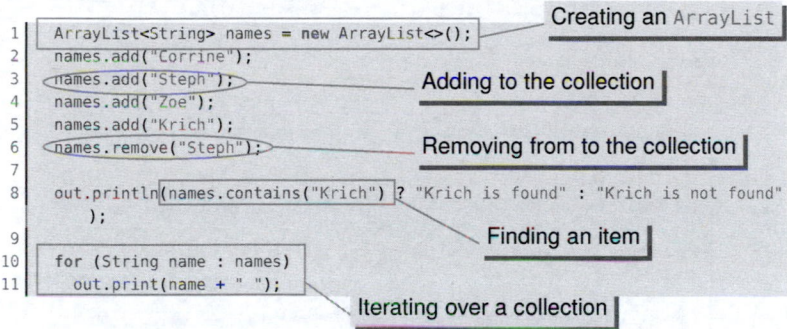

```
1   ArrayList<String> names = new ArrayList<>();          Creating an ArrayList
2   names.add("Corrine");
3   names.add("Steph");                        Adding to the collection
4   names.add("Zoe");
5   names.add("Krich");
6   names.remove("Steph");                     Removing from to the collection
7
8   out.println(names.contains("Krich") ? "Krich is found" : "Krich is not found"
    );
                                               Finding an item
9
10  for (String name : names)
11      out.print(name + " ");
                          Iterating over a collection
```

Exercise Solutions

10.1 This results in a compile-time error:

```
1   ArrayList<String> names = new ArrayList<>();
2   names.add(100);
```

```
ArrayList<String> names = new ArrayList<>();
names.add(100);
       The method add(int, String) in the type ArrayList<String> is not applicable for the arguments (int)
       3 quick fixes available:
          Add argument to match 'add(int, String)'
          Add arguments to match 'add(String, Object[], int)'
          Change to 'addAll(..)'
```

10.2
```
1   // create an ArrayList of ten random numbers
2   ArrayList<Integer> numbers = new ArrayList<>();
3   for (int i = 0; i < 10; i++)
```

```
4      numbers.add((int) (Math.random() * 50 + 1));
5
6   // get the average
7   int sum = 0;
8   for (int number : numbers)
9     sum += number;
10  out.println("The average is " + sum / numbers.size());
```

```
The average is 29
```

10.3
```
1   ArrayList<String> names = new ArrayList<>();
2   names.add("Jacob");
3   names.add("Liz");
4   names.add("Hakeem");
5
6   ArrayList<Integer> grades = new ArrayList<>();
7   grades.add(100);
8   grades.add(97);
9   grades.add(99);
10
11  for (int i = 0; i < names.size(); i++)
12    out.println(names.get(i) + ": " + grades.get(i));
```

```
Jacob: 100
Liz: 97
Hakeem: 99
```

10.4
```
1    ArrayList<Student> students = new ArrayList<>();
2    students.add(new Student("Jacob", 100));
3    students.add(new Student("Liz", 97));
4    students.add(new Student("Hakeem", 99));
5
6    for (int i = 0; i < students.size(); i++)
7      out.println(students.get(i));
8  ...
9  class Student {
10   String name;
11   int grade;
12
13   public Student (String name, int grade) {
14     this.name = name;
15     this.grade = grade;
16   }
17
18   @Override
19   public String toString() {
20     return name + ": " + grade;
21   }
22 }
```

```
Jacob: 100
Liz: 97
Hakeem: 99
```

Interfaces | **11**

11.1 Abstraction

Abstraction is a powerful technique that allows us to simplify our code, making it easier to maintain and change. Suppose we want to write a program that manages a waiting list. We need a collection that holds the list of names in the waiting list. When the program adds a name to the waiting list, the name is added to the collection, and when the program removes a name from the waiting list, the name is removed from the collection. The first name added to the waiting list is the first one removed, and subsequent names are removed from the waiting list in the order in which they were added. This program implements a *queue*. Our initial version of this program is shown in example 11.1,

FIFO is a commonly used acronym describing a *first in, first out* collection of items, where the items are removed from the collection in the order in which they were added.

```java
 1   ArrayList<String> queue = new ArrayList<>();
 2
 3   queue.add("John");
 4   out.println("Added John to queue");
 5
 6   queue.add("George");
 7   out.println("Added George to queue");
 8
 9   if (!queue.isEmpty()) {
10     String name = queue.remove(0);
11     out.println("Removed " + name + " from queue");
12   }
13
14   queue.add("Elizabeth");
15   out.println("Adding Elizabeth to queue");
16
17   while (!queue.isEmpty()) {
18     String name = queue.remove(0);
19     out.println("Removed " + name + " from queue");
20   }
```

Example 11.1. Managing a waiting list.

```
Added John to queue
Added George to queue
Removed John from queue
Adding Elizabeth to queue
Removed George from queue
Removed Elizabeth from queue
```

The queue is implemented as an `ArrayList` of strings. Adding a name to the queue is implemented with a call to the `ArrayList`'s `add` method, which adds the new name to the end of the list. Removing a name from the queue is done with a call to the `ArrayList`'s `remove` method, passing it the index zero, which removes the first item from the list, and returns it so that it can be printed out. The queue is checked, though, before removing a name from the waiting list, to make sure that it's not empty.

Although the program works, it's better to implement the waiting list using a specialized class. So we'll rewrite example 11.1 to add a `Queue` class which has methods for adding a queue item, removing a queue item, and checking whether the queue is empty. The `Queue` class is also generic so that it can hold a queue of items of any type. This second version is shown in example 11.2,

Example 11.2. Adding a `Queue` class.

```
1   public static void main(String[] args) {
2     Queue<String> queue = new Queue<>();
3
4     queue.enqueue("John");
5     out.println("Added John to queue");
6
7     queue.enqueue("George");
8     out.println("Added George to queue");
9
10    if (!queue.isEmpty()) {
11      String name = queue.dequeue();
12      out.println("Removed " + name + " from queue");
13    }
14
15    queue.enqueue("Elizabeth");
16    out.println("Adding Elizabeth to queue");
17
18    while (!queue.isEmpty()) {
19      String name = queue.dequeue();
20      out.println("Removed " + name + " from queue");
21    }
22  }
23  ...
24  class Queue<E> {
25
26    private ArrayList<E> list = new ArrayList<>();
27
28    public void enqueue(E object) {
29      list.add(object);
30    }
31
32    public E dequeue() {
33      return list.remove(0);
34    }
35
36    public boolean isEmpty() {
37      return list.isEmpty();
38    }
39  }
```

```
Added John to queue
Added George to queue
Removed John from queue
Adding Elizabeth to queue
Removed George from queue
Removed Elizabeth from queue
```

The point of abstraction is to hide implementation details so that the interface is intuitive and easy to use. A good abstraction has several characteristics:

- Its public interface is simple and minimal. In the case of the Queue class, its public interface consists of only three methods, enqueue, dequeue and isEmpty. These methods correspond to the conceptual way that a queue works—you can add an item, you can remove an item, and you can check whether the queue is empty.
- Each item in the public interface should be named to reflect its purpose. In the case of the Queue class, the public methods are enqueue, dequeue and isEmpty. These are clear and reflect the common terminology of queues.
- The implementation details aren't available to the caller. In the case of the Queue class, the inner ArrayList object is private, so it's unavailable to the consumer of the Queue class. That's an advantage, not a limitation. It helps the programmer avoid missteps and makes it clear how to use the Queue class. If the inner ArrayList could be accessed by the caller, it would be distracting and confusing to the programmer consuming the Queue class.

Data hiding is a commonly used term referring to a class hiding its internal implementation in order to simplify its interface.

Technique 18. Use abstraction to simplify your code

Using abstraction makes your code simpler and more maintainable.

Exercises

11.1 Use example 11.2 as a starting point, and make a Stack class, which implements a LIFO (*last in, first out*) data structure. Use the standard stack terms *push* and *pop* for the method names.

11.2 Interfaces

An interface in Java specifies a particular set of functionality which can be implemented by a class. It contains declarations for a set of methods without their bodies. In addition, all methods in an interface are implicitly public. A class can implement any number of interfaces. When a class implements an interface, it must provide a definition for each method in that interface.

Interfaces typically define common features that are implemented by more than one class. For example, the `Comparable` interface defines the `compareTo` method which is called by Java's `sort` method. Collections of a class can be sorted if the class implements the `Comparable` interface, and we'll see an example of that later in this chapter.

To illustrate interfaces, consider example 11.3 which updates example 11.2 to add a `Queue` interface. In example 11.3, the `Queue` class is renamed `MyQueue`,

Example 11.3. The `Queue` interface.

```java
public class Test {
  public static void main(String[] args) {

    MyQueue<String> queue = new MyQueue<>();

    queue.enqueue("John");
    out.println("Added John to queue");

    queue.enqueue("George");
    out.println("Added George to queue");

    if (!queue.isEmpty()) {
      String name = queue.dequeue();
      out.println("Removed " + name + " from queue");
    }

    queue.enqueue("Elizabeth");
    out.println("Adding Elizabeth to queue");

    while (!queue.isEmpty()) {
      String name = queue.dequeue();
      out.println("Removed " + name + " from queue");
    }
  }
}

interface Queue<E> {
  void enqueue(E object);
  E dequeue();
  boolean isEmpty();
}

class MyQueue<E> implements Queue<E> {
```

```
35    private ArrayList<E> list = new ArrayList<>();
36
37    public void enqueue(E object) {
38      list.add(object);
39    }
40
41    public E dequeue() {
42      return list.remove(0);
43    }
44
45    public boolean isEmpty() {
46      return list.isEmpty();
47    }
48 }
```

```
Added John to queue
Added George to queue
Removed John from queue
Adding Elizabeth to queue
Removed George from queue
Removed Elizabeth from queue
```

The example above defines the `Queue` interface, which specifies queue functionality. Multiple classes could implement that interface, in which case we would have a choice of which queue class to use in the above example.

The UML diagram for example 11.3 is shown in figure 11.1. Note that while inheritance is denoted in UML class diagrams with an arrow and solid line, implementing an interface is denoted with an arrow and dashed line.

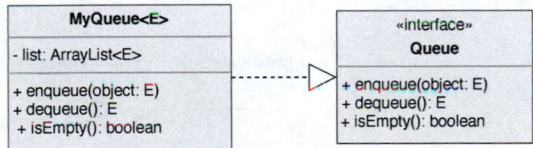

Figure 11.1: UML class diagram for example 11.3.

An interface offers a great way to implement an abstraction, since you can use it to specify needed functionality as a contract implemented by a class and utilized by code in another class.

Exercises

11.2 Create an interface called `Animal` that has a `speak` method, which prints a message to the console. Create a `Dog` class which implements the `Animal` interface. Its `speak` method should write "Bark" to the console. Create a `Cat` class which implements the `Animal` interface. Its `speak` method should write "Meow" to the console. Test the implementation with your `main` method.

11.3 Collection Class Hierarchy

Now that we know about interfaces, we can look at `ArrayList` and some of the classes and interfaces surrounding it in the hierarchy of collection classes. Figure 11.2 shows a partial UML class diagram for this hierarchy.

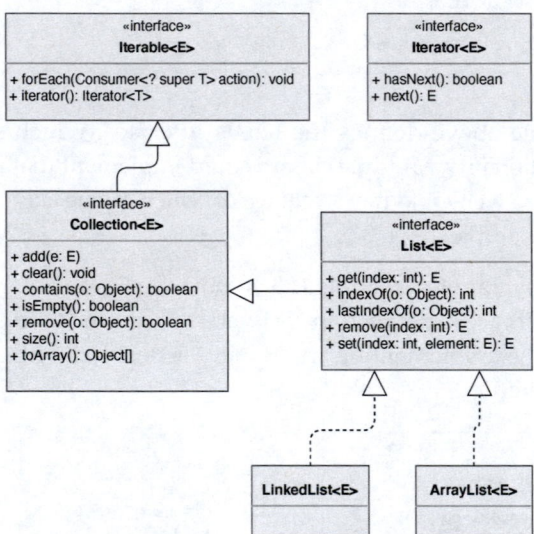

Figure 11.2: Partial collection class hierarchy in Java. For brevity, not all methods are listed.

As you can see in figure 11.2, both `ArrayList` and `LinkedList` implement the `List` interface, which extends the `Collection` interface, which in turn extends the `Iterable` interface, all of which are generic.

- `Iterator<E>` contains the methods `hasNext` and `next`, which were demonstrated in example 10.8.
- `Iterable<E>` contains the `iterator` method, which returns an object that implements `Iterator<E>` as demonstrated in example 10.8.
- `Collection<E>` contains methods that pertain to using collections, such as `add` and `contains`. A collection can contain duplicate data elements, but is inherently unordered.

- `List<E>` imposes a specific order on the elements within a collection, and adds methods that pertain to dealing with an ordered list, such as getting the data element at a specific index (`get`) and replacing the data element at a specific index (`set`).
- `ArrayList<E>` implements `List<E>` and maintains the list's data in an array. The array is initially small, but when it becomes full, the `ArrayList` class replaces it with another array that is larger than the previous one, and copies all the data to the new one. The new array is much larger than the old one, so that this time consuming operation of expanding the array isn't executed too often.
- `LinkedList<E>` implements `List<E>` by keeping each data element of type `E` in a node object. In addition to housing the data of type `E`, the node object has a pointer to the next node in the list. Thus, all elements of type `E` are kept in a specific order.

Different classes implement the same interface in different ways, and these different implementations each have their own pros and cons. For the `LinkedList` class to find the data element at a specific index, the list of node objects is walked from the beginning. This way of keeping a list within `LinkedList` has drawbacks since finding an element by index is slow, but other operations are fast, such as removing the first element of the list. We'll further discuss the performance of `ArrayList` versus `LinkedList` in chapter 13.

Example 11.4 creates two lists of numbers, one in an `ArrayList` and one in a `LinkedList`, then computes the sum of each list and prints it out,

```
public static void main(String[] args) {

  ArrayList<Integer> arrayList = new ArrayList<Integer>();
  for (int i = 0; i < 100; i++)
    arrayList.add(i);
  out.println("Sum of ArrayList is " + sumOfArrayList(arrayList));

  LinkedList<Integer> linkedList = new LinkedList<Integer>();
  for (int i = 0; i < 100; i++)
    linkedList.add(i);
  out.println("Sum of ArrayList is " + sumOfLinkedList(linkedList));
}

private static int sumOfArrayList(ArrayList<Integer> list) {
  int sum = 0;
  Iterator<Integer> iterator = list.iterator();
  while (iterator.hasNext())
    sum += iterator.next();
  return sum;
```

Example 11.4. Computing the sum of elements in a list.

```
20 }
21
22 private static int sumOfLinkedList(LinkedList<Integer> list) {
23   int sum = 0;
24   Iterator<Integer> iterator = list.iterator();
25   while (iterator.hasNext())
26     sum += iterator.next();
27   return sum;
28 }
```

```
Sum of ArrayList is 4950
Sum of LinkedList is 4950
```

Observe that `sumOfArrayList` and `sumOfLinkedList` contain the same code and only use the `list` variable to call methods that are provided by the `List` interface or interfaces that it extends. So, we can easily consolidate the two methods as in example 11.5,

Example 11.5. Using more general types.

```
 1 public static void main(String[] args) {
 2
 3   List<Integer> list = new ArrayList<Integer>();
 4   for (int i = 0; i < 100; i++)
 5     list.add(i);
 6   out.println("Sum of ArrayList is " + sumOf(list));
 7
 8   list = new LinkedList<Integer>();
 9   for (int i = 0; i < 100; i++)
10     list.add(i);
11   out.println("Sum of ArrayList is " + sumOf(list));
12 }
13
14 private static int sumOf(List<Integer> list) {
15   int sum = 0;
16   Iterator<Integer> iterator = list.iterator();
17   while (iterator.hasNext())
18     sum += iterator.next();
19   return sum;
20 }
```

```
Sum of ArrayList is 4950
Sum of LinkedList is 4950
```

Notice in example 11.5 that `sumOf` now takes a parameter of type `List<Integer>`, which is an interface type, but can still be used as the type of the `list` parameter, as long as the `list` parameter is only used to access methods provided by `List` or interfaces that `List` extends.

Because the `sumOf` method's `list` parameter can refer to an `ArrayList`, a `LinkedList`, or any other class that implements the `List` interface, it can take on many forms at runtime. This is referred to as *polymorphism*.

Polymorphism is derived from the latin *poly*, meaning many, and *morph* meaning form.

Note also that `List<Integer>` is used as the `list` variable's type in `main`. `list` is assigned a reference to an `ArrayList<Integer>`, which implements `List<Integer>`. This is preferred, since the reference `list` is only used to invoke methods of the `List` interface. Later in `main`, we assigned a `LinkedList<Integer>` to the `list` variable in the same way. Holding and passing around references to a more general class or interface is preferred since this allows code to apply to more situations.

Variables can hold references to interfaces.

> **Technique 19. Hold references to more general classes or interfaces when possible**
>
> Holding and passing around references to a more general class or interface is preferred since this allows code to apply in more situations.

11.4 **Comparable** and Sorting

Sorting a list of numbers can be done with the `Collections.sort` method, as shown in example 11.6,

```
1   // Generate 20 random numbers between 1 and 20
2   List<Integer> list = new ArrayList<Integer>();
3   for (int i = 0; i < 20; i++)
4     list.add((int) (Math.random() * 20) + 1);
5
6   out.println("Before sorting: " + list);
7   Collections.sort(list);
8   out.println("After sorting: " + list);
```

Example 11.6. Sorting a list of numbers.

```
Before sorting: [5, 8, 16, 2, 7, 8, 13, 2, 17, 5, 10, 19, 20, 11, 5, 10, 3, 7, 3, 7]
After sorting:  [2, 2, 3, 3, 5, 5, 5, 7, 7, 7, 8, 8, 10, 10, 11, 13, 16, 17, 19, 20]
```

The `Collections.sort` method is able to sort the list because the type of data held in the list (`Integer` in this case) implements the `Comparable` interface, which contains the `compareTo` method that allows its caller to compare two data elements. If you want your own class to support sorting, you'll have to update it to implement the `Comparable` interface. Consider example 11.7 where we define an `Employee` class and sort a list of employee objects,

Example 11.7. Sorting a list of employees.

```
 1  ...
 2    List<Employee> employees = new ArrayList<>();
 3    employees.add(new Employee("Ina", "Brown", 10121));
 4    employees.add(new Employee("John", "Forsyth", 10029));
 5    employees.add(new Employee("Laura", "Smith", 10089));
 6    employees.add(new Employee("Tim", "Edwards", 10041));
 7
 8    out.println("Before sorting: " + employees);
 9    Collections.sort(employees);
10    out.println("After sorting: " + employees);
11  ...
12  class Employee {
13    String firstName;
14    String lastName;
15    int id;
16
17    public Employee (String firstName, String lastName, int id) {
18      this.firstName = firstName;
19      this.lastName = lastName;
20      this.id = id;
21    }
22  }
```

```
out.println("Before sorting: " + employees);
Collections.sort(employees);
out.println("    The method sort(List<T>) in the type Collections is not applicable for the arguments (List<Employee>)

                 1 quick fix available:
                    Cast argument 'employees' to 'List<T>'
nployee {
ing firstName
```

The compile error we get isn't too specific, but the reason is that we haven't implemented `Comparable` in our `Employee` class. Eclipse provides a convenient way to implement placeholder methods for an interface. First we revise the `Employee` declaration to add `implements Comparable<Employee>`,

```
 1  class Employee implements Comparable<Employee> {
```

```
    class Employee implements Comparable<Employee> {
25      St
26      St    The type Employee must implement the inherited abstract method Comparable<Employee>.compareTo(Employee)
27      in   2 quick fixes available:
28
29      pu      Add unimplemented methods
30              Make type 'Employee' abstract
```

Hovering over the error message and choosing the "add unimplemented methods" option will add placeholder methods, as in example 11.8,

Tip 8. Don't use Eclipse convenience features until you're able to write the code without them.

```
 1  class Employee implements Comparable<Employee> {
 2    String firstName;
 3    String lastName;
 4    int id;
 5
 6    public Employee (String firstName, String lastName, int id) {
 7      this.firstName = firstName;
```

```
 8        this.lastName = lastName;
 9        this.id = id;
10      }
11
12      @Override
13      public int compareTo(Employee o) {
14        // TODO Auto-generated method stub
15        return 0;
16      }
17  }
```

Example 11.8. Placeholder method added by Eclipse.

The `compareTo` method is meant to compare the current object with the object passed in as a parameter, and return a positive number if the current object should be considered larger, a negative number if the current object should be considered smaller, and zero if they're equal. Our implementation of `compareTo` is shown in example 11.9 (we've also added a `toString` method),

```
 1      @Override
 2      public String toString() {
 3        return firstName + " " + lastName;
 4      }
 5
 6      @Override
 7      public int compareTo(Employee o) {
 8        if (!lastName.equals(o.lastName))
 9          return lastName.compareTo(o.lastName);
10        if (!firstName.equals(o.firstName))
11          return firstName.compareTo(o.firstName);
12        return 0;
13      }
```

Example 11.9. Custom `compareTo` implementation.

```
Before sorting: [Ina Brown, John Forsyth, Laura Smith, Tim Edwards]
After sorting: [Ina Brown, Tim Edwards, John Forsyth, Laura Smith]
```

The above implementation of `compareTo` compares the two objects' last names. If the last names aren't the same, the result of comparing the last names is returned as the result of comparing the two employees. This has the effect of sorting employees by last name. If the last names are equal, it will sort by first name, and if the last and first names are the same, the employee records are considered equal. Similar logic can be used with non-string data members.

Exercises

11.3 Update example 11.9. Add the employee's street address, city, state and zip code. Change the `compareTo` method to sort by state, then city, then street address.

Chapter Summary

- An interface specifies a set of methods that can be implemented by one or more classes.
- A variable can have an interface as its type, while referring to an instance of a class implementing the interface.
- The Java collection classes implement the generic Collection interface.
- When a class implements the `Comparable` interface, collections of that class can be sorted.

```
1   public static void main(String[] args) {
2       Dog fido = new Dog();
3       out.print("Fido says ");
4       fido.speak();                         Calling interface method
5       Cat whiskers = new Cat();
6       out.print("Whiskers says ");
7       whiskers.speak();
8   }
9   ...
10  interface Animal {                        Interface definition
11      void speak();
12  }
13
14  class Dog implements Animal {             Declaring interface implementation
15      public void speak() {
16          out.println("Bark!");
17      }
18  }
19
20  class Cat implements Animal {
21      public void speak() {
22          out.println("Meow!");             Implementing interface method
23      }
24  }
```

Exercise Solutions

11.1
```java
public static void main(String[] args) {

    Stack<String> stack = new Stack<>();

    stack.push("John");
    out.println("Pushed John onto the stack");

    stack.push("George");
    out.println("Pushed George onto the stack");

    if (!stack.isEmpty()) {
        String name = stack.pop();
        out.println("Popped " + name + " from the stack");
    }

    stack.push("Elizabeth");
    out.println("Pushed Elizabeth onto the stack");

    while (!stack.isEmpty()) {
        String name = stack.pop();
        out.println("Popped " + name + " from the stack");
    }
}
...
class Stack<E> {

    private ArrayList<E> list = new ArrayList<>();

    public void push(E object) {
        list.add(object);
    }

    public E pop() {
        return list.remove(list.size() - 1);
    }

    public boolean isEmpty() {
        return list.isEmpty();
    }
}
```

```
Pushed John onto the stack
Pushed George onto the stack
Popped George from the stack
Pushed Elizabeth onto the stack
Popped Elizabeth from the stack
Popped John from the stack
```

11.2
```java
public static void main(String[] args) {
    Dog fido = new Dog();
    out.print("Fido says ");
    fido.speak();
    Cat whiskers = new Cat();
    out.print("Whiskers says ");
    whiskers.speak();
```

```
 8   }
 9  ...
10  interface Animal {
11    void speak();
12  }
13
14  class Dog implements Animal {
15    public void speak() {
16      out.println("Bark!");
17    }
18  }
19
20  class Cat implements Animal {
21    public void speak() {
22      out.println("Meow!");
23    }
24  }
```

```
Fido says Bark!
Whiskers says Meow!
```

11.3

```
 1      List<Employee> employees = new ArrayList<>();
 2      employees.add(new Employee("Ina", "Brown", 10121, "100 Main St",
          "Cleveland", "OH", 44101));
 3      employees.add(new Employee("John", "Forsyth", 10029, "19
          Brookline Place", "Boston", "MA", 2109));
 4      employees.add(new Employee("Laura", "Smith", 10089, "3105 12th
          Ave", "Tucson", "AZ", 85706));
 5      employees.add(new Employee("Tim", "Edwards", 10041, "526 Gerard
          St.", "New Orleans", "LA", 70013));
 6
 7      out.println("Before sorting: " + employees);
 8      Collections.sort(employees);
 9      out.println("After sorting: " + employees);
10  ...
11  class Employee implements Comparable<Employee> {
12    String firstName;
13    String lastName;
14    int id;
15    String address;
16    String city;
17    String state;
18    int zipCode;
19
20    public Employee (String firstName, String lastName, int id, String
          address, String city, String state, int zipCode) {
21      this.firstName = firstName;
22      this.lastName = lastName;
23      this.id = id;
24      this.address = address;
25      this.city = city;
26      this.state = state;
27      this.zipCode = zipCode;
28    }
29
30    @Override
31    public String toString() {
32      return firstName + " " + lastName + " (" + address + ", " + city
          + ", " + state + ")";
33    }
34
```

```
35    @Override
36    public int compareTo(Employee o) {
37      if (!state.equals(o.state))
38        return state.compareTo(o.state);
39      if (!city.equals(o.city))
40        return city.compareTo(o.city);
41      if (!address.equals(o.address))
42        return address.compareTo(o.address);
43      return 0;
44    }
45  }
```

```
Before sorting: [Ina Brown (100 Main St, Cleveland, OH), John Forsyth
After sorting: [Laura Smith (3105 12th Ave, Tucson, AZ), Tim Edwards
```

File I/O | 12

12.1 Exceptions

As seen in section 3.3, integer division by zero at runtime causes an exception. There are a variety of runtime errors that cause different types of exceptions. When a runtime exception occurs, we say that an exception is *thrown*. Your code can handle such an occurrence, and in this case, we say that the exception is *caught*.

To do this, you would add a *try-catch* block to your code. The **try** block contains code that might throw an exception. The **catch** block is placed directly after the **try** block, and handles the exception, if it's thrown. Consider example 12.1, where we revise example 3.2 by placing the integer division within a try-catch block, and printing a warning if the code attempts to divide by zero,

```
1   Scanner input = new Scanner(System.in);
2
3   out.print("Please enter the rectangle's area: ");
4   int area = input.nextInt();
5   input.nextLine();
6   out.print("Please enter the rectangle's height: ");
7   int height = input.nextInt();
8   input.nextLine();
9
10  try {
11    int width = area / height;
12    out.print("The rectangle's width is: " + width);
13  }
14  catch (Exception ex) {
15    out.print("An error occurred: " + ex.getMessage());
16  }
17
18  input.close();
```

Example 12.1. Catching an exception.

```
Please enter the rectangle's area: 12
Please enter the rectangle's height: 0
An error occurred: / by zero
```

The `catch` block receives a parameter, the exception that was thrown. It can use this parameter to access information pertinent to the exception, such as a specific error message. In example 12.1, the `catch` block prints out the exception's error message. Execution then continues and the `Scanner` object is closed before the `main` method returns. Contrast this to the output of example 3.2 where the standard exception output was displayed, followed by the program immediately terminating. The `try-catch` statement allows us to handle exceptions in a graceful way and continue with normal program execution. How an exception is handled depends on the particular situation.

If not caught in a `catch` block, an exception causes the current method to return immediately to the calling method. The calling method, in turn, will return immediately unless it catches the exception with its own `catch` block, and so on. If no method in the call stack catches a thrown exception, the standard exception error message is displayed in the console and the program terminates.

Exception Class Hierarchy

In example 12.1, the `catch` block received a parameter of type `Exception`. In reality though, the exception thrown was an `ArithmeticException`, which indirectly extends `Exception`. Accepting an `Exception` parameter in the `catch` block works because all exception classes are ultimately derived from `Exception`. Figure 12.1 displays a partial hierarchy of the exception classes in Java.

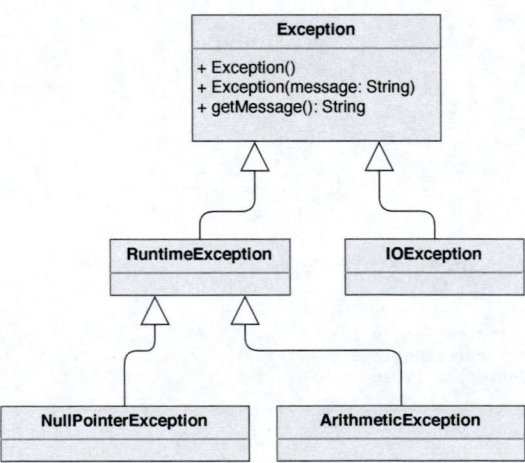

Figure 12.1: Partial exception hierarchy in Java.

Multiple `catch` Blocks

You can specify multiple `catch` blocks to catch the different types of exceptions that may be thrown in the `try` block. To do this, the `catch` blocks have to be in order from the more specific to the more general, since the first `catch` block that matches a thrown exception will be executed. This technique allows you to handle different exception types in different ways. If none of the `catch` blocks matches the type of exception thrown, it won't be caught and will proceed up the call stack to be caught at a higher level.

The `finally` Block

After all `catch` blocks, an optional `finally` block can be included to perform any needed cleanup. The code in the `finally` block is executed whether an exception is thrown within the `try` block or not. Example 12.2 illustrates this,

Example 12.2. Finally block.

```java
import static java.lang.System.out;
import java.util.Scanner;

public class Test {
  public static void main(String[] args) throws Exception {

    Scanner input = null;
    try {
      // arbitrary computation
      int players = 3;
      int goals = 4;
      int goalsPerPlayer = goals / players;
      out.println("Goals per player: " + goalsPerPlayer);

      // declare Scanner
      input = new Scanner(System.in);

      // get input from user
      out.print("Enter rectangle area: ");
      int area = input.nextInt();
      input.nextLine();

      out.print("Enter rectangle height: ");
      int height = input.nextInt();
      input.nextLine();

      // compute result
      int width = area / height;
      out.println("The rectangle's width is: " + width);
    }
    catch (Exception ex) {
      int lineNumber = ex.getStackTrace()[0].getLineNumber();
      out.println("An error occurred: " + ex.getMessage() + " at line " +
      lineNumber);
    }
```

```
35     finally {
36       // Scanner is closed if it has already been initialized
37       if (input != null) {
38         input.close();
39         out.println("(closed Scanner object)");
40       }
41     }
42   }
43 }
```

```
Goals per player: 1
Enter rectangle area: 12
Enter rectangle height: 3
The rectangle's width is: 4
(closed Scanner object)
```

```
Goals per player: 1
Enter rectangle area: 12
Enter rectangle height: 0
An error occurred: / by zero at line 28
(closed Scanner object)
```

The code within the `try` block has several distinct sections:

- An initial computation occurs. This is meant to illustrate some code that *may* throw an exception.
- A `Scanner` object is created. Note that the scanner is declared before the `try` block, and initialized to `null`.
- The `Scanner` is used to get input from the keyboard.
- A result is computed and output to the console. This computation may also throw an exception.

If an exception occurs, the `catch` block prints the exception's cause and the line number at which it occurred. The `finally` block closes the `Scanner` object, but only if it's already been created. The first run shown above illustrates a normal control flow where no exception occurs. But if the user entered a zero value for the rectangle's height, a divide by zero occurs. At that point, the exception's information is displayed by the `catch` block, and the `Scanner` object is closed in the `finally` block. This is shown in the second run above.

Now let's suppose that the initial code within the `try` block causes an exception. This can be simulated by changing the number of players to zero:

```
1    . int players = 0;
```

```
An error occurred: / by zero at line 12
```

As you can see in the program's output, when an exception occurs in the first section of code in the `try` block, the exception is handled in the `catch` block, and the `Scanner` object isn't closed since its value was still null when the exception was thrown. The `finally` block is always executed whether an exception occurs or not, and cleanup code can be placed there to handle any cleanup no matter which path the control flow has taken. Note also that the `finally` block is executed if an exception occurs but isn't handled by any of the `catch` blocks.

Rethrowing Exceptions

After an exception is caught, it can be processed appropriately in a `catch` block and then re-thrown. This allows your `catch` block to process the error that occurred, while allowing the exception to continue in order to be caught by one of the methods further up the call stack. If a `finally` block is present, it's executed even if an exception occurs and is re-thrown. Re-throwing an exception in a `catch` block is done with the syntax "`throw ex;`", where `ex` is the exception.

Throwing Exceptions

Your code can throw an exception. When you do this, you're actually throwing an object of the `Exception` class, or one of its subclasses. Example 12.3 shows how to create and throw an exception containing a particular error message,

```
1  import static java.lang.System.out;
2  import java.util.Scanner;
3
4  public class Test {
5    public static void main(String[] args) throws Exception {
6      out.println("The result is " + compute(4507.3910));
7    }
8
9    private static double compute(double inputValue) throws Exception {
10     boolean error = true; // simulate an unexpected error
11     if (error) {
12       Exception exception = new Exception("Something unexpected happened in
         compute()");
13       throw exception;
```

Example 12.3. Throwing an exception.

```
14        }
15
16        return Math.sqrt(inputValue);
17    }
18 }
```

```
Exception in thread "main" java.lang.Exception: Something unexpected happened in compute()
        at Test.compute(Test.java:12)
        at Test.main(Test.java:6)
```

Any time a method *may* throw a particular exception type, it must append a "throws" clause to the method's declaration, as seen on lines 5 and 9 of example 12.3. While it's possible to use an exception to handle any error situation, this should only be done in exceptional error conditions. Exceptions shouldn't be used for normal flow of control, or for expected errors. There are two reasons for this,

- Since a thrown exception can skip up several levels in the call stack, it can obfuscate the flow of control.
- Exception processing is less efficient at runtime than normal control flow, so it shouldn't be a common occurrence.

Technique 20. Throw exceptions only in exceptional error situations

Exceptions should only be thrown in exceptional error situations. They shouldn't be used for normal control flow or expected errors. A method should respond to expected errors such as an invalid parameter value by returning an error code instead of throwing an exception.

You can define your own exception class, which must extend `Exception` or one of its subclasses. This can help to indicate specific error conditions and catch them easily by giving the specialized exception class its own `catch` block.

Now that we know how to catch and process exceptions, we can revise example 10.13 to handle invalid input in the entry of flight departure and arrival times. That section of code is reproduced here as example 12.4,

```
1   out.print("Departure time (hour:minute): ");
2   String departure = input.nextLine();
3   int colonIndex = departure.indexOf(':');
4   int departureHour = -1, departureMinute = -1;
5   if (colonIndex > 0) {
6     departureHour = Integer.parseInt(departure.substring(0, colonIndex));
7     departureMinute = Integer.parseInt(departure.substring(colonIndex + 1));
8   }
9
10  if (departureHour == -1 || departureMinute == -1) {
11    out.println("Invalid departure time");
12    return;
13  }
```

Example 12.4. Getting departure time from the user.

```
(A)dd flight
(D)elete flight
(C)hange a flight
(L)ist all flights
(1)Search by airline and flight number
(2)Search by destination
(E)xit
a
Airline: Delta
Flight Number: 312
Origin: JFK
Destination: LAX
Departure time (hour:minute): 10:30x
Exception in thread "main" java.lang.NumberFormatException: For input string: "30x"
        at java.base/java.lang.NumberFormatException.forInputString(NumberFormatException.java:68)
        at java.base/java.lang.Integer.parseInt(Integer.java:652)
        at java.base/java.lang.Integer.parseInt(Integer.java:770)
        at Example_Flights.addFlight(Example_Flights.java:78)
        at Example_Flights.main(Example_Flights.java:32)
```

The user's input is assigned to the **departure** string on line 2. If it doesn't contain a colon character, an error message is displayed and the **addFlight** method returns. If a colon does exist, but two valid integers don't exist before and after it, an exception is thrown and the program terminates as seen in the above screen shot. We can handle invalid input, and allow the user to re-enter the departure time by putting the code within a *try-catch* block and enclose it in a loop to allow the user to keep trying until the input's format is valid. Example 12.5 shows the revised code,

```
1   boolean valid = false;
2   int departureHour, departureMinute;
3   do {
4     out.print("Departure time (hour:minute): ");
5     String departure = input.nextLine();
6     int colonIndex = departure.indexOf(':');
7     departureHour = -1;
8     departureMinute = -1;
9     if (colonIndex > 0) {
10      try {
11        departureHour = Integer.parseInt(departure.substring(0, colonIndex));
12        departureMinute = Integer.parseInt(departure.substring(colonIndex + 1))
      ;
13        valid = true;
14      }
15      catch (NumberFormatException ex) {
16        // ignore this error
17      }
```

Example 12.5. Handling invalid user input.

```
18      }
19
20      if (departureHour == -1 || departureMinute == -1)
21        out.println("Invalid departure time");
22    } while (!valid);
```

```
a
Airline: Delta
Flight Number: 312
Origin: JFK
Destination: LAX
Departure time (hour:minute): 1030
Invalid departure time
Departure time (hour:minute): 10:30x
Invalid departure time
Departure time (hour:minute): 10:30
Arrival time (hour:minute): 13:55
```

The `while` loop and `valid` flag in example 12.5 allow repeated user input of the flight departure time until a valid time is entered. In case the numbers before or after the colon character are invalid, the `catch` block catches the exception and the loop is allowed to repeat.

12.2 Writing to a File

Now that we know about exceptions, we can learn how to write to a text file. In order to do this, we'll need to create two objects, one of the `File` class and another of the `FileWriter` class. The `File` object receives the path of the file that we want to write to as a parameter to its constructor. The `FileWriter` class receives the `File` object as a parameter to its constructor. After creating both objects, we can use the `print` method of the `FileWriter` class to write lines to the file, and when we're done we call the `FileWriter`'s `close` method. Example 12.6 shows this sequence of events, and writes the first fifteen powers of 2 to a file called `powers_of_2.txt` in the user's home directory.

```
1  import static java.lang.System.out;
2  import java.io.File;
3  import java.io.FileWriter;
4  import java.io.IOException;
5
6  public class Test {
7    public static void main(String[] args) throws IOException {
8
9      String filePath = System.getProperty("user.home") + "/powers_of_2.txt";
10     File file = new File(filePath);
11     FileWriter writer = new FileWriter(file);
12     for (int i = 0; i <= 15; i++)
13       writer.write((int) Math.pow(2, i) + "\n");
14     writer.close();
15     out.println("Done writing to " + filePath);
16   }
17 }
```

```
1
2
4
8
16
32
64
128
256
512
1024
2048
4096
8192
16384
32768
```

Example 12.6. Writing to a file.

```
Done writing to /Users/marwan/powers_of_2.txt
```

The output of the program is shown above, and the contents of the new file, that is, the powers of 2, are shown in the margin. The "\n" notation denotes a newline character which causes the output to advance to a new line. The following sections discuss the above example in further detail.

File Paths

After running the code in example 12.6, you should be able to find the file that was written by the program in your home directory. Your home directory is retrieved by the Java program using the syntax `System.getProperty("user.home")`, and then stored in the `directory` string. The file path consists of the directory name followed by a slash, followed by the file name. The file extension in our case is ".txt", but you can specify any extension that you want, or no extension at all.

If you're on Windows, your home directory is under "c:\users". If you're on a Mac, it's under "/Users".

Relative paths are allowed as well, and if used, will be relative to your project's root directory in Eclipse. To see this in action, you can just use the file name as the file path, without the directory name or slash. After the program runs, right-click on the project's root in Package Explorer and choose "Refresh", after which you'll see the "powers_of_2.txt" file in the project's file tree alongside the "src" directory. You can even double click on it in Package Explorer to open the file in Eclipse.

Exceptions

Since creating a `FileWriter` object may throw an exception, either the `FileWriter` creation has to be placed in a `try` block, or the method declaration has to include a "throws" clause. In example 12.6 we've added the `throws` clause to the `main` method, but you can choose to wrap file I/O in try-catch blocks if that's your preference.

Appending to a File

To append to an existing file instead of creating a new file, add another parameter to the `FileWriter`'s constructor with the value `true`. This tells the `FileWriter` to keep the existing file if it's already there, and append to the file's existing contents.

Exercises

12.1   Write a program that prompts the user for a recipe's name, its ingredient list and preparation instructions, then creates a text file containing the information that was entered by the user.

12.2   Use exercise 8.2 as a starting point. After creating the NewsStory class, create a NewsStory object using data entered by the user, then save the story record to a file.

12.3 Reading from a File

Reading from a file in Java is very similar to writing to a file. You would create a `File` object, passing its constructor the path to the file that you want to read. Then you'd create a `FileReader` object, passing its constructor the `File` object. We'll go a step further and create a `BufferedReader` object, passing its constructor the `FileReader` object, and this allows us to use the `readLine` method of the `BufferedReader` class to easily read each line of the file. Example 12.7 shows how to read the file that was written in example 12.6,

```java
import static java.lang.System.out;
import java.io.BufferedReader;
import java.io.File;
import java.io.FileReader;
import java.io.IOException;

public class Test {
  public static void main(String[] args) throws IOException {

    String filePath = System.getProperty("user.home") + "/powers_of_2.txt";
    File file = new File(filePath);
    FileReader reader = new FileReader(file);
    BufferedReader bufferedReader = new BufferedReader(reader);
    do {
      String line = bufferedReader.readLine();
      if (line == null)
        break;
      out.println(line);
    } while (true);
    bufferedReader.close();
  }
}
```

Example 12.7. Reading from a file.

```
1
2
4
8
16
32
64
128
256
512
1024
2048
4096
8192
16384
32768
```

note that the program doesn't make any assumption with regard to the length of the file. It keeps looping until the `readLine` method returns null, at which point it exits from the "do-while" loop. It's also possible to use `Scanner` to read from a text file, which allows us to use the convenient methods `nextInt`, `nextDouble`, and so on. Example 12.8 shows how to use the `Scanner` class to read numbers from the "powers_of_2.txt" file, add them up and display the total,

```java
import static java.lang.System.out;
import java.io.File;
import java.io.IOException;
import java.util.Scanner;

public class Test {
  public static void main(String[] args) throws IOException {

    String filePath = System.getProperty("user.home") + "/powers_of_2.txt";
    File file = new File(filePath);
```

Example 12.8. Reading from a file using `Scanner`.

```
11    Scanner reader = new Scanner(file);
12    int sum = 0;
13    while (reader.hasNext())
14      sum += reader.nextInt();
15    reader.close();
16    out.println("The sum of the first fifteen powers of 2 is " + sum);
17  }
18 }
```

```
The sum of the first fifteen powers of 2 is 65535
```

Note the use of `hasNext` in example 12.8, which allows the concise loop syntax as opposed to the loop in example 12.7.

`BufferedReader` and `Scanner` are higher level classes which use the lower level `FileReader` class under the hood. They're both good examples of abstraction. Reading with `FileReader` in our program would entail more code because it doesn't have `nextLine`, `hasNext`, `nextInt` and other convenient methods. Abstractions usually allow more concise syntax, but with that benefit comes hidden danger. You should always think about runtime performance when using abstractions because you usually don't know exactly how they're implemented.

Tip 9. Be cautious when using abstractions. Although using abstractions is encouraged, you should investigate the runtime performance characteristics of classes or methods that you utilize. Unless you wrote it yourself, you aren't usually aware of what the code is doing under the hood.

Exercises

12.3 Download a text file that contains a list of English words, for example search for "Google 10000 words" to find `google-10000-english.txt`. Write a program that reads this file and prints out the word containing the most vowels.

12.4 Repeat exercise 12.3 and find the word that ends with the most vowels.

12.4 Binary I/O

Binary input and output are similar to text-based I/O, but the data you're reading or writing is stored within the file in its native format. For example, a signed integer would be stored in the standard two's compliment format and occupies four bytes in the file. Binary format is useful in some situations to reduce the file size and also speed up input and output, since numeric data doesn't need to be converted to and from a text format. Example 12.9 shows how to write the first fifteen powers of 2 to a binary file, while example 12.10 shows how to read the same numbers from a binary file,

```java
import static java.lang.System.out;
import java.io.DataOutputStream;
import java.io.FileOutputStream;
import java.io.IOException;

public class Test {

  public static void main(String[] args) throws IOException {
    String filePath = "powers_of_2.bin";
    DataOutputStream stream = new DataOutputStream (new FileOutputStream(
      filePath));
    for (int i = 0; i <= 15; i++)
      stream.writeInt((int) Math.pow(2, i));
    stream.close();
    out.println("Done writing to " + filePath);
  }
}
```

Example 12.9. Writing to a binary file.

```
Done writing to powers_of_2.bin
```

```java
import static java.lang.System.out;
import java.io.DataInputStream;
import java.io.FileInputStream;
import java.io.IOException;

public class Test {

  public static void main(String[] args) throws IOException {
    String filePath = "powers_of_2.bin";
    DataInputStream stream = new DataInputStream(new FileInputStream(filePath))
      ;
    int sum = 0;
    while (stream.available() > 0)
      sum += stream.readInt();
    stream.close();
    out.println("The sum is " + sum);
  }
}
```

Example 12.10. Reading from a binary file.

```
The sum is 65535
```

The code is similar to the text-based examples, but writing binary data uses the **DataOutputStream** class with its **writeInt** method, while reading binary data uses the **DataInputStream** class with its **readInt** and **available** methods. The binary file is 64 bytes in size, with each of the sixteen integers using four bytes.

Exercises

12.5 Write a program that saves the numbers 1 to 10 to a binary file. Download a free hex editor and view the file. Identify the bytes that represent each of the ten integers. Look up hexadecimal format online if you're not familiar with it.

12.6 Repeat exercise 12.5 with a short string.

12.7 Repeat exercise 12.5 with the integers -1 through -10. Look up two's compliment format online to learn more about it.

12.8 Repeat exercise 12.5 with the floating point numbers 1, 1000 and 0.001. Look up the IEEE 754 format online to learn more about it.

12.5 Object Serialization

To *serialize* an object is to write it to a file. To *deserialize* an object is to read it from a file. Serialization is sometimes called *persistence*.

When writing objects to a file, or reading them from a file, you can use the techniques shown in the previous section to write and read each of the object's fields separately. But, there's a more convenient way to write objects to files and read them from files. It involves the object's class implementing the `Serializable` interface. Once this is done, the `ObjectOutputStream` and `ObjectInputStream` classes can be used to write an object to a file in one step, and read it from a file in one step. Example 12.11 shows a class named `Language`, which implements the `Serializable` interface. This interface doesn't include any methods, but lets the serialization methods know that the class can be serialized.

Example 12.11. Implementing a serializable class.

```
1  import java.io.Serializable;
2
3  class Language implements Serializable {
4
5    private String name;
6    private char[] firstFewLetters;
7    private int speakers;
8
9    public Language (String name, char[] firstFewLetters, int speakers) {
10     this.name = name;
11     this.firstFewLetters = new char[firstFewLetters.length];
```

```
12      for (int i = 0; i < firstFewLetters.length; i++)
13        this.firstFewLetters[i] = firstFewLetters[i];
14      this.speakers = speakers;
15    }
16
17    @Override
18    public String toString() {
19      String result = name + ", " + speakers + " speakers: [";
20      for (char ch : firstFewLetters)
21        result += ch + ",";
22      result += "...]";
23      return result;
24    }
25 }
```

Note that the `firstFewLetters` character array in example 12.11 is copied from an array that's passed in, as opposed to copying the array reference. This means the **Language** object has its own copy that won't be affected in case the array that was passed into its constructor is later modified by the caller.

The `main` method in the next example (12.12) creates several **Language** objects, writes them to a file, then reads the language data from the file and prints it out.

```
1  import static java.lang.System.out;
2  import java.io.FileInputStream;
3  import java.io.FileOutputStream;
4  import java.io.IOException;
5  import java.io.ObjectInputStream;
6  import java.io.ObjectOutputStream;
7
8  public class Test {
9
10   public static void main(String[] args) throws IOException,
         ClassNotFoundException {
11
12     Language english = new Language ("English", new char[] { 'a', 'b', 'c', 'd'
         , 'e' }, 510_000_000);
13     Language japanese = new Language ("Japanese", new char[] { '\u3041', '\
         u3042', '\u3043', '\u3044', '\u3045' }, 127_000_000);
14     Language urdu = new Language ("Urdu", new char[] { '\u0627', '\u0628', '\
         u067e', '\u062a', '\u0679' }, 104_000_000);
15
16     ObjectOutputStream outputStream = new ObjectOutputStream(new
         FileOutputStream("languages.bin"));
17     outputStream.writeInt(3); // write number of objects being saved
18     outputStream.writeObject(english);
19     outputStream.writeObject(japanese);
20     outputStream.writeObject(urdu);
21     outputStream.close();
22
23     ObjectInputStream inputStream = new ObjectInputStream(new FileInputStream("
         languages.bin"));
24     int count = inputStream.readInt();  // read number of objects to load
25     for (int i = 0; i < count; i++) {
26       Language language = (Language) inputStream.readObject();
27       out.println(language);
```

Example 12.12. Serializing objects.

If foreign language characters don't appear properly in the output, go into the Run Configurations dialog, choose the current run configuration, then go to the Common tab, and change the encoding to UTF-8 in the Encoding section.

```
28      }
29        inputStream.close();
30    }
31 }
```

```
English, 510000000 speakers: [a,b,c,d,e,...]
Japanese, 127000000 speakers: [あ,ぁ,い,ぃ,う,...]
Urdu, 104000000 speakers: [ش,ت,پ,ب,ا,...]
```

Syntactic sugar is alternate syntax that doesn't change the meaning of code, but makes it easier to read.

Java allows you to add underlines to in an integer constant to make it easier to read, thus `127_000_000` is the same as `127000000`.

In Java, characters hold data in the Unicode format, which represent letters in any language. Non-English characters typically occupy two bytes or more, and may be represented as a hexadecimal constant such as `\u3041`. Each byte is represented by two hex digits.

It's important for you to be familiar with the binary and hexadecimal number systems, and to be able to convert numbers between binary, hexadecimal and decimal. There are many good online tutorials on number systems.

In example 12.12, three `Language` objects are created. An `ObjectOutputStream` object is created, the number of languages (three) is written to the output stream, then each of the languages is written and the stream is closed. The code then creates an `ObjectInputStream` object and reads the number of languages from the file. Finally, each language is read and printed to the console.

Exercises

12.9   Start with example 8.8. Save a few `Car` objects to a file, then write another program that reads the `Car` objects from the file and prints them to the console.

12.6 Example: Flight Database

Now that we know how to write to, and read from files, we'll update the flight database example from chapter 10. When the program starts up, it reads flights from a data file. If the file doesn't exist, it creates the sample flights. When the program exits, it writes the flights to the data file, so the data is preserved until the next run.

```
1  ...
2  import java.io.FileInputStream;
3  import java.io.FileOutputStream;
4  import java.io.IOException;
5  import java.io.ObjectInputStream;
6  import java.io.ObjectOutputStream;
7  import java.io.Serializable;
8  ...
9    public static void main(String[] args) {
10 ...
11     ArrayList<Flight> flights = new ArrayList<>();
12     readFlights(flights);
13
14     boolean done = false;
15     while (!done) {
16 ...
17     }
18
19     writeFlights(flights);
20     input.close();
21   }
22 ...
23   private static void readFlights(ArrayList<Flight> flights) {
24     try {
25       ObjectInputStream inputStream = new ObjectInputStream(new FileInputStream
          ("flights.dat"));
26       int count = inputStream.readInt();  // read number of objects to load
27       for (int i = 0; i < count; i++) {
28         Flight flight = (Flight) inputStream.readObject();
29         flights.add(flight);
30       }
31       inputStream.close();
32     }
33     catch (IOException ex) {
34       out.println("An error occurred reading flight data: " + ex.getMessage());
35
36       // add default sample data
37       flights.add(new Flight("JFK", "MCO", "Delta", 1100, 13, 30, 16, 11));
38       flights.add(new Flight("LGA", "LAX", "United", 29, 6, 0, 9, 21));
39       flights.add(new Flight("CLE", "PDX", "Delta", 412, 9, 59, 11, 15));
40       flights.add(new Flight("SAT", "BWI", "American", 11, 20, 42, 1, 2));
41       flights.add(new Flight("LFT", "ATL", "Delta", 90, 12, 0, 15, 57));
42       flights.add(new Flight("SNA", "CVG", "Southwest", 170, 10, 30, 12, 28));
43     }
44     catch (ClassNotFoundException ex) {
45       out.println("An error occurred reading flight data: " + ex.getMessage());
46     }
47   }
48
49   private static void writeFlights(ArrayList<Flight> flights) {
50     try {
51       ObjectOutputStream outputStream = new ObjectOutputStream(new
          FileOutputStream("flights.dat"));
52       outputStream.writeInt(flights.size()); // write number of flights being
          saved
53       for (Flight flight : flights)
54         outputStream.writeObject(flight);
55       outputStream.close();
56     }
57     catch (IOException ex) {
58       out.println("An error occurred writing flight data: " + ex.getMessage());
59     }
```

Example 12.13. Adding serialization to the flight management application.

```
60    }
61 ...
62 class Flight implements Serializable {
63 ...
64 }
```

```
l
Delta 1100 (JFK 13:30 -> MCO 16:11)
United 29 (LGA 06:00 -> LAX 09:21)
Delta 412 (CLE 09:59 -> PDX 11:15)
American 11 (SAT 20:42 -> BWI 01:02)
Delta 90 (LFT 12:00 -> ATL 15:57)
Southwest 170 (SNA 10:30 -> CVG 12:28)

(A)dd flight
(D)elete flight
(C)hange a flight
(L)ist all flights
(1)Search by airline and flight number
(2)Search by destination
(E)xit
d
Airline: delta
Flight number: 1100
Deleted

(A)dd flight
(D)elete flight
(C)hange a flight
(L)ist all flights
(1)Search by airline and flight number
(2)Search by destination
(E)xit
e
```

```
(A)dd flight
(D)elete flight
(C)hange a flight
(L)ist all flights
(1)Search by airline and flight number
(2)Search by destination
(E)xit
l
United 29 (LGA 06:00 -> LAX 09:21)
Delta 412 (CLE 09:59 -> PDX 11:15)
American 11 (SAT 20:42 -> BWI 01:02)
Delta 90 (LFT 12:00 -> ATL 15:57)
Southwest 170 (SNA 10:30 -> CVG 12:28)
```

The code in example 12.13 to write and read flights mirrors the serialization of language objects in example 12.12. The flight database is read upon startup, and written when the program exits. The sample output shows deleting one flight, exiting, restarting, and listing the flights again to verify the change was saved.

Chapter Summary

- An exception occurs in case of an exceptional error. Code can catch such an exception and handle it appropriately.
- A Java program can write text to, and read text from a text file.
- A program can read and write data in its native format to a binary data file.
- Objects of a Java class can be written to a binary data file if the class implements the `Serializable` interface.

Creating `File` object

`throws` block

Creating `FileReader` object

Creating `BufferedReader` object

Reading a line

Closing reader

```java
1  public static void main(String[] args) throws IOException {
2
3    File file = new File("datafile.txt");
4    FileReader reader = new FileReader(file);
5    BufferedReader bufferedReader = new BufferedReader(reader)
6    List<String> lines = new ArrayList<>();
7    do {
8      String line = bufferedReader.readLine();
9      if (line == null)
10       break;
11     lines.add(line);
12   } while (true);
13   bufferedReader.close();
14 }
```

Exercise Solutions

12.1
```java
1  import static java.lang.System.out;
2  import java.io.File;
3  import java.io.FileWriter;
4  import java.io.IOException;
5  import java.util.Scanner;
6
7  public class Test {
8
9    public static void main(String[] args) throws IOException {
10
11     Scanner input = new Scanner(System.in);
12     out.print("Enter recipe name: ");
13     String name = input.nextLine();
14     out.print("Enter ingredient list: ");
15     String ingredients = input.nextLine();
16     out.print("Enter preparation instructions: ");
```

```
17      String instructions = input.nextLine();
18      input.close();
19
20      FileWriter writer = new FileWriter(new File("recipe.txt"));
21      writer.write(name + "\n");
22      writer.write(ingredients + "\n");
23      writer.write(instructions + "\n");
24      writer.close();
25      out.println("Done");
26    }
27  }
```

```
Enter recipe name: Easy Tuna Casserole
Enter ingredient list: 3 cups cooked macaroni, 1 can tuna, 1 can cream of chicken soup, 1 cup
Enter preparation instructions: Preheat oven to 350 degrees, combine the macaroni, tuna and so
Done
```

12.2

```
1   import static java.lang.System.out;
2   import java.io.File;
3   import java.io.FileWriter;
4   import java.io.IOException;
5   import java.io.Serializable;
6   import java.util.Scanner;
7
8
9   public class Test {
10
11    public static void main(String[] args) throws IOException {
12
13      Scanner input = new Scanner(System.in);
14
15      NewsStory story = new NewsStory();
16      out.print("Enter title: ");
17      story.title = input.nextLine();
18      out.print("Enter summary: ");
19      story.summary = input.nextLine();
20      out.print("Enter author: ");
21      story.author = input.nextLine();
22      out.print("Enter publication year: ");
23      story.publicationYear = input.nextInt();
24      input.nextLine();
25
26      input.close();
27
28      FileWriter writer = new FileWriter(new File("story.txt"));
29      writer.write(story.title + "\n");
30      writer.write(story.summary + "\n");
31      writer.write(story.author + "\n");
32      writer.write(story.publicationYear + "\n");
33      writer.close();
34      out.println("Done");
35    }
36  }
37
38  class NewsStory {
39    String title;
40    String summary;
41    String author;
42    int publicationYear;
43  }
```

```
Enter title: How fast is the universe expanding? Galaxies provide one answer
Enter summary: Determining how rapidly the universe is expanding is key to un
Enter author: Robert Sanders
Enter publication year: 2021
Done
```

12.3

```java
1  import static java.lang.System.out;
2  import java.io.File;
3  import java.io.IOException;
4  import java.util.Scanner;
5
6  public class Test {
7
8    public static void main(String[] args) throws IOException {
9
10       Scanner dictionary = new Scanner(new File("google-10000-english.
         txt"));
11
12       String result = "";
13       int resultVowels = 0;
14       while (dictionary.hasNext()) {
15         String word = dictionary.nextLine();
16         int vowels = wordVowels(word);
17         if (vowels > resultVowels) {
18           result = word;
19           resultVowels = vowels;
20         }
21       }
22
23       dictionary.close();
24       out.println("The word with the most vowels is " + result);
25    }
26
27    private static int wordVowels (String word) {
28      int count = 0;
29      for (int i = 0; i < word.length(); i++) {
30        char ch = word.charAt(i);
31        if (ch == 'i' || ch == 'o' || ch == 'e' || ch == 'u' || ch ==
         'a')
32          count++;
33      }
34      return count;
35    }
36  }
```

```
The word with the most vowels is telecommunications
```

12.4

```java
1  import static java.lang.System.out;
2  import java.io.File;
3  import java.io.IOException;
4  import java.util.Scanner;
5
6  public class Test {
7
8    public static void main(String[] args) throws IOException {
9
10       Scanner dictionary = new Scanner(new File("google-10000-english.
         txt"));
11
12       String result = "";
```

```java
13      int resultVowels = 0;
14      while (dictionary.hasNext()) {
15        String word = dictionary.nextLine();
16        int vowels = trailingVowels(word);
17        if (vowels > resultVowels) {
18          result = word;
19          resultVowels = vowels;
20        }
21      }
22
23      dictionary.close();
24      out.println("The word that ends with the most vowels is " +
          result);
25    }
26
27    private static int trailingVowels (String word) {
28      int count = 0;
29      for (int i = word.length() - 1; i >= 0; i--) {
30        char ch = word.charAt(i);
31        if (ch != 'i' && ch != 'o' && ch != 'e' && ch != 'u' && ch !=
            'a')
32          break;
33        count++;
34      }
35      return count;
36    }
37  }
```

```
The word that ends with the most vowels is ieee
```

12.5
```java
1   import static java.lang.System.out;
2   import java.io.DataOutputStream;
3   import java.io.FileOutputStream;
4   import java.io.IOException;
5
6   public class Test {
7
8     public static void main(String[] args) throws IOException {
9       String filePath = "data.bin";
10      DataOutputStream stream = new DataOutputStream (new
          FileOutputStream(filePath));
11      for (int i = 1; i <= 10; i++)
12        stream.writeInt(i);
13      stream.close();
14      out.println("Done writing to " + filePath);
15    }
16  }
```

```
00000000  00 00 00 01 00 00 00 02  00 00 00 03 00 00 00 04  |................|
00000010  00 00 00 05 00 00 00 06  00 00 00 07 00 00 00 08  |................|
00000020  00 00 00 09 00 00 00 0a  10                        |........|
00000028      1
```

12.6
```java
1   import static java.lang.System.out;
2   import java.io.DataOutputStream;
3   import java.io.FileOutputStream;
4   import java.io.IOException;
5
6   public class Test {
7
```

```
8     public static void main(String[] args) throws IOException {
9       String filePath = "data.bin";
10      DataOutputStream stream = new DataOutputStream (new
        FileOutputStream(filePath));
11      stream.writeBytes("Make a long story short.");
12      stream.close();
13      out.println("Done writing to " + filePath);
14    }
15  }
```

```
00000000  4d 61 6b 65 20 61 20 6c  6f 6e 67 20 73 74 6f 72  |Make a long stor|
00000010  79 20 73 68 6f 72 74 2e                           |y short.|
00000018
```

12.7
```
1   import static java.lang.System.out;
2   import java.io.DataOutputStream;
3   import java.io.FileOutputStream;
4   import java.io.IOException;
5
6   public class Test {
7
8     public static void main(String[] args) throws IOException {
9       String filePath = "data.bin";
10      DataOutputStream stream = new DataOutputStream (new
        FileOutputStream(filePath));
11      for (int i = -1; i >= -10; i--)
12        stream.writeInt(i);
13      stream.close();
14      out.println("Done writing to " + filePath);
15    }
16  }
```

```
00000000  ff ff ff ff ff ff ff fe  ff ff ff fd ff ff ff fc  |................|
00000010  ff ff ff fb ff ff ff fa  ff ff ff f9 ff ff ff f8  |................|
00000020  ff ff ff f7 ff ff ff f6                           |........|
00000028        -1             -10    -2
```

12.8
```
1   import static java.lang.System.out;
2   import java.io.DataOutputStream;
3   import java.io.FileOutputStream;
4   import java.io.IOException;
5
6   public class Test {
7
8     public static void main(String[] args) throws IOException {
9       String filePath = "data.bin";
10      DataOutputStream stream = new DataOutputStream (new
        FileOutputStream(filePath));
11      stream.writeFloat(1);
12      stream.writeFloat(1000);
13      stream.writeFloat(0.001f);
14      stream.close();
15      out.println("Done writing to " + filePath);
16    }
17  }
```

```
00000000  3f 80 00 00 44 7a 00 00  3a 83 12 6f               |?...Dz..:..o|
0000000c      1          1000        0.001
```

12.9
```
1   import static java.lang.System.out;
2   import java.io.FileInputStream;
```

```java
3  import java.io.FileOutputStream;
4  import java.io.IOException;
5  import java.io.ObjectInputStream;
6  import java.io.ObjectOutputStream;
7  import java.io.Serializable;
8
9  public class Test {
10
11   public static void main(String[] args) throws IOException,
        ClassNotFoundException {
12     Car car1 = new Car(34, "Honda", "Civic", 21);
13     Car car2 = new Car("Ford", "Fiesta");
14     Car car3 = new Car(19, "Toyota", "Corola", 22);
15
16     ObjectOutputStream outputStream = new ObjectOutputStream(new
        FileOutputStream("cars.bin"));
17     outputStream.writeInt(3); // write number of objects being saved
18     outputStream.writeObject(car1);
19     outputStream.writeObject(car2);
20     outputStream.writeObject(car3);
21     outputStream.close();
22
23     ObjectInputStream inputStream = new ObjectInputStream(new
        FileInputStream("cars.bin"));
24     int count = inputStream.readInt();  // read number of objects to
        load
25     for (int i = 0; i < count; i++) {
26       Car car = (Car) inputStream.readObject();
27       out.println(car);
28     }
29     inputStream.close();
30   }
31 }
32
33 class Car implements Serializable {
34   double mpg;
35   String make;
36   String model;
37   double tankCapacity;
38
39   static final double DEFAULT_MPG = 20;
40   static final double DEFAULT_TANK_CAPACITY = 15;
41
42   public Car(double mpg, String make, String model, double
        tankCapacity) {
43     this.mpg = mpg;
44     this.make = make;
45     this.model = model;
46     this.tankCapacity = tankCapacity;
47   }
48
49   public Car(String make, String model) {
50     this(DEFAULT_MPG, make, model, DEFAULT_TANK_CAPACITY);
51   }
52
53   double getRange() {
54     return tankCapacity * mpg;
55   }
56
57   @Override
58   public String toString() {
59     return make + " " + model + " [MPG " + mpg + "]";
```

```
60    }
61 }
```

```
Honda Civic [MPG 34.0]
Ford Fiesta [MPG 20.0]
Toyota Corola [MPG 19.0]
```

Program Performance | 13

13.1 Implementing ArrayList

In this chapter, we'll learn how to analyze program performance. We'll begin our discussion by implementing our own versions of `ArrayList` and `LinkedList`, then we'll analyze their performance characteristics.

The `MyList` Interface

Our own versions of `ArrayList` and `LinkedList` will omit some of the functionality offered by Java's built-in versions, while keeping the implementations realistic and comparable to Java's versions. We begin by defining the generic `MyList` interface which both will implement,

```java
interface MyList<E> {
  public void insert (int index, E object) throws Exception;
  public void add (E object);
  public E get (int index) throws Exception;
  public int indexOf (E object);
  public int lastIndexOf (E object);
  public E remove(int index) throws Exception;
  public E set (int index, E object) throws Exception;
  public int size();
}
```

Example 13.1. The MyList interface.

The Test Program

We also need a program to test our versions of `MyArrayList` and `MyLinkedList`. It tests each method of the `MyList` interface,

Example 13.2. Test program for `MyArrayList` and `MyLinkedList`.

```
1   public class Test {
2
3     public static void main(String[] args) throws Exception {
4
5       MyList<String> names = new MyArrayList<>();
6       names.add("Peter");
7       names.add("Mary");
8       names.add("Heather");
9       names.add("Henry");
10      names.add("Elizabeth");
11      names.add("Mary");
12
13      out.println("Initially, list contents are: " + names);
14
15      names.insert(2, "George");
16      out.println("After inserting George at index 2, list contents are: " +
          names);
17
18      names.insert(0, "Betty");
19      out.println("After inserting Betty at index 0, list contents are: " + names
          );
20
21      out.println("List size is: " + names.size());
22      out.println("Element at index 3 is: " + names.get(3));
23      out.println("Index of Mary is: " + names.indexOf("Mary"));
24      out.println("lastIndexOf Mary is: " + names.lastIndexOf("Mary"));
25
26      String removedName = names.remove(2);
27      out.println("After removing index 2 (" + removedName + "), list contents
          are: " + names);
28
29      names.set(1, "John");
30      out.println("After putting John at index 1, list contents are: " + names);
31    }
32  }
```

`MyArrayList` Constructor and Data Members

We'll begin with an empty version of `MyArrayList`, shown in example 13.3. This just contains a constructor and three private data members,

- `array` is a native array containing the list's data, each element being of the generic type `E`.
- `size` keeps track of the number of array elements in use.
- `capacity` holds the size of `array`, which is always equal to or greater than `size`.

An `ArrayList` is a wrapper around a native array. It lets the caller add elements to the internal array, remove elements from the internal array, and so on. When the array grows past the size of the internal native array, it creates a new, larger, internal array to hold the data, and copies the existing array's contents to the new array.

```
1  class MyArrayList<E> implements MyList<E> {
2
3    private E[] array = null;
4    private int size = 0;
5    private int capacity = 0;
6
7    public MyArrayList() {
8      capacity = 10;
9      array = (E[]) new Object[capacity];
10   }
11 }
```

Example 13.3. Empty version of MyArrayList.

The initial capacity in our implementation is 10. The constructor creates the internal array as an array of `Object` references, and each of the array's elements is able to hold a reference to an object of the generic type `E`, since Object is a superclass of `E`. This roundabout way of creating an array of `E` object references is due to one of the limitations of generics in Java, which is that a generic class can't create an array of the generic type.

MyArrayList.add()

In our implementation, each time the internal array grows, the capacity doubles. Java's version doesn't guarantee a specific increase in capacity beyond stipulating that adding an element has a fixed amortized runtime cost. Growing the internal array too frequently would cause a program using the `ArrayList` to be too slow, since each time the internal array grows, its contents must be copied to the new array. Example 13.4 shows the `toString` method, the `add` method, and the utility method `expandIfNeeded`, which is called from `add`,

```
1  class MyArrayList<E> implements MyList<E> {
2    ...
3    private void expandIfNeeded () {
4      if (size == capacity) {
5        int oldCapacity = capacity;
6        capacity *= 2;
7
8        // allocate new array
9        E[] newArray = (E[]) new Object[capacity];
10
11       // copy everything from the old array to the new array
12       for (int i = 0; i < oldCapacity; i++)
13         newArray[i] = array[i];
14
15       array = newArray;
```

Example 13.4. MyArrayList.add().

```
16        }
17    }
18
19    public void add (E object) {
20        expandIfNeeded();
21        array[size++] = object;
22    }
23
24    @Override
25    public String toString() {
26        String result = "[";
27        for (int i = 0; i < size; i++) {
28            result += array[i];
29            if (i < size-1)
30                result += ", ";
31        }
32        return result + "]";
33    }
34    ...
35 }
```

The `expandIfNeeded` method compares the size with the capacity. If there is no more free space, a new internal array is allocated with twice the capacity of the old one, then the contents of the old internal array are copied to the new internal array. Finally, the array reference is set to the newly-allocated array.

The "plus plus" operator is called the post-increment operator when it's used after a variable. When used before a variable, it increments the variable's value before using the value in the enclosing expression, and is called the pre-increment operator.

The `add` method expands the array if needed, then adds the object passed in to the end of the internal array. Note that the "plus plus" operator increments the `size` variable *after* the expression "array[size++]" is evaluated. That is, "size" is taken as the index into `array`, then "size" is incremented.

Finally, `toString` prints the elements of the array as comma-separated values within square brackets.

We have enough to start testing. We'll just need to add placeholders for the rest of the methods, so we can run a test,

Example 13.5. Placeholders for remaining `MyArrayList` methods.

```
1  public void insert (int index, E object) throws Exception {
2  }
3
4  public E get (int index) throws Exception {
5      return null;
6  }
7
8  public int indexOf (E object) {
9      return -1;
10 }
11
12 public int lastIndexOf (E object) {
13     return -1;
14 }
15
16 public E remove(int index) throws Exception {
```

```
17      return null;
18    }
19
20    public E set (int index, E object) throws Exception {
21      return null;
22    }
23
24    public int size() {
25      return size;
26    }
```

```
Initially, list contents are: [Peter, Mary, Heather, Henry, Elizabeth, Mary]
After inserting George at index 2, list contents are: [Peter, Mary, Heather, He
After inserting Betty at index 0, list contents are: [Peter, Mary, Heather, Hei
List size is: 6
Element at index 3 is: null
Index of Mary is: -1
lastIndexOf Mary is: -1
After removing index 2 (null), list contents are: [Peter, Mary, Heather, Henry
After putting John at index 1, list contents are: [Peter, Mary, Heather, Henry
```

The above screen shot shows that the `add`, `toString` and `size` methods work, while the rest are yet to be implemented. We've started testing as soon as possible in keeping with technique 16 on page 192.

We'll proceed next to implement the remaining six methods. Normally we'd test after adding each method, but here we'll test after all six are added, to save some space.

MyArrayList.insert()

The `insert` method receives an object of type `E` to be inserted, and the index at which to insert it into the list. It performs the following steps,

1. Check that the index is valid. The index must refer to an existing list element. If it's not, an exception is thrown.
2. Expand the internal array if needed.
3. Move each element of the internal array over to the right, starting with the index at which the new data element will be inserted.
4. Set the contents of the array at the specified index to its new data value.
5. Increment the array size.

Example 13.6.
MyArrayList.insert().

```
1   public void insert (int index, E object) throws Exception {
2     if (index < 0 || index > size - 1)
3       throw new Exception ("Invalid index");
4
5     expandIfNeeded();
6     for (int i = size - 1; i >= index; i--)
7       array[i+1] = array[i];
8     array[index] = object;
9     size++;
10  }
```

Inserting an element into an array list.

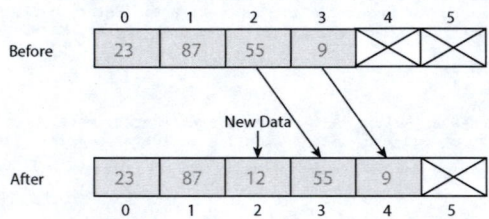

MyArrayList.get()

The **get** method takes one parameter, the index of the list element to be retrieved. It returns the list element of type E that's stored in the array at the specified index. It simply checks that the index is valid (if not, it throws an exception), then returns the element at the specified index.

Example 13.7. MyArrayList.get().

```
1   public E get (int index) throws Exception {
2     if (index < 0 || index > size - 1)
3       throw new Exception ("Invalid index");
4     return array[index];
5   }
```

MyArrayList.indexOf()

The **indexOf** method takes one parameter, an object of type E, and returns the first index at which that object occurs. If the object isn't found, it returns -1. The implementation simply loops from the beginning to the end of the array and returns immediately when the object being searched for is found. If the array terminates, -1 is returned since the object wasn't found. Note that the **equals** method is used to compare the parameter to each element of the array. Had we used the equality operator (==) instead, it would be testing whether the two refer to the *same object instance*.

```
1    public int indexOf (E object) {
2      for (int i = 0; i < size; i++)
3        if (object.equals(array[i]))
4          return i;
5      return -1;
6    }
```

Example   **13.8.**
MyArrayList.indexOf().

MyArrayList.lastIndexOf()

The lastIndexOf method works the same way as indexOf, except that it goes through the array backwards from the end. As with indexOf, it returns immediately if the object being searched for is found.

```
1    public int lastIndexOf (E object) {
2      for (int i = size - 1; i >= 0; i--)
3        if (object.equals(array[i]))
4          return i;
5      return -1;
6    }
```

Example   **13.9.**
MyArrayList.lastIndexOf().

MyArrayList.remove()

The remove method is similar to insert because it has to shift the array's contents starting at a particular index. This time though, it's shifting each element to the left and decrementing the list's size instead of incrementing it. The steps taken by remove are,

The remove method's implementation is a good example of the kind of iteration that you should be comfortable writing.

1. Check that the index is valid. The index must refer to an existing list element. If it's not, an exception is thrown.
2. Save the element that is to be removed in a temporary variable called result.
3. Move each element of the internal array over to the left, starting at the index after that of the list element to be removed, up to the end of the array.
4. Decrement the array size.
5. Return the element of type E that was removed.

```
1    public E remove(int index) throws Exception {
2      if (index < 0 || index > size - 1)
3        throw new Exception ("Invalid index");
4
5      E result = array[index];
6      for (int i = index; i < size - 1; i++)
7        array[i] = array[i+1];
8      size --;
```

Example   **13.10.**
MyArrayList.remove().

```
 9
10      return result;
11    }
```

MyArrayList.set()

The set method takes an index and an element to insert within the list at that index. It follows this procedure,

1. Check that the index is valid. The index must refer to an existing list element. If it's not, an exception is thrown.
2. Save the element that's currently at the specified index of the array in a temporary variable called result.
3. Save the new data within the array at the specified index.
4. Return the element of type E that was overwritten by the new data.

Example 13.11. MyArrayList.set().

```
1    public E set (int index, E object) throws Exception {
2      if (index < 0 || index > size - 1)
3        throw new Exception ("Invalid index");
4
5      E result = array[index];
6      array[index] = object;
7      return result;
8    }
```

Having implemented all the class's methods, we can run the test code again and we get the correct output as shown below,

```
Initially, list contents are: [Peter, Mary, Heather, Henry, Elizabeth, Mary]
After inserting George at index 2, list contents are: [Peter, Mary, George, Heather, Henry, Elizabeth, Mary]
After inserting Betty at index 0, list contents are: [Betty, Peter, Mary, George, Heather, Henry, Elizabeth, Mary]
List size is: 8
Element at index 3 is: George
Index of Mary is: 2
lastIndexOf Mary is: 7
After removing index 2 (Mary), list contents are: [Betty, Peter, George, Heather, Henry, Elizabeth, Mary]
After putting John at index 1, list contents are: [Betty, John, George, Heather, Henry, Elizabeth, Mary]
```

We shouldn't move on without testing the dynamic growth capability of MyArrayList. We'll test that next by adding 100 numbers to a MyArrayList, then printing them out. If all goes well, the internal array will grow as needed from its default capacity of 10 as more elements are added to the array,

Example 13.12. Testing the automatic growth of the MyArrayList's internal array.

```
1    MyList<Integer> countdown = new MyArrayList<>();
2    for (int i = 99; i >= 0; i--)
3      countdown.add(i);
4    for (int i = 0; i < countdown.size(); i++) {
5      if (i % 20 == 0)
6        out.println();
7      out.printf("%4d", countdown.get(i));
8    }
```

99	98	97	96	95	94	93	92	91	90	89	88	87	86	85	84	83	82	81	80
79	78	77	76	75	74	73	72	71	70	69	68	67	66	65	64	63	62	61	60
59	58	57	56	55	54	53	52	51	50	49	48	47	46	45	44	43	42	41	40
39	38	37	36	35	34	33	32	31	30	29	28	27	26	25	24	23	22	21	20
19	18	17	16	15	14	13	12	11	10	9	8	7	6	5	4	3	2	1	0

While our implementation of `ArrayList` lacks the `iterator` method, and a few other details, it's a realistic example of how Java's `ArrayList` is implemented, and has similar performance characteristics. We'll start discussing performance in the next section.

Exercises

13.1 Add the following methods from the `List` interface to the `MyList` interface, then implement them in `MyArrayList`.

    a. void clear(): clears all elements of the list.

    b. boolean isEmpty(): returns `true` if the list is empty, and `false` otherwise.

    c. boolean remove(Object o): removes the first occurrence of the specified object from the list. Returns `true` if an element was removed, and `false` otherwise.

13.2 Program Performance

When we analyze program performance, we aim to find the relative performance of different algorithms on the same computer, not the relative performance of the same algorithm running on different computers. We compare different algorithms that accomplish the same task in order to determine which is the better algorithm. For example, we can compare different sorting algorithms to see which one is faster.

Comparing algorithms, not computers.

Comparing different algorithms that perform the same task, not algorithms that perform different tasks.

In addition, when we analyze program performance, we don't measure performance in seconds. Rather, we measure performance as it relates to the size of the program's input. As the size of the input grows, we observe how the algorithm's runtime grows. For example, an algorithm that has linear runtime is one whose runtime grows proportionally to the size of the input. An algorithm that has constant runtime is one whose runtime doesn't change no matter what the size of its input is.

We compare an algorithm's runtime to the size of its input.

Another thing to keep in mind when analyzing program performance is that we're considering the worst case runtime. An algorithm can have different performance characteristics depending on the input, so it may be fast for some inputs and slow for others. Typically, we're only concerned with the *worst case* performance of the algorithm.

In most cases, we're only interested in the time performance of an algorithm, not how much space it requires to hold its data structures. In some cases though, the space requirements play a role in our decision making when choosing an algorithm.

Keeping in mind what was just said, let's look at an example. The `MyArrayList.indexOf` method in example 13.8 receives a parameter, which is the element we want to find in the list. But the algorithm implemented by this method actually has two inputs:

- The element that we want to find, the `object` parameter.
- The `array` class variable, which holds the internal array of list elements.

We have to think about the time it takes this algorithm to run, as it relates to the size of the input. In our case, the size of the input is the size of the internal array. Recall that the algorithm loops from the start of the array to its end looking for the object that was passed in as a parameter. Once it finds the object in question, the loop terminates even if it hasn't gone all the way to the end of the array.

In the best-case scenario, the object being searched for is at the very start of the internal array. The loop only executes once. Since the object is at the start of the array, it's found right away and the algorithm is done. But we can't consider this case. We have to assume the worst-case scenario. For this algorithm, the worst-case scenario is that the object being searched for isn't in the list, in which case the loop examines every element of the array and then -1 is returned indicating the object wasn't found.

Since the actions taken in each iteration of the loop run in constant time, we now know that the algorithm's runtime is proportional to the size of the input. As the array's size grows, the runtime grows proportionally to it. It's traditional to denote the size of the input with the variable n. When the runtime is proportional to the input's size, we say that it is *on the order of n*, and we denote it as O(n). This notation expresses the runtime as a function of the input size.

Suppose two algorithms perform the same task in O(n) runtime because they both have a loop that iterates once for each element of the input. They may perform the task in different ways, with different operations within the loop for each algorithm. One of the two algorithms may execute a loop iteration faster than the other when running on the same computer. Nevertheless, we consider them equivalent because we're only interested in the *approximate* runtime (hence the expression *on the order of*).

Sequences

Suppose an algorithm has two parts that are run in sequence, and each part runs in O(n) time. The overall runtime is 2*O(n). We discard the constant 2 because we're only interested in the *rough* measure of performance as related to the size of the input. Thus, after discarding the constant, we say that the overall runtime is actually O(n).

When analyzing runtime, we discard constant coefficients (multipliers).

If an algorithm has two parts that run in sequence, one having O(n) runtime and the other having $O(n^2)$ runtime, we discard the part with the smaller runtime and keep the one with the larger runtime. Again, this is because we're only interested in a *rough* measure of the runtime performance as related to the input size. Thus in this case, the overall runtime would be $O(n^2)$.

When analyzing runtime, we discard parts with lower runtime and keep the part with the higher runtime.

For example, suppose a method takes as input a two-dimensional array of grades, one row for each student's grades. Let's suppose this method computes the average grade for each student, then goes through the student list and prints each student's grade average. This method is shown in example 13.13,

```java
public static void main(String[] args) throws Exception {

    int[][] grades = new int[][] {
        { 100,  90,  95,  98, 100,  90,  85 },
        {  77,  94,  95,  95,  81,  93, 100 },
        { 100,  91, 100,  98,  99,  85, 100 },
        {  99,  75, 100,  50,  92,  99,  95 },
    };

    printGradeAverages(grades);
}

private static void printGradeAverages (int[][] grades) {

    double[] averages = new double[grades.length];
    for (int student = 0; student < grades.length; student++) {
        int sum = 0;
```

Example 13.13. Printing student grade averages.

```
Student 1: 94.00
Student 2: 90.71
Student 3: 96.14
Student 4: 87.14
```

```
18      for (int grade = 0; grade < grades[student].length; grade++)
19        sum += grades[student][grade];
20      averages[student] = (double) sum / grades[student].length;
21    }
22
23      for (int student = 0; student < averages.length; student++)
24        out.printf("Student %d: %.2f\n", student + 1, averages[student]);
25    }
```

The `printGradeAverages` method contains two sections. The top section runs in O(nm) time where n is the number of students, and m is the number of grades per student. That's because it has a nested loop, the outer loop processing each student, and the inner processing each grade for the student. The bottom section runs in O(n) time because it loops once per student. So the overall runtime is O(nm) since that is larger than O(n).

Selections

When analyzing runtime of a selection, we add the runtime cost of evaluating the condition to that of the slower of the two alternative sections of code.

When an algorithm contains a selection, such as an if statement with an else clause, one of two sections of code will run, but not both. In this case, as with the cases we discussed above, we have to assume the worst and use the slower section's runtime as the overall runtime. But we should also take into account the time it takes to compute the if statement's *condition*. For example, suppose we have the following section of code,

```
1    if (names.contains(userName)) {
2      out.println("The user " + userName + " is in the list.");
3    }
4    else {
5      out.println("The user " + userName + " is not in the list.");
6    }
```

The notation we've been using is known as *Big-O notation*. An algorithm's runtime expressed in big-O notation is often referred to as its *runtime complexity*, or just its *complexity*. You can use these terms interchangeably.

The `if` clause contains one print statement which runs in constant time (that is, its runtime doesn't vary with the size of the input, which is the length of the name list). Likewise, the else clause also contains a single print statement, also having a constant runtime. But, the `if` condition evaluation takes O(n) time to run because the `contains` method loops over the list. So the overall runtime is O(n) because the slower of the `if` and `else` clauses runs in constant time and evaluating the `if` condition has O(n) runtime.

The runtime of a section of code that runs in constant time is denoted O(1). Note that n doesn't appear in the expression since the runtime is independent of it.

Figure 13.1 shows a visual comparison of the growth rates of some common runtimes, and figure 13.2 shows the same chart in a wider view (note the Y axis values in both figures). These figures illustrate what you already knew intuitively—a runtime that is quadratic grows very fast as the size of the input grows. Most algorithms that you will use frequently have a logarithmic, linear, or O(n log n) complexity. We'll discuss logarithmic complexity and provide an example later on in section 14.1. Table 13.1 lists these common runtimes with an example of each one.

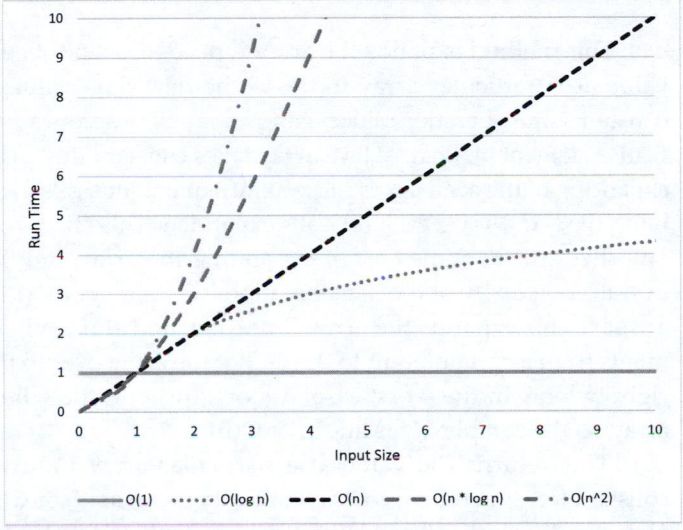

Figure 13.1: Comparing common runtimes.

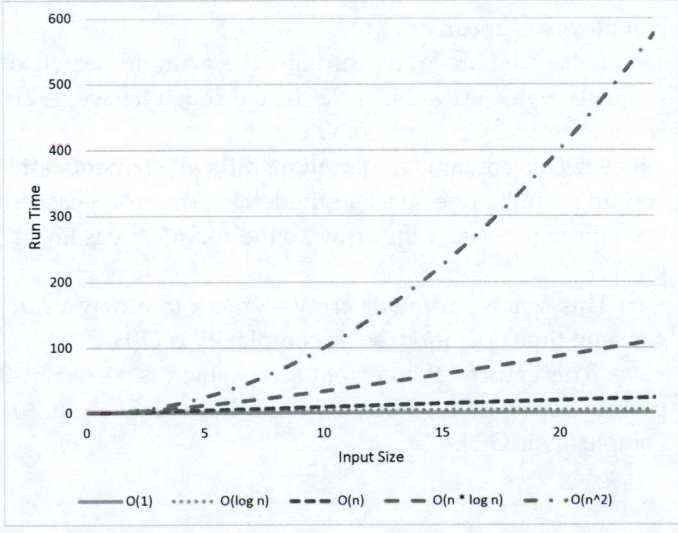

Figure 13.2: Comparing common runtimes (wide view).

Table 13.1: Common runtimes.

Logarithmic complexity, O(log n) is often written as O(lg n) when the logarithm has base 2. In this book, I will use O(log n) to refer to a base 2 logarithm, so you should consider O(log n) and O(lg n) as equivalent.

Runtime	Name	Example
O(1)	Constant	`MyArrayList.get()`
O(log n)	Logarithmic	Binary search (chapter 14)
O(n)	Linear	`MyArrayList.insert()`
O(n log n)	Log-linear	Merge sort (chapter 16)
$O(n^2)$	Quadratic	Bubble sort (chapter 16)

Referring back to the previous section, we can now analyze the complexity of each method of the `MyArrayList` class,

- `add`: This method expands the array if needed, then sets the value at a particular array index to the new data value, a constant-time operation, since using an index to access a particular element of a native Java array takes constant time. The expansion of the array takes place at infrequent intervals, doubling the array's size each time it's expanded. This effectively amortizes the runtime cost of expanding the array and the overall complexity of the `add` operation is constant, or O(1).

- `insert`: This expands the array if needed, and shifts all elements from a certain point to the end of the array over to the right by one. In the worst case, it loops through the whole array, so the complexity is linear, or O(n).

- `get`: This returns the value at a particular array index, a constant time operation, so its complexity is constant, or O(1).

- `indexOf`: This loops through the array in search of a particular value. At worst, it has to go through the whole array, so its complexity is linear, or O(n).

- `lastIndexOf`: This loops through the array in search of a particular value. At worst, it has to go through the whole array, so its complexity is linear, or O(n).

- `remove`: This contains a loop that shifts all elements after a certain point by one space to the left. In the worst case, this goes through most of the array, so the complexity is linear, or O(n).

- `set`: This sets a particular array element to a new value, a constant time operation, so its complexity is O(1).

- `size`: This returns the current size, which is stored in the private `size` data member, a constant time operation, so its complexity is O(1).

Operation	Complexity	Reason
add	O(1)	It just writes to the end of the array.
insert	O(n)	It shifts elements to the right starting at the index inserted into.
get	O(1)	It just gets the array element at a certain index.
indexOf	O(n)	It loops through the array looking for a particular value.
lastIndexOf	O(n)	It loops through the array looking for a particular value.
remove	O(n)	It shifts elements to the left starting after the index removed from.
set	O(1)	It just writes to a particular index in the array.
size	O(1)	It just returns the internal size variable.

Table 13.2: Complexity of each MyArrayList operation.

Exercises

13.2 What is the time complexity of this code?

```java
int addAges(int[] ageArray) {
  int sum = 0;
  for (int i = 0; i < ageArray.length; i++)
    sum += ageArray[i];
  return sum;
}
```

13.3 What is the time complexity of this code?

```java
ArrayList<Integer> doSomething(int[] array) {
  ArrayList<Integer> results = new ArrayList<>();
  for (int i = 0; i < array.length; i++) {
    for (int j = i + 1; j < array.length; j++) {
      results.add(array[i] + array[j]);
    }
  }
  return results;
}
```

13.4 The following method computes a*b. What is its runtime?

```java
int product(int a, int b) {
  int sum = 0;
  for (int i = 0; i < b; i++)
    sum += a;
  return sum;
}
```

13.5 The following method computes a%b, where "a" and "b" are positive integers. What is its runtime?

```
1   int mod(int a, int b) {
2     if (b <= 0)
3       return -1;
4     int div = a / b;
5     return a - div * b;
6   }
```

13.3 Implementing LinkedList

As we did with **ArrayList**, we'll implement our own version of Java's **LinkedList** and analyze its performance. A linked list implements the **List** interface just as the array list does, but the internal structure is completely different, and it has its own pros and cons in terms of performance when compared to an array list. For example, deleting the first element is a constant time operation in a linked list, whereas its complexity is linear in an array list.

The **Node** class

Each data element in a linked list is wrapped in a separate container object, which we'll call a *node*. In addition to the data element, each node has a pointer to the next node in the list. While **MyArrayList** contains an internal native array, **MyLinkedList** doesn't contain an array but a series of nodes, with each node pointing to the next one in the list. The **MyLinkedList** object keeps references to the first and last nodes. Example 13.14 shows the **Node** class and the beginnings of the **MyLinkedList** class.

Example 13.14. Node and MyLinkedList.

```
1   class Node<E> {
2     E element;
3     Node<E> next;
4
5     public Node (E element) {
6       this.element = element;
7     }
8   }
9
10  class MyLinkedList<E> implements MyList<E> {
11
12    Node<E> head = null;
13    Node<E> tail = null;
14    int size = 0;
15
16    public void add (E object) {
17    }
```

```
18
19    public void insert (int index, E object) throws Exception {
20    }
21
22    public E get (int index) throws Exception {
23       return null;
24    }
25
26    public int indexOf (E object) {
27       return -1;
28    }
29
30    public int lastIndexOf (E object) {
31       return -1;
32    }
33
34    public E remove(int index) throws Exception {
35       return null;
36    }
37
38    public E set (int index, E object) throws Exception {
39       return null;
40    }
41
42    public int size() {
43       return size;
44    }
45 }
```

Note that `Node` is generic, and its internal data is of the generic type
`E`. `MyLinkedList` keeps track of the list's size in its `size` variable,
and holds references to the first and last node in the `head` and `tail`
member variables.

We'll use the same test code for `LinkedList` as we did for `ArrayList`.
We just need to change the name list to a linked list,

```
1 │  MyList<String> names = new MyLinkedList<>();
```

Other than the above simple change, the rest of the test program
can be used as shown in example 13.2. This illustrates the power of
polymorphism, defined on page 208.

MyLinkedList.add()

Now that we have the outline of the `MyLinkedList` class and its
testing code, our goal should be to get something minimal working
so that we can start testing, in keeping with technique 16 on page 192.
To do this, we'll just need to override `toString` and implement
either `add` or `insert`. We'll choose `add` since it's simpler.

The `MyLinkedList.add` method adds a new list element to the end of the list by following these steps,

- Create a new `Node` object, initializing it with the data of type `E` being added to the list.
- Increment the internal `size` variable, which keeps track of the size of the list.
- Add the new `Node` object to the end of the linked list. There are two cases to consider:
  - If the list is empty when `add` is called, both `head` and `tail` are null. In this case, both `head` and `tail` will be set to the new node.
  - If the list is not empty, the existing last node will have a `null` value in its `next` reference. Its `next` reference will be changed to point to the new node, and the `tail` reference will also be set to the new node. Note that `tail` will be set to the new node in both of these cases.

The code implementing the above steps is shown in example 13.15,

Example 13.15. `MyLinkedList.add`.

```
1   public void add (E object) {
2
3       // create new node to hold the new data value
4       Node<E> newNode = new Node<E>(object);
5
6       // increment list size
7       size++;
8
9       // insert the new node at the end of the linked list
10      if (head == null)
11          head = newNode;
12      else
13          tail.next = newNode;
14      tail = newNode;
15  }
```

MyLinkedList.toString()

We're almost able to start testing. The only thing we need to do before running the first test is to write the `toString` method. The `toString` method follows the chain of nodes from the head to the tail, adding the data (i.e., the list element) contained in each node to the string that it returns. Following the linked list in this way is sometimes called *walking* the linked list.

The terms *pointer* and *reference* are often used interchangeably, especially by developers who work in both `C` and `Java`. A reference in `C` is called a pointer.

To walk the linked list, we create a new node pointer called `current`, and set its value to the `head`. Then we repeatedly process the current node and increment `current` to point to the next node, terminating once `current` is null at which point we've processed the last node in the chain. This process is illustrated in example 13.16,

```
1   Node<E> current = head;
2   while (current != null) {
3
4       // process the current node. The current node's data is accessed with the
        syntax 'current.element'
5       ...
6
7       // advance to the next node
8       current = current.next;
9   }
```

Example 13.16. Walking a linked list.

It is critical that you understand examples 13.16 and 13.17, especially the way that the `current` reference is dereferenced to access the current node's `element` (its data) and its `next` reference (the pointer to the next node). This kind of code is at the heart of linked lists, and many other data structures.

Loops are the way arrays are often processed. Loops are the algorithmic counterpart of the array data structure. In the same way, the pattern in example 13.16 is the algorithmic counterpart of the linked list data structure. It's a very common way of traversing a linked list to perform some operation on each node, and you'll see examples of this repeatedly throughout the rest of this section starting with example 13.17 that implements the `MyLinkedList.toString` method.

`MyLinkedList.toString` iterates through the linked list, adding each node's data to the string that is ultimately returned. The rest of the methods will be implemented next.

```
1   @Override
2   public String toString() {
3
4       String result = "[";
5       Node<E> current = head;
6       while (current != null) {
7
8           // add this node's data to the resulting string
9           result += current.element;
10          if (current.next != null)
11              result += ", ";
12
13          // advance to the next node
14          current = current.next;
15      }
16      return result + "]";
17  }
```

Example 13.17. `MyLinkedList.toString`.

At first glance, `MyLinkedList.toString` has linear runtime, but the repeated string concatenations are problematic, since each time a data element is concatenated to the result, a new string is created, and the list's contents 'so far' are copied to it. This technically makes it $O(n^2)$, and the same applies to `MyArrayList.toString`. Section 15.7 reveals the way to fix this.

```
Initially, list contents are: [Peter, Mary, Heather, Henry, Elizabeth, Mary]
After inserting George at index 2, list contents are: [Peter, Mary, Heather, Henry, Elizabeth, Mary]
After inserting Betty at index 0, list contents are: [Peter, Mary, Heather, Henry, Elizabeth, Mary]
List size is: 6
Element at index 3 is: null
Index of Mary is: -1
lastIndexOf Mary is: -1
After removing index 2 (null), list contents are: [Peter, Mary, Heather, Henry, Elizabeth, Mary]
After putting John at index 1, list contents are: [Peter, Mary, Heather, Henry, Elizabeth, Mary]
```

MyLinkedList.get()

The **get** method takes an integer index and returns the data element at that index within the list. It walks the linked list to get to the node at the specified index, then returns the node's data.

Example 13.18.
MyLinkedList.get().

```java
public E get (int index) throws Exception {
  if (index < 0 || index > size - 1)
    throw new Exception ("Invalid index");

  Node<E> current = head;
  int counter = 0;
  while (counter < index) {
    current = current.next;
    counter ++;
  }

  return current.element;
}
```

MyLinkedList.indexOf()

The **indexOf** method takes an object to look for in the list, and returns the index of the first occurrence of the object. It walks the linked list from the beginning until it finds the data it's looking for, or reaches the end of the list, in which case it returns -1.

Example 13.19.
MyLinkedList.indexOf().

```java
public int indexOf (E object) {

  Node<E> current = head;
  int index = 0;
  while (current != null) {
    if (object.equals(current.element))
      return index;
    current = current.next;
    index ++;
  }

  return -1;
}
```

MyLinkedList.lastIndexOf()

The **lastIndexOf** method takes an object to look for in the list, and returns the last index at which the object occurs within the list. It walks the linked list from the beginning to the end, keeping the last index at which it finds the data it's looking for. If the data isn't found, it returns -1.

```
1    public int lastIndexOf (E object) {
2
3      int result = -1;
4      Node<E> current = head;
5      int index = 0;
6      while (current != null) {
7        if (object.equals(current.element))
8          result = index;
9        current = current.next;
10       index ++;
11     }
12
13     return result;
14   }
```

Example **13.20**.
MyLinkedList.lastIndexOf().

MyLinkedList.set()

The **set** method takes an index and a data item of type **E**, and writes the data item to the node at the specified index. It also returns the data that was previously at that index.

```
1    public E set (int index, E object) throws Exception {
2      if (index < 0 || index > size - 1)
3        throw new Exception ("Invalid index");
4
5      Node<E> current = head;
6      int counter = 0;
7      while (counter < index) {
8        current = current.next;
9        counter ++;
10     }
11
12     E result = current.element;
13     current.element = object;
14     return result;
15   }
```

Example **13.21**.
MyLinkedList.set().

MyLinkedList.insert()

The **insert** method takes an index and an object to insert at that index within the list. It walks the list from the beginning until the node prior to the desired index (**previous**), then inserts the new data element into the chain after **previous**. This is done by setting the new node's **next** pointer to **previous.next**, then setting **previous.next** to the new node. Special handling is performed when the new node is inserted at the start or the end of the linked list.

Example   **13.22.**
MyLinkedList.insert().

```java
public void insert (int index, E object) throws Exception {
    if (index < 0 || index > size)
        throw new Exception ("Invalid index");

    Node<E> newNode = new Node<>(object);

    Node<E> current = head;
    int counter = 0;
    Node<E> previous = null;
    while (counter < index) {
        previous = current;
        current = current.next;
        counter++;
    }

    if (previous != null)
        previous.next = newNode;
    newNode.next = current;

    size ++;

    if (index == 0)
        head = newNode;
    if (index == size - 1)
        tail = newNode;
}
```

Inserting an element into a linked list.

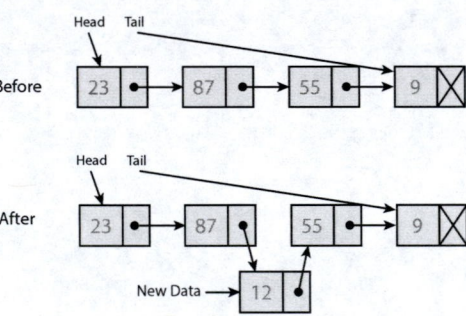

MyLinkedList.remove()

The `remove` method takes an index and removes the object at that index within the list. It walks the list from the beginning, finding the node to be deleted and the one prior to it (`previous`), then deletes the proper node by setting `previous.next` to `current.next`. Special handling is performed when the node to delete is at the start or the end of the linked list. In addition, the deleted data is returned by the `remove` method.

```
1   public E remove(int index) throws Exception {
2     if (index < 0 || index > size - 1)
3       throw new Exception ("Invalid index");
4
5     Node<E> current = head;
6     int counter = 0;
7     Node<E> previous = null;
8     while (counter < index) {
9       previous = current;
10      current = current.next;
11      counter++;
12    }
13
14    if (previous != null)
15      previous.next = current.next;
16    E result = current.element;
17
18    size --;
19
20    if (index == 0)
21      head = current.next;
22    if (index == size - 1)
23      tail = previous;
24
25    return result;
26  }
```

Example   13.23.
MyLinkedList.remove().

```
Initially, list contents are: [Peter, Mary, Heather, Henry, Elizabeth, Mary]
After inserting George at index 2, list contents are: [Peter, Mary, George, Heather, Henry, Elizabeth, Mary]
After inserting Betty at index 0, list contents are: [Betty, Peter, Mary, George, Heather, Henry, Elizabeth, Ma
List size is: 8
Element at index 3 is: George
Index of Mary is: 2
lastIndexOf Mary is: 7
After removing index 2 (Mary), list contents are: [Betty, Peter, George, Heather, Henry, Elizabeth, Mary]
After putting John at index 1, list contents are: [Betty, John, George, Heather, Henry, Elizabeth, Mary]
```

Each method's complexity can be analyzed as was done with
MyArrayList,

- add: This creates a new node and points the existing last node
  to it, which requires constant time, so it runs in O(1) time.
- insert: This method needs to walk the linked list from the
  beginning to the desired index, which takes O(n) time.
- get: This walks the linked list from the start to the desired
  index, so it takes O(n) time.
- indexOf: Walks the linked list looking for a particular data
  item. In the worst case, it takes O(n) time.
- lastIndexOf: Walks the entire linked list and finds the last
  occurrence of a particular data item, so its complexity is O(n).
- remove: Walks the linked list to a specified index, so its complexity is O(n).
- set: Walks the linked list to a specified index, so its complexity
  is O(n).

Table 13.3: Complexity of each operation for both list implementations.

Operation	MyArrayList	MyLinkedList
add	O(1)	O(1)
insert	O(n)	O(n)
get	O(1)	O(n)
indexOf	O(n)	O(n)
lastIndexOf	O(n)	O(n)
remove	O(n)	O(n)
set	O(1)	O(n)
size	O(1)	O(1)
Removing first element	O(n)	O(1)
Inserting at beginning	O(n)	O(1)

- size: Returns the internal size data member, requiring constant time, so its complexity is O(1).

Table 13.3 shows the complexity of each operation for each of MyArrayList and MyLinkedList. A couple more rows have been added to show the relative performance of removing the first list element, and adding a new list element at the start of the list. The table highlights the pros and cons of ArrayList and LinkedList. ArrayList is a good choice in most cases, but LinkedList is very handy in certain cases. For example, the queue implementation shown in example 11.2 uses a list to hold the queue's elements. It uses add to add a new item to the queue, and remove(0) to remove an item from the queue. Both of those operations run in constant time when using a linked list, while an array list adds an item in constant time but requires O(n) time when removing the first element of the list.

Exercises

13.6 Repeat exercise 13.1 for MyLinkedList. Write the remove method's loop manually to get more coding practice (i.e., don't use the indexOf or remove(int) methods in the implementation of remove(Object)).

13.4 Timing Tests

To corroborate the above performance analysis, example 13.24 adds numbers to a `MyLinkedList`, then repeatedly deletes the first element until the list is empty. This is repeated with different list sizes and the time it takes to delete the numbers from the list is reported. Then, the process is repeated with a `MyLinkedList`. The results are charted in figure 13.3, and show that deleting the first element from a linked list has constant runtime, while deleting the first element from an array list runs in time linear in the array size.

```java
public static void main(String[] args) throws Exception {

  for (int size = 0; size <= 100000; size += 10000)
    doTest(size, false);
  for (int size = 0; size <= 100000; size += 10000)
    doTest(size, true);
}

public static void doTest(int size, boolean useArrayList) throws Exception {

  MyList<Integer> list = useArrayList ? new MyArrayList<>() : new
  MyLinkedList<>();

  for (int i = 0; i < size; i++)
    list.add((int) (Math.random() * 100));

  long startTime = System.nanoTime();
  while (list.size() != 0)
    list.remove(0);
  long endTime = System.nanoTime();

  out.printf("Removing elements from %s of size %d took %d microseconds\n",
    useArrayList ? "array list" : "linked list", size, (endTime - startTime)
    /1000);
}
```

Example 13.24. Testing runtime of `remove(0)`.

```
Removing elements from linked list of size 0 took 2 microseconds
Removing elements from linked list of size 10000 took 906 microseconds
Removing elements from linked list of size 20000 took 1220 microseconds
Removing elements from linked list of size 30000 took 368 microseconds
Removing elements from linked list of size 40000 took 383 microseconds
Removing elements from linked list of size 50000 took 483 microseconds
Removing elements from linked list of size 60000 took 595 microseconds
Removing elements from linked list of size 70000 took 758 microseconds
Removing elements from linked list of size 80000 took 401 microseconds
Removing elements from linked list of size 90000 took 449 microseconds
Removing elements from linked list of size 100000 took 454 microseconds
Removing elements from array list of size 0 took 1 microseconds
Removing elements from array list of size 10000 took 169067 microseconds
Removing elements from array list of size 20000 took 714610 microseconds
Removing elements from array list of size 30000 took 1566097 microseconds
Removing elements from array list of size 40000 took 2772301 microseconds
Removing elements from array list of size 50000 took 4265944 microseconds
Removing elements from array list of size 60000 took 6151599 microseconds
Removing elements from array list of size 70000 took 8379022 microseconds
Removing elements from array list of size 80000 took 10922787 microseconds
Removing elements from array list of size 90000 took 13825244 microseconds
Removing elements from array list of size 100000 took 17107247 microseconds
```

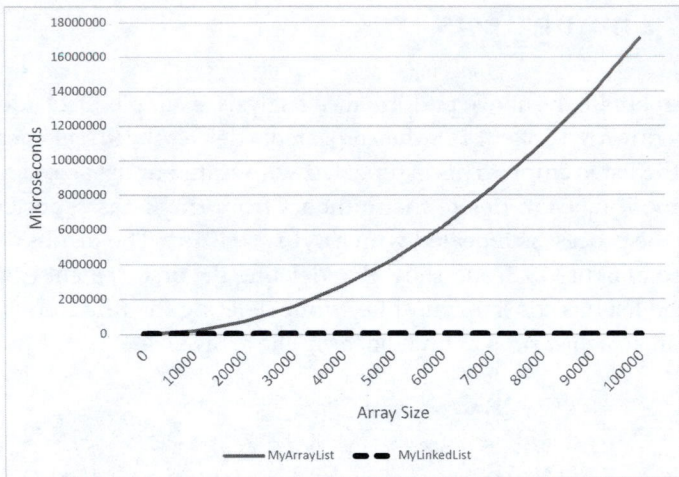

Figure 13.3: Runtime comparison of `ArrayList` and `LinkedList` when deleting first list element.

Finally, we'll run a similar timing test comparing `MyArrayList` and `MyLinkedList`, but this time the test will retrieve array elements by index. The results are charted in figure 13.4, and show that getting an element by index from an array list has constant runtime, while doing so with a linked list runs in time linear in the array size.

Example 13.25. Testing runtime of `get`.

```java
public static void main(String[] args) throws Exception {

  for (int size = 0; size <= 100000; size += 10000)
    doTest(size, false);
  for (int size = 0; size <= 100000; size += 10000)
    doTest(size, true);
}

public static void doTest(int size, boolean useArrayList) throws Exception {

  MyList<Integer> list = useArrayList ? new MyArrayList<>() : new
    MyLinkedList<>();

  for (int i = 0; i < size; i++)
    list.add((int) (Math.random() * 100));

  long startTime = System.nanoTime();
  for (int i = 0; i < size; i++)
    list.get(i);
  long endTime = System.nanoTime();

  out.printf("Getting elements from %s of size %d took %d microseconds\n",
    useArrayList ? "array list" : "linked list", size, (endTime - startTime)
    /1000);
}
```

```
Getting elements from linked list of size 0 took 0 microseconds
Getting elements from linked list of size 10000 took 93462 microseconds
Getting elements from linked list of size 20000 took 361789 microseconds
Getting elements from linked list of size 30000 took 881576 microseconds
Getting elements from linked list of size 40000 took 1499290 microseconds
Getting elements from linked list of size 50000 took 2310426 microseconds
Getting elements from linked list of size 60000 took 3498410 microseconds
Getting elements from linked list of size 70000 took 4723476 microseconds
Getting elements from linked list of size 80000 took 6150266 microseconds
Getting elements from linked list of size 90000 took 7646067 microseconds
Getting elements from linked list of size 100000 took 9688306 microseconds
Getting elements from array list of size 0 took 0 microseconds
Getting elements from array list of size 10000 took 839 microseconds
Getting elements from array list of size 20000 took 153 microseconds
Getting elements from array list of size 30000 took 246 microseconds
Getting elements from array list of size 40000 took 299 microseconds
Getting elements from array list of size 50000 took 375 microseconds
Getting elements from array list of size 60000 took 449 microseconds
Getting elements from array list of size 70000 took 523 microseconds
Getting elements from array list of size 80000 took 607 microseconds
Getting elements from array list of size 90000 took 719 microseconds
Getting elements from array list of size 100000 took 840 microseconds
```

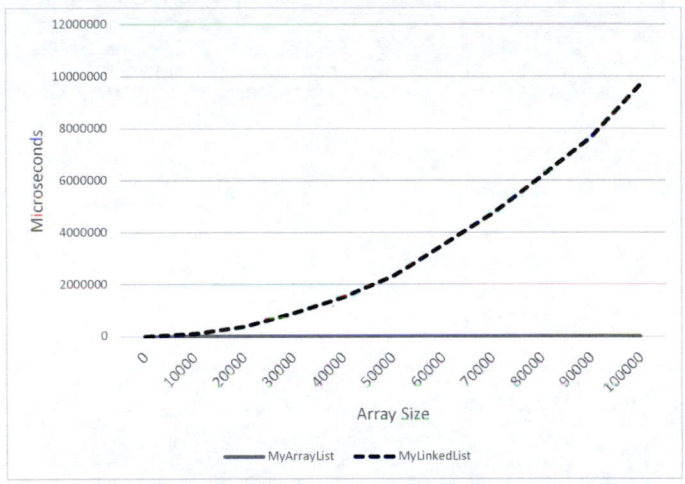

Figure 13.4: Runtime comparison of `ArrayList` and `LinkedList` when getting an element by index.

Chapter Summary

- `ArrayList` and `LinkedList` each implement the `List` interface, but have different performance characteristics, and each is appropriate to use in certain situations.
- When analyzing program performance, we focus on comparing different algorithms with respect to the size of the input.
- When analyzing program performance, we're concerned mainly with worst-case running time.

- Big-O notation summarizes runtime performance by expressing the runtime as a rough function of the input size.
- Timing tests can be used to verify performance analysis by measuring the runtime as the size of the input increases.

```
1  class MyLinkedList<E> implements MyList<E> {
2
3    Node<E> head = null;
4    Node<E> tail = null;
5    int size = 0;
6
7    public int indexOf (E object) {                    Start at the head
8
9      Node<E> current = head;                          Loop until end of list
10     int index = 0;
11     while (current != null) {
12       if (object.equals(current.element))            Process each node
13         return index;
14       current = current.next;
15       index ++;                              Advance current reference
16     }
17
18     return -1;
19   }
20 }
```

Exercise Solutions

13.1
```
1  interface MyList<E> {
2    ...
3
4    public void clear();
5    public boolean isEmpty();
6    public boolean remove(Object o) throws Exception;
7  }
8
9  class MyArrayList<E> implements MyList<E> {
10   ...
11
12   public void clear() {
13     size = 0;
14   }
15
16   public boolean isEmpty() {
17     return size == 0;
18   }
19
20   public boolean remove(Object o) throws Exception {
21     int index = indexOf((E) o);
22     if (index == -1)
23       return false;
24     remove(index);
25     return true;
```

```
26    }
27  }
28
29  public class Test {
30    public static void main(String[] args) throws Exception {
31
32      MyList<String> names = new MyArrayList<>();
33      names.add("Peter");
34      names.add("Mary");
35      names.add("Heather");
36      names.add("Mary");
37      out.println("names = " + names);
38      out.println("names.isEmpty() = " + names.isEmpty());
39      names.remove("Mary");
40      out.println("After removing Mary, names = " + names);
41      names.clear();
42      out.println("After clearing, names = " + names);
43    }
44  }
```

```
names = [Peter, Mary, Heather, Mary]
names.isEmpty() = false
After removing Mary, names = [Peter, Heather, Mary]
After clearing, names = []
```

13.2 It loops once for each element of the array, so the complexity is O(n).

13.3 The outer loop iterates once for each element of the array. The inner loop iterates from i to the end of the array. The first time through the outer loop, the inner loop iterates n times. The last time through the outer loop, the inner loop iterates one time. On average, the inner loop iterates $n/2$ times. So the overall complexity is $O(n^2/2)$, or $1/2\ O(n^2)$. Discarding the constant (1/2), the complexity is O(n).

13.4 It loops from 0 to b, so the complexity is O(n) where n is the *value* of b.

13.5 Each operation in the method runs in constant time, so the complexity is O(1).

13.6
```
 1  interface MyList<E> {
 2    ...
 3
 4    public void clear();
 5    public boolean isEmpty();
 6    public boolean remove(Object o) throws Exception;
 7  }
 8
 9  class MyLinkedList<E> implements MyList<E> {
10    ...
11
12    public void clear() {
13      head = tail = null;
14      size = 0;
```

```
15    }
16
17      public boolean isEmpty() {
18        return size == 0;
19      }
20
21      public boolean remove(Object o) throws Exception {
22
23        Node<E> current = head;
24        Node<E> previous = null;
25        while (current != null) {
26
27          // if object is found, remove it
28          if (current.element.equals(o)) {
29
30            size --;
31
32            // take the current node out of the chain
33            if (previous != null)
34              previous.next = current.next;
35
36            // if this is the first node, special handling is needed
37            if (current == head)
38              head = current.next;
39
40            // if this is the last node, special handling is needed
41            if (current == tail)
42              tail = previous;
43
44            return true;
45          }
46
47          previous = current;
48          current = current.next;
49        }
50
51        // object not found
52        return false;
53      }
54    }
55
56    public class Test {
57      public static void main(String[] args) throws Exception {
58
59        MyList<String> names = new MyLinkedList<>();
60        names.add("Peter");
61        names.add("Mary");
62        names.add("Heather");
63        names.add("Mary");
64        out.println("names = " + names);
65        out.println("names.isEmpty() = " + names.isEmpty());
66        names.remove("Mary");
67        out.println("After removing Mary, names = " + names);
68        names.clear();
69        out.println("After clearing, names = " + names);
70      }
71    }
```

```
names = [Peter, Mary, Heather, Mary]
names.isEmpty() = false
After removing Mary, names = [Peter, Heather, Mary]
After clearing, names = []
```

Maps and Hashing 14

14.1 Binary Search

Maps are efficient collection classes that allow us to store key/value pairs, where the key and value are both generic types. We begin our discussion of maps with an example of looking up a record using its name. For this, we'll use a publicly available database of asteroids, and get an asteroid's information by name. Any other data set can be used for this example, as long as it's in text format and has enough rows. We'll begin by downloading the data set from `http://www.minorplanet.info/lightcurvedatabase.html` (LCDB; Warner et al., 2009). On that web page, we locate the link to LCLIST_-PUB_CURRENT.zip and download it. After unzipping the file, we copy the data file "LC_SUM_PUB.TXT" to the root of our Eclipse project (this can be done by dragging it onto the project root in Eclipse's Package Explorer view). After doing this, it will appear alongside the "src" folder in the Package Explorer, as shown in figure 14.1.

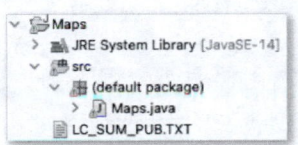

Figure 14.1: Data file under the project root in the Package Explorer window.

The data file has about 34,000 records, one row for each record, with columns for the various data fields. It can be opened in Eclipse as shown in figure 14.2.

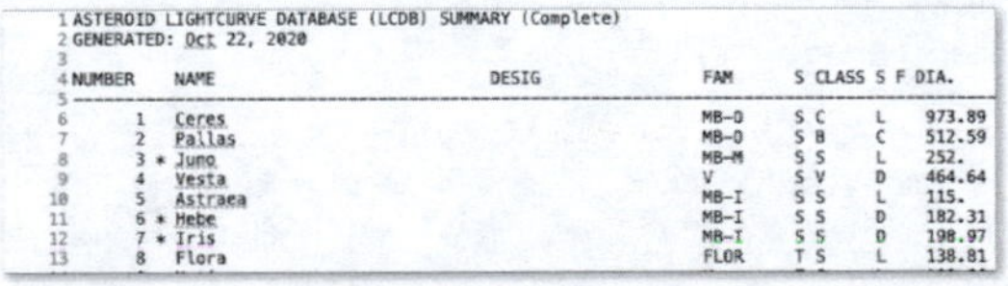

```
ASTEROID LIGHTCURVE DATABASE (LCDB) SUMMARY (Complete)
GENERATED: Oct 22, 2020

NUMBER     NAME                               DESIG              FAM     S CLASS S F DIA.
------------------------------------------------------------------------------------------
       1   Ceres                                                 MB-O    S C       L   973.89
       2   Pallas                                                MB-O    S B       C   512.59
       3 * Juno                                                  MB-M    S S       L   252.
       4   Vesta                                                 V       S V       D   464.64
       5   Astraea                                               MB-I    S S       L   115.
       6 * Hebe                                                  MB-I    S S       D   182.31
       7 * Iris                                                  MB-I    S S       D   198.97
       8   Flora                                                 FLOR    T S       L   138.81
```

Figure 14.2: Asteroids data file opened in Eclipse.

We'll write a program that reads the data from this file, line by line, using the techniques we learned in chapter 12. We'll use the

Scanning goes through a string, separating its components. *Parsing* is similar, but can handle nested structures that are arbitrarily deep. Colloquially, the term *parsing* is often used in place of the term *scanning*.

string manipulation techniques we learned in chapter 2 to scan each line, extracting the relevant data fields (we'll only read some of the data fields that are of interest to us). And, we'll use the techniques we learned in chapter 8 to create an `Asteroid` class that holds each asteroid's data. We'll also use the techniques we learned in chapter 10 to hold the asteroid objects in an `ArrayList`. The `Asteroid` class implements `Comparable` as discussed in chapter 11 to facilitate sorting the list of asteroids. Our first version is shown in example 14.1,

Example 14.1. `Asteroid` class and its test program.

```java
import static java.lang.System.out;
import java.io.File;
import java.io.FileNotFoundException;
import java.util.ArrayList;
import java.util.Collections;
import java.util.List;
import java.util.Scanner;

public class Maps {

  public static void main(String[] args) throws FileNotFoundException {

    List<Asteroid> asteroids = new ArrayList<>();

    File file = new File("LC_SUM_PUB.TXT");
    Scanner input = new Scanner(file);

    // ignore first 5 lines (the header)
    for (int i = 0; i < 5; i++)
      input.nextLine();

    // process each asteroid (one line)
    while (input.hasNext()) {
      String line = input.nextLine();

      int number = Integer.parseInt(line.substring(0, 8).trim());
      String name = line.substring(10, 40).trim();
      float diameter = readFloat (line, 84, 91);
      float reflectivity = readFloat(line, 109, 115);
      float period = readFloat(line, 118, 129);
      Asteroid asteroid = new Asteroid(number, name, diameter, reflectivity, period);
      asteroids.add(asteroid);
    }

    out.println("Read " + asteroids.size() + " asteroids...");

    // sort asteroid list
    Collections.sort(asteroids);

    // display first and last (alphabetically)
    out.println("The first asteroid is: " + asteroids.get(0));
    out.println("The last asteroid is: " + asteroids.get(asteroids.size()-1));

    input.close();
  }

  private static float readFloat(String line, int startIndex, int endIndex) {
```

```
48      float num = 0;
49      String str = line.substring(startIndex, endIndex).trim();
50      if (!str.isEmpty())
51        num = Float.parseFloat(str);
52      return num;
53    }
54  }
55
56  class Asteroid implements Comparable<Asteroid> {
57
58    int number;
59    String name;     // name or designation
60    float diameter;   // diameter in kilometers
61    float reflectivity; // Albedo ranges from 1 (perfectly reflecting) to 0 (
          perfectly absorbing)
62    float period;    // rotation period in hours
63
64    public Asteroid (int number, String name, float diameter, float reflectivity,
          float period) {
65      this.number = number;
66      this.name = name;
67      this.diameter = diameter;
68      this.reflectivity = reflectivity;
69      this.period = period;
70    }
71
72    @Override
73    public String toString() {
74      return name + " (ID " + number + "), reflectivity: " + reflectivity + ",
          diameter: " + diameter + " km, period: " + period + " hours";
75    }
76
77    @Override
78    public int compareTo(Asteroid other) {
79      return name.compareToIgnoreCase(other.name);
80    }
81  }
```

```
Read 34190 asteroids...
The first asteroid is: 05s07 (ID 0), reflectivity: 0.1, diameter: 122.3 km, period: 6.54 hours
The last asteroid is: Zyskin (ID 2098), reflectivity: 0.2, diameter: 8.91 km, period: 3.92 hours
```

Next, we'll search for a particular asteroid in two different ways, while comparing the speed of this search in a way similar to the timing tests you saw in the last chapter. The first method will look for an asteroid by examining each element of the asteroid list. This is referred to as a linear search. The second method is more efficient, and is called a binary search. Let's look at the code first, then we'll discuss how binary search works,

```
1   public static void main(String[] args) throws FileNotFoundException {
2   ...
3     // display first and last (alphabetically)
4     //out.println("The first asteroid is: " + asteroids.get(0));
5     //out.println("The last asteroid is: " + asteroids.get(asteroids.size()-1))
          ;
6
7     input.close();
```

Example 14.2. Comparing linear search and binary search.

```
 8
 9    // linear search
10    Asteroid asteroid = null;
11    long start = System.currentTimeMillis();
12    for (int i = 0; i < 50000; i++) {
13      asteroid = linearSearch(asteroids, "Pluto");
14    }
15    long end = System.currentTimeMillis();
16    out.println("Linear search: Pluto's record is " + asteroid);
17    out.println("Linear search: Time to find Pluto: " + (end-start) + "
        milliseconds");

18
19    // binary search
20    Collections.sort(asteroids);
21    start = System.currentTimeMillis();
22    int index = -1;
23    for (int i = 0; i < 50000; i++) {
24      index = Collections.binarySearch(asteroids, new Asteroid(0, "Pluto", 0,
        0, 0));
25    }
26    end = System.currentTimeMillis();
27    out.println("Binary search: Pluto's record is " + asteroids.get(index));
28    out.println("Binary search: Time to find Pluto: " + (end-start) + "
        milliseconds");
29  }
30
31  private static Asteroid linearSearch (List<Asteroid> asteroids, String
        asteroidName) {
32    for (int i = 0; i < asteroids.size(); i++)
33      if (asteroids.get(i).name.equals(asteroidName))
34        return asteroids.get(i);
35    return null;
36  }
```

```
Read 34190 asteroids...
Linear search: Pluto's record is Pluto (ID 134340), reflectivity: 0.65, diameter: 339.0 km,
Linear search: Time to find Pluto: 13751 milliseconds
Binary search: Pluto's record is Pluto (ID 134340), reflectivity: 0.65, diameter: 339.0 km,
Binary search: Time to find Pluto: 21 milliseconds
```

The timing results reveal that finding Pluto 50,000 times in the list of asteroids using binary search takes about 21 milliseconds, while finding it using the brute force method (linear search) takes about 13,000 milliseconds, so binary search is about 500 times faster in this case.

A binary search is like the children's game where you guess an unknown number between 1 and 100. After each guess, you are told whether the unknown number is higher or lower than the number you guessed. Your first guess is likely to be the number 50. If you are told the unknown number is higher, your next guess is likely to be 75, and so on.

Binary search only works when searching for an item in a sorted list. It works by keeping track of the range of items within the list where the desired record might be, then looking at the middle of that range. Since the list is sorted, comparing the middle item of the range to the desired item will tell whether the desired item is in the upper or lower half of the range. Then the new range is set accordingly and the process is repeated. When starting the binary search process, the range is initially set to the entire list. If we were to write this algorithm as pseudocode, it could look something like this,

1. *Let the list be T, and the desired item be I*
2. *Set the upper index U to the topmost index of T, and the lower index L to 0*
3. *Repeat until I is found, or the upper index U and lower index L are the same,*

   a) *If U = L, and the list item at index U isn't the desired item I, we're done (I is not found)*
   b) *Get the index at the middle of the current range: let M = (U + L) / 2*
   c) *Get the item at index M. If it's the desired item I, we're done*
   d) *If the item at index M is larger than the desired item I, set the lower index L to M*
   e) *Otherwise, the item at index M is smaller than the desired item I, so set the upper index U to M*

Suppose we're looking for the number 58 in the list (-22, 0, 3, 3, 4, 4, 11, 12, 58, 99, 101). The binary search process for these inputs, following the above pseudocode, is illustrated in figure 14.3. The search terminates by finding the number 58 after 3 steps, cutting the range to search by half in each step. Note that the algorithm still works if the list contains duplicate elements.

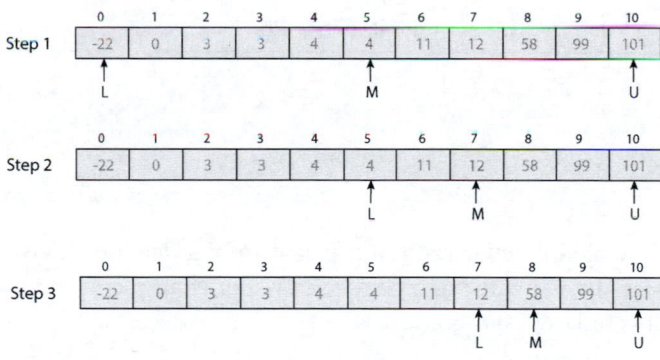

Figure 14.3: Binary search.

The observant reader may wonder how much overhead sorting the list causes, and whether it's worthwhile. Sorting a list runs in O(n log n) time, which makes it worthwhile to sort the list if binary search is used many times. If only one search operation is needed, linear search is faster than having to sort and then do a binary search.

Binary search cuts the current search range by half in each step. At most, the number of steps required is the base 2 logarithm of n, where n is the size of the list. This represents the number of times a list can be cut in half before narrowing down to one element. For example, a list of size 8 can be cut in half three times before reaching size 1. The base 2 log of n is the power of 2 that yields n. In the example just mentioned, raising 2 to the power 3 is 8. Table 14.1 shows the base 2 log for various values of n. As the list's size grows larger and larger, the value of binary search becomes more and more apparent. To find an item in a sorted list with a million numbers using binary search, it only takes 20 steps. To put it in big-O terms, linear search runs in O(n) time, while binary search runs in O(log n) time (refer to table 13.1 on page 256).

Table 14.1: Base 2 logarithms.

n	$log_2(n)$	n	$log_2(n)$
1	0	1,024	10
2	1	2,048	11
4	2	4,096	12
8	3	8,192	13
16	4	16,384	14
32	5	32,768	15
64	6	65,536	16
128	7	131,072	17
256	8	262,144	18
512	9	524,288	19
		1,048,576	20

Exercises

14.1 Download stellar data and put it in a collection. Look up stars by name using binary search. For example, try the file "hygfull.csv" at this address: https://github.com/astronexus/HYG-Database.

14.2 Maps

A map is a collection that stores key/value pairs where both the key and value are generic types. The map can only hold one value for each unique key, and looking up a value by its key is very fast. In Java, the `Map` interface defines methods such as `put` and `get`, and is analogous to the `List` interface for lists because multiple map classes implement `Map` just as multiple list classes implement `List`. The `HashMap` class implements the `Map` interface, and is used frequently. The `TreeMap` class also implements `Map` but is specialized and less often used (it holds the keys in sorted order, but is slower when looking up a value by its key). Just like `ArrayList` is your go-to list class, `HashMap` is your go-to class for storing key/value pairs and looking up values by their keys.

We'll illustrate maps by updating example 14.2, adding a new way of looking up astroids by name. In example 14.3, we add a new collection, `asteroidMap` of type `HashMap<String, Asteroid>`. This maps string values to `Asteroid` objects.

Example 14.3. Using `HashMap`.

```
1   ...
2   import java.util.HashMap;
3   import java.util.Map;
4
5     public static void main(String[] args) throws FileNotFoundException {
6
7         List<Asteroid> asteroids = new ArrayList<>();
8         Map<String, Asteroid> asteroidMap = new HashMap<>();
9   ...
10        // process each asteroid (one line)
11        while (input.hasNext()) {
12  ...
13          asteroids.add(asteroid);
14          asteroidMap.put(asteroid.name, asteroid);
15        }
16
17  ...
18        // map search
19        start = System.currentTimeMillis();
20        for (int i = 0; i < 50000; i++) {
21          asteroid = asteroidMap.get("Pluto");
22        }
23        end = System.currentTimeMillis();
24        out.println("Map search: Pluto's record is " + asteroid);
25        out.println("Map search: Time to find Pluto: " + (end-start) + "
              milliseconds");
26    }
27  ...
```

```
Read 34190 asteroids...
Linear search: Pluto's record is Pluto (ID 134340), reflectivity: 0.65, diameter: 339.0 km,
Linear search: Time to find Pluto: 13266 milliseconds
Binary search: Pluto's record is Pluto (ID 134340), reflectivity: 0.65, diameter: 339.0 km,
Binary search: Time to find Pluto: 21 milliseconds
Map search: Pluto's record is Pluto (ID 134340), reflectivity: 0.65, diameter: 339.0 km, per
Map search: Time to find Pluto: 2 milliseconds
```

Note the following details about the code in example 14.3,

- The map is created on line 8, as a `HashMap<String, Asteroid>`. The key type is `String` and the value type is `Asteroid`.
- Each time an asteroid is added to the list (line 13), it's also added to the asteroid map (line 14), mapping the asteroid's name to the asteroid object using the `put` method of the `HashMap` class.
- The `get` method of the `HashMap` class is used on line 21 to retrieve an `Asteroid` object from the map using its key, the asteroid's name.

The output shows that looking up an asteroid using the map is about ten times faster than the binary search method, in this case. Each time the code in example 14.3 adds an asteroid to the list of asteroids, it also adds it to the asteroid map, mapping the asteroid's name to the asteroid object. In this way, the asteroid map functions as an index into the asteroid list. We create `Asteroid` objects and add them to two separate collections, each holding separate references to the same objects.

The speed of looking up a value in `HashMap` is one of two things in programming that feel like magic (the other is recursion, discussed in chapter 15), and it's thanks to hashing, which we discuss in the next section.

Looking up a value using its key in a `HashMap` is so fast that it approaches constant runtime, O(1), as opposed to logarithmic runtime for binary search and linear runtime for linear search.

Technique 21. Use a `HashMap` as an index to speed up lookups

You can use a separate `HashMap` collection as an index to speed up looking up objects by a specific key, such as an ID or a name. This separate index has to be updated when a new object is added or removed from the main collection, so there is overhead, but it's often much faster in the end to add this separate index.

Occasionally, you'll need to iterate through a map's entries. The `Map` interface provides a way for you to do this,

Example 14.4. Iterating through a Map's entries.

```
1  import java.util.Map.Entry;
2  ...
3    // iterate through the map's entries
4    for (Entry<String, Asteroid> entry : asteroidMap.entrySet())
5      out.println("key = " + entry.getKey() + ", value = " + entry.getValue());
```

```
key = Amelia, value = Amelia (ID 986), reflectivity: 0.1183, diameter
key = 2000 RW50, value = 2000 RW50 (ID 92967), reflectivity: 0.21, di
key = Cosicosi, value = Cosicosi (ID 2129), reflectivity: 0.24, diame
key = 2013 GU92, value = 2013 GU92 (ID 368116), reflectivity: 0.1, di
```

The `Map.entrySet` method returns a collection of `Map.Entry` objects, each of which allows retrieval of the key and value of a single entry using the `getKey` and `getValue` methods. Note that `HashMap`'s implementation of `entrySet` doesn't provide the entries in a particular order.

Exercises

14.2   Use the dictionary file that you downloaded for exercise 12.3. Read each word and add it to a map, mapping the word to *true* (the `HashMap` will map `String` to `Boolean`). This will allow fast lookup of dictionary words. Use this dictionary to spell check a file of the user's choosing and output words that aren't capitalized and don't appear in the dictionary.

14.3 Hashing

Hashing is a technique that boils down the data in an object to a number. The hash code of any object is returned by the `hashCode` method, which takes no parameters. Every class has this method since every class is ultimately derived from Object, and `Object` provides a default implementation. Classes that might be used as keys in a `HashMap` need to override `hashCode`. The number returned by `hashCode` should be different for each instance of an object containing different data. Example 14.5 shows some objects with their hash codes,

```
1    Integer number = 123;
2    out.println("hashCode of " + number + " is " + number.hashCode());
3
4    String str = "To be or not to be";
5    out.println("hashCode of '" + str + "' is " + str.hashCode());
6    str = "To be or not to bee";
7    out.println("hashCode of '" + str + "' is " + str.hashCode());
8
9    Boolean bool = true;
10   out.println("hashCode of " + bool + " is " + bool.hashCode());
11
12   Float decimalNumber = 3.141f;
13   out.println("hashCode of " + decimalNumber + " is " + decimalNumber.hashCode
         ());
14   decimalNumber = 3.142f;
15   out.println("hashCode of " + decimalNumber + " is " + decimalNumber.hashCode
         ());
```

Example 14.5. Hash code examples.

```
hashCode of 123 is 123
hashCode of `To be or not to be' is 557539254
hashCode of `To be or not to bee' is 103847791
hashCode of true is 1231
hashCode of 3.141 is 1078527525
hashCode of 3.142 is 1078531719
```

The `hashCode` implementation for each class essentially maps the class data's possible values to the set of integers. Obviously, this can't be a one-to-one mapping, since a class has an arbitrary number of data elements. But, it should perform this mapping in such a way that ensures good distribution of its set of possible data values to the set of integers. When two instances of a class that have different data result in the same number returned by `hashCode`, it's called a hash value collision. Since collisions are inevitable (because it's not a one-to-one mapping), the goal of `hashCode` is simply to minimize collisions and get an even distribution of internal data values to integer hash codes. It's also desirable for objects with similar data values to produce hash codes that aren't close together, as this produces less clustering of hash codes. Note in example 14.5's output that adding a letter to the end of a string produced a very different hash code.

Without overriding `hashCode`, a custom class inherits the default implementation provided by `Object`. This returns the memory address at which the object resides. In this case, two instances that have the same data will produce different hash codes, which is usually not the desired behavior. Example 14.6 shows this,

Example 14.6. Default `hashCode` implementation.

```
1   import static java.lang.System.out;
2
3   public class TestFilm {
4
5     public static void main(String[] args) {
6
7       Film film1 = new Film("Gone with the Wind", "Victor Fleming", 1939);
8       Film film2 = new Film("Gone with the Wind", "Victor Fleming", 1939);
9       out.println("Film1's hash code is " + film1.hashCode());
10      out.println("Film2's hash code is " + film2.hashCode());
11    }
12  }
13
14  class Film {
15    String title;
16    String director;
17    int year;
18
19    public Film(String title, String director, int year) {
20      super();
21      this.title = title;
22      this.director = director;
23      this.year = year;
24    }
```

```
25
26    @Override
27    public String toString() {
28      return "Film [title=" + title + ", director=" + director + ", year=" + year
            + "]";
29    }
30 }
```

```
Film1's hash code is 225534817
Film2's hash code is 1878246837
```

As mentioned earlier, if you intend for your class to be used as a key in a `HashMap`, you should override `hashCode` and ensure it has a good distribution of hash codes, as well as producing the same hash code for two instances with the same data. The standard technique for doing this is shown in example 14.7,

```java
1  import java.util.HashMap;
2  import java.util.Map;
3  import java.util.Map.Entry;
4  ...
5    public static void main(String[] args) {
6
7      Film film1 = new Film("Gone with the Wind", "Victor Fleming", 1939);
8      Film film2 = new Film("Gone with the Wind", "Victor Fleming", 1939);
9      out.println("Film1's hash code is " + film1.hashCode());
10     out.println("Film2's hash code is " + film2.hashCode());
11
12     Map<Film, Float> ratings = new HashMap<>();
13     ratings.put(film1, 5f);
14     ratings.put(film2, 4.5f);
15
16     for (Entry<Film, Float> entry : ratings.entrySet())
17       out.println(entry.getKey() + " (" + entry.getValue() + " stars)");
18   }
19 ...
20   @Override
21   public int hashCode() {
22     final int prime = 31;
23     int result = 1;
24     result = prime * result + ((director == null) ? 0 : director.hashCode());
25     result = prime * result + ((title == null) ? 0 : title.hashCode());
26     result = prime * result + year;
27     return result;
28   }
29
30   @Override
31   public boolean equals(Object object2) {
32
33     // if second film is null or not a film object, return false
34     if (object2 == null || object2.getClass() != getClass())
35       return false;
36
37     Film film2 = (Film) object2;
38
39     // if titles aren't equal, return false
40     if ((title == null && film2.title != null) ||
```

Example 14.7. Overriding `hashCode`.

As noted on page 64, shortcut operators can be used to avoid errors. We're using that technique in `equals`.

```
41        (title != null && film2.title == null) ||
42        !title.equals(film2.title))
43        return false;
44
45    // if directors aren't equal, return false
46    if ((director == null && film2.director != null) ||
47        (director != null && film2.director == null) ||
48        !director.equals(film2.director))
49        return false;
50
51    // if years aren't equal, return false
52    if (year != film2.year)
53        return false;
54
55    return true;
56 }
```

```
Film1's hash code is 830722461
Film2's hash code is 830722461
Film [title=Gone with the Wind, director=Victor Fleming, year=1939] (4.5 stars)
```

We're assuming that `String.hashCode` runs in constant time. The observant reader may ask how it does this. The answer is that the hash code is computed once with linear time complexity and saved so that `String.hashCode` just needs to return the saved value. Strings are immutable, which guarantees that the hash code only needs to be computed once.

The standard `hashCode` implementation shown in example 14.7 starts with a result of 1, then factors in the hash code of each data element of the class. When factoring in the hash code of each data element, the existing result is multiplied by a prime number, and added to the hash code of the data element. This method was developed over time and generally produces a good distribution with minimal collisions. Note that this implementation of `hashCode` runs in constant time.

We also override the `Object.equals` method, which receives a `Film` parameter and returns true or false depending on whether the data in this instance matches the data in the `Film` instance passed in. Without overriding *both* `hashCode` and `equals`, a class can't be used properly as a key within a `HashMap`. Removing the `equals` override from `Film` results in the hash map not recognizing `film1` and `film2` as the same film, causing two entries to be output as shown below,

```
Film1's hash code is 830722461
Film2's hash code is 830722461
Film [title=Gone with the Wind, director=Victor Fleming, year=1939] (5.0 stars)
Film [title=Gone with the Wind, director=Victor Fleming, year=1939] (4.5 stars)
```

Now that we understand how hashing works, we can discuss how `HashMap` stores key/value pairs and performs `get` operations in constant time. The `HashMap` contains an array of linked lists called chained buckets, with each linked list node containing a pair (a key and a value), as shown in figure 14.4. Each key's hash code is mapped to an index of this array by computing its modulus with respect to the array's length. For example, if the array's length is 9, the hash

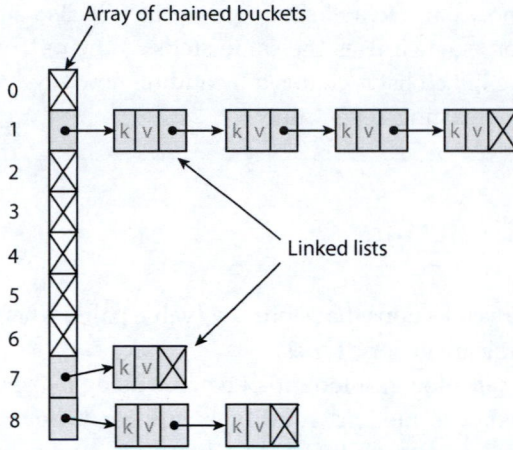

Figure 14.4: Internal structure of HashMap.

code 830722461 maps to the index 6 because 830722461 mod 9 is 6. When adding a key/value pair with that key, the `HashMap` creates a new linked list node containing that key/value pair and adds it to the linked list at index 6 of the array. The array is expanded periodically as more key/value pairs are added to the map, similar to the way that `ArrayList` grows. This periodic growth ensures that the chains are short (assuming that the hash codes aren't clustered). When the array grows, each existing key/value pair is re-mapped so that it's in the right chain. Too many hash code collisions result in some of the array indexes having much longer chains than other indexes.

The `HashMap.get` method performs the following steps to find a key's value in this internal structure,

- Call the key's `hashCode` method to get its hash code. This is a constant-time operation.
- Compute the modulus of hash code with respect to the array length, to find the array index. This is a constant-time operation.
- Traverse the linked list at that array index to find the key, and if it exists, return its value. This is a constant-time operation as long as the chains are short.

When the key's `hashCode` method produces an even distribution of hash codes, the internal structure is well balanced, the chains are short, and the `get` method runs in constant time, O(1). Finally, note that adding new pairs to a `HashMap` (using `put`) is also a constant-time operation, since it uses the same steps as the `get` operation, except that the linked list is changed by adding new key/value pair or updating an existing key's value.

Chapter Summary

- Maps are collections that store key/value pairs, where the key and value are generic types.
- A `HashMap` allow fast lookup of a value using its key.
- The `hashCode` method returns an integer, where different internal data map to different hash integers.
- To use a custom class as a key within a `HashMap` requires overriding `equals` and `hashCode`.

Create `HashMap` collection

```
1   Map<String, Asteroid> asteroidMap = new HashMap<>();
2
3   // read data
4   while (input.hasNext()) {
5       ...
6       asteroidMap.put(asteroid.name, asteroid);
7   }
8
9   asteroid = asteroidMap.get("Pluto");
```

Add key/value pair to the map

Get a value using its key

Recursion $\Big|$ # 15

15.1 Recursion

Recursion is when a method calls itself. Let's consider for example the mathematical definition of a factorial. The factorial of a positive integer n is the product of integers from 1 to n,

$$f(n) = \prod_{i=1}^{n} i$$

Computing factorial is simple using a loop,

```
1   public static void main(String[] args) {
2
3       int n = 6;
4       int factorial = 1;
5       for (int i = 1; i <= n; i++)
6           factorial *= i;
7
8       out.println("The factorial of " + n + " is " + factorial);
9   }
```

Example 15.1. Computing factorial with a loop.

```
The factorial of 6 is 720
```

Another mathematical definition of factorial is the following,

$$f(n) = \begin{cases} 1, & n = 1 \\ n * f(n-1), & n > 1 \end{cases}$$

In this recursive definition, the factorial of an integer n is computed by multiplying n by the factorial of $n - 1$. Every recursive definition has at least one *recursive case*, where the function is used within its own definition with a different parameter value, and at least one *base* case. Here, the base case is when $n = 1$, and the recursive case is when $n > 1$.

Recursive case: The set of inputs causing a function to refer to itself.

Base case: The set of inputs that don't cause a function to refer to itself.

With the recursive definition of factorial, we can compute the factorial of 6 as follows,

$$f(6) = 6 \times f(5)$$
$$f(6) = 6 \times 5 \times f(4)$$
$$f(6) = 6 \times 5 \times 4 \times f(3)$$
$$f(6) = 6 \times 5 \times 4 \times 3 \times f(2)$$
$$f(6) = 6 \times 5 \times 4 \times 3 \times 2 \times f(1)$$
$$f(6) = 6 \times 5 \times 4 \times 3 \times 2 \times 1$$
$$f(6) = 720$$

Note that this computation required the factorial function to be evaluated six times. The recursive definition of factorial is implemented as a recursive method in example 15.2,

Example 15.2. Computing factorial recursively.

```
1   public static void main(String[] args) {
2
3       int n = 6;
4       out.println("The factorial of " + n + " is " + factorial(n));
5   }
6
7   public static int factorial(int n) {
8
9       // base case
10      if (n == 1)
11          return 1;
12
13      // recursive case
14      return n * factorial (n - 1);
15  }
```

```
The factorial of 6 is 720
```

By the time execution reaches line 11, the `return` statement belonging to the base case, several nested calls from `factorial` to itself have occurred. The invocation of `factorial` with parameter value 6 waits for the invocation with parameter value 5 to return, which in turn waits for the invocation with parameter 4 to return, and so on. Each of these method calls has a corresponding stack frame. To see this in action, we place a breakpoint on line 11 and run the program in debug mode. When the program stops at the breakpoint (figure 15.1), the Debug view shows the call stack with the most recent stack frame at the top. Each frame on the call stack corresponds to one method call—the `main` method is seen at the bottom of the stack, followed

When a recursive method calls itself, the method invocation that made the call waits for the nested call to return, and its local data is saved in its stack frame on the call stack.

by the six calls to `factorial`, with parameter values ranging from 6 to 1. You can click on each stack frame in the Debug view to select it, showing the local variables for that frame in the Variables view on the right of the Eclipse window. Figure 15.2 shows the same program with the second-to-last frame selected, where `factorial` has been called with the parameter value 2.

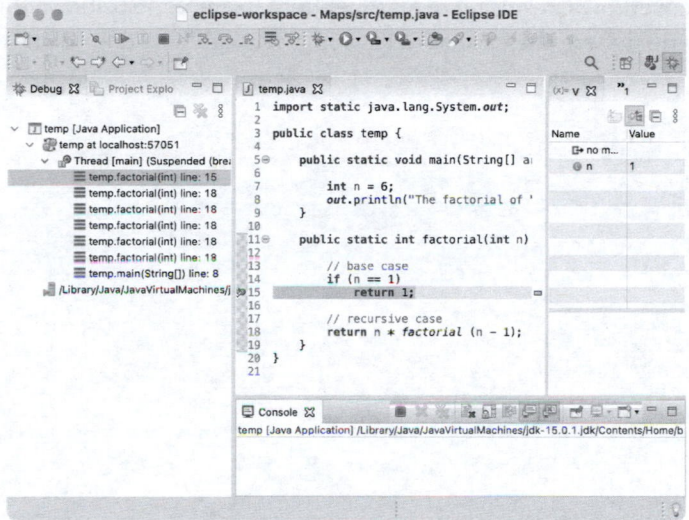

Figure 15.1: Debug view with call stack.

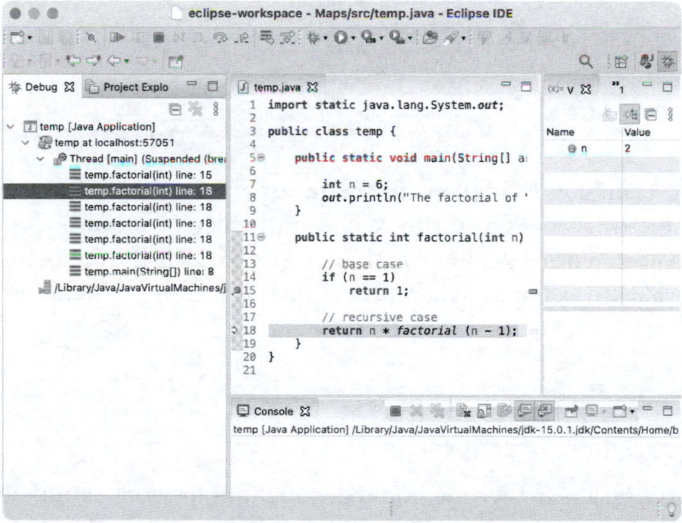

Figure 15.2: Selecting a different stack frame in the debugger.

Examples 15.1 and 15.2 implement factorial in different ways, one using a loop and the other using recursion. Iteration and recursion accomplish the same thing, just in different ways, and they each

Iteration and recursion are equivalent in the sense that each recursive implementation can be made iterative, and vice versa. But each is more natural and preferable to the other in certain situations.

have different pros and cons. In some cases, iteration is easier to implement and in other cases recursion is.

The call stack's memory is large enough that you don't need to worry about the number of nested calls. But the call stack's memory is finite, so if a bug in the recursive method keeps it from terminating, the recursion doesn't terminate and continues until the call stack overflows, resulting in an exception. Example 15.3 shows this scenario, where the base case tests for "n == 10" instead of "n == 1",

Example 15.3. The stack overflow exception.

```
1   public static void main(String[] args) {
2
3     int n = 6;
4     out.println("The factorial of " + n + " is " + factorial(n));
5   }
6
7   public static int factorial(int n) {
8
9     // base case
10    if (n == 10)
11      return 1;
12
13    // recursive case
14    return n * factorial (n - 1);
15  }
```

```
Exception in thread "main" java.lang.StackOverflowError
        at temp.factorial(temp.java:18)
        at temp.factorial(temp.java:18)
        at temp.factorial(temp.java:18)
        at temp.factorial(temp.java:18)
        at temp.factorial(temp.java:18)
        at temp.factorial(temp.java:18)
        at temp.factorial(temp.java:18)
        at temp.factorial(temp.java:18)
```

Using recursion to implement the factorial function isn't a good example of recursion in the real world, since factorial is better implemented using iteration. In the next section we'll introduce trees, and we'll see examples where recursion is preferable to iteration.

Exercises

15.1 Write a recursive method that computes the sum of numbers in an integer array.

15.2 Write a recursive method that concatenates the strings in a list of strings.

15.2 Trees

A tree is a data structure where each node can have multiple child nodes. The tree data structure can model many real-world hierarchical structures. In this section we'll model the organizational structure of the Department of Energy, using information from the DOE's website as seen in figure 15.3.

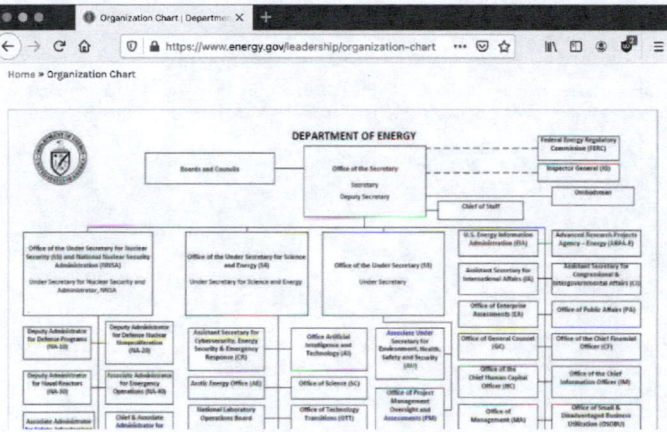

Figure 15.3: Organizational structure of the Department of Energy.

The Java class that will represent a department is `DepartmentNode`, and is shown in example 15.4. It has fields for the department's name, the number of employees, the department budget and a list of child departments. The `DepartmentNode` class resembles the `Node` class in example 13.14, except that a `DepartmentNode` can have multiple children, while `Node` can only have one child.

Example 15.4. The `DepartmentNode` class and test code.

```
1  import static java.lang.System.out;
2  import java.util.ArrayList;
3  import java.util.List;
4
5  public class Trees {
6
7    public static void main(String[] args) {
8
9      DepartmentNode node1 = new DepartmentNode("Bonneville Power Administration"
         , 21, 150000);
10     DepartmentNode node2 = new DepartmentNode("Southeastern Power
         Administration", 11, 190000);
11     DepartmentNode node3 = new DepartmentNode("Southwestern Power
         Administration", 15, 110000);
12     DepartmentNode node4 = new DepartmentNode("Western Area Power
         Administration", 14, 120000);
13
14     DepartmentNode node5 = new DepartmentNode("Assistant Secretary for
         Electricity", 12, 191000, node1, node2, node3, node4);
15     DepartmentNode node6 = new DepartmentNode("Assistant Secretary for Fossil
         Energy", 10, 100000);
```

```
16    DepartmentNode node7 = new DepartmentNode("Assistant Secretary for Nuclear
          Energy", 10, 100000);
17    DepartmentNode node8 = new DepartmentNode("Assistant Secretary for Energy
          Efficiency and Renewable Energy", 10, 100000);
18
19    DepartmentNode node9 = new DepartmentNode("Office of the Undersecretary of
          Energy", 10, 100000, node5, node6, node7, node8);
20
21    DepartmentNode node10 = new DepartmentNode("Office of Science", 15, 110000)
          ;
22    DepartmentNode node11 = new DepartmentNode("Office of Artificial
          Intelligence and Technology", 14, 120000);
23    DepartmentNode node12 = new DepartmentNode("Office of the Undersecretary
          for Science", 12, 191000, node10, node11);
24
25    DepartmentNode node13 = new DepartmentNode("Chief of Staff", 1, 50000);
26    DepartmentNode node14 = new DepartmentNode("Ombudsman", 1, 50000);
27
28    DepartmentNode root = new DepartmentNode("Office of the Secretary", 12,
          191000, node12, node9, node13, node14);
29  }
30 }
31
32 class DepartmentNode {
33
34    String name;
35    int employees;
36    int budget;
37    List<DepartmentNode> children = new ArrayList<>();
38
39    public DepartmentNode (String name, int employees, int budget, DepartmentNode
          ... departmentNodes) {
40       this.name = name;
41       this.employees = employees;
42       this.budget = budget;
43       for (DepartmentNode child : departmentNodes)
44          this.children.add(child);
45    }
46 }
```

In addition to the department name, employee count and budget, the **DepartmentNode**'s constructor receives a varargs parameter containing a list of child department nodes. The test code adds several nodes to the tree, with fictitious numbers for the employee count and budget of each department. The lower nodes are created first so that each can be passed into its parent node's constructor. Once the root node is created, it represents the entire tree.

15.3 Traversing Trees with Iteration

To traverse a tree is to process each of its nodes, applying some action to each node such as printing it out. We can use a loop to do this using the following algorithm,

- Create an empty stack of nodes.
- Push the tree's root onto the stack.
- Repeat the following steps until the stack is empty:
  - Pop a node n from the stack.
  - Process the node n, e.g., print it out.
  - Push each of n's children onto the stack.

Example 15.5 applies the above algorithm to print the tree,

```
1   public static void main(String[] args) {
2   ...
3       DepartmentNode root = new DepartmentNode("Office of the Secretary", 12,
            191000, node12, node9, node13, node14);
4       printTreeIterative(root);
5   }
6
7   private static void printTreeIterative(DepartmentNode root) {
8       Map<DepartmentNode, Integer> nodeLevelMap = new HashMap<>();
9       List<DepartmentNode> stack = new ArrayList<>();
10
11      stack.add(root);
12      nodeLevelMap.put(root, 0);
13
14      while (!stack.isEmpty()) {
15
16          // pop a node from the stack
17          DepartmentNode currentNode = stack.remove(stack.size() - 1);
18
19          // process the node
20          int currentNodeLevel = nodeLevelMap.get(currentNode);
21          for (int i = 0; i < currentNodeLevel; i++)
22              out.print("  ");
23          out.println(currentNode.name);
24
25          // push each of the current node's children onto the stack
26          for (DepartmentNode child : currentNode.children) {
27              stack.add(child);
28              nodeLevelMap.put(child, currentNodeLevel + 1);
29          }
30      }
31  }
```

Example 15.5. Printing a tree using iteration.

```
Office of the Secretary
  Ombudsman
  Chief of Staff
  Office of the Undersecretary of Energy
    Assistant Secretary for Energy Efficiency and Renewable Energy
    Assistant Secretary for Nuclear Energy
    Assistant Secretary for Fossil Energy
    Assistant Secretary for Electricity
      Western Area Power Administration
      Southwestern Power Administration
      Southeastern Power Administration
      Bonneville Power Administration
  Office of the Undersecretary for Science
    Office of Artificial Intelligence and Technology
    Office of Science
```

In example 15.5, the tree traversal algorithm is used to print the tree:

- Create an empty stack of nodes (line 9).
- Push the tree's root onto the stack (line 11).
- Repeat the following steps until the stack is empty (lines 14-30):
  - Pop a node n from the stack (line 17).
  - Process the node n by printing it out (lines 20-23).
  - Push each of n's children onto the stack (lines 26-29).

We've added a map to store the level of each node. The first node pushed onto the stack has level 0, and each further node pushed onto the stack is one level deeper than its parent. The level is used when processing each node to indent it properly. The output shows the tree structure of the department hierarchy.

We'll show one more example of traversing the tree iteratively, this time adding up the departmental budgets for all departments in the tree, and printing out the total budget,

Example 15.6. Summation over a tree using iteration.

```java
public static void main(String[] args) {
...
    DepartmentNode root = new DepartmentNode("Office of the Secretary", 12,
        191000, node12, node9, node13, node14);
    out.println("Total budget is " + totalBudget(root));
}

private static int totalBudget(DepartmentNode root) {

    List<DepartmentNode> stack = new ArrayList<>();
    stack.add(root);
    int totalBudget = 0;

    while (!stack.isEmpty()) {

        // pop a node from the stack
        DepartmentNode currentNode = stack.remove(stack.size() - 1);

        // process the node
        totalBudget += currentNode.budget;

        // push each of the current node's children onto the stack
        for (DepartmentNode child : currentNode.children)
            stack.add(child);
    }

    return totalBudget;
}
```

```
Total budget is 1873000
```

The same pattern is used in example 15.6—the stack is created, the root is pushed onto the stack, then a loop repeatedly pops a node from the stack and processes it, then pushes its own children onto the stack. This time, the act of processing a node is simply adding its budget to the total budget.

Exercises

15.3   Modify example 15.6 to print the number of departments in the tree.

15.4 Traversing Trees with Recursion

Traversing a tree is simpler and more natural using recursion than it is using iteration. There's no need for a queue of nodes. Processing a node consists of performing an operation, e.g., printing the node, then recursively processing each of its subtrees. Example 15.7 prints the department tree and sums the department budgets using recursion,

```
1   public static void main(String[] args) {
2   ...
3      DepartmentNode root = new DepartmentNode("Office of the Secretary", 12,
          191000, node12, node9, node13, node14);
4      root.PrintSubtree(0);
5      out.println("Total budget is " + root.totalBudget());
6   }
7   ...
8   public void PrintSubtree(int level) {
9      for (int i = 0; i < level; i++)
10        out.print("  ");
11     out.println(name);
12
13     for (DepartmentNode child : children)
14        child.PrintSubtree(level+1);
15  }
16
17  public int totalBudget () {
18     int answer = budget;
19     for (DepartmentNode child : children)
20        answer += child.totalBudget();
21     return answer;
22  }
```

Example 15.7. Traversing a tree with recursion.

```
Office of the Secretary
  Office of the Undersecretary for Science
    Office of Science
    Office of Artificial Intelligence and Technology
  Office of the Undersecretary of Energy
    Assistant Secretary for Electricity
      Bonneville Power Administration
      Southeastern Power Administration
      Southwestern Power Administration
      Western Area Power Administration
    Assistant Secretary for Fossil Energy
    Assistant Secretary for Nuclear Energy
    Assistant Secretary for Energy Efficiency and Renewable Energy
  Chief of Staff
  Ombudsman
Total budget is 1873000
```

The recursive versions are simpler, more intuitive and easier to maintain. The `printSubtree` method receives the node's level as a parameter, prints out the node (lines 9-11), then recursively processes each of the node's children while incrementing the level (lines 13-14). The `totalBudget` method adds the node's budget (line 18) to the total budgets of each of its children (lines 19-20), and returns the sum (line 21).

Exercises

15.4 Modify example 15.7 to print the number of departments in the tree.

15.5 Extend exercise 15.4 to print the average budget of a department.

15.5 Graphs

Graph: A tree that can have cycles.

As you have seen, trees are represented by nodes that have references from parent to child. A graph is a tree that can have cycles. To see that in action, we'll look at a program that navigates a maze. Figure 15.4 shows a maze with one entrance and one exit.

To represent this as a graph, we'll number the squares, as shown in figure 15.5,

Each square is connected to an adjacent square if there is no wall between them. Thus, square 2 is connected to squares 1 and 3, but

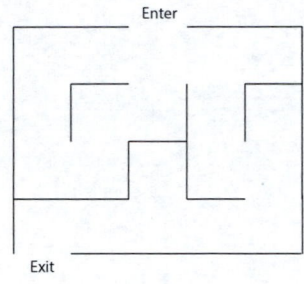

Figure 15.4: Maze example.

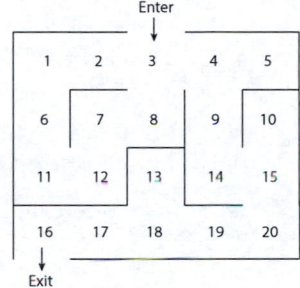

Figure 15.5: Maze example with numbered squares.

not square 7. Each square can be represented in Java as a node, just as we did with trees. The connections between adjacent squares are bidirectional, so two adjacent nodes will each have a reference to the other. Note that the graph representing this maze has a cycle because the player can move from square 3 to 8, then to 7, 12, 11, 6, 1, 2 and back to 3. Square 3 is special because it's the starting point, and square 16 is special because it's the only exit. Example 15.8 shows the Node class and a test program that constructs the graph shown in figure 15.5,

Example 15.8. Representing a maze as a graph in Java.

```java
import static java.lang.System.out;
import java.util.ArrayList;
import java.util.List;

public class Test {

  public static void main(String[] args) {

    // make 20 nodes
    List<Node> nodes = new ArrayList<>();
    for (int i = 0; i < 20; i++)
      nodes.add(new Node(i+1));

    // node 16 (with index 15) is an exit
    nodes.get(15).isExit = true;

    // connect the nodes to represent the maze
    connect(nodes, 1, 2);
    connect(nodes, 2, 3);
```

```
20      connect(nodes, 3, 4);
21      connect(nodes, 4, 5);
22      connect(nodes, 1, 6);
23      connect(nodes, 3, 8);
24      connect(nodes, 4, 9);
25      connect(nodes, 7, 8);
26      connect(nodes, 6, 11);
27      connect(nodes, 7, 12);
28      connect(nodes, 9, 14);
29      connect(nodes, 10, 15);
30      connect(nodes, 11, 12);
31      connect(nodes, 14, 15);
32      connect(nodes, 13, 18);
33      connect(nodes, 15, 20);
34      connect(nodes, 16, 17);
35      connect(nodes, 17, 18);
36      connect(nodes, 18, 19);
37      connect(nodes, 19, 20);
38      }
39
40    private static void connect(List<Node> nodes, int nodeId1, int nodeId2) {
41      // point the first node to the second node, and the second to the first
42      nodes.get(nodeId1 - 1).children.add(nodes.get(nodeId2 - 1));
43      nodes.get(nodeId2 - 1).children.add(nodes.get(nodeId1 - 1));
44    }
45  }
46
47  class Node {
48    int id;
49    List<Node> children = new ArrayList<>();
50    boolean isExit = false;
51
52    public Node(int id) {
53      this.id = id;
54    }
55
56    @Override
57    public String toString() {
58      return ((Integer) id).toString();
59    }
60  }
```

The code to find a path through the maze will perform a traversal, similar to the code that traverses trees, but we need to add logic that prevents getting stuck in a loop when a cycle is encountered in the graph. This is done by keeping a list of nodes that have already been visited, which is checked when processing each child of the current node. If a child node has already been visited, it isn't processed again. In addition, the code checks whether the current node is an exit, and if so, prints a message saying that the exit has been found. This is shown in example 15.9,

Example 15.9. Traversing a graph.

```
1  public static void main(String[] args) {
2  ...
3
4      List<Node> visited = new ArrayList<>();
5      solve(nodes.get(2), visited);
```

```
6    }
7
8    private static boolean solve(Node node, List<Node> visited) {
9
10       System.out.print(node.id + " ");
11       visited.add(node);
12
13       if (node.isExit) {
14          System.out.print("Found exit!");
15          return true;
16       }
17
18       for (Node child : node.children)
19          if (!visited.contains(child))
20             if (solve(child, visited))
21                return true;
22
23       return false;
24    }
```

```
3 2 1 6 11 12 7 8 4 5 9 14 15 10 20 19 18 13 17 16 Found exit!
```

The `solve` method processes one node at a time, and passes the `visited` list to itself when it recurses. The `visited` list contains the list of nodes that have already been seen. `solve` returns true when the exit has been found, in which case the traversal is cut short. Otherwise it returns false. The output shows the order in which nodes are visited. It starts at node 3, and shows the traversal to nodes 2, 1, 6, 11, 12, 7, then 8. While processing node 8, no unvisited child nodes are found, so backtracking occurs until the current node is 3 again, at which point node 4 is the only unvisited child, so the traversal resumes with node 4, and so on.

It is instructive to walk through this traversal in your head, on paper or using the debugger, and you should do this until you're comfortable with the way the traversal works.

Note that traversal is cut short once the exit is found, even if not all nodes have been visited. You can see this if you set node 18 as an exit,

```
1    public static void main(String[] args) {
2    ...
3       nodes.get(17).isExit = true;
4
5       List<Node> visited = new ArrayList<>();
6       solve(nodes.get(2), visited);
7    }
```

Example 15.10. Adding a second exit.

```
3 2 1 6 11 12 7 8 4 5 9 14 15 10 20 19 18 Found exit!
```

The output above shows the list of nodes that are visited, and the order in which they're visited. What if we just want to print out the path from the entrance to the exit? We can do this by adding another list that contains the path from the first node to the last. You can think of this new 'path' list as a stack. When a node is processed, it's pushed onto the stack. When the algorithm is done processing the node, it's popped from the path, unless the exit has been found. As the traversal reaches each node, the `path` list contains the path from the entrance to that node. The code to do this is shown in example 15.11,

Example 15.11. Displaying the path from entrance to exit.

```
 1  ...
 2      List<Node> visited = new ArrayList<>();
 3      List<Node> path = new ArrayList<>();
 4      solve(nodes.get(2), visited, path);
 5  ...
 6
 7    private static boolean solve(Node node, List<Node> visited, List<Node> path)
      {
 8
 9      visited.add(node);
10      path.add(node);
11
12      if (node.isExit) {
13        System.out.print("Found path: ");
14        for (Node pathNode : path)
15          System.out.print(pathNode.id + " ");
16
17        return true;
18      }
19
20      for (Node child : node.children)
21        if (!visited.contains(child))
22          if (solve(child, visited, path))
23            return true;
24
25      path.remove(path.size() - 1);
26      return false;
27    }
```

```
Found path: 3 4 9 14 15 20 19 18
```

15.6 Example: Letter Combinations

As another example of using recursion, we'll look at a program that takes a word and finds the set of words that can be formed using the original word's letters. In this example, not all letters in the original word need to be used to make a new word.

```
1  import static java.lang.System.out;
2  import java.io.File;
3  import java.io.FileNotFoundException;
4  import java.util.ArrayList;
5  import java.util.HashMap;
6  import java.util.List;
7  import java.util.Map;
8  import java.util.Scanner;
9
10 public class Words {
11
12   public static void main(String[] args) throws FileNotFoundException {
13
14     String word = "epidemics";
15     WordFinder wordFinder = new WordFinder();
16
17     long start = System.currentTimeMillis();
18     List<String> words = wordFinder.getWords(word);
19     long end = System.currentTimeMillis();
20
21     out.println("Done in " + (end-start) + " microseconds");
22     out.println("Words contained in '" + word + "': " + words);
23   }
24 }
25
26 class WordFinder {
27
28   private Map<String, Boolean> dictionary = new HashMap<>();
29
30   public WordFinder() throws FileNotFoundException {
31
32     // read dictionary
33     File file = new File("corncob_lowercase.txt");
34     Scanner fileScanner = new Scanner(file);
35     while (fileScanner.hasNext()) {
36       String word = fileScanner.nextLine();
37       dictionary.put(word, true);
38     }
39     fileScanner.close();
40   }
41
42   // Returns words that can be composed from the letters in a word. Not all
         letters need to be used
43   public List<String> getWords (String word) {
44     return getWordsInternal("", word);
45   }
46
47   private List<String> getWordsInternal(String word, String remainingLetters) {
48     List<String> words = new ArrayList<>();
49
50     // Base case: if there are no more letters to add, test the word
51     if (remainingLetters.isEmpty()) {
52       if (dictionary.containsKey(word) && !words.contains(word))
53         words.add(word);
54       return words;
55     }
56
57     // Recursive case: try adding each letter from the remaining letters to the
         word, and recurse
58     for (int i = 0; i < remainingLetters.length(); i++) {
59
60       char letter = remainingLetters.charAt(i);
```

Example 15.12. Letter Combinations.

```
61
62        // Remove this letter from remaining letters
63        String remainder = remainingLetters.substring(0, i) + remainingLetters.
          substring(i+1);
64
65        List<String> newWords = getWordsInternal(word + letter, remainder);
66        for (String newWord : newWords) // merge results
67          if (!words.contains(newWord))
68            words.add(newWord);
69
70        // Also try without the letter
71        newWords = getWordsInternal(word, remainder);
72        for (String newWord : newWords) // merge results
73          if (!words.contains(newWord))
74            words.add(newWord);
75      }
76
77      return words;
78    }
79  }
```

```
Done in 19876 milliseconds
Words contained in 'epidemics': [epidemics, epidemic, epics, epic, ems, em
```

The main method (line 12) creates an instance of the WordFinder class and calls its getWords method, which returns a list of words found. The main method then prints the resulting words as well as the time it took to perform the computation.

The WordFinder class contains a dictionary, which is a map of strings to boolean values. The dictionary is loaded by the WordFinder constructor. Each word from the dictionary file is loaded into the map as a key, with true as the boolean value. The dictionary we use here contains about 50,000 English words, and can be downloaded by searching for 'corncob dictionary file' and downloading 'corncob_-lowercase.txt'. Alternatively, the 'google-10000-english.txt' file from chapter 12 can be used.

The HashSet class, which we haven't mentioned yet, can be used to store the dictionary. A HashSet is similar to a HashMap but only stores the keys without mapping them to values.

The WordFinder.getWords method (line 43) calls an internal version, getWordsInternal, that accepts two parameters. The helper method getWordsInternal is recursive.

The getWordsInternal method (line 47) implements the following algorithm,

It's common for a recursive method to be be called from another method that passes a default initial value for one of its parameters, like we've done in example 15.12 with getWords and getWordsInternal.

- getWordsInternal takes two parameters, a string containing part of a word being constructed, and a second string containing letters that haven't been used yet, and can potentially be used in building the word.

- Base case (lines 51-55): If the list of remaining letters is empty, test the first parameter (the word). If it's a proper word, add the word to the result list and return the result list.
- Recursive case (lines 58-77): Create empty list for the result word list. For each letter L in the list of remaining letters, perform the following steps,

    - Remove the letter L from the list of remaining letters (lines 60-63).
    - Add the letter L to the end of the word, and recursively get a list of results from the new word and new list of remaining letters. Add the results to the result list. (lines 65-68).
    - Recursively get a list of results from the original word and the new list of remaining letters. Add the results to the result list (lines 71-74).

The essence of the algorithm is to construct the possible candidate words by repeatedly taking each possible letter from the input and adding it to the candidate word. Each recursive call uses one more letter from the input, so the depth of recursion will equal the length of the input. The looping performed in each recursive invocation ensures each possible letter is used to construct the next part of the candidate word. Figure 15.6 shows the recursive control flow for the input 'put'.

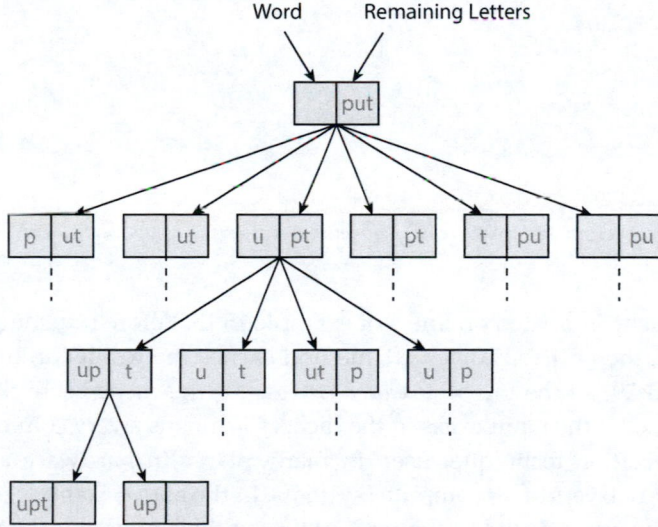

Figure 15.6: Recursive control flow for `getWordsInternal`.

Cache: A set of key/value pairs that's used to remember the results of a computation for particular input values. When the computation needs to be done later with the same set of input values, the result can be retrieved quickly from the cache.

Example 15.13. Letter Combinations with cache.

The cache is created as a static variable on line 4 of example 15.13. Technique 15 on page 184 cautions against using global variables, but the use of a static variable for this purpose is fine, since the cache is *meant* to be shared by multiple invocations of getWordsInternal. If your program is multithreaded, be aware that Map isn't thread safe. Instead, use ConcurrentHashMap.

To speed up the algorithm, a cache can be added to remember previous computations performed by the getWordsInternal method. The Map collection is perfect for such a cache. The key would be the inputs into the method, and the values are the corresponding outputs. This will speed up the program by eliminating all the duplicate calls with the same input values,

```java
class WordFinder {

  private Map<String, Boolean> dictionary = new HashMap<>();
  private Map<String, List<String>> cache = new HashMap<>();
  ...

  private List<String> getWordsInternal(String word, String remainingLetters) {

    // check cache
    if (cache.containsKey(word + "_" + remainingLetters))
      return cache.get(word + "_" + remainingLetters);

    List<String> words = new ArrayList<>();

    // Base case: if there are no more letters to add, test the word
    if (remainingLetters.isEmpty()) {
      if (dictionary.containsKey(word) && !words.contains(word))
        words.add(word);

      // cache the result
      cache.put(word + "_" + remainingLetters, words);

      return words;
    }

    // Recursive case: try adding each letter from the remaining letters to the
      word, and recurse
  ...
    // cache the result
    cache.put(word + "_" + remainingLetters, words);

    return words;
  }
}
```

```
Done in 1117 milliseconds
Words contained in 'epidemics': [epidemics, epidemic, epics, epic, ems, em
```

The cache is created on line 4 of example 15.13. Before returning a result, the getWordsInternal method caches the results on lines 21 and 29. At the top of getWordsInternal, the cache is checked and used if the input exists in the cache. Caching is a very common optimization technique, used in many places in hardware and software layers of all computer systems. In the above example, the runtime was reduced to about 6% of the runtime without using the cache. The difference gets much more pronounced as the size of the input grows. The runtime for the input 'electronic' with the use of caching is about 3% of the runtime without it.

```
Done in 10452 milliseconds
Words contained in 'electronic': [electronic, electron, electro, electric, el
```

```
Done in 380505 milliseconds
Words contained in 'electronic': [electronic, electron, electro, electric, el
```

Technique 22. Use caching to speed up your program

Caching can be used to speed up runtime performance dramatically. The `HashMap` class is a good choice for cache implementation.

Since we're discussing runtime performance, we'll present one more important performance enhancement technique in the next section.

15.7 StringBuilder

Strings in Java are immutable. This means they can't be directly modified. When we add two strings together, a new string is made to hold the result. This can cause performance issues if there is a lot of string manipulation in your program. Java offers a special class for this, called `StringBuilder`. The `StringBuilder` class allows you to modify a string without having to allocate a new string to hold the result. Once you're done with your changes to the string, you can copy the final string from the `StringBuilder` object to a `string` object.

The next example (15.14) eliminates punctuation and numbers from a string, with two implementations, one using `String` and the other using `StringBuilder`,

```
1  import static java.lang.System.out;
2
3  public class TestStrings {
4
5    public static void main(String[] args) {
6
7      String result = "";
```

Example 15.14. Using StringBuilder.

```
 8    String input = "The Olympic Games are on the way with Japan set to host the
          29th edition of the modern games. Over 11,000 competitors from 206
          nations will descend on Tokyo in 2021 to aim for glory in their
          respective fields. A total of 33 sports will be shown at the Olympics
          including five new sports for fans to sink their teeth into.";
 9
10    long start = System.currentTimeMillis();
11    for (int i = 0; i < 1000000; i++)
12      result = eliminatePunctuation(input);
13    long end = System.currentTimeMillis();
14
15    out.println("String - Done in " + (end-start) + " milliseconds");
16    out.println("String - Result: " + result);
17
18    start = System.currentTimeMillis();
19    for (int i = 0; i < 1000000; i++)
20      result = eliminatePunctuation2(input);
21    end = System.currentTimeMillis();
22
23    out.println("StringBuilder - Done in " + (end-start) + " milliseconds");
24    out.println("StringBuilder - Result: " + result);
25  }
26
27  private static String eliminatePunctuation(String input) {
28    String result = "";
29    for (int i = 0; i < input.length(); i++) {
30      char ch = input.charAt(i);
31      if ((ch >= 'a' && ch <= 'z') ||
32        (ch >= 'A' && ch <= 'Z') ||
33        ch == ' ')
34        result += ch;
35    }
36    return result;
37  }
38
39  private static String eliminatePunctuation2(String input) {
40    StringBuilder result = new StringBuilder();
41    for (int i = 0; i < input.length(); i++) {
42      char ch = input.charAt(i);
43      if ((ch >= 'a' && ch <= 'z') ||
44        (ch >= 'A' && ch <= 'Z') ||
45        ch == ' ')
46        result.append(ch);
47    }
48    return result.toString();
49  }
50 }
```

```
String - Done in 16682 milliseconds
String - Result: The Olympic Games are on the way with Japan set to host the th edition o
StringBuilder - Done in 1566 milliseconds
StringBuilder - Result: The Olympic Games are on the way with Japan set to host the th ed
```

The `String` implementation of `eliminatePunctuation` builds a string one character at a time. Punctuation characters and digits are filtered out using the `if` condition on lines 31-33. Each time a character is added to the string result on line 34, a new string object has to be allocated, copying the old string to the new one. This slows down processing and also puts pressure on the memory system since strings are allocated on the heap.

In contrast, the `eliminatePunctuation2` implementation allocates a `StringBuilder` object that doesn't cause this repeated allocation of new strings. Text can be appended to a `StringBuilder` without allocating a new object or copying the previous contents of the `StringBuilder`. The timing test with this particular test data show that the `StringBuilder` implementation uses about 10% of the time that the `String` implementation does.

Technique 23. Use `StringBuilder` to speed up string processing

`StringBuilder` can be used to speed up string operations that require the string to be modified, such as adding to the string, or deleting part of it.

Chapter Summary

- Recursion is when a method calls itself. Problems that require iteration can also be solved using recursion. In some situations, recursive code is much simpler and more maintainable than its iterative counterpart.
- Every recursive method has a base case, which tests for a termination condition, and a recursive case, where the recursive method calls itself.
- Caching is a common technique for increasing the runtime performance of a program.
- The `StringBuilder` class allows manipulation of string data that's faster than using the `String` class.

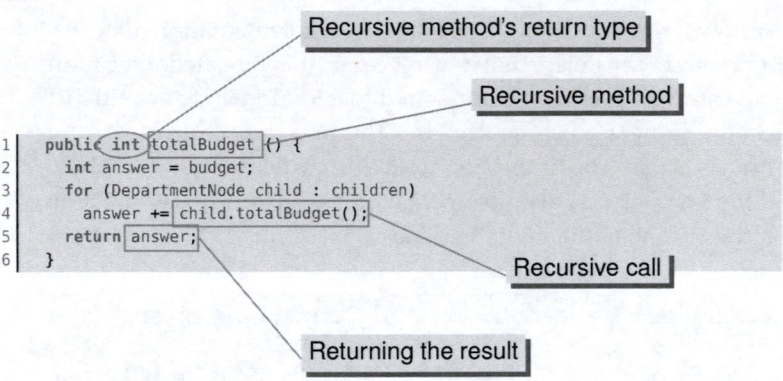

```
1  public int totalBudget () {
2    int answer = budget;
3    for (DepartmentNode child : children)
4      answer += child.totalBudget();
5    return answer;
6  }
```

Recursive method's return type

Recursive method

Recursive call

Returning the result

Exercise Solutions

15.1

```
The sum is 24
```

```
1  public static void main(String[] args) {
2
3    int[] array = { 10, 12, -3, 5 };
4    out.print("The sum is " + sumArray(array));
5  }
6
7  public static int sumArray(int[] array) {
8    return sumArray(array, 0);
9  }
10
11 public static int sumArray(int[] array, int index) {
12
13   // base case
14   if (array.length == index)
15     return 0;
16
17   // recursive case
18   return array[index] + sumArray(array, index + 1);
19 }
```

15.2

```
The merged string is MondayTuesdayFriday
```

```
1  public static void main(String[] args) {
2
3    List<String> days = new ArrayList<>();
4    days.add("Monday");
5    days.add("Tuesday");
6    days.add("Friday");
7    out.print("The merged string is " + concatenateStrings(days));
8  }
9
```

```
10    public static String concatenateStrings(List<String> strings) {
11      return concatenateStrings(strings, 0);
12    }
13
14    public static String concatenateStrings(List<String> strings, int
          index) {
15
16      // base case
17      if (index == strings.size())
18        return "";
19
20      // recursive case
21      return strings.get(index) + concatenateStrings(strings, index +
          1);
22    }
```

15.3

```
1     public static void main(String[] args) {
2  ...
3       DepartmentNode root = new DepartmentNode("Office of the
          Secretary", 12, 191000, node12, node9, node13, node14);
4       out.println("Number of departments in the tree is: " +
          countDepartments(root));
5     }
6
7     private static int countDepartments(DepartmentNode root) {
8
9       List<DepartmentNode> stack = new ArrayList<>();
10      stack.add(root);
11      int totalDepartments = 0;
12
13      while (!stack.isEmpty()) {
14
15        // pop a node from the stack
16        DepartmentNode currentNode = stack.remove(stack.size() - 1);
17
18        // process the node
19        totalDepartments ++;
20
21        // push each of the current node's children onto the stack
22        for (DepartmentNode child : currentNode.children)
23          stack.add(child);
24      }
25
26      return totalDepartments;
27    }
```

`Number of departments in the tree is: 15`

15.4

```
1     public static void main(String[] args) {
2  ...
3       DepartmentNode root = new DepartmentNode("Office of the
          Secretary", 12, 191000, node12, node9, node13, node14);
4       out.println("Number of departments is: " + root.countNodes());
5     }
6
7  class DepartmentNode {
8  ...
9    public int countNodes () {
10     int answer = 1;
```

`Number of departments is: 15`

```
11       for (DepartmentNode child : children)
12         answer += child.countNodes();
13       return answer;
14     }
15   }
```

15.5

```
Average budget is: 124866
```

```
1    public static void main(String[] args) {
2  ...
3      DepartmentNode root = new DepartmentNode("Office of the
         Secretary", 12, 191000, node12, node9, node13, node14);
4      out.println("Average budget is: " + root.totalBudget() / root.
         countNodes());
5    }
6
7  class DepartmentNode {
8  ...
9    public int totalBudget () {
10     int answer = budget;
11     for (DepartmentNode child : children)
12       answer += child.totalBudget();
13     return answer;
14   }
15 }
```

Sorting 16

16.1 Bubble Sort

As you saw in section 11.4, a list can be sorted using `Collec-`
`tions.sort` as long as the list holds elements of a type that implements `Comparable`. We'll repeat example 11.6 here as example 16.1,

```
1  import static java.lang.System.out;
2  import java.util.ArrayList;
3  import java.util.Collections;
4  import java.util.List;
5
6  public class SortTest {
7
8    public static void main(String[] args) {
9
10     // Generate 10 random numbers between 1 and 20
11     List<Integer> list = new ArrayList<Integer>();
12     for (int i = 0; i < 10; i++)
13       list.add((int) (Math.random() * 20) + 1);
14
15     out.println("Before sorting: " + list);
16     Collections.sort(list);
17     out.println("After sorting: " + list);
18   }
19  }
```

Example 16.1. Sorting a list of numbers.

```
Before sorting: [10, 9, 7, 19, 8, 4, 7, 14, 9, 16]
After sorting: [4, 7, 7, 8, 9, 9, 10, 14, 16, 19]
```

What if we wanted to sort the list ourselves without using Java's
built-in **sort** method? A simple sort algorithm called bubble sort can
be used instead of the sort operation on line 16 of example 16.1. The
bubble sort algorithm works by repeatedly swapping two numbers
that are in the wrong order, until the list is sorted. This is shown in
example 16.2,

```
1    public static void main(String[] args) {
2  ...
3      out.println("Before sorting: " + list);
4      bubbleSort(list);
5      out.println("After sorting: " + list);
6    }
```

Example 16.2. Bubble sort.

```
7
8    public static void bubbleSort(List<Integer> list) {
9
10       // loop 'n' times, where n is the size of the list
11       for (int counter1 = 0; counter1 < list.size(); counter1++) {
12
13          // loop 'n' times, where n is the size of the list
14          for (int counter2 = 0; counter2 < list.size() - 1; counter2++) {
15
16             // if we see two elements out of order, swap them
17             if (list.get(counter2) > list.get(counter2 + 1)) {
18                int temp = list.get(counter2);
19                list.set(counter2, list.get(counter2 + 1));
20                list.set(counter2 + 1, temp);
21             }
22          }
23       }
24    }
```

```
Before sorting: [19, 3, 18, 14, 3, 20, 18, 4, 7, 2]
After sorting:  [2, 3, 3, 4, 7, 14, 18, 18, 19, 20]
```

The sort method makes multiple passes, and during each pass examines successive pairs of numbers in the list. When a pair is in the wrong order, i.e., the first number is bigger than the second, the two numbers are swapped before the next pair is examined. After each pair is examined, the larger one is part of the next pair that is examined. Figure 16.1 shows the first three steps of the inner loop, within the first pass of the outer loop:

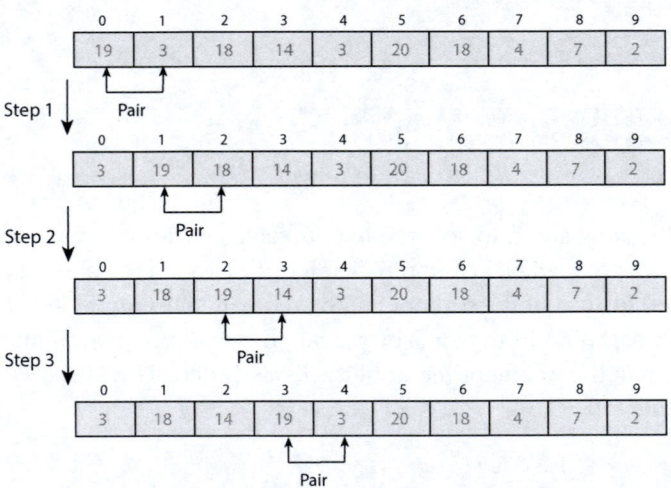

Figure 16.1: The first few steps of the inner loop of the Bubble sort algorithm.

- In step 1, the first pair is examined, with indexes 0 and 1. They're swapped since they're in the wrong order.

- In step 2, the second pair is examined, with indexes 1 and 2. They're swapped.
- In step 3, the third pair is examined, with indexes 2 and 3. They're swapped.

Once the inner loop goes through all pairs, the first pass of the outer loop is over. Note that after the first pass of the outer loop, the largest number, 20, will have been moved to the end of the array. After the second pass of the outer loop, the second-largest number, 19, will be in the right place, and so on. The numbers bubble over to their correct positions, hence the algorithm's name. Figure 16.2 shows the array's contents after the first three passes of the outer loop.

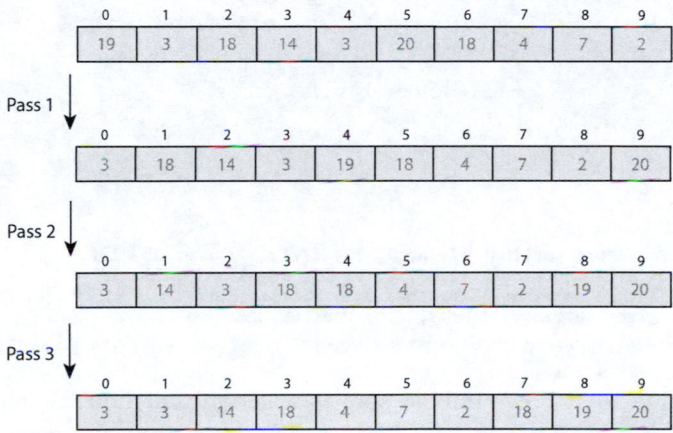

Figure 16.2: The first few steps of the outer loop of the Bubble sort algorithm.

Applying the techniques we learned in chapter 13, it's clear since the outer and inner loop both loop from 1 to n, where n is the list's size, that the algorithm's time complexity is $O(n^2)$.

We're not quite done, because the bubble sort in example 16.2 takes a list of integers as a parameter, so it's not capable of sorting a list of strings or other `Comparable` types. It can be converted to accept a generic type, stipulating that the type implements the `Comparable` interface, as shown in example 16.3,

Example 16.3. Generic bubble sort.

```
1  public static void main(String[] args) {
2
3      List<Integer> numbers = new ArrayList<>();
4      for (int i = 0; i < 10; i++)
5          numbers.add((int) (Math.random() * 20) + 1);
6      out.println("Numbers before sorting: " + numbers);
7      bubbleSort(numbers);
8      out.println("Numbers after sorting : " + numbers);
9
```

```
10      List<String> names = new ArrayList<>();
11      names.add("Samantha");
12      names.add("Jon");
13      names.add("Pierre");
14      names.add("Chris");
15      out.println("Names before sorting: " + names);
16      bubbleSort(names);
17      out.println("Names after sorting : " + names);
18   }
19
20   public static <E extends Comparable<E>> void bubbleSort(List<E> list) {
21
22      // loop 'n' times, where n is the size of the list
23      for (int counter1 = 0; counter1 < list.size(); counter1++) {
24
25         // loop 'n' times, where n is the size of the list
26         for (int counter2 = 0; counter2 < list.size() - 1; counter2++) {
27
28            // if we see two elements out of order, swap them
29            if (list.get(counter2).compareTo(list.get(counter2 + 1)) > 0) {
30               E temp = list.get(counter2);
31               list.set(counter2, list.get(counter2 + 1));
32               list.set(counter2 + 1, temp);
33            }
34         }
35      }
36   }
```

```
Numbers before sorting: [7, 6, 9, 19, 17, 2, 13, 16, 19, 18]
Numbers after sorting : [2, 6, 7, 9, 13, 16, 17, 18, 19, 19]
Names before sorting: [Samantha, Jon, Pierre, Chris]
Names after sorting : [Chris, Jon, Pierre, Samantha]
```

Example 16.3 shows bubble sort as a generic method. Generic methods, which we haven't discussed yet, are similar to generic types in that they accept a type as a parameter. The generic type is shown in angle brackets after the `static` keyword on line 20 of example 16.3, and stipulates that the generic type `E` implements the `Comparable<E>` interface (the `extends` keyword is used here instead of `implements`). The other changes we had to make were to change the `temp` variable on line 30 from `int` to `E`, and to use `compareTo` instead of an arithmetic comparison operator to compare two instances of `E` on line 29.

A common optimization of bubble sort is to end the inner loop at `list.size() - counter1`, which allows it to avoid looking at numbers that have already reached their proper position in the list. Another common optimization is to terminate the outer loop if the previous iteration didn't result in any pairs being swapped, which helps if the list was nearly sorted to begin with. Neither of these optimizations change the algorithm's time complexity.

Sort algorithms generally fall in two categories, slow ones that perform in quadratic time, $O(n^2)$, and fast ones that perform in log-linear time, O(n log n). In the next section, we'll look at one of the faster ones.

Exercises

16.1   Update example 16.3 to implement the following optimization. Have the outer loop terminate if the previous iteration didn't result in any pairs being swapped.

16.2 Merge Sort

One of the faster sorting algorithms is merge sort. It's a recursive algorithm that can be summarized as follows,

- Take the input list L, of size n, and break it into two halves, $H1$ and $H2$, each of size $n/2$.
- Recursively sort each of the two halves, $H1$ and $H2$.
- Merge the sorted halves, $H1$ and $H2$, by looping through both halves in parallel and repeatedly moving the smaller number from either half to a new list, which will contain the sorted contents of the original list L.

The first part is just to break the list into two halves, and there's no re-arranging of list items in that part. The real work of sorting happens during the second phase which merges the two sorted halves. Figure 16.3 illustrates the merge sort algorithm sorting a list of four numbers.

As seen in figure 16.3, the input list has four numbers, which is split into two lists of size 2. Each of the two smaller lists is further split into lists of size 1. The lists of size 1 are sorted by definition, and therein lies the base case of the recursive algorithm. Each two sorted lists of size 1 are merged into a list of size 2, and the two lists of size 2 are merged into the result which has a size of 4. Note that each point where a list is split into two lists represents one invocation of the recursive merge sort algorithm, and there are three such invocations in this example. Each of those three invocations performs a merge,

Note that the recursion depth is the log of the input size.

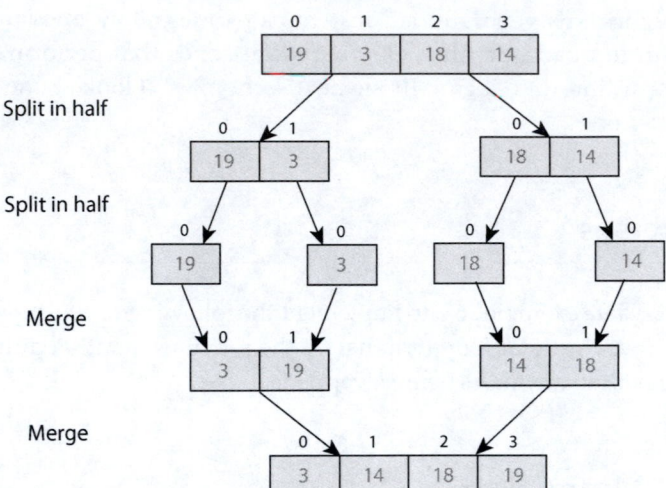

Figure 16.3: Sorting a list using the Merge sort algorithm.

seen in figure 16.3 where two lists are merged into one. The merge sort implementation is shown in example 16.4,

Example 16.4. Merge sort.

```
1   public static void main(String[] args) {
2   ...
3      out.println("Before sorting: " + list);
4      list = mergeSort(list);
5      out.println("After sorting: " + list);
6   }
7
8   public static List<Integer> mergeSort(List<Integer> list) {
9
10     // base case - nothing to do if the list is empty or has just one element
11     if (list.size() < 2)
12       return list;
13
14     // partition the list into two halves, and recurse
15
16     // copy first half of the input list into 'half1', and sort 'half1'
17     List<Integer> half1 = new ArrayList<>();
18     for (int i = 0; i < list.size() / 2; i++)
19       half1.add(list.get(i));
20     half1 = mergeSort(half1);
21
22     // copy second half of the input list into 'half2', and sort 'half2'
23     List<Integer> half2 = new ArrayList<>();
24     for (int i = list.size() / 2; i < list.size(); i++)
25       half2.add(list.get(i));
26     half2 = mergeSort(half2);
27
28     // merge the two sorted halves
29     return merge(half1, half2);
30   }
31
32   public static List<Integer> merge(List<Integer> half1, List<Integer> half2) {
33
34     List<Integer> result = new ArrayList<>();
```

```
35    int index1 = 0;
36    int index2 = 0;
37
38    // loop until both halves are depleted
39    while (index1 < half1.size() || index2 < half2.size()) {
40
41      // if half1 is depleted, take from half2
42      if (index1 == half1.size())
43        result.add(half2.get(index2++));
44
45      // if half2 is depleted, take from half1
46      else if (index2 == half2.size())
47        result.add(half1.get(index1++));
48
49      // if neither half is depleted, take the smaller list element from half1
      or half2
50      else {
51        if (half1.get(index1) > half2.get(index2))
52          result.add(half2.get(index2++));
53        else
54          result.add(half1.get(index1++));
55      }
56    }
57
58    return result;
59  }
```

```
Before sorting: [11, 4, 16, 7, 10, 12, 13, 18, 5, 6]
After sorting:  [4, 5, 6, 7, 10, 11, 12, 13, 16, 18]
```

Example 16.4 contains two methods, `mergeSort` which splits the input into two halves and calls itself recursively, and `merge` which merges two sorted lists into one. These two methods implement the algorithm summarized in the beginning of this section. Note that the algorithm still works when the input's size is odd, in which case one of the two halves is larger than the other by one element. The merge method walks through both input lists in parallel which requires two indexes, one for each list. In each iteration of the main merge loop, the smaller number at the index point of each input list is moved to the output list.

To illustrate the speed difference between the two sorting algorithms, we'll modify the main method to repeatedly test both with different input sizes. Figure 16.4 shows the relative speed as the input grows.

```
1  public static void main(String[] args) {
2
3    for (int i = 8000; i <= 64000; i += 8000)
4      runTest(i);
5  }
6
7  private static void runTest (int size) {
8
```

Example 16.5. Comparing bubble sort and merge sort.

```
9      // Generate random numbers between 1 and 1000000
10     List<Integer> list1 = new ArrayList<Integer>();
11     List<Integer> list2 = new ArrayList<>();
12     for (int i = 0; i < size; i++) {
13       int number = (int) (Math.random() * 1000000) + 1;
14       list1.add(number);
15       list2.add(number);
16     }
17
18     long start = System.currentTimeMillis();
19     bubbleSort(list1);
20     long end = System.currentTimeMillis();
21     out.println("List size " + size + ", Bubble sort took " + (end-start) + "
         milliseconds");
22
23     start = System.currentTimeMillis();
24     list2 = mergeSort(list2);
25     end = System.currentTimeMillis();
26     out.println("List size " + size + ", Merge sort took " + (end-start) + "
         milliseconds");
27   }
```

```
List size 8000, Bubble sort took 453 milliseconds
List size 8000, Merge sort took 16 milliseconds
List size 16000, Bubble sort took 1839 milliseconds
List size 16000, Merge sort took 11 milliseconds
List size 24000, Bubble sort took 4332 milliseconds
List size 24000, Merge sort took 19 milliseconds
List size 32000, Bubble sort took 8050 milliseconds
List size 32000, Merge sort took 19 milliseconds
List size 40000, Bubble sort took 13543 milliseconds
List size 40000, Merge sort took 33 milliseconds
List size 48000, Bubble sort took 19495 milliseconds
List size 48000, Merge sort took 42 milliseconds
List size 56000, Bubble sort took 26959 milliseconds
List size 56000, Merge sort took 48 milliseconds
List size 64000, Bubble sort took 40264 milliseconds
List size 64000, Merge sort took 48 milliseconds
```

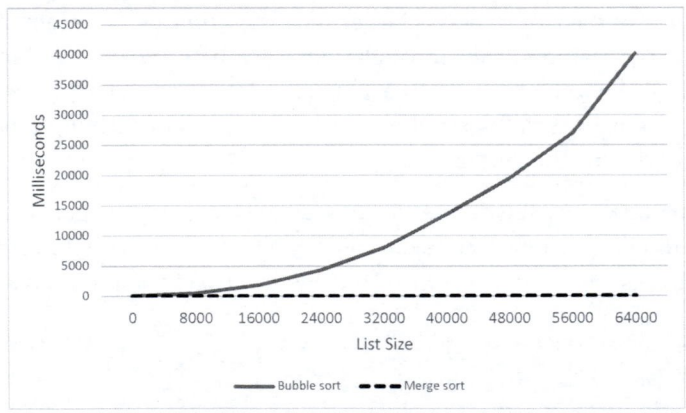

Figure 16.4: Comparing bubble sort and merge sort.

Exercises

16.2 Change the merge sort method in example 16.4 so that it's generic, as was done with bubble sort in the last section.

16.3 Recurrence Relations

Let's discuss the runtime performance of merge sort. There are three parts to the merge sort algorithm,

- Splitting the input list into two lists. This is O(n) since it loops once through the input.
- Recursively calling merge sort on each of the two lists, each containing half of the original input.
- Merging the two sorted lists, each of size $n/2$. This is O(n) since it's done with one pass through both of them simultaneously.

In the second step above, the algorithm calls itself twice, each time with an input size that's half the original input size n. The rest (steps 1 and 3 above) is done in O(n) time. The following recurrence relation describes the runtime:

$$T(n) = 2T(n/2) + O(n) \quad \Rightarrow \quad O(n \ log \ n)$$

A recurrence relation describes the runtime of an algorithm with an input size of n using its own runtime with a smaller input, and in this case the smaller input size is $n/2$. The equation shown above tells us that the runtime of a method that does O(n) work in addition to calling itself twice, each time with half the original input size, is equal to O(n log n). Recall from table 13.1 that O(n log n) is known as log-linear time, and from figure 13.2 that log-linear algorithms are far faster than those that are quadratic. This explains the results seen in figure 16.4 illustrating the difference in runtime between merge sort and bubble sort.

Recurrence relations are useful in analyzing the time complexity of recursive algorithms. Table 16.1 shows some common recurrence

[2] explains recurrence relations in detail and describes three different ways of solving recurrence relations.

Table 16.1: Common recurrence relations.

Recurrence	Complexity	Example
$T(n) = T(n/2) + O(1)$	$O(log\ n)$	Binary Search
$T(n) = T(n-1) + O(1)$	$O(n)$	Traversing a list
$T(n) = 2T(n/2) + O(1)$	$O(n)$	Traversing a tree
$T(n) = T(n-1) + O(n)$	$O(n^2)$	Bubble sort
$T(n) = 2T(n/2) + O(n)$	$O(n\ log\ n)$	Merge sort

relations with an example algorithm for each. Let's think about each one,

- Imagine binary search, first explained in section 14.1 implemented recursively. The middle of the list is found and compared to the item in question. That's the fixed cost which is O(1). Then the recursive call occurs, with search bounds narrowed down to half of the original range. So we've got $T(n) = T(n/2) + O(1)$, and the binary search terminates in a logarithmic number of iterations since the input size is cut in half in each iteration.

- Imagine the list traversal in example 13.17 implemented in a recursive way. Instead of a `while` loop to construct the string result of `toString`, the string is constructed by concatenating the current node in the linked list to the result of a recursive call with the next node as input. That's $O(1)$ fixed cost (using a `StringBuilder`) plus a recursive call to process the rest of the list. Thus we have $T(n) = T(n-1) + O(1)$. Traversing a list visits each node and has overall time cost of $O(n)$.

- Tree traversal is done by processing the current node, then recursively processing each of the node's children. Processing the current node takes $O(1)$ time, and processing each child takes $T(n/m)$ time where n is the size of the node's subtree and m is the branching factor. Thus we have $T(n) = 2T(n/2) + O(1)$ in the case of a binary tree, or $T(n) = m\ T(n/m) + O(1)$ in the case of a tree with a branching factor of m. Traversing a tree visits each node and has $O(n)$ overall time cost.

- Imagine bubble sort implemented recursively. The inner loop is performed once, with cost $O(n)$, resulting in one number bubbling to its proper location, then a recursive call is made to perform another iteration of the outer loop. That's still effectively a nested loop, with both the outer and inner loops repeating n times, performing bubble sort in $O(n^2)$ time where the recurrence relation is $T(n) = T(n-1) + O(n)$.

- The final item in table 16.1 is $T(n) = 2T(n/2) + O(n)$, exemplified by merge sort with the splitting and merging both using $O(n)$ time and two recursive calls, each processing half the input size. Merge sort runs in $O(n\ log\ n)$ time.

Sometimes memory requirements (space complexity) play a big role in deciding which algorithm to use. The merge sort algorithm allocates a new list to store the merge operation's result, and this is done in each nested call. To take pressure off the Java memory management system, for several years the internal sort algorithm used by `Arrays.sort` wasn't one of the $O(n\ log\ n)$ algorithms, but rather quick sort, which is $O(n^2)$ in the worst case, but is $O(n\ log\ n)$ in the *average* case. The big advantage of quick sort is that it sorts a list *in place* without needing to allocate space to copy the list.

Exercises

16.3   Update example 13.17 to implement `MyLinkedList.toString` using recursion instead of iteration. See the above description of list traversal with recursion.

16.4 Where To From Here?

Did you follow my advice in the introduction's "How to use this book" section? If you've internalized what this book covers, and can write the code for the book's examples on your own, I believe the hard part is over for you. Everything else that you'll encounter in the world of software development will either be easier than what you learned here, or will be a variation on the concepts you learned here. Either way, you should be able to pick it up without too much trouble, whether it's "process stuff" such as source control, tooling such as databases, infrastructure such as cloud, or platform-specific programming such as web application development. And, until you get your first full-time developer job, remember to keep practicing!

Tip 10. Until you get your first full-time developer job, remember to keep practicing!

Chapter Summary

- Sorting algorithms generally have $O(n^2)$ or $O(n\ log\ n)$ time complexity.
- Bubble sort has $O(n^2)$ time complexity, and works by making successive passes, examining each pair of numbers in each pass, and swapping them if they're out of order.
- Merge sort has $O(n\ log\ n)$ time complexity, and works by partitioning the list into two parts, recursively sorting each part, then merging the two sorted parts.
- Recurrence relations help to analyze the time complexity of recursive algorithms.

Outer loop

```java
 1    public static void bubbleSort(List<Integer> list) {
 2
 3        // loop 'n' times, where n is the size of the list
 4        for (int counter1 = 0; counter1 < list.size(); counter1++) {
 5
 6            // loop 'n' times, where n is the size of the list
 7            for (int counter2 = 0; counter2 < list.size() - 1; counter2++) {
 8
 9                // if we see two elements out of order, swap them
10                if (list.get(counter2) > list.get(counter2 + 1)) {
11                    int temp = list.get(counter2);
12                    list.set(counter2, list.get(counter2 + 1));
13                    list.set(counter2 + 1, temp);
14                }
15            }
16        }
17    }
```

Inner loop

Check each pair

Swap two numbers

Exercise Solutions

16.1

```
1   public static void bubbleSort(List<Integer> list) {
2
3     boolean swapOccurred = true;
4     while (swapOccurred) {
5
6       swapOccurred = false;
7       for (int counter2 = 0; counter2 < list.size() - 1; counter2++)
      {
8
9         // if we see two elements out of order, swap them
10        if (list.get(counter2) > list.get(counter2 + 1)) {
11          int temp = list.get(counter2);
12          list.set(counter2, list.get(counter2 + 1));
13          list.set(counter2 + 1, temp);
14          swapOccurred = true;
15        }
16      }
17    }
18  }
```

```
Before sorting: [19, 17, 3, 6, 16, 5, 19, 14, 19, 9]
After sorting:  [3, 5, 6, 9, 14, 16, 17, 19, 19, 19]
```

16.2

```
1   public static void main(String[] args) {
2
3     List<Integer> numbers = new ArrayList<>();
4     for (int i = 0; i < 10; i++)
5       numbers.add((int) (Math.random() * 20) + 1);
6     out.println("Numbers before sorting: " + numbers);
7     numbers = mergeSort(numbers);
8     out.println("Numbers after sorting : " + numbers);
9
10    List<String> names = new ArrayList<>();
11    names.add("Samantha");
12    names.add("Jon");
13    names.add("Pierre");
14    names.add("Chris");
15    out.println("Names before sorting: " + names);
16    names = mergeSort(names);
17    out.println("Names after sorting : " + names);
18  }
19
20  public static <E extends Comparable<E>> List<E> mergeSort(List<E>
      list) {
21
22    // base case - nothing to do if the list is empty or has just
      one element
23    if (list.size() < 2)
24      return list;
25
26    // partition the list into two halves, and recurse
27
28    // copy first half of the input list into 'half1', and sort '
      half1'
29    List<E> half1 = new ArrayList<>();
```

```
30        for (int i = 0; i < list.size() / 2; i++)
31          half1.add(list.get(i));
32        half1 = mergeSort(half1);
33
34        // copy second half of the input list into 'half2', and sort '
           half2'
35        List<E> half2 = new ArrayList<>();
36        for (int i = list.size() / 2; i < list.size(); i++)
37          half2.add(list.get(i));
38        half2 = mergeSort(half2);
39
40        // merge the two sorted halves
41        return merge(half1, half2);
42      }
43
44      public static <E extends Comparable<E>> List<E> merge(List<E>
           half1, List<E> half2) {
45
46        List<E> result = new ArrayList<>();
47        int index1 = 0;
48        int index2 = 0;
49
50        // loop until both halves are depleted
51        while (index1 < half1.size() || index2 < half2.size()) {
52
53          // if half1 is depleted, take from half2
54          if (index1 == half1.size())
55            result.add(half2.get(index2++));
56
57          // if half2 is depleted, take from half1
58          else if (index2 == half2.size())
59            result.add(half1.get(index1++));
60
61          // if neither half is depleted, take the smaller list element
             from half1 or half2
62          else {
63            if (half1.get(index1).compareTo(half2.get(index2)) > 0)
64              result.add(half2.get(index2++));
65            else
66              result.add(half1.get(index1++));
67          }
68        }
69
70        return result;
71      }
```

```
Numbers before sorting: [19, 20, 18, 8, 9, 15, 2, 10, 5, 19]
Numbers after sorting : [2, 5, 8, 9, 10, 15, 18, 19, 19, 20]
Names before sorting: [Samantha, Jon, Pierre, Chris]
Names after sorting : [Chris, Jon, Pierre, Samantha]
```

16.3
```
1     @Override
2     public String toString() {
3       StringBuilder sb = new StringBuilder();
4       toString(sb, head);
5       return "[" + sb + "]";
6     }
7
8     private void toString(StringBuilder sb, Node<E> node) {
9
10      // base case - node is null
```

```
11      if (node == null)
12        return;
13
14      // base case - this is the last node in the list, no comma added
15      if (node.next == null) {
16        sb.append(node.element.toString());
17        return;
18      }
19
20      // recursive case
21      sb.append(node.element);
22      sb.append(", ");
23      toString (sb, node.next);
24    }
```

```
names = [Peter, Mary, Heather, Mary]
```

Bibliography & Further Reading

[1] ABELSON, H., AND SUSSMAN, G. J. *Structure and Interpretation of Computer Programs*, 2nd ed. The MIT Press, Cambridge, MA, USA, 1996.

[2] CORMEN, T. H., LEISERSON, C. E., RIVEST, R. L., AND STEIN, C. *Introduction to Algorithms*, 2nd ed. The MIT Press, Cambridge, MA, USA, 2001.

[3] ECLIPSE FOUNDATION. Eclipse documentation. https://www.eclipse.org/documentation, 2020. Accessed: 2020-12-17.

[4] FOOTE, B., AND YODER, J. Big Ball of Mud. In *Pattern Languages of Program Design* (1999), Addison-Wesley, pp. 653–692.

[5] GAMMA, E., HELM, R., JOHNSON, R., AND VLISSIDES, J. *Design Patterns: Elements of Reusable Object-Oriented Software*. Addison-Wesley Longman Publishing Co., Inc., USA, 1995.

[6] KNUTH, D. E. *The Art of Computer Programming, Volume 1 (3rd Ed.): Fundamental Algorithms*. Addison Wesley Longman Publishing Co., Inc., USA, 1997.

[7] ORACLE. Java documentation. https://docs.oracle.com/en/java/index.html, 2020. Accessed: 2020-12-17.

[8] SEDGEWICK, R., AND WAYNE, K. *Computer Science: An Interdisciplinary Approach*, 1st ed. Addison-Wesley Professional, 2016.

Glossary

abstraction	One of the main techniques used to organize computer programs.
algorithm	A series of steps that define how a program will accomplish its task.
argument	A data value that is passed to a method's parameter.
big-o notation	A notation relating the runtime performance of an algorithm to the size of its input.
bug	A mistake in the code that results in incorrect output for certain inputs.
caching	The act of temporarily storing computed values, or storing data from slower memory within a faster memory space, for faster retrieval later.
casting	Converting a value from one type to another.
class	A type defined by Java or by the programmer.
code block	Curly braces containing lines of code.
collection	A built-in Java class that contains objects and grows as needed when you add objects to it.
compiler	A program that translates source code in a high-level language into machine code.
compile-time	When the programmer is entering the source code (compared to run-time).
compiling	Translating source code in a high-level language into machine code.
complexity	A measure of the performance (time or space) of a program or an algorithm.
constant	A named data item defined in a Java program that can't be changed at runtime.
encapsulation	When data related to an object and methods that operate on the object are bundled in a class.
enumeration	A type whose instances can only have a certain set of possible values.
exception	An unexpected error condition.
expression	A Java formula that can include data and operators, producing a result of a certain type.

generic class
: A class that requires another type as a parameter.

global variable
: A variable that is available to all the code within a program.

graph
: A tree data structure that can contain cycles.

hardcoded value
: A constant value of a particular type, used in the program's source code.

hashing
: The process of converting a class's data to an integer.

heap memory
: The area of memory where objects and arrays reside when allocated using the `new` keyword.

high-level language
: A computer language that is easily readable by humans.

IDE
: The Integrated Development Environment, a program that allows the programmer to enter the program and debug it.

immutable
: Immutable data is data that can't be directly changed.

infinite loop
: When a loop doesn't terminate because its termination condition is never met.

inheritance
: When one class extends another, inheriting its data elements and methods.

integer division
: When an integer is divided by another integer.

interface
: Specifies a particular set of methods that can be implemented by one or more classes.

iteration
: Performing an operation repeatedly to accomplish a task or compute a result.

local variable
: A variable that's defined in a local scope, such as a method.

low-level language
: A computer language that is closer to the computer's native machine language.

machine language
: The native language of a CPU.

map
: A collection that maps keys to values, where the key and value are arbitrary classes.

method
: A named block of code that can be executed as a unit.

null reference
: Using an object or array reference before it's initialized, resulting in an exception.

operator precedence	The order in which operators are evaluated within an expression.
parameter	A variable defined by a method that is initialized by the code that calls it, in order to pass information into the method.
polymorphism	When a reference to a base class or interface can refer to more than one derived class at runtime.
primitive type	A native type defined by the Java language.
program	A compiled version of the source code that is executed by the computer.
project	In Eclipse, a project is a collection of classes that, when compiled, produce an executable program.
pseudocode	An English description of the steps that make up a program's algorithm.
recurrence relation	A mathematical description of an algorithm's runtime expressed in terms of its own runtime with a smaller input.
recursion	When a method calls itself.
refactoring	Reorganizing a program so that it's more maintainable.
run-time	When a software program is running (compared to compile-time).
scope	The part of the program where an identifier can be accessed.
serialization	Saving an object to a file.
shortcut evaluation	Evaluating an expression where part of the expression isn't evaluated because it doesn't need to be.
software	A sequence of instructions that tell the computer how to perform a useful task.
stack memory	The area of memory where local variables are stored.
stack overflow	When the call stack runs out of memory because of too many nested method invocations.
ternary operator	An operator that takes three arguments, such as the ?: operator.
tree	A data structure representing hierarchical data.
type casting	Converting a value from one type to another.

UML	The Unified Modeling Language, which defines many types of useful diagrams that help to specify software components and their interactions.
unary operator	An operator that takes one argument, such as the negation operator.
variable	A named data item defined in a Java program.
workspace	A collection of projects in Eclipse.
wrapper class	A class that wraps a native Java type, and provides extra functionality for convenience.

Index

About the Author

Marwan Shaban received his B.S. in computer engineering from N.C. State University in 1988, and Ph.D. in computer science from Boston University in 1996. Subsequently, he worked as a partner, software developer, software architect and in management at companies ranging from startups to large corporations, with diverse technologies such as database, cloud, mobile and web.

During his twenty-year tenure in industry, while not writing code he could be found providing technical direction and mentoring to software teams, hiring software developers, conducting secure coding reviews, managing remediation efforts, working with QA, BA and PM teams, and myriad similar activities. He has created extensive architectural documentation and always promoted code simplicity and efficiency as primary goals.

In 2008, he was profiled in the Microsoft publication "Heroes Happen Here," which highlights 115 IT professionals from 18 countries who all share a passion for adopting the latest technologies.

From 2011 to 2015, he led the enterprise architecture team at SeaWorld Parks & Entertainment, with responsibility for high-level architecture of corporate and park software systems, including the corporate division and ten parks, with 22,000 workers, and dozens of systems and databases across eight data centers, in all lines of business such as HR, finance, park operations, ticketing and customer-facing websites.

Dr. Shaban has published work in computational linguistics and virtual reality. He is currently professor of computer programming and analysis at Seminole State College in Orlando, Florida, where he encourages students to ignore fads and focus on the fundamentals.

THE UNION
AT RISK

*Jacksonian Democracy,
States' Rights, and
the Nullification Crisis*

Richard E. Ellis

OXFORD UNIVERSITY PRESS
New York   Oxford

Oxford University Press

Oxford   New York
Athens   Auckland   Bangkok   Bombay
Calcutta   Cape Town   Dar es Salaam   Delhi
Florence   Hong Kong   Istanbul   Karachi
Kuala Lumpur   Madras   Madrid   Melbourne
Mexico City   Nairobi   Paris   Singapore
Taipei   Tokyo   Toronto

and associated companies in
Berlin   Ibadan

Library of Congress Cataloging-in-Publication Data
Ellis, Richard E.
The Union at risk.
Includes index.
1. Nullification. 2. United States—Politics and
government—1829–1837. I. Title.
E384.3.E466   1987   973.5'61   86-16277
ISBN 0-19-503785-5 (alk. paper)
ISBN 0-19-506187-X (Pbk.)

10 9 8 7 6 5 4 3

Printed in the United States of America
on acid-free paper

For Sharon

The significance of political and constitutional history has long been recognized by scholars. Although it is one of the oldest approaches to the American past it continues to remain an extremely resilient and useful one. Even in recent years, when numerous kinds of new techniques have been developed, the study of constitutional issues has brought forth several big books that have shed important new light on the Revolutionary era and the Civil War and Reconstruction periods. But strangely, relatively little has been done on the constitutional issues of the Jacksonian era. Why should this be?

Part of the explanation may be found in the historiography of the Jacksonian period. Far more than for most periods of American history, the Jacksonian era was a battleground for the debate between the Progressive historians and their consensus critics that so dominated American scholarship during the 1950s and 1960s. This debate, moreover, had an ironic twist to it, for at the same time a similar debate, and in some ways an even more important one, was taking place between Progressive and consensus historians over the meaning of the American Revolution and the significance of the adoption of the United States Constitution. In this debate the consensus historians were able to argue effectively that Progressive scholars had been anti-intellectual, that is, they had not taken the rhetoric and ideas of the Revolutionary generation seriously enough, and had looked for reality exclusively below the surface, usually in terms of sordid self-interest. But in the Jackson period the big book that touched off the debate of the 1950s and 1960s was Arthur M. Schlesinger

Jr.'s *The Age of Jackson* (Boston, 1945), a major piece of scholarship clearly in the Progressive tradition. Schlesinger, who at that time taught intellectual history at Harvard University, did take the rhetoric and the ideas of the period seriously—perhaps too seriously. For reasons that are not altogether clear, Schlesinger's critics, to an extraordinary extent, have down-played the various constitutional and ideological considerations of the Jacksonian era. For example, Bray Hammond, in a view that was endorsed by Richard Hofstadter, decried the Jacksonian ignorance of the usefulness of the Second Bank of the United States and dismissed their rationale for attacking it as nonsense (in Jackson's case) and hypocritical cant (in the case of the Jackson advisers) and saw the state banking interests, operating behind the scenes and below the surface, as the real and dynamic element of the Jacksonian assault.[1] Similarly, two other scholars, Richard P. McCormick and Edward Pessen, in their treatment of the politics of the Jacksonian period, have viewed it primarily as a struggle for power between ins and outs rather than one involving fundamental issues.[2] Also, the "New Political Historians," led by Lee Benson and his students, while they cannot be precisely described as consensus historians, have tended to be strongly critical of Progressive Scholarship in the way they have presented their findings and have picked up on the anti-intellectual biases of the consensus historians.[3] They have looked at issues mainly in terms of their symbolic importance and have ignored the various constitutional and ideological considerations of the period. Moreover, they have not really offered any explanation of why it was that the politicians of the 1820s and 1830s, on both the state and national level, were so concerned with issues such as internal improvements, the role of banks, the tariff, and the Supreme Court of the United States, when voters, as they claim, were supposed to be divided along ethnic, religious, and life-style lines.[4]

Since it has been these consensus historians who have dominated the writing of the history of Jacksonian America in recent years it is really not surprising that constitutional-ideological issues have generally been ignored. For example, the nullification crisis that occurred during the fall and winter of 1832–33 has been a topic that in many ways has brought forth an unusually fine literature.[5] But for the most part these works tend to examine the controversy mainly from the perspective of internal developments within South Carolina or as a prologue to the coming of the Civil War. Something of an exception to this has been the obligatory but generally perfunctory chapter on the event in the numerous biographies of Andrew Jackson. Moreover, none of the more recent works on the general question of the meaning of Jacksonian Democracy have given the nullification controversy more than cursory treatment.

In this book I have taken the political rhetoric of the Jackson period seriously. In particular I have focused on the constitutional and ideological issues raised by the nullification crisis and have tried to explain why Jackson and many of those closest to him took such a strong states' rights position on such issues as a federal program of internal improvements, the Georgia Indian question, and the Second Bank of the United States, and still so vigorously opposed nullification. In doing this I have argued that Andrew Jackson was a clear, coherent, forceful, and even a formidable constitutional thinker. His differences with the nullifiers were real and profound, and in certain ways irresolvable. One cannot explain the Old Hero's opposition to South Carolina's actions during the winter of 1832–33 simply in terms of his hatred for Calhoun, as is often done. To stress the importance of issues and principles, however, is not to deny the role of political considerations or personalities. These, too, were important, and I have also examined them and have tried to put them into perspective.

While I have benefited enormously from the work of previous scholars on nullification, I differ from them on a number of important points. In addition to treating nullification as one of the central events that shaped Jacksonian Democracy, I have taken issue with the claim that South Carolina was completely isolated during the controversy. This is not true. Although no other state endorsed the concept of nullification, there was considerable support among well-placed individuals throughout the South for the nullifiers. There also was an enormous reaction to Jackson's famous Proclamation of December 10, 1832, denouncing nullification, which changed the whole nature of the controversy and eventually led to a major setback for the President. The nullifiers, on the other hand, emerged from the controversy secure and unrepentant.

I have also de-emphasized the traditional way of looking at the constitutional issues involved in the controversy as a struggle between the advocates of nationalism and of states' rights. To be sure, this was a dimension of the debate, but there was also another debate, one that scholars have generally overlooked, although a very important one to the participants. It was between proponents of different kinds of states' rights thought. It was between those advocates of *states' rights* who believed in a perpetual Union and decentralization of power as the best way to fulfill the democratic promise of the American Revolution and keep government responsible to the wishes of the people, and those who advocated that a state had a constitutional right to withdraw from the Union and believed the doctrine of *states' rights* provided the best way to protect the rights of the minority from the tyranny of the majority. An important result of the nullification crisis was that the doctrine of states' rights became fatefully entwined with the concepts of slavery and secession. Finally, I have eschewed making use of the currently fashionable concept of "republicanism." Although the term was certainly part of the vocabulary of the times its meaning was so vague and its use so widespread that use of it obscures the real and specific issues involved in the controversy and reveals very little about the origins, the nature, the direction, and the results of that controversy.

In the course of writing this book I have incurred a substantial number of obligations. It is a pleasure to acknowledge them. The extensive travel necessary to complete the research was financed in part by several small travel grants from the University of Virginia and a Grant-in-Aid from the American Council of Learned Societies. Additional research and time to reflect on the subject occurred when I spent a year at Harvard University as a member of the

Charles Warren Center for Studies in American History and as a Liberal Arts
Fellow at the Law School. Support for this venture came from the John Simon
Guggenheim Memorial Foundation and a University of Virginia Sesquicenten-
nial Fellowship. The initial writing of the book began several years later while I
was a National Endowment for the Humanities Fellow at the American Enterprise Institute in Washington, D.C. Help in financing this opportunity also
came from the State University of New York at Buffalo. I am particularly
indebted to David Grimsted, who opened his home to me during my year in
Washington. I am also very grateful to the staffs of the numerous research
libraries where I have worked. The book has benefited from careful readings of
the manuscript and useful suggestions by Alfred Konefsky, J. Roger Sharp,
Raymond Wolters, and Sheldon Meyer. Daniel Feller of *The Papers of Andrew
Jackson* made available several documents for my use. Special thanks are due
to Charles Sellers who helped make me aware of the wonders and complexities
of the Age of Jackson and who has always been a source of encouragement and
support; I owe him a great deal.

My children, Jonathan, Daniel, Rebekah, and Deborah, who I am sure will
enjoy seeing their names in print, have been a continuing source of inspiration
and enjoyment. To my wife Sharon, who typed the final manuscript and who is
responsible for whatever stylistic virtues my prose might have, I lovingly dedicate this book.

Snyder, New York   R.E.E.
January 1986

CONTENTS

1

An Ambiguous Heritage: States' Rights in America, 1776–1828

For nearly a full century following independence in 1776 the central constitutional issue in America was the problem of the distribution of power between the states and the national government. In one form or another the issue of states' rights permeated almost all ideological and political discussions of the antebellum era. Scholars have long recognized this, and there has been considerable work done on the specific events in which the concept of states' rights has manifested itself: the writing of the Articles of Confederation, the debate over the creation and adoption of the United States Constitution, the Kentucky and Virginia Resolutions, Federalist opposition during the administrations of Thomas Jefferson and James Madison, the various criticisms of the Supreme Court's nationalist decisions during the 1820s, Andrew Jackson's numerous vetoes, South Carolina's nullification of the tariffs of 1828 and 1832, the problem of slavery, and the secession crisis culminating in the Civil War and the Reconstruction of the Union. Yet surprisingly little has been done to look at the states' rights argument itself very closely, to try to explain its origins and its evolution in early American history, or the different ways in which the argument has been used at different points in time.

I

The sources of the states' rights argument that emerged in the years immediately after 1776 were complex and many. In part it can be traced back to the colonists' cultural heritage, since throughout the sixteenth, seventeenth, and even eighteenth centuries, opposition to the centralizing tendency of the monarchy was a way of life for many people. Also of great significance were the separate and independent ways in which the individual colonies were settled and developed and the various commercial rivalries, political jealousies, and other petty hostilities that undermined almost all attempts to get them to cooperate with each other before the Revolutionary crisis began. Looking back at the successful rebellion against British authority that began in 1776, John Adams viewed it as something of a miracle, since before that—

> The colonies had grown up under constitutions of government so different, there was so great a variety of religions, they were composed of so many different nations, their customs, manners, and habits had so little resemblance, and their intercourse had been so rare, and their knowledge of each other so imperfect, that to unite them in the same principles in theory and the same system of action, was certainly a very difficult enterprise. The complete accomplishment of it, in so short a time and by such simple means, was perhaps a singular example in the history of Mankind. Thirteen clocks were made to strike together. A perfection of mechanism, which no artist had ever before effected.[2]

The Revolution both undermined and reinforced the centrifugal heritage of the colonial period. It undermined it by forcing Americans to band together successfully to fight a common foe, and, of course, in the process many people from different parts of the country came to realize that they had a great deal in common. Unquestionably, a spirit of nationalism and with it a desire to see the creation of a strong and active central government were real and dynamic results of the Revolution and suffused the feelings and thoughts of such important figures as George Washington, Alexander Hamilton, John Marshall, Robert Morris, John Adams, Thomas Jefferson, and James Madison.[3] But just as strong were those dimensions of the Revolution that did not lend support to any program that would weaken local authority, particularly by the creation of a strong central government. The debate between Americans and Englishmen in the years immediately before 1776 focused on the rights of the colonies as opposed to those of the imperial government.[4] The Revolution, after all, was fought to deny the authority of the only central government that the colonists had ever known: Great Britain. For most Americans, therefore, in the years immediately following independence, it was natural to associate the idea of a central government with England's arbitrary actions during the 1760s and 1770s.

Buttressing and giving direction to this experience was the ideology of the Revolution, which stressed the tension and essential incompatibility between liberty and power.[5] The weak central government created by the Articles of Confederation, despite the objections of some spokesman from the Middle Atlantic states, seemed to flow almost naturally from the heritage of the colonial period and the intellectual thrust of the Revolution.[6]

After 1776 a related but nonetheless distinct source of support for the decentralization of authority came from those who wished to see the democratic potential of the Revolution fulfilled. Viewing government as at best a necessary evil, determined to protect the rights of the governed from subversion by their rulers and suspicious of any kind of institutional arrangement that placed excessive power in the hands of the few, many people believed government should be made as weak, as simple, and as immediately and directly responsible to the will of the majority as possible. For these reasons eighteenth-century democrats favored such devices as broad suffrage, annual elections, rotation of office, legislative supremacy, and the diffusion of political power through decentralization in order to prevent its consolidation in a few hands.[7]

Although the colonial heritage of particularism, the ideology of the Revolution, and the burgeoning of democratic thought all contributed significantly to the creation of a political persuasion that stressed the importance of local autonomy, it was the actual social and economic conditions under which many people lived during the 1780s that sustained the perspective of localism and made it especially meaningful to a large number of Americans. This is because a very substantial portion of the people at this time were small farmers who lived in simple, isolated, and provincial communities. Since at best they had only a tangential connection with the market economy, it was in the interest of these people to want a weak, inactive, and frugal government which would require few taxes and for the most part leave them alone, and for them to believe that whatever government was necessary should be kept as close to home as possible. It was in these marginally commercial or agrarian areas that the fear of a remote central government was greatest, and that the proponents of democracy and the constitutional concept of states' rights found their firmest supporters.[8]

It does not follow from this that everyone who supported the philosophy of states' rights underlying the Articles of Confederation was necessarily an agrarian or a democrat. New Englanders and Southerners, who felt secure about being able to control the democratic impulses unleashed by the Revolution in their home states but who distrusted each other and who disliked each other's life styles, also supported the adoption of the Articles of Confederation rather than enter into a strong national government where they might be subject to each other's influence. Others undoubtedly favored local rule simply because it was where they had power and not because it was where the popular will could best be expressed. And still others, although fearful and critical of democracy, believed republicanism could only operate in a small and homogeneous area. But as the 1780s developed and the state governments tended to be susceptible to democratic and popular pressures, many people began to change their minds and rethink and even restructure the ideology of the Revolution.[9] To a very considerable extent it was the concern over the vulnerability of the state governments to popular control and to what was viewed as the vices of the people that was at the heart of the movement for the creation of a strong national government. No doubt the struggle over the adoption of the Constitution was a very complicated one, but once overriding political considerations and local and particularistic interests are accounted for, the most basic division appears to have been between cosmopolitan, commercial, and elite-minded Americans on the one hand, and provincial, agrarian, and democratic Americans on the other.[10]

By creating a national government with the authority to act directly upon individuals, by denying to the states many of the prerogatives that they formerly had, and by leaving open to the central government the possibility of claiming for itself many powers not explicitly assigned to it, the Constitution and Bill of Rights as finally ratified substantially increased the strength of the central government at the expense of the states. But the Constitution did not make the states clearly subservient to the federal government. It did not, for example, provide as James Madison and others wanted, for the central government to have a formal negative on all state laws.[11] In fact, the framers of the Constitution in Philadelphia in 1787 were fearful that if they went too far in reducing the power of the states the Constitution would not be ratified. Consequently, many of the provisions dealing with state-federal relations were ambiguous, and in the debate over ratification the Constitution's supporters went out of their way to emphasize the federal nature of the newly created government. Further, by failing to provide for an ultimate arbiter to interpret the Constitution, the new frame of government became open to the logical, although controversial, interpretation that this power rightly belonged to the states. Although most states' rights advocates in the late eighteenth century would have much preferred the kind of central government provided for in the Articles of Confederation, they could nonetheless continue to argue their position under the Constitution by using the Tenth Amendment to claim that the powers granted to the new government should be strictly interpreted.

The political discord that developed on the national level during the early 1790s did not correspond to the divisions that had taken place over the adoption of the United States Constitution. Although in opposing Alexander Hamilton's financial program, Thomas Jefferson and James Madison made some appeal to the need for a strict interpretation of the Constitution, they were not thinking in the agrarian and democratic terms of the Antifederalists. Only after John Adams led the country into an undeclared naval war with France, and Hamilton and his supporters, with the initial cooperation of Adams, passed the Alien and Sedition Acts and began to place the country on a war footing did Jefferson and Madison adopt an extreme states' rights position with the Kentucky and Virginia Resolutions.[12]

There were both similarities and differences between the way the Republicans used the states' rights argument in the Kentucky and Virginia Resolutions and the way the Antifederalists had used it. Since the Kentucky and Virginia Resolutions was above all else a political platform, a rallying call for support to overthrow the Federalists in the election of 1800, it was grounded in the same majoritarian sentiment that had made the Antifederalist persuasion attractive to so many advocates. But by formulating their states' rights position in terms of a legal procedure or "rightful remedy" by which the states could "interpose" or "nullify" an act of Congress, and by formulating the compact theory of the Constitution in such a way that it could be used (as it eventually was by a later generation) to argue the unqualified sovereignty of the states and their right to withdraw from the Union, Jefferson and Madison added new elements to the states' rights argument. For the proponents of the agrarian and majoritarian Antifederalist persuasion the concept of states' rights was really that part of a vague political philosophy concerned with the correct and safe distribution of power between the states and the federal government; and since the Antifederalists saw the proper kind of central government as having only explicitly defined and limited powers they had not been concerned with the problem of how to "correctly interpret" a federal constitution. Nor had the Antifederalists, for all their particularism, ever doubted the need, value, and permanency of some kind of central government and did not think in terms that even implied a right of secession. Most Antifederalists were in total agreement with the assertion in the Articles of Confederation "that the Union shall be perpetual."

Once in power, much to the chagrin of Antifederalist types and states' rights advocates, Jefferson and Madison during the period of their extended ascendancy, 1800–1817, did little to advance the cause of states' rights and much to weaken it. Jefferson, for example, refused to countenance any amendments to the United States Constitution that would formally weaken the federal government, and while he went along with the removal of a number of Federalist judges from office he did not lead an assault upon the authority of the national judiciary. On the other hand, Jefferson expanded the powers of the national government through the purchase of Louisiana and the adoption and enforcement of his controversial embargo policy. Madison was even more of a nationalist than his predecessor. In 1809 he called out troops to uphold the authority of the United States Supreme Court in *United States v. Peters* when the governor of Pennsylvania tried to use the state militia to resist the decision. In 1811, over even Jefferson's objections, he appointed Joseph Story, an extreme nationalist, to the High Court. And in 1816 he requested and signed into law the bill creating the Second Bank of the United States and called for an amendment to the United States Constitution to authorize a federal program of internal improvements.[13]

Despite this neither Jefferson nor Madison repudiated the states' rights position their party had adopted in 1798, and for many, probably even a majority of the Democratic-Republicans it remained the true and unfulfilled credo of the party. This is important because as the unsuccessful opponents of the Constitution the Antifederalists and their ideas were viewed as suspect and even seditious during the 1790s. On the other hand the Democratic-Republican victory in 1800 legitimized the principles of the Kentucky and Virginia Resolutions and allowed countless Americans, including Andrew Jackson and John C. Calhoun, who during the 1820s and 1830s were to call for a rebirth of the "principles of '98," to claim they were the true heirs of Jeffersonian principles.[14]

When the Federalists adopted the states' rights argument in the early nineteenth century it was for a purpose essentially antithetical to the one for which it had been used up to that time. For it was clear that the Federalists had more and more hopelessly become a minority party, and that they were using the states' rights argument in a deliberately obstructionist fashion. The Federalists, in opposing the Louisiana Purchase and Jefferson's embargo and the policies of the national government during the War of 1812, tried to use the demand for a narrow interpretation of the Constitution and the states' rights argument as a way to thwart rather than fulfill the idea of majority rule. Moreover, in the course of their opposition to Republican policies, Federalist spokesmen asserted not simply the right of the states to judge the validity of acts of Congress, but also frequently discussed and even espoused disunion. The Federalists after 1800 thus laid bare, in a way the Republicans had not, the disunionist tendencies that might, but also did not have to, be extrapolated from the states' rights argument. It matters not that most of these statements were blustering threats rather than actual plans or that a much more moderate point of view was adopted by the Hartford Convention. In the eyes of most Americans the Federalist party was forever to be considered the party of treason, and its blatant reversal from its nationalist position of the 1790s was viewed as an opportunistic act brought about by a need to protect its interests rather than from any commitment to political and constitutional principles.[15]

Following the end of the War of 1812 the country was swept by a spirit of intense nationalism, and while there were occasional attempts to make use of the states' rights argument to oppose it, they were not very effective. This postwar nationalism, tied as it was to a period of prosperity and sweeping economic growth, came to an abrupt end in 1819, however, when the country underwent its first national depression. The reaction was enormous, and there followed a decade of intense political strife and a tremendous resurgence of agrarian, democratic, and states' rights thought.

Because of the dramatic shift that took place in the thinking of many of its leading statesmen and because of the elaborate and definite procedure that John C. Calhoun provided for state action, what occurred in South Carolina has received so much attention from historians that it has distorted the real significance of the widespread reemergence of states' rights thought in the 1820s. The fact is its development in South Carolina during the 1820s simply was not typical of how the states' rights argument was being used in most other parts, north and south, of the country.

More pervasive and important for giving tone and direction to the 1820s was the opposition to a federal program of internal improvements and the reaction to the numerous nationalist decisions that the Supreme Court under John Marshall's leadership had been handing down since 1810. The main source of the hostility to the High Court is to be found in the reemergence, after 1819, of an extreme democratic and agrarian rhetoric which brought with it a deep hostility to the numerous market-oriented enterprises, particularly banks, corporations, creditors, and absentee landholders whose interests the Supreme Court had generally defended from attack by various states. Closely related to this was the growth, especially on the local level during the 1820s, of demands to make the state governments more immediately and directly responsible to the will of the people. This included demands for an increase in the number of elective officers, a further expansion of the suffrage, a more proportionate form of representation, ways of making judges more responsive to popular sentiment, and a general desire for the weakening of the national government's power. Of course, not all supporters of the states' rights doctrine in the 1820s were necessarily advocates of agrarianism or democracy. John C. Calhoun, as we shall see, did not support either concept, while neither John Taylor nor Spencer Roane of Virginia was terribly interested in democratic reform on the local level. But these were mainly exceptions, very significant exceptions to be sure, but still exceptions, for the main thrust of states' rights thought in the 1820s was in the agrarian and democratic direction that culminated in Andrew Jackson's election to the presidency in 1828.[16]

II

It was within this broader context of the resurgence of an agrarian and democratic kind of states' rights thought that South Carolina and Calhoun, concerned that the South was becoming a minority section and looking for a way to bring about tariff reduction and also indirectly to protect the institution of slavery from outside interference, took up the states' rights argument.

Throughout the colonial and early national periods, South Carolina had sustained substantial economic growth and prosperity. This had created an extremely wealthy and extravagant low country aristocracy whose fortunes were based first on the cultivation of rice and indigo, and then on cotton. Then the state was devastated by the Panic of 1819. The depression that followed was more severe than in almost any other state of the Union. Moreover, competition from the newer cotton producing areas along the Gulf Coast, blessed with more fertile lands that produced a higher crop-yield per acre, made recovery painfully slow. To make matters worse, in large areas of South Carolina slaves vastly outnumbered whites, and there existed both considerable fear of slave rebellion and a growing sensitivity to even the smallest criticism of the "peculiar institution."

Most South Carolinians blamed their difficulties on the high tariff legislation and other nationalist policies of the federal government. And they were extremely critical of the role Calhoun and his closest followers had played in bringing about the adoption of the Tariff of 1816 and their support for a national program of internal improvements even in the early 1820s. By the mid-twenties these states' rights advocates, led by William Smith and Thomas Cooper, were on the verge of capturing political control of South Carolina. To avoid political annihilation Calhoun and his friends retreated from the early nationalism. Reacting to their Tariff of Abominations passed in 1828, they adopted an even more extreme version of the states' rights doctrine than their rivals.

The famous doctrine of nullification, or state interpretation as Calhoun preferred to call it, was first promulgated as a state legislative report secretly drafted by Calhoun and entitled *The South Carolina Exposition and Protest*.

Building upon the premises of the Kentucky and Virginia Resolutions of 1798, Calhoun maintained that the Constitution was a compact among the states that had delegated only specifically defined powers to the national government and that the states had completely retained their own sovereignty. According to the nullifiers, should the federal government exceed its delegated powers by, for example, enacting a protective tariff, a state had the power to declare such an action unconstitutional and therefore null and void within its boundaries. Should this occur, the federal government had either to accept the act of nullification and refrain from enforcing the objectionable law or it could go the difficult route of trying to obtain the consent of two-thirds of the members of both houses of Congress and three-fourths of the states to amend the Constitution and specifically grant to the national government the powers in question. Only in this way, Calhoun believed, would it be possible to protect the rights of a minority from the tyranny of a numerical majority.[17]

It is always difficult to find the sources of ideas and to trace their transmission. Scholars, generally following Calhoun's lead, have stressed the connection that existed between the doctrine of nullification and the states' rights assertions of the Virginia and Kentucky Resolutions. That the nullifiers should have emphasized this connection is understandable: The Federalist party had been thoroughly discredited by its opposition to the War of 1812 while the Jeffersonian heritage, however ambiguous, was a necessary mantle with which any political cause had to be covered in the 1820s if it was to have any chance of success. Yet for their part most nullifiers never subscribed to the localist and anti-government Old Republican values at the heart of the "Spirit of 1798." Before their conversion to states' rights in the 1820s, the most important nullifier leaders had been New Republicans, that is, proponents of a strong and active national government and the American System with its emphasis on a protective tariff, the Second Bank of the United States, and a federal program of internal improvements; and when they shifted to nullification in the late 1820s what they advocated in place of the American System was a strong and active state government. Further, to trace the source of the nullifiers' ideas only to the Kentucky and Virginia Resolutions is to underestimate the very real relationship that existed between Calhoun and the Federalists before 1828. The great spokesman for nullification had always had close ties with the Federalists, both in his home state of South Carolina, where they had been an important political force in the 1790s, and in New England, dating back to the time he spent at Yale and the Litchfield Law School. Although Calhoun certainly never endorsed, and at times even openly criticized, Federalist actions during the War of 1812, he was also more sympathetic than most other Republicans to the difficulties the Federalists faced after the war. Finally, Calhoun drew considerable support from northern Federalists in his unsuccessful bid for the presidency in 1824, and it was through the Calhoun wing of the party that many Federalists joined Jackson's ranks in 1828.[18]

While the evidence directly linking Calhoun's ideas on nullification and secession to what many Federalists did and espoused during the War of 1812 may be only circumstantial, the similarities of the two positions were frequently noted by contemporaries. In South Carolina the Old Republicans—who came in large part from the small-farmer dominated upcountry area in the northwest part of the state, and who had originally and consistently been the proponents of states' rights during the early nationalist period—formed themselves into the "Union and State Rights Party" to oppose the nullification movement. They denied that nullification had anything to do with the older Republican tradition of states' rights, and they regularly retold the story of Calhoun's nationalist past and of his and his closest followers' sudden and opportunistic conversion to states' rights.[19] Similarly, in Virginia the ideas of the nullifiers were denounced by Thomas Ritchie, the influential editor of the Richmond *Enquirer,* himself a traditional states' rights advocate, who repeatedly compared what South Carolina was advocating to the disunionist tendencies which had earlier been associated with the Federalists. Replying to this criticism, Calhoun and his supporters continued to try to legitimize their position by tracing it back to the "principles of '98." But they were only partially successful in this. For the Kentucky and Virginia Resolutions had been so loosely conceived that they did not offer a firm or clear precedent. The discovery and publication in 1832 of Jefferson's original draft of the Kentucky Resolutions, revealing that he had actually used the term "nullification," worked in their favor, but many remained unconvinced.[20]

III

The publication of the *South Carolina Exposition and Protest* touched off a major debate among leading politicians and constitutional scholars between 1828 and 1833. During this time criticism of the doctrine of nullification came from two very different sources. From one side nationalists took issue with the most basic assumptions and conclusions of the nullifiers. Denying completely the compact theory of the origin of the federal Union, the nationalists argued that the United States Constitution had been created by the people and not the states, and that, therefore, the states were subordinate to the federal government. Also, in deciding constitutional questions it was the United States Supreme Court and not the states that was to be the final arbiter. Finally, according to this interpretation, secession was not a legal or constitutional right, for the Union as created by the United States Constitution was perpetual, and certainly not dissolvable by the actions of a single party to the original agreement. The leading spokesmen for this point of view included Joseph Story, William Duer, John Quincy Adams, Nathaniel Chipman, Nathan Dane, and it was this point of view that Daniel Webster articulated in his famous debate with Robert Y. Hayne of South Carolina.[21]

Traditional proponents of states' rights also were critical of nullification. Although they usually subscribed to some form of the compact theory of the Union, they denied South Carolina's claim that the states were completely sovereign entities. Traditional states' rights advocates generally believed instead in the concept of divided sovereignty. They argued that the people in creating the United States Constitution had given the federal government sovereignty in certain clearly defined areas, where its authority had to be recognized as supreme, while the powers not specifically delegated to the federal government belonged to the states. Most importantly, they were critical of the South Carolina doctrine on the grounds that it subverted the democratic assumptions that underlay the states' rights thought that had been associated with the Jeffersonian tradition. For example, Kentucky, long a center of hostility to the Second Bank of the United States and a vigorous critic of a number of the Supreme Court's nationalist decisions as well as a Jacksonian stronghold in the election of 1828, took issue in 1830 with the underlying assumption of the *Exposition and Protest* on the following grounds:

> The General Assembly of Kentucky cannot admit the right of a minority, either of the state or the people to set up their opinion not only in opposition, but to overrule that of the majority . . . the consequences of such a principle, if practically enforced, would be alarming in the extreme. Scarcely any important measure of the general government is ever adopted, to which one or more of the States are not opposed. If one State have a right to obstruct and defeat the execution of a law of Congress because it deems it unconstitutional, then every State has a similar right. When the dissatisfied State opposes to the Act of Congress its measures of obstruction, the alternative is presented, shall the act be enforced within the particular State, or be abandoned by Congress? If enforced there is a civil war; if abandoned, without being repealed, a virtual dissolution of the Union. As the successful exercise of the power of resisting an Act of Congress by one State, would naturally stimulate other States, disapproving other acts of that body, to similar resistance, the practical result would be, that Congress could adopt and enforce no measure whatever, to which any one of the twenty-four States might be opposed. . . .
>
> Nor can the state of South Carolina derive the smallest aid in sustaining its doctrine of resistance to the federal authority, from the manner in which the Constitution was formed; whether it was the work of the people of the United States collectively, or is to be considered as a compact between sovereign States, or between the people of the several States with each other, there can be, there ought to be, but one rule, which is, that the majority must govern.[22]

Strong support for this point of view came from the venerable James Madison who was himself a long-time student of the problem of how to protect the rights of a minority in a republic. The former President had carefully avoided taking sides on public issues since his retirement in 1817. But the nullifiers' attempt to legitimize their controversial doctrine by claiming it was a logical extension of the principles embodied in the Kentucky and Virginia Resolutions upset him. In a private letter he deliberately wrote for publication, Madison denied many of the assertions of the nullifiers and lashed out in particular at South Carolina's claim that if a state nullified an act of the federal government it could only be overruled by an amendment to the United States Constitution.

> Can more be necessary to demonstrate the inadmissibility of such a doctrine than that it puts in the power of the smallest fraction over ¼ of the U.S.—that is of 7 states out of 24—to give the law and even the Constitution to 17 states, each of

the 17 having as parties to the Constitution an equal right with each of the 7 to expound it & to insist on the exposition. That the 7 might, in particular instances be right and the 17 wrong, is more than possible. But to establish a positive and permanent rule giving such a power to such a minority over such a majority, would overturn the first principle of free Government and in practice necessarily overturn the Government itself.[23]

A full and clear exposition of these three positions—nullifier, nationalist, and traditional states' rights—on the nature of the federal Union took place early in 1830. The ostensible issue was Samuel Foote's resolution to restrict the sale of public land, but the debate soon focused on the issue of the origin and character of the Union and the Constitution. Best known for the exchange between Daniel Webster of Massachusetts and Robert Y. Hayne of South Carolina, advocates of the nationalist and nullifier positions, respectively, it also produced an additional though less well known but equally incisive speech by Edward Livingston of Louisiana.

Rejecting the nationalist view of the origin of the Union as simply a product of the combined will of the American people, Livingston then proceeded to attack also the concepts of nullification and state sovereignty. With great clarity, Livingston articulated the concept of divided sovereignty. The Constitution had been created by both the states and the people. It had been submitted to the former as sovereign units but had been adopted by the people, by means of special state ratifying conventions, in whom ultimate sovereignty resided. The result was a nation in which each state had surrendered to the nation certain specified rights, but retained those not expressly surrendered. The Union was therefore not simply a compact of the states, it was also a compact between the people of the different states that involved each state's giving up a certain portion of its sovereignty. "The Government," argued Livingston, "is partly popular, acting directly on the citizens of the several States; partly federative, depending, for its existence and action, on the existence and action of the several States."

According to Livingston, if a state believed a federal law was clearly unconstitutional it had a number of options open to it: it could go to the Supreme Court; it could remonstrate to Congress; it could address the other states declaring the act in its opinion to be unconstitutional and void—as had been done by Virginia and Kentucky in 1798—and the people of a state, at election time, could pressure their representatives to alter the law in question; or a state could propose amendments to the Constitution. But a single state could not nullify a law, nor did a state have a legal or constitutional right to unilaterally withdraw from the Union. Secession, Livingston argued, "can be justified only on the supposition that the Constitution has been broken, and the State absolved from its obligation; and that, whenever resorted to, it must be at the risk of all the penalties attached to an unsuccessful resistance to established authority."[24]

The debate over the origins and nature of the Union did not lend itself to a clear or easy resolution in either historical or logical terms. Given the purposeful ambiguity of many aspects of the Constitution it was virtually impossible to provide conclusive proof, one way or the other, of precisely what the framers were intending. In addition, the various theories about the Union were open to numerous permutations. For example, it was logically possible to accept nationalist claims about the nature of the Union and yet be an advocate of states' rights by using the Tenth Amendment to argue that the Constitution should be strictly interpreted. Moreover, people who accepted the compact theory could take different sides on whether secession was a legal or only a revolutionary right as well as argue over whether the powers granted to the federal government had been substantial enough to justify a federal program of internal improvements or a national bank. Similarly, many advocates of states' rights accepted the idea of secession as a constitutional right while rejecting the doctrine of nullification. Doubtless also many people were simply confused by the abstract and inconclusive nature of the debate.

Yet, as many people recognized, the debate also had a special urgency to it since, unlike Virginia or Kentucky in 1798, or the Massachusetts and Connecticut Federalists during the War of 1812, whose rhetoric far outdistanced their actions, South Carolina seemed likely, if it did not get its way on the issue of tariff reform, actually to implement nullification. And when it did, in the fall of 1832, it thereby created the most serious constitutional crisis to take place in the United States in the period between the adoption of the Constitution and the Civil War.

On one level the nullification crisis involved a confrontation between nationalists who believed in the concept of a perpetual Union and the nullifiers of South Carolina who, among other things, claimed that secession was a constitutional right. From this perspective, the nullification crisis was indeed a rehearsal for the South's eventual withdrawal from the Union in 1860–61. But this was not all that was involved, for in 1828 Andrew Jackson was elected the seventh President of the United States. He was neither a nationalist nor a nullifier, but a strong advocate of states' rights who was determined to preserve the Union at all costs. In one form or another these two beliefs influenced almost every important decision during his first administration. Further, as President, Jackson played a crucial role in the nullification crisis itself. In fact, it is not too much to say that the nullification crisis, viewed from the perspective of the President, reveals as much as any other issue of the period 1815–1850 about what was involved in that elusive but nonetheless quite real development known as Jacksonian Democracy.

2

Andrew Jackson, States' Rights, and Majority Rule

The election of Andrew Jackson in 1828 brought to the presidency one of the most ferocious and formidable men ever to occupy the White House. The campaign had been a particularly scurrilous and bitter one, and much of it centered on Jackson's controversial personality. Moreover, before assuming the presidency Jackson did not take a clear stand on a number of the most important issues of the day: the need for a national program of internal improvements, the tariff, the Bank, and the powers of the federal judiciary. Because of this, it has been argued that personalities rather than issues were the key ingredients of the election of 1828, and that Jackson's victory is to be explained mainly in terms of his personal charisma and his party's superior organization. Indeed, this has been stressed almost to the total exclusion of more substantive considerations.[1]

I

Actually, issues and ideological considerations played a real and important part in the election of 1828. For Jackson's opponent, John Quincy Adams, had guided his whole administration and run for reelection on what was, in effect, a platform of the American System, a loose interpretation of the Constitution and the need for a strong and active national government. Adams's constitutional views were a major issue in the election of 1828, and opposition to them explains much of the support that Jackson received. In addition to Calhoun and the nullifiers of South Carolina, Adams also alienated the Old Republicans and their political sympathizers. In 1828 this group was led by William H. Crawford in Georgia, Thomas Ritchie in Virginia, and Martin Van Buren in New York. They had opposed Jackson in 1824, but Adams so alienated them by his support of the Indians in Georgia, the nationalist decisions of the Supreme Court, and his advocacy of a federal program of internal improvements without the need of a constitutional amendment, that they could be counted among Jackson's staunchest supporters in 1828. Writing in 1827, Ritchie believed "the coming election will be the crisis of our Constitution. Principles will then be fixed which will cast their shadows, or their lights, upon years to come."[2]

In addition, Jackson received vigorous support from that group to be found mainly in the Old West, where politics had been shaped by the relief wars that took place on the state level following the Panic of 1819, and where, along with a desire to return the country to the traditional states' rights values that originally brought Jefferson to power—the "Spirit of '98" as many people called it—they also wished to see the federal government made more directly responsive to the people's wishes. Among this group's most important members were Thomas Hart Benton of Missouri, James K. Polk of Tennessee, and Amos Kendall and Francis Preston Blair of Kentucky. Blair, a product of the relief struggle in Kentucky, clearly expressed the feelings of this group when he broke with Henry Clay in 1827 to support Jackson, justifying his disaffection on the grounds: "I never deserted your banner until the questions on which you and I so frequently differed in private discussion—(state rights, the Bank, the power of the Judiciary, etc.)—became the criterion to distinguish the parties, and had actually renewed, in their practical effects, the great division which marked the era of 1798."[3]

Yet Jackson had not taken a firm stand on the issues in 1828. He had shrewdly avoided this in order to put together a winning coalition. This caused Daniel Webster to observe, "His friends have no common principle, they are held together by no common tie."[4] Morever, once Jackson was President, his inexperience with political power, his need to broker between the different and competing wings of his party, the emergence of unforeseen developments like the Eaton affair, and the split with Calhoun as well as the exigencies under which the key issues of his first administration arose, all made him cautious about fully enunciating his views.

Nonetheless, from the beginning, there were some like Kendall, soon to become the President's most important informal adviser, who shrewdly recognized Jackson to be both determined and capable of controlling the course of his administration. Kendall also understood that the Old Hero did indeed have some clear and strong beliefs. Writing to a close associate in Kentucky, he warned about becoming too involved in the power struggle that was developing between the followers of Calhoun and Van Buren over the succession and urged instead that "the ground for us to rally upon is, the support of Jackson's administration, opposition to Clay, state rights and amendments to the Constitution."[5] Kendall was right, for, while it took Jackson almost his entire first administration to formulate his program, its basic direction was clear from the start. Jackson was determined to dismantle the American System and move the country in what he believed was a more democratic direction, and underlying these beliefs was his commitment to states' rights.

Jackson's inauguration set the egalitarian tone of his administration. According to one experienced if biased observer, "thousands and thousands of people, without distinction of rank, collected in an immense mass round the Capitol" to watch him become President. After delivering his inaugural address and taking the oath of office, Jackson bowed "to the people—Yes to the people in all their majesty." Up until now everyone had been orderly and quiet, but the town had been filling up for days with an immense crowd "for it was the peoples President and all would see him." When the ceremonies were over and Jackson tried to make his way up Pennsylvania Avenue to the White House, he was stopped. "The living mass was impenetrable." He was able to continue only after mounting his horse to be followed by a cortège made up of "country men, farmers, gentlemen, mounted and dismounted, boys, women and children, black and white. Carriages, wagons and carts all pursuing him. . . ." The President opened the White House reception to these people and the "*Majesty of the People*" became "a rabble, a mob . . . The President, having been *literally* nearly pressed to death and almost suffocated and torn to pieces by the people in their eagerness to shake hands with Old Hickory, had retreated through the backway and had escaped to his lodgings at Gadsby's," a private inn in town. What remained was cut glass and broken China to the amount of thousands of dollars, ladies who fainted, men with bloody noses "and such a scene of confusion took place as is impossible to describe—those who got in could not get out by the door again, but had to scramble out of windows."[6]

The scene shocked official Washington. "The reign of king 'Mob' seemed triumphant," noted Justice Joseph Story. Yet the crowd seemed delighted about what had happened, observed a bewildered Daniel Webster, who "never saw anything like it before. Persons have come five hundred miles to see General Jackson, and they really seem to think the country is rescued from some dreadful danger."[7]

Jackson, however, was not upset by what occurred. He viewed himself as a democratic tribune representing the people. And what Jackson meant by the people was "the real people," those yeoman farmers, laborers, mechanics, and planters who made up the vast majority of honest Americans, who worked for a living with their hands to produce tangible products, who were self-reliant, who believed in God, and who practiced economy and self-denial. "Always," he wrote shortly after becoming President, "keep in view that economy and industry will overcome any and everything and bring you triumphant over your misfortunes." Opposed to "the real people" as Jackson saw it was a small minority of speculators, financiers, promoters, and various other middle men who did not work with their hands and who did not contribute to society in the way that the "real producers" did. Jackson viewed this group, which reaped profits from the labors of others, as immoral, corrupt, extravagant, and

un-republican. He believed this "Moneyed Aristocracy dangerous to the liberties of the Country." It followed inexorably from this, of course, that his
election in 1828 was "a victory indeed of the virtue of the people over
corruption."[8]

Jackson's deeply moralistic view of society had been shaped by his own
experiences as a speculator during the 1790s, which ended in bankruptcy, and
by the impact of the Panic of 1819. This view influenced his thoughts on
politics. The purpose of government, he believed, was to protect honest and
hard working people from being exploited by the "Monied Aristocracy." "I
did believe, and ever will believe," he wrote while governor of Florida in 1821,
"that just laws can make no distinction of privilege between the rich and poor;
and that when men of high standing attempt to trample upon the rights of the
weak, they are the fittest objects for example and punishment. In general, the
great can protect themselves; but the poor and humble require the arm and
shield of the law."[9]

Yet if government was necessary it was also dangerous. It could easily come
under the control of the greedy and the aggressive and be used to obtain special
privileges and monopolies. Therefore, it was best that government be limited
to carefully specified powers. Early in his first administration, Jackson observed: "Experience proves that in proportion as agents to execute the will of
the people are multiplied there is danger of their wishes being frustrated."[10]

Jackson stressed the need to watch the government closely. "All history
tells us," he warned shortly before leaving the presidency, "that a free people
should be watchful of delegated power, and should never acquiesce in a practice that will diminish their control over it."[11] Jackson's faith in the sagacity
and ability of the people to do this was virtually unqualified. "The people," he
wrote at one point, "are honest and firm, and if we do not receive their
ultimate approbation it will be because we do not deserve it."[12] Thomas Hart
Benton recalls that when the political going got tough, Jackson would exclaim:
"We shall whip them yet. The people will take it up after a while."[13]

Jackson also disliked politicians. He viewed them as intriguers, more interested in feathering their own nests than in looking out for the interest of the
public. Jackson had dabbled in politics when he first arrived in Tennessee,
although only for a short while. He did not find it very interesting and preferred instead to pursue his military career and develop his business interests.
Nor was he enthusiastic about being named to the United States Senate in 1823
where he perfunctorily performed his duties. He only became really active in
politics following the election of 1824 when the House of Representatives
chose John Quincy Adams for President, despite the fact that Jackson had
received a plurality of both the popular and electoral vote. When Adams
appointed Henry Clay, the Speaker of the House of Representatives, Secretary
of State, Jackson and his followers shouted "Bargain and Corruption" and
began their four-year campaign to elect Jackson to the White House and
vindicate the will of the people.

One of the first things Jackson did when he became President was to
recommend an amendment to the Constitution to eliminate the House's role in

presidential elections in which no candidate received a majority of the electoral vote, since it is "obvious the will of the people may not be always ascertained, or, if ascertained, may not be regarded . . . Honors and offices are at the disposal of the successful candidate. Repeated ballotings may make it apparent that a single individual holds the cast in his hand. May he not be tempted to name his reward?" If an amendment were not possible then Jackson believed "it is worthy of consideration whether a provision disqualifying for office the Representatives in Congress on whom such an election may have devolved would not be proper." Jackson also favored the election of the President and Vice President to a single term of four or six years and self-government for the District of Columbia.[14]

Jackson's faith in the people, his fear of governmental power, and his hostility to the old political establishment manifested themselves with unusual clarity in his attitude and policies toward incumbent officeholders. His accession to the presidency in 1829 was only the second time under the United States Constitution that the reins of power had been transferred from one political party to another. The first was when Jefferson became President in 1801, and although he removed a number of Federalist officeholders, he was in principle opposed to wholesale removals for party purposes. Madison continued this policy, as did Monroe and Adams. Of course, it was easy for them since they all were generally committed to each other's policies. Jackson, on the other hand, indicated in his inaugural address, that his election "inscribes on the list of Executive duties, in characters too legible to be overlooked, the task of *reform,* which will require particularly the correction of those abuses that have brought the patronage of the Federal government into conflict with the freedom of elections . . . and have placed or continued power in unfaithful or incompetent hands."[15]

Jackson frankly advocated a policy of "rotation in office," whereby each incoming President would make new appointments to the offices under his control. "There are, perhaps, few men," he noted in expressing his fear of government power and its corrupting influence, "who can for any great length of time enjoy office and power without being more or less under the influence of feelings unfavorable to the faithful discharge of their public duties." He believed the holding of offices for long periods of time was undemocratic, for under it: "Office is considered a species of property, and government rather as a means of promoting individual interest than as an instrument created solely for the service of the people. Corruption in some and in others a perversion of correct feelings and principles divert government from its legitimate ends and make it an engine for the support of the few at the expense of the many."[16] Shortly before his election, Jackson made explicit the relationship of this problem to the issue of states' rights:

> The state governments hold in check the federal, and must ever hold it in check, and the virtue of the people supported by the sovereign states, must prevent consolidation, and will put down that corruption engendered by executive patronage, wielded, as it has been lately, by executive organs to perpetuate their own power;

the result of the present struggle between the virtue of the people and executive patronage will test the stability of our government, and I for one do not despair of the Republic.[17]

As Jackson conceived of the policy of "rotation in office" it was a democratic reform designed to make the government more responsive to the will of the people. He believed that in a republic any honest citizen should be able to perform the duties of office as well as any other. If it reduced efficiency somewhat it did not matter, for Jackson was determined "to fill the various offices at the disposal of the Executive with individuals uniting as far as possible the qualifications of the head and heart, always recollecting that in a free government the demand for moral qualities should be made superior to that of talents."[18]

Of course, "rotation in office" in theory was one thing; in practice it was something else. Although Jackson did not justify the idea in terms of partisan politics, some of his supporters did. Jackson's theory of rotation did, in fact, help spawn what was later to be called the "spoils system." Yet Jackson does not deserve to be treated especially harshly on this point. In retrospect, it seems clear that his rhetoric was more extreme than his policy. The removals he actually made were not nearly so great in number as his opponents claimed; they only came to about 20 percent of the officeholders under his authority and many of these removals were for dereliction of duty and not for political reasons. Also, the perversions of the spoils system—the buying of offices, the forced political activity of officeholders, and the collection of party assessments from them, as well as the loss of prestige that the federal civil service suffered—did not really begin until Jackson left office.

Still, Jackson's espousal of a policy of rotation sharply altered the style and tone of politics, and it was denounced during his administration by his opponents and even by some of his more conservative supporters. Many people expressed uneasiness over the unjustness of indiscriminate removals and the replacement of experienced civil servants with party stalwarts. Jackson's opponents vigorously denounced the President's removal power on the grounds that it dangerously increased executive authority, and they argued that it was neither a specifically delegated power nor an inherent part of the President's office. Suspicious of Jackson's military background, they were fearful that, like Caesar, he would continually arrogate power until he put an end to the republic.[19]

One immediate consequence of Jackson's policy of "rotation in office" was that the President was never on good terms with the political establishment in Washington. The two most important members of the Supreme Court, Marshall and Story, were hostile to him, and from the beginning he did not get along with Congress. Nominally, the Democrats held a majority in all of the Congresses that met during Jackson's first term as President, but Jackson never had control. Frightened by Jackson's enormous popularity and his military background, as well as the uncertainties implicit in his patronage policy, which was viewed as an extreme commitment to political democracy, Congress refused to implement many of his recommendations, rejected a number of his appointments, and passed several important acts further implementing the American System. Determined to get his way, Jackson used the veto power more frequently than all of his predecessors combined, and therefore it is to these veto messages, and his attitude toward some key decisions by the Supreme Court that one must look to discover the political philosophy underlying Jackson's commitment to states' rights.

II

Federal aid to internal improvements was the issue on which Jackson made the most frequent use of the presidential veto power. The question was a complex and vexing one, for Jackson did not oppose internal improvements per se. He appreciated the military and commercial value of a system of roads and canals linking the country together. As senator from Tennessee during the middle 1820s he had voted in favor of government support for a number of projects. But, as President, and in spite of his continued expression to be "sincerely friendly to the improvement of our country by means of roads and canals," he moved to circumscribe sharply the federal government's power in this area.[20]

The reasons for Jackson's opposition to a federal program of internal improvements were primarily constitutional, but also involved policy, and political and moral considerations. He believed that much of the money the federal government had already spent and that many of the proposals for future expenditures involved local rather than national projects. As Jackson saw it, these projects infringed upon the rights of the states and boded ill for the future of republican government.

> That this was intended to be a government of limited and specific, and not general powers must be admitted by all, and it is our duty to preserve for it the character intended by its framers. If experience points out the necessity for an enlargement of these powers, let us apply for it to those whose benefit it is to be exercised, and not undermine the whole system by a resort to constructions. . . . The great mass of legislation relating to our internal affairs was intended to be left where the Federal Convention found it—in the state governments. Nothing is clearer, in my view, than that we are chiefly indebted for the success of the Constitution under which we are now acting to the watchful and auxiliary operation of the state authorities. This is not the reflection of a day, but belongs to the most deeply rooted convictions of my mind. I can not, therefore, too strongly or too earnestly, for my own sense of its importance, warn you against all encroachments upon the legitimate share of state sovereignty. Sustained by its healthful and invigorating influence the federal system can never fail.[21]

Closely related to Jackson's concern about federal aid for local improvements was his opposition to the use of public funds to buy stock in privately controlled improvement companies, whose object it was to return a profit. During John Quincy Adams's administration, the federal government bought stock in several companies: the Chesapeake and Delaware Canal Company

(1825), the Louisville and Portland Canal Company (1826), the Dismal Swamp Canal Company (1826), and the Chesapeake and Ohio Canal Company (1828). As senator, Jackson had voted for the purchase of stock in the Chesapeake and Delaware Canal Company. As President, however, he opposed the continuation of this policy, and his reasoning on the matter reveals how tightly his general political philosophy was intertwined with the concept of states' rights:

> Positive experience and a more thorough consideration of the subject have convinced me of the impropriety as well as inexpediency of such investments. All improvements effected by the funds of the nation for general use should be open to the enjoyment of all our fellow-citizens, exempt from the payment of tolls or any imposition of that character. The practice of thus mingling the concerns of the Government with those of the states or of individuals is inconsistent with the object of its institution and highly impolitic. The successful operation of the federal system can only be preserved by confining it to the few and simple, but yet important, objects for which it was designed.
>
> A different practice, if allowed to progress, would ultimately change the character of this Government by consolidating into one the General and State Governments, which were intended to be kept forever distinct. I can not perceive how bills authorizing such subscriptions can be otherwise regarded than as bills for revenue, and consequently subject to the rule in that respect prescribed by the constitution. If the interest of the Government in private companies is subordinate to that of individuals, the management and control of a portion of the public funds is delegated to an authority unknown to the Constitution and beyond the supervision of our constituents; if superior, its officers and agents will be constantly exposed to imputations of favoritism and oppression. Direct prejudice to the public interest or an alienation of the affections and respect of portions of the people may, therefore, in addition to the general discredit resulting to the Government from embarking with its constituents in pecuniary stipulations be looked for as the probable fruit of such associations. It is no answer to the objection to say that the extent of consequences like these cannot be great from a limited and small number of investments, because experience in other matters teaches us—and we are not at liberty to disregard its admonition—that unless an entire stop be put to them it will soon be impossible to prevent their accumulation until they are spread over the whole country and made to embrace many of the private and appropriate concerns of individuals.
>
> The power which the General Government must acquire within the several states by becoming the principal stockholder in corporations, controlling every canal and each 60 to 100 miles of every important road, and giving a proportionate vote in all their elections, is almost inconceivable and in my view dangerous to the liberties of the people."[22]

Jackson believed that a federal program of internal improvements would have adverse political and moral implications. "It promotes a mischievous and corrupting influence upon elections by holding out to the people the fallacious hope that the success of a certain candidate will make navigable their neighboring creek or river, bring commerce to their doors, and increase the value of their property. It thus favors combinations to squander the treasury of the country upon a multitude of local objects, as fatal to just legislation as to the purity of public men." Moreover, log-rolling in Congress would lead to hasty appropriations, undermine the establishment of any kind of systematic plan of action, and encourage the wasteful spending of public funds. "In the best view of these appropriations," Jackson observed, "the abuses to which they lead far exceed the good which they are capable of promoting. They may be resorted to as artful expedients to shift upon the Government the losses of unsuccessful private speculation, and thus, by ministering the personal ambition and self-aggrandizement, tend to sap the foundations of public virtue and taint the administration of government with a demoralizing influence."[23]

Recognizing the value of internal improvements, yet hoping to avoid the difficulties involved in having the national government control the program, Jackson urged that following the retirement of the public debt future surpluses of federal funds be distributed to the states, according to their ratio of representation in Congress, so that the states could spend it on improvements if they so desired. Not only would this prevent congressional log-rolling and corruption, it also would effectively decentralize an enormous power and prevent its abuse.

Economics also played an important role in determining the President's attitude toward a federal program of internal improvements. No other item during Jackson's first administration had a higher priority than the paying off of the national debt, "the unnecessary duration of which is incompatible with real independence and because it will counteract that tendency to public and private profligacy which a profuse expenditure of money by the Government is but apt to engender."[24] In fact, one of the first things Jackson did upon assuming office was to have Secretary of the Treasury Samuel Ingham draw up a schedule of how and when it would be paid off. More was involved than merely wishful thinking on Jackson's part. Considerable progress had been made since the end of the War of 1812 in paying off the national debt and Jackson expected that, if the government followed a policy of retrenchment, reform, and economy, the surplus revenue from the customs receipts and the sale of public lands would allow the government to be out of debt by March of 1833. Further, he was convinced that what the people wanted could best be achieved by a strict interpretation of the federal government's powers. "The Nation expects economy in the disbursement of the public monies," he observed, "and they have a right to expect, nay to *require* their executive officers to execute the law as they find it written and not as they believe it ought to be written." This objective controlled Jackson's attitude on every issue that involved expenditure or receipt of income on the part of the federal government. Consequently, Jackson believed that until the public debt was extinguished it would be inexpedient for the federal government to spend money on public projects, even those for which it had constitutional authority.[25] "Both Governments are the Governments of the people," Jackson declared, "improvements must be made with the money of the people, and if the money can be collected and applied by those more simple and economic political machines, the state governments, it will unquestionably be safer and better for the people than to add to the splendor, the patronage, and the power of the General Government."[26]

In his first annual message to Congress, Jackson urged the passage of an amendment to the Constitution authorizing the adoption of a policy of distribution. If it should be rejected, indicating the wish of the people that the federal government should make appropriations for internal improvements, then it was absolutely necessary that an amendment to the Constitution be adopted "delegating the necessary power and defining and restricting its exercise with reference to the sovereignty of the states. . . ."[27]

What Jackson asked from Congress and what he got were two different things. The question of federal aid to internal improvements was a major question when Congress met during the winter and spring of 1829–30. Congress discussed the building of a national road from Buffalo to New Orleans by way of Washington, but failed to act because no agreement could be obtained on the particular route the road should take. What Congress did pass by a close vote in late April, however, was a bill authorizing the federal government to support the building of a road from Maysville to Lexington in Kentucky. As the President had just aired his views on the federal government's role in internal improvements in his annual address the previous December and the Maysville Road bill, as it was known, was completely within the state of Kentucky, Jackson viewed the measure as a direct challenge perpetrated by Henry Clay and his followers on behalf of the American System. If Jackson allowed the bill to pass it would establish an important precedent for federal aid to local improvements. On the other hand, the measure had the strong support of many of the Old Hero's firmest supporters in the West, including Thomas Hart Benton and Richard M. Johnson of Kentucky; in fact, the latter personally appealed to the President to sign the bill, warning that failure to do so would cost him considerable support in that section of the country. Forced to choose between constitutional and political considerations, Jackson opted for the former. In the first of his great veto messages he rejected the bill on the grounds that he would not allow federal money to be spent on local projects and reiterated his general views on the problems involved in a national program of internal improvements. Throughout the controversy that followed, and during Congress's unsuccessful attempt to override his veto, Jackson consistently maintained that "the opposition . . . is wasting in the common sense of the people. Little sectional interests feel a disappointment, whilst the great body of the people hail the act, as a preservative of the Constitution and the Union." And a short time later he noted, "the veto has become what my enemies neither wished or expected, very popular, I have no doubt but it will be sustained by a large majority of the people."[28]

Other vetoes followed. Only four days after the Maysville Road veto, Jackson rejected, for the same reasons, an act pledging government support for the Washington Turnpike and Road Company. At the end of the session Congress passed a measure for the purchase of additional stock in the Louisville and Portland Canal Company, which Jackson pocket-vetoed because he opposed "instituting a partnership between the Government and private companies."[29]

At that same session Congress also passed a bill entitled "an act for making appropriations for building light-houses, light-boats, beacons and monuments, placing buoys, and for improving harbors and directing surveys." Jackson recognized that the policy and constitutional considerations raised by this bill were of a different order from those raised by the building of roads and canals. "The practice of defraying out of the Treasury of the United States," he noted, "the expenses incurred by the establishment and support of light houses, beacons, buoys and public piers within the bays, inlets, harbors and ports of the United States, to render the navigation thereof safe and easy, is coeval with the adoption of the Constitution and has been continued without interruption or dispute."[30] Every one of his predecessors from George Washington through John Quincy Adams had signed measures of this sort into law. Jackson understood both the value and constitutionality of this kind of spending by the federal government:

> It must not be forgotten that in relation to our foreign commerce the burden and benefit of protecting and accommodating it necessarily go together, and must do so as long as the public revenue is drawn from the people through the custom-house. It is indispensable that whatever gives faculty and security to navigation cheapens imports, and all who consume them are alike interested in whatever produces this effect. If they consume, they ought, as they now do, to pay; otherwise they do not pay. The consumer in the most inland state derives the same advantage from every necessary and prudent expenditure for the faculty and security of our foreign commerce and navigation that he does who resides in a maritime state.[31]

What concerned Jackson was "that these expenses have at times been extravagant and disproportionate." Local pressure and log-rolling had developed to the point where too many lighthouses had been built so "that the security of navigation has in some instances been diminished by the multiplication of light houses and consequent change of lights upon the coast." The result was not only a lack of economy but a dangerous increase in the powers of the national government. Further, Jackson believed that much of the money that had already been spent on making waterways navigable and for the surveys provided for in the present bill related to "improving the navigation of rivers running from navigable streams into a county or neighborhood, or even state. These cannot be considered national. Nothing can be so considered, but those great leading and navigable streams from the ocean, and passing through two or more states, and an obstruction that prevents commerce from passing thro' other states, which when removed will give an uninterrupted passage to those other states, can be viewed as coming within the constitutional powers of congress. If this boundary is once passed then every creek, or small river, emptying into a navigable stream . . . may claim to be surveyed and improved at the national expense. . . ." Jackson pocket-vetoed this bill, and he voted a similar measure for the improvement of harbors and rivers in December 1832 for the same reasons.[32]

But in justifying both of these actions, Jackson clearly indicated that he would sign future measures for the building of lighthouses and for harbor and river improvements if their necessity and national scope were clear. This differed from his position on building roads and canals with federal funds when he had strongly indicated his preference for seeing these projects, even though they were required and truly national in purpose, taken over by the state governments. This distinction is an important one, for it helps explain why so much federal money was spent on internal improvements during Jackson's two administrations, despite his belief in states' rights.

In fact, the federal government spent more money on internal improvements during Jackson's two administrations than during all the previous administrations combined. How is this to be explained? Some historians have interpreted this to suggest the Old Hero's commitment to states' rights was more rhetorical than real, that he vetoed the Maysville Road bill not because the project was confined to a single state, but because it ran through Henry Clay's home town of Lexington, and that he signed numerous bills into law providing federal aid to local projects when political considerations warranted it.[33]

Actually, as we have seen, Jackson was not opposed to all forms of internal improvements but only to those of a local nature, and to those that involved the federal government's buying stock in private corporations. He also believed that canals and roads could best be built by the states, but that federal aid for harbor and river improvements, if truly national in scope, was permissible under the right circumstances. If one examines the specific appropriations made by the federal government during Jackson's two terms of office, his internal improvements policy appears to have been both effective and fairly consistent.[34]

More than ten million dollars were spent by the federal government on internal improvements between 1829 and 1837. A major portion of the money appropriated went for the building of roads, but the money was spent mainly in the territories of Michigan, Wisconsin, Arkansas, Florida, and in the District of Columbia, areas for which the federal government had exclusive jurisdiction. Jackson made this explicit when he approved an act allocating $8,000 for the building of a road from Detroit to Chicago, warning that the money was not to be spent beyond the limits of the territory of Michigan; Illinois already being a state at the time.[35] There were two exceptions to Jackson's policy of denying the use of federal funds to build roads within states. The first was a small appropriation for the building of post and military roads in Maine, Alabama, and Georgia, something the federal government had the constitutional authority to do. The other, a more substantial series of expenditures for the further building of the Cumberland or National Road. Doubtless, Jackson felt it necessary to support these latter measures because of the federal government's long standing commitment to its extension into Ohio, Indiana, and Illinois. But he had reservations about the whole project for he successfully worked to have the completed portions of the road turned over to the states that contained them, thereby reducing the federal government's authority as well as saving it from the burden of future maintenance expenses. In fact, much of the outlay the federal government made on the National Road during Jackson's presidency was for repairs and the building of toll gates to meet the demands of Maryland and Pennsylvania before they would accept control of the road.[36]

The federal government spent substantially less on canals during Jackson's eight years as President than during John Quincy Adams's single term in office. And the money was spent only on projects clearly national in character. Moreover, subscriptions of federal money to the stock of private companies were completely eliminated.

The largest and most frequent expenditure of the federal government on internal improvements during the Jackson years was on lighthouses and river and harbor improvements. But these were areas in which Jackson believed federal action to be justifiable, although even here he was opposed to projects that he considered exclusively local and he did veto some measures on these grounds. Nonetheless, Jackson's critics frequently charged that many of the measures he signed into law contained local projects. There is probably some truth to these charges. In part this was because on the question of lighthouse and river and harbor improvements no clear guidelines existed to determine what were national as opposed to local projects. In part, also, this was because much of the legislation in these areas took the form of omnibus bills where questionable projects were sometimes tacked on for political reasons. Even some of Jackson's severest critics recognized that he, as well as his predecessor John Quincy Adams, could not be held "responsible for all the details of measures presented to them; and it by no means follows, because they signed bills containing objectionable provisions, that they therefore approved of every item in such bills."[37]

Finally, it should be kept in mind that Jackson's two terms in office, and especially the years 1834–1837 when prices rose over 50 percent, occurred during a period of sharp inflation, and this, to a certain extent, also explains the bloated figures of federal spending on internal improvements.[38]

The overall effect of Jackson's policy is to be seen in the fact that most of the expenses for the internal improvements mania of the 1830s were picked up by state and local governments and by private investors, and not by the federal government. It would be too much to argue that Jackson's policy on internal improvements was absolutely consistent. The issue was simply too vague and complex and too political for that to be possible. But it was a carefully thought out and reasonable response to a very complicated issue that reveals fully his deep belief in states' rights.

III

Jackson's belief in states' rights permeated his Indian policy. Moreover, this issue, as it developed, raised, once again, the difficult and still unresolved question of the relative powers of the states and of the United States Supreme Court to be the final arbiter in constitutional questions.

The main issue inherited by Jackson from John Quincy Adams's administration was the Indian claim to sovereign control of various territories then in their possession. This claim, most vigorously put forth by the Cherokee and Creek nations, affected large sections of northwestern Georgia, eastern Alabama, and the southern part of the boundary between Tennessee and North Carolina. If these tribes succeeded in upholding their claims, a similar position would undoubtedly be espoused by the Chickasaw and Choctaw tribes, who occupied lands covering a substantial portion of Mississippi, and by the Seminole, who controlled most of central Florida. The bases for the claims were numerous treaties between the United States and the Cherokee recognizing them "as a nation, capable of making peace and war, of owning the lands within its boundaries, and governing and punishing its own citizens by its own laws."[39] The states, on the other hand, denied that the Indian tribes were sovereign nations and argued instead that they were "dependent tenants" and therefore subject to state law. Desirous of gaining control of Indian lands in order to open them up to settlement by whites, laws were passed extending state jurisdiction over the Indians. Georgia and Alabama took the lead, but the other states watched closely and supported their actions. The situation in Georgia had already reached crisis proportions before Jackson's election. Georgia based its actions on an 1802 agreement whereby the state relinquished western land claims (to the area that became Alabama and Mississippi) in return for a promise from the federal government to extinguish all remaining Indian titles as soon as possible. This, of course, was in direct conflict with the earlier position the federal government had taken in its treaties with the Indians.[40]

Jackson sided with the states. Underlying his decision was a strong belief that it was impossible for Indians to live successfully near whites. Attempts to civilize the Indians had failed, and in Jackson's eyes the Indians remained savages and impeded the advance of civilization. Even more important, Jackson believed it was impossible to protect the Indians from white encroachment on the lands they already inhabited. He observed: "if orders were issued tomorrow one regiment of militia could not be got to march to save them from destruction."[41] Jackson's advice to the Indians, delivered by his Secretary of War and close friend John Eaton shortly after his inauguration, was to give up, voluntarily, claims to all land east of the Mississippi and be relocated at government expense to areas west of the Mississippi, where they could be effectively protected by the federal government, or if they were unwilling to do this then they would have to take their chances under state law.[42]

Jackson rejected completely the Indian claims to sovereignty. To deny to the states control over territory within their own boundaries was simply out of the question. He stated his position clearly in his first annual address to Congress in December 1829:

> Under these circumstances the question presented was whether the General
> Government had a right to sustain those people (the Indians) in their pretensions.
> The Constitution declares that "no state shall be formed or erected within the

jurisdiction of any other State" without the consent of its legislature. If the general government is not permitted to tolerate the erection of a confederate state within the territory of one of the members of this Union against her consent, much less could it allow a foreign and independent government to establish itself there. Georgia became a member of the confederacy which eventuated in our Federal Union as a sovereign state, always asserting her claim to certain limits, which having been originally defined in her colonial charter, and subsequently recognized in the treaty of peace, she has ever since continued to enjoy, except as they have been circumscribed by her own voluntary transfer of a portion of her territory to the United States in the article of cession of 1802. Alabama was admitted to the Union on the same footing with the original states, with boundaries which were prescribed by Congress. There is no constitutional convention or legal provision which allows less power over the Indians within their borders than is possessed by Maine or New York. Would the people of Maine permit the Penobscot tribe to erect an independent government within their State? And unless they did would it not be the duty of the General Government to support them in resisting such a measure? Would the people of New York permit each remnant of the six nations within her borders to declare itself an independent people under the protection of the United States? Could the Indians establish a separate republic in each of their reservations in Ohio? And if they were so disposed would it be the duty of this Government to protect them in the attempt? If the principle involved in the obvious answer to these questions be abandoned, it will follow that the objects of this government are reversed, and that it has become a part of its duty to aid in destroying the States which it was established to protect.[43]

If the Indians decided to remain they would have to submit to state laws. The laws, Jackson observed, would no doubt protect the Indians "in the enjoyment of those possessions which they have improved by their industry. But it seems to me visionary to suppose that in the state of things claims can be allowed on tracts of country on which they have neither dwelt nor made improvements, merely because they have seen them from the mountains or passed them in the chase."[44] Indeed, should state laws turn out to be unduly harsh there was little the federal government would be able to do. "For the justice of the laws passed by the States within the scope of their reserved powers," the President declared, "they are not responsible to the Government. As individuals we may entertain and express our opinions of their acts, but as a Government we have as little right to control them as we have to prescribe laws for other nations."[45]

This warning was clearly meant to intimidate the Indians into relinquishing their land holdings in the existing states and to accept the inevitability of relocation. To facilitate this change, Jackson urged Congress to pass a law "setting apart an ample district west of the Mississippi, and without the limits of any state or Territory now formed, to be guaranteed to the Indian tribes as long as they shall occupy it, each tribe having a distinct control over the portion designated for its use."[46] After a bitter debate and a close vote, Congress complied in the spring of 1830. The law not only provided for an exchange of land, but authorized remuneration for improvements on the property being relinquished, expenses for emigration, and support and subsistence for the first year after arrival. To meet these expenses, Congress appropriated $500,000. Shortly after the passage of the law, Jackson's policy met with partial success as the Choctaw and Chickasaw in Mississippi and western Alabama agreed to removal.[47]

The Cherokee and Creek, on the other hand, refused to give their consent. The Cherokee in particular, whose very real accomplishments—establishing a nation, writing a constitution, and forging a government—the Jackson administration chose to ignore, had a fairly sophisticated understanding of how the American political and legal process worked, and decided to make a fight of it. They received strong support from religious groups and other public figures concerned with the humanitarian implications of Jackson's removal policy. Jackson's opponents stressed the seamy side of his removal policy: the force, deception, corruption, and threats used to obtain land cession treaties from the Indians. And they asked the relevant and difficult to answer question of what guarantees the Indians had that they would be secure on the land they moved to west of the Mississippi. Theodore Frelinghuysen of New Jersey and Pelig Sprague of Maine led the unsuccessful fight against the removal bill in Congress, while the Boston-based American Board of Commissioners for Foreign Missions under the leadership of Jeremiah Evarts offered financial support and advice and took the Indians' case to the public.

Politics quickly became involved. Humanitarian concern for the plight of the Indians and anti-removal sentiment were greatest in New England, the part of the country in which Jackson had the least political support. But it also had strong appeal to religious groups, especially Quakers, in New York, New Jersey, Pennsylvania, and Ohio. During the fight over the removal bill, a number of Jackson men from Ohio and Pennsylvania voted negatively because of the measure's unpopularity with their constituents. This immediately attracted the attention of Jackson's two leading opponents, Daniel Webster and Henry Clay. Clay, who as John Quincy Adams's secretary of state, had been indifferent to the fate of the Indians, was determined to oppose Jackson in the election of 1832. To have any chance of winning he had to carry New York and Pennsylvania. To this end Clay decided to make a campaign issue out of the Indian question. "Its flagitious character, the disgrace which it would bring upon our name and nation," he wrote to a political ally, "and its enormous expense, should be spread fully before the people." Moreover, by linking it up with Jackson's stand on internal improvements and the President's concern for states' rights, it could be turned into a major point of debate.[48]

Meanwhile, the discovery of gold on Cherokee lands made Georgians more eager than ever to exercise control over what they claimed was state land and over those who lived on this land. Confident of Jackson's support, the state in 1829 adopted several harsh and cruel measures extending its authority over the Indians, invalidating all laws adopted by the Indians for their own governance, dividing up the land claimed by the Indians and providing for the sale of large parts of it, denying to the Indians the right to testify in cases involving white persons, and prohibiting any person or group from trying to prevent the Indians from emigrating from the state.[49]

Having failed to get support from Congress, the Indians were advised to take their cause to the Supreme Court. To aid them, William Wirt, a former United States attorney general under James Monroe, was induced to become their chief legal adviser. Totally convinced of the justice of their cause, Wirt became a highly effective propagandist on their behalf. His main problem, however, was how to create a meaningful test case. After giving the matter careful consideration, Wirt decided to by-pass the Georgia state courts and the federal circuit court and go directly to the Supreme Court and file an original bill of equity on behalf of the Cherokee as a foreign nation whose treaty rights had been violated and request an injunction against the state of Georgia restraining it from enforcing its laws against the Indians.[50]

Georgia refused to cooperate. The state's governor, George Gilmer, rejected a request from Wirt for help in establishing a test case. In fact he denounced the idea that the Supreme Court had any authority in the matter at all. "Your suggestion," he wrote to Wirt, is "evidence of the state of the contest in which the advocates of power, are exerting themselves to increase the authority of the departments of the general government, whilst the friends of liberty and the rights of the people are in opposition, endeavoring to sustain the sovereignty of the state."[51]

Georgia's denial of the Supreme Court's authority received concrete illustration in late December 1830. A Cherokee Indian by the name of Corn Tassels was captured, tried, convicted, and sentenced to hang for the murder of another Indian in Indian territory, by a Georgia court. The decision was appealed to the United States Supreme Court on the basis of the illegality of the state's laws, and a writ of error was granted for the purpose of bringing the case before the federal courts. Georgia ignored the order and executed Corn Tassels. Moreover, the governor and the legislature publicly vowed to resist, with force if necessary, any attempt to prevent the execution of the state's criminal laws.[52]

A short time later, in March 1831, the Supreme Court heard Wirt's test case, *Cherokee Nation v. Georgia,* a move for an injunction to stop Georgia from executing its Indian laws. No counsel represented Georgia as the state persisted in its policy of refusing to recognize the Supreme Court's authority in the matter. In addition to Wirt, the Cherokee were represented by John Sergeant, a prominent anti-Jackson politician from Pennsylvania. In his summation Wirt made it clear that the question had come to involve not only the rights of the Indians, but also whether the Supreme Court was going to be the final arbiter of the Constitution. Confronting the unspoken question that hung over the case of what would happen if the Court found for the Indians and issued an injunction which Georgia ignored and the President refused to execute, Wirt observed:

> In pronouncing your decree you will have *declared the law;* and it is part of the sworn duty of the President of the United States, to "take care that the laws be faithfully executed." It is not for him nor for the party defendant, to sit in appeal on your decision. The Constitution confers no such power. He is authorized to call

out the military power of the country to enforce the execution of the laws. It is your
function to say what the law is. It is his to cause it to be executed. If he refuses to
perform his duty, the Constitution has provided a remedy.[53]

The Court refused to accept the challenge. Three opinions were read, that by
Marshall for the majority and separate concurring opinions by Henry Baldwin
and William Johnson. The latter two denied outright the Cherokee claim that
they were a foreign nation and rejected the case as not coming under the Court's
jurisdiction. Marshall, on the other hand, rejected the case exclusively on the
grounds that it involved political and not legal questions and therefore could not
be resolved by the Court. He concluded, however, with a strong hint that a
majority of the justices were sympathetic to the Cherokee's plight by commenting: "The Indians are acknowledged to have an unquestionable . . . right to the
land they occupy . . . ," and could get a favorable decision "in a proper case
with proper parties."[54]

Marshall went still further. After the Court adjourned he encouraged the
two justices who had dissented from the Court's decision not to hear the case,
Smith Thompson and Joseph Story, to publish their opinion in support of the
Cherokee. Written by Thompson it backed the Cherokee on almost every
point. It even suggested the kind of case needed, one involving property rights,
that the Court would be willing to hear and act on. Further, the Court reporter, Richard Peters, published the whole case as a separate pamphlet to be sold
to the public. In this endeavor he received the support of Marshall, Thompson,
and Story, the last noting, "Depend on it there is a depth of degradation in our
National conduct, which will irresistibly lead to better things."[55]

Thus encouraged, and determined to persevere, the Cherokee and their
supporters brought yet another case before the Supreme Court in March 1832.
It arose out of an 1830 Georgia law prohibiting any white men from living in
Cherokee territory without permission from the state. It was directed at the
numerous missionaries working among the Indians and advising them in their
resistance to the state. A number of missionaries refused to obtain a license or
to leave the Cherokee territory when so ordered by state authorities. They were
arrested, convicted by a state court, and sentenced to four years of hard labor.
Shortly thereafter, most of them accepted pardons and agreed to leave the
state, but two, Samuel A. Worcester and Elizer Butler refused and appealed to
the United States Supreme Court.

The Court heard the case in early 1832. As in previous cases, Georgia
denied the Supreme Court's authority to decide the matter and refused to send
counsel to plead its cause. And again, it was Wirt and Sergeant who argued on
behalf of Worcester and Butler and by extension the Indians. By this time the
political implications of the case were more obvious than ever. Wirt had become the Anti-masonic candidate for the presidency and Sergeant had become
Clay's running mate on the National Republican ticket after the party had
made the Indian question and the missionaries' plight a major issue at its
December 1831 convention. Writing for the majority, Marshall took a broad

approach to the case and found for the Indians on almost every point: they were a sovereign nation free from Georgia's control, the state's laws were overturned, and Worcester and Butler were entitled to their freedom.[56]

Both what did and did not happen next has been a source of confusion to many scholars. In large part this is because the technical aspects of the Supreme Court's decision in *Worcester v. Georgia* have been misunderstood. The decision reversed the Georgia court's decree and ordered the release of the missionaries, and if the state refused to take any action the Supreme Court could, at least theoretically, issue a writ of *habeas corpus* on behalf of the prisoners. But before the Supreme Court could take this action it had to have proof that the state court had refused to recognize its authority. Although a special messenger had been sent to Georgia to obtain the necessary documents, he failed to return in time for the Court to consider the question before it adjourned. This meant no official action would be taken by the Court until it reconvened in January 1833. As for Jackson, at this point the Supreme Court's decision did not require him to do anything, and nothing is precisely what Jackson did, although his political enemies did conspire to gather evidence, to be used in the forthcoming political election, to claim that he would refuse to enforce the *Worcester* decision.[57]

Certain other legal technicalities also existed that raised doubts about the ability of the Supreme Court to help Worcester and Butler, even when it reconvened in 1833. The authority for the Court to issue a writ of *habeas corpus* was to be found in Section 25 of the Judiciary Act of 1789. The law had been hastily written and had several defects. It specifically allowed federal judges to issue such writs when prisoners were held under federal authority but made no provision for those incarcerated under state authority. Further, it was doubtful that the Supreme Court would be able to adopt any of the other remedies provided for in these kinds of cases by the Judiciary Act of 1789, because the act also required a written record of the refusal of a state court to carry out its decree. But if a state chose to ignore the Supreme Court, as was Georgia's policy, it was unclear what, if anything, the Court could do for the missionaries under these circumstances. Recognizing the problem, Wirt urged that Congress alter the Judiciary Act of 1789 in such a way as to allow the Supreme Court to act immediately in cases where it seemed likely a state court would resist its decrees. He also advocated tightening up the Militia Act of 1795 in a manner which would have required the President to call out the militia to enforce the High Court's decisions. But as things stood, Wirt recognized that in practical terms, there was little the Supreme Court could do immediately to alleviate the missionaries' situation.[58] Jackson also recognized this for he observed, in April of 1832, "the decision of the Supreme Court has fell still born, and they find it cannot coerce Georgia to yield to its mandate."[59]

Still, what was Jackson's attitude toward the federal judiciary? Is it adequately summed up in the apochryphal statement that has been attributed to him: "John Marshall made his decision, now let him enforce it," a statement which exudes hostility not only to the Chief Justice, but to the Supreme Court as well. To some extent it does reflect Jackson's feelings. The President, to be sure, had no love for Marshall who was reputed to have broken his long abstinence from electoral politics in 1828 to vote against Jackson. Nor did he have much sympathy for the nationalist decisions that the Court had been handing down over the past two decades. He also, as we shall see, rejected the claims of the Court's leading supporters that it was the final arbiter in constitutional questions and that its decisions should be binding upon the President. Further, among Jackson's closest advisers were to be found many advocates of a radical kind of judicial reform: amendments to the Constitution abolishing the provision that federal judges should serve for life tenure during good behavior, requiring unanimity from the Supreme Court in constitutional questions, and denying the Court the right to make decisions in areas that infringed on the rights of the state. As a start many advocated repeal of Section 25 of the Judiciary Act of 1789.[60] Finally, Jackson viewed the decision of the Court in *Worcester v. Butler* as part of an attempt by the Supreme Court to unite with his enemies, Webster, Clay, and Calhoun "to embarass me."[61]

Despite all this Jackson's public pronouncements and his actions where the Supreme Court and the federal judiciary were concerned remained remarkably restrained, perhaps more so than on any other issue he confronted during his two terms as President. For example, nothing he said in his public addresses can be construed as encouraging an assault on the federal courts. In these addresses his main concern seemed to be only the extension of the system of circuit courts to those western states not fully covered by them.[62] Less clear are the reasons why Jackson eschewed a belligerent course toward the federal judiciary. In part it may be that despite his hostility to the decisions and personnel of the Court he nonetheless believed, as he had indicated a number of years earlier in reference to the struggle taking place over the judiciary in Kentucky, "that all the rights secured to the citizens under the constitution is worth nothing, and a mere bubble, except guaranteed to them [the people] by an independent and virtuous Judiciary . . . ".[63] What might have controlled Jackson's attitude toward the Supreme Court therefore, was his expectation that he could alter its course by changing its personnel. This was by no means an unrealistic expectation, for in the course of his presidency he made five appointments to the bench, including Roger Brooke Taney as Chief Justice in 1836, that made the Court more sympathetic to the rights of the states and to popular currents in economic and political matters without necessarily diminishing its influence.[64]

What is clear is that following the Supreme Court's decision in the *Worcester* case, Jackson, despite his obvious annoyance with the decision, did his best to avoid any form of conflict over it. He made this explicit to Wilson Lumpkin, the governor of Georgia, when he indicated "my great desire was that you should do no act which would give the Federal court a legal jurisdiction over a case that might arise with the Cherokees."[65] With an election coming up, and with the President increasingly turning his attention to the question of the Second Bank of the United States, it appears he hoped to avoid becoming embroiled in a struggle with the Supreme Court.

IV

Of all the issues that emerged during Jackson's first term as President, the question of rechartering the Second Bank of the United States was the most important. This has long been recognized by scholars, but they have tended to stress the social, economic, political, and symbolic dimensions of the struggle. Jackson, on the other hand, at least during his first term in office, seems to have been most deeply concerned with the constitutional-ideological issues involved in the contest.[66]

Jackson had long been hostile to banks, both state and national. The source was both his own personal business experiences and his involvement in Tennessee politics during the early 1820s. "Everyone that knows me," he wrote early in his second term, "does know, that I have always been opposed to the U. States Bank, nay all Banks."[67] He also believed that the Bank had used its considerable influence during the election of 1828 to oppose him, and cited in particular its activities in Lexington, Portsmouth, New Orleans, and Charleston. Shortly after Jackson assumed the presidency the word went out that he was determined to prevent the rechartering of the Second Bank of the United States in its current form in 1836.[68]

This attitude was opposed by a number of Jackson's advisers. Support for the Bank came from Secretary of the Treasury Samuel Ingham, Attorney-General John M. Berrien, and William B. Lewis, a close personal friend from Tennessee who lived with Jackson in the White House for a while. They stressed, in particular, the services the Bank performed as the federal government's fiscal agent, in maintaining a sound and uniform currency throughout the country, and in checking the instability of many state banks. There is also some evidence that, at least in the beginning, Van Buren did not share Jackson's hostility to the Bank.[69]

This opposition did not convince Jackson to abandon his objections to the continuance of the Bank under its existing charter, but it did make him cautious. Jackson had originally planned to attack the Bank in his inaugural address, but abandoned the idea at Van Buren's suggestion. An early draft of his first annual address to Congress contained a frontal assault on the institution, but again Van Buren used his influence to have it toned down. Van Buren probably would have been happier if all mention of the Bank had been abandoned, but Jackson refused to do this. He was determined to bring the issue before Congress. But he did so in a very restrained fashion waiting to the end of his address to observe.

> The charter of the Bank of the United States expires in 1836, and its stockholders will most probably apply for a renewal of their privileges. In order to avoid the evils resulting from precipitancy in a measure involving such important principles and such deep pecuniary interest, I feel that I cannot in justice to the parties interested, too soon present it to the deliberate consideration of the Legislature and the people. Both the constitutionality and the expediency of the law creating this bank are well questioned by a large portion of our fellow citizens, and it must be admitted by all that it has failed in the great end of establishing a uniform and sound currency.

Then, in the paragraph that followed, Jackson significantly noted: "if such an institution is deemed essential to the fiscal operations of the Government, I submit to the wisdom of the Legislature whether a national one, founded upon the credit of the Government and its revenues might not be devised which would avoid all constitutional difficulties, and at the same time secure all the advantages to the Government and country that were expected to result from the present bank."[70]

This would seem to indicate that Jackson realized not only that an attack on the Bank might divide his followers, but also that if he managed to destroy the Bank he would have to replace it with another institution or risk serious economic consequences and financial disorder. Despite his hostility to the Bank, therefore, Jackson seems, at least in the early years of his first term, to have been willing to live with some kind of national institution if it could be made constitutionally acceptable. Consequently, most private high-level discussions of the Bank issue in 1829, 1830, and 1831 focused on this issue. For example, when the Bank's president, Nicholas Biddle, went to visit Jackson to discuss the problem, the President indicated that he appreciated the Bank's value but added: "I think it right to be perfectly frank with you. I do not think that the power of Congress extends to charter a Bank out of the ten mile square [the District of Columbia] . . . I have read the opinion of John Marshall [*McCulloch v Maryland*] . . . and could not agree with him."[71]

What kind of national bank would Jackson have found constitutionally acceptable? It is hard to say for sure, because Jackson probably never fully made up his mind on the subject. Certainly a bank located only in the District of Columbia and under the exclusive control of the Treasury Department and acting as the federal government's fiscal agent would have been acceptable. This, however, would not have been as useful as a national bank that had branches throughout the country. But this raised the complicated constitutional question of what kind of control the states would have over branches within their boundaries and whether they could be required to accept a branch even if they did not want one. Further, Jackson wanted control of the Bank, and its profits, to be entirely in the hands of the federal government and therefore opposed having stock in the Bank sold to private investors. Jackson also believed it should be a bank of deposit, which would hold and transfer money and perform other fiscal services, but not one of discount which would create money and make loans and investments, although he recognized that the Bank might have to be given this power in an emergency situation such as a war.[72]

Jackson publicly expressed his feelings on the problem in his second annual message to Congress in December 1830. Again he was very restrained. Calling Congress's attention to the subject he went on:

> Nothing has occurred to lessen in any degree the dangers which many of our citizens apprehend from that institution as at present organized. In the spirit of improvement and compromise which distinguishes our country and its institutions it becomes us to inquire whether it be not possible to secure the advantages

afforded by the present bank through the agency of a Bank of the United States so modified in its principles and structures as to obviate Constitutional and other objections.

It is thought practicable to organize such a bank with the necessary officers as a branch of the Treasury Department, based on the pubic and individual deposits, without power to make loans or purchase property, which shall remit the funds of the Government, and the expense of which may be paid, if thought advisable, by allowing its officers to sell bills of exchange to private individuals at a moderate premium. Not being a corporate body, having no stockholders, debtors or property, and but few officers, it would not be obnoxious to the constitutional objections which are urged against the present bank; and having no means to operate on the hopes, fears, or interests of large masses of the community, it would be shorn of the influence which makes that bank formidable. The States would be strengthened by having in their hands the means of furnishing the local paper currency through their own banks, while the Bank of the United States, though issuing no paper, would check the issues of the State banks by taking their notes in deposit and for exchange only so long as they continue to be redeemed with specie. In times of public emergency the capacities of such an institution might be enlarged by legislative provision.[73]

Despite his strong feelings on the Bank question, Jackson seemed to realize that he might not be able to get his way on it. He introduced his remarks on the issue in December 1830 by referring to "the spirit of improvement and compromise which distinguishes our country," and concluded by saying: "These suggestions are made not so much as a recommendation as with a view of calling the attention of Congress to the possible modifications of a system which cannot continue to exist in its present form without occasional collisions with the local authorities and perpetual apprehensions and discontent on the part of the States and the people."[74] Jackson, at this point, seems to have been torn between his own antipathy to the Bank and his recognition that under Biddle's leadership it was running smoothly and performing useful, even, indispensable, services for the federal government. He undoubtedly was aware that the country had undergone considerable financial chaos between 1811 and 1816 when no national bank existed and that state banks had proliferated and that many had acted irresponsibly during those years. He may not have liked banks, but he seemed to understand that they were here to stay and that the only real option open to him was to control the more pernicious effects of their existence, and that a national bank could serve a useful function in this regard. Jackson also seemed to recognize that by the time he became President the Second Bank of the United States was no longer the unpopular institution it had been following the Panic of 1819. If anything it seems to have been generally respected and popular in 1829–1831. Jackson justified much of his hostility to the Bank on the grounds that it operated to the benefit of the few at the expense of the many, but at this point in his presidency he did not claim that the will of the people demanded that some kind of action be taken against it. In 1829 all he was prepared to claim was, "I have brought it before the people, and I have confidence that they will do their duty."[75]

In addition, although some of those who had become particularly close to

Jackson—Kendall, Blair, Benton, and Roger Brooke Taney—favored making the Bank a major issue, others decidedly opposed such a development. The new cabinet, appointed in 1831, was if anything even more favorably inclined to the Bank than the old one, especially Lewis Mc Lane, the secretary of the treasury; Lewis Cass, the secretary of war; and Edward Livingston, the secretary of state. Further, William B. Lewis remained a firm advocate while neither Levi Woodbury nor Van Buren seemed to have been especially eager to see the Bank made a major issue. The President's nephew, Andrew Jackson Donelson, warned against making it an issue urging his uncle instead to "harmonize the political divisions of the country."[76]

Perhaps, most importantly, Jackson was eager to have the national debt paid off by early 1833. To do this he would need the cooperation of the Bank. He seems to have had hopes of announcing this accomplishment either on the anniversary of his great victory in New Orleans on January 8, 1833, or failing this, in time for his second inauguration on March 4, 1833, for it is clear that by this time he had decided to seek reelection. Indeed, by this time Jackson seemed to be strongly desirous of keeping the Bank issue from becoming involved, in any way, in the presidential election of 1832. Therefore, Jackson seemed to back off from a fight over the Bank in 1831. To Martin Van Buren he wrote "should the people again elect me, the national debt paid, and the Bank question settled, you will see me adopt a course worthy of myself, and the principles I have always advocated." In his third annual address to Congress, Jackson barely referred to the issue, again observing in a restrained fashion and quite briefly "that the attention of the Legislature and the people should be seasonaly directed to that important subject, and that it might be considered and finally disposed of in a manner best calculated to promote the ends of the Constitution and subserve the public interests. Having thus conscientiously discharged a constitutional duty, I deem it proper on this occasion . . . to leave it for the present to the investigation of an enlightened people and their representatives."[77]

What did this mean? That Jackson would be willing to support the rechartering of the Second Bank, with only some minor adjustments, if it did not become a political issue? Perhaps. This is the interpretation that pro-Bank supporters close to the President placed on it. But this is not the only interpretation that could be placed on the President's ambiguous public statements. Particularly ominous signs were the editorials of the *Washington Globe,* the semi-official spokesman of the administration, controlled by anti-Bank Democrats Blair and Kendall, which continued to lash out at the Bank. "What I have always dreaded about this new cabinet," Biddle wrote, "was that the kitchen would predominate over the parlor." Privately, Jackson denied "I had changed my views of the Bank of the United States," and continued to view it as unconstitutional and inexpedient. Jackson also noted that support for the Bank from within the cabinet "springs from convictions much more favorable than mine of the general character and conduct of this institution." The President may have been willing to accept a national bank of some kind, but it would have to be stripped "of the constitutional objections entertained by the Executive." This may have meant that he would refuse to accept one in which private interests held stock, or that made discounts, and would have demanded that it could only have branches with the permission of the states involved. These were substantial modifications and any one of them would have drastically affected the national bank as it then existed under Biddle's direction.[78]

At this point Biddle made an understandable, although fateful decision. Ignoring the advice of pro-Bank Democrats and the warnings of the President, he openly allied himself with Henry Clay, Jackson's chief opponent in the coming presidential election and made rechartering the Bank a political issue. The strategy was simple. Clay and Biddle expected to have no trouble getting Congress to approve a bill to recharter the Bank, and since Jackson seemed to be concerned about the effect of the issue on his reelection bid there seemed to exist a small chance he might sign the bill. If, as seemed probable, he chose to veto it, then it would be made a major issue in the election. No one really thought it likely that Clay would win, but there was hope that the issue would determine the Congressional elections in such a way as to ensure the Bank a two-thirds majority to override the veto at the following session.[79]

Jackson was furious. This brought to an end whatever reservations he may have had about denying the Bank's application for recharter. He now viewed the whole matter primarily in personal terms, as an attempt to intimidate and embarrass him. If Congress passed the bill he was determined to veto it. "I will prove to them that I never flinch," he told a confidant, "that they were mistaken when they expected to act upon me by such considerations." And Van Buren recalls returning from England in July of 1832, after Congress had passed the recharter bill, and going to the White House to see the President who was sick and stretched out on a couch. "Holding my hand in one of his own and passing the other thro' his long white locks he said . . . 'the bank, Mr. Van Buren, is trying to kill me, *but I will kill it.*' "[80]

Van Buren also observed that Jackson said this "with the clearest indications of a mind composed, and in a tone entirely devoid of passion or bluster." From the existing evidence it seems clear that Jackson had given the Bank question considerable thought and that his main objections were constitutional and that his thinking on the issue was greatly influenced by his commitment to states' rights. Shortly before his veto message he commented to Benton, "I have always been opposed to it upon constitutional grounds as well as expediency and policy. . . ."[81]

Jackson vetoed the bill on July 10, 1832. The message was a forceful, even eloquent, statement of his views, directed not only at Congress but also, in anticipation of the coming election, to the people of the United States. It started with the President observing that he had received the bill to "modify and continue," the Second Bank of the United States on July 4 and that he had "considered it with the solemn regard to the principles of the Constitution which the day was calculated to inspire." Jackson admitted that the Bank "is in many respects convenient for the Government and useful to the people." But he also was "deeply impressed with the belief that some of the powers and privileges possessed by the existing bank are unauthorized by the Constitution, subversive of the rights of the states, and dangerous to the liberties of the people." Therefore, he was vetoing the bill to recharter the Bank because its provisions were not adequate "in my opinion, to make it compatible with justice, with sound policy, or with the constitution of our country."

Jackson stressed certain themes in his message. He emphasized that the Bank bill granted exclusive privileges and a monopoly to an institution dominated and controlled by private stockholders. The earnings from this "special favor of the Government," went to people who Jackson variously described as "opulent citizens," "chiefly of the richest class," "the few who have been fortunate," "a designated and favored class of men," and "a privileged order." Further, it created "an interest separate from that of the people" and provided for "a concentration of power in the hands of a few men irresponsible to the people." As Jackson saw it, the Bank was a dangerous institution because it had enormous power and wealth, and once it received its charter was not controllable either by the federal government or the people. It may have provided important services for the federal government, but it was not a servant of the nation.

Jackson also argued at length that much of the Bank's stock was held by foreigners. Aspects of this part of the message had a demagogic tone. But it also provided Jackson with a useful transition to one of the key themes of his veto message: The Second Bank of the United States, as it had existed and would continue to exist under the bill Congress had just passed for its recharter, was not compatible with the rights of the states or with the welfare of the country. The President closely examined a provision in the proposed law that allowed the states to tax that portion of the stock of the Bank held by their own citizens. But in Jackson's view this provision was meaningless and even dangerous because such a substantial portion of the stock was held by foreigners. And since the rest of the stock was controlled mainly by easterners, the southern and western states, where most of the Bank's capital was employed, were at a distinct disadvantage. Indeed, the effect of this ostensible concession to the rights of the states was to make it more profitable for foreigners to hold stock in the Bank than Americans, and would even encourage more of the stock to pass into foreign hands for they would not be liable to this tax. "Controlling our currency, receiving our public moneys and holding thousands of our citizens in dependence," he observed, "it [the Bank of the United States] would be more formidable and dangerous than the military power of the enemy."

Jackson next confronted the question of the Bank's constitutionality. He rejected the idea that it had been settled either by precedent or the Supreme Court. "Mere precedent," the President noted, "is a dangerous source of authority, and should not be regarded as deciding questions of constitutional power except where the acquiescence of the people and the states can be considered as well settled." True, he pointed out, Congress, had passed laws in favor of the Bank in 1791 and 1816, but a Bank bill had been rejected in 1811 and 1815. He also claimed that the preponderence of legislative, judicial, and executive opinions in the states were against the Bank by about four to one.

Turning to the Supreme Court, Jackson presented a clear and forceful statement against the concept of judicial supremacy and the claim that the Supreme Court was to be the final arbiter of constitutional questions:

> If the opinion of the Supreme Court covered the whole ground of this act, it ought not to control the coordinate authorities of this Government. The Congress, the Executive, and the Court must each for itself be guided by its own opinion of the Constitution. Each public officer who takes an oath to support the Constitution swears that he will support it as he understands it, and not as it is understood by others. It is as much the duty of the House of Representatives, of the Senate, and of the President to decide upon the constitutionality of any bill or resolution which may be presented to them for passage or approval as it is of the Supreme judges when it may be brought before them for judicial decision. The opinion of the judges has no more authority over Congress than the opinion of Congress has over the judges, and on that point the President is independent of both. The authority of the Supreme Court must not, therefore, be permitted to control the Congress or the Executive when acting in their legislative capacities, but to have only such influence as the force of their reasoning may deserve.

The remaining two-thirds of the message focused mainly on constitutional issues. Jackson decried a loose interpretation of the Constitution and misuse of the necessary and proper clause for what he called "a palpable attempt to amend the Constitution by an act of legislation." At times Jackson's arguments became strained, but he also dealt with many issues genuinely involving the rights of the states: the power which the act gave to establish up to two branches in any state regardless of whether the state wanted a branch or not, the denial of the right of the states to tax the activities of the branches of the Bank even at the same rate they taxed their own banks, and the right of the Bank to purchase and own lands within the states, a power denied to the federal government itself under the Constitution. In making these points, Jackson reiterated his belief that the Bank was not a truly national institution, but essentially a private one, operated for profit and controlled by private interests, that performed certain useful functions for the federal government.

Jackson concluded the message with an eloquent statement of his social philosophy:

> It is to be regretted that the rich and powerful too often bend the acts of government to their selfish purposes. Distinctions in society will always exist under every just government. Equality of talents, of education, or of wealth cannot be produced by human institutions. In the full enjoyment of the gifts of Heaven and the fruits of superior industry, economy and virtue, every man is equally entitled to protection by the law; but when the laws undertake to add to these natural and just advantages artificial distinctions, to grant titles, gratuities, and exclusive privileges, to make the rich richer and the potent more powerful, the humble members of

society—the farmers, mechanics and laborers—who have neither the time nor the means of securing like favors to themselves, have a right to complain of the injustice of their Government. There are no necessary evils in government. Its evils exist only in its abuses. If it would confine itself to equal protection, and, as Heaven does its rains, shower its favors alike on the high and low, the rich and the poor, it would be an unqualified blessing. In the act before me there seems to be a wide and unnecessary departure from these just principles.

This passage has been quoted by almost all scholars who study Jackson's Bank veto message. What is invariably ignored, however, is the paragraph that follows:

Nor is our Government to be maintained or our Union preserved by invasions of the rights and powers of the several states. In thus attempting to make our General Government strong we make it weak. Its true strength consists in leaving individuals and states as much as possible to themselves—in making itself felt, not in its power, but in its beneficence; not in its control, but in its protection; not in binding the states more closely to the center, but leaving each to move unobstructed in its proper orbit.

This indicates how inextricably intertwined Jackson's belief in states' rights was with his belief in social and political democracy, for in the next and penultimate paragraph of his message he returned again to his concern that: "many of our rich men have not been content with equal protection and equal benefits, but have besought us to make them richer by act of Congress." He concluded by noting: "I have now done my duty to my country."

3

Andrew Jackson, Nullification, and the South

A crucial question remains. If Jackson believed so strongly in states' rights then why did he react to nullification so violently? To answer this question consideration must be given first, to Jackson's attitude toward the tariff, the ostensible issue that led to the formulation of the nullification doctrine; then to his attitude toward the concept of nullification itself; and finally, to the nature of the Jackson-Calhoun relationship, for while personal considerations did not determine the President's attitude toward nullification they did effect, in an important way, the intensity of his reaction and the manner in which he handled the crisis that occurred during the winter of 1832–33.

I

Of all the major issues confronting Jackson during his first administration, the one he had the most difficulty formulating a policy on was the tariff. The economic, political, and constitutional issues raised by the tariff were incongruous with his democratic and states' rights values. As a result, Jackson found the tariff to be an unclear and confusing issue. He issued statements on it which were vague and ambiguous, and he adopted policies that were equivocal and, to a certain extent, even inconsistent. The reasons for this are important for they further reveal Jackson's political and ideological objectives.

The tariff had been fully and furiously debated throughout the 1820s. As the senator from Tennessee and a presidential candidate in 1824, Jackson had

had to confront the highly controversial issue. He voted for the tariff of 1824 on the grounds that "the experience of the late war ought to teach us a lesson, and one never to be forgotten," that the United States should not be dependent upon foreign nations for goods vital to the country's defense. It was too easy for a powerful maritime nation like Great Britain to cut off supplies needed to sustain a war effort. These goods, Jackson believed, had to be produced at home. He also favored the tariff because it produced revenue that could be used to pay off the national debt. "I am one of those," he wrote, "who do not believe that a national debt is a national blessing, but rather a curse to a republic; in as much as it is calculated to raise around the administration a moneyed aristocracy dangerous to the liberties of the Country." In addition, in 1824, like so many others, Jackson also bought the idea of the creation of a home market, as yet another reason why a protective tariff served a useful purpose.[1]

By the time he became President, Jackson had abandoned any faith in the efficacy of the home market argument. But his belief that a tariff was of value for protecting goods "which are of primary necessity in time of war" and for producing a revenue to accomplish the paying off of the national debt remained firm. This latter point was of particular importance to Jackson during his first administration, and he made it clear that until it was accomplished he would not support extensive reduction.[2]

By the time he became President, Jackson also had become concerned about the extreme feelings that had developed on the tariff. They made him uneasy. Shortly after the passage of the tariff of Abominations in 1828 he wrote to one nullifier: "To regulate a Judicious tariff is a subject of great difficulty at all times, and ought to be discussed, with great calmness and due deliberation, with an eye to the prosperity of the whole Union, and not of any particular part, viewing the whole as one great family, and extending impartial Justice to every branch with feelings of mutual concession, extending to all equal benefits, and each bearing a just portion of the burdens the Tariff may impose."[3]

Jackson developed this theme in many of the major state papers of his first administration. For example, in his inaugural address he observed, "it would seem to me that the spirit of equity, caution and compromise in which the Constitution was formed requires that the great interests of agriculture, commerce, and manufactures should be equally favored. . . ."[4] In his first annual address to Congress in December 1829 he referred to regulation of the tariff as "one of the most difficult tasks of Government," and to the "difficulty and delicacy of the operation of placing American goods in fair competition with those of other countries," and called for the abandonment of "local feelings and prejudices . . . in the patriotic determination to promote the great interests of the whole."[5] The following year in his second annual address he described it as "a subject of so much delicacy . . . as to require that it should be touched with utmost caution."[6] And in December of 1831, in his third annual address, Jackson's last public pronouncement on the tariff before the adoption of the Tariff of 1832 and the nullification crisis, he again pleaded for "the exercise of that spirit of concession and conciliation which has distinguished the friends of our Union in all great emergencies."[7]

Underlying Jackson's repeated calls for compromise was a conviction that the effects of protection were overrated. Shortly after taking office he publicly observed: "No very considerable change has occurred during the recess of Congress in the condition of either our agriculture, commerce or manufactures. The operation of the tariff has not proved so injurious to the two former or as beneficial to the latter as was anticipated."[8] He came back to this theme again the following year: "It is an infirmity of our nature to mingle our interests and prejudices with the operation of our reasoning powers, and attribute to the objects of our likes and dislikes qualities they do not possess and effects they cannot produce. The effects of the present tariff are doubtless overrated, both in its evils and its advantages."[9]

On one aspect of the tariff debate, Jackson did take a firm and clear stand. This came in response to the claims of nullifiers and other extreme free traders that a protective tariff was unconstitutional. At the close of his Maysville Road veto, Jackson went out of his way to disagree with nullifier claims that his attack on the power of Congress to appropriate money for internal improvements supported their arguments against protection. The President explicitly denied this: "On the contrary, it appears to me that the supposition of their dependence upon each other is calculated to excite the prejudices of the public against both. The tariff," he argued in May of 1830, "is sustained on the grounds of its consistency with the letter and spirit of the Constitution, of its origin being traced to the assent of all the parties to the original compact, and of its having the support and approbation of a majority of the people on which account it is at least entitled to a fair experiment."[10]

Several months later Jackson elaborated more fully on his view that a protective tariff was constitutional:

> The object of the tariff is objected to by some as unconstitutional. . . . The power to impose duties on imports originally belonged to the several states. The right to adjust these duties with a view to the encouragement of domestic branches of industry is so completely incidental to that power that it is difficult to suppose the existence of one without the other. The states have delegated their whole authority over imports to the General Government without limitation or restriction, saving the very inconsiderable reservations relating to their inspection laws. This authority having thus entirely passed from the states, the right to exercise it for the purpose of protection does not exist in them, and consequently if it be not possessed by the General Government, it must be extinct. Our political system would thus present the anomaly of a people stripped of the right to foster their own industry and to counteract the most selfish and destructive policy which might be adopted by foreign nations. This surely cannot be the case. This indispensable power thus surrendered by the states must be within the scope of the authority on the subject expressly delegated to Congress.[11]

Although Jackson did not doubt the constitutionality of a protective tariff he did have sympathy for its downward revision. In part this was because he was favorably inclined toward free trade ideals, though he remained convinced that they were unrealistic for items vital to the national interest and general welfare, for what he termed goods "essential to our safety" in time of war. He also realized that once the national debt was paid the government would have to find something to do with its surplus income. For his first two years in office he suggested that it be distributed to the states, according to their population, but he eventually abandoned this idea for it ran counter to the heightened agrarian tone of his public statements on federal aid to internal improvements and the national bank. Given his belief that the federal government should be frugal and simple it made more sense, once the national debt was eliminated, to reduce the major source from which it obtained its income: the tariff. Finally, Jackson also recognized that the tariff of 1828 was, in fact, a burden. He observed:

> That many of the taxes collected from our citizens through the medium of imposts have for a considerable period been onerous. In many particulars these taxes have borne severely upon the laboring and prosperous classes of the community, being imposed on the necessaries of life, and this, too, in cases where the burthen was not relieved by the consciousness that it would ultimately contribute to make us independent of foreign nations for articles of prime necessity by the encouragement of their growth and manufacture at home. They have been cheerfully borne because they were thought to be necessary to the support of Government and the payment of the debts unavoidably incurred in the acquisition and maintenance of our national rights and liberties. But have we a right to calculate on the same cheerful acquiescence when it is known that the necessity for their continuance would cease were it not for irregular, improvident and unequal appropriations of the public funds? Will not the people demand, as they have a right to do, such a prudent system of expenditure as will pay the debts of the union and authorize the reduction of every tax to as low a point as the wise observance of the necessity to protect that portion of our manufactures and labor whose prosperity is essential to our national safety and independence will allow?[12]

Where Jackson had trouble, however, was reconciling this attitude with his belief in majority rule. He had admitted in his Maysville Road veto that the tariff had "the approbation of a majority of the people," by which he meant it had been passed in a legitimate manner by the people's representatives. What was Jackson to do, if in spite of his own belief that the tariff should be reduced, a majority of the people's representatives continued to opt for protection which they certainly had a constitutional right to do? It was a tough question and he did not seem eager to deal with it. As one congressman noted shortly after Jackson's election in 1828, "there is a profound silence observed on the subject of the tariff," by those who had any ideas on what the upcoming administration's policies would be on the issues.[13]

Jackson's only real attempt to confront the tariff problems in ideological terms came in his second annual address in December of 1830. After stating that "the present tariff taxes some of the comforts of life unnecessarily high," he went on to observe, in an argument that obviously was influenced by his objection to the log-rolling activities of Congress on internal improvement bills, that:

> The best as well as the fairest mode of determining whether from any just considerations a particular interest ought to receive protection would be to submit the question singly for deliberation. If after due examination of its merits, unconnected with extraneous considerations—such as a desire to sustain a general system or to purchase support for a different interest—it should enlist in its favor a majority of the representatives of the people, there can be little danger of wrong or injury in adjusting the tariff with reference to its protective effect. If this obviously just principle were honestly adhered to, the branches of industry which deserve protection would be saved from the prejudice excited against them when that protection forms part of a system by which portions of the country feel or conceive themselves to be oppressed. What is incalculably more important, the vital principle of our system—that principle which requires acquiescence in the will of the majority—would be secure from the discredit and danger to which it is exposed by the acts of majorities founded not on identity of conviction, but on combinations of small minorities entered into for the purpose of mutual assistance in measures which, resting solely on their own merits, could never be carried.[14]

In sum, Jackson viewed the tariff as constitutional, having the practical benefit of extinguishing the public debt and protecting items necessary for the common good and welfare. He also saw it as a politically complex and dangerous issue, one that in his view brought forth unrealistic and irrational responses and that raised thorny ideological questions when measured against the principle of majority rule. Since, as he made clear numerous times, he had no intention of moving on the tariff until the national debt was eliminated, and since that would not occur until 1833 at the earliest, during his first term Jackson did his best to try to avoid the issue. He, of course, was not entirely successful. The nullifiers, free traders and extreme advocates of protection were unwilling to be ignored. Besides, the tariff of 1828 was such a controversial measure that it called out for attention. Jackson's way of handling this pressure was to throw it back on Congress. On this issue, more than on any other during his first term, he wished Congress to take the initiative and work out a solution, and wherever possible he cooperated with Congress and endorsed its decisions. For Jackson the tariff was essentially a political question. He had successfully finessed the issue during the election of 1828 and tried to do so in those first years following his accession to the Presidency.[15]

In specific terms, what did Jackson's tariff policy look like between 1829 and 1832? In 1829 Jackson suggested to Congress that with the elimination of the public debt in the foreseeable future consideration should be given to the modification of duties on those items not in direct competition with American products. He specifically singled out tea and coffee. Congress responded in 1830 by reducing the duties on these items and on cocoa, cutting in half the duty on molasses, and restoring the drawback on the exportation of rum which had been eliminated in 1828. The following year in his address to Congress, Jackson observed, in what was probably wishful thinking, "much relief will be derived . . . from the measures of your last session."[16] During the 1831–32 session of Congress, Secretary of the Treasury Louis McLane, as well as Henry Clay in the Senate and John Quincy Adams, chairman of the House Committee on Manufactures, presented bills for tariff reform. Out of this complicated situation Congress, on July 14, 1832, finally passed a compromise version of the bill originally introduced by Adams. The tariff slashed some items substantially and abolished the system of minimum valuation, but it retained rates on cottons, woolens, and iron at almost 50 percent. In effect it restored the tariff to what it had been in 1824 when the average rate on dutiable articles was about 33 percent. In no sense was it based on free trade principles; it reduced numerous duties but left the protective principle unimpaired. Jackson, who by this time was fully engaged in his struggle with Biddle and Clay over the recharter of the Second Bank of the United States, was delighted to sign it into law. "The people must now see," he gloated, "that all their grievances are removed, and oppression only existed in the distempered brains of disappointed ambitious men."[17]

Jackson could not have been more wrong, for not only nullifiers but low tariff men generally, including many who had no sympathy with the doctrine of nullification, felt that tariff reform had not gone far enough.

II

Andrew Jackson was vehemently opposed to the doctrine of nullification. His position on this, in sharp contrast to his generally vague and equivocal statements on the tariff, was determined, clear, and straightforward. Moreover, his hostility to the doctrine was firmly grounded in constitutional and ideological considerations.

Two aspects of nullification in particular aroused his ire. First, it was a direct attack on the principle he so deeply believed in: majority rule. The *South Carolina Exposition and Protest* had been explicit on this. "That our industry," it noted at one point, "is controlled by the many, instead of one, by a majority in Congress elected by a majority in the community having an opposing interest, instead of hereditary rulers, forms not the slightest mitigation of the evil. In fact, instead of mitigating, it aggravates." The crucial problem, according to the *Exposition,* was how to control "the unchecked will of the majority." It observed: "No government based on the naked principle, that the majority ought to govern, however true the maxim in its proper sense and under proper restrictions, ever preserved its liberty, even for a single generation. . . . Constitutional government, and the government of a majority are utterly incompatible, it being the sole purpose of a constitution to impose limitations and checks upon the majority. An unchecked majority is a despotism—and government is free, and will be permanent in proportion to the number, complexity and efficiency of the checks, by which its powers are controlled."[18]

This was an attack upon the essence of Jackson's most fundamental beliefs. And he recognized it as such. The President commented directly on the issue in his second annual address to Congress in December 1830:

Acquiescence in the Constitutionaly expressed will of the majority and the exercise of that will in a spirit of moderation, justice and brotherly kindness, will constitute a cement which would forever preserve our Union. Those who cherish and inculcate sentiments like these render a most essential service to their Country, while those who seek to weaken their influence are, however conscientious and praiseworthy their intentions, in effect its worst enemies.[19]

Jackson's fullest and clearest statement on this question came a few months later in a letter to Robert Y. Hayne, one of the leaders of the nullification movement in South Carolina. Nullification, he made clear, was unacceptable because it undercut the principle of majority rule:

For the rights of the state, no one has a higher regard and respect than myself, none would go farther to maintain them: It is only by maintaining them faithfully that the Union can be preserved.

But how I ask is this to be effected? Certainly not by conceding to one state authority to declare an act of Congress void, and meet all the consequences and hazard that such a course would produce, far from it; there is a better remedy, one which has heretofore proved successful in the worst of times, and all must admit its power. If Congress, and the Executive, feeling power, and forgetting right, shall overleap the powers the Constitution bestow, and extend their sanction to laws which the power granted to them does not permit, the remedy is with the people—not by avowed opposition—not thro open and direct resistance, but thro the more peaceful and reasonable course of submitting the whole matter to them at their elections, and they by their free suffrage at the polls, will always in the end, bring about the repeal of any obnoxious laws which violate the constitution. Such abuses as these cannot be of long duration in our enlightened Country where the people rule. Let all contested matters be brought to that tribunal, and it will decree correctly.

This is, in general political questions, the only course that should be pursued, and which the constitution contemplates. That a state has the power to nullify the Legislative enactments of the General Government I never did believe, nor have I ever understood Mr. Jefferson to hold such an opinion. That ours is a Government of laws, and depends on a will of the majority, is the true reading of the Constitution. The time I hope is far distant when the abuse of power on the part of Congress will be so great as to justify a state to stand forth in open violation and resistance to its measures; In all Republics the voice of a majority must prevail, consent to this, and act upon it, and harmony will prevail; oppose it, and disagreement, difference and danger will certainly follow. Assert that a state may declare acts passed by congress inoperative and void, and revolution with all of its attendant evils in the end must be looked for and expected—compromise, mutual concessions, and friendly forbearance between different interests, and sections of our happy Country must be regarded and nourished by all who desire to perpetuate the blessings we enjoy.[20]

The second aspect of nullification Jackson focused on, in his total rejection of the concept, was the assertion made by many of the doctrine's more radical advocates in South Carolina that failure to get tariff reform would lead to a dissolution of the Union. These threats deeply offended Jackson, whose belief in the value of the Union was absolute. Shortly before his election in 1828, Jackson had observed to an important nullifier: "There is nothing that I shudder at more than the idea of a separation of the Union. Should such an event ever happen, which I fervently pray God to avert, from that date, I view our liberty gone."[21]

Jackson totally rejected the idea of secession as a legal or constitutional right that could take place peacefully. He believed: "perpetuity is stamped upon the Constitution by the blood of our Fathers—by those who achieved as well as those who improved our system of free Government. For this purpose was the principle of amendment inserted in the Constitution which all have sworn to support and in violation of which no state or states have the right to secede, much less dissolve the Union." As Jackson viewed it, secession was a revolutionary right, one that had to be fought for and therefore one that could be suppressed. Moreover, he believed nullification and secession were virtually synonymous, for the one verged almost automatically into the other. "Nullification," he wrote, "leads directly to civil war and bloodshed and deserves the execration of every friend of the Country." Indeed, so hostile was he to "this nullifying doctrine, which threatens to dissolve our happy Union," that in his mind support for the nullifiers' cause became synonymous with "Treason against our Government."[22]

Jackson's hostility to nullification manifested itself from the beginning of his presidency. He deliberately exluded any South Carolinian from his first cabinet in 1829 because of the state's reaction to the adoption of the tariff in 1828 and its promulgation of the *Exposition and Protest*. "South Carolinians get nothing," wrote Kendall. "The General told me he should have taken a member of his cabinet from that state but for their movements last summer."[23]

Until South Carolina actually nullified the tariffs of 1828 and 1832, Jackson refrained from commenting directly on the doctrine in his messages to Congress. But when pressed to state his position he responded unequivocally. This occurred with dramatic effect at the famed Jefferson Birthday Dinner of April 13, 1830. Its organizers planned it as an event to do honor to Jefferson's memory and his political philosophy, and to identify them with the Democratic party. For the most part its subscribers favored states' rights and strict construction, opposed an extensive program of federal aid to internal improvements, and were anti-tariff. The latter bias caused the pro-tariff Pennsylvania members to withdraw when they discovered the list of proposed toasts. Jackson had agreed to attend. During the course of the dinner, a close aide reported, the President decided it was "a piece of political management," gotten up by the nullifiers to cover their doctrine with the mantle of Jefferson, and he later indicated that if he had known this beforehand "he should not have gone." One of the official toasts went: "The bane of the Union:—oppression of minorities; unequal taxation; unequal distribution of public benefits." When asked to volunteer a toast, Jackson forthrightly responded: "Our Federal Union: it must be preserved." Shortly after the celebration the President indicated that "he was a Jeffersonian Democrat, but that many sentiments uttered at the dinner were such as Jefferson abhorred. He could not hear the dissolution of the Union spoken of lightly and he meant by his toast that the Federal Union must be preserved *Tariff or no Tariff*." Observing the proceedings Hezekiah Niles noted: "He will resist a *nullification* of the public law—else we much mistake his character."[24]

Jackson's strong feelings on nullification further manifested themselves when he refused to appoint as United States District Attorney for South Carolina a candidate who advocated the doctrine even though he was supported for the position by a clear majority of the South Carolina congressional delegation. Apparently he justified his decision to William Drayton, one of the state's leading Unionists, on the grounds "that he entertains political principles which ought to prevent him from holding an office under the U.S." Upon hearing of the decision, Senator Robert Y. Hayne, one of the more moderate members of the nullification party in South Carolina, wrote to Jackson protesting it. Hayne frankly admitted that the candidate "is a distinguished member of the State Rights Party of So. Ca." who "believes with Thos. Jefferson that a state acting in its sovereign capacity has a right to interpose for the preservation of its rights reserved under the Constitution . . . ". But he added: "Unless therefore it should be considered that *a crisis now exists,* in the relations between South Carolina and the federal government which forbids the appointment to office of any member of the State Rights Party, I must consider the objections to Mr. Finley as altogether groundless." Then Hayne went on to point out that this attitude of proscription from office did not govern the attitude of the Nullification party of South Carolina, which represented the views of a majority of the people in the state, but nevertheless allowed its opponents to hold office. In particular, he singled out the appointment as State Attorney General of "a gentleman not only opposed to nullification and convention, but who acknowledges the supremacy of the federal Judiciary over the Judicial tribunals of the State."[25]

Jackson quickly replied. Although he normally felt no obligation to justify his appointment policy, he made an exception in this case. There followed an assault on nullification: it was undemocratic, and not a legitimate form of states' rights nor part of the Jeffersonian heritage. "These being my opinions religiously entertained," he added, and "situated as I am, charged with the Executive of the laws, and the preservation of the Union and the Constitution, it could not be expected that I would select anyone to prosecute for a violation of them, who holds that a portion of our Revenue laws is not binding, and who would declare that the Union should be dissolved rather than these laws should be permitted to be enforced."[26]

Jackson also made it clear, in no uncertain terms, that he would not allow a state to abrogate a federal law. He believed protection to be constitutional and the existing tariff of 1828, even if a mistake, to have been legitimately adopted, therefore, he also believed it "his constitutional duty," as President to make sure "that the laws be faithfully executed."[27] He expressed this publicly in the late spring of 1831. The nullifiers of Charleston planned a Fourth of July celebration to denounce the tariff and defend their doctrine. The city's Unionist party arranged a separate event and invited Jackson to attend. Jackson declined to come, but sent a letter to be read at the gathering. In it he praised the value of the union, decried the effects of separation and warned "that high and sacred duties which must and will at all hazards, be performed, present an insurmountable barrier to the success of any plan of disorganization."[28]

Both the justice of Jackson's concern about appointing nullifiers to federal office and his determination to enforce federal laws are revealed in an episode that occurred later that summer. Two Charleston lawyers, Isaac E. Holmes and Alexander Mazyck, both supporters of nullification, tried to create a test case to challenge the constitutionality of the tariff of 1828. They imported goods, swore out a bond for the duties, and then declined to pay the bond, arguing that the tariff was invalid. The case was turned over to Edward Frost, the United States district attorney for South Carolina. Frost, however, chose to resign rather than bring suit. Jackson was furious. He first considered refusing the resignation and impeaching the District Attorney "for neglect of duty." But after reconsidering, the President decided to accept the resignation, and appointed a new District Attorney with "instructions to bring the suit and prosecute it with energy." "The Union," he wrote, "*shall be preserved.*"[29]

The case itself, heard late in September, attracted a lot of attention. George McDuffie, waiving his usual fee, agreed to argue the nullifier side. During the trial the presiding judge, a Unionist, refused to allow McDuffie to argue constitutional issues to a jury, which had been called because the sum involved was over $20.00. The judge ruled that juries could only decide questions of fact while all questions of law should be left to judges. McDuffie objected but was overruled, and he withdrew from the case. Following the judge's instructions, the jury found the bond to have been properly executed and ordered it paid. Although the nullifiers had suffered a minor tactical defeat, they did gain a strategic advantage, for it allowed them to argue that the case proved that it would not be possible to get their grievances redressed through the federal courts.[30]

Perhaps Jackson's most serious mistake in dealing with nullification was his failure to perceive that popular support for it grew in South Carolina between 1829 and 1832. He was convinced that the doctrine had been espoused for political purposes and did not really have the support of the people. "The people of South Carolina will not," he wrote in August of 1830, "*nay* cannot sustain such nullifying Doctrines. The Carolinians are a patriotic and high minded people, and they prize their liberty too high to jeopardise it at the shrine of an ambitious demagogue. . . ." And another time he asserted: "The South Carolinians, as a whole, are too patriotic to adopt such *mad projects* as the nullifiers of that state propose."[31]

Until South Carolina actually declared the tariffs of 1828 and 1832 null and void in November of 1832, Jackson was convinced that if he took a firm stand against nullification it would be rejected by the people of the state and the movement would dissipate itself and its leaders become isolated. "Nullification . . . ," he wrote to Van Buren "will ere long be *buried in oblivion,* doing no harm, but carrying with it . . . promoters, exciters and supporters."[32] He fully expected that his decision in 1831 to "recommend to Congress the propriety of taking up the Tariff, and making a judicious reduction of duties to meet the wants of Government after the public debt is paid . . . will annihilate the Nullifiers as they will be left without any pretext of Complaint."[33] Following the passage of the tariff of 1832 he predicted to a close friend: "You may expect to hear from So. Carolina a great noise . . . but the good sense of the people will put it down."[34]

Jackson saw nullification and tariff reform as completely separate issues, and he handled them in different ways. He understood many of the constitutional and ideological implications of nullification and firmly and forthrightly made clear his opposition to the doctrine. At the same time he was vague and evasive on the tariff and treated it mainly as a difficult political question he hoped to avoid having to confront at least until after his reelection in 1832. But the two issues were also related and Jackson seriously miscalculated the nature of that relationship. He never seemed to realize that his failure to push hard for tariff reform served to strengthen the position of the more extreme advocates of nullification in South Carolina. He also badly misjudged the degree of tariff reform that would be needed to satisfy not only South Carolina but the South in general on this issue. And he also failed to appreciate the extent to which widespread hostility to protection in the South would make many people there sympathetic to South Carolina's opposition to the tariffs of 1828 and 1832 even if they did not believe in nullification. As a consequence, when the nullification crisis finally occurred, at the end of his first administration, the President was to suffer the most serious defeat of his two terms in office.

III

What of Calhoun? Jackson's stormy relations with his Vice President dominated much of his first administration. In addition, a struggle between Calhoun and Van Buren over the presidential succession began almost immediately following Jackson's election. The result was a quick victory for Van Buren. In examining how this came about scholars have almost exclusively emphasized the Peggy Eaton Affair and the revelation to Jackson of Calhoun's attempt back in 1818 to punish him for his invasion of Florida. These were dramatic developments, and important ones, but they are only part of the story. Of equal, and probably even more, significance are the constitutional and policy differences that existed between the President and Van Buren on one side, and Calhoun on the other.

In the beginning of the struggle Van Buren appeared to be at a distinct disadvantage. He had supported William H. Crawford for the presidency in 1824 and during the campaign had been harshly critical of Jackson's military record and his lack of political experience. After that election the exigencies of local politics prevented Van Buren's early espousal of Jackson's cause; DeWitt Clinton, Van Buren's chief political rival in New York, had earlier come out for Jackson, and it was not until after Clinton's death in 1827 that Van Buren found it expedient to make his support public. Despite this, following his appointment as secretary of state in 1829 and his move to Washington, Van

Buren quickly became a close friend and confidant of the President. This was because the two men almost immediately discovered they shared much in common in how they viewed the leading political issues of the day. Van Buren had a strong record on states' rights. He and many other members of the Crawford wing of the Jeffersonian party had been critical of the post-1815 nationalist movement. As a senator from New York in the 1820s he opposed a federally sponsored program of internal improvements. On the state level, Van Buren's main political base was in the area east of the Hudson River and north of New York City, extending up into the Adirondack region. This part of the state did not benefit very much from the economic growth and prosperity created by the Erie Canal. Economically stagnant, it was hostile to most entrepreneurial legislation. Van Buren and his closest followers generally opposed the state's going into debt to build feeder canals; and as governor, for a brief period preceding his appointment as Secretary of State, Van Buren helped bring about the passage of the New York Safety Fund Plan, which closely regulated the state's banking activities and controlled and limited the highly profitable privilege of issuing paper money. As much as was politically feasible in the most economically developed and dynamic state of the Union, Van Buren had been a spokesman for agrarian values.[35]

The differences between Jackson and Van Buren tended to be slight. They involved questions of tactics and timing and not substance. Often they had to do with the tone and style with which the much more aggressive and outspoken Jackson wanted to confront the issues. This did not seem to bother the President very much and the high esteem Jackson held for his newfound friend expressed itself in the important role the Secretary of State played in the drafting of the first annual address and the Maysville Road veto. By the end of 1829 Jackson had pretty much decided who was to succeed him. He justified his choice primarily on the grounds that Van Buren was right on the issues. "Permit me here to say of Mr. Van Buren," the President confided to a close friend, "that I have found him everything that I could desire him to be, and believe him not only deserving *my* confidence, but the *Confidence of the Nation.* Instead of his being selfish and intriguing, as has been represented by some of his opponents, I have ever found him frank, open, candid, and manly. As a Counsellor he is *able* and *prudent,* Republican in his principles. . . . He, my dear friend, is not only well qualified, but desires to fill the highest office in the gift of the people who, in him, will find a true friend and safe depository of their rights and liberty."[36] A short time later in a letter to John Coffee, another close friend and confidant, Jackson described Van Buren as a man "whose situation has identified him with the success of the administration," and who "is firm to the core." He also described Van Buren as "a pure Republican who has labored with an eye single to promote the best interests of his country."[37]

Calhoun's experience with Jackson was almost the exact reverse. He began the contest with Van Buren in a very favorable position. He had dropped out of the presidential election in 1824 to run, successfully, for Vice President when his friends in Pennsylvania had been overwhelmed by the Jackson forces, and he helped deliver South Carolina to the General. As Vice President under

John Quincy Adams he had cautiously but effectively used his influence on Jackson's behalf. When Jackson assumed the presidency, the *United States Telegraph*—edited by Calhoun's close friend and eventual son-in-law, Duff Green—became the administration's semi-official national spokesman. With Jackson's election Calhoun expected to play an important, perhaps even dominant, role in the formulation of the new administration's policies.[38]

It was not to be. In the year following Jackson's inauguration, basic policy differences between Calhoun and the President rapidly emerged. Above all else, Calhoun favored tariff reform. He had written to Jackson shortly before the election, stressing the South's hostility to protection. "The belief that those now in power will be displaced shortly," he advised, "and that under an administration formed under your auspices, a better order of things will commence, in which an equal distribution of the burden and benefit of government, economy, the payment of the publick debt, and finally the removal of oppressive duties will be primary objects of policy is what mainly consoles this quarter of the Union under existing embarrassment."[39]

Calhoun went out of his way to let it be widely known that he placed a high premium on reduction. He viewed protection "in its tendency . . . by far the most dangerous question that has ever sprung under our system." It was economically oppressive and the chief source of the South's impoverishment. "I am of the impression," he wrote, "that the industry of the country from its great extent and diversity cannot be regulated by Congress without endangering our liberty. It is an opinion formed on much deliberation, which I fear experience may but too fatally prove to be true, unless the system be restored to what I deem its real intention." He repeatedly stressed his belief that protection in any form other than an incidental benefit from a revenue tariff was unconstitutional. It was crucial, therefore, to return to the true principles of the Constitution. Failure to do so would exacerbate sectional tensions between the North and the South and have the most dangerous consequences. Although Calhoun played down the immediate significance of disunionist sentiment in South Carolina, arguing the real object is "reformation not revolution," he felt "compelled, by a regard to truth, to say, that the sense of injustice has a strong tendency to weaken," the South's commitment to the Union, "and if long continued may finally wholly estrange them from the other sections."[40]

Jackson's refusal to push hard for tariff reform was a very important source of the tension that developed between him and his Vice President. A year after the new administration had taken office Kendall commented that: "Some of Mr. Calhoun's friends (and I have fear he does not discourage them) shew a disposition to throw everything into confusion. They are getting upon their 'high horse' again in relation to the Tariff and letter writers in Washington and newspaper writers in South Carolina, are throwing out their insinuations against Gen. Jackson and those who surround him . . . that there will yet be open war between the anti-tariff Hotspurs and the administration is by no means impossible. Mr. Calhoun is understood to be at the head of that party. You will foresee his fate if he suffers his restless ambition to hurry him into such conflict."[41]

Jackson's refusal to move on tariff reform hurt Calhoun politically in two important ways. First, it cut the ground out from Calhoun's attempt to control the radicals in South Carolina, many of whom, like McDuffie and Hamilton, advocated immediate nullification and talked seriously of secession. As one of the leading members of the moderate wing of the Nullification party, Calhoun had repeatedly offered assurances that once Jackson became President he would move for tariff reform. The President's remarks on the expediency and constitutionality of the tariff in his first annual address and Maysville Road veto message totally belied this, and it decisively strengthened the political position of the extremists in South Carolina.[42]

Second, Jackson's tariff policy clearly worked to Van Buren's advantage. One of the most difficult political problems confronting Van Buren emerged from the fact that his main base of national support came from the old Crawford wing of the Jeffersonian party. This alliance of plain republicans in the North and southern planters shared Jackson's feelings on internal improvements and the national bank, and did not have much problem with his Indian policy. But this alliance, with its strength located in New York, Virginia, North Carolina, and Georgia, was divided deeply on the issue of protection. Van Buren's home state of New York favored protection while his supporters in the South just as strongly opposed it. The formulation of any kind of tariff policy would be politically embarrassing for Van Buren. Therefore, it was to his interest to avoid the issue wherever possible. Jackson's vague position on the tariff allowed him to do this. Calhoun, on the other hand, was looking to the South for political support and was eager to erode Van Buren's influence there. To reduce the tariff, Calhoun hoped for an alliance with the West in return for which the South would support a reduction of the price of land in the federal domain, a high priority for most westerners. Jackson's refusal to push hard for tariff revision clearly indicated that Calhoun was not going to have much influence with the President and undercut his prestige with those uncommited and wavering southerners who had their doubts about Van Buren's tariff policy. It also indicated to westerners that Calhoun's support for bringing the President around on land prices would not be decisive.[43]

Calhoun and Jackson also differed on other issues. An early and intense disagreement developed over Jackson's support, in his early messages to Congress, of a plan eventually to distribute the federal government's surplus revenue to the states after the elimination of the national debt. Jackson favored the measure because "it is the only thing that can allay the jealousies arising between the different sections of the Union, and prevent that flagicious *log rolling legislation,* which must, in the end destroy everything like harmony, if not the Union itself. The moment the people see that the surplus revenue is to be divided among the states (when there shall be a surplus) and applied to internal improvements and education, they will instruct their members to husband the revenue for the payment of the national debt, so that the surplus afterwards may be distributed in an *equal ratio* among the several states."[44]

Calhoun vehemently opposed the measure. He believed distribution made a virtue out of a federal surplus and justified the continuation of a high tariff. As he saw it the two issues were inseparable. To bring about tariff reform it was absolutely crucial, he argued, to "prevent the *distribution of the surplus revenue,* the point in my opinion of the greatest danger. . . ." The measure, he argued, was "most unjust, unconstitutional and dangerous."[45]

Calhoun also did not share Jackson's enthusiasm for an assault on the Second Bank of the United States. He had been one of the prime movers in its establishment back in 1816; and in March of 1830 he wrote that his "every sentiment ever expressed in relation to the bank, remains unchanged." This was not really true, but he unquestionably appreciated the value of the institution, used its services, and remained on good terms with many of its advocates. To some extent his enthusiasm for it had waned a bit as the constitutional justification for the Bank did not square easily with his concern for states' rights. Consequently, it was not an issue he was eager to deal with during Jackson's first term. After Jackson attacked it in his first annual address, Calhoun wrote critically: "There is not the least foundation for the report that I have come out against the bank [of the United States]. I have not moved on it at all, either for or against, as I deem the agitation of the question every way premature. It will be time enough to discuss it four years hence, when we will have full knowledge of the operation of the institution, and will be able to determine what the public interest may demand with a full understanding of all the circumstances. I regret that the subject has been so prematurely brought forward."[46] This differed fundamentally from Jackson's attitude. The Bank, wrote Kendall, at this time "is a question upon which there will be no compromise. It will come to this: whoever is in favor of that Bank will be against Old Hickory. So it is well enough to know as soon as possible whom we shall have to fight."[47]

These differences were central to the split between Jackson and Calhoun and to the President's choice of Van Buren to be his successor. Indicating his preference for the New Yorker, Jackson wrote, "I find Mr. Calhoun objects to the apportionment of the surplus revenue among the several states, after the public debt is paid. He is also, silent on the Bank question, and is believed to have encouraged the introduction and adoption of the Resolution in the South Carolina Legislature relative to the Tariff."[48] In addition, Calhoun also tended to down-play the significance of Jackson's internal improvements policy and its appeal to those concerned with states' rights. There is also some evidence that Calhoun had reservations about the President's "rotation in office" and Indian policy, and secretly worked against the passage of the removal bill. Further, Jackson believed that it was at his Vice President's instigation that McDuffie—who was the chairman of the House Committee considering Jackson's proposal for an amendment to the Constitution providing for the direct election of President and Vice President—killed the measure.[49]

These differences also played a decisive role in Jackson's decision to replace Duff Green's *United States Telegraph* with Francis Preston Blair's *Washington Globe* as the administration's spokesman. Jackson's ascendancy had brought Green luxurious contracts as printer to the House and Senate and, when the new administration first took office, smaller assignments from the various cabinet departments. But as the President formulated his position on the issues he became disillusioned with Green, who was anti-tariff, generally sympathetic to the Bank of the United States, and partisan to Calhoun's presidential aspirations. Further, Jackson suspected Green of conspiring to prevent him from running for a second term. Blair, a close friend and political ally of Kendall, who edited the Frankfort, Kentucky *Argus* got the nod in large part because he was right on the key issues: vehemently anti-Bank and vigorously opposed to nullification. He could be expected, therefore, in Jackson's words, to "announce the policy and defend the administration."[50]

IV

Personal feuds, differences over the President's patronage policy and other political considerations also marred Jackson's first administration. Most of these involved Calhoun in one way or another. Because they occurred simultaneously with the enfolding of policy and constitutional differences between the President and Vice President, it is not always easy to separate cause from effect. Mainly, however, they were a secondary source for the conflict, and their main impact, and it was a very important one, tended to be on the tone, intensity, and focus of Jackson's reaction to the nullification crisis.

A long-standing and particularly bitter feud within the heterogeneous Jackson coalition existed between Calhoun and William H. Crawford of Georgia. It dated back to the time when both men had been members of James Monroe's cabinet, Calhoun as Secretary of War and Crawford as Secretary of the Treasury. Both wanted to become President, and a bitter competition ensued for southern support. Principles became involved, to a certain extent, fairly early as Crawford became the spokesman for those who wanted a return to states' rights and Jeffersonian orthodoxy while Calhoun adhered to his postwar nationalism for a much longer period of time. Each man assiduously cultivated a political following in the other's state, further heightening their mutual dislike, and several duels were fought by their followers. Crawford's presidential ambitions came to an end when he suffered a stroke during the election of 1824. Although he never again held national office, he determined to use his remaining influence to ruin Calhoun. In 1828 Crawford reluctantly threw his support to Jackson. At the same time he and his followers launched an unsuccessful movement to deny Calhoun the vice presidency. In the election Georgia's electors cast their nine votes for Jackson, seven of their ballots for Vice President to William Smith, Calhoun's arch-rival in South Carolina, and only two for Calhoun.[51]

Failing to deny Calhoun the vice presidency, Crawford remained determined to disrupt Calhoun's relationship with Jackson, and to make sure that his political ally from New York, Martin Van Buren, became the heir apparent. He did this by indirectly leaking word that Calhoun had led the unsuccessful movement to discipline Jackson in the secret cabinet meetings of the Monroe administration during the Seminole Indian controversy in 1818. The matter came to Jackson's attention early in 1828 in the form of an old letter from

Monroe to Calhoun implicating the latter. The Vice President claimed this letter had been stolen from his files. Jackson seemed interested and pursued the matter but not very vigorously, probably because he hoped to avoid a schism among his followers that might jeopardize his election chances. The incident, however, made a strong impression on many of Old Hickory's closest friends and political advisers in Tennessee, especially William B. Lewis and John Eaton, who became convinced that it would eventually tilt the succession struggle decisively in Van Buren's favor. And, since Jackson had repeatedly indicated during the campaign that he planned to serve only one term, the implications of the outcome of the struggle were made all the more immediate.[52]

The significance of these developments began to surface when Jackson announced his cabinet appointments. The War Department went to John Eaton, the senator from Tennessee, a close personal friend of the General, and his campaign manager in the elections of 1824 and 1828. Considering Eaton partial to Van Buren's interests, Jackson selected him because he "wanted to have one man about him in whom he had entire confidence."[53] Beyond this the President seems to have made up his mind to use the other positions to pay off the various political debts he had acquired in his quest for the White House; and in many of the decisions that followed Eaton appears to have played a key role. It was pretty much expected that Van Buren would be given the State Department, for he had brought not only New York but also most of Crawford's former supporters into the Jackson camp. No real effort was made to prevent his appointment, although there is some indication that Calhoun hoped it might go instead to Littleton Waller Tazewell of Virginia. What the South Carolinians wanted most was to get control of the Treasury Department, the key cabinet official to deal with tariff reform. The actual appointment almost turned out to be a total disaster for them because the President had made up his mind to use the post to reward Pennsylvania for its strong support in the last two presidential elections, and his first choice was Henry Baldwin, a staunch advocate of protection and one of the leaders of the anti-Calhoun faction of the Keystone State's Democratic party. This was prevented when the influential pro-Calhoun "Family Party" of Pennsylvania strongly protested and managed to have their own leader, Samuel Ingham, appointed instead. Still, it was at most a highly qualified victory for Calhoun. Although Ingham was warmly attached to the Vice President, Calhoun and his followers would have much preferred the position to have gone to a South Carolinian like Langdon Cheves who would push hard for tariff reduction. But Jackson would have none of it. Pennsylvania was an extreme high tariff state and this made Ingham's ability, which was none too highly thought of, to push for reform problematical. The previous year as a member of the House of Representatives voting on the Tariff of 1828 he had resolved his conflicting loyalties by absenting himself. Only the reappointment of John McLean, strongly distrusted by Van Buren and his followers, to the Post-Office was satisfactory to the Calhounites, and this success turned out to be short lived when McLean accepted an appointment to the Supreme Court and was replaced by the more neutral William T. Barry of Kentucky.[54]

John McPherson Berrien of Georgia became attorney general and John Branch of North Carolina, secretary of the navy. Berrien, as a United States senator, had been an effective critic of John Quincy Adams and therefore considered friendly to Jackson's interests. In addition, he was right on the Indian question and came from a state that strongly wanted to have its views on this subject represented in the cabinet. Branch was an original Jackson supporter dating back to 1824, who was sympathetic to the President's views on the Bank and internal improvements, and came from an important state loyal to Jackson which had not been previously represented in the cabinet. Neither man, at this point, was a partisan of Calhoun or Van Buren, rather they owed their appointments to Eaton's influence. They also both came from the South. This was probably an important consideration since Old Hickory was determined to have no one from South Carolina who was in any way tainted with the doctrine of nullification, and he was not high on the various candidates from Virginia who had been suggested for cabinet posts. Since Jackson had taken his other cabinet appointments from the North and West, Berrien and Branch offered sectional balance.[55]

In making these appointments, Jackson consulted with Eaton and Lewis and perhaps some other close friends in Tennessee, but not with any of the other key political leaders in his winning coalition. These appointments reveal his determination to be his own man and his initial desire to try to stay clear of the Calhoun-Van Buren rivalry. The followers of both men expressed consternation when the announcements were made. Van Buren was advised to turn down the offered position because the rest of the cabinet was of such low quality that his membership in it would become a political liability. And the New Yorker, himself, was dismayed that he had not been consulted and had strong reservations about the abilities of Eaton, Branch, and Berrien. At the same time, James Hamilton, Jr., and Robert Y. Hayne of South Carolina, disappointed and angry at their state's not getting the Treasury Department, arranged a special meeting with the President and asked him to reconsider. Following Jackson's refusal, Hamilton commented "in the words of Sir Anthony Absolute, I am perfectly cool—damn cool—never half so cool in my life."[56]

An important second echelon appointment also revealed Jackson's independence. Over Van Buren's strong objections the important post of Collector of Customs for New York City went to Samuel Swartwout who had energetically supported Jackson in the recent campaign, a disastrous decision as Swartwout eventually defaulted. Jackson also followed a policy of generally excluding Virginians from important posts because he felt that the leaders of that state had too long dominated the federal government and were, despite their support for him in 1828, too haughty for their own good. This too caused Van Buren concern because a number of his most important southern allies came from the Old Dominion. Calhoun did no better, although he really pushed hard for only two appointments. He tried to get Eaton to appoint Christopher Van Deventer, who had been the Chief Clerk in the War Department under him during Monroe's administration to the same position. And he made a special effort with the President to obtain the post of Treasurer of the United States for Virgil Maxcy, an old friend and a political ally from Maryland. He was unsuccessful in both cases.[57]

From the moment Jackson announced his cabinet appointments and took office, widespread discontent developed within his party over both his failure to consult properly about his selections and the quality of his appointments. During the presidential canvass in 1828 the National Republicans had argued that Jackson, both by temperament and because of his lack of political experience, was unfit to govern the country properly and if elected would end up being manipulated by unscrupulous politicians. Many Democrats now feared this might prove true. Unwilling to criticize the President directly, they focused their hostility on Eaton and William B. Lewis, Eaton's brother-in-law and Jackson's crony, who had a reputation for being a political intriguer and who was now living in the White House. Several influential Tennessee politicians, James K. Polk, Felix Grundy, and Hugh Lawson White, expressed concern as did the President's secretary and nephew Andrew Jackson Donelson over Eaton and Lewis's influence with Jackson, and the way they controlled access to him. Van Buren also had doubts about Eaton's honesty—"his lax political notions," he called it—and reservations about Lewis's advocacy of the sweeping removal of incumbents from office, but he seemed willing to accommodate himself, in a guarded fashion, to what was in fact a *fait accompli*, and probably also because he received assurances that both Eaton and Lewis were favorable to him in his rivalry with Calhoun.[58]

Calhoun also blamed Eaton and Lewis for his difficulties. He, at first, remained silent, but his failure to obtain a position for Maxcy, despite strenuous efforts soon led him to remark "that it seems to me, that . . . the highest offices, at least, are going too uniformly in a certain direction." In the fall of 1829 he noted: "I see enough in our situation, to cast a gloom on my anticipation of the future course of our affairs," and he complained about "the abuse of the powers and patronage of the government." He went on to observe that support for Jackson in 1828 had been necessitated by the fact that his "Military Reputation" could defeat the alliance between Adams and Clay. Still unprepared to repudiate the President, he added: "that he is in principle true to the grounds on which he was elected I do not doubt, but that he may by the arts and intrigues of him to whom you refer [Van Buren], seconded by some unprincipled individuals [Eaton and Lewis], in whom he had improperly placed confidence, be led to act in opposition to the principles, on which he has been promoted, is not at all improbable. In fact, I see many reasons to fear such may be the fact. . . ."[59]

These developments coincided with the "Eaton-imbroglio," which according to Van Buren started as "a private and personal matter which only acquired political consequences by its adaptation to the gratification of resentments springing out of the formation of the cabinet, and, as we supposed, to the elevation or depression of individuals of high position."[60] It began on New Year's Day 1829, when Eaton had married Peggy O'Neale Timberlake, the daughter of a local innkeeper and widow of a naval officer who had taken his own life the previous fall while on cruise in the Mediterranean. Attractive and socially gregarious, the twenty-nine-year-old Peggy lived at the O'Neale tavern. Eaton, a widower, also resided there, helped her and her father out financially, and many believed had an affair with Peggy. Rumor had it that at one point she had even had an abortion because the baby's timing would prove an embarrassment since her husband had been too long at sea; and some claimed that the general humiliation of her liaison with Eaton had caused her husband's suicide. The new marriage had taken place with Jackson's blessing, and perhaps even at the President-elect's urging.[61]

The marriage scandalized much of Washington society who ostracized the new couple, refusing to return their calls or to incorporate them in their social gatherings. This included Calhoun's wife, Floride, and the wives of Ingham, Branch, and Berrien. It also included the President's niece, Emily Donelson, whom he had brought to Washington to act as his official hostess, Sarah Childress Polk, whose husband, James K., was a Jackson loyalist, the wives of several of the foreign diplomats, and the minister of the President's Washington congregation. In its origins, at least, the Affair was not a political ploy. "It is," wrote one senator loyal to the President, "impossible to force her upon society here."[62]

But the Eaton Affair quickly developed serious political ramifications. Jackson was outraged at the couple's not being received by Washington society, and he immediately came to their defense. In fact, he overreacted. Why? What strong feelings did the messy affair uncover? Undoubtedly part of the explanation is that Jackson had arrived in Washington grief-stricken by his own wife's recent death, and he was embittered by the abuse she had received during the recent election for having married him, as a consequence of a legal technicality, before her divorce from her first husband became final. The President believed these attacks had driven his beloved Rachel to an early grave. In addition to this, Eaton was a friend, and Jackson placed great value on friendship. "I will never abandon an old and well tried friend for new ones, for slight or trivial causes," he wrote, "nor will I ever be silent when female character is wantonly assailed. . . ."[63] At another point he asserted: "The world in truth, cannot say that I ever abandoned a friend . . . unless "they abandoned me without cause." To his confidant John Coffee he explained his defense of the Eatons on the grounds "if it is believed, that I can ever abandon a friend, and that under circumstances with which my friend Eaton is surrounded, they know nothing of me. 'A friend in need is a friend indeed' and I loath the wretch that would abandon his friends for the smiles of a faction. By me it never has or will be done."[64]

The "Eaton Malaria," as some called it, dominated the administration's internal politics during Jackson's first year in office. In large part Old Hickory himself was responsible for this. Whenever possible he confronted and pursued the evidence. He tried to determine the causes of Peggy's first husband's death, sent Lewis to a New York hotel to check out the abortion story, and called a special cabinet meeting to discuss the matter. In addition he went out of his way to pay attention to Peggy, held a special dinner for the Eatons and other cabinet heads and their wives, temporarily broke with the Donelsons on this issue, and in effect ordered his cabinet members to include the Eatons at their private social functions. When Ingham, Berrien, and Branch refused, he stopped holding formal cabinet meetings and instead consulted with an informal and changing group of advisers who became known as the "kitchen Cabinet."

When Van Buren, a widower, arrived in Washington, he quickly sized up the situation. To the President's delight, he went out of his way to be gracious to the Eatons. Barry acted much as did Lewis and Kendall, the fourth auditor of the Treasury, whose influence with the President was sharply on the rise. The Calhouns, on the other hand, continued to snub Peggy and her husband. Although there is little evidence to substantiate the charge that it was the Vice President and his wife who initiated the movement to exclude the Eatons socially, it is clear that they did nothing to try to alleviate the problem. Further, by the fall of 1829, Calhoun had become fully aware that Eaton was politically hostile to him, and he was concerned about Eaton's enormous influence with the President. It is also evident that by this time Calhoun and his friends were becoming increasingly hostile to Kendall and Barry. By the end of 1829, the alignment on the Eaton Affair was beginning to coincide with the Van Buren-Calhoun rivalry.[65]

At first, Jackson blamed Henry Clay and his followers for his administration's social problems. He viewed the situation as a deliberate plot on their part to embarrass him and to prove that he was unfit to govern the country. What he could not understand, therefore, was why so many of his own supporters seemed to be encouraging it.[66] Then, in November, he claimed, "this persecution was founded in political views, looking to the future. Jealousy arose that Eaton might not be a willing instrument to those particular views, that his popularity was growing and it was necessary to put him out of the Cabinet and destroy him regardless what injury it might do me or my administration." By the end of the year he began to suspect that Calhoun was responsible for the Eatons' difficulties. "I have a right to believe," he contended, "that most of the troubles, vexations and difficulties I have had to encounter since my arrival in the city have been occasioned by his friends."[67]

Until this point, despite the intrigues of Crawford and his supporters and the political activities of Eaton and Lewis on Van Buren's behalf, the President himself does not seem to have been hostile to Calhoun. Although his cabinet selections and appointments did not please Calhoun, they had not been noticeably partial to Van Buren, and while the President had made known his dislike for nullification he had not held Calhoun responsible for the doctrine. Why the reversal?

Any explanation must recognize that in November 1829, Jackson was preparing his first annual message to Congress. In it, for the first time, he publicly laid out his views on key political issues, and he began to formulate a legislative program. Van Buren played an important role in drafting the address, for by now both men were fully aware of their shared views on the issues. Calhoun, on the other hand, played no role at all in the writing of the message, since it had also become clear that the two differed fundamentally on the issues. In fact, it is in the very letter where Jackson, for the first time, indicates his preference for Van Buren to succeed him to the presidency and criticizes Calhoun for his opposition to distribution and silence on the Bank and accepts the rumor that the Vice President was responsible for the *South Carolina Exposition and Protest,* that the President, also for the first time, explicitly accuses Calhoun's friends of being responsible for the Eatons' social misfortunes.

This, however, is not all that occurred in November and December of 1829. For it is at this time that Jackson once again took up Calhoun's role in the cabinet discussions that followed his invasion of Florida. Why, after he had earlier chosen not to pursue the matter, he took it up again, has never been adequately determined. Possibly his developing hostility to the Vice President over their policy differences and the Eaton Affair may have convinced him that the whole business was worth re-examination. Perhaps Lewis, who played the key role in reintroducing the subject to Jackson, was able to assure him that new and irrefutable evidence would be forthcoming. It may even have been, though the evidence here is very contradictory, that Jackson was sure of Calhoun's duplicity all the time and simply decided, now that the election was behind him and his relationship with Van Buren adequately secured, that the appropriate moment "to get" Calhoun had arrived. Whatever the reasons, from this point on Jackson pursued the matter with a vengeance.

Several months later, Jackson received a copy of a letter from William H. Crawford that revealed Calhoun's role in the cabinet meetings held following the invasion of Florida in 1818 and his desire to have Jackson punished. The President sent a copy of it to the Vice President and in a brief note demanded an explanation. Calhoun did not deny his role in the cabinet proceedings. But he refused to apologize. Instead, he raised questions about the appropriateness of a discussion of his conduct of the War Department under Monroe, defended himself by taking issue with Jackson's claim that his orders authorized him to pursue the Seminoles across the border, cast doubts upon Crawford's account of what happened in the cabinet and his motivations in raising the whole issue at this time, and suggested that Van Buren was behind the whole episode. "The whole affair," he wrote, "is a political maneuver, in which the design is, that you should be the instrument and myself the victim, but in which the real actors, are carefully concealed, by an artful movement."[68]

There followed a long, and at times angry, and at other times petty and petulant, correspondence. Despite this, the President tried to avoid an open break. Calhoun's allies in Congress, where the administration was already weak, were important and useful, and the administration had been embarrassed enough by the Eaton Affair and did not want to live with a public feud between the President and Vice President also. Late in 1830 an attempt was made to reconcile the two men and Jackson apparently "promised to bury the affair in oblivion, provided the other party will act in good faith," but Calhoun would not agree unless it included full vindication. "Every opening was made for me to renew my intercourse with the President, which I have declined," he noted, "and will continue so to do, till he retracts what he has done." He then added: "His friends are much alarmed." Jackson, however, refused to offer full forgiveness, and in February 1831 Calhoun openly broke with the administration by arranging to have the whole correspondence published by Green in the *United States Telegraph.*[69]

Although the incident was more a manifestation than a cause for the hostility between the President and Calhoun, it did have a profound effect on Jackson's attitude toward the Vice President as an individual. Back in 1824 he had written, "There are none so dangerous as hypocritical friends. . . ." And in making his cabinet appointments, he had remarked, "My first and strong desire, is to have associated with me in the discharge of my Responsible trust, men in whom, under all exigencies I can repose." Early in the correspondence, when he objected to Calhoun's explanation of his role in the cabinet discussions back in 1818, he wrote, "I had a right to believe that you were my sincere friend, and until now never expected to have occasion to say to you, in the language of Caesar, *et tu Brute.*" Jackson now believed "a man who could secretly make the attempt, as he did in the cabinet in 1818, to destroy me and that under the strongest professions of friendship, is base enough to do anything."[70]

Following the publication of their correspondence, which Jackson viewed as a deliberate attempt "to hold me forth to the world in a ludicrous light" and make him look as if he were being manipulated by Van Buren, his feelings toward Calhoun became increasingly intemperate.[71] According to Blair he even regarded Clay "with much more kindness than he does Calhoun."[72] Jackson now had nothing but unrestrained hatred for Calhoun. He held him responsible for all his difficulties, especially the Eaton Affair and his lack of support in Congress. "I now believe him," the President wrote, "one of the greatest intriguers on earth, and the fullest of duplicity and deceit. I know he will *lie,* and knowing this, I know he is fit for any act of human depravity, that his selfish ambition may suggest. . . ." To Jackson, Calhoun had become "one of the basest and most dangerous men living—a man, devoid of principle, and would sacrifice his friend, his country, and forsake his god, for selfish personal ambition." Or as he put it another time: "I have no hesitation in saying that Calhoun is one of the most base hypocritical and unprincipled villains in the United States."[73]

Jackson's opposition to nullification predated his hatred for Calhoun. But his hostility to the Vice President colored his attitude toward the doctrine and is an important consideration in explaining why the President reacted as violently as he did to events in South Carolina during the fall of 1832. So violent, in fact, was his reaction that it transformed the whole nature of the nullification crisis.

V

In the spring of 1831, upon Van Buren's advice, Jackson moved to cleanse his administration completely of Calhoun's influence. The New Yorker and Eaton tendered their resignations, and the President requested the same from Ingham, Berrien, and Branch. Although they complied, they did so unwillingly, and to protect their reputations each man published, in versions highly unfavorable to the President, his own account of their relations with Eaton and his wife, and accused Jackson of trying to regulate their social lives. Infuriated, Eaton challenged Ingham to a duel. Ingham refused, but a little while thereafter fled Washington "in terror" at Eaton's threats of revenge. Shortly afterwards the Eatons left Washington, but by this time the dissolution of the cabinet had turned into a major political scandal and was considered further proof, according to the President's critics, of his unfitness to govern the country.

The reconstituted cabinet consisted of Edward Livingston, formerly of New York and now of Louisiana as Secretary of State and Louis McLane of Delaware as Secretary of the Treasury. Although both men favored rechartering the Second Bank of the United States, they were nonetheless highly able and extremely loyal to the President. Lewis Cass, former governor of the Michigan Territory became secretary of war after Hugh Lawson White of Tennessee declined the post, while Roger Brooke Taney of Maryland became attorney general, and Levi Woodbury of New Hampshire, secretary of the navy. No one in the new cabinet could be considered even faintly partial to the Vice President. Nor could any of them be considered spokesmen for Southern interests, as nobody was openly hostile to protection or committed to a major downward revision of the tariff. So confident was Van Buren that this development augured well for his own political future that he accepted an appointment, after Congress adjourned, as Minister to England, and left for his new post without the Senate's confirmation.

While this was going on, circumstances were forcing Calhoun to clarify his incongruous relationship with the nullification movement in South Carolina. Although he had authored the *Exposition and Protest* in 1828, he had been, up till now, a moderating influence upon the more militant advocates of nullification and disunion, and, fearful of losing national support for his bid for the presidency, had avoided publicly acknowledging his role in the drafting of the nullification doctrine, or "state interposition," as he preferred to label it. Following his break with Jackson he quickly moved to improve his ties with the nullifiers. "Our situation is indeed critical," he wrote to one South Carolina radical shortly before he published his correspondence with the President, ". . . of one thing we may be perfectly assured, that the general government will not relax its hold, unless compelled, and that she cannot be compelled unless the South should unite in one earnest and decided pressure, or some one of the States nullify the unconstitutional tariff acts." Calhoun recognized that as long as Jackson was President there was little hope for a "united effort" on the part of the South, therefore he began to argue, "we must next look to the action of our own State, as she is the only one, that can possibly put herself on her sovereignty."[74]

To a large extent, Calhoun was simply adjusting to the political realities of the situation as the strength of the nullifiers increased sharply in 1831. Among other things this meant that Calhoun's ability to control the course of events in

South Carolina was on the wane. "My friends, out of the State," he wrote, "seem to think . . . that another duty is imposed on me, to step forward in order to arrest the current of events. They appear to take it for granted, that it is in my power. In this they make a great mistake."[75]

Calhoun, after his break with Jackson, was unwilling to either confront or deny the Radicals. "You say that my friends feel anxious about the effects which the course of the State will have on me," he commented as early as September 1830 to one correspondent critical of Radical threats coming out of South Carolina, "and are desirous that the public should have some evidence of my opposition to the ultra measures proposed by the Charleston Hotspurs. Knowing the strong and steady attachment of my friends I cannot regard their solicitude with any surprise, but thinking as I do, both of the intention of my friends in this State, and the character of the remedy which they propose, no earthly consideration would induce me to do an act or utter a sentiment which might countenance an imputation on the purity and patriotism of their motives." He continued to deny, however, that the leading nullifiers intended disunion or the use of force; "on the contrary, right or wrong in their views, they are deeply devoted to the Constitution." He insisted that nullification was a peaceful remedy, "the only means, by which consideration can be prevented, and thereby our liberty, our Union and the Constitution saved."[76]

Calhoun's inability to control developments in South Carolina was clear by the spring of 1831. By that time the Radicals had completely abandoned any hope that Jackson might move to lower the tariff. "As for Old Hickory," James Hamilton, Jr., wrote, "he has fallen below *even contempt* & the only inquiry is what sort of thing is this that we have been worshipping with such stupid blindness."[77] Hamilton and McDuffie were now determined to push the state into open opposition to the administration's tariff policy, and launched their final drive to capture the necessary two-thirds seats in the legislature in the elections of 1832 that would allow them to call a convention and nullify the tariff of 1828. In Charleston on May 19, 1831, McDuffie delivered a "seemingly inspired" speech which contained an extreme statement of the nullifiers' point of view and put the lie to Calhoun's assertions that state interposition was peaceful and constitutional. McDuffie not only denounced the tariff as unconstitutional and called upon the state to nullify it, but also declared, "The Union, such as the majority have made it is a foul monster," and endorsed violence and revolution if necessary to protect the state's sovereign rights.[78] "He has," an alarmed Duff Green wrote, pleading with Calhoun to renounce the address "given to the Globe and Van Buren papers the food upon which they are to keep alive the odium too widely diffused against Nullification, and has done more than Daniel Webster and Henry Clay could do to confirm the tariff & elevate Clay."[79]

Although Calhoun described the speech as "unexpected" and "unprudent" and it upset him, he did not repudiate it. The Radicals had become too strong. In July 1831 Hamilton organized the Charleston States Rights and Free Trade Association to coordinate nullifier activities throughout the state. Its purpose was not only "to make Nullification easy but successful too."[80] In the year that followed, Unionist opposition quickly collapsed, a victim of personality conflicts, poor organizational skills, and a lack of viable alternatives. As the nullifier campaign in South Carolina gained momentum the pressure on Calhoun to declare himself publicly increased. Although he remained uneasy about the intensity of the Radicals' opposition to the federal government and was unhappy with the talk of disunion and revolution, he nonetheless prepared to endorse state interposition openly. "My opinion was decidedly against active operations this summer," he noted. "I saw many and powerful reasons why, as much time should be afforded as was possible, before the State and the Union should be called on to take sides *finally*. Nothing is more dangerous, than to make the issue too soon, with a growing cause, as I believe ours to be. But events have taken another direction; and the most must be made of it. Relaxation now would be fatal."[81]

At the end of July, Calhoun published his famous Fort Hill letter endorsing nullification. By doing this Calhoun indicated that he was first and foremost a South Carolinian, and that he was determined to remain his state's leading spokesman in national politics. He did not support the calls of the more zealous nullifiers for disunion and revolution; in fact his letter stressed his commitment to the Union and his belief that nullification was essentially a conservative remedy that would save the Union from the tyranny of majority rule. But Calhoun had, nonetheless, clearly and openly aligned himself with nullification as both a doctrine and a movement.[82]

Despite all this Calhoun continued to retain hopes of becoming President in 1832. He believed the recent disclosures about the Eaton Affair following the dissolution of the cabinet would finish Jackson. The President, he believed, was now held in contempt by most congressmen, and had lost the confidence of party leaders almost everywhere. "Should he fall, as it appears to me inevitable," he argued, "a new scene would be opened. Our old opponents would be at a loss where to rally. They could not on Clay, and Mr. Van Buren's prospects are hopeless." A union of good and honest men, Calhoun argued, would elect him "to rescue the country from much distraction, and perhaps, even danger." His platform was a sectional alliance between the West and the South. For the West he favored a constitutional amendment allowing a federal program of internal improvements financed by the sale of public lands. In return the South would get a general lowering of the tariff with selective protection so as not to completely alienate the North.[83]

Calhoun's hopes for the presidency were completely undercut by several developments in 1831. To begin with, Jackson made up his mind to run for reelection. The President recognized that many Democratic members of Congress had been alienated by his vetoes, his patronage policies and the messy publicity that surrounded the Eaton Affair, the dissolution of the cabinet and Vice President Calhoun's open break with the administration. Nonetheless he remained convinced that he retained the loyalty of the electorate.

Calhoun also completely miscalculated the extent of Clay's desire to become President in 1832. Although both men were now openly hostile to Jackson, Calhoun, at this time, rejected any kind of alliance with Clay, "who in my opinion has done great mischief to the Country." For while Clay supported a moderate kind of tariff reform, he still remained committed to protection, and opposed to nullification. Clay also favored rechartering the Bank of the United States and had made up his mind to make it the major issue in the coming presidential contest if Jackson vetoed it. Convinced that Clay stood no chance of winning in 1832, Calhoun unsuccessfully tried to convince his Kentucky rival to abandon the presidential contest, at least in the South. Clay refused, which Calhoun believed effectively prevented him from opposing Jackson in the South because the people of that section would not abandon Jackson to support him and risk the chance that Clay and the American System might triumph.[84]

Finally, it was essential to Calhoun's strategy to be able to continue to pose as a moderate in his opposition to the tariff so as not to alienate, totally, his support in the North. But the Radical nullifiers of South Carolina would not cooperate. Hamilton, then governor, rejected Duff Green's suggestion that they compromise with the manufacturing interests on the tariff as part of an attempt to get Calhoun the presidency. "I have replied very explicitly to him," Hamilton confided, "that in no shape lot or scot would we be included in the arrangement, that we would take no part in the presidential election and that I was quite sure that Mr. C's prospects were as hopeless as his Ruin would be certain if he was brought to give his countenance to such a compact." Green had also "civilly asked if we were all crazy" when McDuffie had delivered his May 19 speech advocating disunion and revolution. Hamilton responded "that as for surrendering nullification . . . this was as impossible as his proposed league between the nullifiers and the manufacturers which in itself was as practicable as a confederation between the Pole and the Cossack." Hamilton also added, "I have no doubt he [Green] moves in this matter with Calhoun's sanction." Radicals like Hamilton were determined to force Calhoun "to see the essential weakness of his occupying a double position, Janus faced, with one expression of countenance for one side of the Potomac and another expression for the other—."[85] Hamilton got his way when Calhoun issued his Fort Hill letter, for it effectively destroyed whatever chances he had to be a viable presidential candidate in 1832.

Nonetheless Calhoun continued to remain an important and in some ways a highly prescient political figure. He perceptively criticized Clay for being unrealistic in his continued commitment to the values of the American System: "He appears to me to be where he was 10 years ago, on all questions of political economy, with this disadvantage, that his system then was in the flood but is now in the ebb."[86] He correctly viewed Clay as an ineffective presidential candidate and conceded Jackson victory in 1832, but nevertheless insisted that widespread disaffection existed in the South and predicted that a crisis would soon occur, and while concerned about the dangers it would unleash, believed it would ultimately benefit the country. "Our situation," he wrote, "is a strange one. Jackson is losing ground, without his opponent gaining. Disgust and uneasiness and discontent are gradually taking hold of the public, which if they take the right direction, if they shall cause the people to look into the real cause of our present alarming condition, and to apply the proper remedy, will end in a great and salutary reform, which may perpetuate our liberty and prosperity to the latest generation."[87]

VI

What merit was there to Calhoun's claims that widespread opposition to the Jackson administration existed in the South? Some historians have tended to dismiss these claims arguing that Calhoun was grasping at straws to further his own political ambitions, others that he simply was deluding himself. They point, in particular, to his unrealistic assessment of his own chances for the presidency in 1832 and the unwillingness of any other state formally to support nullification. This argument is not so much wrong as it is inaccurate, for it does not sufficiently take into account the concern that existed among important political leaders in the South over a number of Jackson's political decisions and policies or the sympathy that existed for South Carolina's opposition to the tariff and the nullifiers' grappling with the thorny question of how to protect minority rights in the face of majority tyranny. Anti-tariff and anti-Van Buren and to a lesser extent anti-Jackson feeling was real and intense in certain parts of the South. Because it did not automatically convert into support for Calhoun's political ambitions and for nullification does not mean it did not exist.

These attitudes were manifested in several different ways. First, there was a group, particularly strong in the United States Senate, over which Calhoun as Vice President presided, who were willing to cooperate openly with him in his opposition to the administration. The group included Littleton Waller Tazewell and John Tyler of Virginia, George Poindexter of Mississippi, and Gabriel Moore of Alabama. Combined with the two senators from South Carolina, Robert Y. Hayne and Stephen Miller, who recently deserted the Unionist faction in his state to join the nullifiers, they could on certain key issues cooperate effectively with the National Republicans to harass the administration. A demonstration of their power came in January 1832 when they arranged a tie vote in the Senate allowing Calhoun to defeat Van Buren's appointment as Minister to England. Although in the long run this may have been a political mistake because Jackson retaliated by insisting that the New Yorker be given the Vice Presidency in 1832, it nonetheless was a clear demonstration of strength on the part of those Southern Democrats hostile to Jackson and partial to Calhoun.[88]

Less overt, but nonetheless real, was the lack of enthusiasm on the part of many of the members of the congressional delegation from Jackson's home state of Tennessee for the President's policies. In particular they were unhappy over the extent of Eaton and Lewis's influence, the administration's tariff policy, and Van Buren's ascendancy. This group included the state's two senators, Felix Grundy and Hugh Lawson White, and Representatives Cave Johnson, James K. Polk, Robert Desha and Pryor Lea. Closely associated with them were George M. Bibb, senator from Kentucky, and two representatives from

that state, Henry Daniel and Charles A. Wickliffe. During the cabinet controversy that dominated so much of Jackson's first two years in office they con-
spired to convince the President to abandon Eaton, only to be sharply rebuffed.
They also attended the Jefferson Birthday Dinner and favored Calhoun's plans
for a South-West alliance that would be based on a bargain involving low land
prices for some kind of tariff reform. But a mixture of personal loyalty to
Jackson combined with political caution arising from a fear of the political
consequences of openly opposing the President, forced them, for the time
being, to muffle their criticism.[89]

The political course of Felix Grundy and Hugh Lawson White during
Jackson's first administration well illustrate the tenuous nature of this group's
support for the President's policies. Grundy started out as a strong Calhoun
supporter. During the debate between Hayne and Webster on Foote's resolution, Grundy openly endorsed nullification, and he tried to effect a reconcilia-
tion between Jackson and his Vice President when the split occurred over the
revelation of Calhoun's role in the Seminole Indian controversy. But he soon
got into political trouble for his efforts when Eaton resigned from the cabinet
and began to express interest in running for Grundy's Senate seat in 1832.
With Jackson's backing Eaton would be a formidable opponent. In addition,
Ephraim Foster, a nominal Jackson man, but really a representative of the
Nashville commercial interests, and incipient Whig, also was planning to challenge Grundy, and he had rapidly growing support, especially among those
sympathetic to the Second Bank of the United States.[90]

Faced with the charge of being a nullifier and unfriendly to the President,
Grundy backed away from overtly supporting Calhoun. In fact, immediately
after he heard about McDuffie's rousing May 19 speech equating nullification
with disunion and revolution, he wrote Calhoun requesting a letter that would
attest to his loyalty to the President. Still, his position on the tariff—"it is
constitutional but is unequal unjust & oppressive"—showed that despite his
unwillingness to any longer endorse nullification he retained considerable sympathy for the spirit and focus of South Carolina's opposition.[91]

White was an old personal and professional friend of the President's. Nonetheless he had strong reservations about many of the developments that took
place during Jackson's first administration. He distrusted Eaton and Lewis's
influence and was unhappy with the way the President handled the social and
political problems arising from Eaton's marriage. More careful than Grundy,
he never endorsed nullification, but he was strongly anti-tariff and critical of
Jackson's hostility to South Carolina's course. "The censure," he observed,
"bestowed upon Hayne, . . . Hamilton and others is *unkind* and I think, un-
wise—we have always had, and still need, the aid of these people, and if we
cannot *approve* all their opinions, we ought to let *their* enemies find fault with
them." When Eaton resigned, Jackson offered White the position of secretary
of war, but, much to the President's disappointment, he declined offering as an
excuse the recent death of his wife and several children and the contraction of
consumption by another daughter. More was involved, however, for he continued to remain active in politics. His refusing the cabinet post also seems to

have been motivated by a reluctance to become too closely associated with the administration. But at this point he also was unwilling to openly criticize Jackson. Calhoun described him as "intelligent & pure," but "cautious to timidity." Although White claimed to be neither "a Calhoun Jackson man, or a Van Buren Jackson man," both his sympathies and most of his friends belonged with the former group.[92]

Throughout the South there were important political leaders who were both disgusted by the politics of the Jackson administration and sympathetic to Calhoun and South Carolina's stand on the tariff. Most of them did not endorse nullification but believed, as John Quitman of Mississippi put it, that "Carolina tho' she may be wrong has taken the field in our cause." In addition to Quitman, Abraham Scott, a close political ally of Poindexter's, and governor of Mississippi was understood to be sympathetic to nullification as was John Floyd, the governor of Virginia who was rabidly anti-Jackson and anti-Van Buren.[93]

John Branch of North Carolina had not started out as a Calhoun supporter when appointed to the cabinet in 1829, but he distrusted Eaton and strongly favored tariff reduction. The "Eaton-imbroglio" made him an open sympathizer of the Vice President and a bitter opponent of Van Buren. Following his resignation from the cabinet he returned to North Carolina and was elected a member of the United States House of Representatives. His political allies included Samuel P. Carson, also a member of the House, and less overtly Willie P. Mangum in the United States Senate. Within the Tar Heel state Branch's opposition to the Jackson administration had strong support from such state leaders as Governor James Iredell, and William Polk, Charles Fisher, Edward B. Dudley and John Owen as well as several important newspapers.[94]

After leaving the cabinet, Berrien returned to Georgia and led the opposition to the administration. Although he never endorsed nullification as a proper constitutional remedy, he was vigorously anti-tariff, openly critical of Jackson and Van Buren, and very sympathetic to Calhoun and South Carolina's determination to defy the federal government. He had an important ally in Augustin S. Clayton, prominent member of the state bar, former judge, and one of Georgia's representatives in Congress.[95]

In Alabama there also existed a strong faction, "still professing the greatest devotion to" the President, but who really were determined "to promote the views & wishes of the nullifiers, & to embarrass Gen. Jackson's administration, by every, indirect, means. . . ." In December 1830 they managed to prevent the reelection of John McKinley, a staunch defender of the President, to the United States Senate, and selected instead Gabriel Moore who openly sided with Calhoun. Other important leaders of the group included Dixon H. Lewis, a member of the House of Representatives, and James M. Calhoun, the Vice President's nephew, who was active in the state's General Assembly.[96]

Even more pervasive was southern hostility toward the tariff. The senators and representatives of the section had cast their votes overwhelmingly against the measure in 1828. Although the tariff of 1832 had more support among southern congressmen this did not signify satisfaction or even acceptance as it did a recognition that it was the best that could be gotten at the time and that it was less offensive than the one adopted in 1828. Louisiana, dominated by sugar planters, and parts of western North Carolina and western Virginia and the northeastern part of that state, around Alexandria, were the only parts of the South that favored any kind of protection. By the early 1830s the tariff had become extremely unpopular in the South and its opponents included not only sympathizers to South Carolina who were now becoming openly critical of the President, but also those uncompromisingly hostile to nullification and Calhoun who were strong partisans of the President. Included in this latter group were Senators John Forsyth of Georgia, William King of Alabama, Bedford Brown of North Carolina, and Thomas Hart Benton of Missouri, plus many members of the House of Representatives, the most important of whom were Jesse Speight of North Carolina, Franklin Plummer of Mississippi, Andrew Stevenson and William S. Archer of Virginia, James K. Polk and Cave Johnson of Tennessee, and James M. Wayne and Richard Wilde of Georgia. Jackson's tariff policy, or perhaps it would be more accurate to say his lack of policy on the tariff, was extremely unpopular in the South, and this worked to South Carolina's advantage because it could be used to create serious political problems for the administration.[97]

Southern anti-tariff sentiment tended to translate into anti-Van Buren feeling. The New Yorker had voted for the widely detested law of 1828, and much was made of this fact. His course following Jackson's election, whereby he avoided taking any kind of stand on the tariff, made many people suspicious. It gave credence to the charge made by Calhoun and his followers that Van Buren was a wily and self-serving politician not to be counted on to protect southern interests. In particular they argued that New York congressmen generally supported protection and claimed that if Van Buren were right on the tariff he would use his influence to get New York to endorse reduction. Van Buren was particularly vulnerable on the tariff issue and his friends and supporters in the South stressed the importance of his publicly coming out against protection.[98]

Anti-tariff and anti-Van Buren sentiment merged in an attempt to deny the New Yorker the Vice Presidency and to substitute in his place someone clearly committed to reduction. An effort to do this at the Democratic National Convention held in Baltimore in May 1832 failed because Jackson insisted on having the former secretary of state as his running mate and many others felt it was a just revenge against Calhoun and his supporters for their actions in defeating Van Buren's appointment as Minister to England. Undeterred, many southern Democrats, condemned the convention's decision and launched a movement to run a separate ticket with Jackson for President and P. P. Barbour of Virginia, a long-time opponent of protection and traditional states' righter, who did not have close ties to the nullifiers, for Vice President. For a while the movement gained considerable strength, however, it fizzled out when Barbour, fearful of alienating Jackson and dividing his party, withdrew. But this did not occur until Van Buren in a widely reprinted public letter indicated his opposition to a tariff that operated with "oppresive inequality upon any portion of our citizens, or for the advantage of one section of the Union at the expense of another," and committed himself to "a more equitable adjustment of the tariff."[99] Even so, and despite Barbour's withdrawal, the Jackson-Barbour ticket attracted a fair-sized protest vote in many parts of the South. As John Marshall noted: "Some of the friends of Barbour are secretly for Calhoun; but though attached to nullification in principle they dare not favor the name."[100]

Jackson easily won reelection in 1832, and he ran particularly well in the South. Above all, the result reflected Jackson's enormous personal popularity with the voters, something even his bitterest enemies could not deny. Moreover, while there was considerable unhappiness in the South over his tariff policy and hostility to Van Buren's growing influence, the administration's Indian policy was extremely popular, especially in Georgia, Alabama, and Mississippi, and most people in the South endorsed his policy on internal improvements. Nor were many upset by his veto of the bill rechartering the Second Bank of the United States. If anything it worked to Jackson's advantage since its rechartering was strongly supported by Clay and Webster who also vigorously advocated protection. The fact that the Bank eventually became the dominant issue of the campaign of 1832 probably seriously undermined the impact of southern anti-tariff feeling on the election.[101]

Jackson's victory, however, did nothing to alleviate anti-tariff feeling in the South, and it certainly did not assuage the nullifiers of South Carolina. The political situation on these issues remained extremely fluid, and it was unclear what would happen if South Carolina went ahead, in the fall of 1832, and actually nullified the tariffs of 1828 and 1832 as many expected would happen. Jackson's popularity was quite real, but since no election would be held to determine what the proper course of the federal government should be it might be difficult to channel this popularity to advantage should a crisis occur. Even more important, should a crisis come, it was very unclear what kind of cooperation the President could count on either from Congress or from local political leaders in the South. Thomas Ritchie, an important Virginia ally of Van Buren's, but an uneasy supporter of Jackson, indicated as much when he wrote at the time of the debate over the tariff of 1832: "Should Congress rise without adjusting the tariff in liberal principle, Hamilton & Hayne, Calhoun & McDuffie will help S. Carolina to adopt nullification. . . . The whole South is indignant at the opposition & obduracy of the Tariffites. Virginia is now cool; but very excitable, and determined not to send a man or musket to put down S. Carolina. Events may hurry us further. In fact . . . many of our most sagacious patriots are now beginning to tremble for the Union. It is on all hands admitted to be the most alarming state of things, which has existed since the Revolution."[102]

South Carolina nullifiers recognized that much more was involved than simply being for or against nullification. Without being sure of what the outcome of their course would be they realized that a great deal could occur during the dynamics of a crisis that would operate to their advantage. As one member of the convention that actually declared the tariffs of 1828 and 1832 null and void put it:

> I will therefore only add my most confident belief that the state will maintain the position she has assumed, let the consequences be what they may. She has taken her stand against usurpation & oppression, single handed, not having the positive assurance that any of her sisters will support her. We however have such information as induces us to believe that Georgia & Alabama will finally sustain us, the State Right Party in those states are daily gaining strength & altho they have not all united on the doctrine of nullification, yet they are determined to resist the tariff laws passed for protection & should South Carolina be involved in difficulty about the matter they will support her! . . .
>
> I can imagine no good reason why North Carolina should assist in riveting chains upon So. Carolina, which ultimately reduces her likewise to a state of colonial bondage. If South Carolina is put down or driven out of the Union upon the principles she has adopted, will not all future resistance to the prohibitive system or the exercise of any other power by the general government be useless and unavailing? Will it not establish the right in Congress to pass and compel obedience to any laws which she may think proper to enact and renders ours instead of a confederate, a consolidated government?
>
> These are subjects which our sister states of the South should reflect maturely upon before they make up an opinion against us. I believe that nothing is wanting in order to insure our success and the establishment of the principles we are advocating, but the simple declaration of the other southern states, that they will not see South Carolina put down by military force. Would it be to their interest thus to act? If to get rid of a protecting tariff, a noxious system of internal improvements & other wasteful expenditures of the public funds are desirable objects with them, it surely would. And finally if to avoid the horrors of a civil war, to preserve the public liberty, the Constitution and the Union be desirable objects, then will it become every patriot, every lover of his country, and all who cherish the principles and the memory of the sage of the revolution to step forward and interpose in favor of a peaceful settlement of the matter.[103]

No less a personage than Chief Justice John Marshall, a shrewd politician himself, agreed, for he remarked, "insane as South Carolina unquestionably is, I do not think her so absolutely mad as to have made her declaration of war against the United States had she not counted on uniting the South. . . ."[104]

4

The Proclamation

The nullifiers of South Carolina denounced and rejected the Tariff of 1832, and during the late summer and fall of 1832 launched a final successful campaign to implement their controversial doctrine. Meanwhile, in Washington, President Jackson, never one to back away from a fight, carefully watched these developments and firmly resolved to honor his oath of office and enforce the laws, even if it meant using force. What followed was one of the most serious and dramatic confrontations in American history. It also was a complex one, involving much more than simply being for or against nullification. In addition to a continually shifting interplay of constitutional-ideological issues, it involved clashing personalities and myriad political considerations. And perhaps most important of all, it involved the legitimacy and the practicality of the federal government's use, under the leadership of a man many viewed as a dangerous military chieftain, of force against a state government.

I

South Carolina could not support Henry Clay and the American System in the election of 1832, so it demonstrated its opposition to Andrew Jackson by casting the state's eleven electoral votes for John Floyd of Virginia for President and Henry Lee, a free trader from Massachusetts, for Vice President. In the state legislative elections held on October 8 and 9, despite strong resistance by the Unionists, the nullifiers won a decisive victory giving them the necessary two-thirds control of the legislature. Governor James Hamilton immediately called a special session of the new legislature which met on October 22. He requested that a convention be called as soon as possible, and the legislature quickly concurred, passing a law providing for the election of delegates on November 12 and for the convention to convene on November 19. The state's Unionists did not offer much resistance in the ensuing election of convention delegates, and when the convention convened the nullifiers were in complete control.[1]

The convention contained almost every nullifier of note with the exception of Calhoun, who probably did not allow himself to be nominated as a delegate because of his current position as Vice President of the United States. Governor Hamilton was elected president of the convention and he immediately appointed a committee of twenty-one to prepare an Ordinance of Nullification and a series of reports. Hayne, McDuffie, Robert J. Turnbull, Robert Barnwell, and William Harper controlled its proceedings. The crucial policy questions debated involved the timing of a Nullification Ordinance and whether or not it should include a threat of secession. Some argued that nullification of the tariffs of 1828 and 1832 should go into effect immediately. Others favored giving Congress one more chance to lower the tariff. The committee finally agreed upon a compromise date of February 1, 1833. On the secession question, McDuffie and Hayne wanted the state to assert that it would immediately be out of the Union if the federal government attempted to use force. Another group wanted to avoid the issue entirely, while Barnwell suggested merely threatening secession as a response to coercion. Hayne and McDuffie got their way as the committee of twenty-one declared for immediate secession as a response to the use of force by the federal government.[2]

The committee of twenty-one did its work quickly and reported back to the convention on November 22 with several documents. These consisted of a report drafted by Hayne, the actual Ordinance of Nullification, an "address to the People of South Carolina," authored by Turnbull, and an "Address to the People of the United States," prepared by McDuffie who revised a draft submitted by Calhoun. Collectively, these documents stressed the unfair effects of federal tariff legislation, asserted the constitutional and peaceful nature of nullification, professed friendship for the Union, and indicated that a return to a strictly revenue tariff with equal duties on all items at a rate of no more than 12 percent, to provide an adequate revenue to run the federal government, would meet the state's demands. However, if force were used to enforce the existing tariff laws, the convention warned, "we would infinitely prefer that the territory of the state should be the cemetery of freemen than the habitation of slaves."[3]

The Ordinance itself, penned by Harper, declared the tariffs of 1828 and 1832 "utterly null and void" in South Carolina. It went on to assert that "it shall be the duty of the Legislature to adopt such measures, and pass such acts as may be necessary to give full effect to the Ordinance, and to prevent the enforcement and arrest the operation of the said acts and parts of acts of the Congress of the United States, within the limits of this State," after February 1,

1833. It required all residents of the state "to obey and give effect to the Ordinance," and the acts of the legislature passed to enforce it. Further, it prohibited any appeals to the Supreme Court of the United States against the Ordinance or acts of the legislature adopted to implement it, and it prescribed that all military and civil officers of the state, legislators excepted, take an oath to uphold the Ordinance and sustaining legislation; failure to do so would mean removal from office. Jurors hearing cases under the Ordinance, and state officials elected after its passage, had to take the oath immediately—again, legislators excepted. The Ordinance concluded by warning that if any form of coercion were adopted by the federal government against South Carolina "the people of this state will thenceforth hold themselves absolved from all further obligation to maintain or preserve their political connection with the people of the other states, and will forthwith proceed to organize a separate government, and do all other acts and things which sovereign and independent states may of right do."[4]

On November 24 the convention adopted the report, the two addresses and the Ordinance by an overwhelming 136 to 26 vote, and ordered the printing of twenty thousand copies of each document. Before adjourning, Hamilton was given the right to reconvene the convention at his discretion, and January 31, 1833, the day before the Ordinance was to go into effect, was declared "a day of solemn fasting, humiliation and prayer."

Three days later, when the legislature reconvened, Governor Hamilton called upon it to pass the enabling legislation necessary to put the Ordinance into effect. He also called for a complete revision of the state's militia laws. Although maintaining that nullification was peaceful in intent, he urged the legislature to raise a volunteer army of 12,000 to thwart any attempt to coerce the state. At the same time a caucus of nullifiers agreed that Hayne would resign as United States senator and succeed Hamilton as governor, and Calhoun would resign as Vice President and be elected to the United States Senate.[5]

Although the nullifiers had finally gotten their way, the state's Unionist party continued to remain a problem. The test oath alarmed them; if vigorously implemented it could lead to their total proscription from the political process with the only alternative being the swearing of allegiance to an Ordinance that they viewed as an act of treason. Given the perilous course they had embarked upon, the nullifiers could hardly afford not to enforce it vigorously. Even Calhoun, one of the most moderate of nullifiers acknowledged past "divisions might be excused, but opposition after the State has acted will be of a very different character from a mere division of opinion." Hamilton, in his address to the legislature, recommended passage of a law defining "what shall constitute Treason against the state, and by a bill of pains and penalties, compel obedience and punish disobedience to your own laws."[6]

The Unionists, for their part, vowed allegiance to the federal government and denounced the Ordinance. In particular, they singled out the threat of a test oath as hypocritical and unfair, and asked the embarrassing question of how a convention that had been "called together for the avowed purpose of protecting minorities, could have been capable of passing an act so palpably calculated to oppress them." The Unionists held their own convention at Columbia on December 10, and although it accomplished little because of division over the means and extent of how opposition to the Ordinance should manifest itself, it is clear that some favored military resistance. This group was led by Joel Poinsett, who was in constant touch with Jackson and was one of the President's main sources of information about developments in South Carolina. In return for this allegiance, Jackson vowed to protect the Unionists, to supply them with arms, and to crush nullification, and he generally praised Poinsett's activities as representing "the true spirit of patriotism."[7]

Unionist determination raised some thorny problems. On the one hand if fighting should break out between South Carolina and the federal government the nullifiers would be faced with the threat of civil war as well as outside invasion. On the other hand any attempt to defuse the situation by a compromise acceptable to both sides would have to deal with the difficult issue of what the future role of the Unionists should be in South Carolina politics. For Jackson, always fiercely loyal to faithful subordinates, this would prove to be a particularly important consideration.

Having achieved political hegemony in South Carolina and implemented their ideas, the nullifiers next turned their attention to the important task of attracting support for their cause from other southern states and the development of a strategy for the confrontation with Andrew Jackson that many viewed as inevitable. They criticized the administration's tariff policy, which they blamed on Van Buren, and argued that they were fighting the battle of all those opposed to protection. Duff Green, despite his lack of enthusiasm for the nullification Ordinance, issued a warning "to the people of Virginia, North Carolina, and especially to those of Georgia and Alabama 'have a heed lest you seal your own destiny in denouncing South Carolina.'"[8] Nullifiers and those sympathetic to their cause also argued that the principle involved in Georgia's denial of the Supreme Court's authority in the Cherokee cases and in South Carolina's Ordinance of Nullification were essentially identical, and that South Carolina had only preached nullification while Georgia had actually practiced it. Why then had Jackson sworn "to enforce the laws" against South Carolina but generally supported Georgia's course of action? The answer, they asserted, lay not in matters of principle but in politics and the President's deep personal hatred of Calhoun. These arguments were developed at length by the nullifiers during the winter of 1832–33.[9]

The nullifiers and their supporters also vociferously argued that South Carolina's resistance to the enforcement of the tariffs of 1828 and 1832 would be peaceful. Why then had the Governor called for the raising of an army of 12,000 men? Because, the answer came, the President had repeatedly sworn to enforce the laws, using coercion if necessary, and to hang the leading nullifiers as traitors. This, too, was an effective theme, for it played upon the President's reputation of acting precipitously and even violently when dealing with his enemies, a trait that was a source of much concern even for many of Jackson's strongest supporters. From the beginning, most nullifiers recognized that whether or not they received support from the other southern states hinged on the question of which side used force first.[10]

Perhaps, most important of all, in early December 1832, as the South Carolina legislature prepared to adopt the laws necessary to put the Ordinance into effect, the nullifiers shrewdly perceived that the next move was Andrew Jackson's, and that his response, as much as anything else would determine what would subsequently occur.

II

As events in South Carolina unfolded, Jackson's rage mounted. His dislike for the nullifiers remained unabated, and he clearly expected a violent resolution to the crisis. With one congressman about to leave for home, the President reportedly sent the following message: "Tell them from me that they can talk and write resolutions and print threats to their heart's content. But if one drop of blood be shed there in defiance of the laws of the United States, I will hang the first man of them I can get my hands on to the first tree I can find."[11] To another South Carolina congressman he indicated "that he would be pained to see the State which gave him birth covered with blood, the fruit of their own folly."[12] Similarly, to Van Buren, Jackson explicitly endorsed the view that Calhoun "ought to be hung as a traitor," further expressing his belief "these are and must be the feelings and sentiments of all honest men who love our happy country and who wish to hand down to their posterity the liberty we enjoy." Another time he described South Carolina as "in a state of perfect excitement and the nullifiers in a state of insanity," and expressed the "hope the Unionists will have strength to check them in their mad and wicked course, and preserve the state from civil war and bloodshed."[13]

The intensity of Jackson's hatred for Calhoun and nullification and his determination to use force to crush South Carolina should the state prevent the collection of the tariff duties was widely known. Van Buren, who generally discounted claims about the President's violent temper admitted "he had at this time . . . one feeling which approached to a passion and that was an inclination to go himself with a sufficient force . . . and arrest Messrs. Calhoun, Hayne, Hamilton, and McDuffie. . . ."[14] Roger Brooke Taney, who was Jackson's attorney general at the time, later recalled: "all knew that a man of imperious will held the sword of the country. They knew, too, that a personal dislike of Mr. Calhoun . . . influenced General Jackson's feelings . . . the worst forebodings filled the country. . . ."[15] When Hayne of South Carolina said to Thomas Hart Benton, the important Jacksonian senator from Missouri, "I don't believe he would really hang anybody do you?" Benton replied: "Well before he invaded Florida on his own hook, few people could have believed that he would hang Arbuthnot and shoot Ambrister—also on his own authority—could they? I tell you, Hayne, when Jackson begins to talk about hanging, they can begin to look out for ropes." And, in similar fashion, Daniel Webster wrote: "I am prepared any day to hear that matters have come to blows in Charleston. . . . I have not the slightest doubt, that both General

Jackson and Governor [James] Hamilton Jr. fully expect a decision by the sword."[16]

Throughout late November and early December, Washington buzzed with discussions about "the menaces uttered by the President against South Carolina," his "threatening the gallows," and his frequent assertion "that he considers himself authorized by the *existing* laws, to use military force against South Carolina if he deemed it expedient so to do." Although at this point the administration had not settled on any specific plan of action it was generally believed that the crisis would occur as soon as the Ordinance went into effect on February 1. From that day forward the Collector at Charleston would be ordered to demand the payment of duties in cash. If the importer refused to pay, his goods would be impounded and sent, by the Collector, to the federal warehouse. The importer would then go to a South Carolina court to replevin them. The Collector would refuse to abide by the state court's order. The state court would then order his imprisonment. At this point the state's Unionists would rally to the Collector's defense and forcibly resist his imprisonment, and blood probably would be shed. With South Carolina enthralled in civil war the President would call out various state militias and march down in person to restore order and punish the nullifiers.[17]

The *Globe,* speaking for the administration, stridently condemned the proceedings in South Carolina and stressed the most ominous implications. Nullification, it argued, was not in any sense a peaceful remedy but the work of "the ambitious politicians of South Carolina," who "have rushed into a war against the union, and have taken up arms and are mustering troops to put down the authority of the General Government within the state." The Ordinance, it pointed out, treated the Unionists in an intolerable fashion dooming them to "summary vengeance." It is the evident purpose of the nullifiers to force the Union men to submission or drive them into exile. . . . It is impossible that the Union men in South Carolina should submit to this tyranny, nor is it expected that they will abandon the land of their fathers without a struggle." In other words, civil war in South Carolina was a real possibility, indeed a likelihood. Further, the *Globe*'s editor asserted, it was out of the question for the federal government to submit to a doctrine whereby one state could stop the operation of any or all laws adopted by Congress. The federal government would fall apart, it would become powerless and ineffectual, worse even than in its pre-1788 days. South Carolina was precipitating a crisis that threatened the existence of the Union, and *"the Union must be preserved,* and it will be preserved, peaceably if we can, but it must be preserved."[18]

Throughout the late summer and fall of 1832 Jackson prepared for action. He checked out the loyalty of the naval and army officers and customs officials already in South Carolina, sent reinforcements, alerted the naval authorities in Norfolk to be prepared to send aid if needed, and ordered General Winfield Scott to supervise military preparations. In addition, he sent George Breathitt, a brother of the governor of Kentucky down as a postal agent with instructions to spy on the military activities of the nullifiers. He also made arrangements for arms to be delivered to the Unionists to whom he asserted: "Nullification . . . means insurrection and war; and the other states have a right to put it down: and you also and all other peaceable citizens have a right to aid in the same patriotic object when summoned by the violated laws of the land."[19]

To his trusted adviser, Amos Kendall, Jackson gave the responsibility of organizing political support for the administration's position. Even before the election results were known, Kendall, confident of the President's success argued that now "a question which may be made the leading one, is arising out of the Acts of South Carolina." The Union, he stressed, had to be preserved, "*at all hazards,*" and while he hoped to avoid bloodshed he warned, "temporizing with the mischief may extend it and lead to consequences all must deplore." Recognizing the administration's weakness in Congress, and especially in the Senate, Kendall hoped for the collaboration of National Republicans from the northern, middle, and western states "*upon the question of the Union against Nullification.*" To this end he favored the *Globe's* adopting "a tone of moderation" in relation to the National Republicans and the bank question focusing instead on "the importance of the Union . . . and the consequences of its dissolution." For, he noted, "this would be an indication that no men who should rally around the Union would be excluded from the pale of friends of the administration."[20] This strategy quickly proved to be a complicating factor in an already complicated situation, one that significantly affected the political contours of the nullification crisis.

Jackson also moved to isolate South Carolina from the rest of the South by coming out for a major downward revision of the tariff, and the abandonment of protection. This differed fundamentally from the position he had taken only a few months earlier when he had pronounced the Tariff of 1832 to be a more than adequate reform measure. When Congress convened in December 1832, Jackson's supporters scrambled to gain control of the key committees, especially in the House of Representatives where the tariff bill had to originate. Andrew Stevenson of Virginia, Speaker of the House and an administration loyalist, appointed Gulian C. Verplanck, a New York free trader, head of the Committee of Ways and Means. Stevenson also switched James K. Polk of Tennessee, a firm partisan of the President, from the Foreign Affairs committee to Ways and Means and placed Michael Hoffman of New York, a Van Buren follower in favor of tariff reform, on the Committee of Manufactures in order to ensure a favorable report from that source.[21]

But controlling committees was one thing, getting the House to go for a major reform of the tariff, before the recently adopted 1832 tariff had a chance to be adequately tested, was an entirely different matter. In addition, most National Republicans were committed to protection and many northern Democrats shared this feeling. Jackson's strategy to conciliate both National Republicans and Southern Democrats, in order to isolate South Carolina, involved putting together a highly unstable coalition whose only real common bond was hostility to South Carolina's actions and whose essentially irreconcilable attitudes on most issues could preclude agreement on any positive kind of legislation.

III

On December 4, the President submitted his annual message to Congress. Delighted by his reelection, Jackson viewed it as a popular mandate to continue to pursue vigorously his policy of dismantling the American System. Looking forward to the imminent elimination of the national debt, sharply reducing the federal government's need for an income, Old Hickory took this opportunity to state, with great clarity, both the program and underlying political philosophy of his administration. The *Globe* heralded it as "probably the most important document of the kind which has been submitted to Congress and the country since the organization of the General Government."[22]

The message revealed Jackson's deep commitment to agrarian values. In it he asserted: "The wealth and strength of a country are its population, and the best part of the population are the cultivators of the soil. Independent farmers are everywhere the basis of society and the true friends of liberty." He repeated his frequently stated belief that the federal government should be uncomplicated and parsimonious and that the needs of the people should, wherever possible, be left to the state governments. "Both Governments," he observed, "are the Governments of the people; improvements must be made with the money of the people, and if the money can be collected and applied by the more simple and economical political machines, the state governments, it will unquestionably be safer and better for the people than to add to the splendor, the patronage, and the power of the General Government."[24]

More specifically, in his message Jackson rejected the idea of "perpetual protection," and recommended that the tariff be reduced to a revenue standard as quickly as feasible, with high rates limited only to those objects absolutely necessary to the security of the country. "Experience," he argued, ". . . makes it doubtful whether the advantages of this system are not counterbalanced by many evils, and whether it does not tend to beget in the minds of a large portion of our countrymen a spirit of discontent and jealousy dangerous to the stability of the Union." Jackson went on to attack protection in much the same terms that he had opposed an extensive program of federal aid to internal improvements and the Bank of the United States, characterizing its proponents as greedy for special privileges and motivated mainly by self-interest. He warned "those who have vested their capital in manufacturing establishments cannot expect that the people will continue permanently to pay high taxes for their benefit, when the money is not required for any legitimate purpose in the administration of the Government. Is it not enough that the high duties have been paid as long as the money arising from them could be applied to the common benefit in the extinguishment of the public debt?"[25]

Jackson also called upon the federal government to dispose of all the stock it held in private corporations. "As a source of profit," he observed, "these stocks are of little or no value; as a means of influence among the states they are adverse to the purity of our institutions." In addition, he criticized the Bank of the United States for failing to perform adequately its duties in helping the federal government pay off the national debt, questioned the safety of the public deposits in the Bank and suggested that Congress consider their removal.[26]

The President, at this time, also unveiled a comprehensive policy for the disposal of the national domain. Totally rejecting the plan he had advocated during the first two years of his administration, of distributing to the states the surplus revenue in the federal treasury after the payment of the national debt, he now argued that the public lands should cease to be used as a source of revenue and that they should be sold to actual settlers at a "price barely sufficient" to cover the government's expense in administering them. "It cannot be doubted," he asserted, "that the speedy settlement of these lands constitutes the true interests of the republic." He also favored, wherever practicable, following the clearing of titles and the making of accurate surveys, that the federal government's machinery be withdrawn from the states, and that the right of soil, of the unsold part of the national domain, "and the future disposition of it be surrendered to the states respectively in which it lies."[27]

In other parts of the message he restated his position on the removal of the Indians, opposed an extensive federal program of internal improvements without a constitutional amendment, and advocated the direct election of President and Vice President. The message was vague on only two points. First, while the President noted that the dispute between Georgia and the Cherokee remained unsettled, he completely avoided commenting on the Supreme Court's recent decision, stressing instead the generous inducements offered by the federal government to convince the Indians to resettle west of the Mississippi. He also quickly passed over developments in South Carolina, observing only "that the laws themselves are fully adequate to the suppression of such attempts as may be immediately made," adding that if this should not be so he would lay the whole matter before Congress.[28]

The message was stridently states' rights and agrarian in its tone and thrust. Although these qualities had marked administration policy on internal improvements and the Bank from the very beginning, they had not been very evident in Jackson's handling of the question of protection and the disposal of income from the sale of public lands. On these latter two issues the administration's earlier position had tended to reinforce the inherent nationalism of the American System. By late 1832 this had changed and Jackson's position on almost all the issues now involved a strong and consistent commitment to a traditional form of states' rights as well as being totally antithetical to all the values of the American System. The message concluded:

> We should bear constantly in mind the fact that the considerations which induced the framers of the Constitution to withhold from the General Government the power to regulate the great mass of the business and concerns of the people have been fully justified by experience, and that it cannot now be doubted that the genius of all our institutions prescribes simplicity and economy as the characteristics of the reform which is yet to be effected in the present and future execution of the functions bestowed upon us by this constitution.
>
> Limited to a general superintending power to maintain peace at home and abroad, and to prescribe laws on a few subjects of a general interest not calculated

to restrict human liberty, but to enforce human rights, this Government will find its strength and its glory in the faithful discharge of these plain and simple duties. Relieved by its protecting shield from the fear of war and the apprehension of oppression, the free enterprise of our citizens, aided by the state sovereignties, will work out improvements and ameliorations which cannot fail to demonstrate that the great truth that the people can govern themselves is not only realized in our example, but that it is done by a machinery in government so simple and economical as scarcely to be felt.[29]

Reaction to Jackson's message broke along predictable party lines. High tariff men and advocates of the American System denounced it. "It recommends a total change in the policy of the Union with reference to the bank, manufactures, internal improvement and the public lands," complained John Quincy Adams who also believed: "it goes to dissolve the Union into its original elements, and is in substance a complete surrender to the nullifiers of South Carolina." The message was viewed as being "decidedly conciliatory" to southern interests and even Duff Green and George Poindexter had kind words for it, although they also criticized the President for taking so long to abandon protection and for failing to endorse explicitly the concept of state interposition. Although the President had taken a clear and firm stand on almost all the issues, his treatment of developments in South Carolina, "with peculiar delicacy," bothered many who did not know what to make of it; however, James H. Pleasant, the knowledgeable editor of the pro-Clay Richmond *Constitutional Whig* presciently commented, "the President has so little to say of Nullification, that we are persuaded to think he has reserved the question for a more elaborate discussion in a separate message. . . ."[30]

The separate message came six days later, on December 10, in the form of a special Proclamation. In this powerful and cogently argued statement, Jackson made clear his uncompromising opposition to nullification: "I consider, then, the power to annul a law of the United States, assumed by one state, *incompatible with the existence of the Union, contradicted expressly by the letter of the Constitution, unauthorized by its spirit, inconsistent with every principle on which it was founded, and destructive of the great object for which it was formed.*"[31]

The President denied nullification had any legitimacy in "our constitutional history." The discovery of this important feature in our Constitution, he argued, was reserved for the present day. To the statesmen of South Carolina belongs the invention of what was an "impracticable absurdity," a "sophistical construction," a "metaphysical subtlety, in pursuit of an impracticable theory." Throughout, Jackson stressed the danger of allowing "one state" or what was really only "a small majority of the voters of a single state," the power to declare a congressional act void. In particular, the President focused on South Carolina's claim that secession was a legal right that could take place peacefully. Rejecting this argument he stressed that nullification was "subversive" of the Constitution and had "for its object the destruction of the Union—
. . . that sacred Union, hitherto inviolate, which perfected by our happy Constitution, has brought us, by the favor of Heaven, to a state of prosperity at

home and high consideration abroad rarely, if ever, equalled in the history of nations . . . ".[32]

In no uncertain terms he warned the leaders of South Carolina that secession was not "a peaceable remedy" but involved "insurrection and treason" and "that the duty imposed on me by the Constitution 'to take care that the laws be faithfully executed,'" would be carried out even if "on your unhappy State will inevitably fall all the evils of the conflict you force upon the Government of your country."[33]

The Proclamation, however, involved more than simply a sweeping attack on nullification and secession and a threatening tone. For, in taking issue with South Carolina's assertion that in creating the Constitution the states had "reserved an undivided sovereignty," Jackson also offered a theory about the origins and nature of the Union that in many ways differed radically from the states' rights position he had taken less than a week earlier in his annual address. In the Proclamation he strongly implied that the Union came before the states and asserted that within its sphere of power the federal government was sovereign. He also explicitly claimed that "the people of the United States formed the Constitution." In arguing against the concept of undivided state sovereignty, Jackson pointed out that in the offices of the President and Vice President and in the House of Representatives "the people of all the states, collectively, are represented," and stressed "The Constitution of the United States, then, forms a *government*, not a league; and whether it be formed by compact between the States or in any other manner, its character is the same. It is a government in which all the people are represented, which operates directly on people individually, not upon the states. . . ." Although he added that the states "retained all the power they did not grant," he did not, in the Proclamation, elaborate on what or how extensive these reserved powers were or try to develop meaningfully the concept of divided sovereignty. He also denied and down-played the compact theory of the origins of the Constitution and the rights of a state to secede or to pronounce upon the constitutionality of acts of Congress. Instead, he concluded the Proclamation with an appeal to his fellow citizens: "On your undivided support of your Government depends the decision of the great question it involves—whether your sacred Union will be preserved and the blessings it secures to us as one people shall be perpetuated." The message tilted strongly in the direction of the nationalist theories of the Union that had been variously espoused by Daniel Webster, Joseph Story, John Quincy Adams, Nathan Dane, and others, and while it was an effective reply to nullification it also tended to undercut the constitutional-ideological underpinnings of states' rights in general.[34]

So different in content was the Proclamation from anything else the President had previously espoused that some people expressed disbelief when they first saw it. "One short week," Henry Clay wrote, "produced the message and the proclamation—the former ultra on the side of state rights, and latter ultra on the side of consolidation." As to "How they can be reconciled?" Clay simply had no answer. "Its principles and doctrines," one editor wrote, "are directly at variance with all the political statements bearing the signature of the

President, since he came into power." The Proclamation received Joseph Story's blessings. He pronounced it "excellent" and asserted it "contains the true principles of the Constitution." Story also confided to his wife: "Since his last proclamation . . . the Chief Justice and myself have become his warmest supporters, and shall continue so just as long as he maintains the principles contained in them. Who would have dreamed of such an occurrence?" The virulently anti-Van Buren *Albany Evening Journal* commented, "its doctrines are so unexpected, from whence it came, it is so contrary to former experience, it holds out so much more than anyone dared hope for. . . ." And Daniel Webster, according to one report, "as soon as he received the Proclamation, declared his fullest and unqualified approbation of it. . . ."[35]

On the other hand, Jackson's Nullification Proclamation caused considerable chagrin among administration supporters and proponents of states' rights. "Its principles," a Virginia congressman observed, "you will perceive are at war with all our opinions of state power and the character of our Confederacy." Willie P. Mangum, a senator from North Carolina, noted: "I have been most deeply mortified at public events here. . . . His proclamation is violent and danger[ou]s in its principles." Another observer commented, "General Jackson's proclamation will not satisfy the South. It is thought to be an abandonment of the rights of the states," and administration stalwart Thomas Hart Benton noted he "could not concur in some of the doctrines of the Proclamation." Similarly, C. C. Cambreleng, an administration supporter from New York City, mentioned "the broad errors of doctrine on some of the fundamental principles of the Constitution" that the Proclamation contained.[36]

How does one explain the difference between the annual message and the Proclamation? Various explanations were offered by contemporaries, and a number of them are worth examining because by doing so it is possible to gain some further understanding of what was going on in Jackson's mind during the crisis, of what his intentions were, and of how his administration was functioning in the winter of 1832–33.

Many of those hostile to Jackson viewed it as just another example of his unfitness to govern, for, incapable of drafting his own state papers, they claimed he called upon his various advisers to write them and then would sign them without understanding their content. "The President," claimed a Clay partisan, "has no certain or fixed opinions of his own upon these grave questions . . . he employs not an amanuensis merely, but trusts to some one of his advisors to supply the thought as well as hold the pen; and that the radical conflict which is observable between his different papers, can be accounted for on no other supposition than the chance ascendancy of this or that counsellor—Parlor or kitchen as accident determines."[37]

This interpretation, which views Jackson as a bumbling old fool, manipulated by his advisers, does not hold up under careful scrutiny of the existing evidence which overwhelmingly indicates that on this, as on almost all other issues, Old Hickory was very much his own man. But this interpretation does have a virtue. It highlights the fact that the President did, indeed, depend very heavily on the aid of his advisers in the preparation of his state papers, usually expressing to them his opinions and feelings on a subject and with "that point secured," according to Van Buren, "he cared little . . . as to the form of words in which they were expressed."[38]

To help prepare the Nullification Proclamation Jackson turned to his secretary of state, Edward Livingston. What does not exist is hard evidence to indicate precisely why the President used Livingston to draft the message, but the choice was in many ways a natural one since Livingston in his speech on the debate over Foote's Resolution, in early 1830, had adopted a position on the nature of the Union and the role of the states that was generally compatible with Jackson's views on states' rights. Moreover, Madison had explicitly praised Livingston's effort, remarking, "you have succeeded better in your interpretation of the Virginia Proceedings of '98–99 than those who have seen in them a coincidence with the nullifying doctrine so-called."[39]

What makes this important is that, according to one usually accurate source, at a cabinet meeting discussing the developments in South Carolina "it was resolved to consult the oracle of Montpelier—the venerable Madison. The course was taken; and the argumentative portion of the proclamation is believed to be derived from thence."[40] In the narrow and literal sense this claim is wrong, for Madison was not directly consulted on the drafting of the Proclamation, and, indeed, had reservations about some of its doctrinal implications.[41] But it is correct in the sense that it focuses on the importance that the administration, and especially Livingston, placed upon Madison's various forceful and elaborate criticisms of nullification and how it reinforced their own view which was that the South Carolina doctrine was not to be seen as a legitimate expression of states' rights or the "Spirit of 1798," but rather that nullification was illegitimate and treasonous and that treason had to be suppressed.[42]

Equally important, there is strong circumstantial evidence to indicate that both Jackson and Livingston did have frequent but indirect contact with Madison on the theoretical questions involved in nullification. The intermediary was Nicholas P. Trist, who was married to Thomas Jefferson's granddaughter and who served as Jackson's personal secretary during the period of the Eaton Affair when the President's nephew and secretary, Andrew Jackson Donelson, was banished from Washington, and who, at the time of the nullification crisis, was an assistant clerk in the State Department under Livingston.[43]

Trist frequently visited Madison at Montpelier and engaged in an extensive private correspondence in which they often discussed the question of nullification and the general issue of states' rights and their relationship to the Virginia Resolutions, a subject on which Trist published several newspaper articles. Daniel Webster, a strong supporter of the administration during the nullification crisis, who at the time was developing both political and personal ties with the President, wrote to Joseph Story: "I believe I have found out the authorship of the Proclamation. It is the work I have no doubt, of Mr. [Nicholas Philip] Trist. . . . He never occurred to me, till his name was mentioned; but I have no doubt it is so; as I know him well and know him to be both sound and able, on that point. The discussion of 1830 led to an acquaintance with him, which has since cont[inue]d. He has written other very good things."[44]

Although Trist, in his capacity as Livingston's clerk in the State Department, played a role in transcribing parts of the Proclamation and was involved in the discussion of various aspects of the argument it contained, he nonetheless cannot be viewed as the author, although he may have influenced some of its content, for Trist did not approve of the Proclamation in the form in which it was finally issued. In particular he objected to its failure to endorse explicitly the theory of the Union developed by Madison and Jefferson in the Kentucky and Virginia Resolutions and the Virginia Report of 1799–1800 which viewed the Union as a compact between the different states. Of special relevance here is the reason Livingston chose to avoid discussing the compact theory in the Proclamation, even though he had endorsed it in his speech on Foote's resolution in 1830. According to Trist, the secretary of state argued "that if our [Madison and Trist's] doctrines as to the nature of the parties to the compact be sound, the right of secession *must exist,* as a peaceable right."[45]

Jackson, too, it is clear, had strong feelings on this matter and also rejected the compact theory of the origins of the Union because he believed it led logically to the doctrine of secession. He called it "the Virginia doctrine" and believed it lent support to those who claimed a state had a legal right to withdraw from the Union. As he put it:

> The absurdity of the Virginia doctrine is too plain to need much comment. . . . The preservation of the Union is the supreme law. To show the absurdity, Congress have the right to admit new states. When territories, the[y] are subject to the laws of the Union, the day after the admission they have the right to secede and dissolve it. We gave five million for Louisiana, we admitted her into the Union, she too has the right to secede, close the commerce of six states, and levy contributions both upon exports and imports. A state cannot come into the Union without the consent of Congress, but it can go out when it pleases. Such a Union as this would be like a bag of sand with both ends open—the least pressure and it runs out at both ends. It is an insult to the understanding of the sages who form it, to believe that such a Union was ever intended—it could not last a month. It is a confederate perpetual union, first made by the people in their sovereign state capacities, upon which we the people of the United States, made a more perfect Union, which can only be dissolved by the people who formed it, as in the way pointed out in the instrument, or by revolution.[46]

What seems to have been involved in the writing of the Proclamation was a joint effort on the part of the President and his secretary of state, whereby Jackson "drew up the heads of what he wanted" and Livingston drafted the actual argument. Both men had long since rejected the South Carolina doctrine as a legitimate expression of states' rights thought. Jackson indicated as much when, following his exchange of letters with Hayne in 1831 over why he would not appoint a nullifier to public office, he wrote on the back of Hayne's letter: "Note—I draw a wide difference between states rights and the advocates of them, and a nullifier."[47] Undoubtedly Jackson and Livingston were encouraged in this view by Madison's pointed denunciation of nullification. Neither man therefore was willing, in December 1832, to take seriously any longer, although both men understood what was involved, the theoretical challenge that the South Carolina doctrines posed for the proponents of a traditional form of states' rights. As a consequence, the Proclamation ignored the need for distinguishing between states' rights and state sovereignty.[48]

Instead, Jackson and Livingston focused on nullification as a doctrine "*incompatible with the existence of the Union.*" To their minds, nullification meant secession and treason, and since their understanding of states' rights did not include a belief in secession, it followed, of course, that nullification had nothing to do with states' rights. Four days after Jackson issued the Proclamation, he wrote a letter to his old friend John Coffee which reveals both the President's concerns and his sharp separation of states' rights from secession: "when a faction in a state attempt to nullify a constitutional law of Congress, or to destroy the Union, the balance of the people composing this Union have a perfect right to coerce them to obedience. This is my creed, which you will read in the proclamation which I sent you the other day. No man will go farther than I will to preserve every right reserved to the people or to the states; nor no man will go farther to sustain the acts of Congress passed according to the express grants to Congress. The Union must be preserved, and it will now be tested, by the support I get by the people. I will die for the Union."[49] One Virginia congressman who was critical of the Proclamation and saw it as being "in antithesis to the whole of President Jackson's political opinions heretofore expressed" added, "The Old man is against secession, and I grieve to say, talks about, we the people, whenever he encounters one bold enough to suggest the possibility of his being in error."[50]

A group of Jackson loyalists from Maine explained the apparent differences between the President's previous statements and the Proclamation in these terms:

> The proclamation was written in view of the attitude assumed by the nullifiers of South Carolina, AND IN THAT VIEW ALONE; it was not intended as a general exposition of the PRINCIPLES OF THE PRESIDENT or the Democratic Party, on any other than the main subject on which it was written; and its great principles, thus viewed, are in accordance with those which characterized the messages of President Jackson.[51]

A Virginia supporter put it differently but meant much the same thing when he argued "the purpose of the Proclamation was to stress those aspects of the nature of the Union that undercut South Carolina's claims to total sovereignty. The President's object was to show that the government was not exclusively federal; but in some of its branches, the *People* in contradistinction to the State *Governments*, were represented—that it was in regard to those branches, essentially a popular government."[52]

IV

But these were generous interpretations of the President's Nullification Proclamation, and they were exceptions. Generally, the Proclamation upset most Democrats, and the furor was especially intense among the Southern wing of the party. According to a report from Richmond, "The President's proclamation is openly denounced by his former supporters—his attachment to state rights derided as hollow and hypocritical—and his doctrines denounced as Ultra Federal. Perhaps the same space of time has never exhibited so marked a Revolution of political sentiment as that which we have witnessed among the Virginia state right politicians, since the receipt of the Proclamation. It at one blow prostrates all their fine spun theories of state sovereignty and compels them either to Renounce Gen. Jackson or surrender all their former and long cherished principles."[53] Another account noted: "The proclamation is considered by southern politicians, generally as *ultra federal,* and rightly so considered. A distinguished Jackson senator of the South stated, this day, that it was almost entirely an *anti-Jeffersonian* document."[54]

A mixture of several factors, ideological and political, explain the extremely hostile reception the Proclamation received from Jacksonian Democrats. First, there was genuine concern over its doctrinal implications:

> As a body the South with the exception of South Carolina is decidedly opposed to *Nullification,* as it is to *consolidation;* but the executive has not appreciated their feeling on this head, and in endeavoring to check nullification, he has unfortunately arrayed himself against the Democracy of the country and espoused the Old Federal doctrines which the people of the United States have so repeatedly put down. In consequence of this error—an error which was not, could not be anticipated from a Republican President—the very men who at the South are most opposed to nullification find themselves led to countenance it to a certain extent, in order to pursue their own principles and not lend themselves to consolidation.[55]

This concern was reinforced by the warm reception Jackson's Proclamation received from nationalists and supporters of the American System, especially high tariff advocates and Federalists. Indeed, so substantial and enthusiastic was the support from these sources that one observer believed the Proclamation had "laid the foundation for a new organization of parties." In Boston, at a widely reported meeting held at Faneuil Hall, Daniel Webster, Harrison Gray Otis, Franklin Dexter, and Thomas Handasyd (the latter three members of the Hartford Convention) spoke and passed resolutions denouncing nullification, praising the Proclamation, and pledging their support for the President's effort to save the Union and crush the insurrection in South Carolina.[56]

In New York, Philip Hone described the Proclamation as "just such a paper as Alexander Hamilton would have written and Thomas Jefferson condemned," and James Kent and Peter A. Jay presided over a public meeting pledging support for its principles. A similar meeting in Baltimore was led by William Patterson and Robert Oliver. While in Philadelphia a low tariff partisan reported that although "no public meeting has been held here to sustain the Proclamation the doctrines it contains, it is true, are well received by the whole federal party." And in Ohio, a critic of the President noted "that document like a month of charity has covered a multitude of Jackson's sins."[57]

The administration, looking for allies to help in its confrontation with South Carolina, embraced this development although it created widespread resentment among Jacksonians. This was true not only of Southerners concerned over the protectionist leanings of the new converts, but also of Northern Democrats who viewed with suspicion and discomfit the rallying of their 'old enemies' to the President's cause. The *United States Telegraph* noted with some pleasure the "strong marks of repugnance shown by some of the Jacksonian editors" in New Hampshire and Pennsylvania to these new allies. In Ohio a local politician observed "there seems to be some regret among the leaders of the [Democratic] party, that the opposition so decidedly approve the principal doctrines in the proclamation."[58]

The President's determination to use force against South Carolina also significantly contributed to the hostile reception of the Proclamation by many Democrats. An Ohio Jacksonian, for example, wanted "the difficulties settled without giving to the Federalists the opportunity of acquiring their fame by cutting the throats of Southern brethren." But more was involved than party feelings. Many Democrats, on the basis of Jackson's past reputation, cringed at the thought of his heading an army. Van Buren recalled "that among the admirers and sincere friends of General Jackson, there were in every state not a few who, confiding fully in his integrity, believing him engaged in continual struggles for the public good with a reckless opposition and sincerely wishing him success, yet distrusted his prudence . . . and were kept in constant apprehension that he would, through passion or ill advisement, commit some rash act." He noted in particular that Thomas Ritchie "scarcely ever went to bed in these exciting times without apprehension that he would wake up to hear of some *coup d'état* by the General. . . ."[59]

This feeling was not limited to Democrats. Nationalists, who vigorously denounced nullification and were unsympathetic to states' rights, also made clear their concern that a confrontation between Jackson and South Carolina could easily get out of hand. Webster, in a speech to the National Republican Convention in Worcester, Massachusetts, in October 1832 responded to the various reports that the President planned to employ military force against the nullifiers. He warned, "there is no little reason to think that this suggestion is true. We cannot be altogether unapprehensive for the future . . . I raise my voice beforehand against the unauthorized employment of Military power, and against superseding the authority of the laws, by an armed force, under pretence of putting down Nullification." Webster believed a peaceful solution to be possible, but if a military remedy were necessary then he felt it was absolutely essential that the President be given the power by Congress and not simply assume it. Similarly, the *National Intelligencer,* advocate of the American System and Henry Clay's election in 1832, and a vocal opponent of nullification, commented on the use of force: "We trust that no such views are entertained by the Executive. If they are, we are satisfied they will not be sustained by Congress under existing circumstances."[60]

Many people believed civil war would occur if Jackson used force. Moreover, not only would South Carolina resist, but it would receive support from other states. Following the issuance of the Proclamation a well-informed newspaper correspondent wrote, "A distinguished Virginian, opposed to nullification and *Clayism* said to me—'The Executive can never march troops against South Carolina, through eastern Virginia, *but over our dead bodies.*' . . . I now repeat with perfect and entire confidence what I have heretofore said, and solemnly believed—if coercion is attempted against South Carolina, she will not be alone in her opposition to the 'standing army.' "[61]

Virginia was not the only state in which large numbers of Democrats opposed the use of force against South Carolina and openly expressed disapproval of the President's excessively militant attitude. Widespread reports existed of volunteers from Georgia, North Carolina, and Alabama offering their services to South Carolina, and even from the President's home state an important politician wrote "public sentiment in Tennessee is strongly in favor of the admin., yet I am well satisfied that the actual array and application of military force by the Genl Govt., upon Carolina would divide even our people . . . ".[62] Michael Hoffman, a New York representative connected with the Albany Regency believed "the question of the use [of force] will alienate the whole South," and Thomas Hart Benton warned Van Buren, "You see the difficulties in the South, and nobody can tell what turn things may take if blood is once spilt."[63]

Genuinely fearful of the future of the Union, many important Democrats believed that the crisis should be defused quickly and peacefully through a substantial reduction of the tariff. Among others, this group included Van Buren, Benton, Isaac Hill, C. C. Cambreleng, and George M. Troup. "To carry off the storm quietly," wrote Benton, "will be our GREATEST endeavor. . . ." Another hoped that tariff reduction "will tranquilize the South . . . and make all smooth hereafter." And still another argued, "The Union saved by reasonable concession and a just regard to the RIGHTS OF ALL, will strengthen the fraternal bond; and draw closer the cords of affection between the states. In that case, it will be worth preserving and enjoying. But the Union, saved by the sword, by the butchery of its citizens—and the states kept in their places by military coercion—will be a mere mockery of the Union. It will be a Union whose scourge will equal the unhappy effects of disunion."[64]

V

Despite the consternation of his fellow Democrats, Jackson had no intention of backing down. If anything, the various attitudes and pronouncements of the President in the weeks following the issuance of the Proclamation alienated many of his supporters even further.

The administration's initial response to criticism of the Proclamation was silence, but then in late December and early January it started to defend itself in the pages of the *Globe*. It claimed, "The Proclamation is by some misunderstood, and by others perverted in the hope that a more extended party may be rallied in the South against the speculative views contained in that paper, than can be brought to the support of the principles of nullification as practically carried out in the ordinance." It launched a counterattack against nullification and reiterated the President's position, taking issue with the doctrine's anti-majoritarian assumptions, describing it as a threat to the future of the union, rejecting the idea of peaceful secession and denying that nullification was either a peaceful remedy or a legitimate form of states' rights.[65]

But most importantly, Jackson refused to recant in any way on the Proclamation's controversial doctrinal points. Responding to Ritchie's influential Richmond *Enquirer* which suggested "that the President may not have considered with care due so important a measure as his Proclamation, all the consequences that *legitimately* flow from it," the *Globe* declared: "we feel authorized in saying that that document, both in its argument and its practical views reflects as truly the settled opinions of the President as any which ever proceeded from him . . . ".[66]

Similarly, Jackson continued to express his determination to use force against South Carolina, and Washington was filled with reports to this effect. One observer noted that despite criticism of the Proclamation, "the president stands firm, and talks openly to everyone about his administration. 'God,' he says, 'May stop him, but Andrew Jackson will not be stopped by any power on earth!' He swears, South Carolina shall be brought under." Another newspaper correspondent wrote, "General *Jackson's* violence against South Carolina has rather increased than diminished within a few days. Last evening he declared to a Souther [*sic*] member of Congress, of the *Union* party, that he had already an offer, from Virginia of twenty regiments of volunteers to put down the nullifiers. The member looked grave. 'Sir,' said the President, 'don't knit your brows at me; I tell you South Carolina may raise her ten or twelve thousand men but Andrew Jackson will raise thirty thousand." And according to still another report: "His determination to execute the laws is not a *silent* one. I am told that the subject occupies his mind continually, and that he speaks of his purposes with great freedom, frequency and emphasis. The gathering clouds portend a coming storm of more than ordinary fearfulness."[67]

Verification of these reports comes from Silas Wright, a New York Democrat and Van Buren protégé who spent thirty minutes talking with the President on January 12, and a "few moments" with Secretary of War Cass. He wrote to his political mentor that the President had indicated "that instead of a diminution of the probabilities of force at Charleston those probabilities had been constantly increasing" and that the President was "very firm and decided as to the use of force." To another congressman, Jackson noted that while he expected to use civil authorities to implement the law should force be used by Governor Hamilton to obstruct "the Marshal in the execution of process . . . February will be a month long remembered." Jackson himself wrote to Van Buren less than a week after he issued his Proclamation: "If the assembly [of South Carolina] authorises twelve thousand men to resist the law, I will order thirty thousand to execute the law. . . . It will not do *now* to temporise, or falter, or it undermines the stability of your Government and might shake it to its centre, when by crushing the wicked faction in its bud, you strengthen our Republican government, both at home and abroad." Another letter to the Vice President-elect, nearly a month later, shows that Jackson continued to expect, indeed even was counting on, a violent conclusion. "The parties in So. C. are arming on both sides . . . and I expect soon to hear that a civil war of extermination has commenced. I will meet all things with deliberate firmness and forbearance, but woe, to those nullifiers who shed the first blood."[68]

The President also continued to exasperate Democrats by persevering in his policy of seeking aid from National Republicans during the crisis. The particular National Republican whose support most interested Jackson was Daniel Webster. During the debate with Hayne, Webster had proven himself an eloquent, formidable, and effective opponent of nullification. Moreover, Webster was available. Despite his popularity and influence in New England and his general national prominence, he had never been part of the inner circle of the National Republican leadership. To a large extent this was because he remained tainted by his early affiliation with the Federalist party. Although genuinely concerned by the constitutional issues involved, Webster, who was politically ambitious and strongly desirous of becoming President, also saw the nullification crisis as an opportunity to effect a political revolution that would perhaps make him Jackson's heir apparent.[69]

Webster had responded very favorably to the President's Proclamation. In a speech at Fanueil Hall he fully endorsed Jackson's argument that nullification was rebellion, declaring "It is nothing more nor less than resistance by *force*— it is disunion by force—it is secession by *force*—it is Civil War!"[70] "This information," according to one observer of the Washington scene, ". . . afforded Gen. Jackson great satisfaction."[71] When Webster returned to Washington in late December, he immediately entered a period of warm relations with the President. As a consequence, it was noted, "the Jackson men are unreasonably jealous of the progress Mr. Webster is making in the affections of the executive."[72] This development especially alarmed Van Buren's supporters who feared that if the nullification crisis continued to take on cataclysmic proportions its political dynamics would make Webster into "the main prop of the administration" and he would indeed become a rival to succeed Jackson.[73]

The President also did not do very much to support the policy of the many important Democrats who hoped to defuse the crisis by abandoning protection. His call for tariff reduction in his recent annual message seems to have been a ploy mainly to isolate South Carolina from the rest of the South, and he probably did not want or expect it to take place at the present session of Congress or at least not before the nullifiers backed down. Jackson's feelings on the subject were probably clearly expressed by his very close personal friend, John Coffee, who had only recently arrived in Washington for the ostensible purpose of guiding an Indian treaty through the Senate. "Every day brings some news from there [South Carolina]," he wrote, "and all goes to show their determination to resist the Govt., and to make war, provided the Govt. does not yield to them—and that that is altogether out of the question, the Govt. never can yield to them—but they must submit, and be governed by the laws of the union, or they must be drubbed into it, and the ring leaders, be made an example of, if they can be caught, and then we shall have peace and tranquility."[74] In early January, Webster predicted that any immediate tariff reform was unlikely, in large part, "because it may be doubted whether the President desires to furnish such occasion for triumph to the leaders of nullification."[75]

On January 16, Jackson sent to Congress what is usually referred to as his Force Bill Message, because in it he appealed for official sanction, through legislation, of his policy toward South Carolina. In particular he requested the power to close the custom houses at Beaufort and Georgetown which could not be adequately protected from the state's replevin process and use instead "floating custom houses" on United States ships placed off each port, to remove the Charleston custom house to the federally controlled fortresses at Castle Pinckney or Fort Moultrie in the harbor, to collect duties instead of bonds, and to establish jails for lawbreakers the state refused to incarcerate. These measures would both make it more difficult for the nullifiers to implement their Ordinance and laws and make it easier for Jackson to place upon them the blame for any conflict that might occur. Also, in order to protect more effectively the property and persons of agents of the federal government in South Carolina and citizens of the state opposed to nullification, he requested the right to remove causes "without any copy of record," from state to federal courts. Finally, in what was to be the most controversial part of the message, he requested Congress to revise and update laws passed in 1795 and 1807 empowering the President to use the militia and United States army and navy to enforce the laws of the federal government.[76]

In his Proclamation of December 10, Jackson had claimed that the existing laws were sufficient to allow him to enforce the tariff in South Carolina. Now he was calling on Congress for new legislation and for support. Reacting to the furor the Proclamation had created among Democrats, the President, this time, avoided becoming involved in the complicated debate over the origins and nature of the union. Beyond this, however, the message exuded the President's uncompromising hostility to nullification and opposition to conciliating South Carolina. "While a forbearing spirit may, and I trust will, be exercised toward the errors of our brethren . . . duty to the rest of the Union demands that organized resistance to the laws should not be executed with impunity," he said, and he concluded by asking Congress to proclaim to the present and the future "that the constitution and the laws are supreme and the *Union indissoluble*."[77]

After reading the message, Henry Clay pronounced it as "able and elaborate, freer from passion than the proclamation, but not more compatible with the doctrines which prevail at Richmond." Calhoun wrote, "It will do our cause much good; more than the Proclamation. It has caused much excitement already among the Southern members, which has extended even to the Jackson portion. I do not doubt, that he wants force, tho he has not asked it; but he will not be gratified. Congress will not trust him, unless I am much deceived."[78] And one commentator noted:

It's [*sic*] language though plain, is neat, guarded, and at first blush unoffending. Yet I fear on a close and critical inspection, will be found to be, not the words of wisdom in the tone of persuasion, or conciliation; but rather those of unrelenting determination to persevere in the course chalked out in the Proclamation, utterly regardless of consequences. To me, it sounded not as a warning voice of the father of his country, raised to lead back to the path of duty its *erring,* but honest sons; but that of stubborn sterness, resolutely bent on punishing all who dared think otherwise than as it pronounced, or act but as it prescribed.[79]

VI

The nullifiers moved quickly to take advantage of the confusion caused by the Proclamation and the widespread apprehension of Jackson's determination to use force against South Carolina. "I think," wrote one, "his rash denunciation and reckless and arbitrary doctrines afford the means of prostrating him if used with skill." Another nullifier, commenting on the general unhappiness of Democrats with the Proclamation wrote, "Thank God, we are again Federalists and Republicans." And Duff Green immediately went on the offensive, arguing that now the crucial "question is whether the principles of the Proclamation are not directly opposed to the principles which have been advocated by the Democratic Republican party ever since they existed as a party."[80]

Immediately upon receipt of Jackson's Proclamation, the South Carolina legislature authorized Governor Hayne to issue a counter proclamation which he did on December 20. It succinctly restated the case for nullification, stressing its doctrinal ties to the Jeffersonian tradition, and warned against the dangers involved in allowing the federal government, or any branch of it, to determine exclusively whether its own actions are constitutional or not. But mainly it attacked, in a restrained but effective manner, the President's pronouncement, stressing Jackson's lack of concern for the rights of the states and his nationalist views of the origins and nature of the Union.[81]

The Proclamation allowed South Carolina's leaders to shift attention away from the legitimacy of nullification and focus instead on Jackson's reaction to what they had done. Further, it allowed them to move off the narrow question of the unjustness of the tariff and the technical right of a state to declare an act of the federal government unconstitutional and to broaden their appeal to state's righters in general. "It is not *now,* whatever it may heretofore have been, a doubtful question of political economy. It is now a question of right on one side and power on the other."[82] Or as one writer in South Carolina put it:

The great question now is not nullification and the tariff only—it is not the issue merely between Carolina and Congress—it is not only whether Carolinians, by wavering and yielding shall prove that chains are their appropriate declarations, words their only weapons, murmurs and complaints and scoundrel supplications their befitting language, and bondage their proudest condition—but it is whether the States shall preserve their individuality as sovereign, or be merged into one wide imperial realm, whether the people are hereafter to govern themselves, or to be the serfs of whatever combination of politicians shall acquire sway at Washington; whether any dotard or miscreant from chance or trickery, or popular delusion may elevate to the presidential chair, may lord over us, and write his vengeance against his opponents in blood; whether the United States shall be free, sovereign and independent states, or provences; whether they deserve *freedom*. It is a question of liberty or despotism.[83]

Nullifiers and their supporters argued that the "entire abandonment of the principle of state rights" by the Proclamation revealed "the despotic principles of the Executive," and saw it as Jackson's "attempt to appoint himself a *dictator,* to place himself above the laws as the *sole* expounder of the Constitution. . . ." Only this, they asserted, could explain the President's total abandonment of the principles he had laid out a week earlier in his fourth annual address. Moreover, this development, they claimed, proved their earlier charge that Jackson's hostility to South Carolina involved not a difference in principles and constitutional interpretation but an "insane rashness of personal feelings." In an argument that clearly was finding resonance among Democrats in general and even among many National Republicans they warned, all this:

will bring the states everywhere, and the representative of every state, to a solemn consideration how far such hands as these, are to be trusted with military power. . . . Calhoun is not the only man in the nation whom he abhors and detests; and So. Carolina is not the only state in the Union that he would seek and find pretexts for crushing and exterminating, in order that he might reach and destroy the victims of his insatiable wrath if you once clothe him with adequate military force. It cannot be doubted that he is the most ferocious and arbitrary tyrant in existence in the present day . . . Drunk as many have been with Jacksonianism, it is utterly impossible but the instinct of self preservation will awaken in them, and compel them to pause.[85]

Reaction to the Proclamation had clearly worked to South Carolina's advantage. "I may almost say to you," wrote John Tyler in early January 1833, "that the battle is fought and won . . . and the bold avowal of a determination to strike one of the *old 13* out of existence, by military force, will be rebuked and chided."[86] One observer, describing the warm reception Calhoun received when he arrived in Washington to take up his duties as United States senator noted he "appears to be in good spirits . . . it is the opinion of many that the South will make common cause with Carolina and that Calhoun will be the person around whom they will rally to support the Democratic doctrines of '98."[87]

Recognizing that support for their cause was rapidly growing, it quickly became, as one newspaper correspondent put it, "a great object for South Carolina to gain time." What the state planned to do, according to McDuffie, was to repel "the President's calumny by proving that our remedy is peaceable. Unless General Jackson announces war upon the state by an indiscriminate attack upon men, women and children there can be no military violence used, for the state will proceed calmly on in the civil tribunals without paying the slightest attention to the military parade or the mad ravings of this drivelling old dotard."[88] This strategy manifested itself in several important developments.

First, despite the militancy of the original Ordinance of late November, the nullifiers acted with extreme caution in implementing it. With things going their way, they wanted to avoid a confrontation with the Unionists that would give the President an opportunity to intervene. Although they could do nothing about the convention's order that following the enactment of the Ordinance all elected officials be immediately required to take the test oath, this affected only a small number of minor officials. Most had been elected *before* the Ordinance was enacted, and to avoid antagonizing these Unionists the legislature chose to interpret its charge from the convention in narrow terms by requiring those officials to take the oath only when their duties involved the actual enforcement of nullification. Since many officials of Unionist sympathies held posts that had nothing to do with the collection of tariff duties, and since nullification was not to go into effect until February 1, this interpretation both reduced the number of officials that might be involved in the taking of a test oath, and put off, at least for a while, the need to move against most Unionist officeholders. At this time the South Carolina legislature also chose not to act on a bill giving it broad powers to imprison almost any Unionist for treasonous activities.[89]

The nullifier dominated South Carolina legislature also exercised considerable restraint when it adopted legislation for the actual implementation of nullification. It eschewed making the convention's nullification of the tariffs of 1828 and 1832 compulsory for everyone importing goods into the state, although this is clearly what the convention had intended. Instead, the legislature made it voluntary, allowing those merchants wishing to pay duties to do so. This had the dual purpose of letting the Unionists go their own way and, hopefully, of giving the nullifiers the choice of when and how they would confront the federal government after February 1.

For merchants sympathetic to nullification the legislation provided an elaborate form of legal recourse. Instead of paying duties in cash they would obtain a tariff bond from the customs office when they brought in the goods. They could then refuse to pay their bonds on the grounds that the imposts were null and void. If the matter came to trial it would be before a local judge and jurors who had already sworn to uphold the Ordinance, and who therefore would find for the importing merchant. Should the federal customs collector decline to issue a customs bond and demand a cash payment, the importing merchant could refuse to pay the duties and allow his goods to be seized, whereupon he could go to a state court and ask for a writ of replevin authorizing the sheriff to recover the goods for the importing merchant. To contest the writ the customs collector would again have to go into a court made up of a judge and jurors who had sworn to uphold the Ordinance. Should the customs collector remove the confiscated goods to a fort under federal control, the recourse provided was *a capias* in *withernam,* a process whereby a local sheriff could seize the private assets of the customs collector to an amount up to twice the sworn value of the impounded goods. Or they could simply pay the duties and sue to recover them plus interest on an action of assumpsit.[90]

The strategy behind this was to clothe the actual process of nullifying the tariffs of 1828 and 1832, as much as possible, in legal procedure so as to make it appear peaceful. The Charleston *Mercury* assured its readers: "Our remedy will go on peaceably through our courts; and committing no act of violence ourselves, even ANDREW JACKSON will be unable to make a pretext for commencing a battle. We will not give him a chance to fight us. He may make faces and shake his fist and snap his fingers at us as much as he pleases; we'll walk into the Court House and leave him bullying on the green." It did warn, however, that should the President coerce the state by blockading its harbors and cutting off its trade "we will secede—and if he resolves to fight out the right of secession, why on that score he'll find more states in his way than he expected to meet."[91]

Finally, and most significantly, with the approach of February 1, the nullifiers moved to prevent the Ordinance from going into effect. Under the leadership of James Hamilton, Jr., and William C. Preston they held a large pubic meeting in Charleston on January 21. After condemning Jackson's threats and reaffirming the peaceable right of secession, the likelihood of tariff reform was noted, and it was observed that this combined with "expressions of sentiment in both branches of Congress, as well as in other quarters," made it important that "all occasion of collision between the federal and state authorities should be sedulously avoided . . . ". The meeting thereupon decided that the voluntary system of nullification adopted by the legislature not be put into effect until after Congress adjourned in early March.[92]

The actions of both the legislature and the January 21 meeting at Charleston were questionable and arbitrary for neither had a legal or even theoretical right to alter the decisions of the November convention which had become part of the state's fundamental law. They also were unpopular with many radical nullifiers for Hamilton a short time later confided "the convention . . . could not have been called . . . without great hazards." The usually militant Hamilton recognized, however, that the ideological and political confusion that followed Jackson's proclamation had turned the tide in South Carolina's favor. To an important Virginia ally he wrote, "we shall . . . put our opponents in the wrong. My life upon it, if a conflict does occur, he strikes the first blow."[93]

VII

During this same period the congressional Democratic plan to defuse the crisis through tariff reform had run into trouble. The Constitution required that any change in revenue laws had to originate in the House of Representatives. Therefore a measure was hastily put together by the House Ways and Means Committee. It was known as the Verplanck tariff bill, named after the chairman of the committee where it had been drafted with considerable input from Polk and Secretary of the Treasury Louis McLane. The bill provided for a substantial cut in duties back to the level of 1816, and to take place in the very short period of two years; it did not, however, involve abandonment of the principle of protection. Debate on the measure began in early January. In the course of introducing the bill, Verplanck observed the committee had conducted their deliberations "in the spirit of justice, conciliation, and of peace; and it is in this spirit that they now invite this body to the examination of the bill before them."[94]

This did not happen. Strong opposition to the bill came from an assortment of sources. Anti-Jackson protectionists opposed any reduction at all. They argued that the proposed measure was premature since the 1832 tariff had not been given a chance to go into effect and that the reductions contemplated were too sharp and would cause widespread distress and even ruin and would prostrate American manufacturers. They also condemned the measure as "an undignified truckling to the menaces and blustering of South Carolina," that would encourage other states to try to intimidate the federal government on various issues. As one Pennsylvanian put it, "the stability of our institutions and the permanency of the Union must some day be tested. That day may as well be now as tomorrow." The strategy of these protectionists, led by Webster, and finding encouragement from Jackson's strong stand against nullification in his Proclamation and January 16 message, was to consume as much time in debate as possible so that no action could be taken on the measure at the present session of Congress.[95]

Opposition to the Verplanck bill also came from many northern Democrats. The tariff had always been more of a sectional than a party issue and numerous pro-tariff Jacksonians from Connecticut, New York, New Jersey, Maryland, Pennsylvania, and Ohio also were unhappy over the measure's economic implications and feared political repercussions. Their strategy was generally not to oppose the tariff per se, but to amend the bill to raise specific duties to protect their constituents. Not only did this upset southerners who wanted to see all duties sharply reduced, but it also involved Congress in seemingly endless political maneuvering and roll call votes strengthening the hand of those protectionists who wanted the tariff of 1832 to be allowed to go into effect.[96]

Additional opposition came from the nullifiers and their allies. This group, led by Calhoun, wanted an abandonment of the principle of protection, something not provided for in the Verplanck proposal. In return they offered to support a more gradual reduction of duties to cushion the impact on the manufacturing interests. Prudence as well as politics clearly played a role here. If the decrease in duties were spread out over a longer period of time it would perhaps make tariff reform more palatable to the manufacturing interests and irate voters in the North as well as gain the support of fearful and wavering pro-tariff Jacksonians. Further, killing the Verplanck bill would rob the administration of credit for resolving the volatile tariff question and embarrass Van Buren and his southern supporters who would hold him responsible for the bill's failure.[97]

This combination of anti-Jackson protectionists, pro-tariff Jacksonians, and nullifiers proved too much to overcome and by mid-January it was clear that the Verplanck bill had no chance of passage. The attempt by congressional Democrats to develop an alternative to Jackson's policy of confrontation with South Carolina had failed and many feared that the failure to reduce the tariff would unite the South behind South Carolina and lead to Civil War, and they did not know what to do next. "In Congress all is confusion and uncertainty," wrote Silas Wright. Daniel Webster described the mood of congressional Democrats as "heartless & desponding", and a politically astute New Englander passing through Washington noted "the Jackson party as a party is broken to pieces, and the fragments have not yet adjusted themselves."[98]

Jackson's problems also continued to mount. His failure to become involved personally in tariff reform was the source of much concern and criticism as was his general unwillingness to adopt a more conciliatory stance toward South Carolina. Obviously disappointed by the harsh tone of the January 16 message and the President's preoccupation with military preparations, one previously staunch administration supporter from New York remarked, "the argument by which his conclusion is sustained is as dangerous to liberty as the subject itself . . . ". Moreover, in Congress Calhoun's influence clearly was on the rise. According to one visitor from Virginia, "he makes converts, aye, open converts who have avowed the fact, while others more cautious only wait a favourable opportunity to follow after," and then added: "There is more Nullification here, I fear, than many are aware of."[99]

The President also was running into difficulties with his Unionist allies in South Carolina. He had expected them to recruit volunteers to form a posse to help the federal marshals and customs officials collect the tariff duties; and if fighting should break out he would, of course, have an excuse to call out the various state militias and federal army and march down with them to restore peace and seize the leaders of the rebellion whom he would have tried for treason. On the very day Jackson sent his Force Bill message to Congress he wrote Poinsett: "You can rely on every aid that I can give—only advise me of the action of the nullifyers. The moment they are in hostile array in opposition to the execution of the laws, let it be certified to me by the atty for the *district,* or the *judge,* and I will forthwith order the leaders prosecuted and *arrested*—if the marshal is resisted by 12,000 bayonets I will have his posse 24,000 . . . ".[100]

But on that very day Poinsett, concerned among other things about the various offers of volunteers from Georgia and North Carolina to support the nullifiers' cause, wrote to inform the President that the Unionists were unwilling to form a posse merely upon the authority of a federal marshal because they feared if taken prisoner they would be subject to prosecution under the laws of the state. Instead, they wanted Jackson to call out the state militia so they would be acting directly upon a presidential order. This placed Jackson in a difficult, even embarrassing position, for most Democrats and even many National Republicans to whom nullification was abhorrent, had made it clear that Jackson should not act without the support of Congress, and Congress had only just begun to consider the requests he had made in his Force Bill message. Although Jackson still had hopes that Congress would quickly give its approval by a large majority, it is clear that by the end of January this was wishful thinking on the President's part. Unless he were willing to take on Congress and most of his own party as well as the nullifiers, Jackson could not accede to the Unionists' request.[101]

Jackson was now forced to retreat. In early December, disregarding Congress's feelings on the subject and failing to consult with his party's leaders, he had asserted that the existing laws were adequate to enforce the tariff in South Carolina and that he considered the mere raising of troops by the nullifiers as constituting an act of treason. Now, less than two months later, he had been forced to recognize that some kind of overt act was necessary on the part of the nullifiers before they could be accused of treasonable activities. In late January he had his secretary of war, Lewis Cass, instruct Winfield Scott, the general in charge of federal troops in Charleston Harbor, that "it is the most earnest wish of the President that the present unhappy difficulties in South Carolina should be terminated without any forcible collision"; or if this were not possible that there should be no question that "if such collision does occur it shall not be justly imputable to the United States."[102]

Accurately assessing the situation in early January, Calhoun recognized that the battle was going in his favor and only some rash act on the part of South Carolina, that would justify military intervention by the President, could reverse this trend. He, therefore, wrote home: "Let our people go on; be firm and prudent; give no pretext for force, and I feel confident of a peaceable and glorious triumph for our cause and state," and predicted that "a satisfactory adjustment" of the tariff would take place.[103] The nullifier strategy of shifting the focus of debate from their own highly controversial constitutional doctrines to the dangers inherent in Jackson's fierce determination to enforce the laws in South Carolina had succeeded.

To appreciate fully the extent of the nullifier success it is not enough simply to look at Congressional politics important as they were, but it is also necessary to examine closely reaction at the state level. In this arena a number of crucial developments took place that affected, in significant ways, the outcome of the nullification crisis. In addition, what took place on the local level also decisively influenced a number of other developments that by now had become enmeshed in the nullification crisis: the Georgia Indian controversy, the future role of the Supreme Court, tariff reform, and the origins and character of the opposition to Jackson in the South. On the local level, too, important constitutional debates took place during the winter of 1832–33 that further illuminate the differences between nullification and the more traditional form of states' rights that for so long played an important role in American constitutional and ideological development.

5

Georgia and the Nullification Crisis

Georgia was one of the earliest and most important of the southern states to debate the issues raised by the nullification crisis. Its long-standing opposition to a national program of internal improvements, and its confrontation with the Supreme Court on the Cherokee question made it a states' rights stronghold. Opposition to a protective tariff was also widespread and intense. But, as the nullification crisis unfolded, it soon became clear that, in many people's minds, states' rights was one thing, and the right of a single state to declare an act of the federal government unconstitutional and to withdraw from the Union was something else. On the other hand, there also existed an influential and growing minority sympathetic to the cause of nullification. Consequently, Georgia quickly became deeply divided between those sympathetic and supportive of South Carolina and those who wanted to see the doctrine of nullification condemned and resisted. Jackson's Proclamation strongly influenced the outcome of the ensuing struggle which, in turn, effected both the final resolution of the Cherokee question and the course of Georgia politics for the rest of the decade.[1]

I

Georgia politics in 1831 and 1832 were in a confused and fluid state: the older political alignments were in the process of breaking down but had not been effectively replaced by a new political formation. For a decade and a half

102

preceding the nullification crisis state politics had been dominated by a series of sharp political struggles. During the late 1820s and early 1830s the dominant group was known as the Troupites. This group traced its origins back to the 1790s when, in the wake of the infamous Yazoo scandals, the Jeffersonian-Republicans under the leadership of James Jackson effectively eliminated the Federalists as a force in Georgia politics. Jackson died in 1806 and control of his political machine was passed on to William H. Crawford, who, until illness and a failed presidential bid in 1824, mainly involved himself in national politics, and to George M. Troup who ran things on the state level and was elected governor in 1823 and 1825. Their main opposition came from a group led first by General Elijah Clark and then by his son General John Clark who won the governorship in 1819 and again in 1821.[2]

Part of the struggle between the Troupites and the Clarkites has to be explained in terms of personal feuds, the control of patronage, and the pursuit of power. But more substantial issues also were involved, and during the 1820s the groups fought bitterly over relief legislation following the Panic of 1819, state taxation policies, financial and banking legislation, and the question of constitutional reform. The two factions also had different constituencies. Troup and his followers tended to be strongest in the older and more commercially developed eastern and central portions of the state where the plantation economy had taken hold, while support for the Clarkites tended to come mainly from the western and northern parts of the state, containing areas with poor soil, mountains, and piney woods and characterized as economically backward, thinly populated, and having few slaves.[3]

A particularly important contest occurred in 1825 when Troup defeated John Clark for the governorship. Shortly therafter Clark quietly retired from the Georgia political scene by moving to Florida. This left his followers leaderless and disorganized, and for the next several years they were unable to agree upon a gubernatorial candidate, although they occasionally managed to achieve ineffective control of the legislature. In other words, the Clarkites continued to be an important, if generally unsuccessful, force in the state's politics. Meanwhile, the Troupites began to squabble among themselves. Crawford, who had suffered a stroke in 1823 from which he never fully recovered, returned to Georgia and intermittently became involved in local politics; Troup, who was getting old, went to the United States Senate in 1829. As a result a struggle began to take place among the younger members for control of the party, and in 1829 two rival factions openly contested for the governorship.[4]

In national politics both the Clarkites and Troupites supported Jackson. But there was a difference. Clarkite support for Jackson dated back to the election of 1824, and they often referred to themselves as "the original Jackson men." The Troupites, on the other hand, had supported Crawford in 1824 and were very harsh on Jackson during that campaign. Only reluctantly did they move into the Jackson camp during the election of 1828, and then only because they were thoroughly alienated by John Quincy Adams's nationalist policies, especially his refusal to support their efforts to force the removal of the Creek and Cherokee Indians from the state. As Crawford wrote, "I have opposed the re-election of Mr. Adams rather than advocated that of General Jackson who I have voted for rather as a choice of evils, than as a matter of political preference."[5]

Further effecting political alignments in Georgia was the Van Buren-Calhoun power struggle during Jackson's first administration. In fact, as the struggle became increasingly enmeshed with nullification it triggered a virtual revolution in the state's politics. Crawford had been feuding with Calhoun since they served together in James Monroe's cabinet in 1817. At the same time he had a long-standing political alliance with Van Buren who supported him for the presidency in 1824. Crawford therefore quickly threw his support to the New Yorker, and was the main source of the privileged information that exposed Calhoun's opposition to Jackson during the Seminole Indian controversy. For his part, Calhoun did what he could to cultivate an alliance with the Clarkites in an effort to neutralize Crawford's influence in Georgia.

Then, in 1831, the Clark party staged a successful comeback under the leadership of Wilson Lumpkin, who captured the governorship. As a congressman between 1827 and 1831, Lumpkin, who was hostile to Crawford, had been a Calhoun ally and supported the Vice President in his contest with Van Buren. But he also was openly critical of nullification. Writing of "the true principles of our Constitution," Lumpkin described them as "the only principles which can secure our liberty, & perpetuate the blessings of union & confederation. The sovereignty of the states and the union of the states, *are one and indivisible*."[6] This reflected the feelings of most of the Clarkites, for while they strongly favored the removal of the Creek and Cherokee from Georgia and had supported Troup and his successors in their controversies with the federal government, they also were very critical of inflammatory rhetoric threatening disunion and secession.

Lumpkin and his followers watched unhappily as the strength of the nullifiers grew in South Carolina. In the spring of 1831 one Clarkite wrote to Calhoun: "The party which has heretofore supported you in Georgia has made a sincere devotion to the union one of the main articles of its political creed . . . ," and warned "many of your friends believing you to be identified in feeling & principle with Messrs. Hayne, Hamilton & Miller on the subject of nullification, are almost prepared to abandon you."[7] A short time later, Tomlinson Fort, editor of the influential *Federal Union* of Milledgeville, informed Calhoun that among the Clarkites "a widespread opinion prevails there is at work in South Carolina a powerful passion of disloyalty to the government of the United States . . ." and cautioned "it will be impossible to unite them in support of any one who is tainted with nullification. No! not even against Mr. Van Buren, odious to them as he is." Fort went on to argue against the doctrine of nullification on the grounds that it violated the concept of majority rule:

None know better than we do the unjust operation of the tariff of '28. To frame laws operating equally on a vast empire, with interests so diversified as ours is

> impossible. To object to a majority passing laws to favor their own interests is to
> object to our system altogether. An improvement allowing the minority to govern,
> would last only long enough for the promulgation of laws enacted by them.[8]

When Calhoun refused to disassociate himself from developments in South Carolina and then openly embraced nullification, his Georgia allies began to desert him.[9] As early as 1829 the Clark party, in a clear reflection of its opposition to nullification, started to refer to itself as the Union party. Unionist concern over South Carolina's threat of secession was shared by several important Troupites. Of these one of the most significant was John Forsyth, governor of Georgia from 1827 to 1829 and United States senator between 1831 and 1834, who was a close personal friend and political ally of Van Buren and ardent supporter of Andrew Jackson. Also included in this group was Congressman James M. Wayne from Savannah.[10]

Most of the Troupites, however, remained at best unenthusiastic supporters of the Jackson administration. Although no longer holding political office, Crawford continued to speak out on the issues. He was critical of the President's handling of the tariff issue, but his long-term enmity to Calhoun made it impossible for him to endorse developments in South Carolina. Troup himself, now in the United States Senate, also strongly favored tariff reform and had many close friends among the nullifiers of South Carolina, although he remained wary of Calhoun. While Troup never endorsed nullification, he also avoided criticizing it and did make clear his belief that a state had a constitutional right to secede from the Union. Declining an invitation to attend a public meeting and dinner sponsored by the friends of nullification in Columbia, South Carolina, because of ill health, he wrote:

> Whatever the people in South Carolina, in convention shall resolve for their safety, interest and happiness, will be right, and none will have the right to question it. You can change your government at pleasure; and, therefore, you can throw off the government of the Union, whenever the same safety, interest and happiness require it.[11]

Troup, however, remained circumspect about expressing his opposition to the President and his sympathy toward South Carolina, for he recognized that both Jackson and his Indian policy were extremely popular in Georgia. Writing in 1832, he noted, "the cause of nullification is so generally connected with hostility to the President, that, even if it were more tenable, it would expose to jealousy any politican in Georgia who would seem to favor it."[12]

Of the younger Troupites the most important was John M. Berrien. He was Troup's protégé as well as a close personal friend. Bitter over being forced to resign his position as attorney general in the wake of the Eaton Affair, Berrien was more openly anti-Jackson than his mentor. Further widening the gap was the fact that Berrien had long been a bitter enemy of Forsyth within the Troup party, and was further alienated by the latter's growing influence with the Jackson administration. Returning to Georgia in 1831, Berrien engaged in various anti-administration political activities, labored hard to harness the state's intense anti-tariff feeling to political advantage, and in 1832 he urged the state legislature to adopt a resolution in support of the Second Bank of the United States. Although never prepared to openly endorse nullification, Berrien had clearly become sympathetic to Calhoun and was considered a friend and ally by Duff Green. Within Georgia, Berrien formed a political alliance with Augustin S. Clayton, a former state judge and a leader in the state's struggle with the federal government on the Cherokee matter. Clayton was at that time the congressman from the Athens district and also one of the few leading politicians in the state to openly endorse nullification and advocate that Georgia formally ally itself with South Carolina. Seaborn Jones and Robert Augustus Beall were two other important Georgians sympathetic to nullification.[13]

Although these disruptive developments were playing an increasingly important role within Georgia politics in 1831 and 1832 they did not effect Jackson's bid for reelection. The Clarkites, who with only a few exceptions, had pretty much gone *en masse* into the Union party, continued to support the Old Hero enthusiastically; but many of them remained suspicious of Van Buren because of his long-standing association with Crawford and therefore supported P. P. Barbour for the vice presidency. The Troupites, including Berrien, on the other hand, unable to come up with a viable alternative, continued reluctantly to support the Jackson-Van Buren ticket. Personal feuds and party loyalties still played a dominant role in Georgia politics in the fall of 1832. But in the months following South Carolina's nullification, the tariffs of 1828 and 1832 and constitutional principles and issues became the focal point around which new political alignments formed.

II

During the late spring and throughout the summer of 1832 the nullifiers of South Carolina made a sustained effort to cultivate support for their cause in Georgia. Although there was some resistance to this because of widespread personal dislike of Calhoun and because of varous long-standing rivalries between the two states, considerable progress was made. In May of 1832 a dinner given at Hamburg on the South Carolina side of the Savannah River in honor of Governor Hamilton and nullification was attended by a large number of enthusiastic Georgians. The alliance was cemented when a short time later a huge dinner (more than two thousand attended, it was claimed) was given at Augusta on the Georgia side of the river at which the governor of South Carolina was present as well as a large number of that state's leading nullifiers.

The significance of these developments became apparent at the August commencement exercises of the University of Georgia. Over time this had evolved into much more than an occasion for the granting of degrees to graduating students; it had become an annual opportunity for the state's leading politicians to caucus and engage in their various machinations. William H. Crawford called a meeting of those who supported President Jackson and opposed South Carolina and nullification to be held at the University's chapel. But the opposition, led by Berrien and Clayton, also called a meeting for the same time and place and came in such numbers that they overwhelmed Crawford and his supporters and used the meeting to attack protectionism and Jackson's tariff policy. Among other things, this group called for a statewide anti-tariff convention to be held in Milledgeville in November that should have "full powers, in behalf of the good People of Georgia, to maintain, preserve, and defend the rights and privileges of the free citizens of this state."[14]

The Athens meeting also established a Committee of Correspondence to coordinate activities with other states and within Georgia and sent a letter to all the counties of the state authorizing elections in October for delegates to the Milledgeville convention. At first the Unionists tried to boycott the convention, hoping that the movement would collapse through a lack of popular support. But as it became clear that the Troupites had initiated an energetic campaign, which included the holding of numerous local meetings, and were generating considerable popular enthusiasm for the Milledgeville convention, the Unionists reversed themselves and launched their own campaign to elect delegates openly opposed to nullification. The debate that followed was a far-ranging one. The Unionists, who openly praised Andrew Jackson, stressed the dangers involved in holding a convention that claimed for itself "full powers to act" on behalf of the state. They warned also that support for South Carolina and nullification would inevitably lead to secession, the destruction of the Union, and bloodshed.

On the other side, while most of the supporters of the convention were unwilling to endorse nullification openly, they refused to condemn South Carolina. One writer argued, "Let us remember . . . however inefficient or defective the system of Nullification may be the objects for which it contends are objects dear to freemen, and for which the whole South is now raising its voice in a way that must be heard, and upon the attainment of which, depends our prosperity and honor." As another writer put it, South Carolina's nullifiers are to be praised for the "boldness about their demands for their rights, which has carried conviction to the minds of all who have heard them, that however mistaken in their plan, there was sterling honesty in their intentions!" The convention's supporters made it clear that they opposed the coercion of any state by the federal government. They denounced the tariffs of 1828 and 1832, denied that the latter represented an equitable compromise, and argued instead that these measures were arbitrary and unconstitutional. To the argument of majority rule they countered: "Our government was established to promote the general good—to advance our prosperity as a nation—and not for the majority in power to legislate for self-aggrandizement, to the extermination of those in the minority."[15]

The Milledgeville convention convened on November 12, 1832. Leading the Unionist forces, which were determined to prevent the convention from either criticizing President Jackson or supporting South Carolina, was Senator Forsyth. In recent months he had been attacked by the more extreme Troupites for having voted for the Tariff of 1832. Forsyth justified this action on the grounds that it reduced the duties from the previous tariff and therefore was a "reduction of the burdens of the people; and he would continue the uncompromising incessant enemy of the system, till it was totally abrogated by Congress."[16] But Forsyth was also totally opposed to nullification. Earlier in the year in a speech before the Senate he indicated that his own view of the doctrine clearly was congruent with the President's.

> He would, indeed, oppose the protective system by all fair, legal and constitutional means. He would go that far, but not one step farther. Should the majority overrule us—should the system be continued—he would not on that account, sanction any course of opposition that would endanger the Union, or be contrary to the spirit of the Constitution. God forbid that, on account of any erroneous legislation, he should be betrayed into measures that would tend to the destruction of the constitution. He would continue to urge upon Congress, in every proper constitutional form, the necessity and propriety of an abandonment of a policy which, to a portion of the Union, is odious and oppressive; and he would rely upon the intelligence of the people, and upon their sense of justice, for an ultimate adjustment of the tariff, upon fair, equal and constitutional scruples.[17]

Early in the Milledgeville convention it was moved to select a committee of twenty-one to draft a set of resolutions. At this point the Unionists, led by Forsyth, "finding ourselves in a minority at the convention and knowing ourselves to be a majority with the people" moved for the appointment of a special committee to examine the credentials of the delegates, the methods by which they were selected, and the number of votes cast at the various local elections.[18] It was an attempt to discredit the convention by showing that it did not represent the true sentiments of the people of Georgia and had usurped the power of the state legislature. Forsyth also moved that the Athens committee's entire correspondence be laid before the convention because he was convinced that it would reveal a secret attempt on the part of South Carolina's nullifiers to control events in Georgia. These motions were opposed by Berrien and Clayton, who defended the legitimacy of the convention and the selection of the delegates and charged the Unionists with obstructionism. After a sharp debate that lasted three days, Forsyth's first motion was rejected and he withdrew his second. Following this, Forsyth and fifty-three other delegates walked out of the convention.[19]

Berrien and Clayton now controlled the convention. Clayton and his supporters wanted an open avowal of support for nullification and South Carolina, but many of the delegates, including Berrien, were not willing to go that far. Instead a series of resolutions was adopted that indicated the convention strongly sympathized with, if it did not endorse, the principles of the nullifiers. These resolutions endorsed the compact theory of the origins of the federal government and asserted that the federal government was a government of limited powers and that the power to interpret the Constitution "cannot belong to the agent, since that would be to substitute his judgment for the constitutional limitation, and that in the absence of a common arbiter expressly designated by the Constitution for this purpose, each state as such, and in virtue of its sovereignty is necessarily admitted to the exercise of that right." The convention also declared the Tariff of 1832 unconstitutional and called upon the people of the state to resist it "to the end." Hoping for a peaceful resolution of differences the convention called for a reduction of duties at the next session of Congress and proposed the calling of a convention made up of all the southern states to meet in March. To legitimize their proceedings and to attract public support, the convention adopted a plan to submit their proceedings for public approval. It also provided that in every county the opinions of the citizens were to be registered by elected superintendents, and the results reported back to the convention which would reconvene early in July.[20]

The Unionists denounced the convention's work. Before withdrawing, Forsyth and his followers submitted a document protesting the meeting. It was not read to the convention nor was it included in the published proceedings, of which twenty thousand copies were printed and distributed throughout the state. But it did appear in Unionist newspapers and as a circular. It argued that "all the delegates together convened at Milledgeville were far from representing a majority of the people of Georgia." It pointed out that of the state's eighty counties twenty counties had no representatives at all when the convention convened; and that after Forsyth and his followers seceded, forty-three counties were unrepresented. Moreover, the resolutions of this "minority convention" were really only supported by the delegates of thirty-four counties for the representatives of three of the counties were divided. Attacking the convention's rejection of their demands that the credentials of the delegates be carefully examined, Forsyth and his followers asked, "if they are to try so vital a question in their own forum, by their own agents, and to be themselves the final judges of the decision, what is there which a minority may not assume." A short time later Forsyth and his allies issued another address charging that the real purpose of the Milledgeville convention was "to bring Georgia into the coils of South Carolina, and deliver her people *en masse* to the demon of nullification."[21]

Strong support for the efforts to prevent Georgia from aligning itself with South Carolina came from Governor Lumpkin who, even before the Milledgeville convention met, used his annual address to the legislature on November 6 to make clear his opposition to nullification: "The mystical doctrine of nullification, as contended for by its advocates, has only tended to bewilder the minds of the people, inflame their passions, and prepare them for anarchy and revolution. . . . I believe nullification to be unsound, dangerous and delusive in practice as well as theory." He further argued that he was "unable to comprehend or conceive of a peaceable, constitutional harmony which would attend a measure emanating from one twenty-fourth part of the sovereign power of the Union," and rejected the claim that nullification by a single state was a legitimate part of the Jeffersonian tradition. Lumpkin concluded by denying that Georgians had ever "veiled ourselves in the flimsy garment of peaceable constitutional nullification," and advised the state to continue to rely as it "has always relied on her own population, the justice of her cause, and the virtue and intelligence of the people of the United States, to sustain her unquestionable constitutional rights."[22]

Following Lumpkin's lead the General Assembly, with the Unionists in control, condemned the proceedings at Milledgeville. In a series of resolutions introduced by Dennis Ryan, and passed by large majorities in both houses, the activities of the convention were censured as likely "if persisted in, materially to disturb the public harmony," and as being the work "of delegates from a minority of the people . . ." that "would establish an alarming precedent for usurping the rights of the majority, and might alternatively expose us to all the horrors of discord and anarchy." Finally, the Ryan resolutions also praised Andrew Jackson's recent reelection, which was described as "the happiest augury of better things," and pointedly denounced South Carolina:

> We abhor the doctrine of Nullification as neither a peaceful, nor a constitutional remedy, but on the contrary, as tending to civil commotion and disunion; and while we deplore the rash of revolutionary measures, recently adopted by a Convention of the people of South Carolina, we deem it a paramount duty to warn our fellow citizens against the danger of adopting her mischievous policy.[23]

The Georgia legislature's repudiation of the proceedings at Milledgeville by no means ended the matter. For Berrien, Clayton, and others sympathetic to South Carolina continued to agitate. They charged that the Ryan resolutions played into the hands of northern protectionists by showing "the tariff states that we are a divided people, and that the General Assembly of Georgia is willing to oppose South Carolina."[24] They further argued that the condemnation of South Carolina was a serious mistake for not only had the Georgia legislature "wantonly insulted a large portion of their fellow citizens," but it had also denounced "a sovereign state, and in the exercise of her sovereign rights; it was neither becoming in us, nor rightful, nor politic for us to denounce her for exercising her own rights, in any manner she might think right and just." They also continued to point out "the cause of South Carolina is the cause of Georgia. They both stand upon the principles of everlasting justice—both should hand in hand strive for the maintenance of this exalted position."[25]

This then was the political situation in Georgia when Jackson issued his controversial Nullification Proclamation: although the extreme Troupites had been thwarted in their attempt to unite forces with South Carolina, they nonetheless remained an active and articulate minority. Moreover, the Proclamation, with its strong nationalist implications, clearly worked to their advantage, for most people in the state probably agreed with the claim: "the President goes alike against unionists and nullifiers; and is directly at war with all the state Right defenders. . . ."[26] One observer predicted that the Proclamation would be "repudiated by the great Republican parts of the union, as utterly at war with some of the fundamental principles of their political creed." Or as another writer argued: "No state paper since the foundation of the government, we believe, has produced a sensation so deep and universal . . . as this has." Although the writer praised Jackson as well intentioned, he nevertheless added, "it is not his motives, however just they may be, but to the paper we are to look; and we find there doctrines to which we never can subscribe, till we become advocates of consolidation."[27]

The unfavorable reaction to the Proclamation in Georgia allowed the extreme Troupites to feel secure enough to begin to attack the President directly, something they had been reluctant to do up to this point. "Jackson has done much for the country," wrote one, ". . . but if he had done ten thousand times as much, this Proclamation should not be submitted to. All that he ever did for the country, or ever can do, if he were to live as old as Methusalah, will not be the slightest remuneration for the destruction of our state sovereignty. He denies the sovereignty of the states—he asserts the power of enforcing, at the point of the bayonett, an *unconstitutional* law upon a sovereign state, whose people in solemn convention, have declared that they never granted to Congress the power to enact such a law."[28] Using stronger language, another writer asserted that the President's Proclamation "stamps upon him indelibly the character of hypocrite, usurper and tyrant—the meanest and most palpable of hypocrites—the most daring, reckless and dangerous of usurpers—and the most self-willed, heartless and bloody of tyrants."[29]

Numerous local meetings were held in various parts of the state to attack the President and the Proclamation. One such meeting at Augusta charged that "the principles set forth in the President's Proclamation assailed as much the rights and interests, liberties and sovereignty of Georgia, as of Carolina. . . ." A meeting held in Monroe County and reportedly attended by over five hundred people passed resolutions opposing almost every aspect of the Proclamation. These resolutions criticized the Proclamation's consolidationist tendencies, denied its view of the origins of the Union, rejected the argument that a private citizen could be guilty of treason "whilst acting in obedience to the sovereign authority of his own state," dissented from the view that the tariffs of 1828 and 1832 were constitutional, and opposed the use of any kind of military force against South Carolina. In Newton County a Free Trade and States Rights Association was formed that condemned both the Proclamation and the Ryan resolutions adopted by the legislature in early December. A Clark County meeting denounced the Proclamation as "tending directly to the destruction *of the rights and liberties of the people,*" as well as representing "a high-handed assumption of unconstitutional power" on the part of the President."[30]

Focusing on the Proclamation also allowed the radical Troupites to successfully shift attention away from the question of whether or not nullification was a proper constitutional and legal remedy and onto the dangers involved in allowing the President to use the powers of the federal government to coerce a single state. The President's critics also stressed that South Carolina was struggling to protect not only her own interests and rights but also the interests and rights of Georgia and the entire South. In an appeal to a distinctive southern consciousness one writer argued, "Nullification is no longer a mooted question with us; it is no time now to quibble about small matters.—The question is, are you for southern rights and southern liberty; or for consolidation and northern manufactories? . . . . With noble South Carolina rise or fall—live or die. Her cause is our cause; it is the cause of the whole South; it is the cause of Liberty."[31]

The hostile reception accorded to the Proclamation in Georgia also allowed the radical Troupites to concentrate with rapidly increasing stridency and effectiveness on the President's determination to use force against South Carolina. They stressed, in particular, the dangers this posed for Georgia. One writer maintained, "it ill becomes us to throw obstacles in the path of South Carolina, whose success is an advantage to our cause, whose defeat, death to our hopes. . . . When South Carolina is reduced into subjection . . . Georgia may be looked upon as the next victim for immolation at the altar of consolidation."[32] Another indicated "crush Carolina now, and you crush forever the spirit of freedom. No state, after her fall, would have the spirit to resist any encroachment upon her rights. Usurpation would be added to usurpation until a consolidated government arose from the ruins of that beautiful system of the Union of the Independent sovereignties."[33] It was absolutely essential to make clear to the President, it was argued, "that Georgia will not permit Carolina to be sacrificed, but that shoulder to shoulder, Georgia and Carolina will maintain their freedom, or side by side they will feel a common grave."[34]

What all this means is that it is a mistake to explain, as many scholars have, Georgia's attitude during the nullification crisis simply in terms of the legislature's adoption of the Ryan resolutions in early December. This took place before Jackson issued his Proclamation on December 10, the reaction to which "incalculably strengthened the before growing party for Nullification."[35] Moreover, throughout the rest of December 1832 and into the early months of the following year there were widespread reports that volunteers were being raised to go to the aid of South Carolina should that state be made to fight for its rights. Although it is not possible to state with any kind of precision how many people in Georgia would have either actively supported or opposed a Presidential attempt to use force against South Carolina, there is much impressionistic and indirect evidence to lend credence, despite its hyperbole, to the following report about popular feeling in Georgia:

> The "signs of the times" in our state is rapidly changing. Since the *proclamation* of the President, *thousands* who immediately before were numbered with those who have called themselves the "Union party" . . . have avowed a favorable change of sentiment, and are now good resistance men . . . the great mass of the people of this state will be true to the principles of freedom and state sovereignty. . . . The puerile efforts of our late weak and misguided Legislature, point not to the *real* feelings of the honest yeomanry of Georgia.[36]

III

Georgia's involvement in the Supreme Court case of *Worcester v. Georgia* also created special problems during the nullification crisis. If the President were allowed to use force against South Carolina, it might establish a dangerous precedent that could be used against Georgia when the Supreme Court reconvened in early 1833 and, as seemed likely, in response to a planned application from the missionaries, formally ordered their release. According to one very knowledgeable source, "many of the friends of the President think that he has now placed himself in a position, where it will become his duty to sustain the Supreme Court in their position against Georgia nullification, and some go as far as to express an opinion that he will do it. A storm is evidently gathering for Georgia, as well as South Carolina, and the Georgia gentlemen, on this subject, are completely in a fog."[37]

Concerned over this development, Georgia congressman and Lumpkin ally James M. Wayne approached Attorney General Roger Brooke Taney and had "a very satisfactory" conversation, during which he was reassured that the administration believed "all our proceedings, lottery and all, entirely constitutional and will be prepared to defend the whole if the Court should call upon the President to execute any order it may issue."[38] But reassuring as this might be it really did not do justice to the fluid and complex political situation in Washington, D.C., in the winter of 1832–33. If Jackson wanted congressional approval for the use of force against South Carolina, he would have to get the support of northern congressmen, many of whom were sympathetic to the cause of the Indians, and determined to protect the authority of the Supreme Court and who openly asserted, it was reported, "on the question of force they will do nothing unless Georgia is included. . . .[39]

The Georgia question attracted considerable national attention throughout the nullification crisis, not only from those supportive of South Carolina, but also from those who had long been critical of the President and sympathetic to the plight of the Indians. The nullifiers went out of their way to stress the similarities between the two situations, explaining Jackson's determination to use force against South Carolina while doing nothing about Georgia's refusal to recognize the authority of the Supreme Court over the Cherokee Indian question, in terms of the President's hatred of Calhoun and anger over his failure to receive nullifier support in the recent presidential election. They warned that if Jackson should be allowed to implement the principles enunciated in the Proclamation it would "level at one blow all the barriers erected to prevent the encroachment of consolidation," and then "woe . . . be to Georgia her fate is decided. . . ." Or, as another writer argued, should the federal government be successful in enforcing her will against South Carolina, then "Georgia must open her prison doors to the missionaries—she must acknowledge the supremacy of the Supreme Court, admit its right to control her criminal jurisdiction—she must stop the wheels of her lottery, command her citizens to evacuate the Cherokee territory, or become the next victim and share the fate of Carolina." From the other direction nationalists noted, "if the conduct of South Carolina excited regret and disapprobation that of Georgia, instigated as it is by mercenary motives, ought to excite deep detestation, and we do believe that the public sentiments of the Union is thus qualified in regard to the two states." Clearly looking forward to the reconvening of the Supreme Court, it was observed that "the President's sincerity and consistency will be tested at an early day."[40]

By the end of 1832 the Georgia situation had definitely become an embarrassment for Jackson, particularly in his attempt to isolate and use force against South Carolina. For as long as the meaning of the Supreme Court's ruling in *Worcester v. Georgia* remained unclear, it would cause problems for the President both with those partial to the plight of the Indians and the missionaries and with his own supporters in Georgia, where the nationalist implications of the Proclamation concerned many, who, if critical of nullification, nonetheless feared that if South Carolina were abandoned to her fate their state might next be subject to the President's wrath.

In an attempt to deal with the problem, traditional states' rights advocates made an effort to distinguish, in constitutional terms, between Georgia's refusal to obey a decision by the Supreme Court and South Carolina's claim of the right to nullify a federal law and secede from the Union. Governor Lumpkin clearly expressed the essence of this position when he argued that:

> It cannot be believed . . . that any honest man of common sense will be at a loss to draw the proper distinction between the destructive heresies and acts of South Carolina obviously tending to the destruction of the Federal Union, and those acts of Georgia which have been resorted to in defence of her local jurisdictional rights over her own citizens and territory. South Carolina has not only avowed her determination to resist the execution of the revenue laws of the country, but has openly assumed a position tending to disunion, and has actually commenced the organization of a separate and distinct government, based on belligerent and warlike principles. Her new form of proposed government is not only founded on principles of hostility to her old confederates, but is arbitrary, despotic and tyrannical in the extreme, to all that own portion of her own citizens who have the honesty and patriotism to dissent from ner novel and wild career of revolution, and to adhere to our admirable and beloved constitutional Federal system. Now, because Georgia has resolved at all hazards to maintain and defend their own local laws, enacted for the punishment of offences committed against them, within their own constitutional limits, shall she therefore be identified with the ambitious disappointed disunionists of other states? I trust not.[41]

A similar argument was presented in a widely reprinted essay from a Savannah newspaper:

> The nullification of South Carolina declares acts of Congress unconstitutional which operate upon the whole UNION; the constituted authorities of Georgia declare a JUDGMENT OF THE SUPREME COURT an *usurpation*—because it denies the right of the state of Georgia to legislate for the WHOLE Territory, within her jurisdictional limit. No state has, in its sovereign capacity, the right or the power, upon the principles of the federal compact, to nullify a supreme law of the land, obligatory upon the whole confederacy. But is that Supreme law which, in the form of a decision of the Supreme Court, interdicts a sovereign state from covering with its legislation its entire domain? . . . . Revolution and secession are not in the dreams of Georgia's philosophy. Her legislature and people are opposed to nullification in its South Carolina acceptation; and in resistance to the decree of

the Supreme Court, Georgia nullifies nothing. She plants herself upon her jurisdictional limits without resistance to congressional legislation.[42]

In the minds of traditional states' rights types the basic difference between South Carolina and Georgia was that the former was resisting an act of Congress, a popularly elected body responsive to the will of the majority and acting in an area where it clearly had constitutional authority, whereas Georgia was disobeying a decision of the Supreme Court, whose members held their positions by appointment for life tenure and who therefore were not accountable to the will of the majority, and whose authority over federal-state relations had not been accepted by many traditional states' rights advocates of the compact theory of the establishment of the United States Constitution.

Interesting as these arguments are for explaining the differences between traditional states' rights advocates and nullifiers, in practical terms this effort came too late to prevent *Worcester v. Georgia* from undercutting the administration's effort to isolate South Carolina. A more direct form of intervention was necessary to somehow prevent the case from coming before the Supreme Court in February 1833. Efforts to accomplish this came from several distinct but converging sources during the late fall and winter of 1833.

First, many who had been among the most important and vociferous supporters of the Cherokee and the missionaries began to talk less about the urgency of resisting Georgia's encroachment on the rights of the Indians or for the need for the Supreme Court's decisions to be enforced by the President, and more about the need for compromise. Thus, in April 1832, David Greene, the secretary of the American Board of Commissioners for Foreign Missions, the Boston-based society that had sent the missionaries to Georgia in the first place and that had advised and underwritten the Cherokee decision to take their cause to the Supreme Court, had indicated to Worcester and Butler that he did not think they should accept Governor Lumpkin's offer of a pardon, in return for which they would have to promise to leave the state, because in light of the Supreme Court's recent decision he did not see why they should bear "the stigma of being *pardoned culprits*."[43] But then, after the commencement of the nullification crisis, at a special meeting of the officers of the Board on Christmas day 1832, a resolution was adopted indicating "that, in view of the changes of circumstances, it is, in the opinion of the Committee, inexpedient for Messrs. Worcester & Butler to prosecute their case further before the Supreme Court of the United States."[44]

Why did the supporters of the Indians and the missionaries reverse themselves? Part of the explanation may be that in the spring of 1832 they hoped popular disgust with Jackson's policies would prevent his reelection and bring in Henry Clay, who was more sympathetic to the Indians and who would be willing to enforce the Supreme Court's decisions. They were, however, staggered by the election results and recognized that it made the removal of the Indians inevitable. William Wirt, chief counsel for the Cherokee and presidential candidate on the anti-Masonic ticket, noted that there already was talk of a third term for Jackson and added, "my opinion is, he may be President for life, if he chooses."[45] Along these lines many of the friends of the Indians and the missionaries may have feared that should Worcester and Butler actually apply and get from the Supreme Court some kind of process to carry into effect its former decision it would be ignored by Jackson, and that this would only serve to embarrass and weaken the Court by highlighting its inability to enforce its decisions. Fearful for the Supreme Court's future, they may have believed it safer to abandon the Indians and back down on the specifics of the case than to risk having so flagrantly denied the broader principle that the Supreme Court had the right to declare state laws unconstitutional. Finally, it seems likely that many of these same people had genuinely come to fear for the future of the Union, and viewing nullification as the greater threat were willing to go along with the administration's general policy of trying to isolate South Carolina. For whatever reasons, it is clear that by the end of 1832 a number of the most important supporters of the Indians and missionaries had become part of a concerted effort to resolve as quickly and as practically as possible Georgia's controversy with the Supreme Court, since "public consideratons connected with the state of the country (particularly the open resistance of South Carolina), and the extremely ticklish predicament of Georgia," might lead that state to end up supporting the nullifiers.[46]

Strong support for this course of action came from Van Buren and his followers in New York, who for a long time had had especially close ties with the Crawford Democrats in Georgia. The work in formulating the compromise was handled by Benjamin F. Butler, a lawyer, member of the Albany Regency, and close personal friend of the Vice President, who had been very outspoken in his defense of Georgia in its controversy with the Supreme Court during the recent presidential election. Butler arranged to have two letters written to Governor Lumpkin. One was signed by a number of the leading citizens of Albany who had been critical of Jackson's Indian policy and opposed to his reelection, and two of whom, Eliphalet Nott and Stephen Van Rensselear, were members of the American Board of Commissioners of Foreign Missions. They urged an immediate pardon for the missionaries while at the same time assuring the governor that the results of the recent presidential election had clearly indicated that the nation favored the removal of the Indians from Georgia, and that they were "of the opinion that very many persons who have counteracted their removal will now deem it their duty to cooperate in bringing it about; and they have reason to believe, and confidently hope that an influence will be applied to reconcile the tribe to such a result by those very persons who have labored to prevent it." The second letter, signed by Silas Wright, Jr., Azariah C. Flagg, and John A. Dix, leading New York Democrats and members of the Regency, also urged a pardon, adding, "we now speak as politicians. From the unpleasant agitations which, at the present time are convulsing . . . another of the independent states of the Union, we feel the deepest interest that all danger of conflict between the authorities of Georgia and any of the authorities of the General Government should be put to rest." These letters were transmitted by Van Buren to Senator Forsyth in Washington, D.C., who, in turn, saw that they got to Governor Lumpkin.[47]

Although Jackson did not become directly involved in these proceedings it is clear that he knew what was going on and supported the various attempts being made to negotiate some kind of settlement that would lead to the missionaries' withdrawing their cause from the Supreme Court. Lewis Cass, the secretary of war, who had been in regular "confidential" contact with Lumpkin about the federal government's military preparations now wrote to alert the governor to the possibility that Georgia might soon be called on for support, and made a request "known to the President and approved by him," that the missionaries be released. Cass justified the request on the grounds that

> through every part of the country an anxiety is felt, that this matter should be closed, amicably and forever. And from other important considerations, which must be apparent to you, it is peculiarly desirable, that this should be now done. For party purposes efforts are making to add this to the other embarrassments of the administration. These efforts cannot have escaped your observation. It has occurred to me, that nothing more can be gained by the continued imprisonment of the missionaries, and that their release would produce a favorable effect upon public opinion.

Among other things Cass also noted that it was inevitable that the Indians would soon be leaving the state. History and public opinion, he believed, were on Georgia's side; and moreover, "efforts are making by some patriotic, well disposed citizens to induce the American Board of Missions to lend their influence towards the formation of a treaty [for the Indians' removal] with the Cherokees."[48]

Despite the pressure for an immediate pardon of the missionaries, Lumpkin moved relatively slowly. Although definitely hostile to nullification, firm in his support of the Jackson administration, and generally recognizing the need for some kind of compromise on the missionary question, he nonetheless was reluctant to embark on any course that might indicate that his state had abandoned the constitutional principles it had been advocating in its controversy with the Supreme Court. What this meant was that Lumpkin would not take the initiative and pardon Worcester and Butler, but would only move in response to a request from them for "relief" that was made "in a becoming manner." The possibility of a pardon, he pointed out to Cass, had been open to the missionaries ever since their imprisonment, but they had persisted in taking the matter before the Supreme Court. "Georgia cannot," he argued in true states' rights fashion, "without disgrace, be coerced by the threatening attitude of the Supreme Court, or any other power under heaven, to liberate those men. But the first moment that Georgia can be relieved from threats and menace, and her authority looked to and respected as it ought to be, by these individuals, they will be set at liberty." Lumpkin further argued, it would be wrong for the President to seek a compromise "destructive to vital constitutional principles," for it would only lend strength to the credibility of those who claim that Jackson was motivated mainly by a desire "to wreak his vengeance against the politicians of South Carolina," and who, in response to his recent

Proclamation, charge "that he is disposed to prostrate the rights of the states. . . ."[49]

Lumpkin's determination to see the principles of states' rights, as espoused by Georgia, sustained in any compromise with the missionaries posed a difficult problem. The missionaries and their supporters, while willing to abandon their cause before the Supreme Court, were not willing to admit that they had been wrong or explicitly recognize the legitimacy of Georgia's actions or compromise in any way the theoretical authority of the Supreme Court in this kind of action. Indeed, the American Board of Foreign Missions, when it requested that the missionaries no longer pursue their case before the Supreme Court also strongly advised that "it will be well for you, in our judgment, to state explicitly, that you have come to this determination, not because any doubts have arisen in your minds as to the propriety of your course hitherto on the justice and equity of the decision of the Supreme Court of the U.S. in your favor, or its binding authority on the Court that condemned you, or the legality of prosecuting your case further, but solely from motives of expediency, resulting from regard to the public good. . . ."[50]

Consequently, when Worcester and Butler informed Governor Lumpkin on January 8, 1833, that they had instructed their counsel not to obtain further process from the Supreme Court or to prosecute their case against Georgia in any other way, they pointed out to the governor, "we have not been led to the adoption of that measure by any change of views in regard to the principles on which we have acted or by any doubt of the justice of our cause, or of our perfect right to a legal discharge in accordance with the decision of the Supreme Court in our favor already given, but the apprehension that the further prosecution of the controversy, under existing circumstances, might be attended with consequences injurious to our beloved country."[51] Lumpkin, however, rejected the request on the grounds that it "was an insult on the authority of the state." After some consultation it was decided that the missionaries would write a second letter the next day. This time after indicating that they were sorry that some of the expressions of the previous day "were regarded by your Excellency as an indignity offered to the state or its authorities," they merely informed the governor "in the course we have now taken it has been our intention simply to forbear the prosecution of our cause; and to leave the question of the continuance of our confinement to the magnanimity of the state."[52]

This satisfied Lumpkin, and five days later, on January 14, 1833, he ordered that Worcester and Butler be discharged from the state's penitentiary. In his order, which was widely reprinted, the governor noted "the triumphant ground which the State finally occupies in relation to this subject, in the eyes of the nation," and stressed that this was attested in various ways but "especially in the overwhelming re-election of President Jackson, the known defender of the State throughout this controversy." He justified his release of the missionaries on the grounds that since "the rights of the state have been fully vindicated and sustained in this matter," it was "the generous and liberal" thing to do, especially since they had appealed "to the magnanimity of the state," a point which he made several times in his letter.[53]

Predictably, the release of Worcester and Butler was vigorously criticized by the nullifiers and their supporters. The American Board of Foreign Missions was excoriated: "Those who have kept the concerns and governed the movements of the missionaries, it will be seen, have thought proper to move them off the political chess board. There is, doubtless, just about as much honesty and patriotism and philanthropy, Christianity, benevolence and kind feeling in this, as there was in putting them on. . . ." There could be no doubt, it was asserted, that the purpose of the pardon was "to release Gen. Jackson from the dilemma in which he was involved by his Proclamation." As for Lumpkin, he was "a two faced double dealer" who in his desire to curry favor with the President was quite prepared to stand by and allow South Carolina to be oppressed."[54]

But perhaps the most serious of all the consequences of the pardoning of Worcester and Butler, it was argued, were constitutional. For while Georgia had triumphed over the missionaries it had abandoned the true cause of states' rights by allowing the Supreme Court to emerge from its controversy with Georgia unscathed:

> The contest was not between Georgia and the missionaries, but between Georgia and the Supreme Court. And the matter in controversy was nothing less than this, whether the most potent instrument of federal usurpation, was from henceforth to claim and exercise the right of preventing a state from passing laws to govern her own people. And whether it could in the plenitude of its authority, summon a sovereign state, to its bar, and punish as for contempt, the refusal to notice such insane proceedings. That controversy is one which concerns everyman in this Union. One upon the proper settlement of which, we conceive the rights of the states to depend, this momentous question is still undecided. This was the term of the Court when this usurping tribunal was to have put forth its powers to declare Georgia in contempt, to their Marshal to execute their decree, and if resisted, to call upon the President to compel its submission, by the power of the federal arm. The court is relieved from its embarrassment, it is saved from defeat; this decision will be recorded as a precedent for future adjudications; Georgia has accepted in the nature of a boon the discontinuance of a suit, which she never acknowledged, and the rights of the states, in this important particular, are as undefined, and unsettled and insecure, as ever. This should not have been; we contended not with two obscure individuals; Georgia's contest was with the highest judicial department of the federal government, involving principles the most important perhaps that have occurred in that Court, and of the most momentous character to the rights and liberties of our people. The Missionaries should at least have remained until the Supreme Court had abandoned their illegal and unconstitutional usurpation; the rights of the states should at least have been permitted to triumph; state sovereignty should at least have been admitted by that tribunal which has already been so ready to annihilate it; then might each Georgian have taken a prouder step, as he trod the loved soil of his state, and remembered that by her moderate,

rational and constitutional course, she had thrown another barrier before constitutional infractions.[55]

IV

The pro-Jackson Union party, which consisted of an amalgam of most of the former supporters of the old Clark party plus several Troupite leaders, emerged from the crisis a united and well-organized political force that generally dominated Georgia politics throughout the rest of the decade. Lumpkin at first had his doubts about Wayne and Forsyth, but after the strong support they gave Jackson during the nullification crisis—both, despite tremendous pressure and criticism, were among a handful of southerners who voted for the Force Act—the Governor quickly recognized the value of "forgetting past petty conflicts and party strifes, and uniting with the patriots of the land in the great cause of our common Country." All three prospered politically in the 1830s as a consequence of their common allegiance to Jackson and Van Buren. Wayne was appointed to the United States Supreme Court in 1835. Forsyth, whom Van Buren described to the President "as one of the truest and best of men," became secretary of state in June 1834, replacing McLane, and held the post through the end of Van Buren's administration in 1840. Lumpkin handily won reelection as governor in the fall of 1833, was appointed a United States Commissioner to the Cherokee in 1836, and was elected to the United States Senate in 1837.[56]

The nullification crisis also fundamentally affected the makeup and policies of the old Troup party in Georgia. Troup, himself, vacillated throughout the crisis. Sharing South Carolina's impatience over the slowness of tariff reform and privately sympathetic to the nullifiers' opposition to President Jackson, he nonetheless believed that South Carolina had acted precipitously by not consulting with the other anti-tariff states before it nullified the tariffs of 1828 and 1832, and he refused to endorse nullification openly. Also, while he was critical of both the Proclamation and the Force Act message, he was not prepared to come out in open opposition to the President. Consequently, he became, according to one observer, "neither a Jackson man . . . or nullifier," but rather "like a boat in the ocean without a compass . . . it is impossible to discover at this moment what is his political creed." Finding unacceptable the alternatives offered on the one hand by Forsyth and Wayne, and by Berrien and Clayton on the other, and in declining health, he withdrew from politics, retiring from the United States Senate in 1833, and devoted the remaining twenty-three years of his life to the management of his several plantations.[57]

Crawford also found himself unable to come up with an alternative to the choices offered by the Unionists and the radical Troupites supportive of South Carolina. And, like Troup, he found himself in an increasingly awkward position politically. Anti-tariff and openly critical of Jackson's Proclamation and Force Act message, he also denounced South Carolina's actions as precipitous and publicly opposed Berrien and Clayton's attempt to align Georgia with the nullifiers. His long-standing opposition to Calhoun, whom he held responsible for the consolidationist direction of the federal government during the Monroe administration, remained strong. He totally rejected nullification as a peaceful and legitimate constitutional remedy. "Although So. Carolina," he noted, "has declared war against the tariff which we also hate, I feel no sympathy for her. Right things may be done in wrong ways and I am not disposed to support wrong even that good may come out of it." As an alternative to nullification, he fruitlessly advocated the calling of a national convention, where he hoped the Constitution would be revised in such a way as to outlaw protection.[58]

Unlike Troup, Crawford did not retire from politics after the nullification crisis, but his influence in Georgia politics was very much on the wane. At a convention called to revise the state's constitution in May of 1833, he was soundly defeated for the presidency of the meeting by Wayne, who was the Unionist candidate. During the summer at the annual Troupite caucus at the University of Georgia commencement exercises, he managed to secure the nomination of his son for the upcoming gubernatorial contest, but this was accomplished only after the younger Crawford conceded to a demand from the radical wing of the party that he not denounce nullification during the campaign. In the ensuing election he was badly defeated by Lumpkin. At this time Crawford served as a judge of the state circuit court, but fearing that the "fluctuating" political situation in the state would prevent his reelection to the post he solicited an appointment to the United States Supreme Court. There is no evidence as to how Jackson reacted to this request, for a few weeks later Crawford died of a heart attack.[59]

During this same period the radical Troupites came to increasingly dominate the party which they were determined to turn into the basis of an anti-Jackson movement in Georgia. Throughout the spring, summer, and fall of 1833 they continued to denounce the "unsound" nationalist doctrines of the President's Proclamation, criticized Forsyth and Wayne, whom they referred to as "collar men" under the control of Jackson, for voting for the Force Act, and praised Henry Clay for bringing about the passage of the compromise Tariff of 1833. Following its defeat in the state gubernatorial election in the fall of 1833, the Troup party reorganized itself, and with the radicals in control changed its name to the "States Rights Party of Georgia," and passed a series of resolutions which showed it to be in clear opposition to Andrew Jackson and the Democratic party.[60]

For their part, the Unionists continued to remain hostile to nullification and to support Andrew Jackson and traditional states' rights values. In his annual address to the legislature in November 1833, Lumpkin observed "that the value of our Federal Union should have become a familiar subject of calculation is truly alarming. . . ." And a short time later in his second inaugural address he defined his constitutional beliefs in the following way that completely endorsed the concept of dual sovereignty: "I shall constantly bear in mind that we are all citizens of Georgia, as well as citizens of the United States. That we owe our allegiance to both governments. That both governments are ours, and are equally indispensable to our happiness and prosperity and liberty. That each should be kept strictly within their respective constitutional spheres, and, finally, that he who would destroy the sovereignty of the states by *consolidation,* or the Federal Union by *nullification,* is a traitor to liberty, and deserves the universal execration of mankind."[61]

Nationalists did not play much of a role in Georgia politics during the nullification crisis. The basic struggle was between traditional states' rights advocates and nullifiers. Nonetheless an important effect of the crisis was to relate state politics more closely to the alignments on the national level.

6

Virginia and the Nullification Crisis

At the time of the nullification crisis, Virginia was generally considered to be the most important of the southern and anti-tariff states, and a likely leader in any kind of sectional crisis. Moreover, should Jackson actually resort to force the state would have great strategic importance since federal troops would have to march through it to get to South Carolina. Further, political leaders in the Old Dominion, in the early nineteenth century, took constitutional issues, and especially the problem of defining the rights of the states, very seriously. In fact many of them believed their state had a special mission to define the nature of American federalism correctly. Therefore, many willingly embraced the opportunity to debate extensively the legitimacy of nullification and the related question of secession as a constitutional right. Developments in Virginia were carefully followed by the entire nation. A writer in South Carolina observed, "What will Virginia do? is in every one's mouth." The *Washington Globe* described it as a key state whose proceedings would have "an *extraordinary degree of importance*." The *United States Telegraph* noted "that upon her depends whether the country is involved in civil war, or the controversy be amicably settled." Although the course Virginia finally chose to pursue was in many ways confusing and inconclusive, it did fully reflect the many problems, both theoretical and practical that South Carolina's Ordinance and Jackson's Proclamation caused for the proponents of the rights of the states in the winter of 1832–33.[1]

I

Party lines within Virginia were not clearly drawn during Jackson's first administration. Instead, the state was dominated by a number of strong personalities—lawyers, planters, and editors—mainly from the tidewater and piedmont areas who maintained their power through an oligarchical governmental structure. Thomas Ritchie, editor of the nationally prominent Richmond *Enquirer* was, in many ways, the most influential political figure in the state. By the early 1830s he was the senior member of the so-called Richmond Junto, a coalition of important politicans which dominated political life in the Old Dominion in the immediate post-War of 1812 years and the early 1820s, but whose cohesiveness and power had declined considerably by the time Jackson was elected President. Despite this, Ritchie remained a major political and intellectual force and always had to be reckoned with. Personally eschewing electoral office, he used his newspaper to define the political issues and to shape political opinion. He also served as secretary of the state's Democratic Central Committee, which determined who would be nominated for important posts. Ritchie had denounced Jackson's invasion of Florida in 1818 and had been very critical of the Old Hero in the election of 1824. A Crawford supporter and consistent advocate of states' rights, he reacted to John Quincy Adams's militant espousal of the American System by supporting Jackson in the election of 1828. But he remained extremely wary of the new President, especially his military background, and hoped that he would reign rather than rule. Although Ritchie praised the President's stand on internal improvements, the Bank, and nullification, he took issue with Jackson's policy of rotation of office and was extremely unhappy about his unwillingness to move for immediate tariff reduction. Nonetheless, like most members of the Crawford wing of the Jeffersonian Republicans, he opposed Calhoun's political ambitions and was a strong ally of Van Buren,[2]

Other important Virginians sympathetic to Van Buren and hostile to nullification and Calhoun included: Peter V. Daniel, lawyer, former member of the legislature, and in 1832–33 lieutenant-governor of the state, and a member of its Democratic Central Committee. An uncompromising states' rights advocate in the traditional sense and an avid supporter of Jackson's banking policy, he declined the President's invitation to become attorney general in 1833, although he eventually did accept an appointment to the United States Supreme Court from Van Buren in 1840. Andrew Stevenson, Speaker of the United States House of Representatives, more a politician than an ideologue, supported all the administration's measures, was deeply committed to the permanency of the Union, and opposed to the idea that secession was a constitutional right. William C. Rives, lawyer, former member of the Virginia House of Delegates and United States House of Representatives, was a protégé of Jefferson and Madison, and made Minister to France by Jackson in 1829, a post he held until the fall of 1832 when he returned to America eager for political advancement, and just in time to play an important role in the nullification crisis. Thomas Jefferson Randolph, favorite grandson of the Sage of

Monticello and executor of his estate, looked out for the national administration's interests in the Virginia House of Delegates. Joseph Carrington Cabell, one of the founders of the University of Virginia, also sat in the state legislature. And, finally, acerbic John Randolph of Roanoke, long-term opponent of nationalism in almost every form, and one of the great proponents of the principles of '98. Jackson had appointed him Minister to Russia, but he resigned his post and returned to the United States where, on the eve of the nullification crisis, he was both dying and making preparations to return to Congress.[3]

Virginia also contained a large number of important Democrats who were hostile to Jackson and Van Buren and generally supportive of Calhoun. The most significant and militant of these was the state's governor, John Floyd. Something of an anomaly in that he came from Montgomery County in the western part of Virginia and believed that the Old Dominion would probably be better off if the institution of slavery did not exist, he also was related by marriage to the powerful and well-connected Preston family of South Carolina, and early on became one of the leading supporters of that state's cause. He had backed Andrew Jackson in 1828, but quickly became critical of the President, whom he described at one point as a "vicious old man" controlled "by passions of the worst kind." He criticized in particular Jackson's failure to appoint a prominent Virginian to his cabinet in 1829 and the President's inaction on the tariff. Floyd was in constant contact with Calhoun, who often stopped in Richmond to discuss politics with the governor during his frequent trips between Washington and his home. By the time of the nullification crisis, Floyd, who had become an inveterate foe of the President, was considered so staunch an ally of South Carolina that he received that state's eleven electoral votes for the presidency in 1832.[4]

Sharing many of these views was Littleton Waller Tazewell, a prominent lawyer from the Norfolk area and one of the most respected members of the bar in Virginia. Tazewell had served in the General Assembly and as a United States senator from 1824 to 1832. Alienated by Adams's nationalism, he unenthusiastically supported Jackson in 1828. He was Calhoun's choice for secretary of state in 1829, but all Jackson offered him was the position of Minister to England, which he declined. Although never an advocate of nullification, he became increasingly critical of many of the President's policies, particularly his handling of patronage matters, the Eaton Affair, and the breakup of the cabinet, all of which confirmed his belief that Jackson was unfit to run the country. Disgusted with these developments, he resigned his Senate seat just before the nullification crisis occurred. Although he no longer held an official position he continued to be a highly respected and influential figure, especially in the eastern part of Virginia.[5]

John Tyler, the other United States senator from the Old Dominion and a future President of the United States, felt much the same way. Long active in state politics, and highly respected as a man of principle and integrity, he served several terms in the House of Delegates, and was elected governor in 1825 and again in 1826. As a member of the United States House of Representatives between 1815 and 1821, the heyday of American nationalism, he established himself as a strict constructionist, favoring a revocation of the charter of the Second Bank of the United States and opposing the Missouri Compromise, the latter because he did not believe the federal government should have the power to control the expansion of slavery into the territories. He did not have a very high regard for Jackson, having voted to censure him for his invasion of Florida, and viewed him as a dangerous military hero who by temperament and training was unfit to govern the country. His election to the United States Senate in 1827 over John Randolph was generally considered to be a victory for the anti-Jackson forces. He supported Jackson in 1828 only because he viewed him as a lesser evil than Adams. He quickly became a critic of the new administration's policies, particularly its handling of the tariff and patronage questions, and what he viewed as the President's imperious and self-willed attitude. Tyler had strong ties to the wealthy slaveholders in the tidewater area of Virginia.[6]

The list of other prominent Virginia Democrats who were becoming increasingly critical of Jackson and hostile to Van Buren's presidential ambitions included: Benjamin Watkins Leigh, a distinguished Richmond lawyer who usually represented eastern planter interests and who was very open about his hostility to the President and his sympathy for South Carolina; Richard K. Crallé, editor of the Lynchburg *Jeffersonian and Virginia Times,* who had personal ties with Duff Green and John C. Calhoun, and who moved his newspaper to Richmond to further the latter's theories on state sovereignty; Thomas Walker Gilmer, a lawyer and editor from Charlottesville, Virginia, and a member of the House of Delegates, who was one of Governor Floyd's leading allies in the state legislature; Abel Parker Upshur, a Richmond lawyer with family connections on the eastern shore, who served in the House of Delegates for several years, was a judge of the Virginia Supreme Court, and a pro-slavery advocate highly partial to Calhoun's interests; and William F. Gordon, planter and lawyer from the piedmont area, and a former governor of Virginia who, in 1832–33, was a member of the United States House of Representatives.[7]

The National Republican party, on the other hand, was weak and ineffective in Virginia before 1832. Its chief leaders were Francis Brooke, president of the Court of Appeals, and John H. Pleasants, energetic and articulate editor of the Richmond *Whig,* both of whom were committed to furthering Henry Clay's interests. The party's main areas of support were to be found in the state's urban areas, especially Alexandria and Norfolk in the eastern part of the state, and in various small commercial centers sprinkled throughout the region west of the Blue Ridge Mountains. But it never added up to much. Aside from its small urban areas, consisting of only a small minority of the people, the great majority of Virginians in the tidewater and piedmont areas were strongly opposed to any policies that strengthened the powers of the national government, while in the west Jackson's popularity, if not always his policies, overwhelmed the Clay forces.[8]

Within the Old Dominion, the basic political division was a sectional one. It pitted the slaveholding tidewater and piedmont areas against the Shenandoah Valley and trans-Allegheny sections which had a rapidly increasing white population generally made up of small farmers with very few slaves. The main issue was the political dominance of the eastern part of the state, maintained through hefty property qualifications for voting which disfranchised a sizable minority of the people, and the denial of adequate representation in the legislature to western sections of the state. Western resentment over these matters in the 1820s culminated in the calling of a constitutional convention in 1831, where the east made some minor concessions.[9]

Despite the sectional antagonism within the state, and the growing unhappiness of many prominent eastern Democrats with developments during his first administration, Jackson easily carried Virginia in 1832. In large part this was because the President's critics were badly divided as to the proper course of action to pursue. Floyd favored open opposition, but Tyler and Tazewell were more cautious. The most serious attempt to oppose Jackson in Virginia was the indirect one of trying to block Van Buren's vice-presidential nomination at Baltimore. This found expression in the unsuccessful effort to nominate a local son, P. P. Barbour, to the post, and failing to do this, a special convention was held at Charlottesville, Virginia, which adopted a Jackson-Barbour ticket. The movement collapsed, however, when Barbour withdrew from the election.[10]

A clear manifestation of Jacksonian strength in the Old Dominion came in early December 1832—after South Carolina had voted to nullify the tariffs of 1828 and 1832, but before the President issued his Proclamation—when the state legislature selected a senator to replace Tazewell. William Cabell Rives, who described himself as "anti-tariff, anti-Bank, anti-Nullification, & a thorough & decided friend of Jackson's administration," was the leading candidate. But there was considerable opposition to him because he only opposed the tariff on policy grounds as "unjust, impolitic, unequal & oppressive," and would not also declare it unconstitutional. Viewed by many as too loyal to the President and hostile to South Carolina, some effort was made to try to block his election with Upshur, John Randolph and P. P. Barbour mentioned as possible alternatives, but when it became clear that none of them had much of a chance they all withdrew. Rives won by an overwhelming 153 to 6 vote. Although the size of the vote does not do justice to the amount of opposition there actually was to Rives or to anyone who claimed he was totally committed to the President, it does clearly reveal the extent of Jacksonian hegemony in Virginia in early December 1832. Moreover, the election had implications beyond simply the substitution of a pro-Jackson man for one who had been critical of the administration, it also was an ominous signal for John Tyler who was coming up for re-election later at the same session of the legislature.[11]

Throughout the summer and fall of 1832, the pro-Jackson forces in Virginia also dominated the debate over nullification. Although they made clear the state's opposition to protection, they denounced South Carolina for not exhausting all constitutional remedies, and for acting alone and precipitously. Nullification was rejected as both a legitimate expression of states' rights and a constitutional remedy. "In fact, it is . . . a revolutionary measure. It is an absurd and dangerous heresy." Virginia, it was asserted, could never support such a doctrine, which "not only . . . strikes at the Union of the States; but threatens to involve the country in all the horrors of revolution and civil war." Much, too, was made of Madison's various assaults on nullification and his attempts to distinguish it from the Virginia and Kentucky Resolutions of 1798 and the Virginia Report of 1799–1800. The opponents of nullification in the Old Dominion elaborated, in particular, on the former President's attack on South Carolina's claim that a single state had the power to declare a law of the federal government unconstitutional, after which that law could only be made constitutional by means of an Amendment. It was argued that this power would make the Union ungovernable, for it would be too easy to make any law passed by the central government inoperative in this manner. Such a power, it was pointed out, "strikes at the very foundation of Republican Government," for it reverses the general rule that the majority should govern and assumes "that the minority will be right and a large majority wrong."[12]

Whatever support existed for nullification in Virginia was at this time mute and indirect. The main attempt to enlist sympathy for South Carolina came in Governor Floyd's speech to the newly assembled legislature on December 4. He stressed various "incendiary" activities in Boston, New York, and Pennsylvania "for the purpose no doubt of inciting our slave population to rebellion and acts of violence." He also observed "the late tariff with its oppressive exactions, has been replaced by another hardly less injurious, which only mocks our sufferings by assuming the shape of modification." Under the general topic of federal relations he framed the issues in terms clearly favorable to South Carolina:

> Heretofore Virginia has watched her liberty with sleepless care, and her reserved rights, the sleeping thunder of the States, with an anxiety which bespoke the inestimable value she placed upon them. Ought we to be less on our guard than at any *former* period? Perpetual vigilance is the price we pay for liberty. Do we not find the defenders of those violations of the Constitution increasing in number and in the boldness of their measures? Constitutions are intended to protect the rights of the minority, by restraining the majority from doing that, which to the minority would be ruinous; but if the majority be permitted to become the interpreters of their own powers, there cease to be any limit to the Government.[13]

Floyd's oblique attempt to lend support to the proceedings in South Carolina did not have any noticeable effect. The President's popularity in Virginia, in early December, was unchallengeable. Jackson's annual message, with its stress upon states' rights and its call for a substantial downward revision of the tariff, effectively defused whatever latent criticism of his administration may have been ready to surface. Ritchie noted "the message has given the highest satisfaction." The ever worried editor was especially pleased that the President had not chosen to confront the questions raised by nullification in an overly aggressive fashion. "His tone about S.C. is precisely what it should be," he commented prematurely.[14]

II

Jackson's Proclamation changed all this. The President's views on the origins and nature of the Union and his desire to use force against the nullifiers were the source of considerable controversy and opposition in Virginia. According to one contemporary observer, the Richmond correspondent of the *National Intelligencer,* "perhaps the same space of time has never exhibited so marked a revolution of public sentiment as that which we have witnessed among the Virginia state-rights politicans since the receipt of the Proclamation. . . ."[15]

The Proclamation's critics charged that it was dangerously nationalist in its interpretation of the formation and character of the federal government. It was, they argued, not simply an attack upon nullification, but on the Constitution itself, particularly upon the rights of the states that would "merge this confederate republic into a great and engulphing consolidation," and represented a sweeping "into annihilation those great adverse principles consecrated in 1801." Even the President's friends admitted that the Proclamation was "dangerously national and unorthodox," and that it contained "doctrinal errors" as "obnoxious as nullification itself." So strong was the reaction to what was viewed as the consolidating tendencies of the Proclamation that the administration's supporters quickly found themselves on the defensive. Describing the situation, Thomas Mann Randolph wrote, "The condition of Va is very critical. The reprobation of S. Carolina would have been decided, but the Proclamation has thrown the nullifiers . . . from utter prostration into a majority. . . ."[16]

Those finding fault with the Proclamation took particular issue with the President's assertion that secession was unlawful rebellion and treason and therefore subject to forcible suppression. South Carolina's actions, it was argued, could not be compared to Shays's Rebellion or the Whiskey Insurrection. There was, they pointed out, a fundamental "difference between a mob and a sovereign state or a sudden explosion of popular discontent, and the deliberate action of a political community through its most solemn tribunal." The states, Jackson's critics asserted, were sovereign, and inherent in this sovereignty was the right of secession:

> This is a natural, inherent and inalienable right, and is the primary principle asserted in the Declaration of Independence. . . . No government or power has a right to enquire the reasons of her conduct when a state secedes, much less whip her back. It is different with counties, individuals and a number of individuals, because they have tribunals to go to for redress; because they are but component parts of one whole, because, in short, they are not *sovereign*. Hence the fallacy of all the comparisons instituted, between counties, co-partnerships, individuals and a sovereign state. . . . A state may *secede* as well for oppressive as unconstitutional legislation.[17]

Most discussions of the Proclamation inevitably led to personal criticism of the President. Jackson was portrayed as a particularly dangerous "man of military habits, of summary character" and a despot who was ever to be distrusted. His sudden conversion to nationalism and willingness to accept the support of northern consolidationists was to be explained primarily by the fact that "everything with him assumes a cast of personality. . . . Personal hate or personal partiality are his only incentives to public measures: all virtue consists in attachment to his person. . . . He pursues enemies with a cruel vengeance, which knows no bounds, and is restrained by no generosity." The Proclamation, another writer claimed, was completely in character for the President: "He is willing to array the military power against what he calls his 'native state' that he may pursue with a 'cruel vengeance' one against whom he entertains the most envenomed hatred."[18]

Seeing that the tide had begun to turn, Governor Floyd quickly submitted South Carolina's Ordinance of Nullification to the Virginia legislature for consideration. In a brief supporting message he made clear his sympathies for South Carolina, though he did not explicitly endorse the doctrine of nullification. South Carolina, the governor stressed, was "acting in her sovereign capacity," and had done so only after it had unsuccessfully and "repeatedly protested and pressed her memorials upon the consideration of Congress, earnestly entreating them to abandon laws so unequal and unjust in their operation. . . ."Floyd also made clear his opposition to the use of force by the federal government, arguing it would have frightful consequences for it was against "the genius and spirit of our institutions," and would lead to Civil War. Calling upon the Virginia legislature to "once more sustain the liberties of the country," Floyd concluded by indicating his belief that the nullifiers were fighting the good fight and the Old Dominion should oppose the President. Privately, Floyd confided to his diary his belief that Jackson's Proclamation "is the most extraordinary document which has ever appeared in the United States. . . . I think I shall be able to check him." Several days later he added, "if he uses force, I will oppose him with a military force. I nor my country, will not be enslaved without a struggle."[19]

Strong support for Floyd's attempt to generate opposition to Jackson came from his allies in the eastern part of the state. The influential and widely respected Tazewell published a series of articles in a Norfolk newspaper that were widely reprinted and issued as a pamphlet that were highly critical of the President's constitutional nationalism. Although Tazewell did not specifically endorse South Carolina's actions, he did express sympathy with nullification as a theoretical remedy and defend the concept that the individual states of the Union were sovereign. Under no circumstances, he argued, could Jackson's assertions be allowed to go unchallenged for "when the occasion that has induced the Proclamation shall have passed away (as pass away it must), the question raised by the President will still remain."[20] In even stronger terms Abel Parker Upshur published a series of essays arguing that nullification was a logical extension of the Virginia and Kentucky Resolutions and a legitimate way to solve conflicts between the federal and state governments. Admitting that South Carolina had acted rashly and perhaps unwisely, he nonetheless denounced "the gross inequality" of the burdens imposed by the tariff and called upon Virginians to openly oppose the use of force against South Carolina, lest an extremely dangerous precedent be established.[21]

The general reaction to the Proclamation placed Jackson's Virginia supporters on the defensive. Many of them shared the widespread uneasiness that existed over the President's newfound constitutional nationalism. Some tried to explain it away. One writer, for example, noted "I felt and still feel assured that these doctrines were advanced not for the purpose of enlarging the powers of the Federal government, or of covering any abuse of power contemplated by those who now administer it, but that they were laid down in the way of *abstract* propositions to sustain a favorite argument." Other writers, admitting they had reservations about the Proclamation, defended the President's overall record on states' rights, warned about over reacting to what was, in effect, only a difference of opinion on the history of the formation of the Constitution and not on its meaning, and they gave assurances that in his coming inaugural address Jackson would declare strongly for states' rights and clear up the various misconceptions that existed over his political creed.[22]

The Proclamation not only put the President's supporters on the defensive, it also divided them. While some tried to defend and excuse Jackson's constitutional excesses and ferocity toward South Carolina, others were critical. The latter group included Thomas Ritchie who, although he continued to denounce Calhoun and nullification, openly declared when he saw the Proclamation that "there are some *doctrinal points* to which . . . we cannot subscribe." He called on Jackson to recant his views and recognize that states have the right to secede in extreme cases and to acknowledge explicitly the nature of the federal compact to be such that the states have a right to pass upon the manner in which the federal government exercises certain specified powers and to interpose as Virginia had done in 1799. When Jackson refused to do this, Ritchie continued to attack the principles of the Proclamation in the *Enquirer*. He came out against the passage of the Force Bill and in favor of an immediate lowering of the tariff so as to compromise the crisis and avoid the "extremes of federal encroachment on the one hand, and to stem the headlong current of nullification on the other." Ritchie and the *Enquirer* had a national reputation, and the President's opponents and the nullifiers made much of his unwillingness to endorse either the Proclamation or the administration's hard-line attitude toward South Carolina.[23]

The Proclamation also caused the disaffection of John Randolph of Roanoke. A feisty, independent, and extremely difficult and eccentric individual, who, aside from his own local constituency, did not have any real power base or any special influence with the Jackson administration, Randolph nonetheless was a national figure as a consequence of his long standing and consistent advocacy of states' rights and opposition to Jeffersonian nationalism and the American System. He supported Jackson in 1828 and was an outspoken critic of Calhoun and nullification. But he did not want to see the federal government use force against South Carolina, and in early December 1832 he urged Jackson to act cautiously.

Literally dying at the time, Randolph was so outraged by the Proclamation that he got off his death bed to campaign against it. He took sharp issue with the President's claim that the states had parted with their sovereignty when they entered the Union, argued that the people's allegiance should first be to their respective states and defended the right of a state to secede "whenever she shall find the benefits of Union exceeded its evils, Union being the Means of securing liberty and happiness and not an END, to which these should be sacrificed." At no point did he defend nullification in the abstract or South Carolina's actions in particular, but he did make clear his belief that simply because Jackson advocated something did not necessarily make it right. Under Randolph's leadership a resolution was adopted at a popular meeting got up at the Charlotte County Court House stating: "that while we utterly reprobate the doctrine of nullification as equally weak and mischievious, we cannot for that reason give our countenance to principles equally unfounded and in the highest degree dangerous to the liberties of the people."[24]

The open estrangement of such prominent states' rights spokesmen as Ritchie and Randolph over the Proclamation was a boon to those who argued that the main threat to the Union was Jackson and not South Carolina. These same people generally hoped to see the issues of the crisis polarized in such a way that the middle of the roaders and the confused would end up supporting the course of the nullifiers if not actually endorsing their doctrine. The effect of the President's Proclamation in Virginia, said one observer, "dissatisfied his friends, and encouraged his enemies. It has given new spirit to the friends of nullification—and drawn many a secret and insidious adder from his hole." A different writer noted "the strong denunciation of the Proclamation shows that Virginia has at length thrown off the nightmare of Jacksonianism, which has been holding her in horrid sleep, while her ancient principles were gradually stolen away. The idolatry of men is superseded by the worship of principle. . . ."Along these lines the people of Virginia were appealed to in the following manner: "the hour of trial has arrived—the hour which is to test the sincerity of your . . . devotion to state rights. You can take no neutral position. Inaction on your part is death to your principles. The cause of South Carolina is your cause. If she sinks you must sink with her." A similar argument was directed at the legislature then in session:

> We beg to remind the Legislature, that the true question is not now, whether nullification be right or wrong; but whether having *nullified*, and in the new state of things. . . . Virginia will consent that South Carolina shall be put to the bayonet; whether that does not involve inevitable consolidation; whether it does not become her to announce in a firm voice, that she will consent to no such course; whether if the Legislature does not take this stand forthwith the blood of S. Carolina will not be on their head and the loss of public liberty fairly chargeable to their pusillanimity. Let the veto of Virginia against military force be pronounced firmly and respectfully, and extremes need not be feared.[25]

III

To a large extent the split within the Virginia Democracy over the Proclamation coincided with the sectional division that dominated state politics on most important issues during the late 1820s and 1830s: the strongest criticism of the President's belligerent stand on nullification came from the slave-dense tidewater and piedmont areas while the small-farmer dominated valley and transmontane areas rallied to Jackson's support.[26]

Various popular meetings were held throughout the state during the winter of 1832–33. Prounouncements critical of Jackson's handling of the crisis emanated from James City, King William, King and Queen, Richmond, Powhatan, Prince Edward, Northampton, Cumberland, Hampshire, Prince George, and Halifax counties. The resolutions of the Amelia County meeting are illustrative of the tone and thrust of these gatherings. They denounced the President's Proclamation on the grounds that "if these doctrines are to be carried into effect, it is evident that the rights of the states are at an end, and that our Federal Government is converted into a consolidated despotism, of the worst form, and with the most unlimited powers . . . ." They also condemned the tariffs of 1828 and 1832, expressed sympathy with South Carolina's grievances, warned that if civil war occurred it would be the fault of the national government, and urged Virginia to use force if necessary to resist any attempt of the federal government to coerce South Carolina. Although the Amelia County resolutions did not explicitly comment on secession, the resolutions of a number of the other county meetings did affirm it as a legal and constitutional right.[27]

In the western part of the state, on the other hand, there was considerable support for Andrew Jackson's hard-line position. One writer, in fact, noted, "I verily believe that there are not 100 men North and West of the Blue Ridge in Virginia," sympathetic to nullification. This point of view emerged at various meetings held in Loudon, Augusta, Washington, Frederick, Monongalia, Botetourt, Page, Fauquier, Rockbridge, Scott, Fluvanna, Montgomery, Jefferson, Kanawaha, Amherst, Patrick, Allegheny, Greenbrier, Smyth, and Westmoreland counties, and in towns like Staunton, Lynchburg, and Wheeling. Typical were the resolutions adopted at a meeting at Lynchburg which argued that the state had given up part of its sovereignty upon entering the Union, described nullification as "an unblushing usurpation of unreserved and unconferred power," and equated the South Carolina doctrine with "Disunion, Anarchy and Despotism." Other resolutions passed at the meeting endorsed Jackson's Proclamation, rejected the concept of secession as a legal right, avowed support for the Union party in South Carolina, and criticized Governor Floyd's various pronouncements of sympathy toward the nullifiers.[28]

Although Jackson's tough stance toward South Carolina did have considerable popular support in the western and northern parts of the state, the strongly sectional nature of this support worked to the President's disadvantage. For, despite changes in the State Constitution of 1829–30, the west remained underrepresented in the legislature. The significance of this became apparent on

December 13 when Governor Floyd transmitted South Carolina's Ordinance to the legislature and urged immediate action. Upon the resolution of William Brodnax of Dinwiddie County, commonly viewed as sympathetic to nullification, the Virginia House of Delegates quickly referred the matter to a Committee on Federal Relations, consisting of thirteen members. However, when it was discovered that a majority of the committee was not prepared to take "such strong measures as the crisis demands" to thwart the President, the committee was enlarged to twenty-one with enough new members to make it a "packed jury" prepared to "defy the efforts of the friends of federal power." Noting these developments, that great proponent of nationalism, Chief Justice John Marshall, wrote: "I look with anxious solicitude to the proceedings of our legislature, and with much more of fear than of hope."[29]

Eastern, and therefore anti-Jackson, control of the Virginia legislature made itself felt on another important issue early in the session. Thomas Walker Gilmer, one of the leaders in the recent attempt to substitute P. P. Barbour for Van Buren as Jackson's running mate, moved that the Virginia Resolutions of 1798 and the Report of 1799 should be reprinted to assist the legislature in the upcoming debate. One of the pro-Jackson delegates then moved that in addition James Madison's letter to Edward Everett published in the October 1830 issue of the *North American Review* also be reprinted. In this letter, it will be recalled, Madison criticized nullification, denied the doctrine was in any way justified by the proceedings of the Virginia legislature in 1798 or 1799, declared the judiciary to be the final interpreter of constitutional questions, and warned that the Constitution "cannot be altered or annulled at the will of states individually." Printing it, clearly, would not serve the interests of those determined to align Virginia with South Carolina in the expected confrontation with Jackson. In a mainly sectional vote the motion to republish the Resolutions of 1798 and the Report of 1800 carried, but the proposal to publish Madison's letter was defeated.[30]

On December 29, 1832, the Committee on Federal Relations, under the leadership of Brodnax, submitted its Report to the legislature. Ostensibly the Report was an attempt to steer a middle course between the extremes of consolidation and the dissolution of the Union. Although the Report criticized South Carolina's actions as precipitous and leading "if persisted in, to political confusion and civil war," its basic slant was to take issue with the nationalist policies of the administration and other opponents of nullification. It reaffirmed the compact theory of the origins of the Union as put forth in the Report of 1799. It denounced protective tariffs as unequal and oppressive and indicated that the state would cooperate with South Carolina in using "all proper means" to reduce the tariff to simply a revenue producing measure. The heart of the Report, however, was a protest against the constitutional principles contained in the President's Proclamation. Describing these principles as representing "a dangerous tendency" it asserted the doctrine that the states and not the people had created the Union and ratified the Constitution. The Report also came out for secession as a final recourse, although it indicated that this should occur only after "every constitutional effort has been tried and every peaceful experiment exhausted, to obviate the supposed injury." The Report further claimed that the states have a right, indeed are duty-bound, to interpose when the federal government exceeds its powers in order to arrest "the progress of evil" and to maintain their own powers as guaranteed by the Constitution. In addition, the Report indicated "we can never recognize the conclusion assumed in the Proclamation that the guilt of treason can be incurred by a citizen of a seceded state, who in the discharge of the allegiance due to said state, violates a law of the remaining Union." The Report called upon both South Carolina and the President to avoid the use of force. It concluded by urging that Virginia send two commissioners to South Carolina as mediators.[31]

Although the Report did not specifically endorse the doctrine of nullification it did tilt strongly in South Carolina's direction. During the next several weeks the Report was debated at great length, and the President's followers and others who supported him in the confrontation with South Carolina made several attempts to amend the Report. Specifically, they wanted the nullifiers denounced in stronger terms, the criticism of the Proclamation softened, and the doctrine of secession condemned as having no basis "either in the Constitution of the United States, in the Resolutions of '98 and Report of '99, or in reason." Although these attempts were easily beaten back, it did become clear during the debate that the anti-Jacksonians were not altogether united, for while they disliked the principles of the Proclamation, and shared a common belief in the compact theory of the origins of the Union and the doctrine of states' rights, as well as a distaste and fear of Jackson personally, there were many who were reluctant to endorse explicitly the doctrine of secession or to indicate that they would support the use of force against the federal government or endanger the existence of the Union in any other way. One observer described the tone of hostility to the President in the following manner: "nothing is more certain than that the Proclamation in its leading tenets is repudiated by a large majority of the Legislature. Difference of opinion among the majority, there is, upon what is precisely the best to be done, and the mode of doing it—but the doctrines themselves are sternly and generally reprobated."[32]

During the discussion of the Report it also became clear that the anti-Jacksonians had no clear-cut leader in the legislature. Consequently, as a group they often were disorganized and confused about what was happening. This became especially significant on January 16, 1833, when one wavering easterner, John T. Brown of Petersburg, made nervous by what appeared to be an increasingly fluid situation in the legislature, unexpectedly moved a complete new set of resolutions as a substitute for those proposed in the original Committee on Federal Relations Report. They were meant to be a compromise between those determined to align Virginia with South Carolina, and those who supported the President. They described the Constitution as a compact between the states, rejected the Supreme Court of the United States as the final arbiter of constitutional questions, denounced protective tariffs, declared nullification to be unconstitutional, praised the value of the Union, and said nothing at all about secession. On the Proclamation the new resolutions took issue with the President's view of the origins of the Union, but added "it is at the same time due to this high functionary to declare, that the firmness with which he announced his purpose to enforce the laws, with the means entrusted him by the Constitution, was justified by the course of public events, and has in no respect diminished that confidence in his integrity and patriotism which the many signal proofs he had given, in the course of his administration of a desire to confine the general government in its practical operation, within the strict limits of the Constitution, had previously inspired." The motion naturally attracted the support of many of Jackson's followers and nationalists, who by now despaired of getting anything better, and to almost everyone's surprise managed to pass by a 67 to 66 vote. It was an unexpected setback for those who wanted to see the Old Dominion openly defy the President.[33]

This modest victory for the pro-Jackson forces was short-lived. Their opponents regrouped and managed to achieve enough unity to introduce and pass a resolution strongly critical of the Proclamation. But the price was complete abandonment of any attempt to get the legislature to sanction the doctrine of secession or take any kind of disunionist or belligerent stand against the federal government. The resolutions as finally adopted by the Virginia legislature in late January indicated that the state was motivated "by an ardent desire to preserve the peace and harmony of our common country." They called for South Carolina to rescind its Ordinance of Nullification, for a gradual reduction of tariff duties to a revenue level, and for both the federal government and South Carolina to refrain from any activities that might disturb the peace or endanger the Union. Commenting upon the constitutional-ideological issues raised by the crisis, a special resolution was adopted, indicating:

> That they continue to regard the doctrines of State Sovereignty and State Rights, as set forth in the Resolutions of 1798, and sustained by the Report thereon of 1799, as a true interpretation of the Constitution of the United States, and of the powers therein given to the General Government; but that they do not consider them as sanctioning the proceedings of South Carolina, indicated in her said Ordinance; nor as countenancing all the principles assumed by the President in his said Proclamation—many of which are in direct conflict with them.[34]

Many people, and especially those sympathetic to South Carolina's cause, were disappointed by the essentially middle of the road quality of the resolutions and the legislature's lack of decisiveness. One observer commented, "my mortification is only equaled by my indignation at the contemptible figure which our Legislature is making—debating, hair splitting, mystifying, deprecating, fearing, hoping and fooling—when they should be acting out the principles which they have so long professed." A disappointed member of the legislature, who had wanted the state to adopt a more defiant course toward the President wrote: "the movements of the House of Delegates have no doubt excited universal disgust throughout the country—I am ashamed of my seat."

Another open sympathizer of South Carolina denounced "the cowardice of Virginia!!" and asserted that the resolutions "will not do. Virginia crouches like a whipt hound under the lash of power."[35]

Governor Floyd was particularly unhappy. He described the resolutions of the legislature as "poor ineffectual affairs." In a final attempt to rouse his state to denounce the President's threats in stronger terms, he submitted to the House and Senate a series of resolutions adopted by the General Assembly of South Carolina calling for a "general convention" of all the states to take up the question of the general government's disputed power to levy a protective tariff. In an accompanying message, Floyd urged the state to participate in the calling of such a convention; he also used the message to attack directly the constitutional views expressed in the Proclamation, warned of the danger to liberty of submitting to "the will of an irresponsible majority," and defended the concept of state sovereignty. The message, Floyd privately confided, "contains the true States Right doctrine, and under no other mode can this Union be permanent." Although the message was the subject of some debate, and the legislature voted to attend such a convention if called, no attempt was made to reconsider the adopted resolutions.[36]

Benjamin Watkins Leigh was selected as the Commissioner to South Carolina. Generally recognized as unfriendly to the Jackson administration, his mission was to convince the nullifiers to rescind their Ordinance, and allow Virginia to mediate on its behalf with the federal government. Although Leigh immediately proceeded to Columbia, the mission turned out to be of no real importance, for the nullifiers had already decided to suspend their Ordinance. Moreover, while Leigh was politely received, the nullifiers in South Carolina made it perfectly clear that the Old Dominion would not be asked by them to play any special role in the crisis, nor would Virginia's request for "moderation" receive any special consideration. "Why should our state give ear to this request?" one writer asked. "Has Virginia given us any intimation that, by doing so, we will be supported in the field by that state, in case Congress should not have repealed the oppressive tariff laws. . . . We venture to predict that Mr. Leigh will leave South Carolina as he found her, firm and unmoved in her course." The nullifiers had expected much more in terms of support from the Old Dominion, and clearly were disappointed by the adopted resolutions. According to the Columbia *Telescope*: "The Legislature of Virginia, after nearly a month's debate, has reached a conclusion, at last. Arguing, most skilfully, in a circle, she has most felicitously ended, just where she began."[37]

IV

The failure of the Virginia legislature to endorse nullification or to openly align itself with South Carolina may have been a disappointment to the nullifiers and their Old Dominion allies, but it was scarcely a victory for the President's supporters. Those loyal to Jackson recognized that they had only just barely managed to keep Virginia neutral during the crisis winter of 1832–33.

One important result of the ideological confusion created by the Proclamation and its disruptive effect upon the Democratic party in Virginia was that the word went out to the state's representatives in Washington, and to important Jacksonians throughout the country, that any attempt to defend the principles of the Proclamation or to use force against South Carolina would in all likelihood be resisted by the state. Reacting to advance warning of Jackson's intention of asking for additional authority to enforce the laws in South Carolina in his Force Bill message of January 16, Ritchie warned, "this blow may prostrate us. His immense popularity in Virginia could not withstand the shock—Even his best friends would condemn it." A loyal supporter of the President in the legislature wrote to Senator Rives advising that the administration "budge not an inch in advance of public opinion; it may follow as close in the rear as it pleases, but it must follow, and any effort to direct or lead *will be fatal to it*." And Van Buren was warned in friendly but firm fashion not to follow blindly Jackson's excessively nationalist and belligerent course in the crisis, for in the Old Dominion "no matter who might say otherwise . . . the old fashioned doctrines would be sustained . . . and that any attempt to resist them would be destructive of your strength in Virginia."[38]

In practical political terms developments in Virginia during the nullification crisis reinforced what was generally the response of most Jacksonians, the President aside, to the nullification crisis: a belief that the matter should be defused through a reduction of the tariff and that the use of force or even the threat of the use of force should be avoided.

Jackson's tough stand on nullification also worked against him on the question of John Tyler's reelection to the United States Senate. At the beginning of the legislative session the President's followers had been confident they would be able to defeat Tyler's bid for another term. They demonstrated their political strength in early December by electing Rives to the other Senate seat. They also had become very vocal in their criticism of Tyler's opposition to the President. Out of desperation, Tyler tried to forge an anti-Jackson coalition with Henry Clay's followers. Still, in the late fall of 1832, Tyler's political future did not look very bright. He was saved by the reaction in Virginia to the President's Proclamation. Rives, who defended Jackson throughout the crisis and actually voted for the Force bill, was severely criticized, while Tyler's course of opposing the President and casting the lone dissenting vote in the Senate against the Force bill was much praised. In the subsequent struggle, the Jacksonians threw their support behind James McDowell, a westerner and critic of slavery, who had endorsed the President's Proclamation. The election itself took place on February 16, only a few days after Tyler delivered a "violent nullification speech" in the United States Senate that was very popular with the Virginia legislature. He was reelected, receiving 81 votes to McDowell's 62, with several ballots being cast for various other candidates. The vote, it was noted, "exemplifies the extraordinary revolution wrought by the Proclamation in the position and temper of parties," and was viewed as a "decisive approval of *his* [Tyler's] *course,* and a disapproval of that of" Rives during the crisis.[39]

The antagonisms within the Democratic party uncovered by the nullification crisis continued to dominate Virginia politics even after a compromise was
arrived at on the national level. Those sympathetic to South Carolina and
critical of Jackson began to refer to themselves as the State-Rights party while
the President's supporters became known as the Union party. Both groups
vigorously contested the state and congressional elections that year. In terms of
the sources of support of the two groups the alignment again had a strong
tendency to be a sectional one. The State-Rights party controlled politics in the
slaveholding eastern and southern parts of the state, and were pretty much able
to elect all their candidates except in the Richmond District where Jackson
stalwart Andrew Stevenson was reelected despite a vigorous attempt to unseat
him. In similar terms, the Unionists dominated the Valley, the trans-montane
area and the northeastern sections of the state.[40]

An important result of the nullification crisis was that the Old Dominion's
response to national issues had come to be dominated by the same sectional
alignments that had existed on local issues in the late 1820s and 1830s. A two-
party system was beginning to dominate Virginia politics. The odd group out
in all this were the adherents of Henry Clay and the American System, small in
number but vocal, to be found mainly in the highly commercial areas in the
western part of the state. With the important exception of James H. Pleasants,
editor of the Richmond *Whig,* most National Republicans supported the President during the crisis, but the alliance was only temporary. It broke down
when Jackson decided to remove the deposits from the Second Bank of the
United States in the fall of 1833. Members of the State-Rights party, who
viewed the Bank as a necessary evil, were also critical of the President's course
on this issue, and a new alliance was forged of anti-Jackson elements that
played a very important role in Virginia politics during the 1830s and 1840s.[41]

There had always existed in Virginia many important people critical of
Andrew Jackson, but the great bulk of them were also Democrats. During the
President's first administration they tended to complain among themselves
about his failure to appoint a prominent Virginian to his cabinet, the low
quality of his advisers, the unseemliness of his patronage policy, and his general unfitness to govern as revealed in the embarrassing Eaton Affair and the
open rift with Vice President Calhoun. Not until the nullification crisis did
these people go into open opposition. Their opposition did not stop when the
crisis was compromised in February 1833. If anything, they were more convinced than ever that Jackson's enormous popularity as well as his willingness
to use all the authority of the President's office, even to the point of exceeding
his authority, made him dangerous, and that he had to be opposed and restrained at all costs. As a result there emerged in Virginia a group of energetic,
articulate, and influential politicians led by Floyd, Tyler, Tazewell, Leigh,
Upshur, Gilmer and Beverley Tucker who went into permanent opposition to
Jackson and his successor Van Buren. To be sure there still remained many
important political leaders who were loyal to the President and the Democratic
party. Headed by Rives, Stevenson, and Ritchie, they continued to play impor-

tant roles in Virginia politics, but it is clear that the group suffered from various internal tensions and a definite wariness and lack of enthusiasm for Jacksonian principles that was to create numerous problems throughout the balance of the 1830s. The effect of the nullification crisis in Virginia had been to confuse, divide, and weaken the President's supporters.

7

New York and the Nullification Crisis

New York played a crucial role in the nullification crisis. It had been a Jacksonian stronghold since 1828, and the President expected, in fact, counted on it to strongly support his militant attitude toward South Carolina. In particular he wanted the New York legislature to endorse formally the Proclamation, and the President anticipated no problems since Van Buren was currently in Albany. But as was the case in a number of other states, Jackson completely underestimated the doctrinal problems the Proclamation created for traditional states' rights advocates. In addition, internal divisions within New York's Democratic party and pressure from Van Buren's Southern allies all converged in such a way as to cause the state to undercut rather than support the President's policies.

I

New York politics in the late 1820s and early 1830s were dominated by the Albany Regency, an informal political and social alliance of a number of the state's leading Democrats. The Regency first emerged in the early 1820s, following revisions of the state constitution in 1821 that made it necessary for any group hoping to capture the governorship and gain control of the legislature to develop some kind of organization to coordinate county elections. Made up of men of considerable energy who stressed the importance of party discipline and self-sacrifice, the Regency perfected the use of the legislative caucus, party newspapers, and the dispensing of patronage to run political campaigns and to make important political decisions.[1]

Regency members came mainly from the eastern and northern parts of the state and were usually of New England stock. The main exception to this, and the group's most visible member, was Martin Van Buren, a Yorker of Dutch origins. Although Van Buren had helped to found the group, throughout the 1820s his main interest was in national affairs and he generally left policy making on the state level to others. These included: Silas Wright, a Van Buren protégé and lawyer from Canton in St. Lawrence County, who served in the state senate from 1823 to 1827, a term in the United States House of Representatives, and then became state comptroller in 1829; William Marcy, an Albany resident and a learned and very ambitious man who served as state comptroller from 1823 to 1829 and as a judge of the New York Supreme Court until he became a United States senator in 1831 and governor in 1833; and Azariah C. Flagg, a man of impeccable integrity, exclusively interested in state politics, who was a newspaperman from Plattsburgh and represented Clinton County in the Assembly from 1823 to 1826, and then assumed the position of secretary of New York State for the next seven years.[2]

These men led the Regency. Supporting them were a number of important second echelon figures: John A. Dix, a lawyer and land agent, who managed the Democratic party's interests around Cooperstown, and who became adjutant-general of the state in 1830; Edwin Croswell, from Catskill, who edited the *Daily Albany Argus,* the chief Regency newspaper; Benjamin F. Butler, a former law partner and close personal friend and adviser of Van Buren, who served in the state legislature from 1827 to 1833, and then entered Jackson's cabinet as the United States attorney general in the fall of 1833, a post he held until 1840; Elam Tilden of New Lebanon, storekeeper and postmaster, a local political stalwart, who frequently entertained Van Buren, Wright, and Croswell at his home, and whose son, Samuel, was just beginning a political career that would eventually make him governor of the state and almost President of the United States; Michael Hoffman, who represented the Herkimer district in the United States Congress; and Churchill C. Cambreleng, United States Representative from New York City, free trade advocate, and an important link for the Regency with the influential downstate Tammany Hall organization.

Others who, for various reasons, often self-interest, tended to ally themselves with the Regency included: Thomas Olcott, cashier and president of the powerful Farmers' and Mechanics' Bank of Albany which played an important, even dominant, role in the financial development of the western part of the state; Benjamin F. Knower, a principal stockholder in the bank, a hat manufacturer, wool speculator, and one of Albany's wealthiest citizens who also was Governor Marcy's father-in-law; Nathaniel P. Tallmadge, a recent convert to the Regency and a high tariff man with close ties to important banking interests in different parts of the state; and Jesse Buel, editor, former state printer, promoter of scientific agriculture, and a strong advocate of protection.[3]

The Regency had its origin in the mutual dislike of its members and allies for DeWitt Clinton, perhaps the single most influential person in New York politics in the decade after the close of the War of 1812. An arrogant, egotistical person, who was derisive and vindictive toward those unwilling to accept his leadership, Clinton was also a magnetic and at times brilliant and far seeing leader whose greatest accomplishment was the building of the Erie Canal. By maintaining strict party discipline, the Regency was able to check and defeat Clinton several times during the 1820s, but in each case he took advantage of his enormous popularity in the southern and western parts of the state, as well as Regency mistakes, to make successful political comebacks. Not until late 1827, when Clinton suddenly died, did the Regency secure effective political control of the state.

There was less unanimity in the Regency when it came to issues. Van Buren, Wright, Flagg, Butler, and Hoffman constituted the agrarian wing. Scrupulously honest and openly suspicious of those engaged in the unbridled pursuit of wealth, they opposed the proliferation of banks, the building of economically questionable feeder canals, and deficit spending by the state. It was this group that enacted the famous Safety-Fund law of 1829, which limited the number of banks and subjected them to legislative control. Marcy, Knower, Croswell, and Olcott made up the entrepreneurial wing. They had close ties to a number of state banks, engaged in numerous speculative activities, and generally took advantage of any opportunity that might offer itself to make a profit. During the 1820s, a decade marked by hard times and a sluggish economy, the differences within the Regency, while real enough, tended to be held in check by the lack of investment opportunities and the need to defeat Clinton, and it was generally the agrarians who held the upper hand. By the early 1830s, with Clinton dead, the growing involvement of Van Buren, Butler, and Wright with national politics, and the return of prosperity and economic opportunity, relations between the two wings became increasingly strained, and it was the entrepreneurial wing that came to dominate Albany.

For the most part these differences were kept below the surface in the early 1830s. In part this was because no one wanted to do anything that might threaten Van Buren's chances for advancement to the presidency. In part also it was because 1829 to 1832 were years of unusual political prosperity for the Regency, which no one wanted to jeopardize. Van Buren was elected governor in 1828. When he went to Washington the following year to become secretary of state, he was succeeded by Lieutenant-Governor Enos Throop, a Regency loyalist but a relatively unimportant politician. Throop was reelected in his own right in 1830, but was replaced in the election of 1832 by the more formidable and effective Marcy. That same year the Regency swept the Assembly elections, carrying most of the state, except the western part, and thereby kept New York safe for President Jackson's reelection bid. "Our opponents," wrote William H. Seward, an important opposition leader, "have achieved so destructive a victory that in common decency they are compelled when in our presence to suppress the expression of their exultation."[4]

What opposition there was to the Regency in the early 1830s was weak, disorganized, and divided. The banking interests on Wall Street, rivals of their counterparts on Chestnut Street in Philadelphia, did not oppose Jackson's veto of the bill to recharter the Second Bank of the United States, and did not rally to Clay's banner in 1832. In the western part of the state, the Anti-masonic movement had definite anti-Regency overtones, but it also refused to ally itself with the Clay forces, and it was internally split among those who had originated the movement and the professional politicians who were trying to take it over. Neither group represented much of a threat to Regency control of the legislature.[5]

II

Regency hegemony during these years coincided with Jackson's first administration. Although he had been a latecomer into the Jackson movement, once there Van Buren was loyal to the President on almost all the crucial issues, and especially on those that involved states' rights. He wholeheartedly supported Jackson's constitutional objections to a federal program of internal improvements and the Second Bank of the United States. Both these policies, to be sure, were in New York's interest, but it is clear that more was involved than self-interest. Van Buren, and those around him in the agrarian wing of the Regency, were men of strong principle, who went out of their way to project the image of being spokesmen for traditional Jeffersonian principles whose origins could be traced back to George Clinton's anti-Federalist opposition to a strong central government and to the "spirit of '98." Moreover, this stance was a popular one as indicated by a despairing opponent who observed, ". . . we cannot succeed so long as the impression goes the round among the common people that the Van Buren party is the old Republican Party."[6]

Under Regency leadership, New York State became an energetic and forceful proponent of states' rights. An important manifestation of this came in the case of *The State of New Jersey v. The People of the State of New York*. The dispute had its origins in the conflicting claims of the two states to Staten Island. In addition, New York claimed exclusive jurisdiction and property on the Hudson River up to the high water mark on the Jersey shore.[7] When New York consistently rejected attempts to negotiate a settlement, New Jersey hired William Wirt to represent it and brought a bill of equity before the United States Supreme Court in 1829. New York, however, refused to send any one to represent it despite the fact that a subpoena had been served. In a letter to the Clerk of the Supreme Court, Green C. Bronson, the attorney general of New York, indicated that his state considered the services "utterly void" and denied that the Supreme Court had jurisdiction in the matter. He added, in a manner that revealed the hostility and growing belligerence of many Jacksonians toward the Supreme Court, that "whether the court has been clothed with power to compel the appearance of a state as defendant in an original suit or proceeding, is a question, among others . . . that had yet to be settled."[8]

In response, on March 8, 1830, the Court ruled that precedent for granting the process had been established during the 1790s, and it issued a further subpoena. Once again the State of New York refused to send a representative to plead its cause. At an official hearing of the case in 1831, New Jersey, represented by Wirt, made a motion that the case be heard despite the absence of New York. Chief Justice Marshall ruled favorably on the motion and set the following term for the case to be heard.[9] This time New York sent Attorney General Bronson and Benjamin F. Butler to represent it. The case was heard in March 1832, the same term the Court ruled on *Worcester v. Georgia*. Bronson filed a demurer again denying the Court's jurisdiction, but the Court rejected it and ruled that the attorney general's presence was to be considered an appearance. The case began in earnest the following day when Bronson and Butler entered into a long argument in defense of New York's actions. According to one account:

> . . . it has brought the Supreme Court into a temper of reflection on the subject of State-Rights, more than any case ever before them. It is the first time in the history of our general legislation that a sovereign state ever consented to employ counsel to contest the jurisdiction of the Court. On the first day in which the case was begun, by Mr. Bronson, he entered into a long and learned argument showing the entire unconstitutionality of the jurisdiction assumed by the Court. I understand from good authority that the array of names and authorities in favor of the ground assumed by the Attorney-General of New York startled, in no small degree, the Supreme Bench, particularly the Chief Justice.

When the Court reconvened the next day, much to Bronson and Butler's surprise, it ruled "that as the case had assumed a more important aspect than had been contemplated, the Court had agreed to postpone any further proceeding till next session."[10]

What the Regency had done in this case was to firmly ally itself on the side of Georgia in its controversy with the federal government. This development deeply concerned Chief Justice Marshall, who already was alarmed by the extent of states' rights thought that existed in the South. He now wrote despairingly, "I yield slowly and reluctantly to the Conviction that our Constitution cannot last. I had supposed that North of the Potomack a firm and solid government to the security of rational liberty might be preserved. Even now that seems doubtful." Moreover, during the election of 1832, Butler, who was soon to be appointed United States attorney general by Jackson, openly defended the President and Georgia's course on the Indian question.[11]

III

The Regency, of course, had little sympathy either for Calhoun, South Carolina, or nullification. But the events of the winter of 1832–33 placed them in a difficult situation. Throughout Jackson's first administration, Van Buren recognized that nullification was a tricky and dangerous issue and looked for a way to effect some kind of compromise. To this end he tried to maintain contact with important South Carolinians and also suggested to the President, at one point, that his public remarks on nullification be "made in a temper of great moderation and entirely exempt from anything that could be construed into personal allusion of a hostile character. . . ."[12]

Nullification also highlighted the tariff, the one issue that threatened the North-South sectional alliance that Van Buren inherited from the Crawford wing of the old Jeffersonian party, and which he so carefully maintained as the political base from which, along with Jackson's support, he hoped to become President in 1836. For while most of his political allies in the South may have shared his opposition to Calhoun, they found protection anathema. New York, on the other hand, was basically a high tariff state. During the 1820s in Jackson's first administration, Van Buren had cleverly managed to avoid the issue, so that as one of his political enemies had observed, "one of two things is plain: he is for the tariff, and wants the south to think he is not; or he is not, and wants the people of New York to think that he is."[13]

But it was all to no avail. Van Buren was not able to prevent the nullification crisis from occurring, and by December 1832 he found himself in the unenviable position of having to try to make the best of a bad situation. Part of the problem was that, as Jackson's heir apparent, Van Buren's non-committal views on the tariff had begun to attract a lot of attention in the South. Pushed by his enemies and a cause of concern among his friends, it had become an important issue in the election of 1832. As the nullification crisis unfolded, Congressman Hoffman wrote of Van Buren, "in one way only can he be prevented from reaching the Supreme Executive power and that is by preventing the South from joining in his support. To do this the tariff must be kept up and all concession must be obstinately refused."[14]

Still hoping to defuse the crisis through some kind of compromise, Van Buren and those closest to him in the Regency opted for tariff reform. Their pragmatic approach to the crisis finds clear expression in the following remarks from the *Daily Albany Argus*:

> The material question is not whether we are the advocates or opponents of Nullification. Upon that question not a shadow of a doubt can exist as to the opinions of the people, in or out of the state. But *what* and *where* is the remedy to complaints, or grievances, which extend beyond the feverish or designing efforts of the partisans of Nullification? It is obvious we think that the "rightful remedy" is not in a dictum "unauthorized by the Constitution of the U.S. and fatally repugnant to all the objects to which it was framed," but in the removal to every reasonable extent, of the causes of complaint and irritation. In other words, in such modification of the tariff as shall be deemed reasonable by reasonable men of the different sections—as shall be consonant to the principles of our government, and the economy and simplicity of its administration—as shall be just and proper in itself—and as shall be suited to the exigencies and urgency of the case. And this remedy, rightful, constitutional and truly "peaceful" as it is, is to be applied by Congress. A thousand conventions—a thousand schemes for the creation of a body of dernier resort, of ultimate appeal or decision—and a thousand speculations as to the origin of the government, and the nature of the compact, will, after all, come to this—is this or the next Congress prepared to reduce the duties on imposts to such a standard as we refer to above?[15]

Despite their coolness to Gulian C. Verplanck, a pro-Bank Democrat from New York City whose reelection they had opposed, the Van Burenites in Congress supported his attempt at tariff reform in December of 1832. But there was much opposition to this course among some New Yorkers. It came not only from anti-Jackson protectionists and advocates of the American System who opposed any reduction of the tariff at all, but also from many Democrats. Throughout December and January 1832–33 the New York congressional delegation in Washington, D.C., remained hopelessly split over the need for tariff reform. Although this Democratic division clearly involved very real differences over the value of protection and the dangers of capitulating to South Carolina's unreasonable demands, this development especially concerned the Van Burenites because it was being taken advantage of by their enemies to "make some progress in pushing the suspicion that this is another of the magician arts of Mr. Van Buren . . . that by the conduct of his friends he may lay claim to both sides of this great interest," and was badly hurting him among southern Democrats.[16]

Jackson's Nullification Proclamation and his Force bill message of January 16 caused additional problems for Van Buren. Their controversial doctrinal points and warm reception by nationalists made many New York Democrats and traditional states' rights men unhappy. One observer opined:

> It may be very proper to place in the hands of the Executive the necessary power to cause the Laws to be respected; but care ought to be taken that no more than what is necessary should be granted. Strong powers and democratic feelings cannot long exist together in the same person. . . . I have heard some of the sincere friends of the President express much apprehension that his fame and popularity may be injured by some of the sentiments promulgated in his writings, when coupled with the disposition evinced by those who but a few weeks since were his most bitter foes, but now his eulogists, applauding him to the skies and willing to place at his disposal the whole force of the union, in order to crush the south— when but two or three months since, they were fearful that the power he then possessed was unsafely lodged in the hands of a military chieftan.[17]

The Proclamation came as a complete surprise to Van Buren. At the time it was issued he was in Albany. He immediately recognized that its doctrinal lapses were going to create serious political problems. During the weeks that followed its issuance, he became increasingly concerned about the hostility of southern Democrats to it, as well as nationalist support for the President's desire to use force against South Carolina, and Webster's growing influence with the administration. This was reflected in the unwillingness of the *Albany Argus,* the Regency newspaper, to endorse the Proclamation. Instead, it warned that the President's newfound friends were less interested in sustaining his principles than they were in using the crises for the self-serving purpose of preventing a much needed downward revision of the tariff. This was a difficult and embarrassing course to follow, however, for as an opposition paper noted, "the delay of the friends of Gen. Jackson in this city, in responding to the Proclamation, begins to excite remark."[18]

No one became more upset about this than Jackson himself. He wanted Van Buren and the New York legislature to endorse formally the principles of the Proclamation. Thus, on the very day he issued it the President sent a copy to Van Buren urging him to "read it, & say how you like it. The union must be preserved."[19] When Van Buren finally responded, nearly two weeks later, he cautiously reported, among other things, that "our people are somewhat restive under the attempts of the opposition to convert some portion of the Proclamation into a condemnation of the state right doctrines of Virginia and the South." He went on to explain that "the safe conduct of our affairs here [New York], requires from the diversity of opinion which exists in regard to the tariff & the violence of feeling which has grown out of the late election, great discretion & good temper."[20]

In another letter, written a short time later, Van Buren urged the President to act circumspectly. "The extent to which the hopes of the people rest upon you and the intense anxiety that nothing should be done that can be avoided, which lessens the chances of an amicable adjustment," he advised, ". . . require the observance of a greater degree of caution than might otherwise be deemed necessary. You will say I am on my old track—caution—caution: but my Dr Sir, I have always thought, that considering our respective temperaments, there was no way perhaps in which I could better render you . . . service. . . ." Specifically, Van Buren urged the President carefully to consult with Congress before taking any action against South Carolina. He also suggested that there were political and legal dangers involved in trying to enforce a "constructive levying of war" theory of treason charge against the nullifiers at this point. In addition, Van Buren made it clear that he too had reservations about Jackson's recently espoused theory of the Union, for he urged the President to respond to Virginia's "discussion of some of the doctrinal points of the Proclamation, the most assailable of which might perhaps have been omitted without weakening the force or probable effect of that document" with "toleration and magnanimity" for it involved "*honest* differences of opinion." Van Buren also indicated he did not think South Carolina intended to secede, but that if it did it would be a matter for the entire country, and especially Congress and the other states, to deal with. He concluded by warning Jackson that "the present is not a season for the settlement or discussion of abstract propositions."[21] It is clear Van Buren did not want to see the President continue to debate the issue in inflammatory constitutional terms, and he certainly did not want to see the nullification crisis continue to be a private confrontation between the Chief Executive and his enemies in South Carolina.

Jackson's response was not reassuring. He urged Van Buren "not to be disturbed" by reports "from the alarmists at this place. Many Nullifiers are here under disguise, working hard to save Calhoun and would disgrace their country and the Executive to do it." Although Jackson indicated he would "act with all the forbearance [I possess]" and would consult Congress, for "was I therefore to act without the aid of Congress, or without communicating to it, I would be branded with the epithet, *tyrant*," he also made it clear that he was not thinking in terms of compromise or the political ramifications of the crisis.

"No my friend," he wrote, "the crisis must be now met with firmness, our citizens protected, and the modern doctrines of nullification and secession put down forever." The President also did not recant on any of the doctrinal points contained in the Proclamation. Nor did he suggest that tariff reduction be used as a way of resolving the crisis. Instead he stressed the need to meet force with force. He warned "wo, to those nullifiers who shed the first blood. The moment I am prepared with proof I will direct prosecutions for treason to be instituted against the leaders, and if they are surrounded with 12,000 bayonets our marshal shall be aided by 24,000 and arrest them in the midst thereof— nothing must be permitted to weaken our government at home or abroad."[22]

Having made it unmistakably clear to Van Buren that he had no intention of backing down or of even seeking a compromise, Jackson now expected his Vice President-elect to get the New York legislature to endorse the principles of the Proclamation and his policy toward South Carolina. When nothing happened by the end of January he became upset. Barely restraining his anger, he wrote Van Buren wanting to know: "Why is your Legislature silent at this eventful crisis. Friendship with candor, compels me to say to you that your friends are astonished at the silence of your Legislature, and give rise to dark innuendoes of your enemies, that you command them, and are awaiting the result of the Virginia Legislature. Believing as you know I do, how unworthy those innuendoes are, as respects your firmness or your principles, I cannot but sincerely regret, that the great state of New York has not come forth in her majesty and strength at this eventful moment."[23]

Van Buren's difficulties were further compounded by the fact that in Albany the Regency itself was split over how New York should proceed during the nullification crisis. Whereas Van Buren, Flagg, Wright, and Hoffman clearly favored some sort of compromise that would involve an abandonment of protection, the entrepreneurial wing opposed any tariff reduction. In this fight they were led by Benjamin Knower, a longtime advocate of protection who had speculated heavily in raw wool and who would probably be ruined if tariff rates came down. Support for protection also came from Governor Marcy, who had only recently observed about his career in the United States Senate: "I went to Washington a friend of protection and I came home a friend of protection."[24]

Some indication that Marcy did not plan to go along with Van Buren's intention of abandoning protection came in his address to the legislature on January 2, 1833. Marcy had discussed the message with Van Buren, and much of its content was agreeable to him. It condemned nullification as "not merely unauthorized by the Constitution of the United States, but fatally repugnant to all the objects for which it was framed." In vague and unspecific terms it indicated that New York would support the President "in all measures which are proper and may be necessary for the preservation of the Union," but it entirely avoided any kind of discussion of the principles contained in the Proclamation. The Governor also went along with Van Buren and Butler's efforts to isolate South Carolina through a compromise of Georgia's controversy with the Supreme Court by indicating that New York would also not pursue its own case against New Jersey, "although our counsel entertain very decided opinions against the jurisdiction of the court," but would directly negotiate a settlement because "the interests of both states, and many other important considerations, concur at this time in recommending an adjustment of this question upon terms of honorable compromise." But on the issue of tariff reform Marcy made it clear that he believed protection to be constitutional and just and that no effort would be made to rally the state in favor of reduction.[25]

In Congress, Van Buren's southern allies had been watching the New York situation very carefully, and Marcy's treatment of the tariff upset them. William King, senator from Alabama, a Jackson supporter and a staunch advocate of the New Yorker's presidential ambitions, wrote that the speech "has in one particular fallen very far short of the hopes and expectations of your friends here," for it made no attempt to "give a direction to public opinion" in New York in favor of reduction and as a consequence many of the New York congressional delegation felt free to oppose the Verplanck bill. Should the attempt to reduce the tariff fail, King warned, Van Buren's political aspirations would suffer:

> It will produce throughout the entire South the most inveterate hostility to every prominent man in that [northern] quarter. Calhoun is (politically), a dead cock in the pit. The father of nullification under no circumstances can ever receive the support of the southern states, but the settlement of this distracting question by an individual cannot fail to bind the South to his interest. I know the tariff question is to be adjusted. It may be defeated at this session by the folly of those who have the power at their hands, but adjusted it will be, and at no distant day. When the danger of a disruption of the Government becomes imminent Clay will step forward as the mediator, the great pacificator, the work will be done, and the Presidency will be his reward. Pardon me for troubling you with these speculations and believe me to sincerely be your friend.[26]

Meanwhile, back in New York a coalition of National Republican and Anti-Masonic protectionists were making a formidable case against tariff reduction. They warned against a precipitous repeal of the Tariff of 1832 before it had been given a chance to go into effect, arguing that many manufacturers would be driven into bankruptcy through the sharp lowering of duties contained in the Verplanck bill because they had invested millions of dollars on the government's recent promise of protection. And, of course, they also warned against the dangers involved in giving in to South Carolina's threats. In the legislature an effort was made to pass a joint resolution instructing the state's senators and requesting its representatives to oppose any kind of tariff reduction at the present session of Congress. In itself, this coalition did not have enough votes to accomplish anything, but it is clear that it expected substantial support from Democrats sympathetic to protection as well as popular approval for its course of action. Writing home, William Seward remarked, "our little force are pursuing a course to conciliate the People and win their favor while we trust the immense power of the dominant party will soon be found so great that its discordant materials cannot adhere."[27]

The differences between the agrarian and entrepreneurial wings of the Regency emerged dramatically when, under the leadership of Knower, Jesse Buel and state Chief Justice John Savage, and probably with the tacit assent of Governor Marcy, Democratic protectionists organized a mass meeting in Albany on January 24. In addition to trying to mold public opinion, its purpose was to demonstrate broad-based opposition to the Verplanck bill or any other attempt by Congress to abandon protection. It was hoped that the Albany meeting would serve as a model for other meetings to be held throughout the state and that in this manner enough public pressure could be generated to force the legislature to pass resolutions against tariff reduction. Recognizing that such a meeting would embarrass Van Buren even further with his southern supporters, the Vice President-elect's followers, led by Dix and Butler, quickly moved to thwart Knower's attempt to make sure that New York remained committed to protection. Thus, when the "greatest public meeting ever assembled in Albany" met at the City Hall and Knower's group introduced resolutions declaring it a mistake to reduce the tariff, Van Buren's partisans offered an alternative set of resolutions which denounced nullification and secession, but kept the door open for some kind of compromise in Washington, stressing the need for "that spirit of amity and mutual conciliation" in which the Union originated, and declared that no attempt should be made to instruct the state's congressional delegation on how to vote on a new tariff bill. What followed is not really clear. Pandemonium appears to have broken out at this point and during the uproar Knower's group called for a vote on the substitute proposals, and declared them defeated and their own resolutions adopted. At this point Dix, Butler, and their supporters bolted from the meeting and reassembled at the Capitol where they proceeded to pass the substitute resolutions. In the weeks that followed, both groups openly campaigned to rally public support for their position on tariff reform.[28]

Up to this point the Regency had almost always managed to resolve its internal differences quietly. This was no longer possible. The differences between the two wings of the Democratic party had begun to surface and with them came the most serious threat to Regency supremacy since the death of Clinton. As one critic wrote, "you must observe there is a deadly feud in the Jackson ranks arising from this sessions tariff question. . . . Knower and Buel, the leaders of the dissidents, are veterans 'trained in the wars of Flanders,' and if they . . . oppose themselves to the Van Buren Regency, the Magician will find far more formidable opponents at home than he has yet encountered."[29]

I V

Up to now Van Buren had used his enormous influence with the New York legislature to prevent it from taking any kind of official position on the nullification crisis. Undoubtedly he was waiting to see what kind of stand Virginia would take. But this had not worked out the way he hoped, for the Old Dominion's response was disappointing: a muddled political compromise that rejected both nullification and the Proclamation while doing little to clarify the

complex constitutional questions involved. His own preference was to compromise the entire question quietly through some kind of tariff reform, but in
early February 1833 this did not seem a realistic possibility. Moreover, the
crisis as it developed was taking on increasingly ominous overtones for his own
political future. The widespread discontent, especially in the South, with the
Proclamation, the growing closeness between Webster and Jackson, the President's unhappiness with New York's failure to close ranks behind him, and the
schism within the Regency all jeopardized the likelihood of his becoming
President in 1836. Van Buren apparently now realized he had to make the best
of a bad situation. He, therefore, proceeded to write the Report on Nullification for the Joint Committee of the New York legislature. In it, Van Buren
took upon himself the task of distinguishing the traditional and democratic
states' rights interpretation of the Constitution from that of the nationalists
interpretation, while at the same time condemning nullification without allowing this distinction to become blurred as Jackson had done in the Proclamation. Commenting on the Report the *Argus* pointed out, "It is the sound
Republican doctrine of '98 and the creed of the Democracy in the old times
and at all times."[30] In the process, Van Buren revealed not only his commitment to states' rights but also an understanding of constitutional-ideological
considerations that went way beyond that of a merely clever politician artfully
manipulating these arguments for self-interested purposes. In fact, it is not too
much to say that the New York Report, drafted by Van Buren, is one of the
most coherent and forceful documents to come out of the nullification crisis, a
document whose importance for clearly stating the point of view of traditional
states' rights Jacksonians has been too long overlooked by scholars.

The Report began by making it clear that it was for states' rights and
against nullification. In doing so it offered a number of trenchant observations
about the nature and history of the Union. The federal government was
intended to be a government of limited powers, "leaving the great mass of the
business of the people, relating as it does mainly to their domestic concerns, to
the legislation of the States." In addition, the country's history since the adoption of the Constitution has made it "apparent that the tendency of the system
is to encroachments by the federal government upon the reserved rights of the
states, rather than an unwillingness on the part of the States to submit to a full
exercise of powers which were intended to be delegated to the General Government." Fortunately, this tendency had been corrected by "the memorable civil
revolution of 1800; and the same sovereign remedy, upon the same impulse,
and, it is hoped, with similar effect, was applied by the people in 1828."
Unfortunately, the Report argued, this was in danger of being forgotten since
"so much discredit is apprehended to the sacred cause of state rights from the
excesses of South Carolina."[31]

With skill and clarity the Report took a stand on a number of controversial
and important constitutional concepts. It rejected the claim "that a single State
has a right to withdraw herself, against the wishes of her co-states, from the
union, whenever, in her sole judgment, the acts of the Federal Government
shall be such as to justify the step."[32] It also rejected the nationalists' in-

terpretation of the origins of the Union and their claim that the United States
Supreme Court was the "exclusive expositor of the Constitution," especially in
areas of conflict between the states and the federal government. Should an
unconstitutional action take place, it argued,

> it is the right of each party to judge for itself; not for the federal government
> exclusively, as was contended by the States which protested against the Virginia
> and Kentucky resolutions in 1799; nor for each state solely, as is now contended.
> No right is reserved to the people of any State to absolve themselves from the
> performance of duties which they have so solemnly assumed, without the consent
> of the other party or parties to the compact. Each state on surrendering a portion
> of its sovereignty, acquired, in consequence thereof, a right to the perpetual ad-
> herence of each of its co-States to that Union which is so necessary to, and was
> established for, the security of all.[33]

The Report subscribed to the compact theory of the Union as enunciated in
the Kentucky and Virginia Resolutions which have "been justly regarded as
the genuine text book of political orthodoxy."[34] It endorsed Madison's recent
assertion that neither the Virginia and Kentucky Resolutions nor the Virginia
Report of 1799 were precedents for South Carolina's actions, because they
assumed the principle of majority rule while the nullifiers would allow a single
state "to govern the majority." The Report also argued, at length, that states'
rights thought and the principles of '98 contained within them a firm belief
that the Union was perpetual and its preservation was an absolutely central
consideration. Disagreements over the powers delegated to the federal government were to be resolved through elections, appeals to public opinion, and the
amendment process.[35]

The Report did not endorse Jackson's Proclamation, but did try to explain
away its "doctrinal errors" by observing that "the manner in which the
Federal Constitution was framed and adopted, has always been a matter of
more or less contention." It went on with intelligence and considerable historical accuracy to confront the difficult question of the origins of the Union in
these terms;

> Differences of opinion upon the subject, have been in some degree fostered by a
> seeming discrepancy between the preamble of the Constitution, and historical
> facts; and perhaps in a still greater degree, by the different senses in which the term
> "States" is used by different persons. If we use the term, not merely as denoting
> particular sections of territory, nor as referring to the particular governments,
> established and organized by the political societies within each, but as referring to
> the people composing those political societies, in their highest sovereign capacity
> (as the Committee think that in this respect the term should be used) it is in-
> controvertible, that the States must be regarded as parties to the compact. For it is
> well established, that, in that sense, the Constitution was submitted to the states;
> that in that sense, the States ratified it. This is the explanation which is given of the
> matter in the report to the Virginia legislature, which has already received the
> sanction of the Committee. It is in this sense of the term "States," that they form

the constituency from which the Federal Constitution emanated, and it is by the States, acting either by their Legislatures, or in Convention, that any valid alterations of the instrument can alone be made. It is by so understanding the subject, that the preamble is reconciled with facts, and that it is a Constitution established by "the people of the United States," not as one consolidated body, but as members of separate and independent communities, each acting for itself, without regard to their comparative numbers. It was in this form that the Constitution of the United States was established by the people of the different States, with the same solemnity that the Constitutions of the respective states were established; and, as the Committee have heretofore insisted, with the same binding force in respect to the powers which were intended to be delegated to the Federal Government.[36]

After arguing that the states as well as the people of the United States created the Constitution, the Report went on to defend President Jackson. It did this not in terms of his handling of the nullification controversy, but in broader agrarian and traditional states' rights terms as a President who "in the general bearing of his official acts," has rejected attempts to expand the power of the central government by "ingenious interpretations" and who has evinced "an unwillingness to exercise authority which was not intended to be granted, and which the states and the people might not, on open application, be willing to grant." It further pointed out that the President "has done all in his power to arrest the increase of monopolies, under all circumstances so adverse to public liberty, and the equal interests of the community," and that Jackson's entire official career has been marked "by unceasing assiduity to promote economy in the public expenditures, to relieve the people from all unnecessary burthens, and generally to preserve our republican system in that simplicity and purity which were intended for it." And it observed: "the people of the United States will not doubt his attachment to the true principles of that Constitution which he has so faithfully administered and so nobly supported."[37]

The Report concluded with what was, in effect, Van Buren's solution to the nullification crisis. It called for a spirit of concession and compromise. It stressed the need for mutual sacrifice, warning "if every man looks only to his own interests, or every State to its own favorite policy and insists upon them, this Union cannot be preserved." Although it recognized protection as constitutional it indicated that "the possession of the right, however, and the manner and extent of its exercise are very different matters." It noted that the imminent paying off of the national debt and popular opinion made tariff reduction "just and practicable," and warned against a high tariff whose purpose is "the sole one of taking money from the pockets of one class of our people to put it into those of another." It declared the tariff reforms of 1832 inadequate and came out in favor of a further lowering of duties in accordance with the desires of the President and what it claimed was the will "of the great body of the people."[38]

The Report was controversial. One anti-Jackson newspaper declared it to be "as wretched a piece of genuine Van Burenism as we have ever been required to place on record, and as particularly objectionable because it reaffirms the celebrated anti-constitutional resolutions of Virginia and Kentucky of 1798–99." Another described it as "a servile effort to soothe the President by flattery, while condemning with a view to Mr. Van Buren's future prospects in the South, the doctrines of the Proclamation." The Report, it was charged, had been "framed with great and, we think, with unnecessary scrupulousness as to the South."[39]

When the Report was submitted to the legislature, Van Buren's opponents moved to embarrass him. They wanted to know, in particular, why the Report had failed to endorse the President's course in the nullification crisis. Led by William H. Seward in the Senate, a resolution was introduced, to be added to the Report, indicating "that the President of the United States, in his late Proclamation, has advanced the true principles upon which only the Constitution can be maintaned and defended." In his supporting speech, Seward caustically noted, "approving the principles contained in the Proclamation, seems absolutely necessary, in as much as the Committee either forgot, or evaded expressing, any approbation in their report. They set out to vindicate the President, but compliments supply the place of vindication, or even approval of the Proclamation."[40] If Van Buren's supporters voted for the resolution it would cost him support in the South; if they opposed it, it would undermine their leader's influence with the President.

By means of some skillfull parliamentary maneuvering, Van Buren's friends managed to table Seward's resolution permanently. But they continued to have problems when they introduced their own resolutions in support of the Report. The most controversial was the first one, endorsing the constitutional principles of the Virginia and Kentucky Resolutions of 1798. These had never been formally approved by the New York legislature as it had been under Federalist control when they were originally received. Again, Seward led the attack. In his speech he argued:

> New York demurely resolves against nullification, but adopts the text-book of the heresy to show that she is *not in earnest!* . . . . Sir, South Carolina and the great party who favor nullification at the South ask nothing more of us than to waive the Constitution, and adopt those resolutions of Virginia and Kentucky. They are written in their heart's core. If we adopt them, the question is no longer whether nullification and secession are constitutional, but it is reduced to a question of construction of your new text-book.[41]

Van Buren's supporters made a valiant effort to defend the need to endorse the Virginia and Kentucky Resolutions. They argued that more was involved than appeasing the South and protecting their leader's presidential ambitions. They stressed that real issues and important constitutional principles were also at stake. One Democratic member of the legislature observed "that while we strengthen the arm of government within all proper bounds, there is also danger of a consolidated government. The danger is probably now more immediate than any other, and if South Carolina shall be arrested in her mad career only by the force of arms, it well behooves every friend to state rights to guard against running from one extreme to the other." A different speaker noted the Report had effectively demonstrated that the Virginia and Kentucky Resolutions did not sanction nullification and secession; "and that rightly understood they were sound and constitutional, the true landmarks of the democracy, designed to preserve the equilibrium between the general and state governments." He went on to argue that they were the bulwark against "the spirit of encroachment and the tendency to consolidation," and "the great and fundamental principles of the Democracy, and those who contended for a strict construction of the Constitution, and for a government *with* a limitation of powers."[42]

But it was to no avail. Seward put together a coalition of Anti-Masons, National Republicans, and dissident Democrats, led by John Sudam, a former Federalist and inveterate personal foe of Van Buren, which prevented the adoption of any kind of resolution that endorsed the Kentucky and Virginia Resolutions. Instead, after much political wrangling a watered-down resolution approving "of the general views and conclusions" of the Report was adopted. Additional resolutions described the Union as indispensable to continued prosperity and happiness, disapproved of nullification and secession, vowed cooperation with the President, and came out in favor of tariff reform.[43]

The long delay by the New York legislature as well as the unwillingness of Van Buren and his friends in the Regency to throw their unqualified support behind Jackson's belligerent attitude toward South Carolina undoubtedly played an important role in making the President realize that he might have to go along, albeit reluctantly, with some kind of compromise.

V

The overall effect of the nullification crisis on New York politics is difficult to gauge accurately. It did not, in the end, seriously alter the close working relationship or the mutual respect that Jackson and Van Buren had developed for each other. But this was maintained only by completely avoiding any kind of discussion about what had happened during the winter of 1832–33. Van Buren reported, many years later, that they never discussed the matter. He did, however, at that time, indicate, although there is no evidence to corroborate this and much to contradict it, that the President had actually approved of the way the New York legislature had handled the matter, and recognized that its Report was a better statement of traditional states' rights thought than the Proclamation had been.[44] At any rate, in the spring of 1833 Van Buren remained, and in 1836 actually became, Jackson's heir apparent.

On the state level the crisis had uncovered the differences between the more traditional and agrarian wing of the Regency on the one hand, and the entrepreneurial business oriented wing on the other. The strength of the Knower-led entrepreneurial wing was made especially clear in early February 1833 when the legislature turned its attention to the election of a United States senator. This was the second time the legislature had engaged in this activity at its present session, for both seats had been open. At the beginning of the session, before the Regency had openly split on the question of tariff reform, Silas Wright had been selected to replace Marcy who had resigned his Senate seat when he became governor. This had taken place with very little opposition, and Wright immediately proceeded to Washington, where he worked to protect Van Buren's interests and to convince the state's congressional delegation to go along with a reduction of the tariff. But after the open division at what became known as the "Great Meeting," Knower and his followers were determined to see that the other Senate seat went to a protectionist. Their candiate was Nathaniel Tallmadge, a recent convert from Clintonianism, and an open opponent of tariff reduction who differed from the agrarian wing of the Regency on a number of other issues as well. Although unhappy with the choice, Van Buren and Flagg were not able to mount an effective opposition. Their own choice for the post, Benjamin F. Butler, for personal reasons did not want to go to Washington, and as a reluctant candidate proved unwilling to engage in the necessary politicking to win. As a consequence Tallmadge won a fairly easy victory.[45]

The willingness of Van Buren and his followers begrudgingly to go along with Tallmadge was probably an attempt to maintain a semblance of unity within the Regency. It worked only in the most superficial fashion. The basic tensions unleashed by the nullification crisis were fundamental, and they did not go away. "The breach of the Jackson ranks here between Knower and his friends on one side," wrote one seasoned observer of New York politics, "and Van Buren's friends on the other, appears I think to widen daily and there is reason to believe that it will before long terminate in a permanent political separation." In the months that followed, relations between Van Buren and Governor Marcy, who discreetly sided with his father-in-law, became noticeably cooler. The compromise Tariff of 1833 pretty much eliminated protection as an issue for the rest of the 1830s, but the two groups soon divided on the question of state banking and monetary policy. Thus more than mere irony was involved when one of the leaders of the conservative opposition to Van Buren during his presidency turned out to be Tallmadge.[46]

8

"The Compromise"

That there was a good deal more criticism of Andrew Jackson's policy toward South Carolina as well as indirect support for the nullifiers than has generally been recognized can be seen from developments in a number of other states, especially in the South.

In early January 1833 the Mississippi legislature issued a report and a series of resolves that criticized South Carolina for acting with "reckless precipitancy" and denounced its Ordinance of Nullification as "contrary to the letter and spirit of the Constitution, and in direct conflict with the welfare, safety and independence of every state in the Union. . . ." Nonetheless, its support for the President was extremely circumspect: it refused to endorse Jackson's Proclamation, indicating instead it would sustain him "in the full exercise of his legitimate powers to restore peace and harmony to our distracted country. . . ." This undoubtedly was a response to a strong minority report which urged that Mississippi remain neutral and not condemn another southern state, reaffirmed the Kentucky and Virginia Resolutions, and denounced the Proclamation for presenting doctrines, "monstrous and startling" and "subversive of the rights of the states as independent political communities." Although the Mississippi house of representatives was hostile to South Carolina, the state's senate was more evenly divided and Governor Abram M. Scott, a Poindexter ally, agreed with the minority report and went on record indicating his belief that the crisis should be resolved, not through a use of force, but through a lowering of the tariff. One staunch supporter of the President summed up Mississippi's stance during the nullification crisis in the following way: the state could not support South Carolina's "mad career of separation," but "You can rest assured S.C. has our sympathies. . . ."[1]

On January 5, 1833, the North Carolina legislature adopted a series of resolves that pronounced nullification to be "revolutionary in its character" and "subversive of the Constitution of the United States. . . ." The resolves, however, also indicated that "a large majority of the people" in the State believed protective tariffs to be unconstitutional. Further, the resolves reflected the view of the many people in the state who believed the President's course to be violent and dangerous by not only failing to endorse the Proclamation but also by instructing the state's senators in the United States Congress and urging its representatives "to procure a peaceable adjustment" of the controversy between the federal government and South Carolina.[2]

On January 12 the Alabama legislature rejected nullification as "unsound in theory and dangerous in practice," an unconstitutional remedy that was "essentially revolutionary, leading in its consequences to anarchy and civil discord, and finally to the dissolution of the Union." But it also failed to endorse the Proclamation and the emphasis of a report and resolves of a special select committee of the house of representatives of the Alabama state legislature was upon the need to compromise the crisis through a reduction of the tariff. In fact, in a special recommendation, separately adopted by the Alabama General Assembly, South Carolina was urged to suspend the operation of its Ordinance and to abandon any attempt to use military power to resist the execution of federal laws while the federal government was requested "to exercise moderation, and to employ only such means as are peaceful and usual to execute the laws of the Union."[3]

In Tennessee, Jackson's home state where he had overwhelming popular support, the legislature unanimously endorsed the Virginia Resolutions of 1798 and Madison's various commentaries "as furnishing a true and safe exposition of the Constitution," and declared nullification to be "wholly unwarranted by the Constitution, dangerous to the existence of the Union, inconsistent with the preservation of the federal government, and tending directly, under the guise of a peaceful remedy to bringing upon our Country all the horrors of civil war." But this took place before Jackson issued his Proclamation. The ensuing complications created by the President's inflammatory rhetoric and his newfound nationalism undermined some of the President's support in Tennessee. And when William Carroll, the governor of the state, addressed the legislature in September 1833 he expressed his strong approbation not only that nullification had been rejected as a doctrine, but that the crisis had been settled "in a spirit of compromise and forbearance."[4]

Jackson's Proclamation was more popular in the North. Several states, Pennsylvania (December 21, 1832), Illinois (December 26, 1832), Indiana (January 9, 1833), and Delaware (January 16, 1833), quickly endorsed it.[5] Others, Maryland (February 9, 1833), New Jersey (February 18, 1833), Ohio (February 25, 1833), Massachusetts (March 11, 1833), and Connecticut (May 1833) also supported it, but for a variety of reasons moved more slowly, and it is doubtful that their actions had any significant impact on the outcome of the crisis.[6]

Further, throughout the North many Jacksonians remained uneasy about the political and constitutional implications of the Proclamation. This surfaced with particular clarity in Maine, where in mid-February a legislature dominated by traditional states' rights Democrats rejected nullification and adopted the following resolution endorsing the President's Proclamation:

> . . . we approve of the principles and policy avowed therein, as expounded, not in accordance with the federal doctrine of consolidation, but with the democratic doctrine of state rights, and a limitation of action of the Federal Government to the powers expressly delegated to it by the Constitution and in accordance with the several messages of President Jackson to Congress, and the uniform tenor of the acts of his administration.[7]

Despite the fact that no other state endorsed nullification, in mid-January 1833 South Carolina was not so isolated and the support for Jackson was not so united or clear cut as has usually been suggested.

I

With his Force bill message of January 16 Jackson had, in effect, asked Congress to become officially involved in the nullification crisis. As soon as the message was read in the Senate, Felix Grundy moved that it be referred to the Judiciary Committee. This committee was heavily weighted against the nullifiers. It consisted of William Wilkins of Pennsylvania, a high tariff Democrat, as chairman; Webster of Massachusetts and Theodore Frelinghuysen of New Jersey, both protectionists and outspoken nationalists; Grundy of Tennessee, who, fearful for his own reelection in the fall, was openly siding with the President; and Willie P. Mangum of North Carolina, the only member of the committee in any way sympathetic to South Carolina.

The committee reported on January 21 and the legislation it proposed gave Jackson virtually everything he asked for. It authorized the President, when it was not possible to collect revenues at a specific port because of interference, to remove the custom house to a secure place, either on land or aboard a vessel. It also vitiated South Carolina's recently passed replevin act allowing a plaintiff to sue out a writ in the nature of *a capias in withernam,* by denying process to any court but a federal one for taking property seized by a customs collector under the authority of the laws of the United States and providing that any person who tried to repossess property held by a federal collector be deemed guilty of a misdemeanor and liable to a fine and imprisonment. Further, any action taken against a federal officer in a state court could, upon petition or affidavit, be removed to the United States Circuit Court, where the proceedings of the state court could be declared null and void and any person held by state authorities could be freed by a federal marshal using a writ of *habeas corpus.* Finally, in what was to be the most controversial part of the bill, it authorized, in vague and general terms, the President to employ land or naval forces should the execution of the laws of the United States or decrees of the federal courts be obstructed.[8]

The proposed legislation came under sharp criticism from the nullifiers and others hostile to the President and fearful of any measure authorizing him to use force. The *United States Telegraph* immediately pounced on the bill, pointing out, "it arms the executive with the entire naval and military force of the country, and thus at once creating him a military dictator." It was further argued that "all the powers delegated in the bill depend on one fatal, monarchical principle, and that is, the President's judgment," and what made this so dangerous is that Jackson "is to possess the dictatorial power of determining what is rebellious opposition to the laws and after having passed judgment in a summary way the same individual executes his process at the head of 50,000 men." In other words, according to this point of view, Jackson's intemperate reaction to nullification had not only gotten out of hand, it had, in itself, become the major problem facing the country. "The Union must be preserved; and yet it cannot and *shall not* be preserved by causing blood to flow at the will and judgment of a single man."[9]

In the Senate, Calhoun maneuvered to focus the debate on the fears many held about the President's propensity to violence. Shortly after Grundy moved that Jackson's Force Bill message be referred to the Judiciary Committee, the newly seated senator from South Carolina delivered his maiden address to that body. Admitting that "what he was about to say" was, "under parliamentary rule . . . entirely out of order," he contested the President's claim that the Union had been endangered by the nullifiers' actions. He asserted that for his part "he knew of no other danger but that of military despotism."[10] When the committee reported its bill, Calhoun introduced a set of three resolutions on the nature and power of the federal government. In his supporting speech he indicated that the purpose of the resolutions was to challenge directly the constitutional theory underlying the proposed legislation. He did not discuss nullification or secession or try to defend them against charges that they were not legitimate expressions of states' rights doctrine; instead he spoke in general terms of the rights of the states and the meaning of state sovereignty, and repeatedly attacked the nationalist interpretation of the origins of the Union contained in Jackson's Proclamation. He concluded by warning: "But two modes of political existence can long endure in our country; the one that [was] formed, by the framers of our admirable Constitution, a federal system, unifying free and independent States in a bond of union for mutual advantages, and to be preserved by the concurrent assent of the parts; or a government by the sword." The resolutions themselves affirmed the compact theory of the origins of the Union and the view that the federal government was one of limited delegated powers and was not the judge of what powers had been delegated to it. They also explicitly denied nationalist claims that the Union had been created by the people and not the states or that the states were not the final judge of what powers had been reserved for themselves when they created the federal government.[11]

On the day Jackson sent his Force bill message to Congress, Calhoun confidently wrote, "I have no doubt the message will do more for us, than the Proclamation. It has roused the Southern members more than any event, which has yet occurred. The excitement extends even to administration men of that quarter. I do not doubt that our cause gains daily . . . if we but act prudently." The accuracy of this statement became clear on January 28, when Senator Mangum of North Carolina moved to postpone debate on the Force bill. The motion was supported by the nullifiers and others sympathetic to South Carolina's plight and was opposed by administration spokesmen and their allies. It was viewed as a test of strength between the two groups. Although the Senate voted 30 to 15 to begin debate immediately, the outcome was actually a victory for the nullifiers. Thirteen of the fifteen votes came from southern senators (the other votes were from George Bibb of Kentucky, a Calhoun partisan, and Samuel Smith of Maryland). Grundy, Forsyth, and Josiah Johnston, a high tariff National-Republican from Louisiana, were the only southern senators to vote with the administration.[12]

The meaning of the vote was clear: despite a lack of enthusiasm for nullification as a theoretical doctrine and a fairly pervasive belief that South Carolina had acted precipitously, there was widespread opposition among southerners to the use of force against the nullifiers. In fact, to do so might well mean civil war on a national scale. On the day the Senate Judiciary Committee reported the Force Bill, it had been noted that if the bill "does pass . . . all must see that another bill must also be passed, and that to raise an army of at least fifty thousand men. Our army is now almost nothing; the southern militia cannot be employed; and if the northern militia is carried round in transports, (for they cannot go through the state of Virginia) a bloody civil war will commence, which must last for years before it reaches South Carolina, the state intended to be coerced." Or, as another writer argued, the Senate vote on the postponement of debate on the Force bill "is equivalent to a declaration of the entire South against the use of force, and will have a moral effect on the entire North. It indicates most clearly, that if the North unite in favor of force, the South . . . will unite against force."[13]

This was a major setback for the administration. Included in the group of fifteen were not simply predictable anti-administration types like Tyler of Virginia, Poindexter of Mississippi, Moore of Alabama, and Mangum of North Carolina, but also middle of the road types like White of Tennessee, Troup of Georgia, and Samuel Smith of Maryland. Most significantly, it also included good administration partisans like Rives of Virginia, John Black of Mississippi, Bedford Brown of North Carolina, and William R. King of Alabama. King, who had supported the President on almost every other policy question during the past four years, explained his opposition on the following grounds: "I am opposed to the doctrine contained in the President's Proclamation. I have opposed throughout the Bill to place the whole military power of the Government at the discretion of the President. I can never consent however great my confidence in the executive to cloth any mortal man with such tremendous and unlimited powers." To a friend, Black wrote, if the administration wanted his support "they must be mum about the Proclamation and the Force Act." John Coffee probably expressed Jackson's feelings on the matter when he wrote, "I am truly disgusted with many of our southern men, who pretend to oppose nullification, and yet they are not willing to give the President power to enforce the laws over South Carolina."[14]

Further, it is clear that there existed strong reservations about the measure even among many of the most important senators who voted for the debate on the Force Bill to begin. Included in this group were Wright of New York and Benton of Missouri. Henry Clay reportedly was unenthusiastic about the bill's military provisions. And even Webster, despite his opposition to nullification, support for the tariff, and hopes of forging an alliance with the President, had written a few days after Jackson had sent over his Force bill message, that where Calhoun and his followers were concerned, "I confess I feel no disposition to treat them with unnecessary harshness or censure."[15]

Recognizing that there existed substantial opposition, both overt and covert, in the Senate to the passage of the Force bill, Grundy admitted that the Judiciary Committee "might have gone, perhaps, too far." In an attempt to mollify some of the opposition in order to save the measure, Grundy and Wilkins offered, shortly after the debate began, to alter the bill in two important ways. First, they would limit the life span of its most controversial provisions until the end of the next session of Congress. Second, they would tighten up the wording of the bill and restrict the President's option to use military power only to suppress riotous assemblies and the actual obstruction of federal law enforcement officials and not to "prevent" these events from occurring as the original bill provided. But these concessions were not enough. By early February it had become clear to many that, under existing political circumstances, the Force bill stood no chance of passing. One congressman suspected that a tacit agreement may have been reached by the leaders of the Senate to debate the bill to the end of the session, but not to vote on it.[16]

If anything the administration was in even worse shape in the House of Representatives. Lacking effective spokesmen on its behalf, it suffered a humiliating setback when the House Judiciary Committee rejected Jackson's request to be able to use military force to enforce the laws in South Carolina. The House Judiciary report indicated that South Carolina's military preparations were essentially defensive, stressed the need for some kind of compromise, and urged a reduction of the tariff as the best way of settling the crisis. In advocating a policy of conciliation toward South Carolina, the report argued: "the interest in the question from which it has originated is not limited to a single state, but extends to an entire section of the country and, among the unhappy results of the application of force, there is reason to fear that from a controversy between the general government and a single state, it would extend to a conflict between the two great sections of our country, and it might terminate in the destruction of the Union itself."[17]

The vote in the House Judiciary Committee on the report was close: four to three. Those in favor of the decision to reject Jackson's request for increased discretion to use force were: Henry Daniel of Kentucky, Thomas F. Foster of

Georgia, William F. Gordon of Virginia, and Richard Coulter of Pennsylvania, the last named being a strong Van Buren partisan. On the other side were William Ellsworth of Connecticut, Samuel Beardsley of New York, and John Bell of Tennessee, the committee's chairman. The vote was probably not as close as it appeared, for the opposition was not especially inclined to support the President's cause and may have voted against the report because it gave such strong support to South Carolina and failed to condemn the doctrine of nullification. In fact, rumor had it that Beardsley had almost gone with the majority, and in his speech presenting the report to the House, Bell, who strongly favored immediate tariff reduction and was soon to break openly with Jackson on his banking policy, indicated that the minority "concurred in some of the sentiments expressed." Nor was there a serious effort in the House itself to repudiate the report. All told it was an embarrassing and serious setback for the President who desired a tough stand against the nullifiers. As one member of the House, South Carolina Unionist William Drayton, commented, "if one of our nullifiers had drawn the Report, he could, hardly, have succeeded better in exercising the sentiments of his party, than does this Report."[18]

In the following week the House delivered two more serious blows to the President's prestige. The first came on financial policy. Following his reelection, Jackson was eager to move further against the Second Bank of the United States. Shortly after he issued his Proclamation he wrote, "the hydra of corruption is only *scotched,* not dead" as a consequence of his veto and urged that it be subjected to a congressional investigation which would question its financial soundness. In this manner he hoped to head off any plans the Bank's supporters might have of trying to muster a two-thirds majority of Congress to override his veto. He also wanted Congress to authorize the sale of the government's stock in the Bank to facilitate the paying off of the national debt and to consent to the removal of the deposits.[19]

The President entrusted this mission to James K. Polk, who was a member of the Ways and Means Committee. Throughout December and much of January the committee was preoccupied with the Verplanck tariff and other appropriations measures. But Polk somehow managed to get through a bill to sell the Bank stock, and the committee reported it to the floor of the House. After the first reading a motion was made to reject it immediately. The motion carried and the result was called "a severe rebuke" to the President. One observer noted "it was literally kicked out of the House not suffering it to go to a second reading. There has never before been but one case when a bill reported by a respectable standing committee met with such a fate."[20]

The second blow was humiliating also. It came on the question of the appointment of an official printer to the House of Representatives. This was an extremely valuable contract and had traditionally gone to the editor of the Washington, D.C., newspaper most closely associated with the administration, in this case Blair's *Globe.* Blair definitely wanted it since he would have a great deal of difficulty if he had to survive simply on advertisements and subscriptions. Therefore, "Jackson was using all his influence with Congress in regard to this matter." But when the final vote was counted, after much political maneuvering, the contract went to Gales and Seaton's *National Intelligencer,* the National Republican paper that had supported John Quincy Adams for reelection in 1828 and Henry Clay in 1832 and that also strongly advocated the rechartering of the Second Bank of the United States.[21]

These two developments revealed the weakness of the President and his supporters in Congress. Whatever advantage and momentum Jackson had gained from his recent reelection triumph had been effectively vitiated by the reaction to his Proclamation and his eagerness to use military force against South Carolina. "We have a strange state of things," wrote an unhappy Senator Benton, "a President re-elected by four to one, and a P. a minority in both houses, and just defeated in two mortifying instances—the election of a printer and the rejection at 2nd reading of the bill to sell bank stock." The Missouri senator went on to argue that Jackson had made a mistake in requesting the Force Bill "which contains more, I think than the exigency requires, and enables the opposition, upon that *score,* to agitate the whole South, and perhaps to unite it."[22]

Jackson's defeat on the Bank stock question and the issue of the printer to the House of Representatives involved more than simply growing southern opposition to the President. It also involved an alliance between the nullifiers and their supporters and many National Republicans. That this coalition was indeed real is indicated by the fact that shortly after the House awarded its printing contract to Gales and Seaton, Blair was defeated by a similar alliance, this time in the Senate, which awarded its printing contract to Duff Green's pro-nullifier *United States Telegraph.*[23] Of course, granting printing contracts was one thing, resolving the dispute between the federal government and South Carolina was something else. How could an alliance between National Republicans and the nullifiers do this?

II

Congress's refusal to go along with Jackson's request for the Force bill played an important role in preventing the crisis from getting out of hand. It did not, however, in itself, resolve the crisis, it only postponed it. For despite the nullifiers' decision to delay the implementation of their Ordinance beyond February 1, they remained adamant in their opposition to the tariffs of 1828 and 1832. The major alternative to the use of force was to abandon the tariff, which is what the Democrat-sponsored Verplanck bill tried to do. By February, however, most knowledgeable observers recognized that the measure had no chance of passing. The political situation was too confused as a consequence of the Proclamation, and the Verplanck bill, too extreme in its abandonment of protection, for its supporters to overcome the resistance to it from pro-tariff interests within the Democratic party as well as the opposition of National Republicans and nullifiers.[24]

By early February it had become clear that the confrontation between South Carolina and the federal government could only be settled through some kind of major and all-encompassing compromise. Many believed that the only man capable of bringing this about was Henry Clay. He had played a central role in resolving the Missouri Crisis in 1820–21, and there were now frequent calls from his supporters to repeat that role and "Save the Union." Unlike his fellow luminaries, Calhoun, Webster, and Jackson, Clay had pretty much kept his own counsel during the early part of the nullification crisis. He had, as one commentator observed, "wrapped himself up in a mystery which no one could penetrate."[25]

To a certain extent this was because Clay was demoralized over the severe defeat he had suffered at the hands of Jackson in the presidential election of 1832. In fact, he was so discouraged that he even considered the possibility of resigning his seat in the United States Senate. But, in large part, he also was unhappy and uncomfortable with the alternatives being offered in the crisis by the President and the nullifiers. As a nationalist, and not very theoretically inclined, he did not believe in the compact theory of the Union, nullification, secession, or any of the other ideas of the various strains of states' rights thought. As a proponent of the American System he was sharply opposed to Jackson's stand on the Second Bank of the United States and a federal program of internal improvements, and unhappy about recent attempts to lower the tariff. But, unlike Webster, he did not endorse the principles of the Proclamation, viewing it as heavy handed and inflammatory "which, I apprehend will irritate instead of allaying any excited feeling." His sympathies, he said, lay with those who "would prevent civil war and save us from the danger of entrusting to Andrew Jackson large armies etc."[26]

Despite all this, Clay recognized that important advantages could be gained from becoming involved in the crisis at the right time and in the right manner. First of all, he had a real and long standing commitment to America as a nation, and if he could successfully intervene with some kind of viable compromise, he might in fact "save the Union." Second, as a traditional high tariff partisan he could accept neither the extremely low duties proposed by the administration-sponsored Verplanck bill or the nullifiers' claim that protection was unconstitutional. Although Clay was satisfied with the Tariff of 1832, describing it as " a law which . . . will be a very good measure of protection," he recognized that any peaceful resolution of the nullification crisis would require a reduction in duties. He hoped, however, to gain time for the manufacturing interests by moderating, as much as possible, the extent and speed with which protection might be abandoned. Finally, Clay and his supporters recognized that there were definite political benefits to be gained from playing a leading role in helping to resolve the crisis. It would reinforce his image as a man capable of mediating between the country's great conflicting interests and reestablish him as an effective political leader who, in the not too distant future, might once again become his party's standard bearer for the highest office in the land.[27]

If Clay should, in fact, opt to become involved directly in the crisis, there still remained the sticky question of how he would go about actually effecting a compromise. He recognized that the recent presidential election had weakened his political prestige and that he had many political enemies, so that "any plan that I might offer would be instantly opposed because I offered it."[28] Beyond that, the extremely complex and continually shifting political alliances that had emerged in Washington, D.C., during the winter of 1832–33 might make it impossible for Clay to put together a successful coalition. Working with Jackson was probably out of the question. The President had given no signal, even to his own party members, that he was interested in some kind of compromise with the nullifiers. Clay and Jackson also were bitter personal enemies as well as political ones. It dated at least as far back as Clay's open condemnation in Congress of Jackson's invasion of Florida in 1818, and it had been further exacerbated by the "bargain and corruption" charges coming out of the election of 1824 and the scurrilous nature of the 1828 campaign, especially the various attacks on the President's wife Rachel, for which Jackson believed Clay to be personally responsible.

Working with Webster would also be very difficult. Although ostensibly he and Clay were members of the same party, Webster's new found favor with the White House, at this time, seemed to offer him better chances for political advancement than any kind of compromise, for which Clay would get most of the credit. Moreover, Webster was adamant in his opposition to giving in to South Carolina on the question of protection. And, of course, there were his obvious constitutional differences with the nullifiers. Although Webster might have been unenthusiastic about the Force Bill and fearful of civil war, he had given no indication, at the time, of thinking in terms of a major compromise.

A strong source of support for some kind of compromise could come from the Van Buren Democrats. Throughout the winter of 1832–33 they had been groping for a political solution to the crisis. But the Proclamation and Webster's growing influence with the President left them confused, disorganized, and fearful. They were also essentially leaderless in Congress. Things might have been different if Van Buren had been in Washington, but he elected to remain in New York throughout the crisis. Besides, on most other issues the Van Burenites had been consistently counted among Clay's enemies, and no real ties existed that might be cultivated. Consequently, as a group, these congressional Democrats might support some kind of reasonable compromise, but they were not likely to be useful in actually forging one.

This left Calhoun and his allies. Clay had very real connections with this coherent and well-organized group. He and Calhoun had been political allies in the events leading up to the War of 1812 and in the establishment of the American System. They went their separate ways during the 1820s, but relations between the two remained cordial. Clay also was on particularly good terms with John Tyler, whose reelection to the Senate he had indicated to his Virginia supporters "would be far preferable to any person that could be sent."[29] An alliance between Clay and Calhoun made sense in that both were now vehemently opposed to Jackson and his policies. Although they may have differed among themselves on certain issues, it had become clear by 1832 that if they continued to go their separate ways neither of them could get their programs adopted or fulfill their political ambitions. Ever since his open breach with Calhoun in the spring of 1831, Jackson had claimed that such an alliance had actually taken place. There is, however, no evidence to substantiate this, at least before the nullification crisis began. But by the winter of 1832–33 there were some indications that the supporters and advisers of both Calhoun and Clay were trying to work something out.

Given the existing evidence it is not possible to date precisely or explain exactly how an alliance was formed between the two men. The earliest firm evidence indicates that, shortly after Jackson issued his Proclamation, Tyler "conversed freely with Clay upon the condition of public affairs and the true glory which he had it in his power now to acquire. Upon his friends I urged similar suggestions, and I begin to flatter myself that they *have* not been entirely disregarded." Tyler did not reveal what specifics, if any, were discussed. He did indicate, however, that on tariff reform the nullifiers were less interested in a sharp reduction of existing rates than they were in the eventual abandonment of the principle of protection. He criticized the Verplanck bill because "it lays a heavy hand on the manufacturer and in a great majority of instances annihilates him. Woolens reduced 60 to 80 pr. cent &c &c. This single measure would excite the bitterest feelings in the hearts of the eastern people. . . . Would mortal man believe it that the manufacturers are safer in the hands of those wicked S. Carolina nullifiers, than in those of the *non descripts;* and yet it is so." During this same period Calhoun openly and repeatedly asserted that he did not want to see the manufacturing interests suffer economically and was prepared to go along with some kind of compromise that provided for a slow but definite reduction of duties.[30]

Still Clay did not move right away. He carefully bided his time, and only after it was clear that the Verplanck bill stood absolutely no chance of passing and Jackson's request for congressional authority to use military force had, in effect, been rejected, did he announce in the Senate, on February 11, that he planned to introduce a bill for a compromise tariff on the following day. His decision to act won immediate praise from the nullifiers. "Mr. Clay, never, at any period of his life," observed Duff Green's *United States Telegraph,* "filled a more important position; and we are satisfied that the peculiar condition of parties is most propitious for a favorable adjustment of this vexed and distressing question."[31]

Clay's compromise tariff provided for a gradual reduction of duties over a nine-year period, at which time they would all be reduced to a uniform 20 percent rate. It used the tariff of 1832 as a base point. All duties in that measure which exceeded 20 percent were to be reduced by one-tenth of the excess at two-year intervals on September 30th of the years 1833, 1835, 1837, and 1838, one-half of the remaining excess in 1841, and the other half in 1842. The proposal also expanded the list of items on the free list and indicated that after 1842 duties were to be "laid for the purposes of raising such revenue as may be necessary to an economical administration of the government."[32]

Clay's proposal was similar to the Verplanck bill in that both ultimately reduced the tariff to the same level. But the latter did so much more quickly, arriving at a simple revenue producing level by 1836, while the former delayed it until 1842. The reason was so "that the manufacturers cannot complain of being taken by surprise, or not having opportunity to accommodate themselves to change." This allowed proponents of the measure to claim that it truly was a compromise, because while it did not repudiate protection it did eventually abandon it in a fashion so "as neither to compromise the dignity of the General Government, nor offend the pride of South Carolina." Additional virtues were claimed on its behalf. Clay's proposal, it was argued, secured legislative stability on the question of the tariff for the next decade. This allowed people to plan ahead. It also would free the country from a vacillating policy that had existed for several decades and that had alternately created manufacturing establishments and then destroyed them. Finally, and perhaps most importantly, it was acceptable to the nullifiers and other anti-tariff elements in the South.[33]

Although the nullifiers and their supporters reacted favorably to Clay's proposal, its passage was not ensured. The western wing of the National Republican party was inclined to go along with the measure, but easterners led by John Quincy Adams and especially Webster opposed it. Webster in particular had been uncompromising in his opposition to tariff reform during the past several months. Upon his instigation, resolutions had been adopted by the legislature of Massachusetts and endorsed by the governor of that state, warning of the "inexpediency, impolicy and ruinous tendency" of a reduction of duties at the present time. Similar resolves were adopted by the legislatures of Rhode Island, Vermont, and Pennsylvania and by various pro-protection special interest groups in New York.[34] Upon learning that some kind of alliance had been formed between Clay and Calhoun, Webster caustically commented "it is understood Mr. C[lay] will agree to almost anything, in order to save the question, save the Nullifiers & obtain the credit of *pacification*." As for himself, Webster wrote, "my wish is, *to do nothing, this session; &* my determination, which will not be shaken is, to do nothing, nor suffer anything to be done, on the subject of the Tariff, by a *Union of Extremes*."[35]

Many congressional Democrats were lukewarm to Clay's proposal. Although they favored some kind of compromise as a way of peacefully resolving the crisis, they wanted Van Buren and not the Kentucky senator to get the political benefits from it. Some were uncomfortable at the idea of deserting the President to support a measure sponsored by his two leading political enemies. Others felt the measure did not reduce the tariff to the 20 percent revenue level quickly enough. And many were fearful of the long range political implications of a Clay-Calhoun political alliance. The influence of this coalition had manifested itself in the recent fight over printer to the House of Representatives, and the selection of Gales and Seaton over Blair had, it was noted, "given so much offense to the administration, that the northern friends of the President had resolved to defeat an adjustment of the tariff."[36]

Nor did Jackson respond warmly to the measure. He continued to make clear through various private conversations his desire to see the Force bill adopted. At the same time he did little to encourage any kind of tariff reduction, even though he had asked for it in his fourth annual address. Jackson's feelings on the measure were probably summed up by comments in the *Globe* deriding the "coalition between the arch tariffite and the arch nullifier of the country," and asserting that Clay was mainly motivated by the desire "to secure himself the credit of reconciling the divided interest of the nation." A clear sign that the administration was unwilling to endorse Clay's compromise tariff came in the Senate, where the bill first came up for consideration, when Grundy and Forsyth, who were particularly closely allied with Jackson at the time, opposed it.[37]

III

How then did Clay orchestrate a compromise in February 1833? Skillful political maneuvering and determination on Clay's part as well as some luck played significant roles. Particularly important, Clay shrewdly recognized that while many congressional Democrats and the President himself were unenthusiastic, even opposed, to his compromise proposal, there also existed various counter pressures that could be effectively harnessed to make them allies, albeit reluctant ones.

Democrats in Congress were in a difficult bind. As long-standing political enemies of Clay and opponents of the American System, they were loathe to cooperate with the Kentucky senator and certainly did not want to see him again receive, as he had in 1820–21, the credit for having saved the Union in its time of crisis. But they had been unnerved by Jackson's Proclamation and Webster's sudden rise to influence with the President. Moreover, the party's southern wing was placing continuous and intense pressure on Van Buren's northern supporters for a downward revision of the tariff. They had tried to do this with Verplanck's bill, but they had failed in part because Clay and his followers did not support their efforts. From their point of view Clay's measure was the only alternative left to relieve an explosive situation. Rejecting the proposal would only further divide the party, and so many congressional Democrats were, however unhappily, forced to go along with it, "like," as one observer put it, "slaves chained to the oar; compelled to propel the boat, though they detest the task master."[38]

Dealing with Jackson was more difficult. Throughout the crisis the President had been thinking in terms of confrontation, not compromise. To be sure, his rhetoric tended to be way in advance of any overt actions, but this was not so much a deliberate policy as it was a tactical response to congressional and southern opposition to the use of force, and the widespread criticism of the Proclamation's nationalist assertions. To obtain popular approval for the use of force, he had to make sure the nullifiers committed the first act of violence so that he could claim the federal government was acting defensively and merely to enforce the laws. Though he had not been able to do this and had, as well, failed to get support from Congress for his policy toward South Carolina, there are no indications that the President was thinking in terms of compromise in mid-February 1833.

There is also no evidence that Jackson and Clay ever met or had any other form of contact with each other at any point during the crisis. Moreover, given the mutual dislike that each had for the other, it is highly improbable that such a meeting took place. On the other hand, Jackson always watched the proceedings of Congress closely and there can be no question but that he was aware of Clay and Calhoun's attempt to work out a compromise. He probably was unhappy with Clay's quick return to prominence so soon after his defeat in the election of 1832, but there was nothing he could do about it. He also was not happy with the Kentucky senator's tariff proposal since he believed it "cannot be satisfactory to the south," and all it really did was give "the nullifiers a pretext to clear their way for a disgraceful retreat." But what upset him the most was that in all the talk of compromise, no provision was made to adopt some kind of law to give the President the power to enforce the collection of the revenues. Jackson made this clear the day after Clay introduced his tariff bill and various rumors were afloat that the Force bill was to be permanently tabled. To Grundy, at this point his chief spokesman in the Senate, he wrote with considerable passion: "Surely you and all my friends will push that bill thro the Senate—this is due to the country—it is due to me, & the safety of this Union . . . lay *all* delicacy on this subject aside and compell every man's name to appear upon the journals that the nullifiers may *all* be distinguished from those who are in support of the laws, & the Union."[39]

Although the President did not participate directly in the formulation of the Compromise of 1833 the way Clay and Calhoun did, in order for it to work it would require his tacit and indirect approval. For one thing, Jackson was a major participant, if not *the* major participant in the crisis and his views simply could not be ignored. For another, if he vehemently opposed Clay's tariff proposal, he might be able to rally enough support to kill the measure; or failing to do that, to veto it. At this critical juncture, Clay appears to have wisely recognized that the President's views would have to be taken into account if he were going to formulate a viable compromise.

A decision was made to drop opposition to the Force Bill in the Senate. During the past month, Clay had done little to support the measure because he believed it to be precipitous and vengeful on Jackson's part, although he also recognized that if South Carolina engaged in overt action against the tariffs of 1828 and 1832 something would have to be done to uphold the authority of the federal government. The nullifiers, of course, vehemently opposed the Force Bill, and while it is by no means clear that they had enough support in the Senate to actually vote it down they had succeeded in dragging out the debate and indefinitely postponing its consideration. Under no circumstances could they vote for the Force Bill, even as part of some compromise, but they could abandon their obstructionist tactics against it.[40]

The final vote in the Senate on the Revenue Collection bill came on February 20. It passed 32 to 1. Only John Tyler of Virginia, independent and belligerent to the end, voted against it. All the other opponents of the bill did not vote. Among the southern senators this included: Calhoun and Stephen D. Miller of South Carolina, George M. Troup of Georgia, Willie P. Mangum and Bedford Brown of North Carolina, William R. King and Gabriel Moore of Alabama, and George Poindexter and Jonathan Black of Mississippi. Among southerners, those who voted for it included: Rives of Virginia, Forsyth of Georgia, Grundy and Hugh Lawson White of Tennessee, and Josiah S. Johnston and George A. Waggaman of Louisiana, a high tariff state at the time which had not even followed the rest of the South into the Jackson camp in 1828. Among the senators from outside the South who chose to absent themselves were: Samuel Smith of Maryland, Benton and Alexander Buckner of Missouri, and Clay and George M. Bibb of Kentucky.[41] Perhaps because he was embarrassed to find himself aligned with the nullifiers and other states' rights southerners and did not want to completely alienate his nationalist friends, and perhaps also because he was trying to maintain a middle of the road position, Clay, the very next day, announced in the Senate that he had not voted for reasons of poor health. He declared that had he not been absent he would have voted in favor of the bill as adopted. In this manner he managed to align himself, by his actions, with those who opposed the Force Bill, and by his declaration with those who supported it. He then turned his attention to his proposed tariff bill and urged that it, too, be adopted by the Senate at the present session.[42]

While this was occurring, important Democratic leaders both throughout the country and in Washington pressured Jackson to accept the fact that Clay was the only one who had the influence and ability to work out an acceptable settlement to the crisis. Still refusing to come to Washington and align himself with the administration, Van Buren wrote from New York urging the President to, in effect, endorse Clay's tariff proposal. He also stressed the need to reconcile the southern wing of the party and requested the President to abandon the military provisions of the enforcement bill. In similar fashion, both Ritchie's Richmond *Enquirer* and Isaac Hill's, *New Hampshire Patriot* openly declared in favor of tariff reduction and compromise and against the use of force.[43] And a number of Democratic congressmen indicated to the President that they wanted him to go along with the compromise. It was widely understood, according to one source, that the Senate's passage of the Force Bill was not in any sense an endorsement of Jackson's handling of the crisis, but "is confessedly passed merely for show, to vindicate the dignity of the government." Hugh Lawson White, one of the few southern senators to have voted for the Force Bill, later claimed, that at the time he directly informed the President, "I voted for the Force bill *as a decision merely that the Government had the power to execute its laws. I never intended it should operate or actually be put in force against my countrymen who happened to differ from me in opinion, and who are as honest and conscientious in their opinions as I am in mine.*"[44]

As the crisis wore on, Jackson found himself increasingly isolated from members of his own party and many of his closest political allies. When the President held a levee it was noted "but very few of the southern members of Congress attended." Although northern Democrats denounced nullification and stressed the need to preserve the Union, very few of them went out of their way to defend the President's policy toward South Carolina. Even Grundy's vigorous advocacy of the administration's cause, it was widely recognized, was to be explained mainly by his pending reelection and not from any conviction that it was the right thing to do.[45] Silas Wright, a frequent visitor to the White House, who had personal contact with the President after it had become clear that Congress had no intention of going along with his request for military power, described him as "a good deal harassed," and also noted "the anxiety of the President is intense." And John Coffee, who, in mid and late February was in almost daily contact with Jackson, wrote home describing Congress as made up of a "contemptible" and "corrupt" set of men. He also observed the situation in Washington "is far worse than I ever anticipated, and don't know how things will terminate—a large majority in Congress profess to be friendly to the President, but their acts do not accord with their professions. The Gen'l has a hard time of it, but he seems determined to persevere to the end; and I hope he will save the Union—but it is now to be seen here, that the *seeds* of Nullification is sown throughout all the southern country. . . ."[46]

At this point, Jackson really had no choice but to give in. Failure to do so would split the Democratic party, render him ineffective as a leader during his second term and, perhaps, bring on a civil war. By late February a much subdued Jackson had stopped making belligerent statements about how he intended to crush the nullifiers. Embarrassed, even humiliated, by the fact that the Force Bill had been adopted by the Senate only with the acquiescence of Clay and Calhoun, Jackson decided to go along with the Kentucky senator's attempt to formulate a workable compromise. The President's consent did not take the form of a public announcement, but came in a private "frank conversation" he held with Wright the day after the Senate passed the collection bill. At that time the New York Senator signified that he intended to vote for Clay's tariff bill, and was pleased to report "the President . . . thinks as I do upon the subject."[47]

Having convinced the administration and a significant number of congressional Democrats to support his proposal, Clay next turned his attention to garnering some support from the numerous advocates of protection in Congress. Webster and Adams and other New Englanders remained adamant in their opposition to the abandonment of the Tariff of 1832, but others were more pliant. Particularly important in this regard was John M. Clayton of Delaware, who in his freshman term as a United States senator had quickly established himself as an articulate advocate of the American System and a defender of the powers of the Supreme Court as well as a critic of nullification and a leader of the anti-administration forces. Coming from Delaware, he had close ties with E. I. du Pont, one of the most important industrialists of the early nineteenth century. If Clayton and the group he represented could be brought to favor the compromise tariff, Clay would have succeeded in effectively separating the Middle Atlantic manufacturing interests from those in New England. Clayton was inclined to do this, for he was much closer politically to Clay than he was to Webster, and he recognized that failure to lower the tariff, at the present session of Congress, would further unite the anti-tariff states and might even lead to "a southern convention—a thing infinitely more dangerous than nullification."[48]

But Clayton was not entirely happy with the compromise bill as proferred by Clay. Specifically, Clayton wanted the bill to provide that in 1842 a "home evaluation" would be substituted for a foreign evaluation as a basis on which duties were to be collected. This meant freight, insurance, and other shipping charges to specific ports would be added to the value of the goods on which the tariff was levied. It would, among other things, make it more difficult for shippers and importing merchants to present fraudulent invoices to customs officials. It would also have the effect of raising duties on imported goods. Clay bowed to Clayton's demands and on February 21 introduced an amendment providing for "home evaluation" to his compromise tariff bill. Calhoun immediately opposed it. But Clayton made it clear that the amendment was a *sine qua non* for his support of the compromise bill. Clayton also insisted that Calhoun and Stephen D. Miller, the two senators from South Carolina, both actually vote for the compromise Tariff of 1833 as well as the amendment, as an indication of their commitment to it, and not simply "allow" it to pass as they had done with the Force bill. There followed a long night of intense caucusing, during which Calhoun conceded to the Delaware senator's demands, for the very next day he reversed himself and indicated that while he regretted the amendment he would support and vote for it.[49]

Like Jackson, Calhoun did not have much choice but to go along with the compromise, even after the "home evaluation" provision was tacked on. Had he refused to give in to Clayton's demands, the compromise bill might have been permanently tabled. This would have left the nullifiers in the position of once again confronting Andrew Jackson. Although they had done well up to this point, it had been a harrowing and draining experience. Throughout the crisis, various accounts described Calhoun as "excessively uneasy or agitated," as well as extremely tense and harried.[50] He had good reason to be this way. For, while he was engaged in an intense and dangerous confrontation with a forceful and vengeful President, he also was trying to prevent the situation from getting out of hand in South Carolina. From the vantage point of nationalists, the administration, and other traditional states' rights thinkers, Calhoun was the most articulate and important advocate of nullification, but within the nullifier camp he had been, and continued to be, a moderate. While he was in Washington he had not only to deal with Jackson, but also to be concerned that back home in South Carolina some of the more radical nullifiers might act rashly and actually engage in the use of force. This would not only give the President the excuse he was looking for to take some kind of military action, but it would also put in jeopardy all the political gains that had been made in other parts of the South, in certain Jacksonian strongholds in the North, and in Congress as a result of the President's appearing the aggressor in the crisis.

Both Calhoun and Miller recognized the importance of achieving a compromise at this time. The day after Clay introduced his tariff in the Senate it was reported, "the South Carolina Senators appear like men from whose shoulders an intolerable load has been removed. Their air, countenances, their step and conversation are all lively, buoyant and expressive of life and satisfaction." Calhoun recognized that he had achieved about as much as he could have hoped for, at this time, from the confrontation between his state and the national government. Given Calhoun's consistently held view that he did not want to see any blood shed or the Union destroyed, he really had no choice but to capitulate to Clayton's demands and support the "home evaluation" amendment, for if the crisis were to continue indefinitely, anything might happen.[51]

Although Clay had brilliantly managed to bring about the passage of the Force Bill by the Senate and to put together an incongruous but broad enough coalition to ensure the eventual passage of his proposed tariff, he still had to deal with an important technical objection that had been raised about his quest for an all encompassing compromise to the nullification crisis. The United States Constitution specifically provided that all revenue measures had to originate in the House of Representatives. Clay, however, had introduced his tariff in the Senate. When the point was first raised by the opponents of the compromise tariff, Clay had brushed it aside, but the point was an important one and could not be totally ignored.[52]

Having consolidated his position in the Senate, Clay turned his attention to the House of Representatives. The situation there was very confused. In part this was because there were considerably more congressmen to deal with there than in the Senate, and in part because there were no strong leaders or dominant personality types through which one could work. But Clay was an experienced Washington politician who had been Speaker of the House of Representatives for many years before becoming a senator, and he knew how to deal with that body. In late February, Robert Letcher of Kentucky, an important Clay ally, moved to recommit the Verplanck bill, still being half-heartedly debated by the House, to the committee of the whole, and substitute in its entirety the compromise measure before the Senate. Attempts to block the maneuver were "in vain: it swept like a hurricane" through the House, garnering support from Democrats, southerners of all stripes, the nullifiers and their allies, and almost all of Clay's western supporters; only the representatives of the New England and Middle Atlantic manufacturing interests opposed it, and even a substantial minority of the latter group supported the new tariff proposal. It passed the House on February 26 by a vote of 119–85.[53]

This meant that the Senate had now adopted the Force Bill and the House the tariff. This accomplished, the advocates of the compromise in the Senate, as a way of meeting the constitutional objections to Clay's tariff proposal, successfully moved to substitute the House bill for the one before their own body, even though they were identical. A final problem remained. In the House, the opponents of the Force Bill, under the leadership of the unpredictable and volatile McDuffie, announced their intention to prevent its passage by continually calling for adjournment and insisting on roll call votes on their motions until the end of the session. The Senate responded by refusing to give its assent to the tariff until the House first passed the revenue collection bill, and an angered Jackson reportedly warned he would call the Congress into extra sessions if necessary to ensure the bill's passage. Clay supported these moves not only because it was necessary to save the compromise he had labored so hard to achieve, but also because, once the crisis had been resolved and the need and opportunity for Jackson to use the military no longer existed, he believed it was not a bad idea to have the Force Act on the books since it might dampen the disunionist sentiments of extremists like McDuffie and Hamilton.[54]

The Senate's threat not to adopt the compromise tariff effectively squelched the attempt to kill the Revenue Collection bill in the House. On March 1 at 1:00 a.m. the House passed the Force Bill 111 to 40. Among the opponents were a number of pro-administration southerners: William Archer, Joseph Chinn, Nathaniel H. Claiborne, and John Y. Mason of Virginia; Franklin E. Plummer of Mississippi; C. C. Clay and Samuel W. Mardis of Alabama, and Henry W. Connor and Thomas H. Hall of North Carolina. That same day the Senate by a 29 to 16 vote adopted the tariff.[55]

Almost immediately after it adopted the tariff and the revenue enforcement act, the House passed a third law. It appropriated, for a fixed period of time, the income derived from the sale of the public lands to the different states of the Union according to their population. The measure known as the distribution bill had been introduced earlier in the session by Clay. It was supported by protectionists and easterners who, often but not always, were the same people. The former wanted the tariff to become the exclusive source of revenue for the federal government, and by eliminating the main alternative source of federal income, the public domain, they believed they were keeping the door open for an eventual increase in import duties. The latter opposed western demands that the public lands be ceded to the particular states in which they were to be found, a demand that would take on increasing potency at the next Congress since the reapportionment of seats according to the 1830 census would then go into effect, substantially increasing western representation. Calhoun and the other nullifiers had consistently opposed distribution, but they were apparently forced to go along with it now as part of the deal for the compromise tariff. As Clayton bluntly put it, they had "to yield something to us who have saved them from infamy and blood."[56] This done, Henry Clay referred to the final adoption of "the Compromise bill [the tariff], the land bill and the Enforcing bill," all on March 1 as "perhaps the most important Congressional day that ever occurred."[57]

Jackson did not participate in the distribution part of the compromise. Although he had earlier advocated such a policy, he had entirely abandoned it by the time of his reelection, and had essentially adopted the western position in his recent and important fourth annual message. Opposed to the measure and fearful that a formal veto would probably be overridden, the President pocketed it after Congress adjourned.[58]

The final act of "the Compromise of 1833," occurred in Columbia, South Carolina, when the convention that had nullified the tariffs of 1828 and 1832 reassembled on March 11. A short time later, by an overwhelming vote, it rescinded its earlier Ordinance. Then, in a move that reflected the convention's self-confidence on having successfully foiled what one member referred to as "the barbarian fury" of Andrew Jackson, the reconvened assembly formally nullified the Force Act.[59]

The Nullification Crisis and Jacksonian Democracy

The nullification crisis certainly was not simply, and perhaps not even mainly, a struggle between the proponents of nationalism and states' rights. In a very fundamental way it also involved a struggle between advocates of different kinds of states' rights thought. It also was not an isolated, if dramatic, episode that took place during Andrew Jackson's presidency. Nor should it be viewed only as a precursor of what was to occur on a much broader and even more serious scale in 1860–61. Rather it was an integral event of the Jacksonian era that both reflected and had an enormous impact upon various ideological, constitutional, political, and even economic aspects of the 1820s and 1830s. The importance of the Bank War and the struggle over state banking and financial policy for understanding what was involved in Jacksonian Democracy has long been recognized by scholars.[1] Not so the nullification crisis. This is unfortunate, for while the confrontation between Jackson and South Carolina on the issue of nullification took place over a much shorter time span than the struggle over the rechartering of the Second Bank of the United States, the removal of the deposits, and the attempt to implement a hard money policy, it was a much more intense and volatile crisis, and it had equally far reaching consequences.

I

Andrew Jackson's attitude toward nullification is the necessary starting point for understanding the significance of the crisis. For, like almost everything else

178

during his two terms as President, it was how the Old Hero responded to a particular issue or development that determined the context in which that matter was to be handled and discussed, so powerful was his personality. Although sincerely committed to states' rights himself, Jackson was deeply hostile to Calhoun and South Carolina's version of the doctrine because it was a way of thwarting majority rule and because he believed the claim that secession was a legal right that could be peacefully exercised threatened the existence of the Union. Personal and political considerations also contributed to Jackson's dislike of Calhoun. These, however, were less a cause for his hostility to nullification than they were factors that determined the fierceness of his reaction to South Carolina's actions in the winter of 1832–33.

Jackson's official response to the Ordinances that declared the tariffs of 1828 and 1832 unconstitutional came on December 10, 1832, in a document that is known as the Nullification Proclamation, a powerful and cogently argued statement denying to any state the right to disobey a federal law and denouncing secession as treason. The Proclamation was also more than simply an attack upon the specific actions of South Carolina. Determined to assert the power of the national government and to march down to South Carolina to hang Calhoun and his co-conspirators for treasonous activities, Jackson, in the Proclamation, focused on nullification as a doctrine *"incompatible with the existence of the Union,"* rejected the compact theory of the origins of the Union, and generally downplayed the states' rights position he had taken throughout his first administration. Further, in the process of attacking the concept of secession, Jackson seemed now to be endorsing a nationalist theory of the origins of the Union: the nation came before the states and the national government was sovereign, and that sovereignty was indivisible because it was granted by the people and not the states.

So different in content was the Nullification Proclamation from anything the President had previously espoused that a number of people expressed disbelief when they first saw it. Moreover, it immediately won the warm endorsement of nationalists like John Quincy Adams, John Marshall, Joseph Story, and most important of all, Daniel Webster, while at the same time causing consternation among traditional states' rights advocates and loyal Jacksonians like Martin Van Buren, Thomas Hart Benton, and Thomas Ritchie. In fact, so confusing was the alignment on the reception of the Proclamation that many people during the next few months believed they were in the midst of a major political revolution. As a result ideological confusion and division spread through the Democratic party. Across the country Jacksonians were either uneasy with or were outright critical of the Proclamation, with especially vociferous opposition to the President during the crisis coming from the southern wing of the party.

Conventional wisdom would have it that South Carolina was completely isolated during the nullification crisis. This is true only in the narrow sense that no other state formally endorsed its controversial doctrines. This, however, is only part of the story. In addition to shrill criticism of the Proclamation, there was widespread opposition, an opposition that prevailed in the end, to Jack-

son's repeated threats to use force against South Carolina. The unwillingness
to going along with the use of force extended not only to traditional states'
rights Jacksonians, who favored an immediate and sharp reduction of the tariff
as the best way to compromise the crisis, but also to many nationalists and
high tariff supporters. Webster, the great spokesman for a nationalist interpretation of the origins of the Constitution and opponent of any kind of
tariff reduction in the face of South Carolina's threats, never explicitly endorsed the use of force during the crisis. Young Henry Barnard, who was to
become the famous educator, was traveling through Washington at the time. A
New Englander and a nationalist, he was very critical of South Carolina's
actions. Nonetheless, he expressed the belief "Jackson is the most abandoned
tyrant at heart on earth, and I am not sure if he gets the power, but what he
would seize upon any occasion to hang Hayne etc.-etc."[2] And Massachusetts
congressman Edward Everett, a hard-line opponent of nullification and a
strong protectionist who believed the nullifiers should be tried for treason,
nonetheless also indicated that after a fair trial and conviction they should be
pardoned. He separated himself from Jackson's more bloody-minded approach to the problem by observing, "I do not wish them to die, in the first
ditch nor the last; nor in fact in any ditch at all."[3] In many ways, by the end of
the crisis it was Jackson, not the nullifiers, who was isolated.

An unwillingness to authorize Jackson to use force and a fear of civil war
were the underlying concerns that dominated the country during the winter of
1832–33.[4] As a consequence it soon became clear to the President that he was
not going to get his own way during the nullification crisis, and he reluctantly
agreed to accept the compromise of 1833, upon the terms of which he was only
marginally influential.

The resolution of the crisis in this manner had important political ramifications. In several ways the crisis turned out to be a victory for the nullifiers, and
especially for Calhoun. South Carolina, as a consequence of the crisis, had
forced the federal government to lower the tariff, succeeded in nullifying the
Force Act, and was not required to recant on any aspect of its controversial
theory of the nature of the Union. Furthermore, in the years following the
crisis, the nullifiers effectively consolidated their political control of South
Carolina. They did this by accusing their Unionist opponents of having been
"disloyal" and by adopting a test oath in 1834 which required state militia
men and civil officeholders to, in essence, swear primary allegiance to the state
and only conditional allegiance to the federal government, something most
Unionists could not do in good conscience, and which, therefore, effectively
proscribed them from holding key offices. Calhoun, in particular, emerged
from the crisis in a strong political position. During the 1820s, despite his
national prominence, Calhoun had all kinds of political problems in his home
state: traditional states' rights types opposed him because of his earlier nationalism while the more extreme nullifiers distrusted him. But he proved
himself, at least where most of the nullifiers were concerned, by his successful
advocacy of South Carolina's cause during the crisis. As a result, in the years
after 1833 Calhoun was able to pursue his presidential ambitions, albeit un-

successfully, and various other stratagems, like trying to unite the South on the issue of slavery from an extremely secure political base, something he had lacked in the earlier part of his career.[5]

For Jackson, on the other hand, the nullification crisis, in a number of important ways, turned into a serious political setback, although the President made much of the fact that the Force Act had been adopted by what he called an "unparalleled majority" and claimed it vindicated his position during the crisis.[6] But this could not obscure the fact that, in the end, it was the President who had backed down or been defeated on the most important points. Jackson at the beginning of the crisis had been extremely combatative and argued openly and belligerently that the mere raising of troops on the part of a state to resist the laws of the federal government was rebellion and in itself justified the use of force on his part. Yet when it became clear that this point of view did not have either popular or congressional support, and that it frightened many people and was widely criticized as dangerous, the President formally requested Congress to authorize his using force should South Carolina actually oppose the authority of the federal government. Again, however, Jackson was re-buffed, and in the end the Force act was passed, mainly as a face-saving device for the President, only after it had become clear that the crisis had already been effectively resolved through the adoption of a tariff acceptable to the nullifiers. By the end of February 1833, although Jackson continued to denounce the doctrine of nullification, he had dropped all threats of military coercion and, like everybody else, had become eager to compromise the issue as quickly as possible in order to get out of an adverse political situation.

The resolution of the nullification crisis by compromise was an embarrassing defeat for Jackson in yet another sense: he had to abandon the Unionists of South Carolina. They had been among the President's most loyal supporters before and during the crisis, and Jackson had frequently assured them that he would protect not only their lives and property but their political rights as well. Throughout the crisis the *Globe* defended Jackson's harsh attitude toward the nullifiers in part on the grounds that they did not really represent the will of the people of South Carolina and that they had intimidated the Unionists and violated their constitutional rights. But when the end of the crisis left the nullifiers in total control of the state, and they proceeded to proscribe and reduce the political influence of the Unionists, Jackson, with the exception of singling out a few individuals for federal appointment, could do nothing about it. As a military commander Jackson had always demanded the utmost loyalty from his subordinates and in return was protective and generous with those who stood by him. By going along with compromise in 1833, the President, in practical terms, deserted the Unionists and left them to the mercy of their opponents.[7]

The nullification crisis also adversely affected the other crucial issue of Jackson's presidency: the Bank War. Here the timing of the controversy with South Carolina is especially important. It occurred shortly after Jackson's veto of the bill to recharter the Second Bank of the United States, and right after his successful conclusion of a reelection campaign in which the Bank had been the main issue, and the results of which Jackson viewed as a popular mandate for further action against the Bank. In fact, in the midst of the nullification crisis, one congressman noted, "I have it from a good source that the President rails against the bank as bitterly as against his nullifiers."[8] But whatever gains the President made against the Bank as a consequence of his reelection victory were vitiated by his highly controversial and divisive handling of the nullification crisis. Traditional states' rights Democrats were now wary of the administration, especially of giving it any more power, while many nullifiers and their sympathizers openly supported the Second Bank of the United States after 1833. To be sure, Biddle eventually overplayed his hand by trying to use the Bank's enormous economic power to create a financial crisis to intimidate the federal government and alienated his more responsible supporters, and he never did get the Bank a new national charter. But Jackson also had his share of defeats between 1833 and 1837 when it came to dealing with Congress on such issues as the removal of the deposits, the implementation of a hard money policy, and the adoption of legislation to regulate state banking activities.[9]

The nullification crisis hurt Jackson politically, for it helped create an uneasy but nonetheless real alliance between his two most powerful enemies: Clay and Calhoun. This was offset for a short while by Webster's support for the administration, but when it became clear that Democratic party stalwarts were opposed to giving him any position of leadership and Jackson returned to his attack on the national bank, the alliance collapsed and Webster rejoined the opposition. Moreover, the President's frequently expressed desire to use force during the winter of 1832–33 and to throw the country into civil war provided his enemies with a focal point for their criticism of the administration and buttressed their claims that Jackson was unfit to run the country. "Such are the consequences," it was averred, "of having a President of narrow understanding and violent passions, incapable of surveying consequences with the eye of a statesman, ever obeying the impulse of feeling. and ever taking counsel of his passions, of his hatreds or his favoritism." Long suspicious of Jackson's military background, aghast over his removal policy, and critical of the frequency of his vetoes, the President's critics argued that, like Julius Caesar, he would continually arrogate power to himself until he put an end to the republic. After 1833 the President's opponents complained constantly of the "reign of King Andrew I" and called themselves "Whigs" after the English party that had opposed monarchical authority in the eighteenth century. Fear of the President and the use to which he might put the powers of the executive office proved to be an effective rallying point for Jackson's enemies, regardless of how much they might differ among themselves on specific policy questions.[10]

I I

The nullification crisis also had significant constitutional ramifications. It was the single most important time in American history when the two different conceptions of states' rights—one democratic and committed to the idea of a perpetual union and the other providing a mechanism for the protection of minority interests and espousing secession as a constitutional right—confronted each other.

For their part, the nullifiers claimed that their doctrines flowed naturally and inexorably from the Jeffersonian heritage as manifested in the Kentucky and Virginia Resolutions, and they did their best to avoid any discussion of how their controversial doctrine might differ from the more traditional and democratic kind of states' rights. These differences were precisely what the traditional states' rights spokesmen, critical of nullification, stressed. Between 1828, when the doctrine of nullification was first announced in the *South Carolina Exposition and Protest,* and the beginning of the crisis in December 1832, these spokesmen, led by the likes of James Madison, Edward Livingston, Levi Woodbury, Martin Van Buren, Thomas Ritchie, William Cabell Rives, and Andrew Jackson, denied that any legitimate connection existed between nullification and states' rights. Then, in his zeal to crush the nullifiers and to preserve the Union, Jackson issued his famous Proclamation which tended to endorse a nationalist interpretation of the origins and nature of the Constitution, and which embarrassed most traditional states' rights advocates. Ideological and political confusion followed, after which the crisis was resolved through a political compromise that failed to provide answers to the complex constitutional questions that had been raised in the debate over the legitimacy of nullification.

The seemingly inconclusive outcome of the nullification crisis, especially where constitutional issues are involved, should not obscure the fact that it basically worked to the advantage of the nullifiers. Calhoun and his supporters may have made some concessions on the tariff in 1833, but they had not been forced to back down in any way on their controversial assertions about the relationship of nullification and states' rights. Moreover, during the nullification crisis Jackson and his followers failed to articulate adequately the difference between their own commitment to states' rights and what South Carolina advocated. Their most serious attempt to do this came in speeches by Grundy and especially Rives on the Force bill, but its significance was lost in the political maneuverings that dominated Congress during February of 1833. For their part, in their speeches, Calhoun and his followers ignored the issues raised by the traditional advocates of states' rights; instead they focused on the nationalists' interpretation of the nature of the Union as advocated by Daniel Webster, John Quincy Adams, and others. In other words, the inability of the Jackson administration to articulate its own constitutional position effectively during the crisis allowed Calhoun to polarize the debate in terms of a struggle between a nationalist and states' rights interpretation of the Constitution, and for South Carolina to emerge as the advocate of states' rights thought in general and not just a particular variety of the doctrine. The significance of this became clear to Chief Justice Marshall early on in the crisis. "Our people," he wrote, "will be inextricably entangled in the labryinth of their state right theories, and the feeble attachment they still retain for the union will be daily weakened. We have fallen on evil times."[11]

Immediately following the conclusion of the crisis, traditional states' righters urged the President to make use of his second inaugural address to clarify
the confusion on constitutional questions, and especially the role of the states
in the federal system of government, that had concerned so many Democrats in
recent months. Although the President obliged, the results were disappointing.
It was a very brief speech, and while it acknowledged the rights of the states it
did not contain a creed like his fourth annual message; moreover, it also
stressed the importance of maintaining the Union at all costs, thereby indicating the President was unwilling to recant on the principles of the Proclamation.
The fact of the matter is that Jackson emerged from the nullification crisis
extremely unhappy over the manner in which it had been settled. He was angry
over the failure of key Democrats to give him their unqualified support in the
confrontation with South Carolina, and was unwilling to admit that there was
any justice in the criticism of the Proclamation. He refused to discuss the
matter with Van Buren, and as for the extensive debate on the issue of states'
rights going on in the Old Dominion he is reported to have observed "what has
Virginia to do with this matter? It is no business of hers. And there is Tom
Ritchie talking about *state rights*. I have no patience to read *such stuff*. I fling
his paper against the wall."[12]

A major exception to the President's reluctance to discuss the nullification
crisis and its ramifications took place in an exchange of letters between him
and Nathaniel Macon. Macon, a former Speaker of the House of Representatives and a retired North Carolina senator was, like John Randolph, highly
regarded by Jackson and other important Democrats as a long-standing critic
of the nationalist tendencies of the American System.[13] A vigorous advocate of
states' rights, Macon had been openly critical of nullification and a strong
defender of most of Jackson's policies. But he did not like the Proclamation
and was openly critical of it. Specifically, he took issue with the President's
unwillingness to recognize South Carolina's claim that secession was a constitutional right. "Sovereign power," Macon asserted, "cannot commit treason or rebellion or be subject to the laws relating to either. . . . If South
Carolina would not permit the laws of the United States to be enforced within
her limits, she was out of the Union and ought to have been treated as a foreign
power." Jackson's strongly worded response to Macon indicated that the right
of secession continued to remain a central issue in his debate with the
nullifiers:

> In my opinion the admission of the right of secession is a virtual dissolution of the
> Union. . . . If the federal government and its laws are to be deprived of all authori-
> ty in a state by its mere declaration *that* it *secedes,* the union and all its attributes,
> depend upon the breath of every faction which may maintain a momentary ascen-
> dancy in any one state of the confederacy. To insist that secession is a reserved
> right, is to insist, that each state reserved the right to put an end to the government
> established for the benefit of all and that there are no common obligations among
> the states. I hold that the states expressly gave up the right to secede when they
> entered into the compact binding them in articles of "perpetual union" and more

especially when the present constitution was adopted to establish "a more perfect union" equally unlimited as to duration.[14]

Ironically, it was on the issue of secession, on which Jackson had such strong feelings, that South Carolina emerged triumphant from the nullification crisis. Prior to the espousal of the doctrine by the South Carolina nullifiers, most assertions of secession had taken the form of rhetorical flourishes, political ploys, and logical extensions of arguments not fully understood or thought out. Moreover, secession before 1828–1833 was not a doctrine that was associated with a particular interest group or section of the country. A number of the more vociferous New England opponents of the War of 1812 had spoken of it, but the moderates who controlled the Hartford Convention rejected the doctrine, and the entire movement was soon disgraced and lost in the nationalist fervor that swept the country after 1815. By the time of the nullification crisis most New Englanders were either nationalists or strong Union supporters. In the South, however, as a consequence of South Carolina's being able to more than hold its own in the constitutional debate with Jackson, the doctrine of secession gained both converts and respectability after 1833, and included many who were critical of nullification. The long-range implications of the linking up of secession with states' rights were clear to one particularly prescient congressman: "It is quite remarkable to witness the composure with which a dissolution of the Union is spoken of here—I think the present disturbances will be settled, or got over; but it seems to me that the sound feeling which the Union ever inspired, is irrevocably gone."[15] The doctrine of secession was asserted with great vigor and clarity during the nullification crisis; and since the Compromise of 1833 did not deal with it in any way, it came to play an increasingly important role in the political and ideological culture of the country during the second third of the nineteenth century.

On the other side of the political spectrum, those who argued that the Supreme Court of the United States should be the final arbiter of constitutional questions were also inadvertent beneficiaries of the various compromises that brought an end to the nullification crisis. This had been the nationalist position since the adoption of the United States Constitution in 1788; however, it was rejected by states' rights spokesmen, both traditionalists and nullifiers. Although the Supreme Court had declared part of a federal law unconstitutional in 1803 in *Marbury v. Madison,* the decision was in many ways very ambiguous. While the United States Supreme Court claimed for itself the right to oversee the Constitution, it did not claim that its power to do so was either exclusive or final. Moreover, the actual holding of the case worked to the advantage of the Republican administration, for the Court turned down the request of the disappointed Federalist appointees for a *writ of mandamus* ordering the secretary of state to hand over the commissions of several justices of the peace that had been signed by Federalist President John Adams, but which Thomas Jefferson refused to deliver. After the Civil War the decision in *Marbury v. Madison* took on enormous significance as triumphant nationalists pointed to it as an important first precedent in their successful drive to, in fact, make the Supreme Court the final arbiter in constitutional disputes, but at the time the decision was handed down it was considered, if anything, a defeat for the more belligerent members of the Federalist party and a conciliatory gesture on the part of the Supreme Court toward the new administration.[16]

This conciliatory gesture worked, for Jefferson and especially Madison successfully headed off attempts by radicals and states' rights Old Republicans to dismantle the federal judiciary. During the four administrations of Madison and his successor James Monroe, the Supreme Court handed down a series of important decisions that significantly tilted the distribution of powers between the states and the federal government in a nationalist direction. There was a strong reaction to this development during the 1820s, when states' rights advocates vigorously denied any claims that the Supreme Court should be viewed as the final arbiter of constitutional disputes, especially those involving the state and federal governments. Proponents of states' rights also sponsored various pieces of legislation and even amendments to the Constitution to circumscribe the Supreme Court's power but without much success, for at no time did these measures have the support of an incumbent President. Most critics of the Supreme Court supported Andrew Jackson for the presidency in 1828, and his election was a definite victory for the concept of states' rights over a strong and active national government. Despite this, Jackson did not go out of his way to seek a confrontation with the Supreme Court, at least not in the same way that he tended to with the issues of a federal program of internal improvements or the Bank. Still, the general states' rights thrust of most of his other policies made it highly likely that some kind of confrontation with the Supreme Court would eventually have to take place. The specific issue that emerged was the High Court's decision in *Worcester v. Georgia* that directly contradicted the President's Indian removal policy. An actual confrontation, however, was avoided at the last minute by the intervention of the nullification crisis, when ideological confusion and political expediency required both sides in that controversy—nationalists and traditional states' rights spokesmen—to work out a compromise.

This was an important development for the Supreme Court's long-term well being. For should an actual crisis have occurred, that is, should an attempt have been made to force Jackson's hand in the Worcester case, it is highly probable that he would have refused on the grounds that the President of the United States was not bound by the Court's decisions, as he had indicated in his Bank veto message when he rejected the argument that *McCulloch v. Maryland* had established the Bank's constitutionality. This would have exposed, for all to see, the Supreme Court's lack of political power and its dependency upon the other branches of the government to enforce its decisions. It also would have created a very important and dangerous precedent, for until this point no incumbent President had explicitly refused to uphold the Court's authority. It might even have so angered Jackson as to cause him to initiate, as many of his closest advisers favored, legislation or an amendment to the Constitution restricting the authority of the Supreme Court in cases dealing with federal-state relations.

The various political and ideological issues raised by the nullification crisis were the main cause for the compromise that took place on the *Worcester* decision. The compromise allowed the Court to emerge from the Jacksonian era relatively unscathed. This, of course, in no sense established what we today term judicial supremacy: the idea that the Supreme Court is the final arbiter of constitutional questions. But it was an important step in the long and arduous journey that the Court made during the *antebellum* period to emerge with its various powers and claims to powers virtually intact. The significance of this became clear after the Civil War, when with states' rights thought in general thoroughly discredited, the Supreme Court in fact as well as theory began to become the final arbiter in all constitutional matters.

III

In addition to having important political and constitutional results, the nullification crisis also sheds light on the separate but related questions of the meaning of Jacksonian Democracy and the emergence of slavery as a political issue during the 1830s.

The problem of the meaning of Jacksonian Democracy has been the source of much debate by scholars. In recent years there has been a definite tendency to reject, as totally wrong, the traditional view that saw the 1820s and 1830s as a period of democratic change and the rise of the common man in politics, especially small farmers and working men, who displaced an entrenched political and moneyed aristocracy. This is a mistake, for while the traditional view may be incomplete and imprecise, it contains useful insights and is not fundamentally wrong. It should not be discarded, but rather needs to be refined, corrected, and built upon.[17]

As seen by contemporaries of the period, the great political and constitutional question of the Jacksonian era, and not just simply of the nullification crisis, was the problem of determining what rights and remedies existed for a minority in a country that was becoming increasingly committed to the principle of majority rule. Alexis de Toqueville, who toured the United States from May 1831 to February 1832, eighteen months before the nullification crisis, and who went on to write one of the more perceptive commentaries ever written about American society and institutions, also saw this as one of the fundamental problems facing Americans, and he recognized as well the intricate connection that existed between majority rule and democracy in America. In his famous chapter "The Unlimited Power of the Majority" he observed:

> In my opinion the main evil of the present democratic institutions of the United States does not arise, as is often asserted in Europe, from their weakness, but from their irresistible strength. I am not so much alarmed at the excessive liberty which

reigns in the country as at the inadequate securities which one finds there against tyranny.

When an individual or a party is wronged in the United States, to whom can he apply for redress? If to public opinion, public opinion constitutes the majority; if to the legislature, it represents the majority and implicitly obeys it; if to the executive power, it is appointed by the majority and serves as a passive tool in its hands. The public force consists of the majority under arms; the jury is the majority invested with the right of hearing judicial cases; and in certain states even the judges are elected by the majority. However iniquitous or absurd the measure of which you complain, you must submit to it as well as you can.[18]

More than any other political figure in early nineteenth-century politics, Andrew Jackson built his political career on the belief that he represented the will of the people and was a forceful advocate of the importance of majority rule, especially after the election of 1824. Calhoun, on the other hand, starting in the late 1820s, spent much of his time articulating the need to define and defend the needs of minority interests in a republic (though he was shockingly indifferent to the problems of the South Carolina Unionists who had become a definite minority within their own state) as well as proposing numerous constitutional solutions to the problem. "The Government of the absolute majority," Calhoun asserted in the midst of the nullification crisis, "instead of the Government of the people, is but the Government of the strongest interests; and when not efficiently checked, is the most tyrannical and oppressive that can be devised. . . ."[19]

Only if one recognizes that the important issues of majority rule and minority rights were central to the dispute between Jackson and the nullifiers is it possible to understand why, despite the fact that many thought South Carolina had acted rashly in nullifying the tariffs of 1828 and 1832 and were suspicious of Calhoun, Hayne, and Hamilton because of their former nationalism, they were nonetheless sympathetic to the nullifiers' cause. It is not enough simply to argue that what united the critics of Jackson, especially in the South, was opposition to his high tariff policy or hostility to Van Buren's rise to prominence or fear of Old Hickory's propensity to resort to the use of force to deal with his enemies, although these were certainly real and important issues. To understand fully the opposition to Jacksonian Democracy, at perhaps its deepest level, it is necessary to recognize that the country was convulsed during the 1820s and 1830s by a series of pitched battles on the state level. Many of these involved the economic issues that arose from the Panic of 1819: the need to control banking activities and to regulate the granting of special privileges through the chartering of corporations, and to adjust generally to the rapidly changing economic conditions that swept the country after 1815.[20]

But just as importantly the same years saw a whole series of struggles over constitutional reform. Constitution-making was an important and bitterly fought-over issue in every new state that entered the Union between 1800 and 1840; Ohio (1803), Louisiana (1812), Indiana (1816), Mississippi (1817), Illinois (1818), Alabama (1819), Maine (1820), Missouri (1820), Arkansas (1836), and Michigan (1836). In the older states of the North in these same years—1800 to 1840—Connecticut (1818), New York (1821), Delaware (1831), and Pennsylvania (1838) wrote new constitutions, while Massachusetts held a convention to revise its constitution by means of amendments in 1820. Similarly, in the South, three states, Virginia (1830), Mississippi (1832), and Tennessee (1834) wrote new constitutions. A convention was held in Georgia in 1833, and in North Carolina in 1835 major changes were made in that state's fundamental law by means of an elaborate amendment. In Alabama, during the early 1830s, substantial pressure developed for the writing of a new constitution that was only partly diffused by an amendment altering the tenure of state judges from life to six years.[21]

Although the specific issues varied from state to state, they involved the elimination of property qualifications for officeholding and voting, demands for the popular election of governors, more equitible representation in the legislatures, and provisions for periodic reapportionment in accordance with population shifts, as well as the desire to elect rather than to appoint judges and county officials. On a more fundamental level the central struggle was the same in all the states: between those who wished to see their state governments become more immediately and directly responsible to majority rule and those who feared this tendency. Even among those opposed to nullification there existed the belief, as Madison put it, that "in republics, the great danger is, that the majority may not sufficiently respect the rights of the minority." Wilson Lumpkin, the governor of Georgia and former Calhoun ally, who deserted him because Jackson's Indian policy was so favorable to his state and because he disagreed with many of the assertions of the nullifiers, nonetheless recognized that by effectively linking states' rights with the important problem of how to protect the rights of a minority in a republic the nullifiers were dealing with a subject that in one form or another already was on the minds of a great many people. As Lumpkin put it: "The General Government must keep within its constitutional sphere. Exercise the specific powers granted by the states, and then stop. The moment *they* go further, the *consolidation* principle enters. The majority can do no wrong. The minority has no rights. Doctrine like this is despotism. . . ." No wonder then that many (but certainly not all) who were concerned about the tyranny of the majority ended up sympathetic to, if not in agreement with, the nullifiers. For example, John Quitman, who had been the leader of the forces in the Mississippi state constitutional convention that unsuccessfully tried to blunt the demands of democratic reformers in November 1832, essentially allied himself with the nullifiers on the grounds that "Carolina tho' she may be wrong has taken the field in our cause."[22]

IV

Although the struggle over constitutional reform took place in all sections of the Union, it took on an added dimension in the South, where there existed a definite tendency for those sections of a state with the heaviest slave populations to be opposed to making their constitutions more responsive to the majoritarian will, while it was mainly the small, non-slaveholding farmers of the South who were among Andrew Jackson's earliest and strongest supporters, that wanted these kinds of changes. Moreover, to a very high degree, the spokesmen of these high density slave areas proved to be the most vocal critics of Jackson's Proclamation and the leaders of the opposition to his attempt to use force against South Carolina.[23]

This raises the important question of the relationship of the slavery issue to politics during the Jacksonian era, an area in which the various claims of scholars are particularly confusing. There seems to be no question but that the institution of slavery was becoming more widespread and that attitudes toward it began to harden after 1815. But the relationship of this to political developments between 1815 and 1854 is murky. It has been argued that the tensions uncovered by the Missouri Compromise were the basis of Van Buren's alliance between the plain republicans of the North and the planters of the South.[24] But this avoids the fact that the commitment of Van Buren and his allies to states' rights can be dated to a period well before slavery became a national political issue. It also ignores the fact that Van Buren's chief ally in this alliance, Ritchie of Virginia, aligned himself with the anti-slavery forces in that state in the fight over constitutional reform in 1829–30. Nor does it take into account the findings of the most thorough student of the Missouri Compromise who argues that the event was of secondary importance when compared with the impact of the Panic of 1819 on popular attitudes. While the debate on the Missouri controversy was bitter, and revealing in many ways of people's attitudes on slavery, it does not seem to be particularly important for explaining political alignments in the twenty years that followed.[25]

It is a mistake to equate the reaction to the nationalism of the American System in the 1820s with the formation of a distinctive southern nationalism predicated upon the protection of slavery. The one did not flow logically, automatically, or naturally from the other. If anything, they were based on very different and in some ways even diametrically opposed political, constitutional and ideological assumptions.

It is also an oversimplification to claim, as some scholars have done, that the Jacksonians were proslavery.[26] Basically, Jackson and his followers viewed slavery as an unfortunate institution that they had inherited from a previous generation, and that they expected would eventually die out. "On principle," the Globe asserted, "slavery has no advocates North or South of the Potomac. The present generation finds the evil entailed on it. . . ." It predicted that God "will, no doubt in the course of time, relieve the American people of their share in the misfortune." Although the Jackson administration viewed the abolitionists as fanatics and was insensitive to the moral issues raised by the institution of slavery and indifferent to its impact on those who had been enslaved, it was also hostile to proslavery types who wished to make the defense of slavery a major political issue. To follow this course, the President and his closest advisers believed, would divide the Democratic party and take attention away from what was for them the more important issue of dismantling the American System and returning power to the state governments.[27]

Actually, the true proslavery position in the 1830s was that adopted by

Calhoun and his followers, and a number of other southern intellectuals like Thomas Cooper and Beverley Tucker. They abandoned the older Jeffersonian view of slavery as an inherited evil that eventually would be eliminated. Instead, they embraced the peculiar institution as a positive good that deserved to be defended from its critics. They also abandoned the older approach of avoiding, as much as possible, any discussion of the merits of slavery. On the contrary, they were prepared to defend the institution of slavery openly, and to make this defense an important political issue. Proslavery types strongly supported South Carolina during the nullification crisis, and many of them deserted the Democratic party to become Whigs in the 1830s.[28] Moreover, under the leadership of various proslavery advocates the defense of the peculiar institution emerged as a significant, although by no means the dominant, political issue in the 1830s.

The desire for an aggressive defense of slavery was shaped by the convergence of several important developments. First, there was the growing strength of the anti-slavery movement both in Europe and in the northern United States. Prior to 1830, abolitionism had been a small and ineffectual movement that drew its support mainly from Quakers and intellectuals. But beginning in the late 1820s and early 1830s it became a major force in England, and culminated in 1833 with the abolition of slavery in Britain's Carribean colonies. These feelings carried over to the United States where, under the leadership of William Lloyd Garrison and Theodore Dwight Weld, American abolitionists began to have a major impact on public opinion. The aggressive and uncompromising denunciation of slavery by northern abolitionists on moral and humanitarian grounds concerned and angered many southerners. Despite the assurances of northern politicians that the great majority of their constituents were unsympathetic to the abolitionists, a growing number of southerners, it is clear, were unconvinced. This worked to the nullifiers' advantage. As one Virginian put it: "altho' I am for the *Union* & no *Nullifier,* yet my southern feelings & prejudice are so strong, that I know I should hate to see a Southern man vanquished by a northern one—I'm for the 'Niggers' you know & the East are not."[29] Another critic of the abolitionists revealed the strong emotions that criticism of slavery could evoke among some southerners:

> they have dared to interfere in the most dangerous and delicate relations which can possibly subsist, to demand universal emancipation, even to appeal to the "physical force" of the blacks, as a means of coercing it, to call upon those blacks to right themselves, and to expose the throats of the women and children of a large portion of their country to the knife of the rebel slave. . . . They have done and are doing more to alienate the south from their northern brethren, than the tariff or any or all political causes, that we complain about.[30]

During the 1820s and early 1830s there also was considerable hostility to slavery from within the South. A few Quaker abolitionist types in Virginia, North Carolina, and eastern Tennessee opposed slavery on moral grounds. Others argued the institution was a burden on whites as well as blacks, having a pernicious effect on southern economic and social development. "Our black population," one North Carolina congressman pointed out, "will hang like a mill stone about our necks and render our exertions, even in a good cause, comparatively ineffectual."[31] Chief Justice John Marshall agreed with those who claimed "that nothing portends more calamity & mischief to the southern states than their slave population," and he could not understand why so many in the South "cherish the evil and . . . view with immovable prejudice & dislike everything which may tend to diminish it."[32]

Perhaps the most important source of opposition to slavery within the South during the 1820s and 1830s came from those who, while essentially hostile to the Negro, did not own any slaves themselves, or at best only a very few, and complained about the special advantages and powers the peculiar institution endowed upon the slaveholder. Most slaves in the Old South were held by a minority of whites. This was true not only of the upper and older parts of the South, but also of the lower and more recently settled areas of the South, with the possible exception of South Carolina. During the 1820s and early 1830s there were relatively few slaveholders in northern, central, and western Georgia, northern Alabama with the exception of the Tennessee Valley, and eastern and northern Mississippi. Moreover, even with the further spread of the cotton culture during the prosperous 1830s, which saw an increase in the number of slaves, the relative number of slaveholders, if anything, tended to decline until the Civil War.[33]

Opposition to slavery, on the state level in the South during the 1820s and 1830s, manifested itself in various ways. Sometimes it took the form of direct criticism as in the debates that took place in the Virginia legislature in 1831–32 following Nat Turner's rebellion. Usually it was more indirect. Many non-slaveholding whites simply emigrated from the South. There were also attempts to restrict the growth of the number of blacks by colonizing free Negroes and by preventing the introduction of any new slaves into a state by means of the domestic slave trade. There also was much criticism of the use, in the older parts of the South, of the "federal ratio" as a basis for representation in state legislatures. By this method, following the provision in the United States Constitution, five slaves were counted as the equivalent of three whites for the purpose of apportioning seats. Since, of course, slaves were not allowed to vote, this served mainly to give their owners a disproportionate voice in the selection of members of the state legislature. The attempt to establish a white only basis for representation was a particularly important issue in the movements for constitutional reform in Georgia, North Carolina, Virginia, and Maryland.[34]

Whatever else may have motivated him, Calhoun, earlier and better than any of the other major political figures of his day, recognized that planter insecurity over the future of slavery could be put to political use. Having jettisoned his earlier nationalism and having just lost an important and bitter intraparty struggle to Van Buren, but retaining, nonetheless, his presidential ambitions, Calhoun in the early 1830s was eager to form a new kind of political alliance through which he could further his career. In September of 1830 he made the link explicit:

> I consider the tariff act as the occasion, rather than the real cause of the present unhappy state of things. The truth can no longer be disguised, that the peculiar domestick institution of the Southern States and the consequent direction which that and her soil and climate have given to her industry, has placed them in regard to taxation and appropriations in opposite relation to the majority of the Union, against the danger of which, if there be no protective power in the reserved rights of the states they must in the end be forced to rebel, or, submit it to have their paramount interests sacrificed, their domestick institutions subordinated by Colonization and other schemes, and themselves and children reduced to wretchedness. Thus situated, the denial of the right of the State to interpose constitutionally in the last resort, more alarms the thinking, than all the other causes; and however strange it may appear, the more universally the state is condemned, and her right denied, the more resolute she is to assert her constitutional powers lest the neglect to assert should be considered a practical abandonment of them, under such circumstances.[35]

Calhoun and the nullifiers were not the first southerners to link slavery with states' rights. At various points in their careers, John Taylor, John Randolph, and Nathaniel Macon had warned that giving too much power to the federal government, especially on such an open-ended issue as internal improvements, could ultimately provide it with the power to emancipate slaves against their owners' wishes. But for the most part these arguments tended to take the form of ad hoc defensive responses to appeals for increasing the power of the federal government, and logical extensions of other arguments. Old Republicans never made the defense of slavery a central political concern the way Calhoun and his followers began to do after 1833. Further, people like Randolph and Macon were strong supporters of Jackson (except on the Proclamation), and this included the President's hostility to Calhoun and even his stress on the importance of the majoritarian principle. It was the advocates of nullification and not the Old Republicans who first effectively merged the concern for minority rights and the defense of slavery with states' rights. As one writer argued:

> If a state has no right to *interpose* and protect its citizens against unjust and oppressive laws . . . what security have the people of the south for their liberty and property? We are in the minority in Congress, and must forever continue so. We cannot control Congress. Every member from the South may hang together, and vote against their oppressive measures, and yet they cannot stop them, for the reason that they are in a minority. Let us suppose a case, and it is by no means an improbable one. Suppose the Congress should pass an act, declaring that all the *slaves* should be set *free*. We could not prevent this by our votes in Congress; for there the non-slaveholding states have two to one against us. No! We would have either to submit to this unjust or unconstitutional law, or resort to state *interposition*.[36]

Concern over the future of slavery combined with a recognition that the slave-holding states were going to be in the minority for the foreseeable future to create a nascent southern nationalism, at least among some people. Predicated upon the belief that the South was different from the rest of the country and fueled by various free vs. slave state tensions, it stressed the need for southerners to stick together. Most southerners in the 1820s and 1830s did not think in these terms. But for those southerners and slaveholders who did, and they were an influential and growing minority, South Carolina's actions attracted a sympathetic response, even from those who did not accept the concept of state interposition. Alexander Barrow, a Louisiana planter, expressed the feelings of many when he wrote:

> I am no nullifier . . . but all my sympathies are with theirs; and as the nullifiers are contending against laws which are unconstitutional, unjust, oppressive, and ruinous to the South, I will never consent to see them put down by military force, and before I would take part in a crusade by the Yankees to put South Carolina to the sword, I would be hung for treason.[37]

The Jacksonians, on the other hand, even those from slave states, did not think in sectional terms or of the South becoming a conscious minority. Their response to the nullification crisis was straightforward and directed almost exclusively to the specific issues that had been raised: the constitutionality of a protective tariff, the right of a single state to declare an act of the federal government unconstitutional, the relationship of nullification to earlier states' rights assertions, and the need to preserve the Union. Only at the end of the crisis, when the divisions in the South became clear, and they started to assess the ramifications of what had taken place, did the Jacksonians begin to perceive that the slavery question had indeed been very much involved. When the compromise that effectively ended the crisis was being adopted by Congress, one of its members, an administration supporter from New York observed, "But there is no *peace*. The South will suffer and still rave. And we must go over to the Negro question. That is the rock on which the ship Union will split."[38] The President himself did not explicitly make the connection between slavery and nullification until April 1833, when he noted that despite the fact that "nullification is dead . . . the South intend to blow up a storm on the subject of the slave question."[39] And by June it was widely recognized, as one Cincinnati public figure wrote, "that the Southern men have determined upon a separation. That as the tariff no longer affords them an apology they have taken up the slave question, and broadly and boldly avow their belief, that the northern and western men are currently carrying on public measures, with the ultimate object of depriving them of their property."[40]

V

If the nullification crisis in particular and politics in general below the Mason-Dixon line during the 1820s and 1830s reveal anything about the antebellum

South, it is that the section was deeply split on the related questions of democratic change and slavery. On one side were those who enthusiastically and quite early supported Jackson and who saw his advocacy of decentralization and states' rights as a way of making government in general more responsive to the people, a point of view that found its strongest support in the small farmer, non-slaveholding, and relatively backward and less commercial areas of the South. On the other side were those who only reluctantly supported Jackson in 1828, as the only viable alternative to the nationalism of John Quincy Adams. It consisted of a growing number of planters and slaveholders who were becoming, for a variety of reasons, increasingly concerned about their political hegemony and the future of their peculiar institution. While not all slaveholders necessarily thought this way, it was a concern that linked the nullifiers of South Carolina with their allies in the rest of the South. Even though this group represented only a minority of southerners, perhaps even only a minority of slaveholders, it was a very important minority. influential well beyond its numbers. Its members were extremely well placed. They were governors, and they served in state legislatures and in both houses of Congress. Energetic, articulate, and determined to make the defense of slavery a central political issue, they became an increasingly significant political force as the 1830s wore on, particularly on the Texas question, the abolitionist use of the mails, and the "gag rule" adopted in 1836. They also helped deny Richard M. Johnson the vice-presidential nomination in 1840.

While the pro-slavery interests were a growing and dynamic minority, the proponents of the more traditional form of states' rights were in relative decline, undercut by the profound social and economic changes that affected American society in the years following 1815. The United States at the time the Constitution was adopted in 1788 was above anything else a rural society in which many, perhaps even a majority, of the people lived in areas far from cities and other commercial centers and lacked access to inexpensive forms of transportation. These people were self-sufficient farmers who at best had only sporadic and irregular contact with the marketplace. Most of them tended to be uneducated, provincial, and unprogressive. They also tended to be democratic and egalitarian, at least where white Protestant males were concerned. These people had a deep mistrust of government, often thinking of it in Old World terms of corruption and class rule. As Van Buren put it "Many of them had so vivid a recollection of cruelties practiced upon their fathers [the European experience], and had themselves seen and felt so much of the tyranny of the Mother Country [the Revolution], as to destroy all hope on their part that political power could be vested in remote hands, without the certainty of its being abused."[41]

Further, it made sense for these people, North and South, living in what was essentially a non-commercial economy to favor a weak, inactive, and frugal government which would leave them alone and which would not engage in grandiose social and economic programs that would cost a great deal of money. Recognizing that some kind of authority was "a necessary evil" they believed power should be placed in the hands of local officials who could be closely watched. Deeply suspicious of a strong, active, and distant central government, the beliefs and feelings of these people were summed up in such aphorisms as "that government is best, which governs least," and "the world is too much governed." From this, of course, it followed naturally that on the question of the distribution of power between the states and the federal government, they wanted most of the power to be placed in the hands of the states. States' rights had its origins in the way the separate colonies developed in the seventeenth and eighteenth centuries, and the experiences of the American Revolution reinforced this hostility to a strong central government. But it was the existing social and economic conditions of the United States in the late eighteenth and early nineteenth centuries that made the belief in decentralization and localism socially realistic and popular for so many people.

These social and economic conditions underwent abrupt change after 1815. Foreign demand for America's agricultural products, the growth of a national economy, and innovations to lessen the cost of transporting goods to market all combined to entice increasing numbers of Americans into the market economy. As the desire to make money spread throughout the nation, people became increasingly concerned with what government could do to help them get ahead. Americans did not abandon their faith in democracy, but in their pursuit of progress they became increasingly nationalist in outlook. Late in the eighteenth century, nationalism and democracy tended to be antagonistic beliefs; by the 1830s they had become compatible.

Also, by the 1830s the static and simple agrarian society of the early republic was rapidly being replaced by a more complex, progressive, and interconnected one. This meant the social and economic realities that had once made states' rights an important part of their value system no longer existed for many people. During the 1820s, as the country writhed through the chaos and dislocation brought on by the Panic of 1819, and as John Quincy Adams continued to assert the nationalist values of the American System, the agrarian and states' rights ideal proved to be a reassuring and politically effective rallying cry. But once the Jacksonians were in power—and Jackson and those closest to him were the first group of an agrarian persuasion ever to hold the reins of power on the national level—the limitations of their weak government attitudes became apparent. For one thing, it was based on the assumption that the central government would always be controlled by special interests that would use it for their own ends. But Jackson's victory in 1828 and his reelection in 1832 had demonstrated that it could be controlled and made responsible to the will of the people. For another, by viewing the government's role in simply negative terms it ruled out the possibility of the national government's actively working to defend the rights of the people as it was beginning to do in its assault on the Second Bank of the United States and its attempt to implement a hard money policy.

It is doubtful that the Jacksonians ever fully comprehended the extent to which the economic and social changes of the previous two decades had rendered many of their ideas about society and politics obsolete. Nevertheless, the Jacksonians did accommodate themselves to these changes, although more out of instinct than in a fully understanding way. Perhaps it was for this reason that despite his belief in weak government Jackson proved to be one of the strongest Chief Executives in American history. Perhaps, also, it was for this reason that the one real time in American history when the two different views of states' rights confronted each other it was the agrarian version that faltered and became confused since the social realities that at one time had made its appeal so compelling for many people no longer prevailed.

The nullifiers and those who sympathized with their aims, if not always with their methods, did not share the anti-governmental and anti-commercial biases of the traditional agrarian states' rights spokesmen. In recent years slaveholders have been portrayed as a pre-bourgeois ruling class, committed to a paternalistic and anti-commercial ideology that distinguished them from the men of the North, where the ethos of capitalism had become increasingly dominant. To be sure, some intellectuals in the development of the proslavery argument denigrated the materialism of the North, and some planters to be found in the older and economically declining areas of the South that had been bypassed by the developing economy opposed the further commercialization of the country and denounced the growing influence of the cash nexus.[42] Other southerners had mixed feelings, as did many in the North, about the economic changes taking place. They denounced the pursuit of material well being that engaged so much of the country at the same time that they partici-pated in it. Most southerners, and especially most slaveholders, however, were dominated by the values of the marketplace. They actively and willingly en-gaged in the money making process: raising crops for market, speculating in land ventures, borrowing and lending money on credit, buying and selling slaves, and investing in internal improvement projects, banks, and other finan-cial institutions. In brief, most southerners participated as fully as did norther-ners in the emerging market culture of the second third of the nineteenth century.[43]

The differences in the social and economic backgrounds of traditional states' rights supporters and the advocates of state interposition is reflected in their attitudes toward the other great issue of Jackson's presidency: the Bank War. Traditional states' rights partisans, without much wavering, warmly endorsed the Bank veto and supported the President's policy of removing the deposits as well as his desire to move in a hard money direction. Although nullifier attitudes toward the Second Bank of the United States were more complex, and at times inconsistent, they were over the long run essentially pro-Bank. Before his open break with Jackson in 1832, Calhoun's closest allies, led by Ingham and McDuffie, were among the Bank's strongest advocates in the Democratic party. Most nullifiers, led by Calhoun and Hayne, with the excep-tion of McDuffie, chose to remain neutral in the fight over rechartering in 1832. In large part this was because they were upset that the Bank's spokesmen in Charleston had sided with the Unionists in opposing nullification; in part also it was because the leading South Carolina nullifiers did not want to further antagonize President Jackson in the spring and early summer of 1832 when they still had hopes he would repudiate protection. But by February of

1833, most nullifiers were firmly on the side of the Bank and played an important role in the pro-Bank coalition that fought the President throughout his second administration.[44]

The difference in the social and economic backgrounds of the traditional states' rights advocates and the nullifiers also helps explain the antithetical ways in which they used the doctrine. Traditional states' rights proponents wanted a weak, inactive, and frugal government that would require few taxes and basically would leave them alone. The nullifiers, on the other hand, had a strong commercial outlook. Their involvement in the market economy had made them sensitive to the benefits of governmental activism. Consequently, starting in the 1830s, they used the concept of states' rights not simply as a way of denying the authority of the federal government, but also as a way of getting the federal government to protect and even endorse the institution of slavery, particularly on the question of its expansion into the territories and on matters involving comity. In the years leading up to the Civil War the nullifiers and their proslavery allies used the doctrine of states' rights and state sovereignty in such a way as to try to expand the powers of the federal government so that it could more effectively protect the peculiar institution. And this, in turn, laid the groundwork for the charge that the South was an aggressive slavocracy, an argument that was to play an extremely important role in galvanizing anti-southern feeling in the North during the 1850s.[45]

In short, in certain very important ways the nullification crisis marked the beginning of a new era. For a definite result of the crisis was the emergence of a forceful and determined pro-slavery interest in politics, better organized and more articulate than any other group that had risen to the defense of the peculiar institution. There are strong constitutional and ideological ties between the nullifiers and their supporters in 1832–33 and the fireeaters of 1860–61 since both groups advocated states' rights as a device to protect the interests of minorities. More so than any other event that occurred in the half-century or so following the adoption of the United States Constitution, the nullification crisis created the concepts and some of the political conditions that eventually led to the Civil War.

NOTES

Preface

1. Bray Hammond, *Banks and Politics in America from the Revolution to the Civil War* (Princeton, 1957); Richard Hofstadter, *The American Political Tradition: And the Men Who Made It* (New York, 1948), 56–85.

2. Richard P. McCormick, *The Second American Party System: Party Formation in the Jacksonian Era* (Chapel Hill, 1966); Edward Pessen, *Jacksonian America: Society Personality and Politics* (Homewood, 1978).

3. Lee Benson, *The Concept of Jacksonian Democracy: New York as a Test Case* (Princeton, 1961)Ronald P. Formisano, *The Birth of Mass Political Parties: Michigan, 1827–1860* (Princeton, 1971).

4. Important exceptions to this criticism are: Marvin Meyers, *The Jacksonian Persuasion: Politics and Belief* (Stanford, 1957); John William Ward, *Andrew Jackson: Symbol for an Age* (New York, 1955); James R. Sharp, *Jacksonians versus the Banks: Politics in the States After the Panic of 1837* (New York, 1970); Harry L. Watson, *Jacksonian Politics and Community Conflict: The Emergence of the Second American Party System in Cumberland County North Carolina* (Baton Rouge, 1981); Daniel Feller, *The Public Lands in Jacksonian Politics* (Madison, 1984).

5. Frederic Bancroft, *Calhoun and the South Carolina Nullification Movement* (Baltimore, 1928); Chauncey Boucher, *The Nullification Controversy in South Carolina* (Chicago, 1916); William W. Freehling, *Prelude to Civil War: The Nullification Movement in South Carolina, 1816–1836* (New York, 1966); David Franklin Houston, *A Critical Study of Nullification in South Carolina* (New York, 1896).

1   An Ambiguous Heritage: States' Rights in America, 1776–1828

1. For much that follows both in this chapter and in the entire book I am particularly indebted to: Merrill D. Peterson, *The Jefferson Image in the American Mind* (New York, 1960), 36–66; Charles Sellers (ed.), *Andrew Jackson, Nullification, and the State-Rights Tradition* (Chicago, 1963); Andrew C. McLaughlin, "Social Compact and Constitutional Construction," *American Historical Review*, V (1 April 1900), 467–90; Arthur M. Schlesinger, Jr., *The Age of Jackson* (Boston, 1945), 510–18. For different versions from those offered above of what was involved in the states' rights tradition and in Andrew Jackson's handling of the nullification crisis, see: Arthur Schlesinger, "The State Rights Fetish," *New Viewpoints in American History* (New York, 1922), 220–44; Charles A. Beard, "The Constitution and States' Rights," *Jefferson, Corporations and the Constitution* (Washington, D.C., 1936), 61–84; Edward Payson Powell, *Nullification and Secession in the United States* (New York, 1897); James J. Kilpatrick, *The Sovereign States* (Chicago, 1957); Major Wilson, "Andrew Jackson: The Great Compromiser," *Tennessee Historical Quarterly*, XXVI (Spring 1967), 64–78; Wilson, "'Liberty and Union': An Analysis of Three Concepts Involved in the Nullification Controversy," *Journal of Southern History*, XXXIII (Aug. 1967), 331–55; Wilson, *Space, Time and Freedom* (Westport, Conn., 1974), 73–93; Richard B. Latner, "The Nullification Crisis and Republican Subversion," *Journal of Southern History*, XLIII (Feb. 1977), 19–38.

2. John Adams to Hezekiah Niles, 13 Feb. 1818, Charles Francis Adams (ed.), *The Work of John Adams* (10 vols., Boston, 1850–56), X, 283.

3. For example see: John Stokes Adams (ed.), *An Autobiographical Sketch by John Marshall* (Ann Arbor, 1937), 9–10.

4. Thomas Jefferson, *A Summary View of the Rights of British America* . . . (Williamsburg, 1774); James Wilson, *Considerations on the Nature and the Extent of the Legislative Authority of the British Parliament* (Philadelphia, 1774); Daniel Leonard and John Adams, *Novanglus and Massachusettnsis; or Political Essays Published in the Years 1774 and 1775* . . . (Boston, 1819); Alexander Hamilton, *The Farmer Refuted* . . . (New York, 1775). See also: Andrew C. McLaughlin, "The Background of American Federalism," *American Political Science Review*, 12 (May 1918), 215–40, and *Foundations of American Constitutionalism* (New York, 1932), 129–56.

5. Bernard Bailyn, *The Ideological Origins of the American Revolution* (Cambridge, 1967), 55–93.

6. For various versions of the drafting of the Articles of Confederation, see: Merrill Jensen, *Articles of Confederation: An Interpretation of the Social-Constitutional History of the American Revolution* (Madison, 1940 and 1963); H. James Henderson, *Party Politics in the Continental Congress* (New York, 1974); Jack N. Rakove, *The Beginnings of National Politics* (New York, 1979).

7. Merrill Jensen, "Democracy and the American Revolution," *Huntington Library Quarterly*, XX (Aug. 1957), 312–41; Elisha P. Douglass, *Rebels and Democrats* (Chapel Hill, 1955), 10–33; Richard E. Ellis, *The Jeffersonian Crisis: Courts and Politics in the Young Republic* (New York 1971), 250–53.

8. Jackson T. Main, *The Anti-Federalists, Critics of the Constitution, 1781–1788* (Chapel Hill, 1961) and *Political Parties Before the Constitution* (Chapel Hill, 1973); Lee Benson, *Turner and Beard* (Glencoe, 1960), 214–38; Van Beck Hall, *Politics Without Parties: Massachusetts 1780–1791* (Pittsburgh, 1972); Ellis, *The Jeffersonian Crisis*, 256–59; Norman K. Risjord, *Chesapeake Politics, 1781–1800* (New York, 1978).

9. Gordon S. Wood, *Creation of the American Republic, 1776–1787* (Chapel Hill,

1969), 391–467; Robert A. East "The Massachusetts Conservatives in the Critical Period," Richard B. Morris (ed.), *The Era of the American Revolution* (New York, 1939), 349–91; Jerome J. Nadelhaft, *The Disorders of War: The Revolution in South Carolina* (Orono, 1981).

10. Main, *The Anti-Federalists,* Conclusion. The most important critic of this point of view has been Cecelia Kenyon, "Men of Little Faith: The Anti-Federalists on the Nature of Representative Government," *William and Mary Quarterly,* XII (Jan. 1955), 3–43. But in recent years Miss Kenyon has retreated from her earlier position. See the perceptive review of her *The Anti-Federalists* (Indianapolis, 1966), by Gordon S. Wood in *William and Mary Quarterly,* XXIV (Oct. 1967), 632–37.

11. Charles F. Hobson, "The Negative on State Laws: James Madison and the Crisis of Republican Government," *William and Mary Quarterly,* XXXVI (April 1979), 215–23.

12. Adrienne Koch and Harry Ammon, "The Virginia and Kentucky Resolutions: An Episode in Jefferson and Madison's Defense of Civil Liberties," *William and Mary Quarterly,* V (April 1948), 147–76; James M. Smith, "The Grass Roots Origins of the Kentucky Resolutions," *ibid.,* XXVII (April 1970), 221–45; Ellis, *The Jeffersonian Crisis.* 144–46, 273–75.

13. Ellis, *The Jeffersonian Crisis,* 19–107, 237–42; Kenneth Treacy, "The Olmstead Case, 1778–1809," *Western Political Quarterly,* 10 (Sept. 1957), 175–91; Sanford W. Higginbotham, *The Keystone in the Democratic Arch: Pennsylvania Politics, 1800–1816* (Harrisburg, 1952), 177–204; William O. Douglas, "Interposition and the *Peters* Case, 1778–1809," *Stanford Law Review,* 9 (Dec. 1956), 3–12; Morgan D. Dowd, "Justice Story and the Politics of Appointment," *The American Journal of Legal History,* IX (Oct. 1965), 265–85.

14. Merrill D. Peterson, *The Jefferson Image in the American Mind,* 17–66.

15. Federalist activities at the time of the War of 1812 may be traced in: Frank M. Anderson, "A Forgotten Phase of the New England Opposition to the War of 1812," Mississippi Valley Historical Association, *Proceedings,* VI (1912–13), 176–89; James M. Banner, *To the Hartford Convention* (New York, 1970).

16. Frederick Jackson Turner, *Rise of the New West, 1819–1829* (New York, 1906 and 1962); Paul W. Gates, "Tenants of the Log Cabin," *Mississippi Valley Historical Review,* XLIX (June 1962), 3–31; Charles Warren, "Legislative and Judicial Attacks on the Supreme Court of the United States—A History of the Twenty-fifth Section of the Judiciary Act," *American Law Review,* XLVII (Jan. and Feb. 1913), 1–34 and 161–89, and Warren, *The Supreme Court in United States History* (2 vols., Boston, 1922), I, 474–564, 633–87; Charles G. Haines, *The Role of the Supreme Court in American Government and Politics: 1789–1835* (Berkeley, 1944), 427–535.

17. For the developments in South Carolina leading up to the nullification crisis see: William W. Freehling, *Prelude to Civil War: The Nullification Movement in South Carolina, 1816–1836* (New York, 1966); Frederic Bancroft, *Calhoun and the South Carolina Nullification Movement* (Baltimore, 1928); Chauncey S. Boucher, *The Nullification Controversy in South Carolina* (Chicago, 1916); David F. Houston, *A Critical Study of Nullification in South Carolina* (New York, 1896); James M. Banner, "The Problem of South Carolina," Stanley Elkins and Eric McKitrick (eds.), *The Hofstadter Aegis: A Memorial* (New York, 1974), 60–93; Pauline Maier, "The Road Not Taken: Nullification, John C. Calhoun, and the Revolutionary Tradition in South Carolina," *South Carolina Historical Magazine,* 82 (Jan. 1981), 1–19; James Brewer Stewart, " 'A Great Talking and Eating Machine': Patriarchy, Mobilization and the Dynamics of Nullification in South Carolina," *Civil War History,* 27 (Sept. 1981), 197–220.

18. George C. Rogers, Jr., "South Carolina Federalists and the Origins of the Nullification Movement," *South Carolina Historical Magazine,* 71 (Jan. 1970), 17–32; Patrick Stone Brady, "Political and Civic Life in South Carolina, 1787–1833" (unpublished doctoral dissertation, University of California, Santa Barbara, 1971); Shaw Livemore, *The Twilight of Federalism: The Disintegration of the Federalist Party, 1815–1830* (Princeton, 1962), 151–54, 246; Arthur B. Darling, *Political Change in Massachusetts, 1824–1848* (New Haven, 1925), 55–71, 78–84, 272; Herbert Ershkovitz, "The Election of 1824 in New Jersey," New Jersey Historical Society *Proceedings,* LXXXIV (April 1966), 115–17.

19. There is no really first-rate study of the Old Republican and Unionist tradition in South Carolina, but valuable material can be found in: Lillian Kibler, *Benjamin F. Perry South Carolina Unionist* (Durham, 1946); Harvey T. Cook, *The Life and Legacy of David Rogerson Williams* (New York 1916); J. Fred Rippy, *Joel R. Poinsett, Versatile American* (Durham, 1935); Herbert Everett Putnam, *Joel Roberts Poinsett: A Political Biography* (Washington, D.C., 1935); James Griffin Campbell, "James Louis Petigru: A Rhetorical Study," (unpublished doctoral dissertation, University of South Carolina, 1961); Caroline P. Smith, "South Carolina 'Radical': The Political Career of William Smith to 1826" (unpublished M.A. thesis, Auburn University, 1971) and "Jacksonian Conservative: The Later Years of William Smith, 1826–1840" (unpublished doctoral dissertation, Auburn University, 1977). Also see: Gerald M. Capers, *John C. Calhoun: Opportunist, A Reappraisal* (Chicago, 1960 and 1969), 91–109; Capers, "A Reconsideration of John C. Calhoun's Transition from Nationalism to Nullification," *Journal of Southern History,* XIV (Feb. 1948).

20. Peterson, *Jefferson Image,* 51–59; Agricola, *Virginia Doctrines not Nullification* (Richmond, 1832).

21. John Quincy Adams, *An Oration Delivered to the Citizens of the Town of Quincy, on the Fourth of July, 1831 . . .* (Boston, 1831); Joseph Story, *Commentaries on the Constitution of the United States . . .* (3 vols., Boston, 1833); Nathan Dane, *General Abridgement and Digest of American Law* (9 vols., Boston, 1823–29), IX, Appendix; Nathaniel Chipman, *Principles of Government, A Treatise on Free Institutions . . .* (Burlington, 1833); William A. Duer, *A Course of Lectures on the Constitutional Jurisprudence of the United States . . .* (New York, 1843). See also: Elizabeth Kelley Bauer, *Commentaries on the Constitution, 1790–1860* (New York, 1952), 212–331; Kenneth M. Stampp, "The Concept of a Perpetual Union," *Journal of American History,* LXV (June 1978), 5–33.

22. "Extract from Report of Kentucky in reply to South Carolina—January 27, 1830," Herman V. Ames (ed.), *State Documents on Federal Relations* (New York, 1970), 158–59.

23. James Madison to Edward Everett, 28 Aug. 1830, printed in *North American Review,* 31 (Oct. 1830), 537, in Gaillard Hunt (ed.), *The Writings of James Madison* (9 vols., New York, 1900–1910), IX, 383–403.

24. *Register of Debates in Congress,* 21:1, 247–72, esp. 268–72. A similar point of view was also expressed by Levi Woodbury the senator from New Hampshire, *ibid.,* 179–96. See also: William B. Hatcher, "Edward Livingston's View of the Nature of the Union," *Louisiana Historical Quarterly,* 24 (July 1941), 698–728.

2 Andrew Jackson, States' Rights, and Majority Rule

1. Important works deemphasizing the constitutional and ideological issues involved in the election of 1828 are: Richard P. McCormick, *The Second American Party*

System: Party Formation in the Jacksonian Era (Chapel Hill, 1966); Edward Pessen, *Jacksonian America: Society, Personality, and Politics* (rev. ed., Homewood, 1978); Robert V. Remini, *The Election of Andrew Jackson* (Philadelphia, 1963); Thomas P. Abernethy, "Andrew Jackson and the Rise of Southwestern Democracy," *American Historical Review,* XXXIII (Oct. 1927), 64–77. Two valuable pieces of scholarship which, in different ways, recognize that real issues were involved in the election of 1828 are: Charles G. Sellers, "Banking and Politics in Jackson's Tennessee, 1817–1827," *Mississippi Valley Historical Review,* 41 (June 1954), 61–84; John William Ward, *Andrew Jackson: Symbol for an Age* (New York, 1955).

2. Thomas Ritchie to Littleton Waller Tazewell, 28 Feb. 1827, Tazewell Papers, Virginia State Library (VSL).

3. Francis P. Blair to Henry Clay, 3 Oct. 1827, Mary W. M. Hargreaves and James F. Hopkins (eds.), *The Papers of Henry Clay* (7 vols., Lexington, 1959–), 6, 1106–7. See also Hugh Lawson White to Andrew Jackson, 20 April 1831, John Spencer Bassett (ed.), *Correspondence of Andrew Jackson* (7 vols., Washington, D.C., 1926–35), IV, 267. For a useful account of what groups supported Jackson in 1828 and why, see: Richard B. Latner, *The Presidency of Andrew Jackson: White House Politics, 1829–1837* (Athens, 1979), 7–30.

4. Daniel Webster to Ezekial Webster, 23 Feb. 1829, Charles Wiltse and Harold D. Moser (eds.), *The Papers of Daniel Webster: Correspondence* (4 vols., Hanover, 1974–), II, 401.

5. Amos Kendall to Francis Preston Blair, 9 Jan. 1829, Blair-Lee Papers, Princeton University Library (PUL).

6. Gaillard Hunt (ed.), *The First Forty Years of Washington Society in the Family Letters of Margaret Bayard Smith* (New York, 1906; reprinted 1965), 290–96.

7. Joseph Story to Sarah W. Story, 7 March 1829, W. W. Story (ed.), *Life and Letters of Joseph Story* (2 vols., Boston, 1851), I, 563; Daniel Webster to Mrs. Ezekiel Webster, 4 March 1829, Fletcher Webster (ed.), *The Private Correspondence of Daniel Webster* (2 vols., Boston, 1856), I, 473.

8. Andrew Jackson to John Coffee, 11 Dec. 1828, John Spencer Bassett (ed.), *Correspondence of Andrew Jackson,* III, 452; Andrew Jackson to Richard G. Dunlap, 29 Aug. 1831, *ibid.,* IV, 341; Andrew Jackson to Robert J. Chester, *ibid.,* IV, 96. My view of Jackson has been influenced greatly by Marvin Meyers, *The Jacksonian Persuasion: Politics and Belief* (Palo Alto, 1957), 3–32; Vernon L. Parrington, *Main Currents in American Thought: The Romantic Revolution in America, 1800–1860* (New York, 1927), 138–45; Albert Somit, "Andrew Jackson as Political Theorist," *Tennessee Historical Quarterly,* 7 (June 1949), 99–126. Among the many biographies of Jackson the most useful are: James Parton, *Life of Andrew Jackson* (3 vols., New York, 1860); Marquis James, *Andrew Jackson* (2 vols., Indianapolis, 1933, 1937); John Spencer Bassett, *The Life of Andrew Jackson* (2 vols., New York, 1911); James C. Curtis, *Andrew Jackson and the Search for Vindication* (Boston, 1976); Robert V. Remini, *Andrew Jackson and the Course of American Empire, 1767–1821* (New York, 1977) and *Andrew Jackson and the Course of American Freedom 1822–1832* (New York, 1981).

9. Andrew Jackson to John Quincy Adams, 26 Aug. 1821, *American State Papers* (38 vols., Washington, D.C., 1832–61), Miscellaneous Vol. II, 802; Charles G. Sellers, Jr., "Banking and Politics in Jackson's Tennessee, 1817–1827," *Mississippi Valley Historical Review,* XLI (June 1954), 61–84; John Spencer Bassett, *The Life of Andrew Jackson* (New York, 1911, 1931), 448.

10. "First Annual Message," 8 Dec. 1829, James D. Richardson (ed.), *A Compila-*

tion of the Messages and Papers of the Presidents, 1789–1897 (10 vols., Washington, D.C., 1900), II, 447.

11. "Seventh Annual Message," 7 Dec. 1835, Richardson (ed.), *Messages and Papers of the Presidents,* III, 177.

12. Andrew Jackson to John Randolph, 3 Dec. 1830, Bassett (ed.), *Correspondence of Andrew Jackson,* III, 210.

13. Thomas Hart Benton, *Thirty Years' View* (2 vols., New York, 1854–56), I, 424. See also John C. Fitzpatrick (ed.), *The Autobiography of Martin Van Buren* (Washington, D.C., 1920), 625.

14. "First Annual Message," 8 Dec. 1829, Richardson (ed.), *Messages and Papers of the Presidents,* II, 448; "Second Annual Message," 6 Dec. 1830, *ibid.,* 518–19; "Third Annual Message," 6 Dec. 1831, *ibid.,* 557; "Fourth Annual Message," 4 Dec. 1832, *ibid.,* 605; Ames, *Proposed Amendments,* 87–90.

15. "First Inaugural Address," 4 March 1829, Richardson (ed.), *Messages and Papers of the Presidents,* II, 438.

16. "First Annual Message," 8 Dec. 1829, *ibid.,* 448–49.

17. Andrew Jackson to Major James Hamilton, Jr., 29 June 1828, Bassett (ed.), *Correspondence of Andrew Jackson,* III, 411–12.

18. "Rough Draft of the First Inaugural Address," [4 March 1829], *ibid.,* IV, 12.

19. Albert Somit, "Andrew Jackson as an Administrative Reformer," *Tennessee Historical Quarterly,* XIII (Sept. 1954), 204–33; Leonard D. White, *The Jacksonians: A Study in Administrative History, 1829–1861* (New York, 1954), 300–346; Erik M. Eriksson, "The Federal Civil Service Under President Jackson," *Mississippi Valley Historical Review,* XIII (March 1927), 517–40.

20. "Veto Messages," 27 May 1830, Richardson (ed.), *Messages and Papers of the Presidents,* II, 483. For background on the internal improvements issue, see Carter Goodrich, *Government Promotion of American Canals and Railroads 1800–1900* (New York, 1960), 19–48; Douglas E. Clanin, "Internal Improvements in National Politics, 1816–1830," *Transportation and the Early Nation* (Indianapolis, 1982), 30–60; Carlton Jackson, "The Internal Improvement Vetoes of Andrew Jackson," *Tennessee Historical Quarterly,* XXV (Fall 1966), 261–79.

21. "First Annual Message," 8 Dec. 1829, Richardson (ed.), *Messages and the Papers of the Presidents,* II, 452. See also: Andrew Jackson to James K. Polk, 4[24?] Dec. 1826, Herbert Weaver and Paul H. Bergeron (eds.), *Correspondence of James K. Polk* (5 vols., Nashville, 1969–), I, 63–64. Andrew Jackson to James W. Lanier, [15?] May 1824, Bassett (ed.), *Correspondence of Andrew Jackson,* III, 253.

22. "Second Annual Message," 6 Dec. 1830, Richardson (ed.), *Messages and Papers of the Presidents,* II, 509–10. See also: "Notes for the Maysville Road Veto," [19–26?] May 1830, Bassett (ed.), *Correspondence of Andrew Jackson,* IV, 137–39.

23. "Veto Messages," 27 May 1830, Richardson (ed.), *Messages and Papers of the Presidents,* II, 490–91. See also "Second Annual Message," 6 Dec. 1830, *ibid.,* 511, 513.

24. "First Inaugural Address," 4 March 1829, *ibid.,* 437.

25. Andrew Jackson to John Overton, 30 Sept. 1830, Bassett (ed.), *Correspondence of Andrew Jackson,* IV, 181; Samuel Ingham to Andrew Jackson, 24 Nov. 1829, *ibid.,* 89–93; "First Annual Message," 8 Dec. 1829, Richardson (ed.), *Messages and Papers of the Presidents,* II, 451, 455; "Second Annual Message," 6 Dec. 1830," *ibid.,* 511; "Fourth Annual Message," 4 Dec. 1832, *ibid.,* 597; Andrew Jackson to Martin Van Buren, 15 May 1830, Fitzpatrick (ed.), *Autobiography of Martin Van Buren,* 322.

26. "Fourth Annual Message," 4 Dec. 1832, *ibid.,* 602–3; "First Annual Mes-

sage," 8 Dec. 1829, *ibid.*, 452; "Second Annual Message," 6 Dec. 1830, *ibid.*, 514, 515–16.

27. "Veto Messages," 27 May 1830, *ibid.*, 491–92; "Second Annual Message," 6 Dec. 1830, *ibid.*, 511.

28. "Veto Messages," 27 May 1830, *ibid.*, 483–93; Andrew Jackson to William B. Lewis, 26, 28 June 1830, Bassett (ed.), *Correspondence of Andrew Jackson*, IV, 156–57; "Notes for the Maysville Veto," [19–26?] May 1830, *ibid.*, 137–39; Andrew Jackson to Martin Van Buren, 4 May, 15 May 1830, Fitzpatrick (ed.), *Autobiography of Martin Van Buren*, 321–22.

29. "Second Annual Message," 6 Dec. 1830, Richardson (ed.), *Messages and Papers of the Presidents*, II, 510.

30. *Ibid.*, 508.

31. *Ibid.*, 509.

32. *Ibid.*, 508–9; "Veto Messages," 6 Dec. 1832, *ibid.*, 638–39; Andrew Jackson to Martin Van Buren, 18 Oct. 1830, Bassett (ed.), *Correspondence of Andrew Jackson*, IV, 185–86; Andrew Jackson to Amos Kendall, 23 July 1832, *ibid.*, 465.

33. George Rogers Taylor, *The Transportation Revolution, 1815–1860* (New York, 1951), 20–21; Carter Goodrich, *Government Promotion of American Canals and Railroads, 1800–1890* (New York 1960), 45; Edward Pessen, *Jacksonian America: Society, Personality and Politics,* revised edition (New York, 1969 and 1978), 124.

34. An account of specific expenditures on internal improvements made during Jackson's administration may be found in: E. C. Nelson, "Presidential Influence on the Policy of Internal Improvements," *Iowa Journal of History and Politics,* IV (Jan. 1906), Appendix A, 60–62. See also: Henry G. Wheeler, *History of Congress . . .* (2 vols., New York, 1848), 124–40; Senate Report 450, 26th Cong., 1st Sess. (7 May 1840).

35. "Message to Congress," 30 May 1830, Richardson (ed.), *Messages and Papers of the Presidents,* II, 483.

36. "Veto Messages," 27 May 1830, *ibid.*, 485, 492; James Simeon Young, *A Political and Constitutional Study of the Cumberland Road* (Chicago, 1904), 85–89; Philip D. Jordan, *The National Road* (Indianapolis, 1948), 166–71.

37. *Congressional Globe,* 30:1, XIX, Appendix E, 105.

38. Peter Temin, *The Jacksonian Economy* (New York, 1969), 68–112; Walter Buckingham Smith and Arthur H. Cole, *Fluctuations in American Business, 1790–1860* (Cambridge, 1935), 37–84.

39. *Cherokee Nation v. State of Georgia,* 5 Peters 15 (1831).

40. For a fine treatment of Jackson's Indian policy, one that takes into acocunt the constitutional problems involved see: Francis Paul Prucha, "Andrew Jackson's Indian Policy: A Reassessment," *Journal of American History,* LVI (Dec., 1969), 527–39. See also Richard Latner, *The Presidency of Andrew Jackson,* 86–98; Remini, *Andrew Jackson and the Course of American Freedom,* 200–201, 220–22, 227–29, 303; William S. Hoffman, "Andrew Jackson, State Rightist: The Case of the Georgia Indians," *Tennessee Historical Quarterly,* XI (Dec. 1952), 329–45; Ronald N. Satz, *American Indian Policy in the Jacksonian Era* (Lincoln, 1975), 1–96; Arthur H. DeRosier, Jr., "Andrew Jackson and Negotiation for the Removal of the Choctaw Indians," *Historian,* XXIX (May 1967), 343–62; Arthur H. DeRosier, *The Removal of the Choctaw Indians* (Knoxville, 1970), 3–99; Theodore H. Jack, "Alabama and the Federal Government: The Creek Indian Controversy," *Mississippi Valley Historical Review,* III (Dec. 1916), 301–17. For a much harsher view of Jackson's Indian policy, one that completely ignores constitutional considerations and views Jackson primarily

as a racist, see Michael Paul Rogin, *Fathers and Children: Andrew Jackson and the Subjugation of the American Indian* (New York, 1975).

41. Andrew Jackson to John Coffee, 7 April 1832, Bassett (ed.), *Correspondence of Andrew Jackson,* IV, 430.

42. "First Annual Message," 8 Dec. 1829, Richardson (ed.), *Messages and Papers of the Presidents,* II, 457–59; "Second Annual Message," 6 Dec. 1830, *ibid.,* 519–23; Andrew Jackson to Captain James Gadsden, 12 Oct. 1829, Bassett (ed.), *Correspondence of Andrew Jackson,* IV, 81; Andrew Jackson to John Overton, 8 June 1829, J. M. Dickinson Papers, Tennessee State Library (TSL).

43. Richardson (ed.), *Messages and Papers of the Presidents,* II, 457–58.

44. "First Annual Message," 8 Dec. 1829, *ibid.,* 459.

45. "Second Annual Message," 6 Dec. 1830, *ibid.,* 520.

46. "First Annual Message," 8 Dec. 1829, *ibid.,* 458.

47. United States *Statutes* 4:411–12; Arthur H. DeRosier, *The Removal of the Choctaw Indians* (Knoxville, 1970), 100–28; Anne Heloise Abel, *The History of Events Resulting in Indian Consolidation West of the Mississippi* (Washington, D.C., 1908), 370–413.

48. Henry Clay to Edward Everett, 16 June 1830, Calvin Colton (ed.), *The Works of Henry Clay* (6 vols., New York, 1857), IV, 274. See also: Henry Clay to Francis Brooke, 19, 24 April 1830, *ibid.,* 260–65; Henry Clay to J. S. Johnston, 30 April, 14 June 1830, *ibid.,* 264–65, 278; Daniel Webster to Henry Clay, 29 May 1830, Wiltse and Moser (eds.), *The Papers of Daniel Webster: Correspondence,* III, 78–80.

49. Ulrich B. Phillips, *Georgia and State Rights* (Washington, D.C., 1901), 66–86.

50. Charles Warren, *The Supreme Court in United States History* (2 vols., Boston, 1922), I, 729–79; Joseph C. Burke, "The Cherokee Cases: A Study in Law, Politics, and Morality," *Stanford Law Review,* 21 (Feb. 1969), 500–531. See also John P. Kennedy, *Memoirs of the Life of William Wirt, Attorney General of the United States* (2 vols., Philadelphia, 1849), II, 240–67, 290–95, 303.

51. George Gilmer to William Wirt, 19 June 1830, *Niles' Weekly Register,* XXXIX (18 Sept. 1830), 69–71.

52. *Ibid.,* (8 Jan. 1831), 338; Herman V. Ames, *State Documents on Federal Relations: The States and the United States* (Philadelphia, 1906), 127–28.

53. Kennedy (ed.), *Memoirs of William Wirt,* II, 293. On Sergeant's anti-Jackson bias see: John Sergeant to Thomas W. White, 15 June 1831, Miscellaneous Manuscripts, Virginia Historical Society (VaHS). For Georgia's position in the controversy see: Wilson Lumpkin to Bolling Hall, 1 Feb. 1832, Bolling Hall Papers, Alabama Department of Archives and History (ADAH).

54. *Cherokee Nation v. Georgia,* 5 Peters 1 (1831).

55. Burke, "The Cherokee Cases," *Stanford Law Review,* 21, 516–19; Fitzpatrick (ed.), *Autobiography of Martin Van Buren,* 292–94.

56. *Worcester v. Georgia,* 6 Peters 515 (1832).

57. Warren, *Supreme Court in United States History,* I, 755–69; Somit, "Andrew Jackson as Political Theorist," *Tennessee Historical Quarterly,* VII, 115–18; Burke, "The Cherokee Cases," *Stanford Law Review,* 21, 524–29. See also: Ambrose Spencer to Daniel Webster, 14 March 1832, Wiltse and Moser (eds.), *The Papers of Daniel Webster, Correspondence,* III, 158–59; John Tipton to His Constituents, 19 June 1832, Nellie Armstrong Robertson and Dorothy Riker (eds.), *The John Tipton Papers* (3 vols., Indianapolis, 1942), II, 635.

58. William Wirt to Lewis Williams, 28 April 1832, Wirt Papers, LC; Burke, "The Cherokee Cases," *Stanford Law Review,* 21, 527–28.

59. Andrew Jackson to John Coffee, 7 April 1832, Bassett (ed.), *Correspondence of Andrew Jackson,* IV, 430.

60. House Report No. 43, 21st Cong., 2nd sess. (1831); Joseph Story to Mrs. Story, 28 Jan. 1831, Story (ed.), *Life and Letters of Joseph Story,* II, 43–44; Charles Grove Haines, *The Role of the Supreme Court in American Government and Politics, 1789–1835* (Berkeley, 1944, and New York, 1973), 593–96.

61. Andrew Jackson to Col. Anthony Butler, 16 March 1832, Bassett (ed.), *Correspondence of Andrew Jackson,* IV, 415.

62. "First Annual Message," 8 Dec. 1829, Richardson (ed.), *Messages and Papers of the Presidents,* II, 461; "Third Annual Message," 6 Dec. 1831, *ibid., 558;* "Fourth Annual Message," 4 Dec. 1832, *ibid.,* 605. A careful and useful treatment of Jackson's appointments to the lower federal courts (district and territorial) is to be found in Kermit L. Hall, *The Politics of Justice: Lower Federal Judicial Selection and the Second Party System, 1829–1861* (Lincoln, 1979), 1–26.

63. Andrew Jackson to Andrew Jackson Donelson, 5 July 1822, Bassett (ed.), *Correspondence of Andrew Jackson,* III, 167.

64. During his two terms as President, Jackson made the following appointments to the United States Supreme Court: John McLean (1829), Henry Baldwin (1830), James M. Wayne (1835), Roger B. Taney (1836), Phillip Pendleton Barbour (1830), and John Catron (1837). For an indication that at least some Jacksonians were thinking more in terms of packing than of dismantling the federal judiciary, see Ambrose Spencer to General John Armstrong, Jr., 17 Jan. 1830, Rokeby Collection, New-York Historical Society (NYHS). Also of value on Jackson's attitude toward the judiciary are: Richard P. Longaker, "Andrew Jackson and the Judiciary," *Political Science Quarterly,* 71 (Sept. 1956), 341–46; Curtis P. Nettels, "The Mississippi Valley and the Federal Judiciary, 1807–1837," *Mississippi Valley Historical Review,* 12 (Sept. 1925), 202–26; Robert J. Harris, "Chief Justice Taney: Prophet of Reform and Reaction," *Vanderbilt Law Review,* 10 (Feb. 1957), 227–57.

65. Andrew Jackson to Wilson Lumpkin, 22 June 1832, Bassett (ed.), *Correspondence of Andrew Jackson,* IV, 451.

66. Andrew Jackson to Thomas Hart Benton, [June? 1832] *ibid.,* IV, 445. Standard treatments of the Bank War are: Ralph C. H. Catterall, *The Second Bank of the United States* (Chicago, 1903); Bray Hammond, *Banks and Politics in America from the Revolution to the Civil War* (Princeton, 1957); Robert V. Remini, *Andrew Jackson and the Bank War* (New York, 1967).

67. Andrew Jackson to James K. Polk, 23 Dec. 1833, *ibid.,* V, 236; Andrew Jackson to Capt. John Donelson, 3 Sept. 1821, *ibid.,* III, 117; Andrew Jackson to Andrew J. Donelson, 8 Feb. 1823, *ibid.,* 186–87; Andrew Jackson to William B. Lewis, 16 July 1820, Jackson-Lewis Papers, New York Public Library (NYPL); James A. Hamilton (ed.), *Reminiscences of Men and Events* (New York, 1869), 69; Sellers, "Banks and Politics in Jackson's Tennessee, 1817–1826," *Mississippi Valley Historical Review,* XLI, 61–84.

68. Amos Kendall to Francis Preston Blair, 22 Nov. 1829, Blair-Lee Papers, PUL; Andrew Jackson to John Overton, 8 June 1829, Jacob M. Dickinson Papers, Tennessee State Library (TSL).

69. Samuel Ingham to Andrew Jackson, 26, 27 Nov. 1829, Bassett (ed.), *Correspondence of Andrew Jackson,* IV, 92–94; John Berrien to Andrew Jackson, 27 Nov. 1829, *ibid.,* IV, 94–95; Hamilton (ed.), *Reminiscences,* 150; William B. Lewis to James A. Hamilton, 1 Jan. 1832, *ibid.,* 235–36; William B. Lewis to Nicholas Biddle, 16 Oct. 1829, Biddle Papers, LC.

70. "First Annual Message," 8 Dec. 1829, Richardson (ed.), *Messages and Papers of the Presidents,* II, 462; Hamilton (ed.), *Reminiscences,* 149–50.

71. "Biddle's Memorandum of a Conversation with Andrew Jackson," n.d., Biddle Papers, LC; "Opinion on Bank," [Jan. 1832], Bassett (ed.), *Correspondence of Andrew Jackson,* IV, 389–90.

72. For various discussions of these questions see: Andrew Jackson to Moses Dawson 17 July 1830, *ibid.,* 161–62; Andrew Jackson to James A. Hamilton, 19 Dec., 3 June 1830, Hamilton (ed.), *Reminiscences,* 151–52, 167–68; Amos Kendall to Francis P. Blair, 22 Nov. 1829, Blair-Lee Papers, PUL; Felix Grundy to Andrew Jackson, 22 Oct. 1829, Bassett (ed.), *Correspondence of Andrew Jackson,* IV, 83; Samuel Ingham to Andrew Jackson, 26, 27 Nov. 1829, *ibid.,* 92–94.

73. "Second Annual Message," 6 Dec. 1830, Richardson (ed.), *Messages and Papers of the Presidents,* II, 528–29.

74. *Ibid.,* 529.

75. Andrew Jackson to James A. Hamilton, 19 Dec. 1829, Hamilton (ed.), *Reminiscences,* 151.

76. Andrew Jackson Donelson to John McLemore, 9 Jan. 1831, Donelson Papers, LC; Thomas Cadwalader to Nicholas Biddle, 26 Dec. 1831, Reginald C. McGrane (ed.), *The Correspondence of Nicholas Biddle Dealing with National Affairs, 1807–1844* (Boston, 1919), 160–61; John A. Munroe, *Louis McLane: Federalist and Jacksonian* (New Brunswick, 1973), 296–97, 298, 304–11, 313–17; Latner, *The Presidency of Andrew Jackson,* 199–201.

77. Andrew Jackson to Martin Van Buren, 8 Aug. 1831, Bassett (ed.), *Correspondence of Andrew Jackson,* IV, 329; Richardson (ed.), *Messages and Papers of the Presidents,* II, 558; "Memorandum by Biddle," 19 Oct. 1831, McGrane (ed.), *Correspondence of Nicholas Biddle,* 128–39.

78. Nicholas Biddle to R. M. Gibbes, 13 Dec. 1831, Biddle Papers, LC; Andrew Jackson to John Randolph, 22 Dec. 1831, Bassett (ed.), *Correspondence of Andrew Jackson,* IV, 387; Andrew Jackson to James A. Hamilton, 12 Dec. 1831, Hamilton (ed.), *Reminiscences,* 234; "Opinion on the Bank," [Jan. 1832]; Bassett (ed.), *Correspondence of Andrew Jackson,* IV, 389–90.

79. Thomas Payne Govan, *Nicholas Biddle* (Chicago, 1959), 171–80; Remini, *Andrew Jackson and the Bank War,* 75–77.

80. James A. Hamilton to Friend, 14 March 1832, Hamilton (ed.), *Reminiscences,* 243; Fitzpatrick (ed.), *Autobiography of Martin Van Buren,* 625.

81. "Opinion on the Bank," [Jan. 1832?], Bassett (ed.), *Correspondence of Andrew Jackson,* IV, 389–90; Andrew Jackson to Thomas Hart Benton, [June 1832], *ibid.,* 445–46; "Jackson's Memorandum on the Bank in view of Veto," *ibid.,* 458–59.

82. "Veto Messages," 10 July 1832, Richardson (ed.), *Messages and Papers of the Presidents,* II, 576–91.

3   Andrew Jackson, Nullification, and the South

1. Andrew Jackson to L. H. Coleman, 26 April 1824, Bassett (ed.), *Correspondence of Andrew Jackson,* III, 249–51; Andrew Jackson to James W. Lanier, 26 April 1824, *ibid.,* 253; *Niles' Weekly Register* (Baltimore), XXVI (12 June 1824), 245.

2. "First Annual Message," 8 Dec. 1829, Richardson (ed.), *Messages and Papers of the Presidents,* II, 450, 437; "Veto Messages," 27 May 1830, *ibid.,* 488–89; "Second Annual Message," 6 Dec. 1830, *ibid.,* 523–24; "Third Annual Message," 6 Dec. 1831,

ibid., 555; Andrew Jackson to Martin Van Buren, 14 Nov. 1831, Bassett (ed.), *Correspondence of Andrew Jackson,* IV, 373–74.

3. Andrew Jackson to Major James Hamilton, Jr., 29 June 1828, *ibid.,* III, 411.

4. "First Inaugural Address," 4 March 1829, Richardson (ed.), *Messages and Papers of the Presidents,* II, 437.

5. *Ibid.,* 449–50.

6. *Ibid.,* 525.

7. *Ibid.,* 556.

8. "First Annual Message," 6 Dec. 1829, *ibid.,* 449.

9. "Second Annual Message," 6 Dec. 1830, *ibid.,* 523–24.

10. *Ibid.,* 493; Robert Y. Hayne to Andrew Jackson, 3 Sept. 1828, Bassett (ed.), *Correspondence of Andrew Jackson,* III, 432–35.

11. "Second Annual Message," 6 Dec. 1830, Richardson (ed.), *Messages and Papers of the Presidents,* II, 523.

12. "Veto Message," 27 May 1830, *ibid.,* 489–90.

13. William Smith to Stephen D. Miller, 8 Feb. 1829, Smith Papers, South Caroliniana Collection, University of South Carolina (SC).

14. Richardson (ed.), *Messages and Papers of the Presidents,* II, 524–25.

15. William Smith to David R. Evans, 8 Jan. 1829, Smith Papers, SC.

16. "Second Annual Message," 6 Dec. 1830, Richardson (ed.), *Messages and Papers of the Presidents,* II, 524.

17. Andrew Jackson to John Coffee, 17 July 1832, Bassett (ed.), *Correspondence of Andrew Jackson,* IV, 462–63; John D. Macoll, "Representative John Quincy Adams' Compromise Tariff of 1832," *Capitol Studies,* I (Fall 1972), 41–58; Munroe, *Lewis McLane,* 339–50; Bemis, *John Quincy Adams and the Union* (New York 1956), 240–48; Edward Stanwood, *American Tariff Controversies in the Nineteenth Century* (2 vols., Boston, 1903), I, 320–85; Frank W. Taussig, *The Tariff History of the United States* (New York, 1888), 109–10.

18. "The South Carolina Exposition and Protest," Clyde N. Wilson and W. Edwin Hemphill (eds.), *The Papers of John C. Calhoun* (14? vols., Columbia, 1959–?), X, 489,493.

19. "Second Annual Message," 6 Dec. 1830, Richardson (ed.), *Messages and Papers of the Presidents,* II, 517.

20. Andrew Jackson to Robert Y. Hayne, 8 Feb. 1831, Bassett (ed.), *Correspondence of Andrew Jackson,* IV, 241–42.

21. Andrew Jackson to Major James Hamilton, Jr., 29 June 1828, *ibid.,* III, 411–12.

22. Andrew Jackson to William B. Lewis, 25 Aug. 1830; *ibid.,* IV, 177; Andrew Jackson to Martin Van Buren, 23 July 1831, 17 Dec. 1831, *ibid.,* 316, 384; Andrew Jackson to James A. Hamilton, 12 Nov. 1831, 2 Nov. 1832, Hamilton (ed.), *Reminiscences,* 231, 247.

23. Amos Kendall to Francis Preston Blair, 7 March 1829, Blair-Lee Papers, PUL. See also William B. Lewis to John Overton, 14 Aug. 1830, Overton Papers, Tennessee Historical Society (THS).

24. Andrew Jackson to Samuel J. Hays, 23 April 1831, quoted in Charles G. Sellers, *James K. Polk: Jacksonian, 1795–1843* (Princeton, 1957), 147; Amos Kendall to Francis Preston Blair, 25 April 1830, Blair-Lee Papers, PUL; *Niles' Weekly Register* (Baltimore), XXXVIII (24 April 1830), 154; Daniel Webster to Henry Clay, 18 April 1830, Wiltse and Moser (eds.), *The Papers of Daniel Webster: Correspondence,* III, 58–59; Fitzpatrick (ed.), *Autobiography of Martin Van Buren,* 409–17; Thomas Hart Benton,

Thirty Years' View (2 vols., New York, 1854–56), I, 148–49. For a view that stresses the dinner as an opportunity that Jackson and Van Buren used to "get" Calhoun see: Richard R. Stenberg, "The Jefferson Birthday Dinner, 1830, *"Journal of Southern History,* IV (Aug. 1938), 334–45.

25. Robert Y. Hayne to Andrew Jackson, 4 Feb. 1831, Bassett (ed.), *Correspondence of Andrew Jackson,* IV, 238–39.

26. Andrew Jackson to Robert Y. Hayne, 8 Feb. 1831, *ibid.,* 242.

27. Andrew Jackson to Charles Webb, 5 Sept. 1831, *ibid.,* 345. The Constitution specifically provides: "Before he enters on the Execution of his Office he shall take the following Oath or Affirmation:—I do solemnly swear (or affirm) that I will faithfully execute the Office of President of the United States, and will to the best of my Ability, preserve, protect and defend the Constitution of the United States."

28. Andrew Jackson to John Stoney et al., 14 June 1831, *Niles' Weekly Register* (Baltimore), XL (16 July 1831), 351; Freehling, *Prelude to Civil War,* 223–24; Wiltse, *Calhoun: Nullifier,* II, 112.

29. Andrew Jackson to Martin Van Buren, 23 July 1831, Bassett (ed.), *Correspondence of Andrew Jackson,* IV, 316; Andrew Jackson to James A. Hamilton, 23 July 1831, Hamilton (ed.), *Reminiscences,* 226.

30. *Niles' Weekly Register* (Baltimore), XLI (8 Oct. 1831), 119–25; James Hamilton, Jr., to Little Waller Tazewell, 26 Aug. 1831, Tazewell Papers, Virginia State Library (VSL); Freehling, *Prelude to Civil War,* 245–46.

31. Andrew Jackson to Robert Oliver (Joel R. Poinsett), 26 Oct. 1830, Bassett (ed.), *Correspondence of Andrew Jackson,* IV, 191.

32. Andrew Jackson to Martin Van Buren, 6 Dec. 1831, *ibid.,* 379.

33. Andrew Jackson to Martin Van Buren, 14 Nov. 1831, *ibid.,* 374.

34. Andrew Jackson to John Coffee, 17 July 1832, *ibid.,* 462. See also: W. T. Barry to John Overton, 9 Jan. 1832, Overton Papers, THS; William King to John Coffee, 10 Dec. 1831, Coffee Papers, Alabama Department of Archives and History (ADAH).

35. On Van Buren see: Joseph H. Harrison, Jr., "Martin Van Buren and His Southern Supporters," *Journal of Southern History,* XXII (Nov. 1956), 438–58; Frank O. Gatell "Sober Second Thoughts on Van Buren, the Albany Regency, and the Wall Street Conspiracy," *Journal of American History,* LIII (June 1966), 19–40; Robert V. Remini, *Martin Van Buren and the Making of the Democratic Party* (New York, 1959); Max M. Mintz, "The Political Ideas of Martin Van Buren," *New York History,* XXX (Oct. 1949), 422–48; James C. Curtis, *The Fox at Bay: Martin Van Buren and the Presidency* (Lexington, 1970), 3–51; Meyers, *The Jacksonian Persuasion,* 142–62; Donald B. Cole, *Martin Van Buren and the American Political System* (Princeton, 1984); John Niven, *Martin Van Buren: The Romantic Age of American Politics* (New York, 1983).

36. Andrew Jackson to John Overton, 31 Dec. 1829, Bassett (ed.), *Correspondence of Andrew Jackson,* IV, 108–9.

37. Andrew Jackson to John Coffee, 10 April 1830, 24 April 1831, *ibid.,* 134, 268. See also Andrew Jackson to Hugh Lawson White, 9 April 1831, *ibid.,* 258–60; Andrew Jackson to R. G. Dunlap, 18 July 1831, Jackson Papers, LC; Bassett, *Andrew Jackson.* 432–34.

38. Wiltse, *Calhoun: Nationalist,* I, 337–38, 347–50, 387; Freehling, *Prelude to Civil War,* 118–19, 143–44.

39. John C. Calhoun to Andrew Jackson, 10 July 1828, Wilson and Hemphill (eds.), *The Papers of John C. Calhoun,* X, 396–97.

40. John C. Calhoun to John McLean, 10 July 1828, *ibid.,* 397–98; John C

Calhoun to Duff Green, 1 July 1828, *ibid.*, 392–93; John C. Calhoun to James Monroe, 10 July 1828, *ibid.*, 398–99; John C. Calhoun to Bartlett Yancey, 16 July 1828, *ibid.*, 401; John C. Calhoun to Samuel D. Ingham, 23 July 1828, *ibid.*, 402; John C. Calhoun to Samuel Smith, 28 July 1828, *ibid.*, 403–4; John C. Calhoun to John A. Dix, 1 Sept. 1828, *ibid.*, 413–14; John C. Calhoun to Micah Sterling, 1 Sept. 1828, *ibid.*, 414–15; John C. Calhoun to James Monroe, 5 Sept. 1828, *ibid.*, 416–17; John C. Calhoun to Christopher Vandeventer, 8 Sept. 1828, *ibid.*, 420–22; John C. Calhoun to Micah Sterling, 7 Jan. 1829, *ibid.*, 548–49; John C. Calhoun to John McLean, 22 Sept. 1829, *ibid.*, XI, 77; John C. Calhoun to Samuel D. Ingham, 26 Sept. 1829, *ibid.*, XI, 78–80; John C. Calhoun to Christopher Vandeventer, 9 Nov. 1829, *ibid.*, XI, 85–86. John C. Calhoun to James Monroe, 7 Feb. 1830, *ibid.*, XI, 116–18.

41. Amos Kendall to Francis Preston Blair, 1 March 1830, Blair-Lee Papers, PUL.

42. John C. Calhoun to William Campbell Preston, 6 Nov. 1828, 6 Jan. 1829, Wilson and Hemphill (eds.), *The Papers of John C. Calhoun*, X, 431–32, 545–46; John C. Calhoun to Bartlett Yancey, 16 July 1828, *ibid.*, 401; John C. Calhoun to John D. Gardner, 16 Feb. 1829, *ibid.*, 560.

43. Wiltse, *Calhoun: Nullifier*, II, 39–52; Freehling, *Prelude to Civil War*, 137–42, 186–92.

44. Andrew Jackson to John Overton, 31 Dec. 1829, Bassett (ed.), *Correspondence of Andrew Jackson*, IV, 109.

45. John C. Calhoun to William Campbell Preston, 6 Jan. 1829, Wilson and Hemphill (eds.), *The Papers of John C. Calhoun*, X, 546; John C. Calhoun to James H. Hammond, 15 Jan. 1831, *ibid.*, XI, 299; John C. Calhoun to Patrick Noble, 10 Jan. 1829, *ibid.*, X, 550; John C. Calhoun to James Monroe, 7 Feb. 1830, *ibid.*, XI, 117; John C. Calhoun to Virgil Maxcy, 11 Sept. 1830, *ibid.*, XI, 228; Freehling, *Prelude to Civil War*, 299.

46. John C. Calhoun to Christopher Vandeventer, 20 March 1830, Wilson (ed.), *The Papers of John C. Calhoun*, XI, 140; Tomlinson Fort to John C. Calhoun, 29 Jan. 1830, *ibid.*, 106–7; Marcus Morton to John C. Calhoun, 12 June 1830, *ibid.*, 203–4; House Report No. 358, 21st Cong., 1st sess.; Andrew Jackson to John Coffee, 10 April 1830, Bassett (ed.), *Correspondence of Andrew Jackson*, IV, 134. For Calhoun's use of the Second Bank of the United States see Wilson (ed.), *Papers of John C. Calhoun*, X, 320–60, 390, 411.

47. Amos Kendall to Francis Preston Blair, 1 March 1830, Blair-Lee Papers, PUL; Thomas Hart Benton to F. Ewing, 12 Nov. [1830?], Benton Papers, Missouri Historical Society (MoHS).

48. Andrew Jackson to John Overton, 31 Dec. 1829, Bassett (ed.), *Correspondence of Andrew Jackson*, IV, 109.

49. John C. Calhoun to Virgil Maxcy, 27 June, 6 Aug. 1830, Wilson (ed.), *The Papers of John C. Calhoun*, XI, 208, 214, 228; Andrew Jackson to John Coffee, 10 April 1830, 24 April 1831, Bassett (ed.), *Correspondence of Andrew Jackson*, IV, 134, 269; John C. Calhoun to [Samuel D. Ingham], 13 Jan. 1832, Wilson (ed.), *The Papers of John C. Calhoun*, XI, 542; John C. Calhoun to Bolling Hall, 3 April 1832, *ibid.*, 566.

50. Andrew Jackson to William B. Lewis, 26 June 1830, Bassett (ed.), *Correspondence of Andrew Jackson*, IV, 156; Amos Kendall to Francis Preston Blair, 1, 18 March, 22 Aug., 2 Oct. 1830, Blair-Lee Papers, PUL; Amos Kendall to Andrew Jackson, 3 Dec. 1831, *ibid.*; James A. Hamilton to Andrew Jackson, 29 July 1830, Bassett (ed.), *Correspondence of Andrew Jackson*, IV, 167–68; Andrew Jackson to John Coffee, 26 May 1831, *ibid.*, 285; Smith, *Blair Family*, 1, 52–53; Benton, *Thirty Years' View*, I, 129; William Stickney (ed.), *The Autobiography of Amos Kendall* (Boston,

1872), 371–73; Amos Kendall to Gideon Welles, 10 March 1831, Welles Papers, LC; Duff Green to John C. Calhoun, 19 Nov. 1830; Wilson (ed.), *The Papers of John C. Calhoun*, XI, 261–62; Culver H. Smith, *The Press, Politics and Patronage: The American Government's Use of Newspapers, 1789–1875* (Athens, 1977), 114–35; Amos Kendall to Isaac Hill, 26 Nov. 1830, Misc. Mss. NYHS; William B. Lewis to John Overton, 13 Jan. 1831, Overton Papers, THS; Francis Preston Blair to Duff Green, 13 Oct. 1830, Blair-Lee Papers, PUL.

51. Chase C. Mooney, *William H. Crawford, 1772–1834* (Lexington, 1974), 308–14.

52. Wiltse, *Calhoun*, I, 362–64, II, 76–79; Sellers, *Polk*, I, 135–48; James Monroe to John C. Calhoun, 26 Feb. 1827, Wilson (ed.), *The Papers of John C. Calhoun*, X, 268–70; John C. Calhoun to James Monroe, 30 Feb. 1827, *ibid.*, 221–27; John C. Calhoun to James Monroe, 22 Dec. 1827, *ibid.*, 321–22; James Monroe to John C. Calhoun, 26, 28 Dec. 1827, *ibid.*, 322–26; John C. Calhoun to James Monroe, 3 Jan. 1828, *ibid.*, 330–31; James A. Hamilton to John Forsyth, 29 Jan. 1828, *ibid.*, 341–42; James A. Hamilton to John C. Calhoun, 25 Feb. 1828, *ibid.*, 354; John C. Calhoun to James A. Hamilton, *ibid.*, 355–56; John C. Calhoun to James Monroe, 7 March 1828, *ibid.*, 357–58; James Monroe to John C. Calhoun, 16 March 1828, *ibid.*, 361–65; James A. Hamilton to John C. Calhoun, 20 March 1828, *ibid.*, 365–66; John C. Calhoun to James Monroe, 20 April 1828, *ibid.*, 376–78; John C. Calhoun to Andrew Jackson, 30 April 1828, *ibid.*, 378–79; John C. Calhoun to Henry Lee, 30 April 1828, *ibid.*, 379–80; John C. Calhoun to James Monroe, 1 May 1828, *ibid.*, 380–81; Andrew Jackson to John C. Calhoun, 25 May 1828, *ibid.*, 387–90, John C. Calhoun to Andrew Jackson, 10 July 1828, *ibid.*, 395–97; John C. Calhoun to James Monroe, 10 July 1828, *ibid.*, 398–99; James Monroe to John C. Calhoun, 4 Aug. 1828, *ibid.*, 408–9; Wilson Lumpkin to John C. Calhoun, 27 Jan. 1829, *ibid.*, 554–56.

53. Hamilton (ed.), *Reminiscences*, 97; Amos Kendall to John Pope, 11 Jan. 1829, Blair-Lee Papers, PUL; Amos Kendall to Francis P. Blair, 7 March 1829, *ibid.*; William T. Barry to Mrs. Susan Taylor, 16 May 1829, *William and Mary Quarterly*, XIII (1904–05), 239.

53. Philip S. Klein, *Pennsylvania Politics, 1817–1832: A Game Without Rules* (Philadelphia, 1940), 252–58; Gabriel Lowe, Jr., "John H. Eaton, Jackson's Campaign Manager," *Tennessee Historical Quarterly*, II (1952), 99–147; Wiltse, *Calhoun*, II, 19–23; Hamilton (ed.), *Reminiscences*, 87–103; Bassett, *Andrew Jackson*, 408–19.

55. Royce Coggins McCrary, Jr., "John MacPherson Berrien of Georgia (1781–1856): A Political Biography" (unpublished doctoral dissertation, University of Georgia, 1971), 144–46; Thomas P. Govan, "John M. Berrien and the Administration of Andrew Jackson," *Journal of Southern History*, 5 (Nov. 1939), 447–68; William S. Hoffman, *Andrew Jackson and North Carolina Politics* (Chapel Hill, 1958), 30, 38–39; William S. Hoffman, "John Branch and the Origins of the Whig Party in North Carolina," *North Carolina Historical Review*, 35 (July 1958), 299–315; Nathan Sargent, *Public Men and Events* (2 vols., Philadelphia, 1875), I, 165–66.

56. Fitzpatrick (ed.), *Autobiography of Martin Van Buren*, 231; Richard B. Latner, "The Eaton Affair Reconsidered," *Tennessee Historical Quarterly*, XXXVI (Fall 1977), 330–51; Bassett, *Andrew Jackson*, 415–16; Robert Y. Hayne to Martin Van Buren, 14 Feb. 1829, Van Buren Papers, LC; James Hamilton to Martin Van Buren, 19 Feb. 1829, *ibid.*; James A. Hamilton to Martin Van Buren, 14 Feb. 1829, *ibid.*; Hamilton (ed.), *Reminiscences*, 215; Munroe, *Lewis McLane*, 243–52; John Floyd to Thomas Spalding, 22 Feb. 1829, Misc. Mss., NYHS; Lewis Williams to Willie P. Mangum, 23 Feb.

1829, Henry T. Shanks (ed.), *The Papers of Willie Person Mangum* (5 vols., Raleigh, 1950–56), I, 357.

57. Fitzpatrick (ed.), *Autobiography of Martin Van Buren*, 262–69; Bassett, *Andrew Jackson*, 452; Wiltse, *Calhoun*, II, 24–25; Martin Van Buren to Andrew Jackson, 23 April 1829, Bassett (ed.), *Correspondence of Andrew Jackson*, IV, 25.

58. Sellers, *Polk*, I, 137–43; Bassett, *Andrew Jackson*, 416–19, 445, 460; Fitzpatrick (ed.), *Autobiography of Martin Van Buren*, 231, 340–41, 363; James A. Hamilton to Martin Van Buren, 21, 23 Feb. 1829, Van Buren Papers, LC; C. C. Cambreling to Martin Van Buren, 1 March 1829, *ibid.;* Hugh Lawson White to John Overton, 12 Aug. 1830, Overton Papers, THS.

59. John C. Calhoun to Samuel D. Ingham, 26 July, 26 Sept. 1829, Wilson (ed.), *The Papers of John C. Calhoun*, XI, 63, 78–80; John C. Calhoun to John McLean, 22 Sept. 1829, *ibid.,* 75–76; Virgil Maxcy to John C. Calhoun, 6 April, 7 May, 4 July 1829, *ibid.,* 15–17, 3, 56–61; James Hamilton, Jr., to John C. Calhoun, 10 May 1829, *ibid.,* 43.

60. Quoted in Bassett, *Andrew Jackson*, 458; Fitzpatrick (ed.), *Autobiography of Martin Van Buren*, 339; William T. Barry to Mrs. Susan Taylor, 25 Feb. 1830, *William and Mary College Quarterly, Historical Magazine*, XIV (1905–06), 19–20.

61. Good accounts of the Eaton Affair, although they differ sharply in their interpretation of its significance, are to be found in: Wiltse, *Calhoun*, II, 26–38; Robert V. Remini, *Andrew Jackson* (New York, 1966), 111–16; Richard Latner, "The Eaton Affair Reconsidered," *Tennessee Historical Quarterly*, XXXVI (Fall 1977), 330–51.

62. John McKinley to John Coffee, 25 Jan. 1830, Coffee Papers, ADAH.

63. Andrew Jackson to Richard Keith Call, 5 July 1829; Bassett (ed.), *Correspondence of Andrew Jackson*, IV, 50–53; Andrew Jackson to Samuel Swartwout, 27 Sept. 1829, *ibid.,* 77–79.

64. Andrew Jackson to John Coffee, 6 Dec. 1830, *ibid.,* 211–12. See also Ambrose Spencer to General John Armstrong, 17 Jan. 1830, Rokeby Collection, NYHS.

65. William T. Barry to Mrs. Susan Taylor, 24 Feb. 1830, *William and Mary Quarterly*, XIV (1905–06), 19–20; Amos Kendall to Francis Preston Blair, 28 January 1830, Blair-Lee Papers, PUL; Wiltse, *Calhoun*, II, 36.

66. Andrew Jackson to John Coffee, 19, 22 March 1829, Bassett (ed.), *Correspondence of Andrew Jackson*, IV, 13–15; Andrew Jackson to John C. McLemore, 3 May 1829, *ibid.,* 30–31; Andrew Jackson to John Coffee, 30 May 1829, *ibid.,* 38; Andrew Jackson to Richard Keith Call, 5 July 1829, *ibid.,* 50–53.

67. Andrew Jackson to John McLemore, 24 Nov. 1829, *ibid.,* 88–89; Andrew Jackson to John Overton, 31 Dec. 1829, *ibid.,* 108–9.

68. John C. Calhoun to Andrew Jackson, 29 May 1830, Wilson (ed.), *The Papers of John C. Calhoun*, XI, 189.

69. John C. Calhoun to Lt. James Edward Calhoun, 13 Jan. 1831, *ibid.,* 294; James A. Hamilton to Andrew Jackson, 3 Feb. 1831, Hamilton (ed.), *Reminiscences*, 195.

70. Andrew Jackson to William S. Fulton, 4 July 1824, Bassett (ed.), *Correspondence of Andrew Jackson*, III, 259; Andrew Jackson to John C. Calhoun, 30 May 1830, Wilson (ed.), *The Papers of John C. Calhoun*, XI, 192–93; Andrew Jackson to Martin Van Buren, 14 Feb. 1829, Bassett (ed.), *Correspondence of Andrew Jackson*, IV, 4; Andrew Jackson to John Coffee, 28 Dec. 1830, *ibid.,* 216.

71. Andrew Jackson to John Coffee, 19 June 1831, Coffee Papers (typescript), ADAH.

72. F. P. Blair to Mrs. Gratz, 16 July 1831, Thomas H. Clay (ed.), "Two Years with Old Hickory," *Atlantic Monthly,* LX (Aug. 1887), 196.

73. Andrew Jackson to John Coffee, 24 April, 13 May, 1831, 21 Jan. 1832, Bassett (ed.), *Correspondence of Andrew Jackson,* IV, 269, 282, 400; William B. Lewis to John Overton, 13 Jan. 1831, Overton Papers, THS.

74. John C. Calhoun to James H. Hammond, 15 Jan. 1831, Wilson (ed.), *The Papers of John C. Calhoun,* XI, 298.

75. John C. Calhoun to Virgil Maxcy, 11 Sept. 1830, *ibid.,* 227.

76. John C. Calhoun to Nathan Towson, 11 Sept., 1830, *ibid.,* 230–31.

77. James Hamilton, Jr., to L. W. Tazewell, 26 Aug. 1831, Tazewell Papers, VSL. See also James A. Hamilton, Jr., to James H. Hammond, 21 May 1831, "Letters on the Nullification Movement in South Carolina," *American Historical Review,* VI (July 1901), 745–46.

78. George McDuffie, *Speech . . . at . . . Charleston, S.C., May 19, 1831* (Charleston, 1831); Freehling, *Prelude to Civil War,* 222–23.

79. Duff Green to John C. Calhoun, 31 May 1831, Wilson (ed.), *The Papers of John C. Calhoun,* XI, 398.

80. James Hamilton, Jr. to James Hammond, 21 May 1831, "Letters on the Nullification Movement in South Carolina," *American Historical Review,* VI (July 1901), 745–46.

81. John C. Calhoun to Francis W. Pickens, 1 Aug. 1831, Wilson (ed.), *The Papers of John C. Calhoun,* XI, 445; John C. Calhoun to Samuel D. Ingham, 16 June 1831, *ibid.,* 404–5; John C. Calhoun to Virgil Maxcy, 16 June 1831, *ibid.,* 405; Freehling, *Prelude to Civil War,* 221–25; James Hamilton, Jr., to James Hammond, 11 June 1831, "Letters on the Nullification Movement in South Carolina," *American Historical Review,* VI (July 1901) 746–47.

82. John C. Calhoun to Frederick W. Symmes [Editor of the Pendleton, S.C., *Messenger*], 26 July 1831, Wilson (ed.), *The Papers of John C. Calhoun,* XI, 413–40.

83. John C. Calhoun to Charles J. McDonald, 4 Aug. 1831, *ibid.,* 448–49; John C. Calhoun to Christopher Vandeventer, 5 Aug. 1831, *ibid.,* 450–51; John C. Calhoun to Virgil Maxcy, 6 Aug. 1831, *ibid.,* 451–52; John C. Calhoun to Bolling Hall, 8 Sept. 1831, *ibid.,* 466–67; "Memorandum by James H. Hammond," 18 March 1831, "Letters on the Nullification Movement in South Carolina," *American Historical Review,* VI (July 1901), 741–45.

84. John C. Calhoun to James H. Hammond, 16 May 1831, Wilson (ed.), *The Papers of John C. Calhoun,* XI, 383; John C. Calhoun to Samuel D. Ingham, 31 July, 22 Dec. 1831, 13 Jan., 10 Feb. 1832, *ibid.,* 443, 526–27, 542–43, 547–48; John C. Calhoun to Virgil Maxcy, 6 Aug. 1831, *ibid.,* 451–52; "Memorandum to Richard K. Crallé, 4 Dec. 1831, *ibid.,* 522; John C. Calhoun to Bolling Hall, 13 Feb. 1832, *ibid.,* 553–54; Henry Clay to Francis Brooke, 4 Oct. 1831, 1 April 1832, Colton (ed.), *Henry Clay,* IV, 314–16, 331–33.

85. James Hamilton, Jr., to James H. Hammond, 11 June 1831, "Letters on the Nullification Movement in South Carolina," *American Historical Review,* VI (July 1901), 746–47; James Hamilton to John C. Calhoun, Wilson (ed.), *The Papers of John C. Calhoun,* XI, 607–8.

86. John C. Calhoun to Samuel D. Ingham, 13 Jan. 1832, *ibid.,* 542–43.

87. John C. Calhoun to Richard K. Crallé, 15 April 1832, *ibid.,* 567.

88. Felix A. Nigro, "The Van Buren Confirmation Before the Senate," *The Western Political Quarterly,* XIV (March 1961), 148–59.

89. Sellers, *Polk,* I, 142–52; H. Daniels to Charles A. Wickliffe, 26 Dec. 1831,

Blair-Lee Papers, PUL; Charles A. Wickliffe to Francis P. Blair, 24 Dec. 1831, *ibid.;* George M. Bibb to Charles A. Wickliffe, 22 Jan. 1832, *ibid.;* Charles A. Wickliffe to Hugh Lawson White et al., 24 Dec. 1831, Weaver and Bergeron, *Correspondence of James K. Polk,* I, 430–33; Wickliffe to Hugh Lawson White, Felix Grundy, and James K. Polk, 29 Jan. 1832, *ibid.,* 443–44; James K. Polk to Charles A. Wickliffe, 31 Jan. 1832, *ibid.,* 444–45.

90. Joseph H. Parks, *Felix Grundy, Champion of Democracy* (Baton Rouge, 1940), 204–15; Sellers, *Polk,* I, 142, 145–47, 198–200.

91. John C. Calhoun to Felix Grundy, 8 June 1831, Wilson (ed.), *The Papers of John C. Calhoun,* XI, 401–2; Felix Grundy to John Overton, 22 Jan. 1832, Overton Papers, THS; Felix Grundy to Daniel Graham, 24 Jan. 1831, Grundy Papers, UNC; Felix Grundy to John Eaton, 12 May 1831, *ibid.;* Archibald Yell to John Coffee, 30 May 1831, Coffee Papers, ADAH; Andrew Jackson to John Coffee, 19 June 1831, *ibid.,* Duff Green to Felix Grundy, 25 May 1831, Grundy Papers, UNC; Richard M. Johnson to Felix Grundy, 12 May 1831, Political Papers Collection, Missouri Historical Society (Mo.HS); Hugh Lawson White to Andrew Jackson, 20 April 1831, Bassett (ed.), *Correspondence of Andrew Jackson,* IV, 267; Sellers, *Polk,* I, 142, 145–47, 198–200; Parks, *Grundy,* 204–15.

92. Hugh Lawson White to John Overton, 28 June 1829, 12 Aug. 1830, Overton Papers, THS; John C. Calhoun to James H. Hammond, 16 May 1831, Wilson (ed.), *The Papers of John C. Calhoun,* XI, 382; Nancy N. Scott (ed.), *A Memoir of Hugh Lawson White* (Philadelphia, 1856), 265–70; Hugh Lawson White to Littleton Waller Tazewell, 22, 28 May 1830, 19 Dec. 1832, Tazewell Papers, VSL; Alfred Balch to John McLean, 20 Jan. 1833, McLean Papers, LC; Andrew Jackson to Hugh Lawson White, 9, 29 April 1831, Bassett (ed.), *Correspondence of Andrew Jackson,* IV, 258–60, 271–72; Hugh Lawson White to Andrew Jackson, 20 April, 15 June 1831, *ibid.,* 267–68; 295–96; John Tyler to John Floyd, 4 Dec. 1832, Floyd Papers, LC; Bassett, *Andrew Jackson,* 537.

93. John A. Quitman to Nathan G. Howard, 14 Jan. 1833, Howard Papers, Mississippi Department of Archives and History (MDAH); John C. Calhoun to Lt. James Edward Colhoun, 10 Sept. 1831, Wilson (ed.), *The Papers of John C. Calhoun,* XI, 471; A. Parker to John Quitman, July 1832, J. F. H. Claiborne Papers, MDAH; J. C. Brickler to George Poindexter, 21 Dec. 1831, *ibid.;* E. Turner to John Quitman, 4 July 1830, *ibid.;* John Floyd to John C. Calhoun, 16 April 1831, Wilson (ed.), *The Papers of John C. Calhoun,* XI, 369–71, 536–38; Duff Green to John Floyd, 10 March 1831, *ibid.,* 359–60; John C. Calhoun to John Floyd, 16 Nov. 1831, *ibid.,* 484–85; John Floyd to Littleton Waller Tazewell, 31 May 1832, Floyd Papers, LC.

94. William S. Hoffman, *Andrew Jackson and North Carolina Politics* (Chapel Hill, 1958), 37–46; John Branch to James Iredell, 31 March 1832, Iredell Papers, Duke University (DU); John Branch to Thomas Ruffin, 6 Jan. 1830, J. G. DeRoulhac Hamilton (ed.), *The Papers of Thomas Ruffin* (4 vols., Raleigh, 1918–20), II, 1–2; Nathaniel J. Palmer to Willie P. Mangum, 21 Oct. 1831, Henry T. Shanks (ed.), *The Papers of Willie Persons Mangum* (5 vols., Raleigh, 1950–56), I, 414–15; W. M. Sneed to Willie P. Mangum, 2 Dec. 1831, *ibid.,* 420–22; James Iredell to Willie P. Mangum, 4 Feb. 1832, *ibid.,* 470–73; William S. Ransom to Willie P. Mangum, 8 Feb. 1832, *ibid.,* 470–76; James Iredell to John Branch, 7 March 1832, Branch Family Papers, UNC; Marshall T. Polk to James K. Polk, 19 Dec. 1830, Weaver and Bergeron (eds.), *Correspondence of James K. Polk,* I, 362–63; Augustine H. Shepperd to Charles H. Fisher, 30 Jan. 1830, Fisher Family Papers, UNC.

95. James Hamilton, Jr., to John M. Berrien, 29 July 1831, Berrien Papers, UNC;

Duff Green to John C. Calhoun, 18 July 1831, Wilson (ed.), *The Papers of John C. Calhoun,* XI, 412; John Clark to John C. Calhoun, 4 Aug. 1831, *ibid.,* 447; John C. Calhoun to Charles J. McDonald, 4 Aug. 1831, *ibid.,* 448; McCrary, "John M. Berrien," 137–43, 196–209; Paul Murray, *The Whig Party in Georgia* (Chapel Hill, 1948), 23–26.

96. John McKinley to C. C. Clay, 20 Feb. 1832, C. C. Clay Papers, DU; H. McVay to John Coffee, 4 Dec. 1830, Coffee Papers, ADAH; Charles L. Savage to John Coffee, 5 Feb. 1831, *ibid.;* John McKinley to John Coffee, 2, 29 Jan., 21 Feb. 1831, *ibid.;* Dixon H. Lewis to Richard K. Crallé, 7 May 1832, Crallé Papers, LC; Theodore Henley Jack, *Sectionalism and Party Politics in Alabama, 1819–1842* (Menasha, 1919), 29–30.

97. Frederick Jackson Turner, *The United States 1830–1850* (New York, 1935; reprinted 1965), 399–402; John Forsyth to Martin Van Buren, 7 July 1832, Van Buren Papers, LC; Thomas Ritchie to Martin Van Buren, 10 July 1832, *ibid.;* Peter V. Daniel to Martin Van Buren, 12 July 1832, *ibid.;* H. Bostwick to W. F. Doubleday, 16 June 1832, Blair-Lee Papers, PUL; Charles C. Johnston to David Campbell, 10 June 1832, Campbell Family Papers, DU; Franklin E. Plummer to John A. Quitman, 5 March 1832, J. F. H. Claiborne Papers, MDAH; Joseph George Tregle, Jr., "Louisiana and the Tariff, 1816–1846," *Louisiana Historical Quarterly,* 25 (Jan. 1942), 80–90; John C. Calhoun to James Edward Colhoun, 26 Feb. 1832, Wilson (ed.), *The Papers of John C. Calhoun,* XI, 557; John C. Calhoun to Samuel Ingham, 8 July 1832, *ibid.,* 603; "Extract of letter from William R. King to Governor Gayle [1832]," typescript, William King Papers, ADAH.

98. Littleton Waller Tazewell to John N. Tazewell, 8, 23 May 1832, Tazewell Papers, VSL; James Iredell to John Branch, 7 March 1832, Branch Family Papers, UNC; John Forsyth to Martin Van Buren, 7 July 1832, Van Buren Papers, LC; Thomas Ritchie to Martin Van Buren, 10 July 1832. *ibid.;* C. W. Gooch to Martin Van Buren, 9 Oct. 1832, *ibid.,* James Iredell to Willie P. Mangum, 4 Feb. 1832, *The Papers of Willie P. Mangum,* I, 470–74; R. J. Yancey to Willie P. Mangum, 11 Feb. 1832, *ibid.,* 480; Spencer O'Brien to Willie P. Mangum, 26 Feb. 1832, *ibid.,* 494; John Martin to Willie P. Mangum, 16 March 1832, *ibid.,* 512–13; R. M. Saunders to Willie P. Mangum, 31 March 1832, *ibid.,* 523–24; W. Montgomery to Willie P. Mangum, 6 June 1832, *ibid.,* 550.

99. Martin Van Buren to Joseph H. Bryan et al., 4 Oct. 1832, Samuel Rhea Gammon, *The Presidential Campaign of 1832* (Baltimore, 1922), 163–67, 90–94, 144–45; William T. Barry to John Overton, 5 Aug. 1832, Overton Papers, THS; Charles Savage to John Coffee, 21 Nov. 1831, Coffee Papers, ADAH; C. W. Gooch to C. C. Cambreleng, 3 Nov. 1832, Gooch Family Papers, UVa; Littleton Waller Tazewell to John N. Tazewell, 23 May 1832, Tazewell Papers, VSL; Andrew Jackson to Martin Van Buren, 16 Sept. 1832, Van Buren Papers, LC; Hoffman, *Andrew Jackson and North Carolina Politics,* 47–57. Miles, *Jacksonian Democracy in Mississippi,* 52–53. For a somewhat different interpretation of the significance of the Barbour Movement for southern politics, see: William J. Cooper, Jr., *The South and the Politics of Slavery, 1828–1856* (Baton Rouge, 1978), 17–22.

100. John Marshall to Joseph Story, 24 Aug. 1832, Massachusetts Historical Society, *Proceedings,* 2nd Series, XIV (1900, 1901), 350.

101. Wiltse, *Calhoun,* II, 132–42. General treatments of the election of 1832 are to be found in: Gannon, *The Presidential Campaign of 1832,* passim; Robert V. Remini, "The Election of 1832," Arthur M. Schlesinger, Jr., (ed.), *History of American Presidential Elections, 1798–1968* (4 vols., New York, 1971), I, 495–516; Erik McKinley

Eriksson, "Official Newspaper Organs and Jackson's Re-election, 1832," *Tennessee Historical Magazine,* IX (Jan. 1925), 37–58; Edward Stanwood, *History of the Presidency from 1789 to 1887* (2 vols., Boston, 1928), I, 151–65; Richard G. Miller, "The Tariff of 1832: The Issue That Failed," *The Filson Club Historical Quarterly,* 49 (July 1975), 221–30.

102. Thomas Ritchie to Martin Van Buren, 25 June 1832, Van Buren Papers, LC.

103. Thomas F. Jones to John F. Patterson, 24 Nov. 1832, Jones and Patterson Family Papers, UNC. See also: *Constitutional Whig* (Richmond), 5 Dec. 1832.

104. John Marshall to William Gaston, 20 Dec. 1832, Gaston Papers, UNC.

4 The Proclamation

1. Freehling, *Prelude to Civil War,* 252–61; Wiltse, *Calhoun: Nullifier,* 147–48; Boucher, *The Nullification Controversy in South Carolina,* 164–207; Houston, *A Critical Study of Nullification in South Carolina,* 106–7.

2. "Convention Proceedings," *State Papers on Nullification . . .* (Boston, 1934), 293–320; P. M. Butler to James Hammond, 20, 21, 22 Nov. 1832, Hammond Papers, LC; William Preston to Hammond, 21 Nov. 1832, *ibid.*

3. *State Papers on Nullification,* 71. The three documents are to be found in *ibid.,* 1–27, 33–55, 57–71.

4. *Ibid.,* 28–31.

5. *Ibid.,* 316–21; P. M. Butler to James Hammond, 27 Nov. 1832, Hammond Papers, LC; "Letter of Alfred Huger to the People of Spartinburgh District," 5 Dec. 1832, in *Charleston Courier,* 9 Jan. 1833; *Charleston Mercury,* 3 Nov. 1832.

6. John C. Calhoun to Patrick Noble, 31 Oct. 1832, Wilson (ed.), *The Papers of John C. Calhoun,* XI, 669; *Charleston Mercury,* 30 Nov. 1832; *Charleston Courier,* 9 Jan. 1833; James Henry to Samuel Patterson, 3 Dec. 1832, Jones and Patterson Family Papers, UNC.

7. Joel R. Poinsett to Andrew Jackson, 16 Oct. 1832, Bassett (ed.), *Correspondence of Andrew Jackson,* IV, 481–82; Andrew Jackson to Joel R. Poinsett, 7 Nov. 1832, *ibid.,* 485–86; Joel R. Poinsett to Andrew Jackson, 16, 24, 29 Nov. 1832, *ibid.,* 486–88, 490–92; Andrew Jackson to Joel R. Poinsett, 2, 9 Dec. 1832, *ibid.,* 493–94, 497–98; W. Gilmore Simms to James Lawson, 25 Nov. [1832], Mary C. Simms Oliphant et al. (eds.), *The Letters of William Gilmore Simms* (6 vols., Columbia, 1952–56), I, 46–48.

8. *U.S. Telegraph* (Washington, D.C.), 3 Dec. 1832; *Charleston Mercury,* 1 Dec. 1832.

9. "What is the Question?" *Charleston Mercury,* 5 Dec. 1832; "Letter of Pompilium," *ibid.,* 1 Dec. 1832; *U.S. Telegraph* (Washington, D.C.), 1, 5, 6, 8 Dec. 1832.

10. "Who is for Peace? Who is for War?" *U.S. Telegraph* (Washington, D.C.), 10 Dec. 1832; see also *ibid.,* 1, 4, 6 Dec. 1832.

11. Quoted in Augustus C. Buell, *History of Andrew Jackson* (2 vols., New York, 1904), II, 245.

12. Extract of a Letter from a Member of Congress to Editor of *Ohio Eagle,* dated, Washington City, 9 Dec. 1832, reprinted in *Washington Globe,* 26 Jan. 1833.

13. Andrew Jackson to Martin Van Buren, 30 Aug. 1832, Bassett (ed.), *Correspondence of Andrew Jackson,* IV, 470; Andrew Jackson to Martin Van Buren, 23 Oct. 1832, Van Buren Papers, LC.

14. Fitzpatrick (ed.), *Autobiography of Martin Van Buren,* 544.

15. Samuel Tyler (ed.), *Memoir of Roger Brooke Taney* (Baltimore, 1872), 189.

16. Buell, *History of Andrew Jackson*, II, 246, Daniel Webster to Levi Lincoln, 10 Dec. 1832, Wiltse and Moser (eds.), *The Papers of Daniel Webster*, III, 200. See also: "Spy in Washington," 28 Nov. 1832, in *Courier and Enquirer* (New York), 8 Dec. 1832; *Constitutional Whig* (Richmond), 30 Nov., 4 Dec. 1832; Michael Hoffman to Martin Van Buren, 9 Dec. 1832, Van Buren Papers, LC.

17. "Spy in Washington," 4, 8, 9 Dec. 1832, in *Courier and Enquirer* (New York), 8, 15 Dec. 1832; "From Our Correspondent," Washington, D.C., 8 Dec. 1832, in New York *Commercial Advertiser,* 10 Dec. 1832; "What Will Be Done?" Correspondent from Washington, D.C., 9 Dec. 1832, in *Constitutional Whig* (Richmond), 11 Dec. 1832; Andrew Jackson to Joel R. Poinsett, 7 Nov., 2, 9, Dec. 1832 Bassett (ed.), *Correspondence of Andrew Jackson,* IV, 485–86, 493–94, 497–98.

18. "What Next?" *Washington Globe,* 4 Dec. 1832; "Nullification," *ibid.,* 3, 4 Dec. 1832; "A Peaceful Remedy," *ibid.,* 6 Dec. 1832; "The National Sanction," *ibid.,* 7 Dec. 1832.

19. Andrew Jackson to Joel R. Poinsett, 2 Dec. 1832, Bassett (ed.), *Correspondence of Andrew Jackson,* IV, 494. See also: Andrew Jackson to Secretary of the Navy, Levi Woodbury, 11 Sept. 1832, *ibid.,* 474–75; Andrew Jackson to Andrew Jackson Donelson, 17 Sept. 1832, *ibid.,* 475–76; Joel R. Poinsett to Andrew Jackson, 16 Oct. 1832, *ibid.,* 481–82; Andrew Jackson to Secretary of War Lewis Cass, 29 Oct. 1832, *ibid.,* 483; Andrew Jackson to George Breathitt, 7 Nov. 1832, *ibid.,* 484–85; Andrew Jackson to Joel R. Poinsett, 7 Nov. 1832, *ibid.,* 485–86; Joel R. Poinsett to Andrew Jackson, 16, 24, 29 Nov. 1832, *ibid.,* 486–88, 490–91, 491–92; Lewis Cass to Winfield Scott, 18 Nov. 1832, *American State Papers: Military Affairs,* V, 159; Louis McLane, Secretary of the Treasury to James K. Pringle, Collector of Customs, Charleston (Confidential), 6 Nov. 1832, *Senate Document* No. 45, 22nd Cong. 2nd sess., 92–97; Louis McLane to Robert Gilchrist, District Attorney, United States, Charleston, 19 Nov. 1832, *ibid.,* 97–98; "From Our Correspondent," Washington, D.C., 8 Dec. 1832, in *New York Commercial Advertiser,* 10 Dec. 1832; Leonard D. White, *The Jacksonians* (New York 1954), 512–16.

20. Amos Kendall to Martin Van Buren, 2, 10 Nov. 1832, Van Buren Papers, LC; Amos Kendall to Littleton Dennis, 1 Dec. 1832, Amos Kendall, Misc. Mss., NYHS; Duff Green to John C. Calhoun, 23 Oct. 1832, Wilson (ed.), *The Papers of John C. Calhoun,* XI, 667; *New York Commerical Advertiser,* 4 Dec. 1832; *Washington Globe,* 3 Dec. 1832.

21. "The Spy in Washington," 11 Dec. 1832, in *Courier and Enquirer* (New York), 18 Dec. 1832; Michael Hoffman to Martin Van Buren, 9 Dec. 1832, Van Buren Papers, LC; W. B. Lewis to John Overton, 23 Nov. 1832, Overton Papers, THS; entry of 10 Dec. 1832, Adams (ed.), *Memoirs of John Quincy Adams,* VIII, 504.

22. *Washington Globe,* 5 Dec. 1832; *Constitutional Whig* (Richmond), 5, 7 Dec. 1832; Benton, *Thirty Years' View,* I, 297.

23. Richardson (ed.), *Messages and Papers of the Presidents,* II, 600.

24. *Ibid.,* 602–3.

25. *Ibid.,* 598–99.

26. *Ibid.,* 599–600.

27. *Ibid.,* 600–601.

28. *Ibid.,* 598–605.

29. *Ibid.,* 606.

30. Entry of 4 Dec. 1832, Adams (ed.), *Memoirs of John Quincy Adams,* VIII, 503; *Constitutional Whig* (Richmond), 5, 7 Dec. 1832; "The Message," *U.S. Telegraph*

(Washington, D.C.), 5, 7 Dec. 1832; letter of George Poindexter, Washington, D.C., 4 Dec. 1832, in *Natchez Courier and Adams, Jefferson and Franklin Advertiser*, 8 Feb. 1833; *New York Commercial Advertiser*, 6 Dec. 1832; *Courier and Enquirer* (New York), 8 Dec. 1832.

31. Richardson (ed.), *Messages and Papers of the Presidents*, II, 643.

32. *Ibid.*, 104–5.

33. *Ibid.*, 640–56.

34. *Ibid.*, 648–49, 665. See also *Constitutional Whig* (Richmond), 14 Dec. 1832.

35. Henry Clay to Francis Brooke, 12 Dec. 1832, Colton (ed.), *Private Correspondence of Henry Clay*, 344–45; *New York Commercial Advertiser*, 15 Dec. 1832; Joseph Story to Richard Peters, 22 Dec. 1832, Joseph Story to Mrs. Story, 27 Jan. 1833, Story (ed.), *Life and Letters of Joseph Story*, II, 113; *Albany Evening Journal*, 11 Jan. 1833; C. P. Curtis to Nicholas Trist, 16 Dec. 1832, Trist Papers, LC.

36. General William F. Gordon to Thomas Walker Gilmer, 11 Dec. 1832, *William and Mary Quarterly*, XXI (July 1912), 1; Willie P. Mangum to Charity A. Mangum, 15 Dec. 1832, Shanks (ed.), *The Papers of Willie Person Mangum*, I, 589; William J. Alexander to James K. Polk, 29 Dec. 1832, Weaver and Bergeron (eds.), *Correspondence of James K. Polk*, I, 593; Thomas Hart Benton to Beverley Tucker, 11 Feb. 1833, "Correspondence of Judge Tucker," *William and Mary Quarterly*, XII (Oct. 1903), 86; C. C. Cambreling to Martin Van Buren, [10–18?] and 26 Dec. 1832, Van Buren Papers, LC.

37. *Constitutional Whig* (Richmond), 21 Dec. 1832.

38. Fitzpatrick (ed.), *Autobiography of Martin Van Buren*, 313; *Richmond Enquirer*, 1 Jan. 1833; Richard P. Longaker, "Was Jackson's Kitchen Cabinet a Cabinet?" *Mississippi Valley Historical Review*, XLIV (June 1957), 94–108.

39. James Madison to Edward Livingston, 8 May 1830, in *Washington Globe*, 4 Feb. 1833. On Livingston's speech see *Register of Debates*, 25:1, 247–72, esp. 265–72. See also: Andrew Jackson to Edward Livingston, 4 Dec. 1832, Bassett (ed.), *Correspondence of Andrew Jackson*, IV, 494–95; Fitzpatrick (ed.), *Autobiography of Martin Van Buren*, 424–25, 543–48, 552–57, 705–7; Tyler (ed.), *Memoir of Roger Brooke Taney*, 187–88, *Courier and Enquirer* (New York), 29 Dec. 1832; *New York Commercial Advertiser*, 15 Jan. 1833; *Albany Evening Journal*, 14 Dec. 1832.

40. *New York Commercial Advertiser*, 15 Dec. 1832.

41. James Madison to Nicholas P. Trist, 23 Dec. 1832, Hunt (ed.), *The Writings of James Madison*, IX, 491–92; James Madison to Edward Coles, 29 Aug. 1834, *ibid.*, 538–42.

42. Edward Livingston to James Madison, 29 April 1830, 19 Jan. 1833, Madison Papers, LC; James Madison to Edward Livingston [24 Jan. 1833], *ibid.*

43. J.F.R., "Nicholas Philip Trist," *D.A.B.*, IX, 645–46.

44. Daniel Webster to Joseph Story, 27 Dec. 1832, Wiltse and Moser (eds.), *The Papers of Daniel Webster*, III, 201–2. On the Madison-Trist relationship see James Madison to Nicholas P. Trist, 19 Nov., 4 Dec. 1832, 18 Jan. 1833, Madison Papers, LC; James Madison to N. P. Trist, 15 Feb. 1830, [Dec. 1831], 29 May 1832, 23 Dec. 1832, Hunt (ed.), *Writings of Madison*, IX, 354–58, 471–77, 478–82, 489–92; N. P. Trist to James Madison, 2 May, 17 Sept. 1831, 8 May, 23, 28 Nov. 1832, Trist Papers, VaHS. The relationship between Madison and the Jackson administration is an important but elusive subject that should be more closely examined. Useful along these lines is: Donald O. Dewey, "Madison's Response to Jackson's Foes," *Tennessee Historical Quarterly*, XX (1961), 167–76.

45. N. P. Trist to James Madison, Dec. 1832, Trist Papers, VaHS.

46. Andrew Jackson to Martin Van Buren, 25 Dec. 1832, Bassett (ed.), *Correspondence of Andrew Jackson,* IV, 506.

47. J. Y. Mason to George C. Dromgoole, 24 Dec. 1832, Edward Dromgoole Papers, UNC; Robert Hayne to Andrew Jackson, 4 Feb. 1831, Jackson Papers, LC.

48. A different version may be found in Samuel Tyler (ed.), *Memoir of Roger Brooke Taney,* 188. According to Tyler, Jackson wrote an early draft of the Proclamation and then handed it to Livingston "to be elaborated and put into an appropriate form. When the instrument, as prepared by Mr. Livingston, was presented to General Jackson, he disapproved of the principles and doctrine of centralization contained in it. But as the conclusion suited him, he determined to issue it at once, without waiting to correct the erroneous doctrines contained in it; as promptitude was a cardinal principle of action with him. He authorized Mr. Blair to set forth his [true?] views in an editorial in the Globe which was written by Mr. Blair under his dictation and submitted to General Jackson before it was published." Contemporary evidence does not support this interpretation. It is further undercut by the fact that in the months that followed neither Jackson, in his public and private statements, nor the *Globe,* repudiated any aspect of the Proclamation.

49. Andrew Jackson to John Coffee, 14 Dec. 1832, Bassett (ed.), *Correspondence of Andrew Jackson,* IV, 500.

50. James Y. Mason to George C. Dromgoole, 24 Dec. 1832, Edward Dromgoole Papers, UNC.

51. *National Intelligencer* (Washington, D.C.), 10 Jan. 1833.

52. "The President's Proclamation—No. IV," *Richmond Enquirer,* 14 Feb. 1833.

53. Letter from Richmond, Va., 13 Dec. 1832, in *National Intelligencer* (Washington, D.C.), 17 Dec. 1832; "From Our Correspondent," dated Washington, 17 Dec. 1832, in *New York Commercial Advertiser,* 19 Dec. 1832; *The Herald* (Norfolk, Va.), 17 Dec. 1832; correspondent of *Journal of Commerce* (N.Y.), Washington, 20 Dec. 1832, in *Albany Evening Journal,* 26 Dec. 1832.

54. "The Spy in Washington," 14 Dec. 1832, in *Courier and Enquirer* (New York), 22 Dec. 1832.

55. "The Crisis—Nullification," *Courier and Enquirer* (New York), 22 Dec. 1832. See also C. C. Cambreling to Martin Van Buren, 26 Dec. 1832, Van Buren Papers, LC; "The Proclamation," *U.S. Telegraph* (Washington, D.C.), 18 Dec. 1832; Archibald Yell to James K. Polk, 16 Jan. 1833, Weaver and Bergeron (eds.), *Correspondence of James K. Polk,* I, 27–28; J. L. Bailey to Willie P. Mangum, 25 Dec. 1832, Shanks (ed.), *Papers of Willie P. Mangum,* I, 590–91.

56. C. P. Curtis to Nicholas Trist; 16 Dec. 1832, Trist Papers, LC; Thomas Bulfinch to Nicholas Trist, 18 Dec. 1832, *ibid.; National Intelligencer* (Washington, D.C.), 22, 25 Dec. 1832; Edward Everett to Josiah Johnston, 23 Dec. 1832, Johnston Papers, Historical Society of Pennsylvania (HSP).

57. Entry of 14 Dec. 1832 in Allan Nevins (ed.), *The Diary of Philip Hone* (2 vols., New York, 1927), I, 84–85; *Albany Evening Journal,* 18, 20 Dec. 1832; *National Intelligencer* (Washington, D.C.), 29, 31 Dec. 1832; Condy Raquet to Gulian C. Verplanck, 31 Dec. 1832, Verplanck Papers, NYHS; J. B. Orton to Thomas Erving, 24 Dec. 1832. Ewing Papers, LC; "Proclamation," *U.S. Telegraph* (Washington, D.c.), 17, 21, 22 Dec. 1832; *Constitutional Whig* (Richmond), 21 Dec. 1832; *Courier and Enquirer* (New York), 22 Dec. 1832.

58. *U.S. Telegraph* (Washington, D.C.), 27, 29 Dec. 1832, 1 Jan. 1833; J. B. Orton to Thomas Ewing, 9 Jan. 1833, Ewing Papers, LC.

59. Martin Van Buren, *Inquiry into the Origin and Course of Political Parties in the United States* (New York, 1867), 322.

60. *Speeches of Daniel Webster* (3 vols., Boston, 1850), II, 156–57; *National Intelligencer* (Washington, D.C.), 22, 27 Dec. 1832. See also *Albany Evening Journal*, 19 Dec. 1832.

61. "Spy in Washington," 11 Dec. 1832, in *Courier and Enquirer* (New York), 15 Dec. 1832.

62. Alfred Balch to John McLean, 12 March 1833, McLean Papers, LC; Lewis Williams to William B. Lenoir, 15 Dec. 1832, Lenoir Family Papers, UNC; letter from Washington, D.C., 20 Jan. 1833, *Albany Argus*, 28 Jan. 1833; *National Intelligencer* (Washington, D.C.), 22 Dec. 1832, 3 Jan. 1833; *Constitutional Whig* (Richmond), 18, 21, 25 Dec. 1832; *Richmond Whig and Public Advertiser*, 18 Jan. 1833; *U.S. Telegraph* (Washington, D.C.), 31 Dec. 1832, 9, 14 Jan. 1833; Correspondent from Washington, D.C., 23 Dec. 1832, in *Charleston Mercury*, 1 Jan. 1833.

63. Michael Hoffman to A. C. Flagg, 4 Jan. 1833, Van Buren Papers, LC; Thomas Hart Benton to Martin Van Buren, 16 Dec. 1832, *ibid.*

64. Thomas Hart Benton to Martin Van Buren, 16 Dec. 1832, Van Buren Papers, LC; C. C. Cambreling to Martin Van Buren, 18, 29 Dec. 1832, *ibid.;* letter from Washington, D.C., 1 Jan. 1833, in *Albany Argus*, 8 Jan. 1833; Isaac Hill to Gideon Welles, 14, 30 Dec. 1832, Welles Papers, LC; George M. Troup to Bolling Hall, 21 Jan. 1833, Hall Papers, ADAH; letter from Washington—No. CCCXXXIII, 3 Jan. 1833, *U.S. Gazette* (Philadelphia), 7 Jan. 1833; *Courier and Enquirer* (New York), 22 Dec. 1832, 5 Jan. 1833.

65. "Monstrous" and "South Carolina," *Globe* (Washington, D.C.), 19 Dec. 1832; "Nullification and Secession," Nos. I–III, *ibid.*, 27, 31 Dec. 1832, 3 Jan. 1833; "Governor Hayne's Proclamation," *ibid.*, 28 Dec. 1832, "States' Rights," *ibid.*, 2 Jan. 1833; "President's Message and His Proclamation," *ibid.*, 4 Jan. 1833; "The Proclamation and the Constitution, *ibid.;* "The Proclamation and our Government," *ibid.*, 8 Jan. 1833; "Nullification," *ibid.*, 12 Jan. 1833; "Spirit of Nullification," *ibid.*, 14 Jan. 1833; "The Proclamation and our Government," *ibid.*, 16 Jan. 1833. See also Andrew Jackson to John Coffee, 14 Dec. 1832, Bassett (ed.), *Correspondence of Andrew Jackson,* IV, 500; Andrew Jackson to Martin Van Buren, 15, 23, 25 Dec. 1832, 13 Jan. 1833, *ibid.*, IV, 500–501, 504–6, V, 2–4.

66. *Globe* (Washington, D.C.), 8 Jan. 1833; *National Intelligencer* (Washington, D.C.), 9 Jan. 1833; *Richmond Whig and Public Advertiser*, 11 Jan. 1833.

67. Correspondent, Washington, D.C., 19 Dec. 1832, *American Mercury* [Hartford, Conn.], in *U.S. Telegraph* (Washington, D.C.), 21 Dec. 1832,; "The Spy in Washington," 18 Dec. 1832, *Courier and Enquirer* (New York), 22 Dec. 1832; "From Our Correspondent," Washington, D.C., 20 Dec. 1832, in *Charleston Courier*, 27 Dec. 1832.

68. Silas Wright to Martin Van Buren, 13 Jan. 1833, Van Buren Papers, LC; John Tipton to Calvin Fletcher, 15 Jan. 1833, Robertson and Riker (eds.), *John Tipton Papers* (2 vols., Indianapolis, 1942) II, 777; Andrew Jackson to Martin Van Buren, 15 Dec. 1832, 13 Jan. 1833, Bassett (ed.), *Correspondence of Andrew Jackson,* IV, 500–501, V, 3.

69. Norman D. Brown, "Webster-Jackson Movement for a Constitution and Union Party in 1833," *Mid-America*, 46 (July 1964), 147–71, and *Daniel Webster and the Politics of Availability* (Athens, 1968), 1–28; Sidney Nathans, *Daniel Webster and Jacksonian Democracy* (Baltimore, 1973), 48–61.

70. *Albany Evening Journal,* 21 Dec. 1832.

71. "The Spy in Washington," 21 Dec. 1832, in *Courier and Enquirer* (New York), 26 Dec. 1832. See also William Hammett to Thomas Willis White, 17 Jan. 1833, Hammett Papers, VaHS; John Tyler to John Floyd, 22 Jan. 1833, Floyd Papers, LC.

72. Correspondent of *Journal of Commerce,* Washington, D.C., 31 Dec. 1832, in *Albany Evening Journal,* 7 Jan. 1833.

73. *National Intelligencer* (Washington, D.C.), 18 Dec. 1832; *Albany Argus,* 23 Jan. 1833; "The Spy in Washington," 6 Jan. 1833, in *Courier and Enquirer* (New York), 12 Jan. 1833; Michael Hoffman to A. C. Flagg, 20 Jan. 1833, Flagg Papers, NYPL; Louis McLane to Martin Van Buren, 23 Jan. 1833, Van Buren Papers, LC.

74. John Coffee to Mrs. Coffee, 20 Jan. 1833, Dyas Coll., TSL. Also in Washington at this time was Sam Dale, a sergeant in the Creek and Louisiana campaigns under Jackson, and currently a general of the Mississippi militia. James, *Andrew Jackson,* 310–11; J. F. H. Claiborne, *Life and Times of Sam Dale* (New York, 1860), 178. Was the almost simultaneous arrival in the Capitol of Coffee and Dale, both military men and both close personal friends of the President, merely coincidence, or had Jackson arranged it so they could help him direct the anticipated invasion of South Carolina?

75. Daniel Webster to Warren Dutton, 4 Jan. 1833, Wiltse and Moser (ed.), *The Papers of Daniel Webster,* III, 206. See also: Daniel Webster to William Sullivan, 3 Jan. 1833, Webster (ed.), *Private Correspondence of Daniel Webster,* I, 529; "The Spy in Washington," 3 Jan. 1833, *Courier and Enquirer* (New York), 12 Jan. 1833; Correspondent of *Journal of Commerce,* 9 Jan. 1833, in *Albany Evening Journal,* 16 Jan. 1833; *National Intelligencer* (Washington, D.C.), 9 Jan. 1833; *U.S. Telegraph* (Washington, D.C.), 22 Jan. 1833; William Creighton to Duncan McArthur, 14 Jan. 1833, McArthur Papers, LC; Henry Clay to Francis Brooke, 17 Jan. 1833, Colton (ed.), *Private Correspondence of Henry Clay,* 347.

76. Richardson, *Messages and Papers of the Presidents,* II, 610–32.

77. *Ibid.,* 631–32.

78. Henry Clay to Francis Brooke, 17 Jan. 1833, Colton (ed.), *Private Correspondence of Henry Clay,* 348; John C. Calhoun to Armistead Burt, [16] Jan. 1833, Wilson (ed.), *The Papers of John C. Calhoun,* XII, 15.

79. Letter from Washington, D.C., 16 Jan. 1833, in *Richmond Whig and Public Advertiser,* 22 Jan. 1833. See also entry of 16 Jan. 1833, in Bernard Steiner (ed.), "South Atlantic States in 1833," *Maryland Historical Magazine,* XXII (1918), 283. For the hope that Jackson would use the message to retreat from his earlier extremely belligerent position in the Proclamation, see Martin Van Buren to Andrew Jackson [Jan. 7 or 8] 1833, Van Buren Papers, LC.

80. James Hammond to Robert Y. Hayne, 20 Dec. 1832, "Letters on the Nullification Movement in South Carolina, 1830–1834," *American Historical Review,* VI (July 1901), 751; William C. Preston to James H. Hammond, 31 Dec. 1832, Hammond Papers, LC; *U.S. Telegraph* (Washington, D.C.), 11 Jan. 1833.

81. *Charleston Mercury,* 22 Dec. 1832; *House of Representatives,* 22:2, Doc. 45, No. 13, 99–111.

82. *U.S. Telegraph* (Washington, D.C.), 15 Dec. 1832.

83. "The Crisis," *Charleston Mercury,* 12 Dec. 1832; *U.S. Telegraph* (Washington, D.C.), 1 Jan. 1833.

84. *U.S. Telegraph* (Washington, D.C.), 11, 12, 14, 15, 29, 31 Dec. 1832; *Charleston Mercury,* 20 Dec. 1832.

85. Letter from Columbia, South Carolina, 18 Dec. 1832, in *U.S. Telegraph* (Washington, D.C.), 25 Dec. 1832. See also *ibid.,* 1 Jan. 1833.

86. John Tyler to John Floyd, 10 Jan. 1833, Floyd Papers, LC.

87. Erastus Smith to J. M. Niles, 4 Jan. 1833, Gideon Welles Papers, LC. See also: William Hammet to Thomas Willis White, 22 Dec. 1832, 19 Jan. 1833, Hammet Papers, VaHS; Michael Hoffman to A. C. Flagg, 22 Jan. 1833, Flagg Papers, NYPL.

88. Correspondent, Washington, D.C., 1 Feb. 1833, in *Albany Evening Journal*, 8 Feb. 1833; George McDuffie to Richard R. Crallé, 26 Dec. 1832, Crallé Papers, LC. See also James A. Hamilton to Richard K. Crallé, 15 Jan. 1833, Crallé Pepers, Clemson University (ClU).

89. I have found the discussion in Freehling, *Prelude to Civil War*, 270–73, most useful on this point, although I differ with him over what motivated the nullifiers to act the way they did at this particular time.

90. *Ibid.*, 271–74; *Statutes at Large* (South Carolina), I, 371–74; see also last issue of *Charleston Mercury*, Dec. 1832; "The Replevin Act," *American Beacon* (Norfolk, Va.), 11 Jan. 1833.

91. "The Remedy," *Charleston Mercury*, 1 Jan. 1833.

92. *Niles' Weekly Register*, XLIII (2 Feb. 1833), 380–82; *Charleston Mercury*, 23 Jan. 1833; Freehling, *Prelude to Civil War*, 288.

93. James Hamilton, Jr., to Richard R. Crallé, 6 Feb. 1833, Crallé Papers, ClU.

94. *Register Debates*, 22:2, 960–62, 963. A copy of the bill is to be found in *National Intelligencer* (Washington, D.C.), 28 Dec. 1832. See also Munroe, *Louis McLane*, 367–71; Robert W. July, *The Essential New Yorker: Gulian Crommelin Verplanck* (Durham, 1951), 156–57; Stanwood, *American Tariff Controversies in the Nineteenth Century*, I, 390–96.

95. *New York Commercial Advertiser*, 11 Jan. 1833; Simon Cameron to John C. Bucher, 15 Jan. 1833, MacVeagh Papers HSP; *United States Gazette* (Philadelphia), 18 Jan. 1833; *Albany Evening Journal*, 15 Jan. 1833; "Mr. Verplanck's Report and Bill," *National Intelligencer* (Washington, D.C.), 20 Dec. 1832, 7, 11, 26 Jan. 1833; *Richmond Whig and Advertiser*, 1 Jan. 1833; Daniel Webster to Henry Willis Kinsman, 1 Jan. 1833, Wiltse and Moser (eds.), *Papers of Daniel Webster*, III, 203; Daniel Webster to William Sullivan, 3 Jan. 1833, *ibid.*, 204; Daniel Webster to Stephen White, 18 Jan. 1833, *ibid.*, 207; William Hammet to Thomas Willis White, 11 Jan. 1833, Hammet Papers, VaHS; *Register Debates*, 22:2, 963–98, 1022–1311; Mahlon Dickerson to Gideon Welles, 9 Dec. 1832, Welles Papers, LC; Edward Everett to Josiah Johnston, 23 Dec. 1832, Johnston Papers, HSP.

96. Silas Wright to Martin Van Buren, 13, 29 Jan. 1833, Van Buren Papers, LC; Silas Wright to Azariah C. Flagg, 27, 28 Jan. 1833, Flagg Papers, NYPL; Michael Hoffman to A. C. Flagg, 14, 22 Jan. 1833, *ibid.*; J. Y. Mason to George C. Dromgoole, 8 Jan. 1833, Dromgoole Papers, UNC; A. Judson to Gideon Welles, 21 Jan. 1833, Welles Papers, LC; L. Widman to Gideon Welles, 3 Dec. 1832, *ibid.*; W. Bosworth to Thomas Ewing, 17 Dec. 1832, Ewing Papers, LC; Sellers, *Polk*, I, 158–60; *National Intelligencer* (Washington, D.C.), 7 Jan. 1833; "The Spy in Washington," 13 Jan. 1833, in *Courier and Enquirer* (New York), 19 Jan. 1833; *Register of Debates*, 22:2, 1022–1311.

97. John Tyler to John Floyd, 10, 22 Jan. 1833, Floyd Papers, LC; Thomas Cooper to Gulian C. Verplanck, 15 Jan. 1833, Verplanck Papers, NYHS; Silas Wright to Azariah C. Flagg, 14 Jan. 1833, Flagg Papers, NYPL; Michael Hoffman to A. C. Flagg, 14, 15 Jan. 1833, *ibid.*; Isaac Hill to Gideon Welles, 30 Dec. 1832, Welles Papers, LC; William Hammet to Thomas Willis White, 17 Jan. 1833, Hammet Papers, VaHS; Louis McLane to Martin Van Buren, 23 Jan. 1833, Van Buren Papers, LC; William King to

Martin Van Buren, 9 Jan. 1833, *ibid.;* James Hammond to [William C. Preston], 27 Jan. 1833, Hammond Papers, LC; *Richmond Whig and Public Advertiser* 18 Jan. 1833.

98. Silas Wright to N. P. Tallmadge, 27 Jan. 1833, Tallmadge Papers, Wisconsin Historical Society (WHS); Daniel Webster to [Stephen White], 18 Jan. 1833, Wiltse and Moser (eds.), *Papers of Daniel Webster,* III, 207; entry of 18 Jan. 1833, Steiner (ed.), "The South Atlantic States in 1833 as seen by a Traveller," *Maryland Historical Magazine,* XIII (1918), 284; William Drayton to Joel Poinsett, 13 Jan. 1833, Poinsett Papers, HSP.

99. Michael Hoffman to A. C. Flagg, 17 Jan. 1833, Flagg Papers, NYPL; William Hammet to Thomas Willis White, 19 Jan. 1833, Hammet Papers, VaHS; William Creighton to Duncan McArthur, 14 Jan. 1833, McArthur Papers, LC; Roger Brooke Taney to ? , 22 Jan. 1833, Taney Papers, LC; *U.S. Telegraph* (Washington, D.C.), 22 Jan. 1833; Correspondent, Washington, D.C., 18 Jan. 1833, *Charleston Courier,* 20 Jan. 1833.

100. Andrew Jackson to Martin Van Buren, 23, 25 Dec. 1832, 13 Jan. 1833, Bassett (ed.), *Correspondence of Andrew Jackson,* IV, 504–6, V, 3–4; Andrew Jackson to Joel Poinsett, 16 Jan. 1833, *ibid.,* V, 5.

101. Joel R. Poinsett to Andrew Jackson, 16 Jan. 1833, *ibid.,* V, 6–8; Andrew Jackson to Joel R. Poinsett, 24 Jan. 1833, *ibid.,* V, 11–12.

102. Lewis Cass to Winfield Scott, 26 Jan. 1833, *American State Papers: Military Affairs,* V, 160–61.

103. John C. Calhoun to Lt. James Edward Colhoun, 10 Jan. 1833, Wilson (ed.), *The Papers of John C. Calhoun,* XII, 6–7; John C. Calhoun to Armistead Burt, [16] Jan. 1833, *ibid.,* XII, 15.

5 Georgia and the Nullification Crisis

1. The most important secondary accounts are: Ulrich Bonnell Phillips, *Georgia and State Rights* (Washington, D.C., 1902), 15–142; Paul Murray, *The Whig Party in Georgia, 1825–1853* (Chapel Hill, 1948), 1–58; Jack Nelson Averitt, "The Democratic Party in Georgia, 1824–1837" (unpublished doctoral dissertation, University of North Carolina, Chapel Hill, 1956), 1–439; E. Merton Coulter, "The Nullification Movement in Georgia," *Georgia Historical Quarterly,* V (March 1921), 3–39.

2. Among the more recent treatments of Georgia politics the most useful are: Richard P. McCormick, *The Second American Party System* (Chapel Hill, 1966), 236–46; Ronald W. Faircloth, "The Impact of Andrew Jackson in Georgia Politics, 1828–1840" (unpublished doctoral dissertation, University of Georgia, 1971); Donald Arthur DeBats, "Elites and Masses: Political Structure, Communication and Behavior in Ante-Bellum Georgia" (unpublished doctoral dissertation, University of Wisconsin, Madison, 1973).

3. Phillips, *Georgia and State Rights,* 87, 104–6; Paul Murray, "Economic Sectionalism in Georgia Politics, 1825–1855," *Journal of Southern History,* 10 (Aug. 1944), 293–307.

4. George R. Gilmer to Tomlinson R. Fort, 27 Aug. 1829, Fort Papers, Emory University (EU); Hines Holt to Bolling Hall, 20 June 1828, 21 Oct., 23 Dec. 1829, Hall Papers, ADAH.

5. William H. Crawford to Jesse B. Thomas, 9 Jan. 1828 [1829?], Thomas Papers, Illinois Historical Society (IHS); Hines Holt to Bolling Hall, 30 Aug. 1828, Hall Papers, ADAH; Tomlinson Fort to Andrew Jackson, 1 June 1829, Fort Papers, EU.

6. Wilson Lumpkin to Bolling Hall, 9 April 1830, 29 March 1832, Hall Papers, ADAH. On Lumpkin's relations with Calhoun, see Wilson Lumpkin to John C. Calhoun, 27 Jan. 1829, Wilson ahd Hemphill (eds.), *The Papers of John C. Calhoun*, I, 554–57; Duff Green to John C. Calhoun, 31 May 1831, Wilson (ed.), *ibid.*, XI, 401; Wilson Lumpkin, *The Removal of the Cherokee Indians from Georgia, 1827–41* (2 vols., Wormsloe, privately printed, 1907), II, 297–98; Wilson Lumpkin to Wife, 25 Jan., 14 March 1829, Lumpkin Papers, UGa.

7. Charles J. McDonald to John C. Calhoun, 30 May 1831, Wilson (ed.), *The Papers of John C. Calhoun*, XI, 396.

8. Tomlinson Fort to John C. Calhoun, 15 July 1831, *ibid.*, XI, 409–12.

9. John C. Calhoun to Charles J. McDonald, 29 June [1831], *ibid.*, XI, 406–7.

10. Alvin L. Duckett, *John Forsyth: Political Tactician* (Athens, 1962), 128–66; Alexander A. Lawrence, *James Moore Wayne: Southern Unionist* (Chapel Hill, 1943), 53–76.

11. Edward Jenkins Harden, *Life of George M. Troup* (Savannah, 1859), 510–11.

12. Letter of 29 Aug. 1832, in *ibid.*, 515; George M. Troup to John M. Berrien, 1 Feb. 1830, 16 June 1831, Berrien Papers, UNC.

13. Duff Green to John Pemberton, 5 Aug. 1831, Green Papers, UNC; James Hunter to Nicholas Biddle, 6 Aug., 19 Nov. 1832, Biddle Papers, LC; John M. Berrien to Phillip H. Nicklin, 17 July 1832, *ibid.*; Royce Coggins McCrary, "John MacPherson Berrien of Georgia (1781–1856): A Political Biography" (unpublished doctoral dissertation, University of Georgia, 1971); C. Jay Smith, Jr., "John MacPherson Berrien," Horace Montgomery (ed.), *Georgians in Profile: Historical Essays in Honor of Ellis Merton Coulter* (Athens, 1958), 168–91; Stephen Francis Miller, *The Bench and Bar of Georgia: Memoirs and Sketches* (2 vols., Philadelphia, 1858), I, 21–110, 139–92.

14. Miller, *Bench and Bar of Georgia*, II, 29; E. M. Coulter, *College Life in the Old South* (New York, 1928), 221, 224, 237, 244.

15. *Southern Recorder* (Milledgeville), 4 Oct. 1832; "The Crisis," *ibid.*, 11 Oct. 1832.

16. *Register of Debates*, 22:1, 1290.

17. Duckett, *John Forsyth*, 624–25.

18. John Forsyth to Martin Van Buren, 23 Nov. 1G32, Van Buren Papers, LC.

19. James M. Wayne to Levi Woodbury, 23 Nov. 1832, Woodbury Papers, LC; Duckett, *Forsyth*, 156–59.

20. *Federal Union* (Milledgeville), 29 Nov. 1832; Coulter, "The Nullification Movement in Georgia," *Georgia Historical Quarterly*, V, 28.

21. *Federal Union* (Milledgeville), 6 Dec., 3 Jan. 1832; *Georgia Telegraph* (Macon), 28 Nov. 1832; *Niles' Weekly Register*, 43 (1 Dec. 1832), 231.

22. Lumpkin, *Removal of the Cherokees*, I, 124–25.

23. *State Papers on Nullification*, 271–74.

24. *Georgia Messenger* (Macon), 20 Dec. 1832.

25. "Et Tu Brutus," *ibid.*, 6, 10, 20 Dec. 1832; *Georgia Journal* (Milledgeville), 6 Dec. 1832.

26. *Southern Recorder* (Milledgeville), 27 Dec. 1832.

27. *Georgia Journal* (Milledgeville), 20, 27 Dec. 1832; *Georgia Messenger* (Macon), 20 Dec. 1832.

28. "John Hancock," in *Southern Recorder* (Milledgeville), 3 Jan. 1833.

29. From *Augusta Chronicle*, in *U.S. Telegraph* (Washington, D.C.), 3 Jan. 1833; John Floyd to Governor John Floyd of Virginia, 4 Jan. 1833, Floyd Papers, LC.

30. From *Augusta Chronicle*, in *U.S. Telegraph* (Washington, D.C.), 5 Jan. 1833;

The Times and States' Rights Advocate (Milledgeville), 6 Feb. 1833; *Southern Recorder* (Milledgeville), 3 Jan., 20 Feb. 1833; "Senex," *Georgia Telegraph* (Macon), 2 Jan. 1833; *Georgia Journal* (Milledgeville), 3, 31 Jan. 1833; *Federal Union* (Milledgeville), 17 Jan. 1833.

31. Letter from Hillsboro, Jasper County, Georgia, 20 Jan. 1833, in *The Times and States' Rights Advocate* (Milledgeville), 20 Feb. 1833; "To the People of Georgia," *Georgia Journal* (Milledgeville), 3 Jan. 1833; John Floyd to Governor John Floyd of Virginia, 3 Jan. 1833, Floyd Papers, LC.

32. *The Times and States' Rights Advocate* (Milledgeville), 15 Jan. 1833.

33. *Georgia Messenger* (Macon), 20 Dec. 1832.

34. *Ibid.*, 27 Dec. 1832; *U.S. Telegraph* (Washington, D.C.), 7 Jan. 1833; *The Georgian* (Savannah), 31 Dec. 1832, 1 Jan. 1833; *The Georgia Journal* (Milledgeville), 3 Jan. 1833.

35. *Richmond Whig and Public Advertiser*, 25 Jan. 1833.

36. "Extract of a letter from a highly respectable citizen of Georgia," Milledgeville, 18 Jan. 1833, in *U.S. Telegraph* (Washington, D.C.), 29 Jan. 1833; *The Times and States' Rights Advocate* (Milledgeville), 15 Jan., 20 Feb. 1833; *Georgia Journal* (Milledgeville), 31 Jan. 1833; "Senex," *Georgia Journal* (Macon), 2 Jan. 1833; *The Federal Union* (Milledgeville), 17 Jan. 1833; *Albany Evening Journal*, 4 Jan. 1833; William H. Crawford to Bolling Hall, 17 Jan. 1833, Hall Papers, ADAH: Hines Hall to Bolling Hall, 14 Feb. 1833, *ibid.*

37. "The Spy in Washington," 18 Dec. 1832, in *Courier and Enquirer* (New York), 22 Dec. 1832.

38. James M. Wayne to Governor Wilson Lumpkin, 19 Dec. 1832, Lumpkin Papers, Georgia Department of Archives and History (GDAH).

39. Michael Hoffman to Martin Van Buren, 7 Dec. 1832, Van Buren Papers, LC; Isaac Southard to Samuel L. Southard, 24 Dec. 1832, Southard Papers, PUL; Elias Pitts to Samuel Tilden, 28 Dec. 1832, Tilden Papers, NYPL.

40. "Georgia—The Missionaries—South Carolina," *U.S. Telegraph* (Washington, D.C.), 19 Dec. 1832; "Georgia and the Administration," *ibid.; Georgia Messenger* (Macon), 3 Jan. 1833; *Constitutional Whig* (Richmond), 14, 18 Dec. 1832; *Richmond Whig and Public Advertiser*, 1 Jan. 1833; *National Intelligencer* (Washington, D.C.), 31 Dec. 1832; "Fair Play," *U.S. Telegraph* (Washington, D.C.), 11 Dec. 1832; *ibid.*, 25, 28 Dec. 1832, 2 Jan. 1833; *Missouri Republican* (St. Louis), 25 Dec. 1832; *New York Commercial Advertiser* 12, 15 Jan. 1833; *Courier and Enquirer* (New York), 8 Dec. 1832.

41. Wilson Lumpkin to Lewis Cass, 2 Jan. 1833, Lumpkin, *The Removal of the Cherokee Indians*, I, 196–97.

42. *Daily Albany Argus*, 28 Dec. 1832; *Washington Globe*, 21 Dec. 1832. See also: *New Hampshire Patriot* (Concord), 21 Jan. 1833; *The Georgia Journal* (Milledgeville), 27 Dec. 1832; "South Carolina—Georgia," *Daily Albany Argus*, 15 Dec. 1832; "Georgia—The Missionaries—South Carolina," *Washington Globe*, 17 Dec. 1832.

43. Quoted in Edwin A. Miles, "After John Marshall's Decision: *Worcester v. Georgia* and the Nullification Crisis," *Journal of Southern History*, XXXIX (Nov. 1973), 531. For much that follows in this section I have benefited a great deal from Miles's careful and intelligent article.

44. Quoted in *ibid.*, 539.

45. William Wirt to John T. Lomax, 15 Nov. 1832, John P. Kennedy (ed.), *Memoir of the Life of William Wirt, Attorney General of the United States* (2 vols., Philadelphia, 1849), II, 331.

46. William Wirt to John Sergeant, 28 Dec. 1832, William Wirt Letterbooks, Maryland Historical Society (MdHS); B. B. Wisner, Secretary of the American Board of Foreign Commissioners, to William Wirt, 28 Dec. 1832, *ibid.;* "Messrs. Worcester and Butler's Reasons for Their Course in Relation to the Proceedings of the State of Georgia," Jack Frederick Kilpatrick and Anna Gritt Kilpatrick (eds.), *New Echota Letters: Contributions of Samuel A. Worcester to the Cherokee Phoenix* (Dallas, 1968), 124–28.

47. The two letters: Eliphalet Nott et al., to Wilson Lumpkin, 17 Dec. 1832, and Silas Wright, Jr., A. C. Flagg, and John A. Dix to Wilson Lumpkin, 18 Dec. 1832, are reprinted in *Georgian* (Savannah) 11 July 1833, *Columbus Enquirer* (Columbus, Ga.), 20 July 1833, and a number of other Georgia newspapers. See also: Martin Van Buren to John Forsyth, 18 Dec. 1832, Van Buren Papers, LC; B. F. Butler to Theodore Sedgwick, 22 Dec. 1832, Sedgwick Papers, Massachusetts Historical Society (MHS); William Wirt to John Sergeant, 22 Dec. 1832, Wirt Papers, MdHS; William D. Driscoll, "Benjamin F. Butler: Lawyer and Regency Politician" (unpublished doctoral dissertation, Fordham University, 1965), 240–44.

48. Lewis Cass to Wilson Lumpkin, 14, 24 Dec. 1832, marked "Private and Confidential," Records of the Office of the Secretary of War, Confidential and Unofficial Letters Sent, Record Group 107, Microfilm Series M7 Roll 1, National Archives (NA).

49. Wilson Lumpkin to Lewis Cass, 2 Jan. 1833, and Wilson Lumpkin to Silas Wright et al., 5 Jan. 1833, Lumpkin, *Removal of the Cherokee Indians,* I, 196–207.

50. B. B. Wisner to William Wirt, 28 Dec. 1832, Wirt Papers, MdHS.

51. Quoted in Miles, "After John Marshall's Decision: . . . ," *Journal of Southern History* (Nov. 1973), 540.

52. S. A. Worcester and Elizur Butler to Governor Wilson Lumpkin, 8, 9 Jan. 1833, reprinted in *Daily Albany Argus* 15 Feb. 1833; *Southern Recorder* (Milledgeville), 20 Feb. 1833; Kilpatrick and Kilpatrick (eds.), *New Echota Letters,* 117–18.

53. Wilson Lumpkin to Charles C. Mills, 14 Jan. 1833, Kilpatrick and Kilpatrick (eds.), *New Echota Letters,* 118–20. See also Wilson Lumpkin to Bolling Hall, 12 March 1833, Hall Papers, ADAH.

54. *The Georgia Journal* (Milledgeville), 17 Jan. 1833; "Pardon of the Missionaries," *Georgia Messenger* (Macon), 24 Jan. 1833; "Cassius," *ibid.,* 14 March 1833. See also *U.S. Telegraph* (Washington, D.C.,), 18, 23, 28 Jan. 1833; *Georgia Messenger* (Macon), 17 Jan., 14 Feb. 1833; *The Times and States' Rights Advocate* (Milledgeville), 15, 23 Jan. 1833; *Southern Recorder* (Milledgeville), 30 Jan., 27 Feb. 1833; *Richmond Whig and Public Advertiser,* 25 Jan. 1833; "Letter from Washington No. CCCXI, 19 Jan. 1833, in *United States Gazette* (Philadelphia), 22 Jan. 1833.

55. "The Missionaries" *Southern Recorder* (Milledgeville), 24 Jan. 1833. See also *Courier and Enquirer* (New York), 26 Jan. 1833.

56. Wilson Lumpkin to James M. Wayne, 19 Jan. 1833, Lumpkin, *Removal of the Cherokee Indians,* I, 209; Martin Van Buren to Andrew Jackson, 6 Feb. 1833, Van Buren Papers, LC, and G. W. Owens to Tomlinson Fort, 22 Nov. 1833, Fort Papers, EU; *Federal Union* (Milledgeville), 7 Feb. 1833. On Lumpkin's early distrust of Forsyth, see Wilson Lumpkin to ?, 21 Jan. 1830, Lumpkin Papers, UGa. See also Duckett, *Forsyth,* 89, 176–79; Lawrence, *Wayne,* 77–92.

57. "Franklin," *Federal Union* (Milledgeville), 21 Feb. 1833; *Georgia Journal* (Milledgeville), 7 March 1833; Harden, *Troup,* 510–19. Troup's various public statements during the nullification crisis were muddled attempts to avoid the crucial issues. For example, see: Harden, *Troup,* Appendix, i–xiii; *Federal Union* (Milledgeville), 14 Feb. 1833; *Washington Globe,* 15 Feb. 1833; *U.S. Telegraph,* 28 Feb. 1833; *Georgia*

Journal (Milledgeville), 7 Feb. 1833; George M. Troup to Bolling Hall, 21 Jan. 1833, Hall Papers, ADAH.

58. William H. Crawford to Bolling Hall, 17 Jan. 1833, Hall Papers, ADAH; William H. Crawford to Mahlon Dickerson, 6 Sept. 1832, Dickerson Papers, NJHS; William H. Crawford to Richard Wilde, 16 Jan. 1833, Crawford Papers, LC: William H. Crawford to Richard Wilde, 29 Jan. 1833, Otis Norcross Collection, MHS. For Crawford's public statements see: *Federal Union* (Milledgeville), 1 Nov. 1832; *Southern Recorder* (Milledgeville), 20 Dec. 1832; *Daily Argus* (Albany), 28 Dec. 1832; *The Georgian* (Savannah), 28 Feb. 1, 2 March 1833; *Georgia Chronicle* (Milledgeville), 28 Feb. 1833.

59. Mooney, *Crawford,* 327–41.

60. "Minutes of the States' Rights Party of Georgia," Miller, *Bench and Bar of Georgia,* I, 27–30; *Georgia Journal* (Milledgeville), 16 Nov. 1833; *Southern Recorder* (Milledgeville), 20 Nov. 1833; *Federal Union* (Milledgeville), 20 Nov. 1833.

61. Lumpkin, *Removal of the Cherokee Indians,* I, 127, 142.

6 Virginia and the Nullification Crisis

1. "A Radical" *Charleston Courier,* 24 Dec. 1832; *Washington Globe,* 24 Jan. 1833; *U.S. Telegraph* (Washington, D.C.), 22 Dec. 1832.

2. Charles Henry Ambler, *Thomas Ritchie: A Study in Virginia Politics,* 9–154; Thomas Ritchie to W. C. Rives, 1 Dec. 1832, Rives Papers, LC; Thomas Ritchie to Col. A. Ritchie, 8 June 1830 in *John P. Branch Historical Papers,* III (June 1911), 207–9; Van Buren, *Inquiry into the Origin and Course of Political Parties,* 322; Thomas Ritchie to Martin Van Buren, 25 June 1832, Van Buren Papers, LC; Thomas Ritchie to Littleton Waller Tazewell, 28 Feb. 1827, Tazewell Papers, VSL.

3. John P. Frank, *Justice Daniel Dissenting: A Biography of Peter V. Daniel, 1784–1860* (Cambridge, 1964); Francis Fry Wayland, *Andrew Stevenson, Democrat and Diplomat, 1785–1857* (Philadelphia, 1949); Raymond C. Dingeldine, "The Political Career of William Cabell Rives" (unpublished doctoral dissertation, University of Virginia, 1967); T.P.A. "Thomas Jefferson Randolph," *D.A.B.,* VIII, 369–70; A.C.G., Jr., "Joseph C. Cabell," *D.A.B.,* II, 387–88; Hugh A. Garland, *The Life of John Randolph of Roanoke* (2 vols., New York, 1850); William Cabell Bruce, *John Randolph of Roanoke, 1773–1833* (2 vols., New York, 1922); Robert Dawidoff, *The Education of John Randolph* (New York, 1979).

4. Charles Ambler (ed.), *The Life and Diary of John Floyd* (Richmond, 1918), 123–37, 173–98; *Lynchburg Virginian,* 7 Jan. 1833, in *National Intelligencer* (Washington, D.C.), 15 Jan. 1833; John Floyd to Littleton Waller Tazewell, 24, 31 May 1832, Floyd Papers, LC; John Floyd to Thomas Spalding, 22 Feb. 1829, Misc. Mss., NYHS; John Floyd to Duff Green, 21 Aug. 1831, Green Papers, LC; John Floyd to Abel Parker Upshur, Nov. 1832, Floyd Papers, LC; John Floyd to James Hamilton, Jr., 19 Nov. 1831, *ibid.;* John Floyd to John C. Calhoun, 16 April 1831, 2 Jan. 1832, Wilson (ed.), *The Papers of John C. Calhoun,* XI, 369–71, 536–38; A. S. Garnett to Richard M. T. Hunter, 14 March 1831, R. M. T. Hunter Papers, UVa.

5. Noma Lois Peterson, *Littleton Waller Tazewell* (Charlottesville, 1983); Timothy R. Sawers, "The Public Career of Littleton Waller Tazewell, 1824–1836" (unpublished doctoral dissertation, Miami University, 1972); Littleton Waller Tazewell to John Tazewell, 8, 23 May 1832, Tazewell Papers, VSL; P. P. Barbour to James Barbour, 27 Jan. 1829, Barbour Papers, NYPL; John Wickham to Littleton Waller Tazewell, 24 April

1829, Tazewell Papers, VSL; Martin Van Buren to James A. Hamilton, 1 Feb. 1829, Hamilton (ed.), *Reminiscences,* 91; entries of 11 April 1831, 27 Oct. 1832, Ambler (ed.), *Diary of John Floyd,* 136, 199; entries of 27 March, 26 April 1830, Adams (ed.), *Memoirs of John Quincy Adams,* 209, 222; Andrew Jackson to Andrew J. Donelson, 24 March 1831, Bassett (ed.), *Correspondence of Andrew Jackson,* IV, 253; Andrew Jackson to John Coffee, 24 April 1831, *ibid.,* 269; Andrew Jackson to Martin Van Buren, 18 Nov. 1832, *ibid.,* 489.

6. John Tyler to John Rutherfoord, 8 Dec. 1827, 14 March 1830, Rutherfoord Papers, DU; John Tyler to John Floyd, 4 Dec. 1832, Floyd Papers, LC; John Sherrard to George W. Munford, 5 July 1832, Misc. Mss., VaHS; Oliver Perry Chitwood, *John Tyler: Champion of the Old South* (New York, 1939); Robert Seager, II, *And Tyler Too: A Biography of John and Julia Gardiner Tyler* (New York, 1963).

7. Benjamin Watkins Leigh to Littleton Waller Tazewell, 24 Jan. 1827, Tazewell Papers, VSL; Abel Parker Upshur to Richard Crallé, 22 Feb. [1833], Crallé Papers, ClU; Charles C. Johnston to David Campbell, 10 June 1832, Campbell Family Papers, DU; ["Memorandum by Richard R. Crallé"], Wilson (ed.), *The Papers of John C. Calhoun,* XI, 523; John Floyd to John C. Calhoun, 2 Jan. 1832, *ibid.,* 537; A.C.G., Jr., "Thomas Walker Gilmer, *D.A.B.,* IV, 308–9; John Marshall to Joseph Story, 3 May 1831, "Letters of Chief Justice Marshall," Massachusetts Historical Society, *Proceedings,* 2nd Series, XIV (1900, 1901), 344; Claude H. Hall, *Abel Parker Upshur, Conservative Virginian, 1790–1844* (Madison, 1964); Armisted C. Gordon, *William Fitzhugh Gordon: A Virginian of the Old School* (New York and Washington, 1909).

8. Henry H. Simms, *The Rise of the Whigs in Virginia, 1824–1840* (Richmond, 1929), 11–61; Charles Ambler, *Sectionalism in Virginia from 1776 to 1861* (New York, 1910; reissued 1964), 128, 204–5; William G. Hall to George C. Dromgoole, 6 Aug. 1829, Edward Dromgoole Papers, UNC. Robert Hume Tomlinson, "The Origins and Editorial Policies of the *Richmond Whig and Public Advertiser, 1824–1865*" (unpublished doctoral dissertation, Michigan State University, 1971), 37–66. Results of the 1832 presidential contest between Jackson and Clay, by county, can be found in *The Constitutional Whig* (Richmond), 16 Nov. 1832.

9. Alison Goodyear Freehling, *Drift Toward Dissolution: The Virginia Slavery Debate of 1831–1832* (Baton Rouge, 1982), 11–81; Robert P. Sutton, "The Virginia Constitutional Convention of 1829–1830: A Profile Analysis of Late-Jeffersonian Virginia" (unpublished doctoral dissertation, University of Virginia, 1967); Sutton, "Sectionalism and Social Structure: A Case Study of Jeffersonian Democracy," *Virginia Magazine of History and Biography,* 30 (Jan. 1972), 70–84; Ambler, *Sectionalism in Virginia,* 137–74.

10. John Marshall to Joseph Story, 24 Aug. 1832, "Letters of Chief Justice Marshall," Massachusetts Historical Society *Proceedings,* 2nd Series, XIV (1900, 1901), 350; C. W. Gooch to C. C. Cambreling, 3 Nov. 1832, Gooch Family Papers, UVa; L. W. Tazewell to John N. Tazewell, 8, 23 May 1832, Tazewell Papers, VSL; C. C. Johnston to David Campbell, 10 June 1832, Campbell Family Papers, DU; Peter V. Daniel to Martin Van Buren, 12 July 1832, Van Buren Papers, LC; Thomas Walker Gilmer to John N. Tazewell, 21 Aug., 15 Sept. 1832, Tazewell Papers, VSL; John Floyd to L. W. Tazewell, 31 May 1832, Floyd Papers, LC; John Floyd to Thomas Walker Gilmer, 26 April 1832, *William and Mary Quarterly,* XX (Jan. 1912), 192–95; McCormick, *Second American Party System,* 191–92; Gannon, *Election of 1832,* 144–45.

11. William C. Rives to Charles Yancey, 6 Dec. 1832, Rives Papers, LC; John S. Barbour to James Barbour, 13 Dec. 1832, Barbour Papers, NYPL; J. C. Campbell to Thomas Ewing, 8 Dec. 1832, Ewing Papers, LC; R. Augustine Thompson to George C.

Dromgoole, 17 Nov. 1832, Dromgoole Papers, UNC; Thomas Walker Gilmer to W. C. Rives, 3, 4, 8, 10 Dec. 1832, Rives Papers, LC; Thomas Rutherford to W. C. Rives, 1, 3, 10 Dec. 1832, *ibid.;* Thomas Ritchie to W. C. Rives, 6, 10 Dec. 1832, *ibid.;* Richard H. Baptist to George C. Dromgoole, 8 Dec. 1832, Dromgoole Papers, UNC; *Constitutional Whig* (Richmond), 30 Nov., 4, 11, 14 Dec. 1832; *American Beacon* (Norfolk) 13 Dec. 1832.

12. "Agricola," *Virginia Doctrines Not Nullification* (Richmond, 1832). Possibly written by Philip Norbone Nicholas, this pamphlet reprints essays published in the *Richmond Enquirer* 17 Aug.–15 Sept. 1832. See also "What Next?" *Richmond Enquirer,* 30 Nov. 1832, and *ibid.,* 25, 26 Oct. 1832; *The Herald* (Norfolk) 3 Dec. 1832.

13. Reprinted in *Constitutional Whig* (Richmond), 5 [7?] Dec. 1832.

14. Thomas Ritchie to W. C. Rives, 6 Dec. 1832. Rives Papers, LC; J. C. Campbell to Thomas Ewing, 8 Dec. 1832, Ewing Papers, LC; J. H. Cocke to J. C. Cabell, 8 Dec. 1832, Cabell Deposit, UVa.

15. *National Intelligencer* (Washington, D.C.), 18 Dec. 1832.

16. *U.S. Telegraph* (Washington, D.C.), 21, 22, 31 Dec. 1832; *Richmond Enquirer,* 2 Feb. 1833; *Constitutional Whig* (Richmond), 18 Dec. 1832; *The Herald* (Norfolk), 24 Dec. 1832; Thomas Mann Randolph to W. C. Rives, 21 Feb. 1833, Rives Papers, LC; John Brockenbrough to W. C. Rives, 11 Jan. 1833; *ibid.;* Thomas McCullach to David Campbell, 16 Dec. 1832, Campbell Family Papers, DU.

17. *Richmond Whig and Public Advertiser,* 4 Jan., 8 Feb. 1833. See also *Richmond Enquirer,* 31 Jan., 19 Feb. 1833; *Constitutional Whig* (Richmond), 14 Dec. 1832; *Reporter* (Danville, Virginia), in *U.S. Telegraph* (Washington, D.C.), 4. 9, 12 Jan. 1833.

18. *Constitutional Whig* (Richmond), 14, 21, 25 Dec. 1832; *Richmond Whig and Public Advertiser* (Richmond) 15, 18 Jan. 1833; Beverley Tucker to [Andrew Jackson?] 1 March 1833, Tucker-Coleman Papers, The College of William and Mary (CWM).

19. *Journal of the House of Delegates of the Commonwealth of Virginia* (Richmond, 1832), 30–31; entries of 13, 19 Dec. 1832, Ambler (ed.), *Diary of John Floyd,* 203–4; John Floyd to Littleton Waller Tazewell, 23 Dec. 1832, Tazewell Papers, VSL; John Floyd to Littleton Waller Tazewell, 28 Dec. 1832, Floyd Papers, LC. See also: *Washington Globe,* 18 Dec. 1832; *U.S. Telegraph* (Washington, D.C.), 17, 24 Dec. 1832.

20. *The Herald* (Norfolk), 28 Dec. 1832–30 Jan. 1833; Tazewell, *A Review of the Proclamation of President Jackson . . . Under the Signature* "A Virginian" (Norfolk, 1833); *Albany Argus* 4 Jan. 1833; John Tyler to Littleton Waller Tazewell, 2 Feb. 1833, in Tyler (ed.), *Life and Times of the Tylers,* I, 447–48.

21. *Address of Judge Abel P. Upshur to the People of Northampton County* (Richmond, 1833); Abel Parker Upshur, *An Exposition of the Virginia Resolutions of 1798: A Series of Essays Addressed to Thomas Ritchie . . . Under the Signature of "Locke"* (Philadelphia, 1833); Upshur, *The Essays of Napier* (Norfolk, 1833); Hall, *Upshur,* 89–95.

22. *Richmond Enquirer,* 3 Jan., 2, 19 Feb. 1833; Thomas Jefferson Randolph to Nicholas Trist, 23 Jan. 1833, Trist Papers, LC; Charles Yancey to William C. Rives, 18 Feb. 1833, Rives Papers, LC; C. W. Gooch to W. C. Rives, 16 Feb. 1833, *ibid.;* Henry St. George Tucker to John Randolph, 24 Dec. 1832, Tucker-Coleman Papers, CWM.

23. *Richmond Enquirer,* 13 Dec. 1832, 1, 3, 5, 8, 17, 18, 26 Jan. 1833; *U.S.*

Telegraph (Washington, D.C.), 23 Jan., 6 Feb. 1833; *Richmond Whig and Public Advertiser,* 28 Feb. 1833; Thomas Ritchie to Nicholas Trist, 2 Jan. 1833, Trist Papers, LC; Thomas Ritchie to W. C. Rives, 6 Jan., 2 Feb. 1833, Rives Papers, LC; Thomas Jefferson Randolph to Nicholas Trist, 23 Jan., 26 Feb. 1833, Trist Papers, LC; William Brodnax to Beverley Tucker, 19 Feb. 1833, Tucker-Coleman Papers, CWM; Thomas Mann Randolph to W. C. Rives, 21 Feb. 1833, Rives Papers, LC; Ambler, *Ritchie,* 149–54.

24. *U.S. Telegraph* (Washington, D.C.), 9, 21 Feb. 1833; *Richmond Whig and Public Advertiser,* 15 Feb., 26 March, 1833; *Constitutional Whig* (Richmond), 30 Nov. 1832; *Washington Globe,* 1 Dec. 1832; *Charleston Courier,* 4 Dec. 1832; *Richmond Enquirer,* 9 Feb. 1833; John Randolph to Andrew Jackson 6 Dec. 1832, Bassett (ed.), *Correspondence of Andrew Jackson,* IV, 496–97; William Brodnax to Beverley Tucker, 19 Feb. 1833, Tucker-Coleman Papers, CWM; "Statement of Beverley Tucker of a Conversation of Andrew Jackson with John Randolph," 21 Feb. 1833, Bryan Family Papers, UVa.

25. "Doctrines—Origin of the Government—Secession," *Richmond Enquirer,* 24 Jan. 1833; from the *Columbia Telescope,* reprinted in *U.S. Telegraph* (Washington, D.C.), 12 Jan. 1833; *Constitutional Whig* (Richmond), 21 Dec. 1832; *Richmond Whig and Public Advertiser,* 8 Jan. 1833.

26. Thomas Mann Randolph to W. C. Rives, 21 Feb. 1833, Rives Papers, LC; Thomas McCulloch to David Campbell, 16 Dec. 1832, Campbell Family Papers, DU; *Richmond Whig and Public Advertiser,* 5 Feb. 1833; Herbert E. Wiglis, Jr., "State-Rights in Virginia, 1832–1833: A Study Showing What Men Advanced the State Rights Theory of Government" (unpublished senior thesis, Princeton University, 1957).

27. *Richmond Whig and Public Advertiser,* 8, 22, 31 Jan., 8, 12, 16 Feb., 5, 8, 22 March 1833; *Constitutional Whig* (Richmond), 25 Dec. 1832; *U.S. Telegraph* (Washington, D.C.), 7, 21 Jan. 1833.

28. "R. W.", 6 Jan. 1833 in *Washington Globe,* 23 Jan. 1833; *Richmond Whig and Public Advertiser,* 25 Jan. 1833. For accounts of other pro-Jackson meetings see: *Richmond Enquirer,* 1, 3, 5 Jan. 1833; *Richmond Whig and Public Advertiser,* 8, 11, 15, 22, 25, 31 Jan., 5, 15 Feb. 1833; *National Intelligencer* (Washington, D.C.), 1, 5, 8, 19 Jan., 7 Feb. 1833; *Washington Globe,* 25 Dec. 1832, 2, 5, 23 Jan., 7, 12 Feb. 1833; *The Virginia Herald* (Fredricksburg), 15, 19 Dec. 1832.

29. John W. Murdaugh to John Tazewell, 13, 14 Dec. 1832, Tazewell Papers, VSL; John Marshall to William Gaston, 20 Dec. 1832, Gaston Papers, UNC; *Constitutional Whig* (Richmond), 18 Dec. 1832; "Spy in Washington," 16 Dec. 1832, in *Courier and Enquirer* (New York), 22 Dec. 1832.

30. *Niles' Weekly Register,* supplement to Vol. XLIII (1832–33), i; *Constitutional Whig* (Richmond), 25 Dec. 1832.

31. *Journal, Virginia House of Delegates, 1832–1833* (Richmond, 1833), 79–80; *Constitutional Whig* (Richmond), 21 Dec. 1832; *U.S. Telegraph* (Washington, D.C.), 24 Dec. 1832.

32. *Constitutional Whig* (Richmond), 25 Dec. 1832; *Richmond Enquirer,* 1, 3, 5, 12, 15, 21, 23, 31 Jan., 2, 8 Feb. 1833; *Richmond Whig and Public Advertiser,* 1, 4, 8, 11, 15, 18 Jan. 1833; *The Virginia Herald* (Fredericksburg), 9 Jan. 1833; *Journal, Virginia House of Delegates, 1832–1833,* 82–84, 88–89; J. Wickham to L. W. Tazewell, 8 Jan. 1833, Tazewell Papers, VSL; John W. Murdaugh to John Tazewell, 12 Jan. 1833, *ibid.;* R. Wallace to W. C. Rives, 9 Jan. 1833, Rives Papers, LC; Lawrence Dade to W. C. Rives, 12 Jan. 1833, *ibid.*

33. John W. Murdaugh to John W. Tazewell, 16 Jan. 1833, Tazewell Papers, VSL;

J. T. Brown to W. C. Rives, 16 Jan. 1833, Rives Papers, LC; R. Wallace to W. C. Rives, 16 Jan. 1833, *ibid.; Richmond Enquirer,* 20 Jan. 1833; *Richmond Whig and Public Advertiser,* 18, 22 Jan. 1833; *Journal, Virginia House of Delegates, 1832–33,* 89–91, and Document Number 19; J. C. Campbell to Thomas Ewing, "27 Jan. 1833," Ewing Papers, LC; entry of 15 Jan. 1833, Ambler (ed.), *Diary of John Floyd,* 208.

34. *State Papers on Nullification,* 195–97; *Journal, Virginia House of Delegates,* 95–98; *Richmond Enquirer,* 25, 27 Jan. 1833; *Niles' Weekly Register,* XLIII (9 Feb. 1833), 394–97.

35. *Richmond Whig and Public Advertiser,* 29 Jan. 1833; John W. Murdaugh to John W. Tazewell, 19 Jan. 1833, Tazewell Papers, VSL; Beverley Tucker to Lucy Ann Tucker, 24 Jan., 13 Feb. 1833, Tucker-Coleman Papers, CWM.

36. *Journal, Virginia House of Delegates, 1832–1833,* Document Number 28; entry of 27 Jan. 1833, Ambler (ed.), *Diary of John Floyd,* 210.

37. *Columbia Times,* 8 Feb. in *Richmond Whig and Public Advertiser,* 15 Feb. 1833; *Columbia Telescope,* in *U.S. Telegraph* (Washington, D.C.), 13 Feb. 1833; Freehling, *Prelude to Civil War,* 290; *Journal, Virginia House of Delegates, 1832–1833,* Document Number 29.

38. Thomas Ritchie to W. C. Rives, 6, 18 Jan. 1833, Rives Papers, LC; R. Wallace to W. C. Rives, 24 Jan. 1833; *ibid.;* C. C. Cambreling to Martin Van Buren, 26 Dec. 1832, Van Buren Papers, LC.

39. *Richmond Whig and Public Advertiser,* 16, 19 Feb. 1833; *U.S. Telegraph* (Washington, D.C.), 18 Feb. 1833; Thomas Hart Benton to Martin Van Buren, 16 Feb. 1833, Van Buren Papers, LC; *Richmond Enquirer,* 1, 5, 22 Jan. 1833. The politics of the election may be traced in: J. C. Campbell to Thomas Ewing, 22, 27 Jan. 1833, Ewing Papers, LC; John W. Murdaugh to John W. Tazewell, 19 Jan., 5 Feb. 1833, Tazewell Family Papers, VSL; T. J. Randolph to Nicholas Trist, 23 Jan. 1833, Trist Papers, LC; R. Pollard to W. C. Rives, 19, 20 Feb. 1833, Rives Papers, LC; R. Wallace to W. C. Rives, 11 Feb. 1833, *ibid.;* Charles Yancey to W. C. Rives, 18 Feb. 1833, *ibid.* The vote in the legislature indicated that the delegates from the eastern and southern slaveholding sections of the state supported Tyler while delegates from the north and west voted for McDowell. Ambler, *Sectionalism in Virginia,* 217–18; Sally Campbell Preston Miller (ed.), *Memoir of James McDowell* (Baltimore, 1895), 44–83; James Glen Collier, "The Political Career of James McDowell, 1830–1851" (unpublished doctoral dissertation, University of North Carolina, Chapel Hill, 1963).

40. Ambler, *Sectionalism in Virginia, 1776–1861,* 218; Simms, *Rise of the Whigs in Virginia,* 76–86. Details of Virginia politics in the months immediately after the resolution of the nullification crisis may be followed in: Andrew Stevenson to Francis Preston Blair, 17 March 1833, Blair-Lee Papers, PUL; L. W. Tazewell to John Floyd, [28 March 1833], Floyd Papers, LC; Beverley Tucker to James Hamilton, Jr., 22 March 1833, Tucker-Coleman Papers, CWM; J. A. Davis to N. P. Trist, 25 April 1833, Trist Papers, LC; W. C. Rives to Nicholas Trist, 15 April 1833, *ibid.;* John Floyd to ?, March 1833, Floyd Papers, LC; W. C. Rives to N. Niles, 21 July 1833, Niles Papers, LC; Abel Parker Upshur to Richard Crallé, 19 March 1833, Crallé Papers, ClU; J. C. Cabell to N. Francis Cabell, 5 June 1833, Cabell Deposit, UVa.

41. Simms, *The Rise of the Whigs in Virginia,* 76–86; Ambler, *Sectionalism in Virginia,* 219–50; McCormick, *The Second American Party System,* 193–99; Cole, *The Whig Party in the South,* 28–29, 37–38.

7 New York and the Nullification Crisis

1. There are numerous accounts of the Regency. Among the most useful are: Robert V. Remini, "The Albany Regency," *New York History,* XXXIX (Oct. 1958), 341–55; Frank Otto Gatell, "Sober Second Thoughts on Van Buren, The Albany Regency, and the Wall Street Conspiracy," *Journal of American History* LIII (June 1966), 19–40; Kalman Goldstein, "The Albany Regency: The Failure of Practical Politics (unpublished doctoral dissertation, Columbia University, 1969); Dixon Ryan Fox, *The Decline of Aristocracy in the Politics of New York, 1801–1840* (New York, 1919), 281–86; Herbert D. A. Donovan, *The Barnburners: A Study of the Internal Movements in the Political History of New York State and of the Resulting Changes in Political Affiliation, 1830–1852* (New York, 1925), 7–8. For a different view of the Regency from that offered in this chapter, one that sees it mainly as a well-organized but cynical and self-serving group of politicians see: Alvin Kass, *Politics in New York State, 1800–1830* (Syracuse, 1965); Lee Benson, *The Concept of Jacksonian Democracy: New York as a Test Case* (Princeton, 1960), 10, 26, 39, 44, 47, 51, 53, 91; Richard P. McCormick *The Second American Party System* (Chapel Hill, 1966), 112, 115–17, 122; Michael Wallace, "Changing Concepts of Party in the United States: New York, 1815–1828," *American Hstorical Review,* LXXIV (Dec. 1968), 453–91.

2. John Niven, *Martin Van Buren: The Romantic Age of American Politics* (New York, 1983); Donald B. Cole, *Martin Van Buren and the American Political System* (Princeton, 1984); Edward M. Shepard, *Martin Van Buren* (Boston and New York, 1900); Robert V. Remini, *Martin Van Buren and the Making of the Democratic Party* (New York, 1959); James C. Curtis, *The Fox at Bay* (Lexington, 1970); John A. Garraty, *Silas Wright* (New York, 1949); Ivor D. Spencer, *The Victor and the Spoils: A Life of William L. Marcy* (Providence, 1959); H.W.H.K., "Azariah Cutting Flagg," *D.A.B.,* III, 447.

3. William D. Driscoll, "Benjamin F. Butler: Lawyer and Regency Politician" (unpublished doctoral dissertation, Fordham University, 1965); W.E.S., "Edwin Croswell," *D.A.B.,* II, 571; Morgan Dix, *Memoirs of John Adams Dix* (2 vols., New York, 1883); N.A.C., "Jesse Buell," *D.A.B.,* II 238–39; A.C.F., "Samuel J. Tilden," *D.A.B.,* IX, 537.

4. William H. Seward to ?, 10 Nov. 1832, Frederick W. Seward (ed.), *William H. Seward: An Autobiography* (New York, 1891), 218; Rudolph Bunner to Gulian C. Verplanck, 3 Jan. 1833, Verplanck Papers, NYHS.

5. Jabez Hammond, *The History of Political Parties in the State of New York* (3 vols., Cooperstown, 1846), II, 315–428; McCormick, *The Second American Party System,* 117–21.

6. Salmon G. Grover to William H. Seward, 23 Jan. 1833, Seward Papers, University of Rochester (UR). For Van Buren's version of the issues involved in early 19th century politics, one that stresses his own commitment to Jeffersonian states' rights principles see Van Buren, *Inquiry Into the Origin and Course of Political Parties in the United States* (New York, 1867).

7. Joel Parker, "Brief History of the Boundary Dispute between New Jersey and New York," New Jersey Historical Society *Proceedings,* VII (Jan. 1858), 106–7.

8. Green C. Bronson to William Thomas Carroll, 27 July 1829, 3 Peters 461 (1830).

9. *New Jersey v. New York,* 3 Peters 461 (1830); *ibid.,* 5 Peters 284 (1831).

10. *Courier and Enquirer* (New York), 21 March 1832; *New Jersey v. New York,* 6 Peters 323 (1832); Charles Butler to Harriet Butler, 4 March 1832, Butler Papers,

NYSL; *U.S. Telegraph* (Washington, D.C.), 8 March 1832; *National Intelligencer* (Washington, D.C.), 16 March 1832; Warren, *History of the Supreme Court,* I, 770–72; Driscoll, "Benjamin F. Butler," 223–26.

11. John Marshall to Joseph Story, 22 Sept. 1832, Massachusetts Historical Society *Proceedings,* 2nd Series, XIV (1900, 1901), 351–52; Bates Cooke to Thurlow Weed, 28 Dec. 1832, Weed Papers, UR; *Daily Albany Argus,* 22, 24, 27, 29 Oct., 6 Nov. 1832; *Albany Evening Journal,* 23, 24, 25, 29 Oct., 1832; Driscoll, "B. F. Butler," 233–41.

12. Martin Van Buren to Andrew Jackson, 21 Sept. 1831, Bassett (ed.), *Correspondence of Andrew Jackson,* IV, 351–52; James Hamilton, Jr., to Martin Van Buren, 20 April, 27 May, 8 June, 20 Sept. 1830, Van Buren Papers, LC; Robert Hayne to Martin Van Buren, 20 Oct. 1830, *ibid.*

13. *U.S. Telegraph* (Washington, D.C.), 18 Dec. 1832; Remini, *Martin Van Buren and the Making of the Democratic Party,* 53–55, 147–69; Fitzpatrick (ed.), *Autobiography of Martin Van Buren,* 239–42.

14. Michael Hoffman to A. C. Flagg, 12 Dec. 1832, Flagg Papers, NYPL. For southern concern about Van Buren in regard to the tariff see: Thomas Ritchie to Van Buren, 25 June 1832, Van Buren Papers, LC; William King to Van Buren, 9 Jan. 1833, *ibid.;* Van Buren to Joseph H. Bryant et al., 4 Oct. 1832, Gammon, *Presidential Campaign of 1832,* 163–67.

15. *Daily Albany Argus* 3 Jan. 1833. See also: Azariah C. Flagg to Judge Soule, 22 Dec. 1832, Flagg Papers, NYPL; Silas Wright to N. P. Tallmadge, 27 Jan. 1833, Tallmadge Papers, WHS.

16. Silas Wright to A. C. Flagg, 20 Jan. 1833, Flagg Papers, NYPL; Michael Hoffman to A. C. Flagg, 14, 15, 16 Dec. 1832, 14, 20 Jan., 4 Feb. 1833, *ibid.;* G. Van Sackett to William H. Seward, 7 Jan. 1833, Seward Papers, UR; July, *Verplanck,* 173–77.

17. Stephen Allen to Gulian C. Verplanck, 24 Jan. 1833, Verplanck Papers, NYHS; Bates Cooke to Thurlow Weed, 20 Dec. 1832, Weed Papers, UR; ? to Nicholas Biddle, 27 Dec. 1832, Biddle Papers, LC.

18. *Albany Evening Journal,* 4 Jan. 1833. See also: *ibid.,* 20, 26, 28 Dec. 1832, 5, 7, 11, 12 Jan. 1833; *Courier and Enquirer* (New York), 29 Dec. 1832, *Commercial Advertiser* (New York) 20 Dec. 1832, 17 Jan. 1833; G. Van Sackett to William H. Seward, 7 Jan. 1833, Seward Papers, UR; Francis Granger to Thurlow Weed, 14 Jan. 1833, Granger Papers, LC; *Daily Albany Argus* 15 Dec. 1832, 24 Jan., 20 Feb. 1833; *Utica Sentinel and Gazette* 18 Dec. 1832; Fitzpatarick (ed.), *Autobiography of Martin Van Buren,* 545–49.

19. Andrew Jackson to Martin Van Buren, 10 Dec. 1832, Van Buren Papers, LC; Andrew Jackson to Martin Van Buren 23, 25 Dec. 1832, Bassett (ed.), *Correspondence of Andrew Jackson,* IV, 504–6.

20. Martin Van Buren to Andrew Jackson, 22 Dec. 1832, Van Buren Papers, LC.

21. Martin Van Buren to Andrew Jackson, 27 Dec. 1832, Bassett (ed.), *Correspondence of Andrew Jackson,* IV, 506–8.

22. Andrew Jackson to Martin Van Buren, 13 Jan. 1833, Bassett (ed.), *Correspondence of Andrew Jackson,* V, 2–4.

23. Andrew Jackson to Martin Van Buren, 25 Jan. 1833, *ibid.,* V, 12.

24. William Marcy to D. Cushman, 22 Sept. 1832, Marcy Papers LC. See also: William Marcy to Thomas W. Olcott, 4 Jan. 1832, Olcott Papers, CU; Benjamin Knower to William Marcy, 28 March 1832, Marcy Papers, LC; William Marcy to Benjamin Knower, 6 May 1832, *ibid.;* A. C. Flagg to Silas Wright, 22, 24 January 1833,

Flagg Papers, NYPL; Hammond, *History of Political Parties in New York*, II, 432–33; Fitzpatrick (ed.), *Autobiography of Martin Van Buren*, 549–52, 562–63; Spencer, *Marcy*, 76–77; Garraty, *Wright*, 98–100.

25. Charles Z. Lincoln (ed.), *Messages from the Governors . . .* (11 vols., Albany, 1909), II, 399–430), see especially 420–21, 422–24, 427–30; Martin Van Buren to Andrew Jackson, 27 Dec. 1832, Bassett (ed.), *Correspondence of Andrew Jackson*, IV, 508; *Commercial Advertiser* (New York), 8, 9 Jan. 1833.

26. William King to Martin Van Buren, 9 Jan. 1833, Van Buren Papers, LC.

27. William H. Seward to Samuel Seward, 10 Jan. 1833, Seward Family Papers, NYSL; *Albany Evening Journal*, 29 Dec. 1832, 3, 16, 23 Jan. 1833; *Utica Sentinel and Gazette* 15 Jan. 1833; "A Farmer," *Daily Albany Argus,* 11 Jan. 1833.

28. *Daily Albany Argus*, 26, 28, 29, 30, 31 Jan., 1, 2, 5, 7, 8, 13 Feb. 1833; *Albany Evening Journal*, 25, 26, 29 Jan., 9 Feb. 1833; *New York Commercial Advertiser*, 1 Feb. 1833; *Courier and Enquirer* (New York), 9 Feb. 1833; G. A. Worth to William Marcy, 29 Jan., 3 Feb. 1833, Marcy Papers, LC; A. C. Flagg to Silas Wright, 22, 23, 24 Jan. 1833, Flagg Papers, NYPL; Francis Granger to Thurlow Weed, 19 Feb. 1833, Granger Papers, LC; Erastus Humphreys to William H. Seward, 3 Feb. 1833, Seward Papers, UR; E. Pitts to Samuel J. Tilden, 12 Feb. 1833, Tilden Papers, NYPL; Morgan Dix (ed.), *Memoirs of John Adams Dix* (2 vols., New York, 1883), I, 134–37; Garraty, *Wright*, 99–100.

29. William Kent to Moses Kent, 10 Feb. 1833, James Kent Papers, LC.

30. *Daily Albany Argus*, 1 Feb. 1833.

31. *State Papers on Nullification*, 133–57, quote from 133–37. The Report may also be found in *Daily Albany Argus,* 1 Feb. 1833.

32. *Ibid.,* 138.

33. *Ibid.,* 147.

34. *Ibid.,* 140.

35. *Ibid.,* 144–48.

36. *Ibid.,* 149–50.

37. *Ibid.,* 150–51.

38. *Ibid.,* 152–57.

39. From *New York Commerical Advertiser*, in *Daily Albany Argus* 15 Feb. 1833; *Albany Evening Journal*, 8 Feb. 1833; *Utica Sentinel and Gazette* 12 Feb. 1833.

40. Seward (ed.), *Seward: Autobiography*, 228–29; *The Ontario Freeman* (Canadaigua), 6 March 1833; *Albany Evening Journal*, 19 Feb. 1833.

41. Seward (ed.), *Seward: Autobiography*, 228; Peterson, *Jefferson Image*, 61–62.

42. *Daily Albany Argus*, 13, 26 Feb. 1833. Additional aspects of the debate in the New York legislature may be found in: *ibid.*, 14, 18, 25 Feb. 1833; *The Ontario Freeman* (Canandaigua), 6 Feb. 1833; *Albany Evening Journal*, 19, 23 Feb. 1833.

43. *State Papers on Nullification*, 158–59; Elam Tilden to John W. Edmonds, 14 Feb. 1833, Tilden Papers, NYPL; *New York Commercial Advertiser*, 14, 15, 16 Feb. 1833; entries of 10, 16 Feb. 1833, Diary of Henry Van Der Lyn, NYHS; Fitzpatrick (ed.), *Autobiography of Van Buren*, 27–28.

44. *Ibid.,* 553.

45. *Albany Evening Journal*, 4, 5, 6, 9, 12 Feb. 1833; *New York Commercial Advertiser*, 8, 14 Feb. 1833; *Daily Albany Argus*, 6 Feb. 1833; *Courier and Enquirer* (New York), 23 Feb. 1833; Charles Butler to Bowen Whiting, 4 Feb. 1833, Charles Butler Papers, LC; A. C. Flagg to Silas Wright, 13 Feb. 1833, Flagg Papers, NYPL; E. Pitts to Samuel J. Tilden, 12 Feb. 1833, Tilden Papers, NYPL; Peter B. Porter to Henry

Clay, 11 Feb. 1833, Porter Papers, Buffalo and Erie County Historical Society (BECHS).

46. Peter B. Porter to Henry Clay [?] Feb. 1833, Porter Papers, BECHS: Thurlow Weed to Albert H. Tracy 18 June 1833, Tracy Papers, NYSL; William L. Marcy to Martin Van Buren, 13 Feb. 1833, Van Buren Papers, LC; *Albany Evening Journal,* 26 Feb. 1833; "Correspondent," dated 2 March 1833, in *New York Commercial Advertiser,* 7 March 1833; Schlesinger, *Age of Jackson,* 177–200.

8 "The Compromise"

1. *State Papers on Nullification,* 229–31; Samuel Gwin to Andrew Jackson Donelson, 6 Jan. 1832 [1833], Donelson Papers, LC; Lucie Robertson Bridgforth, "Mississippi's Response to Nullification, 1833," *The Journal of Mississippi History,* XLV (Feb. 1983), 1–21; Miles, *Jacksonian Democracy in Mississippi,* 65–67.

2. *State Papers on Nullification,* 201; William S. Hoffman, *Andrew Jackson and North Carolina Politics* (Chapel Hill, 1958), 58–68.

3. *State Papers on Nullification,* 219–25; J. Mills Thornton, III, *Politics and Power in a Slave Society* (Baton Rouge, 1978), 27–35.

4. *Niles' Weekly Register,* XLIII (1 Dec. 1832), 220; Robert H. White (ed.), *Messages of the Governors of Tennessee* (8 vols., Nashville, 1952, 1972), II, 441–42; Paul H. Bergeron, "Tennessee's Response to the Nullification Crisis," *Journal of Southern History,* XXXIX (Feb. 1973), 23–44. Bergeron, in my opinion, does not give sufficient attention to the impact of Jackson's Proclamation on the political situation in Tennessee. For example, see Alfred Balch to John McLean, 12 March 1833, McLean Papers, LC.

5. *State Papers on Nullification,* 169–71, 190–91, 213–15, 377–81.

6. *Ibid.,* 112–28, 163–66, 205–7, 285–86, 289–92.

7. *Ibid.,* 105–8.

8. *Register of Debates* 2:2, 244–246; *National Intelligencer* (Washington, D.C.), 22, 24 Jan. 1833; *Washington Globe,* 23 Jan. 1833; *U.S. Telegraph* (Washington, D.C.), 22 Jan. 1833; *Charleston Courier,* 28 Jan. 1833; "From Our Correspondent," dated Washington, D.C., 21 Jan. 1833, in *New York Commercial Advertiser,* 24 Jan. 1833; "Spy in Washington," dated 21 Jan. 1833, in *Courier and Enquirer* (New York), 24 Jan. 1833; Silas Wright to A. C. Flagg, 24 Jan. 1833, Flagg Papers, NYPL.

9. "Progress of Consolidation and Despotic Principles," *U.S. Telegraph* (Washington, D.C.), 22 Jan. 1833; "Liberty and the Constitution," *ibid.,* 4 Feb. 1833.

10. Wilson (ed.), *The Papers of John C. Calhoun,* XII, 10–15; *Register of Debates,* 22:2, 100–03; Wiltse, *Calhoun,* II, 177–78.

11. Wilson (ed.), *The Papers of John C. Calhoun,* XII, 18–26; *Register of Debates,* 22:2, 187–92; Wiltse, *Calhoun,* II, 179–80.

12. John C. Calhoun to James C. Hamilton, Jr., 16 Jan. 1833, Wilson (ed.), *The Papers of John C. Calhoun,* XII, 16; *Register of Debates,* 22:2, 246. Voting in favor of postponing the debate on the Force bill were: George M. Bibb (Kentucky), John Black (Mississippi), Bedford Brown (North Carolina), John C. Calhoun (South Carolina), William R. King (Alabama), Willie P. Mangum (North Carolina), Stephen D. Miller (South Carolina), Gabriel Moore (Alabama), George Poindexter (Mississippi), William C. Rives (Virginia), Samuel Smith (Maryland), George M. Troup (Georgia), John Tyler (Virginia), George A. Waggaman (Louisiana), and Hugh Lawson White (Tennessee).

13. Letter dated 21 Jan. 1833, in *Richmond Whig and Public Advertiser,* 31 Jan.

1833; "Correspondence of the Whig," dated 28 Jan. 1833, in *ibid.*, 2 Feb. 1833; "From Our Correspondent," 2 Feb. 1833, in *New York Commercial Advertiser,* 6 Feb. 1833; *U.S. Telegraph* (Washington, D.C.), 6 Feb. 1833; S. Pleasanton to James Buchanan, 30 Jan. 1833, Buchanan Papers, HSP.

14. William R. King to John Gayle, 26 Feb. 1833, King Papers, ADAH; John Black to John A. Quitman, 23 Jan., 2 March 1833, Claiborne Papers, MDAH; John Coffee to Mrs. Coffee, 12, 17 Feb. 1833, Dyas Collection, TSL; See also: Houston G. Jones, "Bedford Brown: State Rights Unionist: Part I: The Senator," *North Carolina Historical Review,* XXXII (July 1955), 321–45; John M. Martin, "William R. King: Jacksonian Senator," *The Alabama Review,* XVIII (Oct. 1965), 243–67; Miles, *Jacksonian Democracy in Mississippi,* 64.

15. Daniel Webster to Stephen White, 18 Jan. 1833, Wiltse and Moser (eds.), *Papers of Daniel Webster,* III, 208; Silas Wright to A. C. Flagg, 27 Jan., 2 Feb. 1833, Flagg Papers, NYPL; Silas Wright to Gideon Welles 13 Feb. 1833, Welles Papers, LC; Thomas Hart Benton to Martin Van Buren, 16 Feb. 1833, Van Buren Papers, LC; Thomas Hart Benton to Beverley Tucker, 11 Feb. 1833, *William and Mary College Quarterly,* XII (Oct. 1903), 86; William Drayton to Joel Poinsett, 9, 11 Feb. 1833, Poinsett Papers, HSP; Simpson Torbett to George M. Wolf, 4 Feb. 1833, Wolf Papers, HSP; Mark Alexander to Beverley Tucker, 6 Feb. 1833, *William and Mary College Quarterly,* XX (Oct. 1911), 115; Willie P. Mangum to Charity A. Mangum, 2 Feb. 1833, Shanks (ed.), *Papers of Willie Person Mangum,* II, 18. On Clay's lack of enthusiasm for the Force act see: *Richmond Whig and Public Advertiser,* 12 Feb. 1833.

16. *Register of Debates* 22:2, 240, 253, 263–64; Michael Hoffman to A. C. Flagg, 4 Feb. 1833, Flagg Papers, NYPL.

17. *House Document 85,* 22nd Cong., 2nd sess.; *Richmond Whig and Public Advertiser,* 12 Feb. 1833; *National Intelligencer* (Washington, D.C.), 11 Feb. 1833; *U.S. Telegraph* (Washington, D.C.), 9 Feb. 1833; *Courier and Enquirer* (New York), 16 Feb. 1833.

18. *Register of Debates,* 2:2, 1053; William Drayton to Joel Poinsett, 9 Feb. 1833, Poinsett Papers, HSP; "Rights of the States," *U.S. Telegraph* (Washington, D.C.), 9 Feb. 1833; "Spy in Washington," 20, 29 Jan. 1833, in *Courier and Enquirer* (New York), 26 Jan., 2 Feb. 1833; "Important from Washington," *Richmond Whig and Public Advertiser,* 2, 12 Feb. 1833; Parks, *John Bell,* 58–65.

19. Andrew Jackson to James K. Polk, 16 Dec. 1832, Weaver and Bergeron (eds.), *Correspondence of James K. Polk,* I, 575; Sellers, *Polk: Jacksonian,* 186–95.

20. Manuel Eyre to Nicholas Biddle, 14 Feb. 1833, Biddle Papers, LC; "Spy in Washington," 17 Feb. 1833, in *Courier and Enquirer* (New York), 23 Feb. 1833; John G. Watmough to Nicholas Biddle, 13 Feb. 1833; Biddle Papers, LC; Lewis Williams to Nicholas Biddle, 17 Feb. 1833, *ibid.;* William Hammett to Thomas Willis White, 15 Feb. 1833, Hammett Papers, VaHS; *National Intelligencer* (Washington, D.C.), 14 Feb. 1833.

21. "Spy in Washington," 17 Feb. 1833 in *Courier and Enquirer* (New York), 23 Feb. 1833; "Correspondence dated Washington 15 Feb. 1833 in *Albany Evening Journal* 21 Feb. 1833; Michael Hoffman to A. C. Flagg, 14, 20 Feb. 1833, Flagg Papers, NYPL; Manuel Eyre to Nicholas Biddle, 15 Feb. 1833, Biddle Papers, LC; *Daily Albany Argus,* 20 Feb. 1833.

22. Thomas Hart Benton to Martin Van Buren, 16 Feb. 1833, Van Buren Papers, LC; Henry Clay to Nicholas Biddle 16 Feb. 1833, Biddle Papers, LC.

23. On Duff Green's election as printer to the U.S. Senate see: *Washington Globe,* 21, 28 Feb. 1833; *Richmond Whig and Public Advertiser,* 23 Feb. 1833; *New Hamp-*

shire Patriot (Concord), 4 March, 1 April 1833; *Albany Evening Journal,* 25 Feb. 1833; *Daily Albany Argus,* 25 Feb. 1833.

24. Silas Wright to A. C. Flagg, 27, 28 Jan. 1833, Flagg Papers, NYPL; *New York Commercial Advertiser,* 13 Feb. 1833; *New Hampshire Patriot* (Concord), 11 Feb. 1833; "The Spy in Washington," 13 Jan., in *Courier and Enquirer* (New York), 19 Jan. 1833; "An Observer," *Richmond Enquirer,* 5 Feb. 1833; Michael Hoffman to A. C. Flagg 1, 6 Feb. 1833, Flagg Papers, NYPL; James Callan to Harmar Denny, 15 Jan. 1833, Harmar Denny Papers, Historical Society of Western Pennsylvania (HSWP).

25. *Richmond Enquirer,* 14 Feb. 1833.

26. Henry Clay to Francis Brooke, 12 Dec. 1832, 17, 23 Jan. 1833, Colton (ed.), *Works of Henry Clay,* IV, 345, 347–48; Henry Clay to Peter B. Porter, 29 Jan., 1, 16 Feb. 1833, Peter B. Porter Papers, BECHS; Glyndon G. Van Deusen, *The Life of Henry Clay* (Boston, 1937), 238, 264–69. The most detailed and the best treatment of Henry Clay's role during the nullification crisis is to be found in Merrill D. Peterson, *Olive Branch and Sword—The Compromise of 1833* (Baton Rouge, 1982). It completely supersedes the older treatment by Frederick L. Nussbaum, "The Compromise Tariff of 1833: A Study in Practical Politics," *South Atlantic Quarterly,* XI (Oct. 1912), 337–49.

27. Henry Clay to Francis Brooke, 29 June 1832, Colton (ed.), *Works of Henry Clay,* IV, 340; Henry Clay to Peter B. Porter, 29 Jan., 1, 16 Feb. 1833, Porter Papers, BECHS.

28. Henry Clay to Francis Brooke, 17 Jan. 1833, Colton (ed.), *Works of Henry Clay,* IV, 347; "Spy in Washington," 10 Jan. 1833, in *Courier and Enquirer* (New York), 19 Jan. 1833; "From a Correspondent in Washington," dated 22 Jan. 1833, in *United States Gazette* (Philadelphia), 28 Jan. 1833.

29. Henry Clay to Francis Brooke, 23 Jan. 1833, Colton (ed.), *Works of Henry Clay,* IV, 348.

30. John Tyler to John Floyd, 10 Jan. 1833, *William and Mary College Quarterly,* XXI (July 1912), 9–10; C. C. Cambreling to Martin Van Buren, 29 Dec. 1832, 3 Feb. 1833, Van Buren Papers, LC; Louis McLane to Martin Van Buren, 23 Jan. 1833, *ibid.;* Michael Hoffman to A. C. Flagg, 4 Jan. 1833, Flagg Papers, NYPL; Silas Wright to A. C. Flagg, 2 Feb. 1833, *ibid.;* Simpson Turbert to George M. Wolf, 4 Feb. 1833, Wolf Papers, HSP; "From Washington," *Daily Albany Argus,* 15 Feb. 1833; *U.S. Telegraph* (Washington, D.C.), 14 Feb. 1833; "From Our Correspondent," Washington, 11, 12 Feb. 1833, in *Charleston Courier* 18, 20 Feb. 1833; "Spy in Washington," 1 Feb. 1833, in *Courier and Enquirer* (New York), 2 Feb. 1833; *National Intelligencer* (Washington, D.C.), 8 Feb. 1833.

31. "Adjustment of the Tariff," *U.S. Telegraph* (Washington, D.C.), 12 Feb. 1833. For a more detailed account of Clay's activities during this period, see Peterson, *Olive Branch and Sword,* 65–67.

32. *Register of Debates* 22:2, Appendix, pp. 810–11; *Courier and Enquirer* (New York), 16 Feb. 1833; Taussig, *Tariff History of the United States,* 110–11; Stanwood, *America's Tariff Controversies,* 397–98; *Richmond Enquirer,* 16 Feb. 1833; William Drayton to Joel Poinsett, 19 Feb. 1833, Poinsett Papers, HSP.

33. *U.S. Telegraph* (Washington, D.C.), 19 Feb. 1833; "Spy in Washington," 12 Feb. 1833, in *Courier and Enquirer* (New York), 16 Feb. 1833.

34. Daniel Webster to Henry Willis Kinsman, Jan. 1833, Wiltse and Moser (eds.), *The Papers of Daniel Webster,* III, 203–4; Daniel Webster to William Sullivan, 3 Jan. 1833, *ibid.,* III, 204–5; House Reports 21, 50, 56, 57, 71, 81, 110, 124, 22nd Cong., 2nd sess.; *New York Commercial Advertiser,* 6 Feb. 1833; *Richmond Whig and Public*

Advertiser, 29 Jan. 1833; *Albany Evening Journal,* 15 Feb. 1833; Henry Clay to Nicholas Biddle, 16 Feb. 1833, Biddle Papers, LC.

35. Daniel Webster to Joseph Hopkinson, 9 Feb. 1833, Wiltse and Moser (eds.), *The Papers of Daniel Webster,* III, 213; *Daily Albany Argus,* 18, 19 Feb. 1833; "From Our Correspondent," Washington, 12 Feb. 1833, in *Charleston Courier,* 20 Feb. 1833; *U.S. Telegraph* (Washington, D.C.), 18 Feb. 1833.

36. "From Washington," 17 Feb. 1833, *Richmond Whig and Public Advertiser,* 19 Feb. 1833; *Daily Albany Argus* 15, 19 Feb. 1833; M. Hoffman to A. C. Flagg, 21 Feb. 1833, Flagg Papers, NYPL; William Hammett to Thomas Willis White, 12 Feb. 1833, Hammett Papers, VaHS; *U.S. Telegraph* (Washington, D.C.), 14, 22 Feb. 1833.

37. *Washington Globe,* 18, 22, 25 Feb. 1833; *U.S. Telegraph* (Washington, D.C.), 13, 19 Feb. 1833; *Richmond Whig and Public Advertiser,* 15 Feb. 1833; "Spy in Washington," 12 Feb. 1833, in *Courier and Enquirer* (New York), 16 Feb. 1833; Daniel Webster to Joseph Hopkinson, 7, 9, 15, 21 Feb. 1833, Wiltse and Moser (eds.), *The Papers of Daniel Webster,* III, 212–15, 219–20; William Hammett to Thomas Willis White, 4 Feb. 1833, Hammett Papers, VaHS.

38. "From Washington," *Richmond Whig and Public Advertiser,* 5 March 1833. See also: *ibid.,* 12, 21, 23 Feb. 1833; *Daily Albany Argus,* 1, 4 March 1833; *U.S. Telegraph* (Washington, D.C.), 8, 18, 28 Feb. 1833; "Spy in Washington," 28 Feb. 1833, in *Courier and Enquirer* (New York), 9 March 1833; Michael Hoffman to A. C. Flagg, 21, 25 Feb. 1833, Flagg Papers, NYPL; Silas Wright to Gideon Welles, 13 Feb. 1833, Welles Papers, LC; John G. Watmough to Nicholas Biddle, 21 Feb. 1833, Biddle Papers, LC; William R. King to John Gayle, 26 Feb. 1833, King Papers, ADAH; Silas Wright to A. C. Flagg, 25 Feb., 1833 Flagg Papers, NYPL.

39. Andrew Jackson to John Coffee, 16 March 1833, Bassett (ed.), *Correspondence of Andrew Jackson,* V, 30–31; Andrew Jackson to Felix Grundy, 13 Feb. 1833, *The American Historical Magazine,* V (April 1900), 137. On Grundy's ties to the administration at this time see: John Coffee to John D. Coffee, 21 Feb. 1833, Dyas Collection, TSL; "Felix Grundy," *Richmond Whig and Public Advertiser,* 8 March 1833.

40. M. C. Hoffman to A. C. Flagg, 8 Feb. 1833, Flagg Papers, NYPL.

41. *Register of Debates,* 22:2, 687; *The Georgia Journal* (Milledgeville), 7 March 1833; *Charleston Courier,* 1 March 1833; *Richmond Enquirer,* 21 Feb. 1833; *Richmond Whig and Public Advertiser,* 23 Feb. 1833.

42. *Register of Debates,* 22:2, 689–90; *Daily Albany Argus,* 26 Feb. 1833.

43. Martin Van Buren to Andrew Jackson, 20 Feb. 1833, Bassett (ed.), *Correspondence of Andrew Jackson,* V, 19–20; *Richmond Enquirer,* 22 Jan., 2, 7, 14, 19 Feb. 1833; *New Hampshire Patriot* (Concord), 7 Jan., 4 March 1833.

44. Scott (ed.), *Memoir of Hugh Lawson White,* 240.

45. *The Georgia Journal* (Milledgeville), 14 March 1833; *Courier and Enquirer* (New York), 16, 23 Feb. 1833; "Felix Grundy," *Richmond Whig and Public Advertiser,* 8 March 1833.

46. Silas Wright to Martin Van Buren, 29 Jan. 1833, Van Buren Papers, LC; Silas Wright to Nathaniel P. Tallmadge, 27 Jan. 1833, Tallmadge Papers, WHS; John Coffee to Wife, 24 Feb. 1833, Dyas Collection, TSL.

47. Silas Wright to A. C. Flagg, 21, 25 Feb. 1833, Flagg Papers, NYPL.

48. John M. Clayton to E. I. du Pont, 13 Feb. 1833, Clayton Papers, Eleutherian Mills Historical Library (EMHL); Richard Arden Wire, "Young Senator Clayton and the Early Jackson Years," *Delaware History* 17 (1976), 104–26; Munroe, *McLane,* 374.

49. *Register of Debates*, 22:2, 690–717; Wilson (ed.), *The Papers of John C. Calhoun*, XII, 96–101; *Washington Globe*, 28 Feb. 1833; *U.S. Telegraph* (Washington, D.C.), 21 Feb. 1833; *Daily Albany Argus*, 28 Feb., 5, 6 March 1833; *Courier and Enquirer* (New York), 23 March 1833. See also Wiltse, *Calhoun*, II, 191–92; Benton, *Thirty Years' View*, I, 342–44.

50. *Albany Evening Journal*, 4 Feb. 1833.

51. Michael Hoffman to A. C. Flagg, 25, 26 Feb. 1833, Flagg Papers, NYPL; *Albany Evening Journal*, 4, 21 Feb. 1833; *Charleston Courier*, 21 Feb. 1833; *Richmond Whig and Public Advertiser*, 21 Feb. 1833; *Daily Albany Argus*, 28 Feb., 5 March 1833.

52. United States Constitution, Article I, Section 7.

53. *Register of Debates*, 22:2, 1771–1807; entries of 25, 26 Feb. 1833, Adams (ed.), *Memoirs of John Quincy Adams*, VIII, 527–28; Daniel L. Barringer to Colonel William Polk, 27 Feb. 1833, Polk-Yeatman Papers, UNC; Michael Hoffman to A. C. Flagg, 25 Feb. 1833, Flagg Papers, NYPL.

54. *National Intelligencer* (Washington, D.C.), 27, 28 Feb., 7 March 1833; *Washington Globe*, 22, 27 Feb., 4 March 1833; *U.S. Telegraph* (Washington, D.C.), 23, 28 Feb. 1833; *Richmond Whig and Public Advertiser*, 5, 8 March 1833; *Courier and Enquirer* (New York), 2, 9 March 1833; *Albany Evening Journal*, 4 March 1833; *Daily Albany Argus* 4 March 1833; entry of 7 March 1833, Diary of Henry Van Der Lyn, NYHS; Michael Hoffman to A. C. Flagg, 25 Feb. 1833, Flagg Papers, NYPL.

55. *Register of Debates*, 22:2, 809, 1897–98; *Washington Globe*, 4 March 1833; *National Intelligencer* (Washington, D.C.), 4 March 1833; *Daily Albany Argus*, 2 March 1833.

56. John M. Clayton to E. I. du Pont, 2 March 1833, Clayton Papers, EMHL; Raynor G. Wellington, "The Tariff and the Public Lands from 1828 to 1833," American Historical Association, *Annual Report* (1911), I, 177–85; Michael Hoffman to A. C. Flagg, 14 Feb. 1833, Flagg Papers, NYPL; *National Intelligencer* (Washington, D.C.), 13 Dec. 1832, 23 Jan., 4 Feb., 2, 4 March 1833.

57. Henry Clay to James Barbour, 2 March 1833, Barbour Papers, NYPL.

58. Henry Clay to Nicholas Biddle, 4 March 1833, Biddle Papers, LC; John Connell to Nicholas Biddle, 1 March 1833, *ibid.*; Silas Wright to Nathaniel P. Tallmadge, 5 March 1833, Tallmadge Papers, WHS; *Richmond Whig and Public Advertiser*, 8 March 1833; Benjamin H. Hibbard, *A History of the Public Land Policies* (Madison, 1965), 171–94. For a different view see: Peterson, *Olive Branch and Sword*, 82–83. Daniel Feller, *The Public Lands in Jacksonism Politics* (Madison, 1984) is the most recent and best treatment of this important issue.

59. *Speeches Delivered in the Convention of the State of South Carolina, held in Columbia in March 1833. To which is Prefixed the Journal of Proceedings* (Charleston, 1833); *State Papers on Nullification*, 373–74.

9 The Nullification Crisis and Jacksonian Democracy

1. There is a large and unusually good, if conflicting, literature on the relationship of the Second Bank of the United States and financial policy in the 1830s to the problem of Jacksonian Democracy. See: Arthur Schlesinger, Jr., *The Age of Jackson* (Boston, 1945); Bray Hammond, *Banks and Politics in America from the Revolution to the Civil War* (Princeton, 1957); Marvin Meyers, *The Jacksonian Persuasion: Politics and Belief* (Palo Alto, 1957); Robert Remini, *Andrew Jackson and the Bank War* (New York,

1967); John M. McFaul, *The Politics of Jacksonian Finance* (Ithaca, 1972); Peter Temin, *The Jacksonian Economy* (New York, 1969); Sellers, *Polk,* I, 168–233.

2. Henry Barnard to Chauncey Barnard, 20 Feb. 1833, Bernard C. Steiner (ed.), "The South Atlantic States in 1833 . . . ," *Maryland Historical Magazine,* XIII (Sept., Dec., 1918), 311.

3. Edward Everett to Josiah Johnston, 23 Dec. 1832, Johnston Papers, HSP.

4. Adam King to John Rankin, 2 Jan. 1833, George M. Wolf Papers, HSP, John C. Bucher to William Ayres, 31 Dec. 1832, 11 Jan. 1833, Society Misc. Collection, HSP; William H. Crawford to Bolling Hall, 17 Jan. 1833, Hall Papers, ADAH; W. C. Rives to Nathanial Niles, 4 March 1833, Niles Papers, LC; Nicholas Trist to James Madison, 5 Feb. 1833, Trist Papers, VaHS.

5. Gerald M. Capers, "A Reconsideration of John C. Calhoun's Transition from Nationalism to Nullification," *Journal of Southern History,* XIV (Feb. 1948), 34–48; Capers, *John C. Calhoun—Opportunist: A Reappraisal* (Gainesville, 1960), 130–254; W. W. Freehling, *Prelude to Civil War,* 301–60; Boucher, *The Nullification Controversy in South Carolina,* 316–66; Houston, *A Critical Study of Nullification in South Carolina,* 131–41; Bancroft, *Calhoun and the South Carolina Nullification Movement,* 168–85.

6. Andrew Jackson to Joel R. Poinsett, 6 March 1833, Bassett (ed.), *Correspondence of Andrew Jackson,* V, 28; Andrew Jackson to John Coffee, 16 March 1833, *ibid.,* 30–31; John Coffee to Robert J. Chester, 3 March 1833, Misc. Collection, THS. See also Andrew Jackson to James Buchanan, 21 March 1833, Buchanan Papers, HSP.

7. William Drayton to Joel Poinsett, 9 Feb. 1833, Poinsett Papers, HSP; *Richmond Enquirer,* 5 Jan. 1833.

8. Edward Everett to Josiah Johnston, 23 Dec. 1832, Johnston Papers, HSP.

9. On the relationship of the nullification crisis and the nullifiers to the Bank War see: Henry Clay to Nicholas Biddle, 4 March 1833, Biddle Papers, LC; John Sergeant to Nicholas Biddle, 2, 4 March 1833, *ibid.;* S. Jaudin to Nicholas Biddle, 19, 21, 23 Jan. 1833, *ibid.;* John Watmough to Nicholas Biddle, 17 Jan., 11 Feb., 2 March 1833, *ibid.;* Manuel Eyre to Nicholas Biddle, 5, 7 Feb. 1833, *ibid.;* J. S. Barbour to Nicholas Biddle, 14 Feb. 1833, *ibid.;* Duff Green to Nicholas Biddle, 14 Feb. 1833, *ibid.;* John Connell to Nicholas Biddle, 2 March 1833, *ibid.;* Nicholas Biddle to Henry Clay, 25 March 1833, *ibid.*

10. *Richmond Whig and Public Advertiser,* 1, 8 March 1833; *Georgia Journal* (Milledgeville), 7 March 1833; Norman D. Brown, "Webster-Jackson Movement for a Constitution and Union Party in 1833," *Mid-America,* 46 (July 1964), 147–71; Sidney Nathans, *Daniel Webster and Jacksonian Democracy* (Baltimore, 1973), 52–70; Edwin A. Miles, "The Whig Party and the Menace of Caesar," *Tennessee Historical Quarterly,* XXVII (Winter 1968), 361–79; William E. Stokes, "Whig Conceptions of Executive Power, "*Presidential Studies Quarterly,* VI (Winter and Spring 1976), 16–34; Cole, *The Whig Party in the South,* 1–38; E. Malcolm Carrol, *Origins of the Whig Party* (Durham, 1925), 91–117. On the divided and confused state of the Democratic party after the nullification crisis see especially: Silas Wright to Nathaniel Tallmadge, 15 March 1833, Tallmadge Papers, WHS; James Hampson to John McLean, 6 March 1833, McLean Papers, LC; W. C. Rives to Nathaniel Niles, 4 March 1833, Niles Papers, LC; John G. Watmough to Nicholas Biddle, 21 Feb. 1833, Biddle Papers, LC.

11. John Marshall to William Gaston, 20 Dec. 1832, Gaston Papers, UNC.

12. Richardson (ed.), *Messages and Papers of the Presidents,* III, 3–5; "Rough Draft of Second Inaugural Address," Bassett (ed.), *Correspondence of Andrew Jackson,* V, 25–27; *Washington Globe,* 16, 27 Feb. 1833; *U.S. Telegraph* (Washington, D.C.),

15, 21 Feb. 1833; *Richmond Enquirer,* 19, 21 Feb., 7 March 1833; *Richmond Whig and Public Advertiser,* 22 Jan., 8 March 1833; *Daily Albany Argus,* 20 Feb., 8 March 1833; Richard E. Parker to Martin Van Buren, 21 March [1833], Van Buren Papers, LC.

13. On Macon and his relation to the Jacksonians, see especially: Benton, *Thirty Years' View,* I, 114–118.

14. Nathaniel Macon to Andrew Jackson, 26 Aug. 1833, Bassett (ed.), *Correspondence of Andrew Jackson,* V, 171–72; Andrew Jackson to Nathanial Macon, 2 Sept. 1833, *ibid.,* V, 176–78; Nathaniel Macon to Martin Van Buren, 2 March 1833, Van Buren Papers, LC; Nathaniel Macon to Samuel P. Carson, 9 Feb. 1833, *John P. Branch Historical Papers,* III (June 1909), 92; "Spy in Washington," 24 Jan. 1833, in *Courier and Enquirer* (New York), 2 Feb. 1833.

15. William Kent to Moss Kent, 10 Feb. 1833, James Kent Papers, LC. See also William Wirt to Judge Carr, 6 Jan. 1833, Kennedy (ed.), *Memoirs of the Life of William Wirt,* II, 347–51; Edward J. Hale to Willie P. Mangum, 30 Jan. 1833, Shanks (ed.), *The Papers of Willie P. Mangum,* II, 14–17; Aaron V. Brown to James K. Polk, 20 Jan. 1833, Weaver and Bergeron (eds.), *Correspondence of Polk,* II, 34–35; Nathaniel Macon to Martin Van Buren, 2 March 1833, Van Buren Papers, LC; J. A. Davis to Nicholas P. Trist, 25 April 1833, Trist Papers, LC; Nicholas Trist to James Madison, 5 Feb. 1833, Trist Papers, VaHS; David Campbell to William B. Campbell, 19 Feb. 1833, Campbell Family Papers, DU; William H. Crawford to Mahlon Dickerson, 6 Sept. 1832, Dickerson Papers, NJHS; William Drayton to Joel Poinsett, 31 Dec. 1832, Poinsett Papers, HSP; S. Pleasanton to James Buchanan, 30 Jan. 1833, Buchanan Papers, HSP.

16. Warren, *Supreme Court,* I, 231–68; Ellis, *The Jeffersonian Crisis,* 58–68; Charles Haskins and Herbert A. Johnson, *History of the Supreme Court of the United States: Foundation of Power: John Marshall 1801–1815* (New York, 1981), 182–204; Donald O. Dewey, *Marshall Versus Jefferson: The Political Background of Marbury v. Madison* (New York, 1970).

17. The debate over the meaning of Jacksonian Democracy may be traced in: Charles G. Sellers, "Andrew Jackson Versus the Historians," *Mississippi Valley Historical Review,* 44 (March, 1958), 615–34; Ronald P. Formisano, "Toward a Reorientation of Jacksonian Politics: A Review of the Literature, 1959–1975," *Journal of American History* 63 (June 1976), 42–65; Edward Pessen, *Jacksonian America: Society, Personality and Politics* (Homewood, 1978), 348–67.

18. Phillips Bradley, ed., *Democracy in America* by Alexis De Toqueville (2 vols., New York, 1945), I, 260–61.

19. Register of Debates, 22:2, 547–49. See also Richard N. Current, *John C. Calhoun* (New York, 1963), 37–105.

20. Charles G. Sellers, "Banking and Politics in Jackson's Tennessee, 1817–1827," *Mississippi Historical Review* 41 (June 1954), 61–84; Charles G. Sellers, "Jackson Men with Feet of Clay," *American Historical Review,* 62 (April 1957), 537–51; Kim T. Phillips, "The Pennsylvania Origins of the Jackson Movement," *Political Science Quarterly,* 91 (Fall 1976), 489; 489–508; Donald J. Ratcliffe, "The Role of Voters and Issues in Party Formation: Ohio, 1824," *Journal of American History,* 59 (March 1973), 847–70; Ruth Ketring Nuermberger, "The 'Royal Party' in Early Alabama Politics," *The Alabama Review,* VI (April, July, 1953), 81–98, 198–212; Sydnor, *The Development of Southern Sectionalism,* 104–56.

21. State Constitutional reform in the post-1815 period remains an area much in need of study. Some help may be obtained from: Merrill D. Peterson (ed.), *Democracy,*

Liberty and Property: The State Constitutional Convention of the 1820's (Indianapolis, 1966), v–vii; George Phillip Parkinson, Jr., "Antebellum State Constitution Making: Retention, Circumvention, Revision" (unpublished doctoral dissertation, University of Wisconsin, 1972); Sydnor, *The Development of Southern Sectionalism,* 104–33, 275–93; Fletcher M. Green, *Constitutional Development in the South Atlantic States, 1776–1860* (Chapel Hill, 1930), 201–53, and "Democracy in the Old South," *Journal of Southern History,* XII (Feb. 1946), 3–23; Winbourne Magruder Drake, "The Mississippi Constitutional Convention of 1832," *Journal of Southern History,* XXIII (Aug. 1957), 554–70; Harold J. Counihan, "The North Carolina Constitutional Convention of 1835: A Study in Jacksonian Democracy," *North Carolina Historical Review,* XLVI (Autumn 1969), 335–64; Malcolm Cook McMillan, *Constitutional Development in Alabama, 1798–1901: A Study in Politics, The Negro and Sectionalism* (Chapel Hill, 1955), 47–63; A. G. Freehling, *Drift Toward Dissolution,* 36–81; Fred Seigel, "The Paternalist Thesis: Virginia as a Test Case," *Civil War History,* 25 (Sept. 1975), 246–61; Chase C. Mooney, "The Question of Slavery and the Free Negro in the Tennessee Constitutional Convention of 1834," *Journal of Southern History,* XI (Nov. 1946), 487–509.

22. *Proceedings and Debates of the Virginia State Constitutional Convention of 1829–30* (Richmond, 1830), 537–38; Wilson Lumpkin to Bolling Hall, 1 Feb. 1832, Hall Papers, ADAH; John A. Quitman to Nathan G. Howard, 14 Jan. 1833, Howard Papers, MDAH. Quitman's activities at the Mississippi Constitutional Convention in the fall of 1832 may be traced in: John A. Quitman to Eliza Quitman, 12, 16, 23 Sept., 2, 12, 18 Oct. 1832, Quitman Papers, UNC.

23. For the sectional divisions within the Old South see: A. Freehling, *Drift Toward Dissolution,* 36–81; Robert Sutton, "Sectionalism and Social Structure: A Case Study of Jeffersonian Democracy," *Virginia Magazine of History and Biography* 80 (Jan. 1972), 70–84; Paul Murray, "Economic Sectionalism in Georgia Politics, 1825–1855," *Journal of Southern History* 10 (Aug. 1944), 293–307; Edwin A. Miles, *Jacksonian Democracy in Mississippi,* 3–17.

24. Richard H. Brown, "The Missouri Crisis, Slavery and the Politics of Jacksoniansim," *South Atlantic Quarterly,* 65 (Winter 1966), 55–72; William J. Cooper, Jr., *The South and the Politics of Slavery, 1828–1856* (Baton Rouge, 1978); Michael Holt, *The Political Crisis of the 1850's* (New York, 1978), 20–21.

25. Ambler, *Ritchie,* 118–54.

26. Leonard L. Richards, "The Jacksonians and Slavery," Lewis Perry and Michael Fellman (eds.), *Antislavery Reconsidered: New Perspectives on the Abolitionists* (Baton Rouge, 1979), 99–118; Gerald S. Henig, "The Jacksonian Attitude Toward Abolitionism in the 1830's," *Tennessee Historical Quarterly,* XXVIII (Spring 1969) 42–56; Richard H. Brown, "The Missouri Crisis, Slavery and the Politics of Jacksonianism," *South Atlantic Quarterly,* 65 (Winter 1966), 55–72; Pessen, *Jacksonian America,* 301–3.

27. *Washington Globe,* 24 April 1833; *New Hampshire Patriot* (Concord), 7 Jan. 1833; John M. McFaul, "Expediency vs. Morality: Jacksonian Politics and Slavery," *Journal of American History* 63 (June 1975), 24–39; Richard B. Latner, "The Nullification Crisis and Republican Subversion," *Journal of Southern History,* 43, 23–27; Latner, *The Presidency of Andrew Jackson,* 212.

28. Cole, *The Whig Party in the South,* 39–63; U. B. Phillips, "The Southern Whigs," Guy S. Ford, (ed.), *Essays in American History Dedicated to Frederick Jackson Turner* (New York, 1910), 203–30; Thomas Brown, "Southern Whigs and the Politics of Statesmanship, 1833–1841," *Journal of Southern History,* XLVI (Aug. 1980), 361–

80; Murray, *The Whig Party in Georgia, 1825–1853,* 59–88; Simms, *The Rise of the Whigs in Virginia,* 11–86; Dumas Malone, *The Public Life of Thomas Cooper, 1783–1839* (Columbia, 1961); Robert J. Brugger, *Beverley Tucker: Heart over Head in The Old South* (Baltimore, 1978); Drew Gilpin Faust, *James Henry Hammond and the Old South: A Design for Mastery* (Baton Rouge, 1982); Faust, *A Sacred Circle: The Dilemma of the Intellectual—The Old South, 1840–1860* (Baltimore, 1977); Faust (ed.), *The Ideology of Slavery: Pro-Slavery Thought—The Antebellum South, 1820–1860* (Baton Rouge, 1981).

29. Bernard Peyton to W. C. Rives, 21 Jan. 1833, Rives Papers, LC.

30. "The Liberator and Emancipator—Lundy and Garrison," *Richmond Whig and Public Advertiser,* 29 March 1833. See also Bolling Hall to Dennis L. Ryan, 21 Nov. 1832, Hall Papers, ADAH; B. E. Beasley to W. C. Rives, 3 March 1833, Rives Papers, LC; C. C. Clay to Francis P. Blair, 7 May 1833, Blair-Lee Papers, PUL; *Richmond Enquirer,* 16 Feb. 1833.

31. Lewis Williams to William B. Lenoir, 15 Dec. 1832, Lenoir Family Papers, UNC.

32. John Marshall to Timothy Pickering, 20 March 1826, "Letters of Chief Justice Marshall," Massachusetts Historical Society, *Proceedings,* 2nd Series, XIV (1900, 1901), 321.

33. Gavin Wright, " 'Economic Democracy' and the Concentration of Agricultural Wealth in the Cotton South, 1850–1860," *Agricultural History,* 44 (Jan. 1970), 63–94; Wright, *The Political Economy of the Cotton South: Households, Markets and Wealth in the Nineteenth Century* (New York, 1978), 29–37. See also: Lee Soltow, "Economic Inequality in the United States in the Period from 1790 to 1860," *Journal of Economic History,* XXXI (Dec. 1971), 822–39; Lee Soltow, *Men and Wealth in the United States 1850–1870* (New Haven, 1975), 124–46; Jeffrey G. Williamson and Peter H. Lindert, *American Inequality: A Macroeconomic History* (New York, 1980), 33–46.

34. A. G. Freehling, *Drift Toward Dissolution,* 12–169; William H. Crawford to Benjamin Watkins Leigh, 24 Dec. 1829, Leigh Papers, VaHS; William Lucas to J. B. C. Lucas, 26 Sept. 1829, J. B. C. Lucas Papers, MoHS; Robert C. Hynson to John Overton, 9 Nov. 1831, Overton Papers, THS; James C. Bonner, "Legislative Apportionment and County Unit Voting in Georgia Since 1777," *Georgia Historical Quarterly,* XLVII (Dec. 1963), 351–74; Lucien E. Roberts, "Sectional Factors in Movements for Legislative Reapportionment and Reduction in Georgia, 1777–1860," James C. Bonner and Lucien E. Roberts (eds.), *Studies in Georgia History and Government* (Athens, 1949), 94–122; George Ruble Woolfolk, "Taxes and Slavery in the Antebellum South," *Journal of Southern History,* XXVI (May 1960), 180–200; C. C. Mooney, "The Question of Slavery and the Free Negro in the Tennessee Constitutional Convention of 1834," *Journal of Southern History,* XI (Nov. 1946), 486–509; Murray, *The Whig Party in Georgia,* 38–54; Miles, *Jacksonian Democracy in Mississippi,* 25–26, 33–43; T. H. Jack, *Sectionalism and Party Politics in Alabama, 1819–1842,* (Menasha, 1919), 16–20.

35. John C. Calhoun to Virgil Maxcy, 11 Sept. 1830, Wilson (ed.), *The Papers of John C. Calhoun,* XI, 229. In general my own findings support William W. Freehling's argument in *Prelude to Civil War* that links the nullifiers with the defense of slavery. For a different point of view see Paul Bergeron, "The Nullification Controversy Revisited," *Tennessee Historical Quarterly,* 35 (Fall 1976), 263–75; J. P. Ochenkowski, "The Origins of Nullification in South Carolina," *South Carolina Historical Magazine,* 83 (April 1982), 121–53.

36. *U.S. Telegraph* (Washington, D.C.), 25 Feb. 1833.

37. Alexander Brown to William S. Hamilton, 19 Feb. 1833, Hamilton Papers, Louisiana State University, LSU.

38. Michael Hoffman to A. C. Flagg, 26 Feb. 1833, Flagg Papers, NYPL.

39. Andrew Jackson to John Crawford, 9 April 1833, Bassett (ed.), *Correspondence of Andrew Jackson*, V, 56. See also: Andrew Jackson to Andrew J. Crawford, 1 May 1832, *ibid.*, V, 71–72.

40. Edward King to Sarah King, 22 June 1833, King Family Papers, Cincinnati Historical Society (CiHS).

41. Martin Van Buren, *Inquiry into the Origin and Course of Political Parties in the United States* (New York, 1867), 54.

42. Genovese, *The World the Slaveholders Made;* David Donald, "The Proslavery Argument Reconsidered," *Journal of Southern History*, XXXVII (Feb. 1971), 3–19.

43. James Oakes, *The Ruling Race: A History of American Slaveholders* (New York, 1982), 35–150; Gavin Wright, *The Political Economy of the Cotton South* (New York, 1978); Robert W. Fogel and Stanley L. Engerman, *Time on the Cross: The Economics of American Negro Slavery* (2 vols., Boston, 1974).

44. John Sergeant to Nicholas Biddle, 2, 4 March 1833, Biddle Papers, LC; John G. Watmough to Nicholas Biddle, 17 Jan., 11, 26 Feb., 2 March 1833, *ibid.*; S. Jaudon to Nicholas Biddle, 19, 21, 23 Jan. 1833, *ibid.*; Manuel Eyre to Nicholas Biddle, 5, 7 Feb. 1833, *ibid.*; Duff Green to Nicholas Biddle, 4 Feb. 1833, *ibid.*; John Connell to Nicholas Biddle, 2 March 1833, *ibid.*; J. S. Barbour to Nicholas Biddle, 14 Feb. 1833, *ibid.*; P. P. F. Degrand to Nicholas Biddle, 15 Feb. 1833, *ibid.*, Govan, *Biddle*, 164, 221.

45. Arthur Bestor, "State Sovereignty and Slavery: A Reinterpretation of Proslavery Constitutional Doctrine, 1846–1860," *Journal of the Illinois State Historical Society*, LIV (Summer 1961), 117–80; Paul Finkelman, *An Imperfect Union: Slavery, Federalism and Comity* (Chapel Hill, 1981); J. Mills Thornton, III, *Politics and Power in a Slave Society* (Baton Rouge, 1978), 35.

BIBLIOGRAPHY

Manuscripts

Alabama Department of Archives and History (ADAH): Bolling Hall Papers; John Coffee Papers; William King Papers.
Buffalo and Erie County Historical Society (BECHS): Peter B. Porter Papers.
Cincinnati Historical Society (CiHS): King Family Papers.
Columbia University (CU): Thomas W. Olcott Papers.
The College of William and Mary (CWM): Tucker-Coleman Papers.
Clemson University (ClU): Richard Crallé Papers.
Duke University (DU): C. C. Clay Papers; Campbell Family Papers; James Iredell Papers; John Rutherfoord Papers.
Eleutherian Mills Historical Library (EMHL): John M. Clayton Papers; Eleutherian Bradford du Pont Collection.
Emory University (EU): Tomlinson R. Fort Papers.
Georgia Department of Archives and History (GDAH): Wilson Lumpkin Papers.
Historical Society of Pennsylvania (HSP): James Buchanan Papers; George M. Wolf Papers; Josiah Johnston Papers; Isaac Wayne MacVeagh Papers; Joel Poinsett Papers; Society Miscellaneous Collection; George M. Wolf Papers.
Historical Society of Western Pennsylvania (HSWP): Harmer Denny Papers.
Illinois Historical Society (IHS): Jesse B. Thomas Papers.
Library of Congress (LC): Nicholas Biddle Papers; Charles Butler Papers; Richard Crallé Papers; William H. Crawford Papers; Andrew Jackson Donelson Papers; Thomas Ewing Papers; John Floyd Papers; Francis Granger Papers; Duff Green Papers; James H. Hammond Papers; Andrew Jackson Papers; James Kent Pa-

246

pers; James Madison Papers; William H. Marcy Papers; Duncan McArthur Papers; John McLean Papers; Nathaniel Niles Papers; William C. Rives Papers; Roger B. Taney Papers; Nicholas Trist Papers; Martin Van Buren Papers; Gideon Welles Papers; William Wirt Papers; Levi Woodbury Papers.

Louisiana State University (LSU): William S. Hamilton Papers.

Mississippi Department of Archives and History (MDAH): J. F. H. Claiborne Papers; Nathan Howard Papers.

Massachusetts Historical Society (MHS): Otis Norcross Collection; Theodore Sedgwick Papers.

Maryland Historical Society (MdHS): William Wirt Letterbooks.

Missouri Historical Society (MoHS): Thomas Benton Papers; J. B. C. Lucas Papers; Political Papers Collection.

National Archives (NA): Records of the Office of the Secretary of War, Confidential and Unofficial; Letters Sent, Record Group 107, Microfilm Series M7 Roll 1.

New Jersey Historical Society (NJHS): Mahlon Dickerson Papers.

New-York Historical Society (NYHS): Rokeby Collection; Diary of Henry Van Der Lyn; Miscellaneous Manuscripts; Gillian C. Verplanck Papers.

New York Public Library (NYPL): James Barbour Papers; Azariah C. Flagg Papers; Jackson-Lewis Papers; Samuel Tilden Papers; Martin Van Buren Papers.

New York State Library (NYSL): B. F. Butler Papers; Seward Family Papers; Albert H. Tracy Papers.

Princeton University Library (PUL): Blair-Lee Papers; Samuel Southard Papers.

University of South Carolina (USC): William Smith Papers, South Caroliniana Collection.

Tennessee Historical Society (THS): Miscellaneous Collection; John Overton Papers.

Tennessee State Library (TSL): J. M. Dickinson Papers; Dyas Collection.

University of Georgia (UGa): Wilson Lumpkin Papers.

University of North Carolina (UNC): John M. Berrien Papers; John Branch Family Papers; Edward Dromgoole Papers; Fisher Family Papers; William Gaston Papers; Duff Green Papers; Felix Grundy Papers; Jones and Patterson Family Papers; Lenoir Family Papers; Polk-Yeatman Papers; John A. Quitman Papers.

University of Rochester (UR): William H. Seward Papers; Thurlow Weed Papers.

University of Virginia (UVa): Bryan Family Papers; Cabell Deposit; Gooch Family Papers; R. M. T. Hunter Papers.

Virginia State Library (VSL): Littleton Waller Tazewell Papers.

Virginia Historical Society (VaHS): William Hammett Papers; Benjamin Watkins Leigh Papers; Miscellaneous Manuscripts; Nicholas Trist Papers.

Wisconsin Historical Society (WHS): Nathaniel P. Tallmadge Papers.

Newspapers

District of Columbia: *National Intelligencer* (Washington, D.C.); *U.S. Telegraph* (Washington, D.C.); *Washington Globe.*

Georgia: *Columbus Enquirer; Federal Union* (Milledgeville); *Georgia Chronicle* (Milledgeville); *Georgia Journal* (Milledgevile); *Georgia Messenger* (Macon); *Georgia Telegraph* (Macon); *Georgian* (Savannah); *Southern Recorder* (Milledgeville); *The Times and States' Rights Advocate* (Milledgeville).

Maryland: *Niles' Weekly Register* (Baltimore)

Mississippi: *Natchez Courier and Adams, Jefferson and Franklin Advertiser*

Missouri: *Missouri Republican* (St. Louis)
New Hampshire: *New Hampshire Patriot* (Concord)
New York: *Albany Argus; Albany Evening Journal; Commercial Advertiser* (New
    York); *Courier and Enquirer* (New York); *Daily Albany Argus* (Albany); *Jour-
    nal of Commerce* (New York); *New York Commercial Advertiser; The Ontario
    Freeman* (Canandaigua); *Utica Sentinel and Gazette* (Utica).
Pennsylvania: *United States Gazette* (Philadelphia).
South Carolina: *Charleston Courier* (Charleston); *Charleston Mercury* (Charleston);
    Columbia Telescope.
Virginia: *American Beacon* (Norfolk); *Constitutional Whig* (Richmond); *Lynchburg
    Virginian* (Lynchburg); *Richmond Enquirer* (Richmond); *Richmond Whig and
    Public Advertiser* (Richmond); *The Constitutional Whig* (Richmond); *The Her-
    ald* (Norfolk); *The Virginia Herald* (Fredricksburg).

Published Sources

Adams, Charles Francis, ed. *Memoirs of John Quincy Adams* (Philadelphia, 1874–77),
    12 vols.
Adams, Charles Francis, ed. *The Work of John Adams,* (Boston, 1850–56), 10 vols.
Adams, John Quincy, *An Oration Delivered to the Citizens of the Town of Quincy, on
    the Fourth of July, 1831* . . . (Boston, 1831).
Adams, John Stokes, ed. *An Autiobiographical Sketch by John Marshall* (Ann Arbor,
    1937).
Address of Judge Abel P. Upshur to the People of Northampton County (Richmond,
    1833).
Agricola. *Virginia Doctrines not Nullification* (Richmond, 1832).
Ambler, Charles, ed. *The Life and Diary of John Floyd* . . . (Richmond, 1918).
Ambler, Charles, ed. "Unpublished Letters of Thomas Ritchie," *The John P. Branch
    Historical Papers of Randolph Macon College* 3 (1911), 199–252.
American State Papers: Military Affairs, V.
Ames, Herman V. *State Documents on Federal Relations: The States and the United
    States* (Philadelphia, 1906).
Barry, William T. "Letters of William T. Barry," *William and Mary Quarterly,* XIII
    (April 1905), 236–44; XIV (July 1905), 19–23; XIV (April 1906) 230–41.
Bassett, John Spencer, ed. *Correspondence of Andrew Jackson* (Washington, D.C.,
    1926–35), 7 vols.
Benton, Thomas Hart. *Thirty Years' View* (New York, 1854–56), 2 vols.
Bradley, Phillips, ed. *Democracy in America* by Alexis De Toqueville (New York,
    1945), 2 vols.
Chipman, Nathaniel. *Principles of Government, A Treatise on Free Institutions* . . .
    (Burlington, 1833).
Claiborne, J. F. H. *Life and Correspondence of John A. Quitman* (New York, 1860), 2
    vols.
Claiborne, J. F. H. *Life and Times of Gen. Sam. Dale, the Mississippi Partisan* (New
    York, 1860).
Clay, Thomas H., ed. "Two Years with Old Hickory," *Atlantic Monthly* LX (Aug.
    1887).
Colton, Calvin, ed. *Private Correspondence of Henry Clay* (New York, 1855).
Colton, Calvin, ed. *The Works of Henry Clay* (New York, 1857), 6 vols.

Congressional Globe, Containing the Debates and Proceedings, 1833–1873 (Washington, D.C., 1834–73), 109 vols.

Correspondence: "Correspondence of Judge Tucker," *William and Mary Quarterly* XII (Oct. 1903).

Dane, Nathan. *General Abridgement and Digest of American Law* (Boston, 1823–29), 9 vols.

Dix, Morgan, ed. *Memoirs of John Adams Dix* (New York, 1883), 2 vols.

Dodd, William E., ed. "Nathaniel Macon Correspondence," *The John P. Branch Historical Papers of Randolph Macon College*, 3 (1909), 17–93.

Duer, William A. *A Course of Lectures on the Constitutional Jurisprudence of the United States . . .* (New York, 1843).

Fitzpatrick, John C., ed. *The Autobiography of Martin Van Buren* (Washington, D.C., 1920).

Hamilton, Alexander. *The Farmer Refuted . . .* (New York, 1775).

Hamilton, J. G. De Roulhac, ed. *The Papers of Thomas Ruffin* (Raleigh, 1918–20), 4 vols.

Hamilton, James A., ed. *Reminiscences of Men and Events* (New York, 1869).

Hammond, Jabez. *The History of Political Parties in the State of New York* (Cooperstown, 1846), 3 vols.

Hargreaves, Mary W. M., and James F. Hopkins, eds. *The Papers of Henry Clay* (Lexington, 1959–—), 7 vols.

Hunt, Gaillard, ed. *The Writings of James Madison* (New York, 1900–1910), 9 vols.

Hunt, Gaillard, ed. *Letters of Margaret Bayard Smith: The First Forty Years of Washington Society in the Family Letters of Margaret Bayard Smith* (New York, 1906; reprinted 1965).

Jefferson, Thomas. *A Summary View of the Rights of British America . . .* (Williamsburg, 1774).

Journal of the House of Delegates of the Commonwealth of Virginia (Richmond, 1832).

Kennedy, John P., ed. *Memoirs of the Life of William Wirt, Attorney General of the United States* (Philadelphia, 1849), 2 vols.

Kilpatrick, Jack Frederick, and Anna Gritt Kilpatrick, eds. *New Echota Letters: Contributions of Samuel A. Worcester to the Cherokee Phoenix* (Dallas, 1968).

"Letters of Chief Justice Marshall," Massachusetts Historical Society, *Proceedings*, 2nd Series, XIV (1900, 1901), 320–60.

"Letters on the Nullification Movement in South Carolina," *American Historical Review*, VI (July 1901); VII (Oct. 1901), 735–65, 92–119.

Leonard, Daniel, and John Adams. *Novanglus and Massachusettnsis; Massachusettnsis; or Political Essays Published in the Years 1774 and 1775 . . .* (Boston, 1819).

Lincoln, Charles Z., ed. *Messages from the Governors . . .* (Albany, 1909), 11 vols.

Lumpkin, Wilson, *The Removal of the Cherokee Indians from Georgia, 1827–41* (New York, 1907), 2 vols.

McDuffie, George. *Speech . . . at . . . Charleston, S.C., May 19, 1831* (Charleston, 1831).

McGrane, Reginald C., ed. *The Correspondence of Nicholas Biddle Dealing with National Affairs, 1807–1844* (Boston, 1919).

Miller, Sally Campbell Preston, ed. *Memoir of James McDowell* (Baltimore, 1895).

Miller, Stephen Francis. *The Bench and Bar of Georgia: Memoirs and Sketches* (Philadelphia, 1858), 2 vols.

Nevins, Allan, ed. *The Diary of Philip Hone* (New York, 1927), 2 vols.

[Nicholas, Philip Norbone.] "Agricola," *Virginia Doctrines Not Nullification* (Richmond, 1832).

Oliphant, Mary C. Simms, et al., eds. *The Letters of William Gilmore Simms* (Columbia, 1952–56), 5 vols.

Peters, Richard, Jr. *Reports of Cases Argued and Adjudged in the Supreme Court, 1828–1842* (1828–43), 17 vols.

Peterson, Merrill D., ed. *Democracy, Liberty and Property: The State Constitutional Convention of the 1820's* (Indianapolis, 1966).

Proceedings and Debates of the Virginia State Constitutional Convention of 1829–30 (Richmond, 1830).

Register of Debates in Congress, 1825–1837 (Washington, D.C., 1825–37), 29 vols.

Richardson, James D., ed. *A Compilation of the Messages and Papers of the Presidents, 1789–1897* (Washington, D.C., 1900), 10 vols.

Robertson, Nellie Armstrong, and Dorothy Riker, eds. *The John Tipton Papers* (Indianapolis, 1942), 3 vols.

Sargent, Nathan. *Public Men and Events* (Philadelphia, 1875), 2 vols.

Scott, Nancy N., ed. *A Memoir of Hugh Lawson White* (Philadelphia, 1856).

Seward, Frederick W., ed. *William H. Seward: An Autobiography* (New York, 1891).

Shanks, Henry T., ed. *The Papers of Willie Persons Mangum* (Raleigh, 1950–56), 5 vols.

Speeches Delivered in the Convention of the State of South Carolina, held in Columbia in March 1833. To which is Prefixed the Journal of Proceedings (Charleston, 1833).

Speeches of Daniel Webster (Boston, 1850), 3 vols.

State Papers on Nullification.

Steiner, Bernard, ed. "The South Atlantic States in 1833, as Seen by a New Englander," *Maryland Historical Magazine*, XIII (Sept.–Dec. 1918), 267–94, 295–386.

Stickney, William, ed. *The Autobiography of Amos Kendall* (Boston, 1872).

Story, Joseph. *Commentaries on the Constitution of the United States . . .* (Boston, 1833), 3 vols.

Story, W. W., ed. *Life and Letters of Joseph Story* (Boston, 1851), 2 vols.

Tazewell, Littleton W. *A Review of the Proclamation of President Jackson . . . Under the Signature "A Virginian"* (Norfolk, 1833).

Tyler, Lyon G., ed. *The Letters and Times of the Tylers* (Richmond, 1844–96), 3 vols.

Tyler, Samuel, ed. *Memoir of Roger Brooke Taney* (Baltimore, 1872).

Upshur, Abel Parker. *An Exposition of the Virginia Resolutions of 1798: A Series of Essays Addressed to Thomas Ritchie . . . Under the Signature of "Locke"* (Philadelphia, 1833).

Upshur, Abel Parker. *The Essays of Napier* (Norfolk, 1833).

Van Buren, Martin. *Inquiry into the Origin and Course of Political Parties in the United States* (New York, 1867).

Weaver, Herbert, and Paul H. Bergeron, eds. *Correspondence of James K. Polk* (Nashville, 1969–?—), 6 vols.

Webster, Fletcher, ed. *The Private Correspondence of Daniel Webster* (Boston, 1856), 2 vols.

White, Robert H., ed. *Messages of the Governors of Tennessee* (Nashville, 1952–72), 8 vols.

Wilson, Clyde N., and W. Edwin Hemphill, eds. *The Papers of John C. Calhoun* (Columbia, 1959——), 14 vols. to date.

Wilson, James. *Considerations on the Nature and the Extent of the Legislative Authority of the British Parliament* (Philadelphia, 1774).

Wiltse, Charles, and Harold D. Moser, eds. *The Papers of Daniel Webster: Correspondence* (Hanover, 1974——), 7 vols. to date.

Books

Abel, Anne Heloise. *The History of Events Resulting in Indian Consolidation West of the Mississippi* (Washington, D.C., 1908).

Ambler, Charles Henry. *Thomas Ritchie: A Study in Virginia Politics* (Richmond, 1913).

Ames, Herman V. *The Proposed Amendments to the Constitution of the United States During the First Century of Its History* (New York, 1896, 1970).

Bailyn, Bernard. *The Ideological Origins of the American Revolution* (Cambridge, 1967).

Bancroft, Frederic. *Calhoun and the South Carolina Nullification Movement* (Baltimore, 1928).

Banner, James M. *The the Hartford Convention* (New York, 1970).

Bassett, John Spencer. *The Life of Andrew Jackson* (New York, 1911, 1931).

Bauer, Elizabeth Kelley. *Commentaries on the Constitution, 1790–1860* (New York, 1952).

Baxter, Maurice G. *One and Inseparable: Daniel Webster and the Union* (Cambridge, 1984).

Bemis, Samuel Flagg. *John Quincy Adams and the Union* (New York, 1956).

Benson, Lee. *The Concept of Jacksonian Democracy: New York as a Test Case* (Princeton, 1960).

Benson, Lee. *Turner and Beard* (Glencoe, 1960).

Boucher, Chauncey S. *The Nullification Controversy in South Carolina* (Chicago, 1916).

Brown, Norman. *Daniel Webster and the Politics of Availability* (Athens, 1968).

Bruce, William Cabell. *John Randolph of Roanoke, 1773–1833* (New York, 1922), 2 vols.

Brugger, Robert J. *Beverley Tucker: Heart Over Head in the Old South* (Baltimore, 1978).

Buell, Augustus. *History of Andrew Jackson* (New York, 1904), 2 vols.

Capers, Gerald M. *John C. Calhoun: Opportunist, A Reappraisal* (Chicago, 1960, 1969).

Carrol, E. Malcolm. *Origins of the Whig Party* (Durham, 1925).

Catterall, Ralph C. H. *The Second Bank of the United States.* (Chicago, 1903).

Chitwood, Oliver Perry. *John Tyler: Champion of the Old South* (New York, 1939).

Cole, Arthur C. *The Whig Party in the South* (Washington, D.C., 1913).

Cole, B. Donald. *Martin Van Buren and the American Political System* (Princeton, 1984).

Cook, Harvey T. *The Life and Legacy of David Rogerson Williams* (New York, 1916).

Cooper, William J., Jr. *The South and the Politics of Slavery, 1828–1856* (Baton Rouge, 1978).

Coulter, E. M. *College Life in the Old South* (New York, 1928).

Culver H. Smith. *The Press, Politics and Patronage: The American Government's Use of Newspapers, 1789–1875* (Athens, 1977).

Current, Richard N. *John C. Calhoun* (New York, 1963).

Curtis, James C. *Andrew Jackson and the Search for Vindication* (Boston, 1976).

Curtis, James C. *The Fox at Bay: Martin Van Buren and the Presidency* (Lexington, 1970).

Darling, Arthur B. *Political Change in Massachusetts, 1824–1848* (New Haven, 1925).

Dawidoff, Robert. *The Education of John Randolph* (New York, 1979).

DeRosier, Arthur H. *The Removal of the Choctaw Indians* (Knoxville, 1970).

Dewey, Donald O. *Marshall versus Jefferson: The Political Background of Marbury v. Madison* (New York, 1970).

Dictionary of American Biography (New York, 1928–36), 20 vols.

Donovan, Herbert D. A. *The Barnburners: A Study of the Internal Movements in the Political History of New York State and of the Resulting Changes in Political Affiliation, 1830–1852* (New York, 1925).

Douglass, Elisha P. *Rebels and Democrats* (Chapel Hill, 1955).

Duckett, Alvin L. *John Forsyth: Political Tactician* (Athens, 1962).

Ellis, Richard E. *The Jeffersonian Crisis: Courts and Politics in the Young Republic* (New York, 1971).

Faust, Drew, ed. *The Ideology of Slavery: Pro-Slavery Thought—the Antebellum South, 1820–1860* (Baton Rouge, 1981).

Faust, Drew Gilpin. *James Henry Hammond and the Old South: A Design for Mastery* (Baton Rouge, 1982).

Faust, Drew. *A Sacred Circle: The Dilemma of the Intellectual—the Old South, 1840–1860* (Baltimore, 1977).

Feller, Daniel. *The Public Lands in Jacksonian Politics* (Madison, 1984).

Finkelman, Paul. *An Imperfect Union: Slavery, Federalism and Comity* (Chapel Hill, 1981).

Fogel, Robert W., and Stanley L. Engerman. *Time on the Cross: The Economics of American Negro Slavery* (Boston, 1974), 2 vols.

Fox, Dixon Ryan. *The Decline of Aristocracy in the Politics of New York, 1801–1840* (New York, 1919).

Frank, John P. *Justice Daniel Dissenting: A Bibliography of Peter V. Daniel, 1784–1860* (Cambridge, 1964).

Freehling, Alison Goodyear. *Drift Toward Dissolution: The Virginia Slavery Debate of 1831–1832* (Baton Rouge, 1982).

Freehling, William W. *Prelude to Civil War: The Nullification Movement in South Carolina, 1816–1836* (New York, 1966).

Gammon, Samuel Rhea. *The Presidential Campaign of 1832* (Baltimore, 1922).

Garland, Hugh A. *The Life of John Randolph of Roanoke* (New York, 1850), 2 vols.

Garraty, John A. *Silas Wright* (New York, 1949).

Goodrich, Carter. *Government Promotion of American Canals and Railroads, 1800–1890* (New York, 1960).

Gordon, Armisted C. *William Fitzhugh Gordon: A Virginian of the Old School* (New York and Washington, 1909).

Govan, Thomas Payne. *Nicholas Biddle* (Chicago, 1959).

Green, Fletcher. *Constitutional Development in the South Atlantic States, 1776–1860* (Chapel Hill, 1930).

Haines, Charles Grove. *The Role of the Supreme Court in American Government and Politics, 1789–1835* (Berkeley, 1944; New York, 1973).

Hall, Claude H. *Abel Parker Upshur, Conservative Virginian, 1790–1844* (Madison, 1964).

Hall, Kermit L. *The Politics of Justice: Lower Federal Judicial Selection and the Second Party System, 1829–1861* (Lincoln, 1979).

Hall, Van Beck, *Politics Without Parties: Massachusetts 1780–1791* (Pittsburgh, 1972).

Hammond, Bray. *Banks and Politics in America from the Revolution to the Civil War* (Princeton, 1957).

Harden, Edward Jenkins. *Life of George M. Troup* (Savannah, 1859).

Haskins, Charles, and Herbert A. Johnson. *History of the Supreme Court of the United States: Foundation of Power: John Marshall 1801–1815* (New York, 1981).

Henderson, H. James. *Party Politics in the Continental Congress* (New York, 1974).

Hibbard, Benjamin H. *A History of the Public Land Policies* (Madison, 1965).

Higginbotham, Sanford W. *The Keystone in the Democratic Arch: Pennsylvania Politics, 1800–1816* (Harrisburg, 1952).

Hoffman, William S. *Andrew Jackson and North Carolina Politics* (Chapel Hill, 1958).

Holt, Michael. *The Political Crisis of the 1850's* (New York, 1978).

Houston, David F. *A Critical Study of Nullification in South Carolina* (New York, 1896).

Jack, Theodore Henley. *Sectionalism and Party Politics in Alabama, 1819–1842* (Menasha, 1919).

James, Marquis. *Andrew Jackson* (Indianapolis, 1933, 1937), 2 vols.

Jensen, Merrill. *Articles of Confederation: An Interpretation of the Social-Constitutional History of the American Revolution* (Madison, 1940, 1963).

Jordan, Philip D. *The National Road* (Indianapolis, 1948).

July, Robert W. *The Essential New Yorker: Gulian Crommelin Verplanck* (Durham, 1951).

Kass, Alvin. *Politics in New York State, 1800–1830* (Syracuse, 1965).

Kibler, Lillian. *Benjamin F. Perry: South Carolina Unionist* (Durham, 1946).

Kilpatrick, James J. *The Sovereign States* (Chicago, 1957).

Klein, Phillip S. *Pennsylvania Politics, 1817–1832: A Game Without Rules* (Philadelphia, 1940).

Latner, Richard B. *The Presidency of Andrew Jackson: White House Politics, 1829–1837* (Athens, 1979).

Lawrence, Alexander A. *James Moore Wayne: Southern Unionist* (Chapel Hill, 1943).

Livemore, Shaw. *The Twilight of Federalism: The Disintegration of the Federalist Party, 1815–1830* (Princeton, 1962).

Main, Jackson T. *Political Parties Before the Constitution* (Chapel Hill, 1973).

Main, Jackson T. *The Anti-Federalists, Critics of the Constitution, 1781–1788* (Chapel Hill, 1961).

Malone, Dumas. *The Public Life of Thomas Cooper, 1783–1839* (Columbia, 1961).

McCormick, Richard P. *The Second American Party System: Party Formation in the Jacksonian Era* (Chapel Hill, 1966).

McFaul, John M. *The Politics of Jacksonian Finance* (Ithaca, 1972).

McLaughlin, Andrew C. *Foundations of American Constitutionalism* (New York, 1932).

McMillan, Malcolm Cook. *Constitutional Development in Alabama, 1798–1901: A Study in Politics, the Negro and Sectionalism* (Chapel Hill, 1955).

Meyers, Marvin. *The Jacksonian Persuasion: Politics and Belief* (Palo Alto, 1957).

Miles, Edwin A. *Jacksonian Democracy in Mississippi* (Chapel Hill, 1960).

Mooney, Chase C. *William H. Crawford, 1772–1834* (Lexington, 1974).

Morris, Richard B. (ed.). *The Era of the American Revolution* (New York, 1939).

Munroe, John A. *Louis McLane: Federalist and Jacksonian* (New Brunswick, 1973).

Murray, Paul. *The Whig Party in Georgia, 1825–1853* (Chapel Hill, 1948).

Nadelhaft, Jerome. *The Disorders of War: The Revolution in South Carolina* (Orono, 1981).

Nathans, Sidney. *Daniel Webster and Jacksonian Democracy* (Baltimore, 1973).

Niven, John. *Martin Van Buren: The Romantic Age of American Politics* (New York, 1983).

Oakes, James. *The Ruling Race: A History of American Slaveholders* (New York, 1982).

Parks, Joseph H. *Felix Grundy, Champion of Democracy* (Baton Rouge, 1940).

Parks, Joseph H. *John Bell* (Baton Rouge, 1950).

Parrington, Vernon L. *Main Currents in American Thought: The Romantic Revolution in America, 1800–1860* (New York, 1927), 3 vols.

Parton, James. *Life of Andrew Jackson* (New York, 1860), 3 vols.

Pessen, Edward. *Jacksonian America: Society, Personality and Politics* (New York, 1969, 1978), revised edition.

Peterson, Merrill D. *The Jefferson Image in the American Mind* (New York, 1960).

Peterson, Merrill D. *Olive Branch and Sword—the Compromise of 1833* (Baton Rouge, 1982).

Phillips, Ulrich Bonnell. *Georgia and State Rights* (Washington, D.C., 1902).

Potter, David M. *The South and the Sectional Conflict* (Baton Rouge, 1968).

Powell, Edward Payson. *Nullification and Secession in the United States* (New York, 1897).

Putnam, Herbert Everett. *Joel Roberts Poinsett: A Political Biography* (Washington, D.C., 1935).

Rakove, Jack, N. *The Beginnings of National Politics* (New York, 1979).

Remini, Robert V. *Andrew Jackson* (New York, 1966).

Remini, Robert V. *Andrew Jackson and the Bank War* (New York, 1967).

Remini, Robert V. *Andrew Jackson and the Course of American Democracy, 1833–1845* (New York, 1984).

Remini, Robert V. *Andrew Jackson and the Course of American Empire, 1767–1821* (New York, 1977).

Remini, Robert V. *Andrew Jackson and the Course of American Freedom 1822–1832* (New York, 1981).

Remini, Robert V. *The Election of Andrew Jackson* (Philadelphia, 1963).

Remini, Robert V. *Martin Van Buren and the Making of the Democratic Party* (New York, 1959).

Rippy, J. Fred. *Joel R. Poinsett, Versatile American* (Durham, 1935).

Risjord, Norman K. *Chesapeake Politics, 1781–1800* (New York, 1978).

Risjord, Norman K. *The Old Republicans: Southern Conservatism in the Age of Jefferson* (New York, 1965).

Rogin, Michael Paul. *Fathers and Children: Andrew Jackson and the Subjugation of the American Indian* (New York, 1975).

Satz, Ronald N. *American Indian Policy in the Jacksonian Era* (Lincoln, 1975).

Schlesinger, Arthur M., Jr., *The Age of Jackson* (Boston, 1945).

Seager, Robert, II. *And Tyler Too: A Biography of John and Julia Gardiner Tyler* (New York, 1963).

Sellers, Charles, ed. *Andrew Jackson, Nullification, and the State-Rights Tradition* (Chicago, 1963).

Sellers, Charles. *James K. Polk: Jacksonian, 1795–1843* (Princeton, 1957).

Shepard, Edward M. *Martin Van Buren* (Boston and New York, 1900).

Simms, Henry H. *The Rise of the Whigs in Virginia, 1824–1840* (Richmond, 1929).

Smith, Elbert, *Francis Preston Blair* (New York, 1980).

Smith, Walter Buckingham, and Arthur H. Cole. *Fluctuations in American Business, 1790–1860* (Cambridge, 1935).

Smith, Culver. *The Press, Politics and Patronage: The American Government's Use of Newspapers, 1789–1875* (Athens, 1977).

Smith, William E. *The Francis Preston Blair Family in Politics* (New York, 1933).

Soltow, Lee. *Men and Wealth in the United States 1850–1870* (New Haven, 1975).

Spencer, Ivor D. *The Victor and the Spoils: A Life of William L. Marcy* (Providence, 1959).

Stanwood, Edward. *American Tariff Controversies in the Nineteenth Century* (Boston, 1903), 2 vols.

Stanwood, Edward. *History of the Presidency from 1789 to 1887* (Boston, 1928), 2 vols.

Sydnor, Charles. *The Development of Southern Sectionalism, 1819–48* (Baton Rouge, 1948).

Taussig, Frank W. *The Tariff History of the United States* (New York, 1888).

Taylor, George Rogers. *The Transportation Revolution, 1815–1860* (New York, 1951).

Temin, Peter. *The Jacksonian Economy* (New York, 1969).

Thornton, J. Mills, III. *Politics and Power in a Slave Society* (Baton Rouge, 1978).

Turner, Frederick Jackson. *Rise of the New West, 1819–1829* (New York, 1906, 1962).

Turner, Frederick Jackson. *The United States 1830–1850* (New York, 1935, reprinted 1965).

Van Deusen, Glyndon G. *The Life of Henry Clay* (Boston, 1937).

Ward, John William. *Andrew Jackson: Symbol for an Age* (New York, 1955).

Warren, Charles. *The Supreme Court in United States History* (Boston, 1922), 2 vols.

Wayland, Francis Fry. *Andrew Stevenson, Democrat and Diplomat, 1785–1857* (Philadelphia, 1949).

Wheeler, Henry G. *History of Congress . . .* (New York, 1848), 2 vols.

White, Leonard D. *The Jacksonians: A Study in Administrative History, 1829–1861* (New York, 1954).

Williamson, Jeffrey G., and Peter H. Lindert. *American Inequality: A Macroeconomic History* (New York, 1980).

Wilson, Major. *Space, Time and Freedom* (Westport, 1974).

Wiltse, Charles. *John C. Calhoun.* (Indianapolis, 1944–51), 3 vols.

Wood, Gordon S. *Creation of the American Republic, 1776–1787* (Chapel Hill, 1969).

Wright, Gavin. *The Political Economy of the Cotton South: Households, Markets and Wealth in the Nineteenth Century* (New York, 1978).

Young, James Simeon. *A Political and Constitutional Study of the Cumberland Road* (Chicago, 1904).

Articles and Essays

Abernethy, Thomas P., "Andrew Jackson and the Rise of Southwestern Democracy," *American Historical Review* XXXIII (Oct. 1927).

Anderson, Frank M., "A Forgotten Phase of the New England Opposition to the War of 1812," Mississippi Valley Historical Association, *Proceedings* VI (1912–13).

Banner, James M., "The Problem of South Carolina." In Stanley Elkins and Eric McKitrick (eds.), *The Hofstadter Aegis: A Memorial* (New York, 1974).

Beard, Charles, "The Constitution and States' Rights," *Jefferson, Corporations and the Constitution* (Washington, 1936).

Bergeron, Paul H., "Tennessee's Response to the Nullification Crisis," *Journal of Southern History* XXXIX (Feb. 1973).

Bergeron, Paul, "The Nullification Controversy Revisisted," *Tennessee Historical Quarterly* 35 (Fall 1976).

Bestor, Arthur, "State Sovereignty and Slavery: A Reinterpretation of Proslavery Constitutional Doctrine, 1846–1860, *Journal of the Illinois State Historical Society* LIV (Summer 1961).

Bonner, James C., "Legislative Apportionment and County Unit Voting in Georgia Since 1777," *Georgia Historical Quarterly* XLVII (Dec. 1963).

Bridgforth, Lucie Robertson, "Mississippi's Response to Nullification, 1833," *Journal of Mississippi History* XLV (Feb. 1983).

Brown, Norman D., "Webster-Jackson Movement for a Constitution and Union Party in 1833," *Mid-America* 46 (July 1964).

Brown, Richard H., "The Missouri Crisis, Slavery and the Politics of Jacksonianism," *South Atlantic Quarterly* 65 (Winter 1966).

Brown, Thomas, "Southern Whigs and the Politics of Statesmanship, 1833–1841," *Journal of Southern History* XLVI (Aug. 1980).

Burke, Joseph C., "The Cherokee Cases: A Study in Law, Politics, and Morality,"*Stanford Law Review* XXI (Feb. 1969).

Capers, Gerald M., " A Reconsideration of John C. Calhoun's Transition from Nationalism to Nullification," *Journal of Southern History* XIV (Feb. 1948).

Clanin, Douglas E., "Internal Improvements in National Politics, 1816–1830," In *Transportation and the Early Nation* (Indianapolis, 1982).

Coulter, E. Merton, "The Nullification Movement in Georgia," *Georgia Historical Quarterly* V (March 1921).

Counihan, Harold J., "The North Carolina Constitutional Convention of 1835: A Study in Jacksonian Democracy," *North Carolina Historical Review* XLVI (Autumn 1969).

DeRosier, Arthur H., Jr., "Andrew Jackson and Negotiation for the Removal of the Choctaw Indians," *Historian* XXIX (May 1967).

Donald, David, "The Proslavery Argument Reconsidered," *Journal of Southern History* XXXVII (Feb. 1971).

Dewey, Donald O., "Madison's Response to Jackson's Foes," *Tennessee Historical Quarterly* XXI (1961).

Douglas, William O., "Interposition and the *Peters* Case, 1778–1809," *Stanford Law Review* 9 (Dec. 1956).

Dowd, Morgan D., "Justice Story and the Politics of Appointment," *American Journal of Legal History* IX (Oct. 1965).

Drake, Winbourne Magruder, "The Mississippi Constitutional Convention of 1832," *Journal of Southern History* XXIII (Aug. 1957).

East, Robert A., "The Massachusetts Conservatives in the Critical Period." In Richard B. Morris (ed.), *The Era of the American Revolution* (New York, 1965).

Eriksson, Erik M., "The Federal Civil Service Under President Jackson," *Mississippi Valley Historical Review* XIII (March 1927).

Eriksson, Erik McKinley, "Official Newspaper Organs and Jackson's Re-election, 1832," *Tennessee Historical Magazine* IX (Jan. 1925).

Ershkovitz, Herbert, "The Election of 1824 in New Jersey," New Jersey Historical Society Proceedings LXXXIV (April 1966).

Formisano, Ronald P., "Toward a Reorientation of Jacksonian Politics: A Review of the Literature, 1959–1975," *Journal of American History* 63 (June 1976).

Gatell, Frank Otto, "Sober Second Thoughts on Van Buren, the Albany Regency, and the Wall Street Conspiracy," *Journal of American History* LIII (June 1966).

Gates, Paul W., "Tenants of the Log Cabin," *Mississippi Valley Historical Review* XLIX (June 1962).

Govan, Thomas P., "John M. Berrien and the Administration of Andrew Jackson," *Journal of Southern History* 5 (Nov. 1939).

Green, Fletcher M., "Democracy in the Old South," *Journal of Southern History* XII (Feb. 1946).

Harris, Robert J., "Chief Justice Taney: Prophet of Reform and Reaction," *Vanderbilt Law Review* 10 (Feb. 1957).

Harrison, Joseph H., Jr., "Martin Van Buren and His Southern Supporters," *Journal of Southern History* XXII (Nov. 1956).

Hatcher, William B., "Edward Livingston's View of the Nature of the Union," *Louisiana Historical Quarterly* 24 (July 1941).

Henig, Gerald S., "The Jacksonian Attitude Toward Abolitionism in the 1830's," *Tennessee Historical Quarterly* XXVIII (Spring 1969).

Hobson, Charles F., "The Negative on State Laws: James Madison and the Crisis of Republican Government," *William and Mary Quarterly* XXXVI (April 1979).

Hoffman, William S., "Andrew Jackson, State Rightist: The Case of the Georgia Indians," *Tennessee Historical Quarterly* XI (Dec. 1952).

Hoffman, William S., "John Branch and the Origins of the Whig Party in North Carolina," *North Carolina Historical Review* 35 (July 1958).

Jack, Theodore H., "Alabama and the Federal Government: The Creek Indian Controversy," *Mississippi Valley Historical Review* III (Dec. 1916).

Jackson, Carlton, "The Internal Improvement Vetoes of Andrew Jackson," *Tennessee Historical Quarterly* XXV (Fall 1966).

Jensen, Merrill, "Democracy and the American Revolution," *Huntington Library Quarterly* XX (Aug. 1957).

Jones, Houston G., "Bedford Brown: State Rights Unionist: Part I: The Senator," *North Carolina Historical Review* XXXII (July 1955).

Kenyon, Cecelia, "Men of Little Faith: The Anti-Federalists on the Nature of Representative Government," *William and Mary Quarterly* XII (Jan. 1955).

Koch, Adrienne, and Harry Ammon, "The Virginia and Kentucky Resolutions: An Episode in Jefferson and Madison's Defense of Civil Liberties," *William and Mary Quarterly* V (April 1948).

Latner, Richard B., "The Eaton Affair Reconsidered," *Tennessee Historical Quarterly* XXXVI (Fall 1977).

Latner, Richard B. "The Nullification Crisis and Republican Subversion," *Journal of Southern History* XLIII (Feb. 1977).

Longaker, Richard P., "Andrew Jackson and the Judiciary," *Political Science Quarterly* 71 (Sept. 1956).

Longaker, Richard P., "Was Jackson's Kitchen Cabinet a Cabinet?" *Mississippi Valley Historical Review* XLIV (June 1957).

Lowe, Gabriel, Jr., "John H. Eaton, Jackson's Campaign Manager," *Tennessee Historical Quarterly* II (1952).

Macoll, John D., "Representative John Quincy Adams' Compromise Tariff of 1832," *Capitol Studies* I (Fall 1972).

Maier, Pauline, "The Road Not Taken: Nullification, John C. Calhoun, and the Revolutionary Tradition in South Carolina," *South Carolina Historical Magazine* 82 (Jan. 1981).

Martin, John M., "William R. King: Jacksonian Senator," *The Alabama Review* XVIII (Oct. 1965).

McFaul, John M., "Expediency vs. Morality: Jacksonian Politics and Slavery," *Journal of American History* 63 (June 1975).

McLaughlin, Andrew C., "Social Compact and Constitutional Construction," *American Historical Review* V (April 1900).

McLaughlin, Andrew C., "The Background of American Federalism," *American Political Science Review* 12 (May 1918).

Miles, Edwin A., "After John Marshall's Decision: *Worcester v. Georgia* and the Nullification Crisis," *Journal of Southern History* XXXIX (Nov. 1973).

Miles, Edwin A., "The Whig Party and the Menace of Caesar," *Tennessee Historical Quarterly* XXVII (Winter 1968).

Miller, Richard G., "The Tariff of 1832: The Issue That Failed," *The Filson Club History Quarterly* 49 (July 1975).

Mintz, Max M., "The Political Ideas of Martin Van Buren," *New York History* XXX (Oct. 1949).

Mooney, Chase C., "The Question of Slavery and the Free Negro in the Tennessee Constitutional Convention of 1834," *Journal of Southern History* XI (Nov. 1946).

Murray, Paul, "Economic Sectionalism in Georgia Politics, 1825–1855," *Journal of Southern History* 10 (Aug. 1944).

Nelson, E. C., "Presidential Influence on the Policy of Internal Improvements," *Iowa Journal of History and Politics* IV (Jan. 1906).

Nettels, Curtis P., "The Mississippi Valley and the Federal Judiciary, 1807–1837," *Mississippi Valley Historical Review* 12 (Sept. 1925).

Nigro, Felix A., "The Van Buren Confirmation Before the Senate," *Western Political Quarterly* XIV (March 1961).

Nuermberger, Ruth Ketring, "The 'Royal Party' in Early Alabama Politics," *The Alabama Review* VI (April, July 1953).

Nussbaum, Frederick L., "The Compromise Tariff of 1833: A Study in Practical Politics," *South Atlantic Quarterly* XI (Oct. 1912).

Ochenkowski, J. P., "The Origins of Nullification in South Carolina," *South Carolina Historical Magazine* 83 (April 1982).

Parker, Joel, "Brief History of the Boundary Dispute between New Jersey and New York," New Jersey Historical Society *Proceedings* VII (Jan. 1858).

Phillips, Kim T., "The Pennsylvania Origins of the Jackson Movement," *Political Science Quarterly* 91 (Fall 1976).

Phillips, U. B. "The Southern Whigs." In Guy S. Ford (ed.), *Essays in American History Dedicated to Frederick Jackson Turner* (New York, 1910).

Prucha, Francis Paul, "Andrew Jackson's Indian Policy: A Reassessment," *Journal of American History* LVI (Dec. 1969).

Ratcliffe, Donald J., "The Role of Voters and Issues in Party Formation: Ohio, 1824," *Journal of American History* 59 (March 1973).

Remini, Robert V., "The Albany Regency," *New York History* XXXIX (Oct. 1958).

Remini, Robert V., "The Election of 1832." In Arthur M. Schlesinger, Jr. (ed.), *History of American Presidential Elections, 1798–1968* (New York, 1971), 4 vols.

Richards, Leonard, "The Jacksonians and Slavery." In Lewis Perry and Michael Fellman (eds.), *Antislavery Reconsidered: New Perspectives on the Abolitionists* (Baton Rouge, 1979).

Roberts, Lucien E., "Sectional Factors in Movements for Legislative Reapportionment and Reduction in Georgia, 1777–1860." In James C. Bonner and Lucien E. Roberts (eds.), *Studies in Georgia History and Government* (Athens, 1949).

Rogers, George C., Jr., "South Carolina Federalists and the Origins of the Nullification Movement," *South Carolina Historical Magazine* 71 (Jan. 1970).

Seigel, Fred, "The Paternalist Thesis: Virginia as a Test Case," *Civil War History* 25 (Sept. 1975).

Sellers, Charles G., "The Travail of Slavery." In Charles Sellers (ed.), *The Southerner as American* (Chapel Hill, 1960).

Sellers, Charles G., "Andrew Jackson Versus the Historians," *Mississippi Valley Historical Review* 44 (March 1958).

Sellers, Charles G., Jr., "Banking and Politics in Jackson's Tennessee, 1817–1827," *Mississippi Valley Historical Review* 41 (June 1954).

Sellers, Charles G., "Jackson Men with Feet of Clay," *American Historical Review* 62 (April 1957).

Smith, C. Jay, Jr., "John MacPherson Berrien." In Horace Montgomery (ed.), *Georgians in Profile: Historical Essays in Honor of Ellis Morton Coulter* (Athens, 1958).

Soltow, Lee, "Economic Inequality in the United States in the Period from 1790 to 1860," *Journal of Economic History* XXXI (Dec. 1971).

Somit, Albert, "Andrew Jackson as Political Theorist," *Tennessee Historical Quarterly* 7 (June 1949).

Somit, Albert, "Andrew Jackson as an Administrative Reformer," *Tennessee Historical Quarterly* 13 (Sept. 1954).

Stampp, Kenneth M., "The Concept of a Perpetual Union," *Journal of American History* LXV (June 1978).

Stenberg, Richard R., "The Jefferson Birthday Dinner, 1830," *Journal of Southern History* IV (Aug. 1938).

Stewart, James Brewer, "'A Great Talking and Eating Machine': Patriarchy, Mobilization and the Dynamics of Nullification in South Carolina," *Civil War History* 27 (Sept. 1981).

Stokes, William E., "Whig Conceptions of Executive Power," *Presidential Studies Quarterly* VI (Winter and Spring 1976).

Sutton, Robert, "Sectionalism and Social Structure: A Case Study of Jeffersonian Democracy," *Virginia Magazine of History and Biography* 30 (Jan. 1972).

Treacy, Kenneth, "The Olmstead Case, 1778–1809," *Western Political Quarterly* 10 (Sept. 1957).

Tregle, Joseph George, Jr., "Louisiana and the Tariff, 1816–1846," *Louisiana Historical Quarterly* 25 (Jan. 1942).

Wallace, Michael, "Changing Concepts of Party in the United States: New York, 1815–1828," *American Historical Review* LXXIV (Dec. 1968).

Warren, Charles, "Legislative and Judicial Attacks on the Supreme Court of the United States—A History of the Twenty-fifth Section of the Judiciary Act," *American Law Review* XLVII (Jan. and Feb. 1913).

Wellington, Raynor G., "The Tariff and the Public Lands from 1828 to 1833," American Historical Association *Annual Report* (1911).

Wilson, Major, "Andrew Jackson: The Great Compromiser," *Tennessee Historical Quarterly* XXVI (Spring 1967).

Wilson, Major, "'Liberty and Union': An Analysis of Three Concepts Involved in the Nullification Controversy," *Journal of Southern History* XXXIII (Aug. 1967).

Wire, Richard Arden, "Young Senator Clayton and the Early Jackson Years," *Delaware History* 17 (1976).

Woolfolk, George Ruble, "Taxes and Slavery in the Antebellum South," *Journal of Southern History* XXVI (May 1960).

Wright, Gavin, "'Economic Decmocracy' and the Concentration of Agricultural Wealth in the Cotton South, 1850–1860," *Agricultural History* 44 (Jan. 1970).

Theses and Dissertations

Averitt, Jack Nelson. "The Democratic Party in Georgia, 1824–1837." Unpublished doctoral dissertation, University of North Carolina, Chapel Hill, 1956.

Brady, Patrick Stone. "Political and Civic Life in South Carolina, 1787–1833." Unpublished doctoral dissertation, University of California, Santa Barbara, 1971.

Campbell, James Griffin. "James Louis Petigru: A Rhetorical Study." Unpublished doctoral dissertation. University of South Carolina, 1961.

Collier, James Glen. "The Political Career of James McDowell, 1830–1851." Unpublished doctoral dissertation, University of North Carolina, Chapel Hill, 1963.

DeBats, Donald Arthur. "Elites and Masses: Political Structure, Communication and Behavior in Ante-Bellum Georgia." Unpublished doctoral dissertation, University of Wisconsin, Madison, 1973.

Dingeldine, Raymond C. "The Political Career of William Cabell Rives." Unpublished doctoral dissertation, University of Virginia, 1967.

Driscoll, William D. "Benjamin F. Butler: Lawyer and Regency Politician." Unpublished doctoral dissertation, Fordham University, 1965.

Faircloth, Ronald W. "The Impact of Andrew Jackson in Georgia Politics, 1828–1840." Unpublished doctoral dissertation, University of Georgia, 1971.

Goldstein, Kalman. "The Albany Regency: The Failure of Practical Politics." Unpublished doctoral dissertation, Columbia University, 1969.

McCrary, Royce Coggins, Jr. "John McPherson Berrien of Georgia (1781–1856): A Political Biography." Unpublished doctoral dissertation, University of Georgia, 1971.

Parkinson, George Phillip, Jr. "Antebellum State Constitution Making: Retention, Circumvention, Revision." Unpublished doctoral dissertation, University of Wisconsin, 1972.

Sawers, Timothy R. "The Public Career of Littleton Walter Tazewell, 1824–1836." Unpublished doctoral dissertation, Miami University, 1972.

Smith, Caroline P. "Jacksonian Conservative: The Later Years of William Smith, 1826–1840." Unpublished doctoral dissertation, Auburn University, 1977.

Smith, Caroline P. "South Carolina 'Radical': The Political Career of William Smith to 1826." Unpublished M.A. thesis, Auburn University, 1971.

Sutton, Robert P. "The Virginia Constitutional Convention of 1829–1830: A Profile Analysis of Late-Jeffersonian Virginia." Unpublished doctoral dissertation, University of Virginia, 1967.

Tomlinson, Robert Hume. "The Origins and Editorial Policies of the *Richmond Whig and Public Advertiser*, 1824–1865." Unpublished doctoral dissertation, Michigan State University, 1971.

Wiglis, Herbert E., Jr. "State-Rights in Virginia, 1832–1833: A Study Showing What Men Advanced the State Rights Theory of Government." Unpublished senior thesis, Princeton University, 1957.

INDEX

Abolitionists, 191–92

Adams, John, 2, 4, 185

Adams, John Quincy: advocates nationalist interpretation of U.S. Constitution, 9, 84, 183, 195; and American System, 13; favors federal program of internal improvements, 19–20; and Indian policy, 26; and Georgia, 103–4; opposes Compromise Tariff of 1833, 169, 173; and Nullification Proclamation, 179; mentioned, 16, 46, 165.

Address to the People of South Carolina, 75

Address to the People of the United States, 75

Age of Jackson, The, viii

Alabama: Constitutional reform in, 188; Indians in, 26, 28; opposition to Jackson in, 70; support for South Carolina in, 91; Nullification and, 159; slavery in, 192

Albany Argus, 142, 146

Albany Evening Journal, 85

Albany Regency, 141–44

Alien and Sedition Acts, 4

Amendments to United States Constitution, 8, 16–17, 22

American Board of Commissioners for Foreign Missions, 28, 115, 116, 117, 118

Antifederalists, 191–92

Anti-Masons, 144

Archer, William S., 71, 176

Arkansas, 188

Articles of Confederation, 1, 2, 3, 4

Athens, Georgia, 107

Augusta, Georgia, 106

Baldwin, Henry, 30, 57

Bank of the United States (Second): and Jackson, 33–40, 164–65; and John C. Calhoun, 55, 197–98; and John Tyler, 126; as important issue during Jacksonian era, 178, 196, 197–98; and Nullification crisis, 181–82, 197–98; mentioned, viii, 8

Barbour, P. P., 71, 106, 127

Barnwell, Robert, 75

Barrow, Alexander, 194

Barry, William T., 57, 61

Beall, Robert Augustus, 106

Beardsley, Samuel, 164

Bell, John, 164

Benson, Lee, viii

Benton, Thomas Hart: supports Jackson, 14; opposed Maysville Road Veto, 22; opposed to

Bank of the United States, 36; opposed to protective tariff, 71; and Nullification Proclamation, 85, 179; and Force bill, 163; mentioned, 16, 78, 91, 165

Berrien, John M.: becomes Attorney General, 58; and Eaton Affair, 61; leaves Cabinet, 64; opposed Jackson, 70; and Georgia politics, 105–6; and Milledgeville Convention, 107, 108; supports South Carolina, 110

Bibb, George M., 68, 162, 172

Biddle, Nicholas, 34, 36, 37, 46, 182

Black, John, 162, 171

Blair, Francis P., 14, 36, 55, 164–65, 169

Branch, John, 58, 61, 64, 70

Breathitt, George, 79

Brodnax, William, 134

Bronson, Green C., 144, 145

Brooke, Francis, 126

Brown, Bedford, 71, 162, 171

Brown, John T., 135

Buckner, Alexander, 172

Buell, Jesse, 142, 151

Butler, Benjamin F.: *Worcester v. Georgia*, 116, 145; and New York politics, 142, 143, 151, 157

Butler, Elizer, 30, 31, 115–19

Cabell, Joseph C., 125

Calhoun, Floride, 60

Calhoun, James M., 70

Calhoun, John C: and states' rights, 5; and Federalists, 8–9; rivalry with Van Buren, 14, 51–64, 71; relationship with Jackson, 51, 52–68; and tariff reform, 53; opposes Distribution, 54; and Bank of the United States, 55, 197–98; rivalry with Crawford, 56; critical of Jackson's appointment policy, 59; openly endorses Nullification, 64–68; and Nullification convention proceedings, 75; resigns as Vice President to become U.S. Senator, 76; opposes Verplanck tariff, 99; strategy during Nullification crisis, 101; opposition to in Georgia, 106; support for in Virginia, 125–26; and Force bill, 161–62, 171; relations with Clay, 167–69, 182; forced to vote for Tariff of 1833, 174–75; benefits from Nullification crisis, 180–81; and minority rights, 188; and slavery issue, 192–93; mentioned, 6, 7

Cambreleng, Churchill C., 85, 91, 142

Carroll, William, 159